CW00731536

ISAEUS

202

ISAEUS

WITH AN ENGLISH TRANSLATION BY

EDWARD SEYMOUR FORSTER, M.A.

PROFESSOR OF GREEK IN THE UNIVERSITY OF SHEFFIELD

CAMBRIDGE, MASSACHUSETTS
HARVARD UNIVERSITY PRESS
LONDON
WILLIAM HEINEMANN LTD
MCMLXXXIII

American ISBN 0 674 99222 9
British ISBN 0 434 99202 X

First printed 1927
Reprinted 1946, 1957, 1962, 1983

Printed in Great Britain

CONTENTS

INTRODUCTION

The Life and Writings of Isaeus

WE possess fewer details about the life of Isaeus than about that of any other of the Attic orators. No contemporary writer alludes to him, and our earliest authority is the literary critic Dionysius of Halicarnassus, who wrote in the Augustan age, and supplies us with a meagre biography, to which later writers have nothing substantial to add. His account of the life of Isaeus (*De Isaeo*, § 1, pp. 586-8) [a] is as follows :

" Isaeus, the teacher of Demosthenes—and this is his chief title to fame—was according to some an Athenian by birth, according to others a Chalcidian. He flourished after the Peloponnesian War, as I gather from his speeches, and survived into the reign of Philip. I cannot state the exact date of his birth and death, nor can I give any account of his manner of life or political principles, nor do I know whether he held any particular views ; in fact I am ignorant on all such points, since I have never come across any account of him. Even Hermippus,[b] who wrote about the pupils of Isocrates, though he gives details about the others, has only recorded two facts about Isaeus,

[a] Dion. Hal. *Opuscula*, ed. Usener-Radermacher, pp. 93-4.　　　　[b] H. of Smyrna (*c.* 200 B.C.).

namely, that he was a pupil of Isocrates and that he taught Demosthenes."

There can be little doubt that Isaeus was a native of Chalcis [a] ; had he been an Athenian, it is difficult to see how the tradition of his Chalcidian origin could have originated. It seems likely, therefore, that, like Deinarchus and Lysias, he was a resident alien (μέτοικος) at Athens, a fact which would account for his abstention from politics. It is not impossible, however, that he was of Athenian descent, since in 509 B.C. the Athenians, after their victory over the Chalcidians, sent out 4000 settlers to Chalcis (Herod. v. 77).

The indications given by Dionysius regarding the date of Isaeus are so vague as to be of little value ; more definite results can be obtained from the internal evidence of his surviving speeches, some of which can be more or less accurately dated. The earliest is that *On the Estate of Dicaeogenes* (Or. v.), which can be dated about 389 B.C.,[b] the latest that *On behalf of Euphiletus,* which dates from about 344 B.C.[c] These dates give the approximate limits of his professional activity. We shall probably be not far wrong if we place the date of his birth between 415 and 410 B.C. ; his death must have occurred some time after 344 B.C.

There is no reason to doubt the statement that Isaeus was a pupil of Isocrates, especially as Dionysius, as we have seen, quotes an early authority for it. Isaeus must have been among the earliest of the

[a] Harpocration, *s.v.* Ἰσαῖος, quotes the authority of Demetrius of Magnesia (first century B.C.) in support of the Chalcidian origin of Isaeus.

[b] See p. 157.   [c] See p. 430.

pupils of Isocrates, who opened his school at Athens about the year 392 B.C.

The tradition that Isaeus was the teacher of Demosthenes is repeated by all his biographers. Dionysius (*De Isaeo*, § 4, p. 592) quotes the saying of Pytheas, the enemy of Demosthenes, that he " had swallowed Isaeus whole and all his rhetorical devices," and the internal evidence of the speeches confirms the influence of Isaeus upon Demosthenes. As the latter was born in 384 B.C., he must have begun his studies under Isaeus about 366 B.C., when he came of age and began to contemplate the prosecution of his fraudulent guardians, Aphobus and Onetor, against whom he commenced proceedings in 363 B.C. As Wyse has pointed out,[a] the speeches of Demosthenes against his guardians contain several passages which directly copy or imitate the eighth speech of Isaeus (*On the Estate of Ciron*).

The meagreness of our information about the life of Isaeus is no doubt due to the fact that he took no part in public life, but devoted himself entirely to his profession of speech-writing on behalf of others. According to the pseudo-Plutarchian *Lives of the Ten Orators*, Isaeus left behind him sixty-four speeches, of which fifty were regarded as genuine, and a treatise on rhetoric. Eleven orations, all concerned with cases of inheritance, have come down to us, and a large fragment (Or. xii.), preserved by Dionysius of Halicarnassus, written on behalf of one whose political rights were threatened. The titles and some fragments of forty-three other speeches have survived ; [b] these cover a much wider field, and were

---

[a] *The Speeches of Isaeus*, pp. 591-2, 597-8, 606, 624.
[b] See pp. 445 ff.

INTRODUCTION

delivered in a variety of cases concerned with real property, guardianship, sureties, adoption, assault, and rights of citizenship. The only two lost speeches which can possibly have had any connexion with public affairs are that *Against the Megarians*,[a] the genuineness of which is doubtful, and that *On the Speeches made in Macedonia*.[a] He seems to have been sufficiently well known to the general public to have figured in the *Theseus* of the comic poet Theopompus.[b]

The reputation of Isaeus as a speech-writer rested mainly on his skill in dealing with cases of inheritance (κληρικοὶ λόγοι). No doubt his speeches on this topic came first in the collected *Corpus* of his works, for which our MS. authority ends abruptly in the middle of the eleventh oration. They show an extraordinary grasp of the intricacies of Athenian testamentary law, for which, indeed, they are our chief authority, and a consummate skill in clearly presenting complicated cases often involving intricate family relationships. Isaeus gives us a unique picture of Athenian family life, though certainly not in its pleasantest aspect, since nothing embitters family relations so much as quarrels about money. He appears to have won a reputation for his cleverness in making the worse cause appear the better,[c] —perhaps the strongest testimony which could be given to his skill ; his speeches certainly contain specious arguments and suppressions, and even perversions, of the truth, but, after all, the object of an advocate is to win his case, and the better the

---

[a] See p. 454.
[b] Ps.-Plutarch, *Vita Isaei*.
[c] Dion. Hal. *De Isaeo*, § 4, p. 591.

advocate the more likely is he to be employed in desperate causes.

The Place of Isaeus among the Attic Orators

The place of Isaeus in the development of Greek oratorical prose can be best appreciated by comparing him with his predecessor Lysias on the one hand, and his pupil Demosthenes on the other. With Lysias he has many points in common : both wrote the purest Attic Greek ; both, as Dionysius points out, are simple, concise, clear, and vivid in their style. Isaeus, however, lacks the peculiar charm and grace of Lysias, and his skill in appreciating the psychology of the person for whom he is writing a speech, and in adopting a style and tone suitable to his character and circumstances. Isaeus is less subtle but more vehement, especially in the expression of just indignation and in carefully reasoned remonstrance ; he gets to grips with his adversary as Lysias never succeeds in doing. Again, he is singularly deficient in humour [a] and lightness of touch as compared with Lysias, and on occasions does not scruple to descend to scurrilous abuse and innuendo, from which Lysias, with his more refined nature, would have shrunk. In " composition " (σύνθεσις), though Lysias to a large extent freed himself from the intricate style of his predecessors, he is still in some degree under its influence, particularly in his love of antitheses ; Isaeus, on the other hand, is almost wholly free from the shackles of the periodic style. In the arrange-

[a] The only instance of humour in his surviving speeches is the description of the numerous claimants for the estate of Nicostratus (Or. iv. §§ 7-10), see p. 135.

ment of his subject matter Lysias adheres rigorously to the four conventional divisions of proem, narrative, proof, and epilogue ; Isaeus is a more clever tactician, and arranges his materials in whatever manner he thinks will have the greatest effect on his hearers. While Lysias usually offers only a rhetorical proof, Isaeus is not content unless he can present a proof which is completely systematic and logical.

Demosthenes stands both intellectually and morally on a far higher plane than Isaeus ; but he owed not a little to his teacher. He resembles him in his arrangement of his subject matter so as to produce the greatest effect, in his method of grappling with his opponent, and in his love of exhaustive proof. But Demosthenes in his private orations can meet and defeat Isaeus on his own ground, forensic oratory ; in the wider field of political eloquence his mastery of every tone of which the Greek language is capable, his burning patriotism, and his statesmanlike width of view mark him as an original genius unique in the history of oratory.

The Athenian Laws of Inheritance

For the understanding of the speeches of Isaeus it is necessary very briefly to summarize the Attic laws regulating inheritance :

(a) A citizen who had no legitimate or adopted children might devise his property to anyone he chose, the usual method being to adopt a son (or, less often, a daughter) as his heir. A will could not be upset unless it were proved that the testator was under a disability through insanity or disease, or was a victim of undue influence or duress.

(b) Sons inherited their father's property in equal shares, unless they had been adopted into another family.

(c) In default of sons and their issue, daughters and their issue succeeded ; but a daughter was not, strictly speaking, an heiress, but was attached to the estate (ἐπίκληρος), which, if she were unmarried, the father usually devised to some person on condition that he married her. If there were no such provision by will, the nearest kinsman, who became her guardian, had the option of marrying her and claiming the estate ; otherwise he was under the obligation of providing her with a husband, and the estate devolved on her son, or sons, when they came of age.

(d) If there were no lineal descendants, an intestate estate passed to the nearest collateral relative on the father's side, with a preference in favour of males, as far as the children of first cousins. Failing these, it passed to the collateral relatives on the mother's side under the same conditions.

Three points, which occur frequently in the speeches, call for brief notice. The first is the extensive use made of adoption, which was due to a desire to keep up the continuity of the family, particularly in view of the importance attached to the ceremonies which had to be carried out at the family tomb. Secondly, a curious preference, entirely at variance with modern practice, was shown by Athenian judges for the title of kinship over the rights conferred by testament ; it appears that wills, although admitted to be properly executed, were not infrequently assailed and annulled in favour of kinsmen who had been passed over. Thirdly,

the evidence of slaves could only be given under torture, and, though the elaborate defences of this practice by the orators seems to show that the Athenians thought that it stood in need of apology, such evidence was regarded as the most reliable form of proof.

The Text

The foundation of the text of Isaeus is a thirteenth-century MS. on vellum in the British Museum, the Codex Crippsianus (A) (British Museum Burneianus 95).[a] It contains Andocides, Isaeus, Deinarchus, Antiphon, Lycurgus, Gorgias, Alcidamas, Lesbonax, and Herodes. Originally in the library of the monastery of Vatopedi on Mount Athos, it passed into the hands of the Phanariot Greek Prince Alexander Bano Hantzerli of Constantinople, from whom it was purchased by John Marten Cripps in the first years of the nineteenth century. It subsequently formed part of the collection of Dr. Charles Burney, whose books and MSS. were purchased by the nation in 1827 and placed in the British Museum. It has been frequently collated, in particular by Thalheim in 1880, by Buermann in 1881–2, and by Wyse, who states that his collation produced no important variation from that of Buermann.

It is generally agreed that A shows two classes of corrections. One class, usually called A[1], seems to be due to the original scribe, who compared his copy with the original and corrected any errors which he had made, and very occasionally introduced conjectures of his own. The second class (A[2]) consists

---

[a] For a complete account of this MS. see Wyse, *The Speeches of Isaeus*, pp. viii ff.

of corrections which begin in the 3rd oration, and
are irregularly distributed over the remaining
speeches. Wyse estimates the emendations of A²
at " about 190, of which not more than 25 or 26 are
clearly wrong." It is uncertain whether or no the
corrections of A² are due to the consultation of
another MS. or to the unaided ingenuity of the
corrector himself. Many of them are such as any
ordinary Greek scholar could make ; others show
considerable learning.

Thus A¹ represents a considerable improvement
on A, while A² is usually right, though occasionally
obviously wrong, in its further corrections. This
being so, in order not to overburden the *apparatus
criticus*, the readings of A, A¹, and A² have not been
set out in full, and for details of these the reader
is referred to the editions of Wyse and Thalheim.
While obvious and unimportant corrections of spell-
ings etc. are not noted, any reading adopted in
the text which is not found in the MSS. is noted and
the authority indicated, and is followed by the MS.
reading, which, unless it is otherwise stated, is that
found in A as corrected by A¹.

It is now generally agreed that of the other existing
MSS. of Isaeus, B (Laurentianus), L (Marcianus),
M (Brit. Mus. Burneianus 96), P (Ambrosianus, A 99),
and Z (Vratislauiensis) are all derived from A. The
only independent MS. is Q (Ambrosianus, D 42 sup.),
which contains only the first two orations. Its
independence is proved by the presence of words not
found in A ; it is carelessly written and shows
frequent omissions, and is obviously inferior to A.

In the text square brackets [ ] have been used to
enclose words appearing in the original which are not

INTRODUCTION

translated, and angular brackets <> to indicate words inserted without MS. authority.

BIBLIOGRAPHY

The *editio princeps* of Isaeus was that of Aldus (Venice, 1513), based on the inferior fifteenth-century MS. L (Marcianus) and full of typographical errors. This was followed by the editions of Stephanus (Paris, 1575) and Reiske (Leipzig, 1773) with valuable annotations by the editor, who also incorporated the notes of Scaliger (1540–1609); both these editions contributed greatly to the purgation of the text, but were based on inferior MSS., L, M, Z, P, which do not include Or. i. 22 ἢ ἐκείνῳ to Or. ii. 47 καταστήσητε. The second oration was published in full for the first time by Tyrwhitt from B in 1785. The first edition which made use of the Crippsianus (A) was that of Bekker (Oxford, 1823). This was followed by the editions of Dobson (London, 1828)*, which included the valuable notes of Dobree; Schoemann (Greifswald, 1831)* containing the first comprehensive commentary; Baiter and Sauppe (Zurich, 1840)*; Scheibe (Leipzig 1860)*; Buermann (Berlin, 1883); Thalheim (Leipzig, 1903)*; and W. Wyse (*The Speeches of Isaeus*, Cambridge, 1904)* with the most valuable and exhaustive commentary which has yet appeared.

The speeches have been translated into English by Sir William Jones (1779)*; into French by Dareste and Hassoullier (1898), and Pierre Roussel (1922)*; into Italian by Caccialanza (1901); into German by Schoemann (1830) and Munscher (1919).

For a bibliography of modern theses and articles

INTRODUCTION

the reader is referred to Wyse, *op. cit.* pp. lx-lxi, and
Thalheim, pp. ix-x.[a] For the general study of
Isaeus reference may be made to R. C. Jebb, *The
Attic Orators from Antiphon to Isaeus* (2nd ed., 1893)* ;
J. F. Dobson, *The Greek Orators* (1919) ; L. Moy,
Étude sur les plaidoyers d'Isée (1876) ; and F. Blass,
Die attische Beredsamkeit (2nd ed., 1892)*.

(The asterisk indicates those works which have been prin-
cipally used in the preparation of this translation.)

[a] To the articles by P. S. Photiades, cited by Thalheim,
should be added further articles dealing with the first four
orations published in Ἀθηνᾶ, 1922 and 1923, and Νομικὸν Περι-
οδικόν, 1924. The loss of Dr. Photiades' ms. notes on Isaeus,
which embodied the work of many years, as well as of his
valuable library of books on the Greek orators, in the
destruction of Smyrna, calls for the sympathy of all classical
scholars. It is much to be hoped that he will be able to
reconstruct his notes on the remaining speeches of Isaeus.

I. ON THE ESTATE OF CLEONYMUS

INTRODUCTION

CLEONYMUS, the son of Polyarchus,[a] dying without issue, left a will bequeathing his estate to certain of his relatives who were not his next of kin. There is no evidence of their exact relationship to the testator, nor is it certain how many of them there were. Two of them were Pherenicus (§§ 31, 45) and Poseidippus (as appears from § 23), and it may be inferred from § 45 (Φερένικος ἢ τῶν ἀδελφῶν τις) that they were brothers, and that there was at least one more brother concerned, possibly Diocles mentioned in §§ 14, 23. The author of the Argument prefixed to the Speech (where see note) includes Simon among the beneficiaries, but this is certainly a mistake. The will had been made some years before Cleonymus's death, and had been deposited for safety in official custody.

The claimants under the will were attacked by the next-of-kin, who, in the absence of the will, would

[a] STEMMA

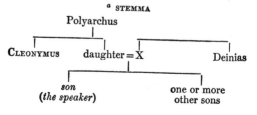

have been the legal heirs, and one of whom is the speaker, acting on behalf of himself and his brother or brothers. They appear to have been the sons of Cleonymus's sister, whose husband's brother, Deinias, acted as their guardian after their father's death.

Before the case came on for trial an attempt had been made to arrive at a compromise by means of arbitration. The arbitrators must have included friends of both parties, but in the speech they are represented as being all friends of the speaker's opponents. The arbitrators suggested that the nephews should receive a third of the estate and abandon any further claim. Encouraged by this offer, and using it as an argument in favour of the justice of their claim, the nephews proceeded to claim the whole estate, relying (§ 41) on the well-known bias of the Athenian judges towards the claims of the next-of-kin in preference to those of legatees under a will.

The claimants, while fully admitting the genuineness of the will and the right of Cleonymus to dispose of his property, rely in the main on the argument that the will does not represent the last wishes of the testator. At the time when it was made they were quite young and under the tutelage of Deinias, with whom Cleonymus had quarrelled. Subsequently, according to their account, after the death of Deinias, Cleonymus had received them into his house and brought them up and protected their interests in every possible way. At the time of his death they were on terms of close intimacy with him, while he was at variance with some at least of the beneficiaries under the will. During his last illness, they allege, he had wished to revoke the will, and had sent

3

Poseidippus to demand it back from the official in whose custody it was, but Poseidippus had not only refused to go, but had also sent away one of the officials who came to the house—obviously because he and the other legatees were afraid that Cleonymus had changed his intentions—and Cleonymus, dying suddenly the next day, had been unable to record his final wishes about the property. They further allege that Cleonymus's father, Polyarchus, had left instructions that, if anything happened to him, he was to leave his property to themselves.

A specious attempt is made to put the judges on the horns of a dilemma by the argument that either Cleonymus, in sending for the will, wished to revoke it in favour of his nephews, or else he was not in his right senses in neglecting their stronger claims both of affinity and of intimacy with him ; in either case, they urge, the judges must decide against the will and award the inheritance to them as next-of-kin.

Though presented with considerable skill the case is obviously a weak one, and no modern jury would have listened for a moment to such arguments in favour of upsetting an admittedly genuine will. The whole question is made to turn upon the intention of the testator ; but if, as the speaker urges, he had intended to alter his will, why should he have let so many years pass by without doing anything, and then, in his last illness, send one of the bene-ficiaries under the will to fetch the will in order that he might revoke it in favour of others ? Moreover, if he had intended to make his nephews his heirs, he would almost certainly have followed the practice so common at Athens of adopting one or more of them as his sons during his lifetime, and so assured

4

the continuity of family upon which the Athenians set so much store.

The speech contains no historical allusions by which its date might be determined, and there is no external evidence regarding any of the persons concerned in it.

I.—ΠΕΡΙ ΤΟΥ ΚΛΕΩΝΥΜΟΥ ΚΛΗΡΟΥ

ΥΠΟΘΕΣΙΣ

Ἀδελφιδοῖ Κλεωνύμου τελευτήσαντος ἐπὶ τὸν κλῆρον ἔρχονται κατὰ γένος, τὰς διαθήκας, ἃς παρέχονται εἰς αὐτοὺς[1] οἱ περὶ Φερένικον καὶ Σίμωνα καὶ Ποσείδιππον, γράψαι, ὡς ἀληθὲς ἦν, καὶ θεῖναι παρὰ τοῖς ἄρχουσιν ὁμολογοῦντες Κλεώνυμον κατὰ τὴν πρὸς Δεινίαν τὸν ἐπίτροπον αὐτῶν ὀργήν, ὕστερον δὲ ἐπιχειρήσαντα λῦσαι καὶ μεταπεμψάμενον τὸν ἀστυνόμον ἐξαίφνης ⟨ἀποθανεῖν⟩[2]· καὶ Πολύαρχον δὲ τὸν πάππον αὐτῶν, Κλεωνύμου δὲ πατέρα, προστάξαι, εἴ τι πάσχοι Κλεώνυμος, δοῦναι αὐτοῖς τὰ ὑπάρχοντα. ἡ στάσις ὅρος διπλοῦς κατὰ ἀμφισβήτησιν· οἱ μὲν γὰρ ἄλλοι ταῖς γενομέναις ἐξ ἀρχῆς διαθήκαις διισχυρίζονται, οἱ δέ, λέγοντες [φησὶν] ὅτι μετεκαλέσατο[3] τὸν ἄρχοντα, ἵνα λύσῃ αὐτάς, τοῖς[4] τελευταῖον παρὰ τοῦ Κλεωνύμου γενομένοις.

1 Πολλὴ μὲν ἡ μεταβολή μοι γέγονεν, ὦ ἄνδρες, τελευτήσαντος Κλεωνύμου. ἐκεῖνος γὰρ ζῶν μὲν ἡμῖν κατέλιπε τὴν οὐσίαν, ἀποθανὼν δὲ κινδυνεύειν περὶ αὐτῆς πεποίηκε. καὶ τότε μὲν οὕτως ὑπ' αὐτοῦ σωφρόνως ἐπαιδευόμεθα, ὥστ' οὐδ' ἀκρασόμενοι οὐδέποτ' ἤλθομεν ἐπὶ δικαστήριον, νῦν δὲ ἀγωνιούμενοι περὶ πάντων ἥκομεν τῶν ὑπαρχόντων· οὐ γὰρ τῶν Κλεωνύμου μόνον ἀμφισβητοῦ-

---

[1] αὐτοὺς Schoemann : καὶ τὰς.
[2] ἀποθανεῖν add. Aldus.
[3] μετεκαλέσατο Q : -αντο.
[4] τοῖς Sauppe : καί.

I. ON THE ESTATE OF CLEONYMUS

ARGUMENT

Cleonymus having died, his nephews claim his estate as
the natural heirs. They admit that the will in favour of
Pherenicus, Simon,[a] and Poseidippus, and produced by
these persons, was the genuine will of Cleonymus, and was
deposited by Cleonymus with the magistrates at a time when
he was angry with their guardian Deinias ; they allege,
however, that he subsequently tried to annul the will, and
after having sent for the police-magistrate, died suddenly.
They further allege that Polyarchus, their grandfather and
Cleonymus's father, instructed the latter, if anything should
happen to him, to leave his property to them. The question
at issue is a decision between the conflicting claims of the
two parties, one basing their claim on the original will, the
other relying on the last acts of Cleonymus, and alleging
that he sent for the magistrate in order to annul the will.

Great indeed, gentlemen, is the change which the
death of Cleonymus has brought upon me. In his
lifetime he devised his property to us ; his death has
exposed us to the danger of losing it. While he lived,
we were so discreetly brought up by him that we
never entered a law court even as listeners ; now we
have come here to fight for all that we possess ; for
our opponents claim not only Cleonymus's property,

[a] The insertion of Simon's name here is a mistake ; he
was only a friend of Cleonymus (see §§ 31, 32).

σιν ἀλλὰ καὶ τῶν πατρῴων, ὀφείλειν ἐπὶ τούτοις
2 ⟨ἡμᾶς⟩[1] ἐκείνῳ φάσκοντες ἀργύριον. καὶ οἱ μὲν
οἰκεῖοι καὶ οἱ προσήκοντες [ἐπὶ τούτοις] οἱ
τούτων ἀξιοῦσιν ἡμᾶς καὶ τῶν ὁμολογουμένων, ὧν
Κλεώνυμος κατέλιπεν, αὐτοῖς τούτων ἰσομοιρῆσαι·
οὗτοι δὲ εἰς τοῦτο ἥκουσιν ἀναισχυντίας, ὥστε καὶ
τὰ πατρῷα προσαφελέσθαι ζητοῦσιν ἡμᾶς, οὐκ
ἀγνοοῦντες, ὦ ἄνδρες, τὸ δίκαιον, ἀλλὰ πολλὴν
ἡμῶν ἐρημίαν καταγνόντες.

3   Σκέψασθε γὰρ οἷς ἑκάτεροι πιστεύοντες ὡς ὑμᾶς
εἰσεληλύθαμεν· οὗτοι μὲν διαθήκαις ἰσχυριζόμενοι
τοιαύταις, ἃς ἐκεῖνος διέθετο[2] μὲν οὐχ ἡμῖν ἐγκαλῶν ἀλλ' ὀργισθεὶς τῶν οἰκείων τινὶ τῶν ἡμετέρων,
ἔλυσε δὲ πρὸ τοῦ θανάτου, πέμψας Ποσείδιππον
4 ἐπὶ τὴν ἀρχήν· ἡμεῖς δὲ γένει μὲν ἐγγυτάτω προσήκοντες, χρώμενοι δὲ ἐκείνῳ πάντων οἰκειότατα,
δεδωκότων δ' ἡμῖν καὶ τῶν νόμων κατὰ τὴν ἀγχιστείαν καὶ αὐτοῦ τοῦ Κλεωνύμου διὰ τὴν φιλίαν
τὴν ὑπάρχουσαν αὐτῷ, ἔτι δὲ Πολυάρχου, τοῦ
πατρὸς ⟨τοῦ⟩[3] Κλεωνύμου, πάππου δ' ἡμετέρου,
προστάξαντος, εἴ τι πάθοι Κλεώνυμος ἄπαις, ἡμῖν
5 δοῦναι τὰ αὐτοῦ. τοσούτων τοίνυν ἡμῖν ὑπ-
αρχόντων οὗτοι, καὶ συγγενεῖς ὄντες καὶ οὐδὲν
δίκαιον εἰπεῖν ἔχοντες, οὐκ αἰσχύνονται καταστή-
σαντες ἡμᾶς εἰς ἀγῶνα περὶ τούτων, περὶ ὧν αἰσχρὸν ἦν ἀμφισβητῆσαι καὶ τοῖς μηδὲν προσ-
6 ήκουσιν. οὐχ ὁμοίως δέ μοι δοκοῦμεν, ὦ ἄνδρες,
διακεῖσθαι πρὸς ἀλλήλους. ἐγὼ μὲν γὰρ οὐχ ὅτι
ἀδίκως κινδυνεύω, τοῦθ' ἡγοῦμαι μέγιστον εἶναι
τῶν παρόντων κακῶν, ἀλλ' ὅτι ἀγωνίζομαι πρὸς

---

[1] ἡμᾶς add. Buermann.
[2] διέθετο Scaliger: δὴ ὑπέθετο.   [3] τοῦ add. Dobree.

but also our patrimony, alleging that we owe his estate money as well. Their own friends and relatives concede our right to an equal share with them even in the undisputed property which Cleonymus left behind him; but our opponents have become so impudent that they are seeking to deprive us even of our patrimony—not because they are ignorant, gentlemen, of what is just, but because they are convinced of our utter helplessness.

For consider the grounds on which the respective parties rely in coming before you. Our opponents insist upon a will which our uncle drew up, not because he had any ground of complaint against us, but through anger against one of our relatives, and which he annulled before his death, sending Poseidippus to the magistrate's office for the purpose. We were Cleonymus's nearest relatives, and lived on terms of greater intimacy with him than did anyone; and the laws have given us the right of succession as next of kin, as also did Cleonymus himself, owing to the affection which subsisted between us. And, further, Polyarchus, Cleonymus's father and our grandfather, gave instructions that, if Cleonymus should die without issue, he was to leave his property to us. Though we have all these claims, our opponents, though they are our relatives and have no justice to urge, are not ashamed to bring us into court in a matter about which it would be disgraceful even for those who are no relatives at all to dispute. But I think, gentlemen, that we and our opponents have not the same feelings towards one another; for I regard it as the worst feature of my present troubles, not that I am being unjustly placed in peril, but that

9

οἰκείους, οὓς οὐδ᾽ ἀμύνεσθαι καλῶς ἔχει· οὐ γὰρ
ἂν ἐλάττω συμφορὰν ἡγησαίμην¹ κακῶς ποιεῖν τούτους ἀμυνόμενος, οἰκείους ὄντας, ἢ κακῶς παθεῖν
7 ἐξ ἀρχῆς ὑπὸ τούτων. οὗτοι δ᾽ οὐ τοιαύτην ἔχουσι
[30] τὴν γνώμην, ἀλλ᾽ | ἤκουσιν ἐφ᾽ ἡμᾶς καὶ τοὺς
φίλους παρακαλέσαντες καὶ ῥήτορας παρασκευασά-
μενοι καὶ οὐδὲν ἀπολείποντες τῆς αὑτῶν δυνάμεως,
ὥσπερ, ὦ ἄνδρες, ἐχθροὺς τιμωρησόμενοι, καὶ οὐκ
ἀναγκαίους καὶ συγγενεῖς κακῶς² ποιήσοντες.
8 τὴν μὲν οὖν τούτων ἀναισχυντίαν καὶ τὴν αἰσχρο-
κέρδειαν ἔτι μᾶλλον γνώσεσθε, ἐπειδὰν πάντων
ἀκούσητε· ὅθεν δ᾽ οἶμαι τάχιστ᾽ ἂν ὑμᾶς μαθεῖν
περὶ ὧν ἀμφισβητοῦμεν, ἐντεῦθεν ἄρξομαι διδάσκειν.
9 Δεινίας γὰρ ὁ τοῦ πατρὸς ἀδελφὸς ἐπετρόπευσεν
ἡμᾶς, θεῖος ὢν ὀρφανοὺς ὄντας. Κλεωνύμῳ³ δ᾽
οὗτος, ὦ ἄνδρες, διάφορος ὢν ἔτυχεν. ὁπότερος
μὲν οὖν αὐτῶν ἦν τῆς διαφορᾶς αἴτιος, ἴσως οὐκ
ἐμὸν ἔργον ἐστὶ κατηγορεῖν· πλὴν τοσοῦτόν γε ἂν
δικαίως αὐτοῖς ἀμφοτέροις μεμψαίμην, ὅτι καὶ
φίλοι τέως ὄντες καὶ προφάσεως οὐδεμιᾶς γενομένης ἐκ λόγων τινῶν οὕτως εἰκῇ πρὸς ἀλλήλους
10 ἔχθραν ἀνείλοντο. τότε⁴ γοῦν ἐκ ταύτης τῆς
ὀργῆς Κλεώνυμος ταύτας ποιεῖται τὰς διαθήκας,
οὐχ ἡμῖν ἐγκαλῶν, ὡς ὕστερον †ἐσώθη†⁵ ἔλεγεν,
ὁρῶν δὲ ἡμᾶς ἐπιτρεπομένους ὑπὸ Δεινίου, καὶ
δεδιὼς μὴ τελευτήσειεν αὐτὸς ἔτι παῖδας ἡμᾶς
καταλιπὼν καὶ τῆς οὐσίας ἡμετέρας οὔσης γένοιτο
κύριος Δεινίας· ἡγεῖτο γὰρ δεινὸν εἶναι τὸν ἔχθιστον τῶν οἰκείων ἐπίτροπον καὶ κύριον τῶν

---

¹ ἡγησαίμην Aldus : -άμην. ² κακῶς Stephanus : κακοὺς.
³ Κλεωνύμῳ Taylor : -ου. ⁴ τότε Schoemann : ὅτι.
⁵ ἐσώθη AQ manifeste corruptum.

10

I am at law with kinsmen, against whom even to defend oneself is not creditable ; for I should not regard it as a less misfortune to injure them, my relatives, in my own defence than to have been originally injured by them. They have no such sentiments, but have come against us after calling all their friends to their aid, and procuring orators and mustering all their forces, as though, gentlemen, they were going to punish foes, and not to harm kinsmen and relatives. You will understand their shamelessness and greed better when you have heard the whole story. I will begin my narrative at a point which will, I think, enable you most readily to understand the matters in dispute.

We were orphans, and our uncle Deinias, our father's brother, assumed the guardianship of us. Now it happened, sirs, that he was at variance with Cleonymus ; which of the two was to blame for this, it is not perhaps my business to determine, but I might justly find fault with both of them alike, inasmuch as, having previously been friends, without any real pretext, as the result of certain words which were spoken, they became so hastily at enmity with one another. It was at this time, under the influence of this anger, that Cleonymus made this will : not because he had any complaint against us, as he subsequently stated, but because he saw that we were under the guardianship of Deinias, and was afraid that he might himself die while we were minors, and that Deinias might obtain control of the property, if it became ours ; for he could not bear to think of leaving his bitterest enemy as the guardian

αὑτοῦ καταλιπεῖν, καὶ ποιεῖν αὐτῷ τὰ νομιζόμενα
τοῦτον, ἕως ἡμεῖς ἡβήσαιμεν, ᾧ ζῶν διάφορος ἦν·
11 ταῦτα διανοηθεὶς ἐκεῖνος, εἴτ' ὀρθῶς εἴτε μή, τὰς
διαθήκας ταύτας διέθετο. καὶ εὐθὺς ἐρωτῶντος
τοῦ Δεινίου παραχρῆμα εἴ τι ἡμῖν ἢ τῷ πατρὶ
ἐγκαλεῖ τῷ ἡμετέρῳ, ἀπεκρίνατο πάντων τῶν
πολιτῶν ἐναντίον ὅτι οὐδὲν πονηρὸν ἐγκαλεῖ, καὶ
ἐμαρτύρησεν ὡς ὀργιζόμενος ἐκείνῳ καὶ οὐκ
ὀρθῶς βουλευόμενος ταῦτα διέθετο. πῶς γὰρ ἂν
εὖ φρονῶν, ὦ ἄνδρες, κακῶς ποιεῖν ἡμᾶς ἐβου-
12 λήθη, τοὺς μηδὲν αὐτὸν ἠδικηκότας; ὕστερον
δὲ τούτων, ὃ μέγιστον ἡμῖν τεκμήριον ὅτι οὐδὲ
ταῦτα ἔπραξεν ἡμᾶς βλάπτειν βουλόμενος· τελευτήσαντος γὰρ Δεινίου καὶ τῶν πραγμάτων ἡμῖν
πονηρῶς ἐχόντων οὐδὲ περιεῖδεν ἡμᾶς οὐδενὸς
ἐνδεεῖς ὄντας, ἀλλ' αὐτοὺς μὲν εἰς τὴν οἰκίαν τὴν
αὑτοῦ κομισάμενος ἐπαίδευε, τὴν δ' οὐσίαν ἀφελέσθαι τῶν χρηστῶν ἐπιβουλευσάντων ἔσωσεν
ἡμῖν, ἐπεμελεῖτό τε ὁμοίως τῶν ἡμετέρων ὥσπερ
13 τῶν αὑτοῦ πραγμάτων. καίτοι χρὴ θεωρεῖν αὐτοῦ
τὴν ἔννοιαν ἐκ τούτων τῶν ἔργων μᾶλλον ἢ ἐκ τῶν
διαθηκῶν, καὶ τεκμηρίοις χρῆσθαι μὴ τοῖς μετ'
ὀργῆς πραχθεῖσιν, ἐν οἷς ἅπαντες πεφύκαμεν ἁμαρ-
τάνειν, ἀλλ' ἀφ' ὧν ὕστερον φανερὰν τὴν αὑτοῦ
ἔννοιαν ἐποίησεν. ἔτι γὰρ μᾶλλον ἐν τοῖς τελευ-
14 ταίοις ἐδήλωσεν ὡς εἶχε πρὸς ἡμᾶς. ἤδη γὰρ
ἀσθενῶν ταύτην τὴν νόσον ἐξ ἧς ἐτελεύτησεν,
ἐβουλήθη ταύτας τὰς διαθήκας ἀνελεῖν καὶ προσέταξε Ποσειδίππῳ τὴν ἀρχὴν εἰσαγαγεῖν. ὁ δὲ οὐ
μόνον οὐκ εἰσήγαγεν, ἀλλὰ καὶ τὸν ἐλθόντα τῶν
ἀρχόντων ἐπὶ τὴν θύραν ἀπέπεμψεν.[1] ὀργισθεὶς

---

[1] ἀπέπεμψεν Stephanus: ἀπ-.

of his relatives and in control of his property, and
of the customary rites being performed over him,
until we grew up, by one with whom he had been
at variance in his lifetime. Such were the sentiments under which, whether rightly or wrongly, he
made this will; and when Deinias immediately
asked him at the time whether he had any grievance
against us or our father, he replied in the hearing of
all that he had no fault to find with us, and so testified
that it was his anger against Deinias and not his calm
judgement which decided him to make this will. For
surely, gentlemen, if he had been in his right senses,
he would never have wished to injure us, who had
never wronged him. His subsequent conduct is the
strongest proof in support of our contention, that
even in acting thus he did not intend to injure
us. For after Deinias's death, when things were
going badly with us, he would not allow us to lack
anything, but took us into his own house and brought
us up, and saved our property when our creditors were
scheming against it, and looked after our interests
as though they were his own. It is from these acts
rather than from the will that his intentions must be
discerned, and inferences must be drawn not from
what he did under the influence of anger—through
which we are all liable to err—but from his subsequent acts, whereby he made his attitude quite clear.
In his last hours he showed still more plainly his
feelings toward us. For, when he was suffering from
the illness of which he died, he wished to revoke this
will, and directed Poseidippus to fetch the magistrate.
Not only did he fail to do so, but he even sent away
one of the magistrates who had come to the door.

δὲ τούτῳ Κλεώνυμος πάλιν ἐς τὴν ὑστεραίαν
Διοκλεῖ καλέσαι τοὺς ἄρχοντας προσέταξε, καὶ
οὐχ οὕτως ὡς ἀσθενῶν διακείμενος· ἀλλ' ἔτι πολλῶν οὐσῶν ἐλπίδων, ἐξαπίνης τῆς νυκτὸς ταύτης
ἀπέθανεν.

15 Πρῶτον μὲν οὖν ὑμῖν παρέξομαι μάρτυρας ὡς
οὐχ ἡμῖν ἐγκαλῶν ἀλλὰ Δεινίᾳ πολεμῶν ταύτας
τὰς διαθήκας διέθετο, ἔπειτα ὡς ἐκείνου τελευτήσαντος ἐπεμελεῖτό τε τῶν ἡμετέρων ἁπάντων, καὶ
αὐτοὺς[1] ἐπαίδευεν εἰς τὴν οἰκίαν τὴν αὐτοῦ κομισάμενος, πρὸς δὲ τούτοις ὡς Ποσείδιππον ἔπεμ-
ψεν ἐπὶ τὸν ἀστυνόμον, οὗτος δ' οὐ μόνον αὐτὸς
οὐκ εἰσεκάλεσεν, ἀλλὰ καὶ ἐλθόντα ἐπὶ τὴν θύραν
16 [ἀρχονίδην] ἀπέπεμψεν. ὡς οὖν ἀληθῆ λέγω, κάλει
μοι τοὺς μάρτυρας.

ΜΑΡΤΥΡΕΣ

Ἔτι τοίνυν ὡς οἱ τούτων φίλοι καὶ Κηφίσανδρος
ἠξίουν νείμασθαι τὴν οὐσίαν καὶ τὸ τρίτον μέρος
ἡμᾶς ἔχειν ἁπάντων τῶν Κλεωνύμου, καὶ τούτων
[37] μοι κάλει | μάρτυρας.

ΜΑΡΤΥΡΕΣ

17 Ἡγοῦμαι μὲν τοίνυν, ὦ ἄνδρες, πᾶσι τοῖς τῶν
κλήρων ἀμφισβητοῦσιν, ὅταν ἀποφήνωσι σφᾶς
αὐτοὺς ὥσπερ ἡμεῖς καὶ τῷ γένει προτέρους ὄντας
καὶ τῇ φιλίᾳ τῇ πρὸς τὸν τετελευτηκότα, περί-
εργον εἶναι τοὺς ἄλλους λόγους λέγειν· ἐπειδὴ δὲ
τούτων οὐδέτερον ἔχοντες οὗτοι[2] τολμῶσι τῶν οὐ
προσηκόντων ἀμφισβητεῖν καὶ ψευδεῖς παρασκευά-
ζονται λόγους, βούλομαι βραχέα καὶ περὶ τούτων

---

[1] αὐτοὺς Reiske: αὐτὸς.　　　[2] οὗτοι Bekker: οὕτω.

14

Cleonymus was enraged at this, and again gave instructions, this time to Diocles, to summon the magistrates for the following day, though he was in no fit state to transact business owing to his illness; but, although there was still good hope of his recovery, he died suddenly that night.

I will now produce witnesses to prove, first, that the motive of Cleonymus in making this will was not any grievance against us, but his enmity towards Deinias ; secondly, that after Deinias's death he looked after all our interests, and took us to his own house and brought us up ; and, thirdly, that he sent Poseidippus for the magistrate, but not only did he himself fail to summon him, but also sent him away when he came to the door. To prove the truth of my statements, please call the witnesses.

WITNESSES

Next call witnesses to testify that the friends of our opponents, including Cephisander, were of opinion that the parties should share the estate, and that we should have one third of all that Cleonymus possessed.

WITNESSES

I think, gentlemen, that in any dispute about an inheritance, if the claimants can prove, as we can, that they are nearer both in affinity and in affection to the deceased, all other arguments are superfluous. But, since my opponents, though they can urge neither of these titles, have the impudence to claim what does not belong to them, and are trumping up false arguments, I should like to say a few words on

15

18 αὐτῶν εἰπεῖν. ἰσχυρίζονται γὰρ ταῖς διαθήκαις,
λέγοντες ὡς Κλεώνυμος μετεπέμπετο τὴν ἀρχὴν
οὐ λῦσαι βουλόμενος αὐτὰς ἀλλ᾽ ἐπανορθῶσαι καὶ
βεβαιῶσαι σφίσιν αὐτοῖς τὴν δωρεάν. ὑμεῖς δὲ
σκοπεῖσθε τὰς διαθήκας τὰς μετ᾽ ὀργῆς γενομένας
πότερα εἰκός ἐστι βουληθῆναι Κλεώνυμον ἀνελεῖν,
ἐπειδὴ πρὸς ἡμᾶς οἰκείως ἔσχεν, ἢ σκοπεῖν ὅπως
ἔτι βεβαιότερον ἡμᾶς ἀποστερήσει[1] τῶν αὐτοῦ.

19 τοῖς μὲν γὰρ ἄλλοις κἀκείνων ὧν ἂν ὀργισθέντες
τοὺς οἰκείους ἀδικήσωσιν ὕστερον μεταμέλει·
οὗτοι δὲ ἐκεῖνον ἀποφαίνουσιν, ἐν ᾧ πρὸς ἡμᾶς
οἰκειότατα διέκειτο, μᾶλλον βεβαιοῦν τὴν διαθήκην βουλόμενον, ἣν ὀργιζόμενος ἐποιήσατο.
ὥστ᾽ εἰ καὶ ἡμεῖς ὁμολογήσαιμεν[2] ταῦτα καὶ ὑμεῖς
αὐτοὶ πιστεύσαιτε,[3] ἐνθυμεῖσθε ὅτι παράνοιαν

20 αὐτοῦ τὴν μεγίστην οὗτοι κατηγοροῦσι. τίς γὰρ
ἂν γένοιτο ταύτης μανία μείζων, ἢ τότε μὲν ὅτε
Δεινίᾳ διάφορος ὢν ἔτυχεν, ἡμᾶς κακῶς ποιεῖν τε
καὶ διατίθεσθαι τοιαύτας διαθήκας, ἐξ ὧν οὐκ
ἐκεῖνον ἐτιμωρεῖτο ἀλλὰ τοὺς οἰκειοτάτους ἠδίκει·
νυνὶ δὲ χρώμενος ἡμῖν καὶ περὶ πλείστου ποιούμενος ἁπάντων, μόνους ἐβουλήθη τοὺς ἀδελφιδοῦς,
ὡς οὗτοί φασιν, ἀκλήρους ποιῆσαι τῶν ἑαυτοῦ.
καὶ τίς ἂν εὖ φρονῶν, ὦ ἄνδρες, τοιαῦτα περὶ τῶν

21 αὑτοῦ βουλεύσαιτο; ὥστ᾽ ἐκ τούτων τῶν λόγων
ῥᾳδίαν ὑμῖν[4] τὴν διάγνωσιν πεποιήκασι περὶ αὐτῶν.
εἰ μὲν γὰρ ἀνελεῖν τὰς διαθήκας βουλόμενος μετεπέμπετο τὴν ἀρχήν, ὥσπερ ἡμεῖς φαμεν, οὐδεὶς
ἔνεστι τούτοις λόγος· εἰ δ᾽ οὕτω παραφρονῶν

---

[1] ἀποστερήσει Baiter-Sauppe : -ρήσειε.
[2] ὁμολογήσαιμεν Reiske : -ομεν.
[3] πιστεύσαιτε Reiske : -οιτε.   [4] ὑμῖν Aldus : ἡμῖν.

these very points. They insist upon the will, declaring that Cleonymus sent for the magistrate because he wished, not to revoke it, but to correct it and to confirm the bequest in their favour. Now consider which is the more likely, that Cleonymus, now that he had become friendly towards us, wished to cancel the will which he had made in anger, or that he was seeking a still surer means to deprive us of his property. All other men afterwards repent of wrongs which they have done to their relatives in moments of anger ; Cleonymus is represented by my opponents as desirous, when he was on terms of the closest affection with us, still further to confirm the will which he made in anger. So, even if we were to admit that he did so and you yourselves were to believe it, my opponents, you must observe, are accusing Cleonymus of utter madness. For what greater act of insanity could be committed than that Cleonymus, when he was at variance with Deinias, should wrong us and make a will whereby he did not punish Deinias but wronged his nearest and dearest, whereas now, when he was on terms of the closest friendship with us and held us in higher esteem than anyone else, he should have wished, as my opponents allege, to leave his nephews alone without any share in his property ? Who, gentlemen, in his right mind would determine so to dispose of his estate ? By these arguments they have made it easy for you to decide their case. For if it was to revoke the will, as we assert, that Cleonymus sent for the magistrate, they have no possible plea to urge ; if he was so mad as always to have the

17

ἔτυχεν ὥσθ' ἡμᾶς ἀεὶ περὶ ἐλαχίστου ποιεῖσθαι,
τοὺς γένει πρωτεύοντας καὶ χρωμένους αὐτῷ
πάντων οἰκειότατα, δικαίως ἂν δήπου τὰς τοιαύτας
διαθήκας ἀκύρους ποιήσαιτε.

22 Ἔτι τοίνυν ἐνθυμεῖσθε ὅτι φάσκοντες καλεῖν
τὴν ἀρχὴν Κλεώνυμον, ἵνα βεβαιώσῃ τὴν αὑτῶν
δωρεάν, προσταχθὲν αὐτοῖς οὐκ ἐτόλμησαν εἰσαγαγεῖν, ἀλλὰ καὶ τὸν ἐλθόντα τῶν ἀρχόντων ἐπὶ
τὴν θύραν ἀπέπεμψαν. καὶ δυοῖν τοῖν ἐναντιω-
τάτοιν θάτερα μέλλοντες, ἢ τὴν οὐσίαν ἕξειν
βεβαιοτέραν ἢ ἐκείνῳ[1] μὴ ποιήσαντες ἀπεχθήσε-
σθαι, τὴν ἀπέχθειαν εἵλοντο μᾶλλον ταύτης τῆς
δωρεᾶς. καίτοι πῶς ἂν ἕτερα τούτων γένοιτο
23 ἀπιστότερα; τοὺς μὲν τηλικαῦτα μέλλοντας ἐκ τοῦ
πράγματος κερδαίνειν, ὥσπερ ζημιωθησομένους, φυ-
λάξασθαι τὴν διακονίαν, Κλεώνυμον δ' ὑπὲρ τῆς τούτων ὠφελείας τοσαύτην ποιήσασθαι σπουδὴν ὥστε
Ποσειδίππῳ μέν, ὅτι κατημέλησεν, ὀργισθῆναι, Διοκλέους δὲ ταὐτὰ[2] πάλιν ἐς τὴν ὑστεραίαν δεηθῆναι;

24 Εἰ γὰρ δή, ὦ ἄνδρες, ὡς οὗτοί φασιν, ἐν ταῖς
νῦν γεγραμμέναις διαθήκαις ἔδωκεν αὐτοῖς τὴν οὐσίαν, καὶ τοῦτ' ἄξιον εἶναί μοι δοκεῖ θαυμάζειν, ὅ
τί ποτε ἐπανορθώσας κυριωτέρας αὐτὰς ἡγεῖτ'[3] ἂν
ποιῆσαι· τοῖς γὰρ ἄλλοις οὗτος ὅρος ἐστίν, ὦ
25 ἄνδρες, τῶν δωρεῶν. ἔτι δὲ καὶ εἴ τι προσγρά-
ψαι τούτοις ἐβούλετο, διὰ τί οὐκ ἐν ἑτέρῳ γράψας
αὐτὰ γραμματείῳ κατέλιπεν, ἐπειδὴ τὰ γράμματα
παρὰ τῶν ἀρχόντων οὐκ ἐδυνήθη λαβεῖν· ἀνελεῖν
μὲν γάρ,[4] ὦ ἄνδρες, οὐχ οἷός τ' ἦν ἄλλο γραμματεῖον ἢ τὸ παρὰ τῇ ἀρχῇ κείμενον· γράψαι δ'

---

[1] ἐκείνῳ Q: ἐκεῖνο.   [2] ταὐτὰ Cobet: ταῦτα.
[3] ἡγεῖτ' Cobet: ἡγοῖτ'.   [4] μὲν γάρ Q: γάρ.

least regard for us, his nearest kinsmen and most intimate friends, you would be justified, I presume, in declaring such a will invalid.

Next remark, that, though they allege that Cleonymus asked for the magistrate to be summoned in order to confirm the bequest to themselves, yet, when they were ordered to do so, they dared not bring him in, and also sent away one of the magistrates who came to the door. Two alternatives lay before them, either to have the inheritance confirmed to them or else to offend Cleonymus by not doing what he asked ; they preferred to incur his enmity rather than to secure this bequest ! Could anything be more incredible than this ? Those who had so much to gain by doing what he asked, avoided rendering this service, as though they were going to lose by it, while Cleonymus showed so much zeal for their advantage that he was angry with Poseidippus for neglecting his wishes, and repeated the request to Diocles for the following day !

If, gentlemen, Cleonymus, as my opponents allege, bequeathed the estate to them by the will in its present form, I cannot help wondering by what alteration he thought he could make it more valid ; for to everybody else, sirs, such a will is the most complete form of bequest. Furthermore, if he wished to add anything to these dispositions, why did he not record and leave behind him his wishes in a codicil, when he found himself unable to procure the original will from the officials? For he could not annul any other document except that which was deposited at the magistrate's office ; but he was at

ἐξῆν εἰς ἕτερον εἴ τι ἐβούλετο, καὶ μηδὲ τοῦθ'
26 ἡμῖν ἀμφισβητήσιμον ἐᾶν. εἰ τοίνυν καὶ τοῦτο
συγχωρήσαιμεν, ὡς ἐκεῖνος ἐπανορθῶσαι τὰς διαθήκας ἐβούλετο, πᾶσι δήπου φανερὸν ὑμῖν¹ ἐστιν
ὅτι οὐκ ὀρθῶς αὐτὰς ἔχειν ἡγεῖτο. καίτοι σκοπεῖτε
καὶ ἐντεῦθεν τὴν ἀναισχυντίαν αὐτῶν, οἵτινες
ταύτας τὰς διαθήκας ἀξιοῦσιν εἶναι κυρίας, ἃς
ὁμολογοῦσι μηδ' αὐτὸν τὸν διαθέμενον [ταῦτα]
ὀρθῶς ἔχειν ἡγεῖσθαι, καὶ πείθουσιν ὑμᾶς ἐναντία
καὶ τοῖς νόμοις καὶ τῷ δικαίῳ καὶ τῇ τοῦ τετε-
27 λευτηκότος γνώμῃ ψηφίσασθαι. ἔτι τοίνυν τούτων ἁπάντων ἀναιδέστατος τῶν λόγων ἐστίν, ὅταν
τολμῶσι λέγειν ὡς Κλεώνυμος οὐδὲν ἡμᾶς τῶν
αὑτοῦ λαβεῖν ἐβούλετο. καίτοι, ὦ ἄνδρες, τίνας ἂν
ἄλλους ταῦτα ἔχειν ἐβουλήθη μᾶλλον ἢ τούτους,
οὓς καὶ ζῶν ἐκ τῶν αὑτοῦ πλεῖστα τῶν οἰκείων
28 ὠφέλει; πάντων δ' ἂν εἴη θαυμασιώτατον, εἰ
Κηφίσανδρος μὲν ὁ τούτων οἰκεῖος δίκαιον ἡγεῖτο
εἶναι μέρος ἕκαστον ἡμῶν ἔχειν τῆς οὐσίας, Κλεώνυμος δ' ὃς ἦν ἡμῖν οἰκειότατος² καὶ ἡμᾶς εἰς τὴν
οἰκίαν τὴν αὑτοῦ λαβὼν ἐθεράπευε καὶ ἐπεμελεῖτο
τῶν ἡμετέρων ὥσπερ τῶν αὑτοῦ πραγμάτων, οὗτος
μόνος ἐβούλετο ἡμᾶς ἀκλήρους εἶναι τῶν αὑτοῦ.
29 καὶ τίς ἂν ὑμῶν πιστεύσειεν εὐνουστέρους καὶ
μετριωτέρους τοὺς ἀντιδίκους ἡμῖν εἶναι τῶν
οἰκειοτάτων; κἀκεῖνον μέν, ᾧ καὶ ἀναγκαῖον εὖ
ποιεῖν ἡμᾶς καὶ αἰσχρὸν ἡμῶν ἀμελῆσαι, μηδὲν τῶν
αὑτοῦ ἡμῖν δοῦναι· τούτους δέ, οἷς οὔτ' ἀνάγκη
ἐστὶν οὔτ' αἰσχύνην οὐδεμίαν φέρει, τῶν οὐ προσηκόντων, ὥς φασιν, ἡμῖν μεταδιδόναι; ἀλλὰ ταῦτα
μέν, ὦ ἄνδρες, πολλὴν ἀπιστίαν ἔχει.

¹ ὑμῖν Q: ἡμῖν.　　² οἰκειότατος Bekker: οἰκειότερος.

liberty to record anything he liked in a codicil, and thus avoid leaving this matter in dispute between us. If we concede also that Cleonymus wished to alter his will, it is, I think, obvious to you all that he was dissatisfied with it. Here, again, mark the impudence of our opponents, who claim that the will should be valid, though they admit that even the testator himself was dissatisfied with it, and are trying to persuade you to give a verdict which is contrary to the laws and to justice and to the intentions of the deceased. Most impudent of all their statements is when they dare to say that Cleonymus did not wish us to have any of his property. Whom, gentlemen, could he have wished to have it rather than those to whom in his lifetime he gave more assistance out of his private means than to any other of his relatives? It would be most extraordinary if, while Cephisander, the kinsman of our opponents, thought it fair that each of us should have a share of the property, yet Cleonymus, who was our nearest relative and received us into his house and cared for us and looked after our interests as though they were his own, was the only person who wished that we should receive no share of his estate. Who of you could possibly believe that our opponents-at-law are kinder and more considerate towards us than our closest kindred; and that he, who was bound to treat us well and in whom it would have been disgraceful to neglect us, left us none of his property, whereas these men, who are under no obligation to us and whose disregard of us involves no disgrace, offered us a share of the property to which, as they say, we have no claim? These suppositions, gentlemen, are perfectly incredible.

21

30 Ἔπειτα, εἰ μὲν καὶ νῦν οὕτω πρὸς ἀμφοτέρους
ἡμᾶς ἔχων ἐτελεύτησεν, ὥσπερ ὅτε τὰς διαθήκας
ταύτας ἐποιήσατο, εἰκότως ἄν τις ὑμῶν πιστεύ-
σειε¹ τοῖς λόγοις τοῖς τουτωνί· νυνὶ δὲ πᾶν τοὐναντίον εὑρήσετε. τότε μὲν γὰρ ἔτυχε Δεινίᾳ, ὃς
ἡμᾶς ἐπετρόπευε, διάφορος ὢν ἡμῖν τε οὔπω²
χρώμενος τούτοις τε ἅπασιν ἐπιτηδείως διακεί-
μενος· νῦν δὲ τούτων μέν τισι διάφορος ἐγένετο,
31 ἡμῖν δὲ πάντων ἐχρῆτο οἰκειότατα. καὶ ἐξ ὧν
μὲν αὐτῷ πρὸς τούτους ἐγένετο ἡ διαφορά, περί-
εργόν ἐστι λέγειν· σημεῖα δ' ὑμῖν³ ἐρῶ μεγάλα, περὶ
ὧν καὶ μάρτυρας ἔξω παρασχέσθαι. πρῶτον μὲν
γὰρ θύων τῷ Διονύσῳ, καὶ τοὺς οἰκείους ἅπαντας
καλέσας καὶ τῶν ἄλλων πολιτῶν πολλούς, Φερένικον οὐδαμοῦ παρεστήσατο. ἔπειτα μικρὸν πρὶν
τελευτῆσαι βαδίζων εἰς Πάνορμον μετὰ Σίμωνος,
καὶ συντυχὼν αὐτῷ, προσειπεῖν οὐκ ἐτόλμησεν.
32 ἔτι δὲ πρὸς τούτοις πυνθανομένου τὴν διαφορὰν
τοῦ Σίμωνος τήν τ' ἔχθραν διηγήσατο, καὶ προσ-
ηπείλησεν ὅτι δηλώσειε⁴ ποτ' ἂν τούτῳ ὡς διά-
κειται πρὸς αὐτόν. καὶ ὡς ἀληθῆ λέγω, κάλει μάρτυρας.

⟨ΜΑΡΤΥΡΕΣ⟩

33 Οἴεσθε οὖν, ὦ ἄνδρες, τὸν οὑτωσὶ πρὸς ἑκατέρους ἡμᾶς διακείμενον ἡμῖν μέν, οἷς οἰκειότατα
ἐχρῆτο, οὕτω ποιεῖν ὅπως μηδὲ λόγον ὑπολείψει,⁵

---

¹ πιστεύσειε Scheibe : πιστεῦσαι.   ² οὔπω Mai : οὕτω.
³ ὑμῖν Q : ἡμῖν.   ⁴ δηλώσειε Dobree : δηλώσει.
⁵ ὅπως μηδὲ λόγον ὑπολείψει Q : ὥστε μ. λ. ὑπολείψειν A :
ὥστε μηδὲν ὅλως ὑπολείψειν Photiades.

Again, if Cleonymus had entertained the same feelings towards both parties at the time of his death as when he made the will, some of you might reasonably believe my opponents' story ; as it is, you will find that the exact contrary is true. *Then* he was at variance with Deinias, who was acting as our guardian, and was not yet on terms of close intimacy with us, and was kindly disposed towards all my opponents ; at the time of his death he had become at variance with some of them, and was living on terms of closer intimacy with us than with anyone else. On the causes of the quarrel between my opponents and Cleonymus it is unnecessary for me to dwell ; but I will mention some striking proofs of its existence, of which I shall be able also to produce witnesses. Firstly, when he was sacrificing to Dionysus, he invited all his relatives and many other citizens besides, but he offered no place to Pherenicus. Again, when, shortly before his death, he was journeying to Panormus [a] with Simon and met Pherenicus, he could not bring himself to speak to him. Furthermore, when Simon asked him about the quarrel, he narrated the circumstances of their enmity, and threatened that some day he would show Pherenicus what were his feelings towards him. Now call witnesses to prove the truth of these statements.

WITNESSES

Do you imagine, gentlemen, that Cleonymus, being thus disposed towards both parties, acted thus towards us, with whom he lived on terms of the closest affection, in order to leave us without a word to say,

[a] A harbour on the south-east coast of Attica between Thoricus and Sunium.

ISAEUS

τούτοις δέ, ὧν τισι καὶ διάφορος ἦν, σκοπεῖν ὅπως
ἅπασαν βεβαιώσει τὴν οὐσίαν; καὶ τούτους μὲν νῦν
περὶ πλείονος ποιεῖσθαι ταύτης ὑπούσης τῆς ἔχθρας, ἡμᾶς δὲ τοσαύτης οἰκειότητος καὶ φιλίας
34 γενομένης πειρᾶσθαι μᾶλλον κακῶς ποιεῖν; ἀλλ'
ἔγωγε, εἰ κατηγορεῖν ἐβούλοντο τῶν διαθηκῶν ἢ
τοῦ τετελευτηκότος, οὐκ οἶδ' ὅ τι ἂν ἄλλο πρὸς
ὑμᾶς εἶπον, οἵ γε τὰς διαθήκας μὲν ἀποφαίνουσιν
οὔτ' ὀρθῶς ἐχούσας οὔτ' ἀρεσκούσας τῷ διαθε-
μένῳ, τοῦ δὲ τοσαύτην μανίαν κατηγοροῦσιν, ὥστε
φασὶν αὐτὸν¹ περὶ πλείονος ποιεῖσθαι τοὺς αὐτῷ
διαφερομένους ἢ τοὺς οἰκείως χρωμένους, καὶ οἷς
μὲν ζῶν οὐδὲ² διελέγετο ἅπασαν δοῦναι τὴν οὐσίαν,
τοὺς δ' οἰκειότατα κεχρημένους³ οὐδὲ πολλοστοῦ
μέρους ἀξιῶσαι. ὥστε τίς ἂν ὑμῶν ταύτας εἶναι
35 κυρίας τὰς διαθήκας ψηφίσαιτο, ἃς ὁ μὲν διαθέμενος ὡς οὐκ ὀρθῶς ἐχούσας ἀπεδοκίμασεν, οὗτοι
δ' ἔργῳ λύουσιν ἐθέλοντες ἡμῖν ἰσομοιρῆσαι τῆς
οὐσίας, πρὸς δὲ τούτοις ἡμεῖς ὑμῖν ἀποφαίνομεν
ἐναντίας οὔσας καὶ τῷ νόμῳ καὶ τοῖς δικαίοις καὶ
τῇ τοῦ τελετευτηκότος διανοίᾳ;
36 Οἶμαι δ' ὑμᾶς τὸ περὶ ἡμῶν δίκαιον σαφέστατ'
ἂν παρ' αὐτῶν τούτων πυνθάνεσθαι. εἰ γάρ τις αὐτοὺς ἔροιτο διὰ τί ἀξιοῦσι κληρονόμοι γενέσθαι τῶν
Κλεωνύμου, τοῦτ' ἂν εἰπεῖν ἔχοιεν, ὅτι καὶ γένει
ποθὲν προσήκουσι καὶ ἐκεῖνος αὐτοῖς χρόνον τινὰ
ἐπιτηδείως διέκειτο. οὐκ ἂν⁴ ἄρα ὑπὲρ ἡμῶν
37 μᾶλλον ἢ ὑπὲρ σφῶν αὐτῶν εἶεν εἰρηκότες; εἴ τε

¹ αὐτὸν Q: αὐτῷ.   ² οὐδὲ Cobet: οὐ.
³ οἰκειότατα κεχρημένους Bekker: οἰκειότητα κεκτημένους.
⁴ οὐκ ἂν Mai: οὐκοῦν.

24

while he sought means to confirm the bequest of his whole property to my opponents, with some of whom he was at variance ? And that, although this enmity subsisted, he thought more highly of them, and, in spite of the intimacy and affection which had sprung up between us, tried rather to injure us ? For my part, if they wished to attack the will or the deceased, I do not know what else they could have said to you, since they represent the will as incorrect and disapproved by the testator, and accuse him of being so insane that, according to them, he set more store by those who were at variance with him than by those with whom he was living on terms of the closest affection, and left all his property to those with whom in his lifetime he was not on speaking terms, while he did not consider those, whom he had treated as his closest friends, as worthy of the smallest share of his estate. Who of you, then, could vote for the validity of this will, which the testator rejected as being incorrect, and which our opponents are actually ready to set aside, since they expressed their willingness to share the estate with us, and which, moreover, we can show to be contrary both to law and to justice and to the intention of the deceased ?

You can best learn, I think, the justice of our plea from the statements of our opponents themselves. If they were asked on what grounds they claimed to inherit the property of Cleonymus, they might reply that they are somehow related to him, and that for some time he was on terms of friendship with them. Would not this statement tell in our favour rather than in theirs ? For if the right of

γὰρ διὰ τὴν τοῦ γένους ἀγχιστείαν δεῖ γενέσθαι
τινὰς κληρονόμους, ἡμεῖς ἐγγυτέρω γένει προσ-
ήκομεν· εἴ τε διὰ τὴν φιλίαν τὴν ὑπάρχουσαν,
ἴσασιν αὐτὸν ἅπαντες ἡμῖν οἰκειότερον διακείμενον. ὥστ᾽ οὐ χρὴ παρ᾽ ἡμῶν, ἀλλὰ [καὶ] παρ᾽
38 αὐτῶν τούτων πυνθάνεσθαι τὸ δίκαιον. πάντων δ᾽
ἂν εἴη δεινότατον, εἰ τοῖς μὲν ἄλλοις ψηφίζοισθε,
ὅταν θάτερα¹ τούτων ἀποφαίνωσι σφᾶς αὐτούς, ἢ
γένει προτέρους ὄντας ἢ τῇ φιλίᾳ τῇ πρὸς τὸν
τετελευτηκότα, ἡμᾶς δ᾽ οἷς ἐστιν ἀμφότερα ταῦτα
παρὰ πάντων ὁμολογούμενα, ἀξιώσετε μόνους
ἀκλήρους ποιῆσαι τῶν ἐκείνου.
39   Καὶ εἰ μὲν Πολύαρχος² ὁ πατὴρ ὁ Κλεωνύμου,
πάππος δ᾽ ἡμέτερος, ζῶν ἐτύγχανε καὶ τῶν ἐπιτηδείων ἐνδεὴς ὤν, ἢ Κλεώνυμος ἐτελεύτησε θυγατέρας ἀπορουμένας καταλιπών, ἡμεῖς ἂν διὰ τὴν ἀγχιστείαν καὶ τὸν πάππον γηροτροφεῖν ἠναγκαζόμεθα καὶ τὰς Κλεωνύμου θυγατέρας ἢ λαβεῖν αὐτοὶ
γυναῖκας ἢ προῖκα ἐπιδιδόντες ἑτέροις ἐκδιδόναι,
καὶ ταῦθ᾽ ἡμᾶς καὶ ἡ συγγένεια καὶ οἱ νόμοι καὶ
ἡ παρ᾽ ὑμῶν αἰσχύνη ποιεῖν ἠνάγκαζεν ἄν, ἢ ταῖς
μεγίσταις ζημίαις καὶ τοῖς ἐσχάτοις ὀνείδεσι περι-
40 πεσεῖν· εἰ δ᾽ οὐσία κατελείφθη, δίκαιον ἡγήσεσθ᾽
εἶναι ταύτης ἑτέρους ἡμῶν μᾶλλον κληρονομεῖν;
οὐκ ἄρα δίκαια οὐδ᾽ ὑμῖν αὐτοῖς συμφέροντα οὐδὲ
τοῖς νόμοις ὁμολογούμενα ψηφιεῖσθε, εἰ τῶν μὲν
συμφορῶν τοὺς ἐγγυτάτω γένει κοινωνεῖν ἀναγ-
κάσετε, χρημάτων δὲ καταλειφθέντων πάντας
ἀνθρώπους κυριωτέρους ἢ τούτους ποιήσετε.
41   Χρὴ δέ, ὦ ἄνδρες, καὶ διὰ τὴν συγγένειαν καὶ
διὰ τὴν τοῦ πράγματος ἀλήθειαν, ὅπερ ποιεῖτε,

¹ θάτερα Mai: θάττερα.   ² Πολύαρχος Mai: ναύαρχος.

succession is based on affinity, we are more closely related to him ; if it is to be based on existing friendship, it is common knowledge that it was to us that he was more closely bound by affection. Thus it is from their lips rather than from ours that you must learn the justice of the case. Now it would be very strange if in all other cases you were to vote in favour of those who prove themselves nearer either in kinship or in friendship to the deceased, but decide that we, who are admitted to possess both these qualifications, alone are to be deprived of all share in his property.

If Polyarchus, the father of Cleonymus and our grandfather, were alive and lacked the necessities of life, or if Cleonymus had died leaving daughters unprovided for, we should have been obliged on grounds of affinity to support our grandfather, and either ourselves marry Cleonymus's daughters or else provide dowries and find other husbands for them— the claims of kinship, the laws, and public opinion in Athens would have forced us to do this or else become liable to heavy punishment and extreme disgrace—but now that property has been left, will you regard it as just that others, rather than we, should inherit it ? Your verdict, then, will not be just or in your own interest or in harmony with the law, if you are going to force those who are next of kin to share in the misfortunes of their relatives, but, when money has been left, give anyone rather than them the right to its possession.

It is only right, gentlemen, that you should—as indeed you do—give your verdicts on grounds of

τοῖς κατὰ γένος ψηφίζεσθαι μᾶλλον ἢ τοῖς κατὰ
διαθήκην ἀμφισβητοῦσι. τὴν μὲν γὰρ τοῦ γένους
οἰκειότητα πάντες ἐπιστάμενοι τυγχάνετε, καὶ οὐχ
οἷόν τε τοῦτ' ἔστι πρὸς ὑμᾶς ψεύσασθαι· διαθήκας
δ' ἤδη πολλοὶ ψευδεῖς ἀπέφηναν, καὶ οἱ μὲν τὸ
παράπαν οὐ γενομένας, ἐνίων δ' οὐκ ὀρθῶς βεβου-
42 λευμένων. καὶ νῦν ὑμεῖς[1] τὴν μὲν συγγένειαν καὶ
τὴν οἰκειότητα τὴν ἡμετέραν, οἷς ἡμεῖς ἀγωνι-
ζόμεθα, ἅπαντες ἐπίστασθε· τὰς δὲ διαθήκας, αἷς
οὗτοι πιστεύοντες ἡμᾶς συκοφαντοῦσιν, οὐδεὶς
ὑμῶν οἶδε κυρίας γενομένας. ἔπειτα τὴν μὲν ἡμετέραν συγγένειαν εὑρήσετε καὶ παρ' αὐτῶν τῶν
ἀντιδίκων ὁμολογουμένην, τὰς δὲ διαθήκας ὑφ'
ἡμῶν ἀμφισβητουμένας· οὗτοι γὰρ τὸ ἀνελεῖν
43 αὐτὰς ἐκείνου βουλομένου διεκώλυσαν. ὥσθ' ὑμῖν,[2]
ὦ ἄνδρες, πολὺ κάλλιόν ἐστι ψηφίσασθαι κατὰ τὸ
γένος τὸ παρ' ἀμφοτέρων ἡμῶν ὁμολογούμενον
μᾶλλον ἢ κατὰ τὰς διαθήκας τὰς οὐ δικαίως γεγε-
νημένας. πρὸς δὲ τούτοις ἐνθυμήθητε ὅτι αὐτὰς
ἔλυσε μὲν Κλεώνυμος εὖ φρονῶν, διέθετο δὲ ὀργισθεὶς καὶ οὐκ ὀρθῶς βουλευόμενος· ὥστε πάντων
ἂν εἴη δεινότατον, εἰ κυριωτέραν αὑτοῦ τὴν ὀργὴν
ἢ τὴν διάνοιαν ποιήσετε.

44 Οἶμαι δ' ὑμᾶς καὶ λαμβάνειν παρὰ τούτων ἀξιοῦν
καὶ μὴ τυγχάνοντας ἀγανακτεῖν, οἷς ἂν ὑπάρχῃ
καὶ παρ' ὑμῶν τῶν αὐτῶν τυχεῖν. εἰ τοίνυν συνέβη
Κλεωνύμῳ μὲν ζῆν, ἐξερημωθῆναι δὲ τὸν ἡμέτερον
οἶκον ἢ τὸν τούτων, σκέψασθε ποτέρων[3] ἐκεῖνος
ἐγίγνετο κληρονόμος· δίκαιον γάρ ἐστι τούτους
ἔχειν τὰ ἐκείνου, παρ' ὧν ὠφείλετο καὶ λαβεῖν

---

[1] ὑμεῖς Mai : ἡμεῖς. [2] ὑμῖν Mai : ἡμῖν.
[3] ποτέρων Mai : πότερον.

affinity and the true facts of the case in favour of those who claim by right of kinship rather than of those who rely on a will. For you all know surely what a family relationship is ; one cannot misrepresent it to you ; on the other hand, many people have produced false wills, some complete forgeries, some made by people not in their right mind. In the present case you are all aware of our kinship and close relations with the deceased, which are the basis of our claim ; but none of you has any knowledge that the will was valid, in reliance upon which our opponents are scheming against us. Further, you will find that our relationship to the deceased is admitted even by our adversaries, whereas the will is contested by us, for they prevented him from annulling it when he wished to do so. So, gentlemen, it is much better that you should give your verdict on the ground of our affinity, which is admitted by both sides, rather than in accordance with the will which was not properly drawn up. Remember also that Cleonymus made the will in a misguided moment of passion, but was in his right mind when he revoked it ; it would, therefore, be an extraordinary proceeding to let his momentary passion prevail rather than his reasoned intention.

I think that you yourselves consider it your right to inherit—and feel a grievance if you do not do so— from those who have a claim to inherit from you. Supposing, therefore, that Cleonymus were alive, and that our family or that of our opponents had become extinct, consider to which family Cleonymus had the prospect of becoming heir ; for it is only fair that those should possess his property from whom

45 αὐτῷ. εἰ μὲν τοίνυν Φερένικος ἢ τῶν ἀδελφῶν τις
ἐτελεύτησεν, οἱ παῖδες οἱ τούτων, οὐκ ἐκεῖνος
ἐγίγνετο κύριος τῶν καταλειφθέντων· ἡμῶν δὲ
τοιαύτῃ τύχῃ χρησαμένων Κλεώνυμος ἁπάντων
ἐγίγνετο κληρονόμος. οὔτε γὰρ παῖδες ἡμῖν ἦσαν
οὔτ᾽ ἄλλοι συγγενεῖς, ἀλλ᾽ ἐκεῖνος καὶ γένει προσήκων ἐγγυτάτω καὶ τῇ χρείᾳ πάντων ἦν οἰκειό-
46 τατος· ὥστε διὰ ταῦτα καὶ οἱ νόμοι δεδώκασιν
αὐτῷ, καὶ ἡμεῖς οὐδέν᾽ ⟨ἂν⟩[1] ἄλλον ἠξιώσαμεν
ταύτης τῆς δωρεᾶς. οὐ γὰρ δήπου ζῶντες μὲν
οὕτως ἂν ἐνεχειρίσαμεν αὐτῷ τὴν οὐσίαν, ὥστε
περὶ τῶν ἡμετέρων κυριωτέραν εἶναι τὴν ἐκείνου
διάνοιαν τῆς ἡμετέρας αὐτῶν, ἀποθνῄσκοντες δὲ
ἄλλους κληρονόμους ἐβουλήθημεν ⟨εἶναι⟩ αὐτῶν
47 μᾶλλον ἢ τὸν πάντων οἰκειότατον. ὥσθ᾽ ἡμᾶς μὲν
ἐν ἀμφοτέροις, ὦ ἄνδρες,[2] καὶ ἐν τῷ δοῦναι καὶ
ἐν τῷ λαβεῖν οἰκείους ὄντας εὑρήσετε, τούτους δὲ
νῦν μὲν ἀναισχυντοῦντας καὶ τὴν οἰκειότητα καὶ
τὴν ἀγχιστείαν λέγοντας, ὅτι λήψεσθαί τι προσ-
δοκῶσιν· ἐν δὲ τῷ δοῦναι πολλοὺς ἂν καὶ συγγενεῖς καὶ φίλους ἐκείνου προείλοντο οἰκειοτέρους.
48 Κεφάλαιον δὲ τῶν εἰρημένων, ὦ πάντας ὑμᾶς
προσέχειν δεῖ τὸν νοῦν· ⟨ἐν⟩ ὅσῳ[3] γὰρ ἂν ταῦτα
λέγοντες ἀποφαίνονται καὶ πειρῶνται πείθειν ὑμᾶς
ὡς ἐκεῖνος διέθετο ταύτας τὰς διαθήκας καὶ οὐδὲ
πώποτε ὕστερον αὐτῷ μετεμέλησε, ⟨ἀλλὰ⟩[4] καὶ
νῦν ἐβούλετο ἡμᾶς μὲν[5] μηδὲν τῶν αὐτοῦ λαβεῖν,
49 σφίσι δ᾽ αὐτοῖς βεβαιῶσαι τὴν δωρεάν, καὶ ταῦτα
πάντα λέγοντες καὶ διισχυριζόμενοι μηδέτερον

[1] οὐδέν᾽ ⟨ἂν⟩ Bekker: οὐδένα.
[2] ἄνδρες Baiter-Sauppe: Ἀθηναῖοι.
[3] ⟨ἐν⟩ ὅσῳ Dobree.   [4] ἀλλὰ add. Blass.
[5] νῦν ἐβούλετο ἡμᾶς μὲν Q: νῦν μὲν ἐβ. ἡμᾶς.

he had a right to inherit. If Pherenicus or one of his brothers had died, their children, and not Cleonymus, had the prospect of becoming entitled to the property which they left behind. If, on the other hand, such a fate had befallen us, Cleonymus had the prospect of becoming heir to everything ; for we had no children or other relatives, but he was a next-of-kin and most closely bound to us by ties of affection ; for which reasons the laws have given him the right of succession, and we should never have thought of making this bequest to anyone else. For we should never, I imagine, have in our lifetime placed our property in his hands in such a way that his wishes prevailed over our own in the matter of what belonged to us, and yet, at our death, have wished others to inherit it rather than our closest friend. Thus, gentlemen, you will find us bound to Cleonymus by the double tie of mutual bequest and inheritance, while you will find my opponents acting impudently and talking of close connexion and affinity, because they expect to profit thereby. If it were a question of giving anything away, there are many kinsmen and friends whom they would have preferred as nearer and dearer than him.

I will now sum up what I have said, and I beg the close attention of you all. As long as my opponents try by these arguments to prove and attempt to persuade you that this will represents Cleonymus's intentions, and that he never subsequently regretted having made it, but still wished us to receive none of his estate and to confirm the bequest to them— yet, while stating and insisting on all these points,

ἀποφαίνωσι[1] μήθ᾽,[2] ὡς ἐγγυτέρω τῷ γένει προσήκουσι μήθ᾽ ὡς οἰκειότερον ἡμῶν πρὸς Κλεώνυμον διέκειντο, ὑμεῖς ἐνθυμεῖσθε ὅτι ἐκείνου κατηγοροῦσιν, ἀλλ᾽ οὐχ ὡς δίκαιόν ἐστι τὸ πρᾶγμα
50 διδάσκουσιν ὑμᾶς. ὥσθ᾽ ὑμεῖς ὅταν μὲν τοῖς τούτων λόγοις πιστεύητε, οὐ τούτους προσήκει ποιῆσαι τῶν ἐκείνου κληρονόμους, ἀλλὰ παράνοιαν
Κλεωνύμου καταγιγνώσκειν, ὅταν δὲ τοῖς ἡμετέροις, ἐκεῖνόν τε νομίζειν ὀρθῶς βεβουλεῦσθαι λῦσαι
τὰς διαθήκας βουλόμενον, ἡμᾶς τε μὴ συκοφαν-
51 τεῖν ἀλλὰ δικαίως τούτων ἀμφισβητεῖν. ἔπειτα, ὦ
ἄνδρες, ἐνθυμεῖσθε ὅτι οὐχ οἷόν τε ὑμῖν[3] ἐστι κατὰ
τοὺς τούτων λόγους γνῶναι περὶ αὐτῶν. πάντων
γὰρ ἂν εἴη δεινότατον, εἰ τῶν ἀντιδίκων γιγνω-
σκόντων ἡμᾶς δίκαιον εἶναι τὸ μέρος αὐτῶν
λαβεῖν, ὑμεῖς ἅπαντ᾽ αὐτοὺς ἔχειν ψηφιεῖσθε,[4]
καὶ τούτους μὲν ἡγήσεσθε χρῆναι πλείω λαβεῖν ὧν
αὐτοὶ σφᾶς αὐτοὺς ἠξίωσαν, ἡμᾶς δὲ μηδὲ τούτων ἀξιώσετε ὧν οἱ ἀντίδικοι συγχωροῦσιν ἡμῖν.

---

[1] ἀποφαίνωσι Schoemann: ἀποφήνωσι.
[2] μήθ᾽ Bekker: μηδ᾽.　　　[3] ὑμῖν Mai: ἡμῖν.
[4] ψηφιεῖσθε Thalheim: ψηφίσεσθε.

they never really prove either that they are nearer of kin to Cleonymus or that they were on terms of closer intimacy with him than we were—remember that they are merely accusing him and are not demonstrating to you the justice of their cause. If, therefore, you believe what they say, you ought not to declare them heirs to Cleonymus's estate but to pronounce Cleonymus insane. If, on the other hand, you believe what we say, you must consider that Cleonymus exercised his proper judgement when he wished to revoke the will, and that we are not bringing a vexatious suit but are making a just claim to the inheritance. Lastly, gentlemen, remember that it is impossible for you to decide the matter on the basis of their arguments ; for it would be extraordinary, when our adversaries decide that we are entitled in justice to part of the estate, if your verdict is to give them the whole of it, and if you shall hold that they ought to receive more than the amount to which they considered themselves entitled, while you do not award us even as much as our adversaries conceded.

II. ON THE ESTATE OF MENECLES

INTRODUCTION

MENECLES [a] had married as his second wife the young daughter of a friend of his, Eponymus. After a short period, during which she bore him no children, he separated from her on friendly terms and she married a certain Elius. Menecles, having no children by either wife, followed the common custom of adopting a son, so that his family should not die out, and chose for this purpose the brother of his second wife. On his death, twenty-three years after the date of the adoption, his own brother, as next-of-kin, challenged the legality of the adoption under a law of Solon, on the ground that it had been made " under the influence of a woman," namely, Menecles' second wife, the sister of the adopted son, and claimed the estate.

A legitimate son, or a son adopted during the lifetime of the person who adopted him, enjoyed by law the right of entering into his inheritance without any application to the court such as had

[a] STEMMA

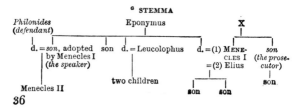

to be made by testamentary and collateral heirs.
If a claim was put forward by any other person who
contested the son's, or the adopted son's, right to
inherit and made application to the archon, this
claim could be met by a special form of protestation
(διαμαρτυρία) to the effect that the estate was not
subject to adjudication (ἐπίδικος), because there
was a direct heir to inherit it. In the present case
the adopted son put in a protestation, supported by
the evidence of his father-in-law, Philonides. The
burden of proving that the adopted son's claim was
invalid thus fell upon the claimant, the brother of
the deceased, whose action took the form of a
prosecution of the witness, Philonides, for perjury.
It is on his behalf that the adopted son made the
present speech. Thus, while nominally the speaker
is defending his father-in-law on a charge of perjury,
he is actually pleading his own right to inherit,
since the result of the acquittal of the witness would
be that his claim as heir would be vindicated, whereas,
if the witness were convicted, he would be forced
to abandon his claim to the estate.

The prosecutor had based his case on the contention that the adoption had been due to the
influence of the sister of the speaker, and seems to
have urged that she had brought no dowry with
her, and that, therefore, the presumption was that
Menecles had never legally married her. Against
this contention the speaker brings evidence that a
dowry of twenty minae had been paid, and he paints
a touching picture of the parting between Menecles
and his young wife, whom he put away out of pity
because she had no children by him. If there had
been any undue influence, surely, he contends, it

would have been exercised in favour of her children by her second husband and not in favour of her brother. The truth, he says, is that Menecles, in his childless and lonely condition, desired to adopt a son, and naturally turned to the family of his old friend, Eponymus, with which he had been connected by marriage. He shows that after his adoption he had acted as a dutiful son to Menecles and had performed all the due rites over him after his death. His only object now is, he says, to vindicate the memory of his adopted father, since from a pecuniary point of view the inheritance is practically worthless owing to the machinations of the prosecutor, who had, during Menecles' lifetime, managed to defraud him of the greater part of his property.

The exact facts on this point are somewhat obscure, but it appears that Menecles had been appointed trustee of the property left by a certain Nicias to his orphan children, and had given, as guarantee for his guardianship, a mortgage on certain land which he held jointly with his brother. When the elder of the orphans came of age, Menecles was called upon to restore to him the capital and interest, for which purpose he was obliged to sell his land. His brother opposed the sale, and Menecles was forced to reserve the portion which he claimed, selling the remainder and paying the money due to the orphans. Menecles subsequently brought an action against his brother for restraint of sale, which was heard before arbitrators, who being, as the speaker alleges, friends of the brother, gave a verdict in his favour to the detriment of the estate. The speech concludes with a contrast between the rapacity of the prosecutor and the dutiful conduct of the adopted son.

The date of the speech can be approximately fixed by the allusion to the absence of the speaker on military service in Thrace under Iphicrates. It seems probable, from the phrase used in § 6 (ἀπεδημήσαμεν μετὰ Ἰφικράτους εἰς Θρᾴκην), that the reference is not to the official Athenian expedition to the Chersonese and Hellespont about 388 B.C., but to a later private expedition, undertaken by Iphicrates about 383 B.C. with a mercenary force on behalf of the Thracian prince Cotys, whose daughter he married. The speaker seems to have been absent for some little time on this expedition, since two children were born to his elder sister during his absence (§ 7). A further period elapsed before the adoption took place (§ 10), so that we must probably allow for a period of about five years between the departure of the speaker to Thrace and the date of his adoption. A further period of twenty-three years elapsed before the death of Menecles, so that the date of the speech would seem to fall about the year 355 B.C.

II. ΠΕΡΙ ΤΟΥ ΜΕΝΕΚΛΕΟΥΣ ΚΛΗΡΟΥ

ΥΠΟΘΕΣΙΣ

Μενεκλέους ποιησαμένου υἱὸν καὶ ἐπιβιώσαντος τῇ ποιήσει εἴκοσι τρία ἔτη, ἀδελφῶν ἀμφισβητησάντων τοῦ κλήρου ἐμαρτύρησέ τις Φιλωνίδης μὴ εἶναι τὸν κλῆρον ἐπίδικον, καταλείψαντος υἱὸν Μενεκλέους. τούτῳ ἐπέσκηψαν ψευδομαρτυρίας οἱ ἀδελφοί, καὶ πρὸς τούτους ὁ παῖς ὑπὲρ αὐτοῦ τὴν ἀπολογίαν εἰσέρχεται. ἔστι δὲ ὁ λόγος οὗτος ἐναντίος τῷ περὶ τοῦ Κλεωνύμου κλήρου· ἐκεῖ μὲν γὰρ ὑπὲρ συγγενείας εἶπεν, ὧδε δὲ ὑπὲρ διαθήκης. ἡ στάσις ἀντίληψις κατὰ στοχασμόν· λέγει γὰρ ὅτι ἐξῆν αὐτῷ ποιεῖν ἑαυτῷ υἱόν. εἶτα τὸ στοχαστικόν, ὅτι οὐ πεισθεὶς γυναικὶ ἐποιήσατό με.

1 Ἡγούμην μέν, ὦ ἄνδρες, εἴ τις καὶ ἄλλος ἐποιήθη ὑπό τινος κατὰ τοὺς νόμους, καὶ ἐγὼ ποιηθῆναι, καὶ οὐκ ἄν ποτε εἰπεῖν οὐδένα τολμῆσαι ὡς ἐποιήσατό με Μενεκλῆς παρανοῶν ἢ γυναικὶ πειθόμενος· ἐπειδὴ δὲ ὁ θεῖος οὐκ ὀρθῶς βουλευόμενος, ὡς ἐγώ φημι, πειρᾶται ἐξ ἅπαντος τρόπου τὸν ἀδελφὸν τὸν αὑτοῦ ἄπαιδα τεθνεῶτα καταστῆσαι, οὔτε τοὺς θεοὺς τοὺς πατρῴους οὔθ᾽ ὑμῶν αἰσχυνόμενος οὐδένα, ἐμοὶ ἀνάγκη ἐστὶ πολλὴ βοηθεῖν τῷ τε[1] πατρὶ τῷ ποιησαμένῳ με

---

[1] τῷ τε Bremi : τε τῷ.

II. ON THE ESTATE OF MENECLES

ARGUMENT

Menecles adopted a son and lived for twenty-three years after the date of the adoption. When his brothers [a] claimed his estate, a certain Philonides attested that the estate was not adjudicable, because Menecles had left a son. The brothers then brought an action for perjury against Philonides, and it is against them that the son undertakes the defence of Philonides. The speech, which is in defence of a will, is the counterpart of that delivered " On the Estate of Cleonymus," [b] which upholds the rights of kindred. The discussion concerns a point of law with a controversy on a point of fact; for the speaker affirms that the deceased had the right to adopt a son, and then deals with the point of fact, saying, " It was not under the influence of a woman that he adopted me."

I think, gentlemen, that, if any adoption was ever made in accordance with the laws, mine was, and no one could ever dare to say that Menecles adopted me in a moment of insanity or under the influence of a woman. But since my uncle, acting, as I assert, under a misapprehension, is trying by every means in his power to deprive his dead brother of descendants, showing no respect for the gods of his family or for any of you, I feel constrained to come to the aid of the father who adopted me, and

[a] This is incorrect ; there was only one brother, whose son was also apparently associated with him in the case.
[b] Oration i.

2 καὶ ἐμαυτῷ. διδάξω[1] οὖν ὑμᾶς ἐξ ἀρχῆς ὡς προσηκόντως τε καὶ κατὰ τοὺς νόμους ἐγένετο ἡ ποίησις, καὶ οὐκ ἔστιν ἐπίδικος ὁ κλῆρος ὁ Μενεκλέους ὄντος ἐμοῦ υἱοῦ ἐκείνου, ἀλλ' ὁ μάρτυς διεμαρτύρησε τἀληθῆ. δέομαι δ' ὑμῶν ἀπάντων καὶ ἀντιβολῶ καὶ ἱκετεύω μετ' εὐνοίας ἀποδέχεσθαί μου τοὺς λόγους.

3 Ἐπώνυμος γὰρ ὁ Ἀχαρνεύς, ὁ πατὴρ ὁ ἡμέτερος, ὦ ἄνδρες, φίλος ἦν καὶ ἐπιτήδειος Μενεκλεῖ, καὶ ἐχρῆτο οἰκείως[2]· ἦμεν δὲ αὐτῷ παῖδες τέτταρες ἡμεῖς, δύο μὲν υἱεῖς, δύο δὲ θυγατέρες. τελευτήσαντος δὲ τοῦ πατρὸς ἐκδίδομεν ἡμεῖς τὴν πρεσβυτέραν ἀδελφήν, ἐπειδὴ εἶχεν ὥραν, Λευκο-
4 λόφῳ, προῖκα ἐπιδόντες εἴκοσι μνᾶς. καὶ ἀπ' ἐκείνου τοῦ χρόνου τετάρτῳ ἔτει ἢ πέμπτῳ[3] ὕστερον ἥ τε ἀδελφὴ ἡμῖν ἡ νεωτέρα σχεδὸν ἡλικίαν εἶχεν ἀνδρὶ συνοικεῖν, καὶ τῷ Μενεκλεῖ ἡ γυνὴ τελευτᾷ ἣν εἶχε πρότερον. ἐπειδὴ οὖν ἐκείνη τὰ νομιζόμενα ἐποίησεν ὁ Μενεκλῆς, ᾔτει τὴν ἀδελφὴν ἡμᾶς, ὑπομιμνήσκων τήν τε φιλίαν τὴν τοῦ πατρὸς καὶ ἑαυτοῦ, καὶ ὡς πρὸς ἡμᾶς
5 αὐτοὺς[4] ἦν διακείμενος· καὶ ἡμεῖς εἰδότες ὅτι καὶ ὁ πατὴρ οὐδενὶ ἂν ἔδωκεν ἥδιον ἢ ἐκείνῳ, δίδομεν αὐτῷ, οὐκ ἄπροικον, ὡς οὗτος λέγει ἑκάστοτε, ἀλλὰ τὴν ἴσην προῖκα ἐπιδόντες ἥνπερ καὶ τῇ πρεσβυτέρᾳ ἀδελφῇ ἐπέδομεν· καὶ ἐκ τοῦ τρόπου τούτου, πρότερον ὄντες αὐτοῦ φίλοι, κατέστημεν οἰκεῖοι. καὶ ὡς ἔλαβεν εἴκοσι μνᾶς ὁ Μενεκλῆς ἐπὶ τῇ ἀδελφῇ προῖκα, τὴν μαρτυρίαν ταύτην πρῶτον βούλομαι παρασχέσθαι.

[1] διδάξω Bekker : διδάσκω. [2] οἰκείως Bekker : οἰκείῳ.
[3] ἢ πέμπτῳ add. Q. [4] αὐτοὺς Sauppe : αὐτὸς.

to my own aid. I intend, therefore, first to show you that my adoption was appropriate and legal, and that there is no question of adjudicating the estate of Menecles, since he had a son, namely, myself, and that the evidence of the witness was true. I beg and entreat and beseech you all to listen with favour to what I have to say.

My father, gentlemen, Eponymus of Acharnae,[a] was a friend and close acquaintance of Menecles and lived on terms of intimacy with him ; there were four of us children, two sons and two daughters. After my father's death we married our elder sister, when she reached a suitable age, to Leucolophus, giving her a dowry of twenty minae. Four or five years later, when our younger sister was almost of marriageable age, Menecles lost his first wife. When he had carried out the customary rites over her, he asked for our sister in marriage, reminding us of the friendship which had existed between our father and himself and of his friendly disposition towards ourselves. Knowing that our father would have given her to no one with greater pleasure, we gave her to him in marriage—not dowerless, as my opponent asserts on every possible occasion, but with the same portion as we gave to our elder sister. In this manner, having been formerly his friends, we became his kinsmen. I should like first to produce evidence that Menecles received a dowry of twenty minae with my sister.

[a] A deme of Attica about seven miles north of Athens.

ISAEUS

6 Ἐκδόντες τοίνυν τὰς ἀδελφάς, ὦ ἄνδρες, καὶ
ὄντες αὐτοὶ ἐν ἡλικίᾳ ἐπὶ τὸ στρατεύεσθαι ἐτρα-
πόμεθα, καὶ ἀπεδημήσαμεν μετὰ Ἰφικράτους εἰς
Θρᾴκην· ἐκεῖ δὲ δόξαντές του¹ εἶναι ἄξιοι περι-
ποιησάμενοί τι κατεπλεύσαμεν δεῦρο, καὶ κατα-
λαμβάνομεν τῇ πρεσβυτέρᾳ ἀδελφῇ ὄντα δύο
παιδία, τὴν δὲ νεωτέραν, ἣν εἶχε Μενεκλῆς,
7 ἄπαιδα. καὶ ἐκεῖνος δευτέρῳ μηνὶ ἢ τρίτῳ, πολλὰ
ἐπαινέσας τὴν ἀδελφήν, λόγους ἐποιεῖτο πρὸς
ἡμᾶς, καὶ ἔφη τήν τε ἡλικίαν ὑφορᾶσθαι τὴν
ἑαυτοῦ καὶ τὴν ἀπαιδίαν· οὔκουν ἔφη δεῖν ἐκείνην
τῆς χρηστότητος τῆς ἑαυτῆς τοῦτο ἀπολαῦσαι,
ἄπαιδα καταστῆναι συγκαταγηράσασαν αὐτῷ·
8 ἱκανὸς γὰρ ἔφη αὐτὸς ἀτυχῶν εἶναι. [καὶ ἐκ
ταύτης τῆς λέξεως δῆλον ὅτι φιλῶν ἀπεβάλετο·
οὐδεὶς γὰρ μισῶν τινα ἱκετεύει αὐτῷ.] ἐδεῖτο οὖν
ἡμῶν δοῦναι χάριν ταύτην αὐτῷ, ἐκδοῦναι ἄλλῳ
αὐτὴν μετὰ τῆς γνώμης τῆς ἑαυτοῦ. καὶ ἡμεῖς
ἐκελεύομεν αὐτὸν πείθειν αὐτὴν περὶ τούτων· ὅ
τι γὰρ ⟨ἂν⟩² ἐκείνη πεισθῇ, τοῦτ' ἔφαμεν ποιήσειν.
9 κἀκείνη τὸ μὲν πρῶτον οὐδ' ἠνέσχετ' αὐτοῦ λέγοντος, προϊόντος δὲ τοῦ χρόνου μόλις ἐπείσθη·
καὶ οὕτως ἐκδίδομεν αὐτὴν Ἠλείῳ Σφηττίῳ, καὶ
ὁ Μενεκλῆς τήν τε προῖκα ἐπιδίδωσιν αὐτῷ, μετα-
σχὼν τοῦ οἴκου τῆς μισθώσεως τῶν παίδων τῶν³
Νικίου, καὶ τὰ ἱμάτια, ἃ ἦλθεν ἔχουσα παρ'
ἐκεῖνον, καὶ τὰ χρυσίδια, ἃ ἦν, δίδωσιν αὐτῇ.

---

¹ δόξαντές του Bremi: δόξαντες τοῦ.
² ἂν add. Dobree.   ³ τῶν Bekker: τοῦ.

EVIDENCE

Having thus settled our sisters, gentlemen, and, being ourselves of military age, we adopted the career of a soldier and went abroad with Iphicrates to Thrace.[a] Having proved our worth there, we returned hither after saving a little money ; and we found that our elder sister had two children, but that the younger, the wife of Menecles, was childless. A month or two later Menecles, with many expressions of praise for our sister, approached us and said that he viewed with apprehension his increasing age and childlessness : she ought not, he said, to be rewarded for her virtues by having to grow old with him without bearing children; it was enough that he himself was unfortunate. [His words clearly prove that he loved her when he put her away ; for no one utters supplications for one whom he hates.][b] He, therefore, begged us to do him the favour of marrying her to someone else with his consent. We told him that it was for him to persuade her in the matter, for we would do whatever she agreed. At first she would not even listen to his suggestion, but in course of time she with difficulty consented. So we gave her in marriage to Elius of Sphettus,[c] and Menecles handed over her dowry to him—for he had become part-lessee of the estate of the children of Nicias [d]— and he gave her the garments which she had brought with her to his house and the jewelry which there

[a] See Introduction, p. 39.
[b] This sentence is inappropriate and has clearly come into the text from a marginal gloss.
[c] A deme south-west of Athens.
[d] See Introduction, p. 38.

10 μετὰ δὲ ταῦτα χρόνου διαγενομένου ἐσκόπει ὁ
Μενεκλῆς ὅπως μὴ ἔσοιτο ἄπαις, ἀλλ' ἔσοιτο
αὐτῷ ὅς τις ζῶντά γηροτροφήσοι καὶ τελευτήσαντα θάψοι αὐτὸν καὶ εἰς τὸν ἔπειτα χρόνον τὰ
νομιζόμενα αὐτῷ ποιήσοι. τούτῳ μὲν οὖν ἑώρα
ἕνα μόνον υἱὸν ὄντα, ὥστε ἐδόκει αὐτῷ αἰσχρὸν
εἶναι ἄπαιδα τοῦτον καθιστάντα ἀρρένων παίδων
11 αὐτῷ κελεύειν δοῦναι τοῦτον εἰσποιήσασθαι. εὑρι-
σκεν οὖν οὐδένα ἄλλον οἰκειότερον ὄνθ' ἡμῶν
ἑαυτῷ. λόγους οὖν πρὸς ἡμᾶς ἐποιεῖτο, καὶ ἔφη
δοκεῖν αὐτῷ καλῶς ἔχειν, ἐπειδὴ οὕτως αὐτῷ ἡ
τύχη συνέβη ὥστε ἐκ τῆς ἀδελφῆς τῆς ἡμετέρας
παῖδας αὐτῷ μὴ γενέσθαι, ἐκ ταύτης τῆς οἰκίας
υἱὸν αὐτῷ ποιήσασθαι, ὅθεν καὶ φύσει παῖδας
ἐβουλήθη ἂν αὐτῷ γενέσθαι· " ὑμῶν οὖν " ἔφη
" βούλομαι τὸν ἕτερον ποιήσασθαι, ὁποτέρῳ ὑμῶν
12 καλῶς ἔχει." καὶ ὁ ἀδελφὸς ἀκούσας ταῦτα
[ἐπειδὴ προετίμησεν αὐτοὺς πάντων], ἐπῄνεσέ τε
τοὺς λόγους αὐτοῦ, καὶ εἶπεν ὅτι δέοιτο ἥ τε
ἡλικία καὶ ἡ παροῦσα ἐρημία ἐκείνου τοῦ θερα-
πεύσοντος αὐτὸν καὶ ἐπιδημήσοντος· " ἐμοὶ μὲν
οὖν " ἔφη " συμβαίνει¹ ἀποδημία, ὡς σὺ οἶσθα·
ὁ δὲ ἀδελφὸς οὑτοσί" ἐμὲ λέγων " τῶν τε σῶν
ἐπιμελήσεται καὶ τῶν ἐμῶν, ἐὰν βούλῃ τοῦτον
ποιήσασθαι." καὶ ὁ Μενεκλῆς καλῶς ἔφη αὐτὸν
λέγειν, καὶ ἐκ τοῦ τρόπου τούτου ποιεῖταί με.
13 Ὡς οὖν κατὰ τοὺς νόμους ἐγένετο² ἡ ποίησις,
τοῦτο ὑμᾶς βούλομαι διδάξαι. καί μοι τὸν νόμον
ἀνάγνωθι, ὃς κελεύει τὰ ἑαυτοῦ ἐξεῖναι διαθέσθαι
ὅπως ἂν ἐθέλῃ, ἐὰν μὴ παῖδες ἄρρενες ὦσι·γνήσιοι.

---

¹ συμβαίνει Q: -ειν.   ² ἐγένετο Dobree: ἐπεγ-.

was. Some time after this Menecles began **to** consider how he could put an end to his childless condition and have someone to tend his old age and bury him when he died and thereafter carry out the customary rites over him. He saw that my opponent had only one son ; so he thought it wrong to ask him to give him his son to adopt and so deprive him of male offspring. Thus he could find no nearer relative than us ; he, therefore, approached us and said that he thought it right, since fate had decreed that he should have no children by our sister, that he should adopt a son out of the family from which he would have wished to have a son of his own in the course of nature ; " I should like, therefore," he said, " to adopt one of you two, whichever is willing." My brother, on hearing this,[a] expressed his approval of Menecles' proposal and agreed that his age and solitary condition required someone who would look after him, and remain at home ; " I," he said, " as you know, go abroad ; but my brother here " (meaning me) " will look after your affairs as well as mine, if you wish to adopt him." Menecles approved of his suggestion and thus adopted me.

I wish next to prove to you that the adoption was carried out in the proper legal manner. So please read me the law which ordains that a man can dispose as he likes of his own property, if he does not possess legitimate male issue. The law-

[a] The words bracketed in the text have certainly come in from a marginal note and are unsuited to the context here.

ὁ γὰρ νομοθέτης, ὦ ἄνδρες, διὰ τοῦτο τὸν *νόμον*
ἔθηκεν οὕτως, ὁρῶν μόνην ταύτην καταφυγὴν
οὖσαν τῆς ἐρημίας καὶ παραψυχὴν τοῦ βίου τοῖς
ἅπασι τῶν ἀνθρώπων, τὸ ἐξεῖναι ποιήσασθαι ὃν
14 τινα ἂν βούλωνται. διδόντων οὖν τῶν νόμων αὐτῷ
ποιεῖσθαι διὰ τὸ εἶναι ἄπαιδα, ἐμὲ ποιεῖται, οὐκ
ἐν διαθήκαις, ὦ ἄνδρες, γράψας, μέλλων ἀπο-
θνήσκειν, ὥσπερ ἄλλοι τινὲς τῶν πολιτῶν, οὐδ᾽
ἀσθενῶν· ἀλλ᾽ ὑγιαίνων, εὖ φρονῶν, εὖ νοῶν,
ποιησάμενος εἰσάγει με εἰς τοὺς φράτορας παρόντων τούτων, καὶ εἰς τοὺς δημότας με ἐγγράφει
15 καὶ εἰς τοὺς ὀργεῶνας. καὶ τότε μὲν οὐδὲν ἀντ-
έλεγον αὐτῷ οὗτοι ὡς ⟨οὐκ⟩[1] εὖ φρονοῦντι· καίτοι πολὺ κάλλιον ἦν ζῶντα πείθειν ἐκεῖνον, εἴ τι
βούλοιντο, μᾶλλον ἢ τελευτήσαντα ὑβρίζειν καὶ
ἐξερημοῦν αὐτοῦ τὸν οἶκον. ἐπεβίω γὰρ ἐκεῖνος
μετὰ τὴν ποίησιν οὐκ ἐνιαυτὸν ἕνα ἢ δύο, ἀλλὰ
τρία καὶ εἴκοσιν ἔτη· καὶ ἐν τούτῳ τῷ χρόνῳ,
τοσούτῳ ὄντι, οὐδὲν ἐκεῖνος μετέγνω τῶν πεπραγμένων ἑαυτῷ, διὰ τὸ παρὰ πάντων ὁμολογεῖσθαι
16 ὅτι ἦν ὀρθῶς βεβουλευμένος. καὶ ὡς ἀληθῆ λέγω
ταῦτα, τῆς μὲν ποιήσεως ὑμῖν[2] τοὺς φράτορας καὶ
τοὺς ὀργεῶνας καὶ τοὺς δημότας παρέξομαι μάρτυρας, ὡς δ᾽ ἐξῆν ποιήσασθαι, τὸν νόμον αὐτὸν
ὑμῖν ἀναγνώσεται, καθ᾽ ὃν ἡ ποίησις ἐγένετο.
καί μοι τὰς μαρτυρίας ἀνάγνωθι ταύτας καὶ τὸν
νόμον.

MARTYRIAI. NOMOΣ

[1] οὐκ add. Dobree.   [2] ὑμῖν Tyrwhitt: ἡμῖν.

giver, gentlemen, legislated thus, because he saw that for childless persons the only refuge for their solitary condition, and the only possible comfort in life, lay in the possibility of adopting whomsoever they wished. The law thus allowing Menecles, because he was childless, to adopt a son, he adopted me, sirs, not by will made at point of death, as other citizens have done, nor during illness; but when he was sound in body and mind, and fully aware of what he was doing, he adopted me and introduced me to his fellow-wardsmen in the presence of my opponents and enrolled me among the demesmen and the members of his confraternity.[a] At the time my opponents raised no objection to his action on the ground that he was not in his right mind, although it would have been much better to have tried to win him over to their point of view during his lifetime rather than insult him now that he is dead and try to desolate his house. For he lived on after the adoption, not one or two years, but twenty-three, and during all this period he never regretted what he had done, because it was universally acknowledged that he had been well advised in what he did. To prove the truth of these statements, I will produce before you, as witnesses of the transaction, the wardsmen, the members of the confraternity, and the demesmen, and, to prove that Menecles was at liberty to adopt me, the clerk of the court shall read you the text of the law in accordance with which the adoption was made. Please read these depositions and the law.

DEPOSITIONS. LAW

[a] A private religious association, cf. Or. ix. 30.

17 Ὡς μὲν τοίνυν ἐξῆν τῷ Μενεκλεῖ ποιήσασθαι
υὸν αὑτῷ ὅν τινα ἐβούλετο, ὁ νόμος αὐτὸς δηλοῖ·
ὡς δὲ ἐποιήσατο, οἵ τε φράτορες καὶ οἱ δημόται καὶ
οἱ ὀργεῶνες ὑμῖν μεμαρτυρήκασιν· ὥστε περιφανῶς
ἀποδέδεικται ἡμῖν,¹ ὦ ἄνδρες, ὁ μάρτυς τἀληθῆ
διαμεμαρτυρηκώς, καὶ οὗτοι πρός γε τὴν ποίησιν
αὐτὴν λόγον οὐδ' ὁντινοῦν δύναιντ' ἂν ἀντειπεῖν.

18 Πραχθέντων δὲ τούτων ἐσκόπει ὁ Μενεκλῆς
γυναῖκά μοι, καὶ ἔφη με χρῆναι γῆμαι· καὶ ἐγὼ
λαμβάνω τὴν τοῦ Φιλωνίδου θυγατέρα. κἀκεῖνός
τε τὴν πρόνοιαν εἶχεν ὥσπερ εἰκός ἐστι πατέρα
περὶ υἱέος ἔχειν, καὶ ἐγὼ τὸν αὐτὸν τρόπον ὥσπερ
γόνῳ ὄντα πατέρα ἐμαυτοῦ ἐθεράπευόν τε καὶ
ᾐσχυνόμην, καὶ ἐγὼ καὶ ἡ γυνὴ ἡ ἐμή, ὥστε
ἐκεῖνον πρὸς τοὺς δημότας ἐπαινεῖν ἅπαντας.

19 Ὅτι δὲ οὐ παρανοῶν οὐδὲ γυναικὶ πειθόμενος ὁ
Μενεκλῆς ἐποιήσατο, ἀλλ' εὖ φρονῶν, ἐνθένδε
ἐστὶν ὑμῖν ῥᾴδιον ἐπιγνῶναι. πρῶτον μὲν γὰρ ἡ
ἀδελφή, περὶ ἧς οὗτος τὸν² πλεῖστον τοῦ λόγου
πεποίηται, ὡς ἐκείνῃ πεισθεὶς ἐμὲ ἐποιήσατο,
πολλῷ πρότερον ἦν ἐκδεδομένη ἤ³ τὴν ποίησιν
γενέσθαι, ὥστ' εἰ γ' ἐκείνῃ πεισθεὶς τὸν υὸν
ἐποιεῖτο, τῶν ἐκείνης παίδων τὸν ἕτερον ἐποιήσατ'
20 ἄν· δύο γάρ εἰσιν αὐτῇ. ἀλλ', ὦ ἄνδρες, οὐχ ὑπ'
ἐκείνης πεισθεὶς ἐμὲ ἐποιήσατο υὸν, ἀλλὰ μάλιστα
μὲν ὑπὸ τῆς ἐρημίας [ἐπείσθη], δεύτερον δὲ διὰ
τὰς προειρημένας αἰτίας καὶ διὰ τὴν εὔνοιαν τὴν
ὑπάρχουσαν πρὸς τὸν πατέρα τὸν ἐμόν, τρίτον δὲ
διὰ τὸ μὴ εἶναι συγγενῆ μηδέν' ἄλλον αὐτῷ,
ὁπόθεν ἂν ἐποιήσατο υὸν. ταῦτα τηνικαῦτα ἐν-

---

¹ ἡμῖν Q: ὑμῖν.   ² τὸν edd.: τὸ.   ³ ἤ Q: πρινή.

The law itself makes it clear that Menecles was free to adopt anyone he liked as his son ; that he did adopt a son, the wardsmen, the demesmen, and the members of the confraternity have provided evidence. Thus we have clearly proved it, gentlemen, the witness [a] has attested the truth of it, and my opponents cannot say a word against the actual fact of the adoption.

After this, Menecles began to look about for a wife for me, and said I ought to marry. So I married the daughter of Philonides. Menecles exercised the forethought on my behalf which a father would naturally exercise for his son, and I tended him and respected him as though he were my true father, as also did my wife, so that he praised us to all his fellow-demesmen.

That Menecles was not insane or under the influence of a woman but in his right mind when he adopted me, you can easily understand from the following facts. In the first place, my sister, with whom most of my opponent's argument has been concerned, and under whose influence he alleges that Menecles adopted me, had remarried long before the adoption took place, so that, if it had been under her influence that he was adopting his son, he would have adopted one of her boys ; for she has two. But, gentlemen, it was not under her influence that he adopted me as his son ; his chief motive was his loneliness, and, secondly, the other causes I have mentioned, and the goodwill which he felt towards my father, and, thirdly, because he had no other relative from whose family he might have adopted a son. These were the motives which at the time

* Philonides.

ἦγεν ἐμὲ ποιήσασθαι· ὥστε οὐ παραφρονῶν φαίνεται οὐδὲ τῇ γυναικὶ πεισθείς, εἰ μὴ ἄρα τὴν
ἐρημίαν αὐτοῦ καὶ τὴν ἀπαιδίαν οὗτος βούλεται
τὸ ὄνομα τοῦτο προσαγορεύειν.

21 Ἡδέως δ᾽ ἄν μοι δοκῶ[1] τούτου πυθέσθαι τοῦ
φάσκοντος εὖ φρονεῖν, τίνα ποιήσασθαι ἐχρῆν
[ἀπὸ] τῶν συγγενῶν; πότερα τὸν υἱὸν τὸν τούτου;
ἀλλ᾽ οὐκ ἂν αὐτῷ ἔδωκεν, ἄπαιδα αὐτὸν καθιστάς·
οὐχ οὕτως οὗτός ἐστι φιλοχρήματος. ἀλλὰ τὸν
τῆς ἀδελφῆς ἢ τὸν τῆς ἀνεψιᾶς ἢ τὸν τοῦ ἀνεψιοῦ;
ἀλλὰ τὴν ἀρχὴν οὐκ ἐγένετο αὐτῷ οὐδεὶς τούτων
22 τῶν συγγενῶν. οὐκοῦν ἐξ ἀνάγκης ἦν αὐτῷ ἄλλον
τινὰ ποιήσασθαι μᾶλλον ἢ ἄπαιδα καταγηρᾶν,
ὥσπερ οὗτος ἀξιοῖ νυνὶ αὐτόν. ἐγὼ τοίνυν πάντας
[ἀνθρώπους] ἂν οἶμαι ὁμολογῆσαι ὑμᾶς ὡς οὐκ ἂν
ποιησάμενος ἄλλον οἰκειότερον ἐμοῦ ἐποιήσατ᾽[2] ἄν.
δειξάτω γὰρ οὗτος ὑμῖν. ἀλλ᾽ οὐκ ἄν ποτε δύναιτο·
ἦν γὰρ οὐδεὶς ἄλλος συγγενὴς αὐτῷ πλὴν τούτων.

23 Ἀλλὰ νῦν οὗτος ἐπιτιμῶν αὐτῷ φαίνεται οὐχ
ὅτι τὸν υἱὸν οὐκ ἐποιήσατο τὸν αὑτοῦ, ἀλλ᾽ ὅτι τὸ
παράπαν ἐποιήσατο καὶ οὐκ ἐτελεύτησεν ἄπαις.
τοῦτ᾽ ἔστιν ὃ ἐπιτιμᾷ, ἐπίφθονον πρᾶγμα καὶ οὐ
δίκαιον ποιῶν· ὄντων γὰρ αὐτῷ παίδων ἐκείνῳ
24 ὄντι ἄπαιδι καὶ ἀτυχοῦντι φαίνεται ἐπιτιμῶν. καὶ
τοῖς μὲν ἄλλοις ἅπασιν ἀνθρώποις καὶ Ἕλλησι
καὶ βαρβάροις δοκεῖ καλῶς οὗτος ὁ νόμος κεῖσθαι,
ὁ περὶ τῆς ποιήσεως, καὶ διὰ τοῦτο χρῶνται
πάντες αὐτῷ· ὁ δὲ θεῖος οὑτοσὶ οὐκ αἰσχύνεται τὸν
αὑτοῦ ἀδελφὸν ταύτης τῆς ἐξουσίας ἀποστερῶν
νῦν, τοῦ ποιήσασθαι, ἧς οὐδὲ τοῖς οὐ γένει προσ-

---

[1] δοκῶ Orelli: ποθῶ.   [2] ἐποιήσατ᾽ Dobree: ποιήσαιτ᾽.

induced him to adopt me; so that it is quite clear that he was not insane or under the influence of a woman, unless, indeed, my opponent wishes to describe his loneliness and childlessness in these terms.

I feel that I should like my opponent, who thinks himself so wise, to tell me whom of his relatives Menecles ought to have adopted? Ought he to have adopted my opponent's son? But he would never have given him up and so rendered himself childless; he is not so avaricious as all that. Well then, the son of his sister or of his male or female cousin? But he had no such relative at all. He was, therefore, obliged to adopt someone else, or, failing that, grow old in childlessness, as my opponent now thinks he ought to have done. I think, therefore, that you would all admit that, when he adopted a son, he could not have adopted anyone who was more closely connected with him than I was. Otherwise, let my opponent indicate such a person. He cannot possibly do so; for he had no other kinsman than those whom I have mentioned.

But my opponent is now clearly blaming Menecles not for failing to adopt his own son but for adopting any son at all and not dying childless. It is for this that he blames him, a proceeding which is as spiteful as it is unjust; for while he has children of his own, he is obviously blaming Menecles for being childless and unfortunate. All other men, whether Greek or barbarians, regard this law about adoption as a good one and therefore all make use of it; but my uncle here is not ashamed to deprive his own brother of this right to adopt a son, the enjoyment of which no one has ever grudged even those

25 ἥκουσιν οὐδεὶς πώποτε ἐφθόνησεν. οἶμαι δὲ κἂν[1]
τοῦτον, εἴ τις ἐρωτήσειεν αὐτὸν τί[2] δή ποτ᾽ ἂν
ἐποίησεν εἰς τὴν αὐτὴν τύχην ἐκείνῳ καταστάς,
οὐκ ἄλλ᾽ οὐδὲν εἰπεῖν ἢ ὅτι ἐποίησατ᾽ ἂν ὅς τις
αὐτὸν ἔμελλε ζῶντα θεραπεύσειν καὶ τελευτήσαντα
θάψειν· καὶ δῆλον ὅτι κατὰ τὸν αὐτὸν τοῦτον
νόμον ἡ ποίησις ἐγένετ᾽ ἄν, καθ᾽ ὅν περ ἡ ἐμή.
εἶτα αὐτὸς μὲν εἰ ἦν ἄπαις, ἐποιήσατ᾽ ἄν· τὸν δὲ
Μενεκλέα ποιήσαντα ταὐτὰ τούτῳ παραφρονεῖν
26 φησι καὶ γυναικὶ πειθόμενον ποιήσασθαι. πῶς οὖν
οὐ σχέτλια λέγων φαίνεται; ἐγὼ γὰρ οἶμαι πολλῷ
μᾶλλον τοῦτον παραφρονεῖν τῷ τε λόγῳ τούτῳ ᾧ
νυνὶ λέγει, καὶ οἷς ποιεῖ.[3] τοῖς τε γὰρ νόμοις καὶ
‹τοῖς ›[4] δικαίοις καὶ οἷς αὐτὸς ἐποίησεν ἂν τἀναντία
λέγων φαίνεται, καὶ οὐκ αἰσχύνεται μὲν αὐτῷ τὸν
νόμον τὸν περὶ τῆς ποιήσεως ποιῶν κύριον, τῷ δὲ
ἀδελφῷ τὸν αὐτὸν τοῦτον ζητῶν ἄκυρον ποιῆσαι.

27 Εἶτα νῦν διὰ τί διαφερόμενος ζητεῖ οὗτος τὸν
ἀδελφὸν τὸν ἑαυτοῦ ἄπαιδα καταστῆσαι, ἄξιόν
ἐστιν, ὦ ἄνδρες, ἀκοῦσαι. εἰ μὲν γὰρ περὶ τοῦ
ὀνόματός μοι διαφέρεται καὶ ἀναίνεται, εἰ ἐγὼ
ἔσομαι υἱὸς Μενεκλέους, πῶς οὐ φθονερός ἐστιν;
εἰ δὲ περὶ χρημάτων ἐστὶν ὁ λόγος αὐτῷ, ἐπιδειξάτω ὑμῖν ὁποῖον χωρίον ἢ συνοικίαν ἢ οἰκίαν
κατέλιπεν ἐκεῖνος, ἃ ἐγὼ ἔχω νυνί. εἰ δὲ μηδὲν
τούτων κατέλιπεν, ἃ δ᾽ ἦν αὐτῷ ὑπόλοιπα, ἐπειδὴ
τῷ ὀρφανῷ τὸ ἀργύριον ἀπέδωκεν, οὗτος ἔλαβε
ζῶντος ἐκείνου ἔτι, πῶς οὐ περιφανῶς ἐξελέγχεται

---

[1] κἂν Gebauer: καί.　　　　[2] τί Tyrrwhitt: ἤ.
[3] ποιεῖ Bekker: ποιεῖται.
[4] τοῖς om. A: τοῖς γὰρ δικαίοις καὶ τοῖς νόμοις Q.

who were no relatives at all. I think that my
opponent, if anyone were to ask him what he would
have done in the same circumstances as Menecles,
would have nothing to say except that he would
have adopted someone who was likely to look after
him while he lived and bury him when he died ; and
it is obvious that the adoption would have been
carried out under the same law as mine was. He
himself, then, if he had been childless, would have
adopted a son ; but when Menecles acted in the
same manner, he declares that he was insane and
under the influence of a woman when he adopted
me. Is it not clear that he is talking in an abominable manner ? I am of opinion that it is much
rather my opponent who is insane by reason of the
line of argument which he employs and the things
which he does. For he is clearly arguing the contrary of the laws and of justice and of what he himself would have done, and is not ashamed of making
the law about adoption valid for himself, while he seeks
to render this same law of no effect for his brother.

Next, it is right, gentlemen, that you should hear
what cause of quarrel my opponent has that he
seeks to make his own brother childless. For if
he has any quarrel with me about my name, and
repudiates the suggestion that I am to be called
Menecles' son, is he not the victim of mean jealousy ?
But if it is a question of money with him, let him
point out to you what land or tenement or house
Menecles left behind of which I am now in possession. But if he left no such property, but my
opponent took from him in his lifetime all that
remained after he had paid off the money due to
the orphan, is he not clearly convicted of shameless

28 ἀναιδὴς ὤν; ὡς δὲ ἔχει, ἐγὼ ἐπιδείξω. ἐπειδὴ
γὰρ ἔδει τῷ ὀρφανῷ τὰ χρήματα ἀποδιδόναι,[1] ὁ
δ᾽ οὐκ εἶχεν ὁπόθεν ἀποδῷ, τόκοι δὲ πολλοῦ
χρόνου συνερρυηκότες ἦσαν αὐτῷ, τὸ χωρίον
ἐπώλει. καὶ οὗτος καιροῦ λαβόμενος καὶ βουλόμενος αὐτῷ ἐπηρεάζειν, ὅτι ἐμὲ ἐποιήσατο, δι-
εκώλυε τὸ χωρίον πραθῆναι, ἵνα κατοκώχιμον[2]
γένηται καὶ ἀναγκασθῇ τῷ ὀρφανῷ ἀποστῆναι.
ἠμφισβήτει οὖν αὐτῷ μέρους τινὸς τοῦ χωρίου,
πρότερον οὐδὲ πώποτε ἀμφισβητήσας, καὶ ἀπ-
29 ηγόρευε τοῖς ὠνουμένοις μὴ ὠνεῖσθαι. κἀκεῖνος
ἠγανάκτει, οἶμαι, καὶ ἠναγκάζετο ὑπολείπεσθαι
οὗ ἠμφισβήτησεν οὗτος. τὸ δὲ ἄλλο ἀποδίδοται[3]
Φιλίππῳ τῷ Πιθεῖ[4] ἑβδομήκοντα μνῶν, καὶ οὕτω
διαλύει τὸν ὀρφανόν, ἑπτὰ μνᾶς καὶ τάλαντον
ἀποδοὺς ἀπὸ τῆς τιμῆς τοῦ χωρίου· τούτῳ δὲ
λαγχάνει δίκην τῆς ἀπορρήσεως. λόγων δὲ πολλῶν
γενομένων καὶ ἔχθρας πολλῆς ἔδοξεν ἡμῖν χρῆναι,
ἵνα μή ποτε εἴπῃ τις ἐμὲ φιλοχρηματεῖν καὶ
ἐχθροὺς ἀδελφοὺς ὄντας αὐτούς[5] καθιστάναι,[6]
ἐπιτρέψαι τῷ τε κηδεστῇ τῷ τούτου καὶ τοῖς
30 φίλοις διαιτῆσαι. ἐκεῖνοι δ᾽ εἶπον ἡμῖν, εἰ μὲν[7] ἐπι-
τρέποιμεν αὐτοῖς ὥστε τὰ δίκαια διαγνῶναι, οὐκ
ἂν ἔφασαν διαιτῆσαι· οὐδὲν γὰρ δεῖσθαι ἀπέχθεσθαι οὐδετέροις ἡμῶν· εἰ δ᾽ ἐάσομεν αὐτοὺς γνῶναι τὰ συμφέροντα πᾶσιν, ἔφασαν διαιτήσειν. καὶ
ἡμεῖς, ἵνα δὴ πραγμάτων ἀπαλλαγῶμεν, ὥς γε δὴ

---

[1] ἀποδιδόναι Bekker : -δίδοσθαι.
[2] κατοκώχιμον Dobree : κατόχιμον.
[3] ἀποδίδοται Bekker : -δίδόναι.
[4] Πιθεῖ Sauppe : πιτθεῖ. [5] αὐτοὺς Bremi : αὐτοῦ.
[6] καθιστάναι Baiter-Sauppe : -άνειν.
[7] μὲν Bekker : μὴ.

conduct ? I will put the facts of the case before you. When it became necessary to pay back the money to the orphan, and Menecles did not possess the requisite sum, and interest had accumulated against him over a long period, he was for selling the land. My opponent, seizing the opportunity and being desirous to pick a quarrel with him because he had adopted me, tried to prevent the land from being sold, in order that it might be held as a pledge, and that Menecles might be obliged to cede the possession of it to the orphan. My opponent, therefore, claimed a part of the property from Menecles, though he had never previously made any such claim, and tried to prevent the purchasers from completing the purchase. Menecles was annoyed, as I can well imagine, and was obliged to reserve the portion which my opponent claimed ; the rest he sold to Philippus of Pithos for seventy minae and thus paid off the orphan, giving him one talent and seven minae out of the price of the property ; and he brought an action against his brother for restraining the sale. After long discussion had taken place and much bad feeling been aroused, we thought it best, in order that no one might say that I was avaricious and that I was setting these men, who were brothers, against one another, to submit the matter to the arbitration of my opponent's brother-in-law and our friends. The latter told us that, if we were to entrust them to decide the rights of the case, they would refuse to act as arbitrators, for they did not wish to quarrel with either party ; if, however, we would allow them to decide what was in the interest of all, they consented to act. So we, in order, as we thought, to get rid of the

31 ᾠόμεθα,¹ οὕτως ἐπιτρέπομεν. καὶ ἐκεῖνοι ὀμόσαντες ἡμῖν πρὸς τῷ βωμῷ τῷ τῆς Ἀφροδίτης
τῆς Κεφαλῆσι² τὰ συμφέροντα γνώσεσθαι, δι-
ῄτησαν ἡμᾶς ἀποστῆναι ὧν οὗτος ἡμφισβήτησε
καὶ δοῦναι δωρεάν· οὐ γὰρ ἔφασαν εἶναι ἄλλην ἀπ-
αλλαγὴν οὐδεμίαν, εἰ μὴ μεταλήψονται οὗτοι τῶν
32 ἐκείνου. ἐκ δὲ τοῦ λοιποῦ χρόνου ἔγνωσαν ἡμᾶς
εὖ ποιεῖν ἀλλήλους καὶ λόγῳ καὶ ἔργῳ, καὶ ταῦτα
ὀμόσαι ἠνάγκασαν ἡμᾶς ἀμφοτέρους πρὸς τῷ
βωμῷ ᾗ μὴν ποιήσειν.³ καὶ ἡμεῖς ὠμόσαμεν εὖ
ποιεῖν ἀλλήλους ἐκ τοῦ ἐπιλοίπου χρόνου, κατὰ
33 δύναμιν εἶναι, καὶ λόγῳ καὶ ἔργῳ. καὶ ὡς ὅ τε
ὅρκος ἐγένετο, καὶ ἔχουσιν οὗτοι ἃ ἐγνώσθη αὐτοῖς
ὑπὸ⁴ τῶν οἰκείων τῶν τούτου, εἶτα νυνὶ ταυτὶ τὰ
ἀγαθὰ ποιοῦσιν ἡμᾶς, τὸν μὲν τεθνεῶτα ἄπαιδα
βουλόμενοι καταστῆσαι, ἐμὲ δ' ἐκβάλλειν ὑβρίσαν-
τες ἐκ τοῦ οἴκου, τοὺς γνόντας αὐτοὺς ὑμῖν παρέξομαι μάρτυρας, ἐὰν ἐθέλωσιν ἀναβαίνειν (εἰσὶ γὰρ
τούτων οἰκεῖοι), εἰ δὲ μή, τοὺς παραγενομένους.
34 καί μοι τὰς μαρτυρίας ἀνάγνωθι ταυτασί· σὺ δ'
ἐπίλαβε⁵ τὸ ὕδωρ.

MAPTYPIAI

Λαβὲ δή μοι τὰς μαρτυρίας ἐκείνας, ὡς τό τε
χωρίον ἑβδομήκοντα μνῶν ἐπράθη, καὶ ὡς ἀπ-
έλαβεν ὁ ὀρφανὸς ἑπτὰ καὶ ἑξήκοντα μνᾶς πραθέντος
τοῦ χωρίου.

¹ ὥς γε δὴ ᾠόμεθα Sauppe: ὥστε δηώμεθα.
² Κεφαλῆσι Schoemann: κεφαλαίωσι.
³ ποιήσειν Q: ποιεῖν.   ⁴ ὑπὸ Q: ἀπὸ.
⁵ ἐπίλαβε Tyrwhitt: ἐπίβαλε.

ᵃ This sanctuary is mentioned on an inscription found
near the E. coast of Attica about 12 miles N. of Sunium.

matter, entrusted the decision to them on these terms. They, after having sworn an oath to us at the altar of Aphrodite at Cephale*a* that they would decide what was to our common interest, gave as their verdict that we should give up what my opponents claimed and hand it to him as a free gift; for they declared that the only way of settling the matter was that my opponent should receive a share of Menecles' property. They decided that for the future we must behave in a proper manner towards one another, both in word and in deed, and they obliged both parties to swear at the altar that they would do so ; so we swore that we would in future behave properly towards one another both in word and in deed, as far as lay within our power. That the oath was sworn and that these men are in possession of the property which was awarded to them by my opponent's friends and that their notion of behaving well towards us is this, to try and make the deceased childless and drive me forth with insult from his family—of all this I will produce before you as witnesses the very men who gave the decision, if they are willing to appear (for they are my opponent's friends), but, if not, those who were present on the occasion. Please read these depositions ; and, you, turn off the water-clock.*b*

EVIDENCE

Now, please, take these depositions to the effect that the land was sold for seventy minae and that the orphan received sixty-seven minae from the proceeds.

b The length of the speeches was regulated by means of a water-clock, which was turned off during the reading of laws and depositions.

ΜΑΡΤΥΡΙΑΙ

35 Ὁ θεῖος τοίνυν οὑτοσί, ὦ ἄνδρες, κεκληρονομη-
κὼς τῶν ἐκείνου ἔργῳ καὶ οὐ λόγῳ ὥσπερ ἐγώ,
καὶ ἔχων ἐμοῦ πολλῷ πλείονα· ἐγὼ γὰρ τὰς τριακοσίας δραχμὰς ἔλαβον τὰς περιλειφθείσας ἀπὸ
τῆς τιμῆς τοῦ χωρίου, καὶ οἰκίδιον ὅ ἐστιν οὐκ
ἄξιον τριῶν μνῶν· οὗτος δὲ πλεῖον ἢ δέκα μνῶν
χωρίον ἔχων, εἶτα προσέτι νῦν ἥκει τὸν οἶκον
36 αὐτοῦ ἐξερημώσων. καὶ ἐγὼ μὲν ὁ ποιητὸς ἐκεῖνόν τε ζῶντα ἐθεράπευον, καὶ αὐτὸς καὶ ἡ ἐμὴ
γυνή, θυγάτηρ οὖσα τουτουὶ Φιλωνίδου, καὶ τῷ
ἐμῷ παιδίῳ ἐθέμην τὸ ὄνομα τὸ ἐκείνου, ἵνα μὴ
ἀνώνυμος ὁ οἶκος αὐτοῦ γένηται, καὶ τελευτήσαντα
ἔθαψα ἀξίως ἐκείνου τε καὶ ἐμαυτοῦ, καὶ ἐπίθημα
καλὸν ἐπέθηκα, καὶ τὰ ἔνατα καὶ τἆλλα πάντα
ἐποίησα τὰ περὶ τὴν ταφὴν ὡς οἷόν τε κάλλιστα,
37 ὥστε τοὺς δημότας ἐπαινεῖν ἅπαντας· οὗτος δὲ
ὁ συγγενής, ὁ ἐπιτιμῶν αὐτῷ ὅτι ὑὸν ἐποιήσατο,
ζῶντος μὲν τὸ χωρίον τὸ περιλειφθὲν αὐτῷ περι-
είλετο, τελευτήσαντα δ' αὐτὸν ἄπαιδα καὶ ἀνώνυμον
βούλεται καταστῆσαι. τοιοῦτός ἐστιν οὗτος. καὶ
ὡς ἔθαψά τ' ἐγὼ αὐτὸν καὶ τὰ τρίτα καὶ τὰ ἔνατα
ἐποίησα καὶ τἆλλα τὰ περὶ τὴν ταφήν, τὰς μαρτυρίας ὑμῖν τῶν εἰδότων ἀναγνώσεται.

---

[a] *i.e.*, seeking to disinherit the adopted son and so deprive
Menecles of a representative to carry on his family.

EVIDENCE

Thus it is my uncle here, gentlemen, who has inherited the property of Menecles—really and not merely nominally, as I have—and has a much larger share than I have ; for I received only the three hundred drachmae which remained over out of the proceeds of the sale and a small house not worth three minae. My opponent, on the other hand, being in possession of land worth more than ten minae, has now, moreover, come into court with the object of rendering desolate the house of the deceased.[a] I, the adopted son, with the aid of my wife, the daughter of Philonides here, tended Menecles while he lived and gave his name to my little son, in order that his family might not lack a representative. On his death, I buried him in a manner befitting both him and myself, and I erected a fine monument to him and celebrated the commemorative ceremony on the ninth day and performed all the other rites at the tomb in the best manner possible, so that I won the praise of all the members of my deme. But my opponent, his kinsman, who blames him for having adopted a son, during his lifetime deprived him of the landed property which remained to him, and, now that he is dead, wishes to render him childless and wipe out his very name ; that is the kind of man he is. In proof that I buried Menecles and performed the ceremonies on the third and ninth days and all the other rites connected with the burial, the clerk shall read you the depositions of those who are acquainted with the facts.

ΜΑΡΤΥΡΙΑΙ

38 "Ὅτι τοίνυν ὁ Μενεκλῆς, ὦ ἄνδρες, ἐποιήσατό
με οὐ παρανοῶν οὐδὲ γυναικὶ πειθόμενος, βούλομαι
ὑμῖν καὶ αὐτοὺς τούτους μάρτυρας παρασχέσθαι,
[καὶ] ἐμοὶ μαρτυροῦντας ἔργῳ καὶ οὐ λόγῳ, ἐξ
ὧν ἔπραξαν αὐτοί, ὅτι ἐγὼ τἀληθῆ λέγω. τὰς
γὰρ διαλύσεις φαίνονται πρὸς ἐμὲ ποιησάμενοι
ἀμφότεροι οὗτοι, καὶ οὐ πρὸς τὸν Μενεκλέα, καὶ
39 ὁμόσαντες ὅρκους ‹ἐμοὶ›¹ καὶ ἐγὼ τούτοις. καίτοι
εἴ γε μὴ κατὰ τοὺς νόμους ἐγεγένητο ἡ ποίησις,
μηδὲ κληρονόμος ἦν ἐγὼ τῶν² Μενεκλέους ὑπ᾽
αὐτῶν τούτων δεδοκιμασμένος, τί ἔδει αὐτοὺς
ὀμνύναι ἐμοὶ ἢ παρ᾽ ἐμοῦ λαμβάνειν ὅρκους;
οὐδὲν³ δήπου. οὐκοῦν ὁπότε ἐποίησαν ταῦτα,
φαίνονται αὐτοὶ οὗτοι ἐμοὶ μαρτυροῦντες ὅτι κατὰ
τοὺς νόμους ἐποιήθην⁴ [ἡ ποίησις] καὶ δικαίως
40 εἰμὶ κληρονόμος τῶν Μενεκλέους. ἐγὼ δ᾽ οἶμαι
καταφανὲς ὑμῖν ἅπασι τοῦτ᾽ εἶναι, ὡς καὶ παρὰ
τούτων αὐτῶν ὁμολογούμενόν ἐστιν ὅτι Μενεκλῆς
οὐ παρεφρόνει, ἀλλὰ πολὺ μᾶλλον οὗτος νυνί, ὅς
γε ποιησάμενος τῆς ἔχθρας διάλυσιν πρὸς ἡμᾶς καὶ
ὀμόσας ὅρκους πάλιν νῦν ἥκει τὰ ὁμολογηθέντα
καὶ ὁμοθέντα παραβάς, καὶ ἀφελέσθαι με ἀξιοῖ
41 ταυτὶ τὰ λοιπά, οὕτως ὄντα μικρά. ἐγὼ δὲ εἰ μὴ
πάνυ τὸ πρᾶγμα αἰσχρὸν εἶναι ἐνόμιζον καὶ ἐπονεί-
διστον, προδοῦναι τὸν πατέρα οὗ εἶναι ὠνομάσθην
καὶ ὃς ἐποιήσατό με, ταχὺ ἂν ἀπέστην αὐτῷ τῶν
ἐκείνου· ἔστι γὰρ ὑπόλοιπον οὐδὲ ἕν, ὡς καὶ ὑμᾶς
42 οἴομαι αἰσθάνεσθαι. νυνὶ δὲ δεινὸν τὸ πρᾶγμα καὶ

---

¹ ἐμοὶ add. Bremi.
² τῶν edd. : τοῦ.
³ οὐδὲν Tyrwhitt: οὐδὲ ἕν.
⁴ ἐποιήθην Cobet: -η.

EVIDENCE

In support of the truth of my assertion, gentlemen, that Menecles, when he adopted me, was not insane or under the influence of a woman, I wish to bring before you my opponents themselves as witnesses, not in word but in deed, by their own conduct. For it is notorious that both of them went through the process of reconciliation with me and not with Menecles, and swore an oath to me, as I did to them. Yet if the adoption had not been carried out in proper legal form and I had not been recognized as heir to Menecles' property by my opponents themselves, what need was there for them to swear to me and to receive an oath from me? Surely none. By so acting then they themselves clearly bear witness that I was legally adopted and am the rightful heir of Menecles. It is clear, I think, to you all that it was acknowledged even by my opponents themselves that Menecles was not insane but that it is much rather my opponent who is insane now, seeing that, after having effected a settlement of his quarrel with us and having sworn oaths, he has now again come forward in violation of his acknowledgements and oaths, and demands that I shall be deprived of these poor remnants of the estate. Were it not that I think it an altogether base and shameful act to betray him whose son I was called and who adopted me, I would have readily abandoned the right of succession to his estate in favour of my opponent; for there is nothing at all left, as I think you realize. But, in the cir-

αἰσχρὸν εἶναι τῇδε νομίζω, εἰ ἡνίκα μὲν ὁ Μενεκλῆς
εἶχέ τι, τότε μὲν ἔδωκα ἐμαυτὸν υὸν αὐτῷ ποιήσασθαι, καὶ ἀπὸ τῆς οὐσίας τῆς ἐκείνου, πρὶν
πραθῆναι τὸ χωρίον, ἐγυμνασιάρχουν ἐν τῷ δήμῳ
καὶ ἐφιλοτιμήθην ὡς υὸς ὢν ἐκείνου, καὶ τὰς
στρατείας, ὅσαι ἐγένοντο ἐν τῷ χρόνῳ τούτῳ,
ἐστράτευμαι ἐν τῇ φυλῇ τῇ ἐκείνου καὶ ἐν τῷ
43 δήμῳ· ἐπειδὴ δὲ ἐκεῖνος ἐτελεύτησεν, εἰ προδώσω
καὶ ἐξερημώσας αὐτοῦ τὸν οἶκον ἀπιὼν οἰχήσομαι,
πῶς οὐκ ἂν δεινὸν τὸ πρᾶγμα εἶναι καὶ κατα-
γέλαστον δοκοίη, καὶ τοῖς βουλομένοις περὶ ἐμοῦ
βλασφημεῖν πολλὴν ἐξουσίαν παράσχοι[1]; καὶ οὐ
μόνον ταῦτ' ἐστὶ τὰ ποιοῦντά με ἀγωνίζεσθαι τὸν
ἀγῶνα τοῦτον, ἀλλ' εἰ οὕτω φαῦλος ἄνθρωπος δοκῶ
εἶναι καὶ μηδενὸς ἄξιος, ὥστε ὑπὸ μὲν εὖ φρονοῦντος μηδ' ὑφ' ἑνὸς ἂν ποιηθῆναι τῶν φίλων, ὑπὸ δὲ
παραφρονοῦντος, ταῦτ' ἐστὶ τὰ λυποῦντά με.

44 Ἐγὼ οὖν δέομαι ὑμῶν πάντων, ὦ ἄνδρες, καὶ
ἀντιβολῶ καὶ ἱκετεύω ἐλεῆσαί με καὶ ἀποψηφίσασθαι τοῦ μάρτυρος τουτουί. ἀπέφηνα δ' ὑμῖν
πρῶτον μὲν ποιηθέντα ἐμαυτὸν ὑπὸ τοῦ Μενεκλέους ὡς ἄν τις δικαιότατα ποιηθείη,[2] καὶ οὐ
λόγῳ οὐδὲ διαθήκῃ τὴν ποίησιν γεγενημένην, ἀλλ'
ἔργῳ· καὶ τούτων ὑμῖν τούς τε φράτορας καὶ τοὺς
45 δημότας καὶ τοὺς ὀργεῶνας παρεσχόμην μάρτυρας·
καὶ ἐκεῖνον ἐπέδειξα τρία καὶ εἴκοσιν ἐπιβιόντα[3]
ἔτη. εἶτα τοὺς νόμους ἐπέδειξα ὑμῖν τοῖς ἄπαισι
τῶν ἀνθρώπων[4] ἐξουσίαν διδόντας υἱεῖς ποιεῖσθαι.

---

[1] παράσχοι Buermann : παράσχομαι.
[2] ποιηθείη Bekker : -θῇ.
[3] ἐπιβιόντα Bamberg : ἐπιβιοῦντα.
[4] τοῖς ἄπαισι τῶν ἀνθρώπων Naber : τοῖς ἄπασι τοῖς ἀνθρώποις.

cumstances, I consider it terrible and disgraceful
that, when Menecles possessed property, I accepted
adoption as his son and out of his property, before
the land was sold, acted as gymnasiarch[a] in his
deme and won credit as his son, and served in his
tribe and deme on all the campaigns which took
place during that period ; and, now that he is dead,
if I shall betray him and go off leaving his house
desolate, would it not seem a strange and ridiculous
proceeding, and give those who wish to do so a good
occasion to speak evil of me ? And these are not
the only motives which induce me to fight this
case ; but what grieves me is the possibility of
being thought so worthless and good-for-nothing
as not to be able to find a friend in his right senses,
but only a madman, to adopt me.

I beg you all therefore, gentlemen, and beseech
and entreat you to pity me and to acquit the witness
here. I have shown you that, in the first place, I
was adopted by Menecles with the strictest possible
legality, and that the form of adoption was not
merely verbal or by will but by very act and deed ;
and of these things I produced before you the
evidence of the wardsmen, the demesmen, and the
members of the confraternity. I further showed that
Menecles lived for twenty-three years after he had
adopted me. Further, I placed before you the
laws which permit those who are childless to adopt
sons. In addition to this I am shown to have tended

[a] The duty of the gymnasiarch was to bear the expense
of the torch-races at certain festivals.

καὶ ἔτι πρὸς τούτοις ζῶντά τε φαίνομαι θεραπεύων
46 αὐτὸν καὶ τελευτήσαντα θάψας. οὗτος δὲ νυνὶ
ἄκληρον μὲν ἐμὲ ποιεῖν τοῦ κλήρου τοῦ πατρῴου,
εἴτε μείζων ἐστὶν οὗτος εἴτε ἐλάττων, ἄπαιδα δὲ
τὸν τελευτήσαντα καὶ ἀνώνυμον βούλεται καταστῆσαι, ἵνα μήτε τὰ ἱερὰ τὰ πατρῷα ὑπὲρ ἐκείνου
μηδεὶς τιμᾷ μήτ᾽[1] ἐναγίζῃ αὐτῷ καθ᾽ ἕκαστον
ἐνιαυτόν, ἀλλὰ ἀφαιρῆται[2] τὰς τιμὰς τὰς ἐκείνου·
ἃ προνοηθεὶς ὁ Μενεκλῆς, κύριος ὢν τῶν ἑαυτοῦ,
ἐποιήσατο ὑὸν ἑαυτῷ, ἵνα τούτων ἁπάντων τυγ-
47 χάνῃ. μὴ οὖν, ὦ ἄνδρες, πεισθέντες ὑπὸ τούτων
ἀφέλησθέ μου τὸ ὄνομα, τῆς κληρονομίας ὃ ἔτι
μόνον λοιπόν ἐστιν,[3] ἄκυρον δὲ τὴν ποίησιν αὐτοῦ
καταστήσητε[4]· ἀλλ᾽ ἐπειδὴ τὸ πρᾶγμα εἰς ὑμᾶς
ἀφῖκται καὶ ὑμεῖς κύριοι γεγόνατε, βοηθήσατε καὶ
ἡμῖν καὶ ἐκείνῳ τῷ ἐν Ἅιδου ὄντι, καὶ μὴ περιίδητε, πρὸς θεῶν καὶ δαιμόνων δέομαι ὑμῶν,
προπηλακισθέντα αὐτὸν ὑπὸ τούτων, ἀλλὰ μεμνημένοι τοῦ νόμου καὶ τοῦ ὅρκου ὃν ὀμωμόκατε
καὶ τῶν εἰρημένων ὑπὲρ τοῦ πράγματος, τὰ δίκαια
καὶ τὰ εὔορκα κατὰ τοὺς νόμους ψηφίσασθε.

---

[1] μήτ᾽ Bremi: μηδ᾽.   [2] ἀφαιρῆται Dobree: -εῖται.
[3] ἐστιν Tyrwhitt: ἔσται.   [4] καταστήσητε edd.: καταστήσετε.

him in his lifetime and to have buried him when he died. My opponent wishes now to deprive me of my father's estate, whether it be large or small, and to render the deceased childless and nameless, so that there may be no one to honour in his place the family cults and perform for him the annual rites, but that he may be robbed of all his due honours. It was to provide against this that Menecles, being master of his own property, adopted a son, so that he might secure all these advantages.

Do not therefore, gentlemen, listen to my opponents and deprive me of my name, the sole remnant of my inheritance, and annul Menecles' adoption of me; but since the matter has come before you for judgement and you have the sovereign right of decision, come to the aid both of us and of him who is in the other world, and do not allow Menecles, by the gods and deities I beseech you, to be insulted by my opponents, but mindful of the law and of the oath which you have sworn and of the arguments which have been used in support of my plea, pass in accordance with the laws the verdict which is just and in conformity with your oath.

III. ON THE ESTATE OF PYRRHUS

INTRODUCTION

PYRRHUS[a] having adopted Endius, his sister's son, made a will leaving his property to him. On the death of Pyrrhus, Endius succeeded without question and, after having enjoyed the estate for twenty years, died without issue. Being an adopted son he had no right to dispose of the property, which on his decease passed by law to Pyrrhus's legal heir.

Two days after Endius's death the estate was claimed by one Xenocles on behalf of his wife, Phile, whom he asserted to be the legitimate daughter of Pyrrhus; he even appears to have attempted to seize a portion of the property. His claim was opposed by Endius's mother, whose name is not known to us, as being sister of Pyrrhus and therefore his next-of-kin. She is represented by her younger son. Xenocles thereupon put in a protestation (διαμαρτυρία) that the estate could not

[a] STEMMA

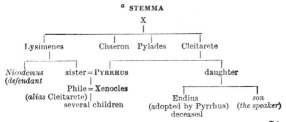

71

legally be claimed by Pyrrhus's sister, because Pyrrhus had left a legitimate daughter, and offered evidence that his wife's mother, the sister of a certain Nicodemus, had been legally married to Pyrrhus, and that Phile was the offspring of their union. A charge of perjury was successfully brought against Xenocles, with the result that the illegitimacy of Phile was established. In order still further to substantiate the claim of Pyrrhus's sister, her son brings a further action for perjury against Nicodemus, the brother of Phile's mother, who had supported Xenocles by bearing witness to his sister's marriage with Pyrrhus. The present speech, therefore, which was delivered on this occasion, though in effect concerned with the "Estate of Pyrrhus," might be more accurately described as "Against Nicodemus for perjury." The object of the speaker being to prove that the testimony of Nicodemus was false when he swore that he had given his sister in legal marriage to Pyrrhus, many of the arguments must be a repetition, before a new panel of judges, of those which had been employed in the earlier action against Xenocles.

The speech provides one of the best examples of the way in which the Attic orators used the topic of probability which Aristotle recommends as the basis of a rhetorical syllogism (*Rhet.* 1357 a 32 ff., 1376 a 18 ff.). Was it likely, the speaker asks, that Pyrrhus would have married Nicodemus's sister in view of her general mode of life and her conduct while she lived in Pyrrhus's house ? Again, he urges, Nicodemus's account of his own action in the matter of the marriage contains inconsistencies which make it improbable : since he was marrying his sister to a man of wealth, he would naturally have summoned as many reputable witnesses as possible; instead of this he alleged the presence of only one witness, Pyretides, who subsequently denied that he had been present or had made any deposition to that effect. It is true that the three uncles of Pyrrhus declared that they were present at the ceremony; but is it likely that they would have countenanced the marriage of their nephew to such a woman? Again, their evidence disclosed the fact that no dowry was settled on the woman; yet, even if Nicodemus had been unable to give her a portion, he would naturally have insisted on a contract in order to make a divorce more difficult. Obviously, the speaker urges, the uncles' evidence is worthless; for example, they told a different story about the name given to the child, saying that she was called not Phile but Cleitarete, after her paternal grandmother. Again, Nicodemus would have insisted on a settlement, because, in event of his sister's death without issue, he would have become heir to any money which had been settled upon her. Supposing for a moment that his sister had been legally married to Pyrrhus and that consequently her child Phile was her father's heiress, why was no opposition offered when Endius succeeded to the estate of his adoptive father, and why did not Nicodemus prosecute Endius when he gave Phile in marriage to Xenocles as the illegitimate daughter of Pyrrhus? In fact all the parties conserned clearly showed by their acts that they regarded Phile as illegitimate; Xenocles, by not claiming his wife's patrimony at Pyrrhus's death or during Endius's lifetime; the uncles, by allowing Phile to marry Xenocles, since, if she had been legitimate, the estate would have passed to her issue instead of to themselves ; and, lastly, Pyrrhus himself, by adopting Endius as his son, which he would not have done if he had had a legitimate daughter, and by his omission of the usual formality of introducing Phile to his fellow-wardsmen and so recognizing her as his legitimate child. The speaker concludes with a summary of his earlier arguments and by calling evidence to prove that Pyrrhus can never have married Nico-demus's sister, since he never offered a marriage feast to the members of his ward and never per-formed on her behalf the public services in his deme which his financial position would have entailed.

Thus, as has already been said, the whole argu-ment is based upon probabilities, and the speaker seems to rely on the cumulative effect of frequent repetition to convince his hearers. On the other hand, the defence was obviously based on testimony, in particular, that of the uncles of Pyrrhus, who were hardly likely to have given evidence in favour of a marriage which was anything but creditable to their nephew, unless it had really taken place ; moreover they gave evidence not only of the mar-riage but also of the fact that Pyrrhus celebrated the naming-festival on the tenth day after Phile's birth, thus acknowledging the child as his own.

It would be interesting to know how the defence met the challenge of the prosecutor to explain, first, why Endius succeeded without question to the estate, and, secondly, the exact circumstances of Phile's marriage to Xenocles. Wyse (*op. cit.* p. 276) suggests that a clue is provided by the 10th Oration, where the speaker is arguing on the other side in favour of an heiress, who, it is alleged, had been defrauded of her just rights by an iniquitous family compact, and whose husband was prevented from claiming the estate due to her by the fear that he would lose his wife, whose hand might be legally claimed by the next of kin. If a similar line of defence was adopted by the supporters of Phile, Endius would certainly have acted illegally, but the uncles and Nicodemus would also be blameworthy for allowing Phile to be the subject of such a bargain if they believed her to be the legitimate child of Pyrrhus.

There is no conclusive evidence of the date of the speech, but it is probably among the later works of Isaeus. The only indications are the mention of Diophantes of Sphettus and Dorotheus of Eleusis (§ 22). The former is probably the orator and politician, who is known to have survived until 343 B.C., when he was called as a witness by Demosthenes in the speech *De falsa legatione* ; Dorotheus is known from inscriptions to have been trierarch in 357/6 B.C. and to have owned property in Athens about 342 B.C. ([Dem.] *In Neaeram*, 39).

III. ΠΕΡΙ ΤΟΥ ΠΥΡΡΟΥ ΚΛΗΡΟΥ

ΥΠΟΘΕΣΙΣ

[38]   Πύρρου τὸν ἕτερον ⟨τῶν⟩ τῆς ἀδελφῆς υἱῶν υἱοποιησα-
μένου Ἔνδιον, καὶ τούτου πλέον ἢ εἴκοσιν ἔτη τὸν
κλῆρον[1] κατασχόντος, εἶτα ἀποθανόντος, Ξενοκλῆς λαχὼν τῶν χρημάτων ὑπὲρ Φίλης, τῆς ἑαυτοῦ γυναικός,
διεμαρτύρησεν εἶναι αὐτὴν γνησίαν Πύρρου θυγατέρα,
ἀμφισβητούσης τοῦ κλήρου τῆς Ἐνδίου μητρός· καὶ ἑάλω
ψευδομαρτυριῶν, Νικοδήμου καὶ αὐτοῦ μαρτυρήσαντος
ἐγγυῆσαι Πύρρῳ τὴν ἀδελφὴν κατὰ τοὺς νόμους, ἐξ ἧς
γεγονέναι τὴν Φίλην. ὁ Ἐνδίου δὲ ἀδελφὸς νόθην
εἶναί φησιν, ἐξ ἑταίρας Πύρρῳ γενομένην, καὶ οὕτως
ὑπὸ Ἐνδίου ἐκδοθῆναι Ξενοκλεῖ. ἡ στάσις στοχασμός,
τὸ δὲ ἔγκλημα ψευδομαρτυριῶν κατὰ τοῦ Νικοδήμου.

1   Ἄνδρες δικασταί, ὁ ἀδελφὸς τῆς μητρὸς τῆς ἐμῆς
Πύρρος, ἄπαις ὢν γνησίων παίδων, ἐποιήσατο Ἔνδιον τὸν ἀδελφὸν τὸν ἐμὸν υἱὸν ἑαυτῷ· ὃς κληρονόμος ὢν τῶν ἐκείνου ἐπεβίω[2] πλείω ἔτη ἢ εἴκοσι,
καὶ ἐν χρόνῳ τοσούτῳ ἔχοντος ἐκείνου τὸν κλῆρον
οὐδεὶς πώποτε προσεποιήσατο οὐδ' ἠμφισβήτησε
2   τῆς κληρονομίας ἐκείνῳ. τελευτήσαντος δὲ τοῦ
ἀδελφοῦ πέρυσιν, ὑπερβᾶσα τὸν τελευταῖον κληρονόμον, γνησία θυγάτηρ τοῦ ἡμετέρου θείου ἥκει
φάσκουσα εἶναι Φίλη, καὶ κύριος Ξενοκλῆς Κό-

---

[1] τὸν κλῆρον Aldus : τοῦ κλήρου.
[2] ἐπεβίω Naber : ἐβίω.

III. ON THE ESTATE OF PYRRHUS

ARGUMENT

Pyrrhus had adopted one of his sister's two sons, Endius, who enjoyed the estate for more than twenty years and then died. Xenocles then sued for the property in the name of Phile, his wife, and declared upon oath that she was a legitimate daughter of Pyrrhus, the succession being claimed by Endius's mother. Xenocles was convicted of perjury. Nicodemus had also borne witness that he had given his sister in legal marriage to Pyrrhus and that Phile was her child. The brother of Endius declares that Phile is illegitimate, having been the child of Pyrrhus by a mistress, and that she was given as such by Endius in marriage to Xenocles. The question at issue is one of fact, and the action a charge of perjury against Nicodemus.

Judges, my mother's brother, Pyrrhus, having no legitimate issue, adopted my brother Endius as his son. The latter inherited his estate and survived him by more than twenty years ; and during all this long period of possession no one claimed the estate or questioned his right of inheritance. My brother having died last year, Phile, ignoring the existence of the last tenant, came forward, claiming to be the legitimate daughter of our uncle, and Xenocles of Coprus,[a] as her legal representative,

---

[a] A deme belonging to the tribe of Hippothontis. A scholiast on Aristophanes, *Equites* 899, states that it was an island off Attica.

πρειος[1] τοῦ Πύρρου κλήρου λαχεῖν τὴν λῆξιν
ἠξίωσεν, ὃς τετελεύτηκε[2] πλείω ἢ εἴκοσιν ἔτη, τρία
3 τάλαντα τίμημα τῷ κλήρῳ ἐπιγραψάμενος. ἀμφισβητούσης δὲ τῆς μητρὸς τῆς ἡμετέρας, ἀδελφῆς δὲ
τοῦ Πύρρου, ὁ κύριος τῆς εἰληχυίας τοῦ κλήρου
γυναικὸς ἐτόλμησε διαμαρτυρῆσαι μὴ ἐπίδικον τῇ
ἡμετέρᾳ μητρὶ τὸν τοῦ ἀδελφοῦ κλῆρον εἶναι, ὡς
οὔσης γνησίας θυγατρὸς Πύρρῳ, οὗ ἦν ἐξ ἀρχῆς
ὁ κλῆρος. ἐπισκηψάμενοι[3] δὲ ἡμεῖς, καὶ εἰς
ὑμᾶς εἰσαγαγόντες τὸν διαμαρτυρῆσαι τολμήσαντα
4 [κατὰ] ταῦτα, ἐκεῖνόν τε ἐξελέγξαντες περιφανῶς
τὰ ψευδῆ μεμαρτυρηκότα τὴν τῶν ψευδομαρτυρίων[4]
δίκην εἵλομεν παρ' ὑμῖν, καὶ τουτονὶ Νικόδημον
παραχρῆμα ἐξηλέγξαμεν ἐν τοῖς αὐτοῖς δικασταῖς
ἀναισχυντότατον τῇ μαρτυρίᾳ ὄντα ταύτῃ, ὅς γε
ἐτόλμησε μαρτυρῆσαι ἐγγυῆσαι τῷ θείῳ τῷ
ἡμετέρῳ τὴν ἀδελφὴν τὴν ἑαυτοῦ γυναῖκα εἶναι
5 κατὰ τοὺς νόμους. ὅτι μὲν οὖν καὶ ἐν τῇ προτέρᾳ
δίκῃ ἡ τούτου μαρτυρία ψευδὴς ἔδοξεν εἶναι, ὁ
τόθ' ἑαλωκὼς μάρτυς σαφέστατα τοῦτον ἐξελέγχει.
εἰ γὰρ μὴ ἐδόκει οὗτος τὰ ψευδῆ τότε μαρτυρῆσαι,
δῆλον ὅτι ἐκεῖνός τ' ἂν ἀποφυγὼν τὴν διαμαρ-
τυρίαν ἀπῆλθε, καὶ κληρονόμος ἂν τῶν τοῦ θείου
ἡ διαμαρτυρηθεῖσα γνησία θυγάτηρ εἶναι, ἀλλ' οὐκ
6 ἂν ἡ ἡμετέρα κατέστη μήτηρ. ἁλόντος δὲ τοῦ
μάρτυρος καὶ ἀποστάσης τοῦ κλήρου τῆς ἀμφι-

---

[1] Κόπρειος Wyse: κύπριος.
[2] τετελεύτηκε Baiter: τετελευτήκει.
[3] ἐπισκηψάμενοι Taylor: ἐπισκεψ-.
[4] ψευδομαρτυρίων Wyse: -τύρων.

demanded to be given possession of the estate of
Pyrrhus, who had died more than twenty years
before, having fixed the value of the estate at three
talents. When our mother, the sister of Pyrrhus,
claimed[a] the estate, the legal representative of the
woman who was suing for the estate audaciously put
in a protestation[b] that her brother's estate was
not adjudicable to our mother, because Pyrrhus,
to whom it originally belonged, had a legitimate
daughter. We denounced his protestation and
brought before you the man who had the audacity
to make it ; and, having clearly convicted him of
having given false evidence, we obtained from you
a verdict for perjury against him. At the same
time we convicted Nicodemus, the present defendant,
before the same judges, of the most shameless lying
in the evidence which he then gave, since he had
the impudence to bear witness that he had given
his sister in marriage to our uncle in the proper
legal manner. That in the former trial Nicodemus's
evidence was recognized as being false, the con-
demnation of the witness[c] on that occasion most
clearly proves. For if the present defendant had
not been recognized as having given false evidence,
the other witness would have been acquitted in
the suit about the protestation, and the woman
whom the protestation affirmed to be my uncle's
legitimate daughter would have been established
as his heiress instead of our mother. But since the
witness was convicted and the woman who claimed

---

[a] She claimed as sister of Pyrrhus, not as mother of
Endius, in which capacity she had no title.
[b] For the meaning of διαμαρτυρία (protestation) see
Oration II. Introduction, p. 37.
[c] *i.e.*, Xenocles.

σβητούσης γνησίας θυγατρὸς Πύρρῳ εἶναι, μεγάλη
ἀνάγκη ἅμα καὶ τὴν τούτου μαρτυρίαν ἑαλωκέναι·
περὶ γὰρ αὐτοῦ τούτου διαμαρτυρήσας τὴν τῶν
ψευδομαρτυριῶν[1] δίκην ἠγωνίζετο, πότερον ἐξ ἐγγυητῆς ἢ ἐξ ἑταίρας ἡ ἀμφισβητοῦσα τοῦ κλήρου
τῷ θείῳ [γυναικὸς] εἴη· γνώσεσθε <δ᾽>[2] ἀκούσαντες
καὶ ὑμεῖς τῆς τε ἀντωμοσίας τῆς ἡμετέρας καὶ τῆς
τούτου μαρτυρίας καὶ τῆς ἁλούσης διαμαρτυρίας.
7 ἀναγίγνωσκε λαβὼν τασδὶ αὐτοῖς.

ΑΝΤΩΜΟΣΙΑ.   ΜΑΡΤΥΡΙΑ.   ΔΙΑΜΑΡΤΥΡΙΑ.

Ὡς μὲν ἔδοξε παραχρῆμα εὐθὺς τότε <πᾶσι>[3] τὰ
ψευδῆ μαρτυρῆσαι[4] Νικόδημος ἐπιδέδεικται [τότε
πᾶσι]· προσήκει δὲ καὶ παρ᾽ ὑμῖν τοῖς περὶ αὐτοῦ
τούτου τὴν δίκην μέλλουσι ψηφιεῖσθαι ἐξελεχθῆναι
8 τὴν τούτου μαρτυρίαν. ἐπιθυμῶ δὲ πρῶτον μὲν
[περὶ αὐτοῦ τούτου] πυθέσθαι, ἥν τινά ποτε
προῖκά φησιν ἐπιδοὺς ἐκδοῦναι τὴν ἀδελφὴν ὁ
μεμαρτυρηκὼς τῷ τὸν τριτάλαντον οἶκον κεκτημένῳ, εἶτα πότερον ἡ ἐγγυητὴ γυνὴ ἀπέλιπε τὸν
ἄνδρα ζῶντα ἢ τελευτήσαντος τὸν οἶκον αὐτοῦ,
καὶ παρ᾽ ὅτου ἐκομίσατο τὴν τῆς ἀδελφῆς προῖκα
οὗτος, ἐπειδὴ τετελευτηκὼς ἦν ᾧ μεμαρτύρηκεν
9 οὗτος αὐτὴν ἐγγυῆσαι, ἢ εἰ μὴ ἐκομίζετο, ὁποίαν
δίκην σίτου ἢ τῆς προικὸς αὐτῆς ἐν εἴκοσιν ἔτεσι

---

[1] ψευδομαρτυριῶν Wyse : -τύρων.
[2] δ᾽ add. Aldus.   [3] πᾶσι add. Roussel.
[4] μαρτυρῆσαι Reiske: διαμαρτ-.

---

[a] The term ἀντωμοσία was given to the " counter-oaths "
taken by the contending parties at the preliminary hearing
in support of their respective declarations.

to be Pyrrhus's legitimate daughter abandoned her pretensions to the estate, it follows by absolute necessity that Nicodemus's evidence has been also condemned ; for, having solemnly sworn to the truth of the same proposition, he was a party to the action for perjury which was to decide whether the woman who claimed my uncle's estate was the issue of a legitimate wife or of a mistress. You, too, will realize that this is so when you have heard our affidavit,[a] the evidence of Nicodemus, and the protestation which was overruled. Please take and read these documents to the court.

AFFIDAVITS. EVIDENCE. PROTESTATION

It has now been shown that it was immediately apparent to all at the time that Nicodemus committed perjury ; but it is proper that the falsity of his evidence should be proved before you also who are about to give your verdict on this very issue. But I desire first to ask some questions. He has deposed that he married his sister to a man who possessed a fortune of three talents ; what dowry does he allege that he gave with her ? Next, did this wedded wife leave her husband during his lifetime or quit his house after his death ?[b] And from whom did the defendant recover his sister's dowry after the death of him to whom he has deposed that he gave her in marriage ? Or, if he did not recover it, what action did he think fit to institute

---

[b] A widow might either remain in her late husband's house, if there were no children, or return to the house of her legal representative (κύριος), and, through him, obtain the return of her dowry or the payment of interest upon it for her maintenance.

[39] τῷ ἔχοντι τὸν | κλῆρον δικάσασθαι ἠξίωσεν,[1] ἢ
εἴ του ἀνθρώπων ἐναντίον προσῆλθεν ἐγκαλῶν τῷ
κληρονόμῳ περὶ τῆς προικὸς τῆς ἀδελφῆς ἐν χρόνῳ
τοσούτῳ. περί τε οὖν τούτων ἡδέως ἂν πυθοίμην,
ὅ τι ποτ' ἦν τὸ αἴτιον τοῦ μηδὲν τούτων γεγενῆσθαι
περὶ τῆς ἐγγυητῆς (ὡς μεμαρτύρηκεν οὗτος) γυναι-
10 κός, καὶ πρὸς τούτοις εἴ τις ἄλλος ἐγγυητὴν ἔσχε
τὴν τούτου ἀδελφὴν γυναῖκα, ἢ τῶν πρότερον χρησαμένων πρὶν γνῶναι τὸν ἡμέτερον θεῖον αὐτήν, ἢ
ὅσοι ἐκείνου γιγνώσκοντος ἐπλησίαζον αὐτῇ, ἢ
ὅσοι ὕστερον ἐπλησίαζον τετελευτηκότος ἐκείνου·
δῆλον γὰρ ὅτι τὸν αὐτὸν τρόπον ὁ ἀδελφὸς αὐτὴν
11 ἅπασι τοῖς πλησιάζουσιν ἐκδέδωκεν.[2] περὶ ὧν εἰ
δεήσειε καθ' ἕκαστον διελθεῖν, οὐκ ἂν πάνυ μικρὸν
ἔργον γένοιτο. ἐὰν μὲν οὖν ὑμεῖς κελεύητε, περὶ
ἐνίων μνησθείην ἂν αὐτῶν· εἰ δέ τισιν ὑμῶν ἀηδὲς
ἀκούειν ἐστίν, ὥσπερ ἐμοὶ λέγειν τι περὶ τούτων,
αὐτὰς τὰς μαρτυρίας ὑμῖν παρέξομαι τὰς μαρτυ-
ρηθείσας ἐν τῇ προτέρᾳ δίκῃ, ὧν οὐδεμιᾷ ἐπισκήψασθαι ἠξίωσαν οὗτοι. καίτοι ὅπου κοινὴν αὐτοὶ[3]
ὡμολογήκασιν εἶναι τοῦ βουλομένου τὴν γυναῖκα,
πῶς ἂν εἰκότως ἡ αὐτὴ γυνὴ ἐγγυητὴ δόξειεν
12 εἶναι; ἀλλὰ μὴν ὁπότε μὴ ἐπεσκημμένοι εἰσὶ ταῖς
περὶ αὐτοῦ τούτου μαρτυρίαις, ὡμολογηκότες εἰσὶ
ταῦτα. ἀκούσαντες δὲ καὶ ὑμεῖς αὐτῶν τῶν
μαρτυριῶν, γνώσεσθε ὡς οὗτός τε περιφανῶς τὰ
ψευδῆ μεμαρτύρηκε, καὶ ὀρθῶς καὶ κατὰ τοὺς
νόμους οἱ δικάσαντες τὴν δίκην ἔγνωσαν τὴν

---

[1] ἠξίωσεν Reiske : -σαν.
[2] ἐκδέδωκεν Reiske : ἐδεδώκει.
[3] αὐτοὶ Schoemann : αὐτὴν.

to obtain her maintenance or the restitution of her dowry against the man who was for twenty years the tenant of the estate ? Or did he ever, during all that long period, go and make any claim upon the heir regarding his sister's dowry in the presence of any witness ? I should be glad to learn what was the reason why none of these steps has been taken in favour of a woman, who, according to the defendant's evidence, was legally married. Furthermore, has anyone else taken this man's sister in legal marriage, either of those who had dealings with her before our uncle knew her, or of those who associated with her during his acquaintance with her, or of those who did so after his decease ? For it is clear that her brother has given her in marriage on the same terms to all those associated with her. If it were necessary to enumerate all these persons one by one, it would amount to no small a task. If you bid me do so, I would mention some of them ; but if it is as unpleasant to some of you to hear as it is to me to mention such matters, I will content myself with producing the actual depositions made at the previous trial, none of which they thought fit to contest. Yet when once they have themselves admitted that the woman was at the disposal of anyone who wished to take her, how can it be reasonably conceived that she was also a wedded wife ? And indeed, since they have never impeached the evidence on this very point, they have in fact admitted all this. You, too, when you have heard the actual depositions, will understand that the defendant has obviously borne false witness, and that those who judged the case gave a proper and a legal sentence when they

κληρονομίαν μὴ προσήκειν τῇ μὴ ὀρθῶς γεγενη-
μένῃ γυναικί. ἀναγίγνωσκε. σὺ δ' ἐπίλαβε[1] τὸ
ὕδωρ.

ΜΑΡΤΥΡΙΑ⟨Ι⟩

13 Ὡς μὲν ἑταίρα ἦν τῷ βουλομένῳ καὶ οὐ γυνὴ
τοῦ ἡμετέρου θείου, ἣν οὗτος ἐγγυῆσαι ἐκείνῳ μεμαρτύρηκεν, ὑπὸ τῶν ἄλλων οἰκείων καὶ ὑπὸ τῶν
γειτόνων τῶν ἐκείνου μεμαρτύρηται πρὸς ὑμᾶς· οἳ
μάχας καὶ κώμους καὶ ἀσέλγειαν πολλήν, ὁπότε ἡ
τούτου ἀδελφὴ εἴη παρ' αὐτῷ, μεμαρτυρήκασι
14 γίγνεσθαι περὶ αὐτῆς. καίτοι οὐ δή πού γε ἐπὶ
γαμετὰς γυναῖκας οὐδεὶς ἂν κωμάζειν τολμήσειεν·
οὐδὲ αἱ γαμεταὶ γυναῖκες ἔρχονται μετὰ τῶν
ἀνδρῶν ἐπὶ τὰ δεῖπνα, οὐδὲ συνδειπνεῖν ἀξιοῦσι
μετὰ τῶν ἀλλοτρίων, καὶ ταῦτα μετὰ τῶν ἐπι-
τυχόντων. ἀλλὰ μὴν τῶν γε μεμαρτυρηκότων οὐδενὶ[2] ἐπισκήψασθαι οὗτοι ἠξίωσαν. καὶ ὡς ἀληθῆ
λέγω, ἀναγίγνωσκε πάλιν αὐτοῖς τὴν μαρτυρίαν.

ΜΑΡΤΥΡΙΑ

15 Ἀνάγνωθι δὴ καὶ τὰς περὶ τῶν πλησιασάντων
αὐτῇ μαρτυρίας, ἵνα εἰδῶσιν ὅτι ἑταίρα τε ἦν τοῦ
βουλομένου, καὶ ὅτι οὐδ' ἐξ ἑνὸς ἄλλου φαίνεται
τεκοῦσα. ἀναγίγνωσκε αὐτοῖς.

ΜΑΡΤΥΡΙΑ⟨Ι⟩

16 Ὡς μὲν τοίνυν ἦν κοινὴ τῷ βουλομένῳ, ἣν οὗτος
ἐγγυῆσαι τῷ ἡμετέρῳ θείῳ μεμαρτύρηκε, μνη-

---

[1] ἐπίλαβε Scaliger: ἐπίβαλλε.
[2] τῶν γε μεμαρτυρηκότων οὐδενὶ Dobree: τῷ γε μεμαρτυρη-
κότι οὐδ'.

decided that the estate could not pass to a woman of irregular birth. Read the depositions; and you, please stop the water-clock.

DEPOSITIONS

That the woman, whom the defendant has deposed that he gave in legal marriage to our uncle, was a courtesan who gave herself to anyone and not his wife, has been testified to you by the other acquaintances and by the neighbours of Pyrrhus, who have given evidence of quarrels, serenades, and frequent scenes of disorder which the defendant's sister occasioned whenever she was at Pyrrhus's house. Yet no one, I presume, would dare to serenade a married woman, nor do married women accompany their husbands to banquets or think of feasting in the company of strangers, especially mere chance comers. Yet, our adversaries did not think fit to make any protest against the evidence of any of those who testified to these things. And to prove that what I say is true, read the deposition to them again.

DEPOSITION

Now read the depositions about those who associated with her, so that they may know she was a courtesan at anyone's disposal and never bore a child to any other man.[a] Read to them.

DEPOSITIONS

I beg you then to bear in mind the number of persons who have given evidence that this woman, whom the defendant has deposed that he gave in

[a] An innuendo that Phile was perhaps a supposititious child.

μονεύειν χρὴ ὑφ᾽ ὅσων ὑμῖν μεμαρτύρηται, καὶ ὅτι
οὐδενὶ ἄλλῳ ἐγγυηθεῖσα οὐδὲ συνοικήσασα φαίνε-
ται· σκεψώμεθα δὲ καὶ ἐξ ὧν ἄν τις ὑπονοήσειεν
ἐγγύην γενέσθαι τοιαύτης γυναικός, εἰ ἄρα καὶ τῷ
17 ἡμετέρῳ θείῳ τοιοῦτόν τι συμβέβηκεν. ἤδη γὰρ
τινες νέοι ἄνθρωποι ἐπιθυμήσαντες τοιούτων γυ-
ναικῶν, καὶ ἀκρατῶς ἔχοντες αὐτῶν, ἐπείσθησαν
ὑπ᾽ ἀνοίας εἰς αὐτοὺς¹ τοιοῦτόν τι ἐξαμαρτεῖν.
πόθεν οὖν ἄν τις σαφέστερον γνοίη περὶ τούτων,
ἢ ἔκ τε τῶν μαρτυριῶν τῶν τούτοις μεμαρτυρημένων ἐν τῇ προτέρᾳ δίκῃ καὶ ἐκ τῶν εἰκότων τῶν
18 περὶ αὐτὸ τὸ πρᾶγμα σκεψάμενος; ἐνθυμεῖσθε δὲ
τὴν ἀναίδειαν ὧν λέγουσιν. ὁ μὲν γὰρ ἐγγυᾶν
μέλλων εἰς τὸν τριτάλαντον οἶκον, ὥς φησι, τὴν
ἀδελφήν, διαπραττόμενος τηλικαῦτα² ἕνα μάρτυρα
παρεῖναι αὐτῷ Πυρετίδην προσεποιήσατο, καὶ
τούτου ἐκμαρτυρίαν ἐπ᾽ ἐκείνῃ τῇ δίκῃ παρέσχοντο
οὗτοι· ἣν Πυρετίδης οὐκ ἀναδέδεκται αὐτοῖς, οὐδὲ
ὁμολογεῖ μαρτυρῆσαι οὐδὲ εἰδέναι τούτων ἀληθὲς
19 ὂν οὐδέν. μέγα δὲ τεκμήριον ὡς περιφανῶς ψευδῆ
τὴν μαρτυρίαν οὗτοι παρέσχοντο ταύτην· ἴστε γὰρ
πάντες ὡς ὅταν μὲν ἐπὶ προδήλους πράξεις ἴωμεν,
ἃς δεῖ μετὰ μαρτύρων γενέσθαι, τοὺς οἰκειοτάτους
[40] | καὶ οἷς ἂν τυγχάνωμεν χρώμενοι μάλιστα, τού-
τους παραλαμβάνειν εἰώθαμεν ἐπὶ τὰς πράξεις τὰς
τοιαύτας, τῶν δὲ ἀδήλων καὶ ἐξαίφνης γιγνομένων
τοὺς προστυχόντας ἕκαστοι μάρτυρας ποιούμεθα.

---

¹ αὐτοὺς Reiske: αὐτάς.   ² τηλικαῦτα Taylor: τηνικαῦτα.

ᵃ When a witness was ill or abroad, his evidence, duly
attested, might be submitted in writing.

marriage to our uncle, was common to all who wished to associate with her, and that she obviously was never married to or lived permanently with anyone else. Let us next consider the circumstances in which it might be conceived that a marriage with such a woman in fact took place, supposing that such a thing really did happen to our uncle ; for young men before now, having fallen in love with such women, and being unable to control their passion, have been induced by folly to ruin themselves in this way. How then can one obtain a clearer knowledge as to what happened than by a consideration of the evidence submitted in favour of our opponents in the former trial and the probabilities of the case itself ? Now consider the impudence of their assertions. The man, who was, according to his own account, about to marry his sister to a man with a fortune of three talents, when he was arranging a matter of such importance, represents that only one witness was present on his behalf, namely, Pyretides, whose written deposition [a] was produced by the other side in the previous trial. This deposition Pyretides has disavowed and refuses to admit that he made any deposition or has any knowledge of the truth of any of the facts which it contains. We have here a striking indication that this deposition produced by our opponents is certainly forged. You all know that, when we are proceeding to a deliberate act which necessitates the presence of witnesses, we habitually take with us our closest acquaintances and most intimate friends as witnesses of such acts ; but of unforeseen acts carried out on the spur of the moment, we always call in the testimony of any chance persons.

20 καὶ ἐπὶ μὲν ταῖς μαρτυρίαις αὐταῖς τοῖς παρα-
γενομένοις αὐτοῖς, ὁποῖοί τινες ἂν ὦσι, τούτοις
μάρτυσι χρῆσθαι ἀναγκαῖόν ἐστιν ἡμῖν· παρὰ δὲ
τῶν ἀσθενούντων ἢ τῶν ἀποδημεῖν μελλόντων ὅταν
τις ἐκμαρτυρίαν ποιῆται, τοὺς ἐπιεικεστάτους τῶν
πολιτῶν καὶ τοὺς ἡμῖν γνωριμωτάτους ἕκαστος
21 ἡμῶν παρακαλεῖ μάλιστα, καὶ οὐ¹ μεθ' ἑνὸς οὐδὲ
μετὰ δυοῖν, ἀλλ' ὡς ἂν μετὰ πλείστων δυνώμεθα
τὰς ἐκμαρτυρίας πάντες ποιούμεθα, ἵνα τῷ τε
ἐκμαρτυρήσαντι μὴ ἐξείη ὕστερον ἐξάρνῳ γενέσθαι
τὴν μαρτυρίαν, ὑμεῖς τε πολλοῖς καὶ καλοῖς κἀγα-
22 θοῖς ταὐτὰ² μαρτυροῦσι πιστεύοιτε³ μᾶλλον. Ξενοκλῆς τοίνυν Βήσαζε μὲν ἰὼν εἰς τὸ ἐργαστήριον τὸ
ἡμέτερον εἰς τὰ ἔργα, οὐχ ἡγήσατο δεῖν τοῖς ἀπὸ
τοῦ αὐτομάτου ἐκεῖ ἐντυχοῦσι μάρτυσι χρῆσθαι
περὶ τῆς ἐξαγωγῆς, ἀλλ' ἧκεν ἔχων ἐνθένδε⁴
Διόφαντον τὸν Σφήττιον μεθ' ἑαυτοῦ, ὃς ἔλεγε τὴν
δίκην ὑπὲρ τούτου, καὶ Δωρόθεον τὸν Ἐλευσίνιον
καὶ τὸι ἀδελφὸν αὐτοῦ Φιλοχάρη καὶ ἄλλους
πολλοὺς μάρτυρας, παρακεκληκὼς ἐνθένδε σταδίους
23 ἐγγὺς⁵ τριακοσίους ἐκεῖσε· περὶ δὲ τῆς ἐγγύης τῆς
τήθης τῶν παίδων τῶν ἑαυτοῦ ἐν τῷ ἄστει ἐκμαρτυρίαν (ὥς φησι) ποιούμενος τῶν μὲν οἰκείων
οὐδένα τῶν ἑαυτοῦ παρακεκληκὼς φαίνεται, Διονύσιον δὲ <τὸν >⁶ Ἐρχιέα καὶ [τὸν] Ἀριστόλοχον τὸν
Αἰθαλίδην· μετὰ δυοῖν τούτοιν ἐν τῷ ἄστει αὐτοῦ τὴν
ἐκμαρτυρίαν ποιήσασθαί φασιν οὗτοι,—τοιαύτην⁷

---

¹ οὐ Bekker: οὐδὲ. ² ταὐτὰ Muretus: ταῦτα.
³ πιστεύοιτε Dobree: πιστεύητε.
⁴ ἐνθένδε Bekker: ἔνθεν. ⁵ ἐγγὺς Dobree: εὐθὺς.
⁶ τὸν add. Dobree. ⁷ τοιαύτην Thalheim: τοιαῦτα.

ᵃ Besa is situated in the extreme south of Attica near

When direct evidence has to be given in court, we are obliged to employ those who were actually present, whosoever they are, as witnesses; but when it is a question of obtaining a written deposition from a witness who is ill or about to go abroad, each of us summons by preference the most reputable among his fellow-citizens and those best known to us, and we always have written depositions made in the presence not of one or two only but of as many witnesses as possible, in order to preclude the deponent from denying his deposition at some future date, and to give his evidence more weight in your eyes by the unanimous testimony of many honest men. Thus, when Xenocles went to our factory at the mines at Besa,[a] he did not think it sufficient to rely on any chance person who happened to be there as witness regarding the eviction, but took with him from Athens Diophantus of Sphettus, who defended him in the former case, and Dorotheus of Eleusis,[b] and his brother Philochares, and many other witnesses, having invited them to make a journey of nearly three hundred stades from here to there; yet when, on the question of the marriage of the grandmother of his own children, he was obtaining, as he declares, a written deposition in Athens itself, he is shown to have summoned none of his own friends but Dionysius of Erchia and Aristolochus of Aethalidae. In the presence of these two men my opponents declare that they obtained the written

Laurium. It appears that the estate of Pyrrhus included a factory at Besa and that Xenocles proceeded thither after the death of Pyrrhus in order to take possession of it: knowing that he would be forcibly prevented from doing so, he took with him witnesses of his eviction.

[b] See Introduction, p. 75.

μετὰ¹ τούτων· οἷς οὐδ' ἂν περὶ ὁτουοῦν πιστεύσειεν
23 ἄλλος οὐδείς. ἴσως γὰρ ἦν νὴ Δία πάρεργον καὶ
φαῦλον, περὶ οὗ τὴν ἐκμαρτυρίαν παρὰ τοῦ Πυρε-
τίδου φασὶ ποιήσασθαι οὗτοι, ὥστε οὐδὲν θαυμαστὸν ὀλιγωρηθῆναι ἦν τὸ πρᾶγμα. καὶ πῶς; οἷς
γε² περὶ αὐτοῦ τούτου ὁ ἀγὼν ἦν ὁ τῶν ψευδομαρτυρίων, ὃν Ξενοκλῆς ἔφευγεν, ἢ ἐξ ἑταίρας ἢ
ἐξ ἐγγυητῆς τὴν ἑαυτοῦ γυναῖκα εἶναι. εἶτα ἐπὶ
ταύτην ἂν τὴν μαρτυρίαν, εἰ ἦν ἀληθής, οὐκ ἂν
ἅπαντας τοὺς οἰκείους τοὺς ἑαυτοῦ παρακαλεῖν
25 ἐκεῖνος ἠξίωσεν; ναὶ μὰ Δία, ὡς ἔγωγε ᾤμην, εἰ
γε ἦν ἀληθὲς τὸ πρᾶγμα. οὐ τοίνυν φαίνεται,
ἀλλ' ὁ μὲν Ξενοκλῆς πρὸς τοὺς ἐπιτυχόντας δύο
ἐκμαρτυρησάμενος τὴν μαρτυρίαν ταύτην, Νικόδημος δὲ οὑτοσὶ³ ἕνα μόνον μάρτυρα παρακαλέσας
μεθ' ἑαυτοῦ τῷ τὸν τριτάλαντον οἶκον κεκτημένῳ
26 ἐγγυῆσαί φησι τὴν ἀδελφήν. καὶ οὗτος μὲν τὸν
Πυρετίδην μόνον, οὐχ ὁμολογοῦντα, προσεποιήσατο
μεθ' ἑαυτοῦ⁴ παραγενέσθαι· ὑπὸ δὲ τοῦ ἐγγυήσασθαι μέλλοντος τὴν τοιαύτην Λυσιμένης καὶ οἱ
ἀδελφοὶ αὐτοῦ, Χαίρων καὶ Πυλάδης, φασὶ παρα-
κληθέντες τῇ ἐγγύῃ παραγενέσθαι, καὶ ταῦτα θεῖοι
27 ὄντες τῷ ἐγγυωμένῳ. ὑμέτερον οὖν ἔργον σκέψασθαι νῦν, εἰ δοκεῖ πιστὸν εἶναι τὸ πρᾶγμα. ἐγὼ
μὲν γὰρ νομίζω, ἐκ τῶν εἰκότων σκοπούμενος,
πολὺ ἂν μᾶλλον τὸν Πύρρον πάντας ἂν τοὺς
οἰκείους βούλεσθαι λεληθέναι, εἴ τι παρεσκευάζετο
ὁμολογεῖν ἢ πράττειν ἀνάξιον τῶν αὐτοῦ, ἢ παρα-

---

¹ μετὰ Dobree: μὲν τὰ.
² οἷς γε Meutzner: ὥστε.
³ οὑτοσὶ Dobree: οὗτος ἦν.
⁴ μεθ' ἑαυτοῦ scripsi, cf. 25. 6: μετ' αὐτοῦ.

deposition—a document of this nature in the presence of men whom no one else would trust in any matter whatsoever ! Perhaps it will be urged that it was a trifling matter of secondary importance about which they say that they obtained the deposition from Pyretides, so that negligence in the affair was not surprising. How so, when the trial for perjury, in which Xenocles was defendant, turned upon this very point, as to whether his own wife was the child of a concubine or of a legitimate wife ? To attest a deposition like this, if it had been really true, would he not have thought fit to summon all his own friends ? Most assuredly he would have done so, I should have thought, if the deposition had been true. We see then Xenocles did not do so, but took this deposition before two chance witnesses ; Nicodemus, however, the present defendant, says that, when he married his sister to a man with a fortune of three talents, he summoned only a single witness to accompany him ! He pretends that the only person present with him was Pyretides, who denies his assertion ; on the other hand, Lysimenes and his brothers, Chaeron and Pylades, declare that they were summoned by Pyrrhus when he was about to make this brilliant match and were present at the ceremony, in spite of the fact that they were uncles of the bridegroom. It is a matter for you to consider now whether their story seems to be credible. It appears to me, judging from probabilities, that Pyrrhus would have been much more likely to wish to keep the matter secret from all his friends, if he was meditating the making of a contract or the commission of an act discreditable to his family, rather than summon his

καλέσαι μάρτυρας τοὺς θείους τοὺς ἑαυτοῦ ἐπὶ
ἁμάρτημα τηλικοῦτον.

28 Ἔτι δὲ καὶ περὶ ἐκείνου θαυμάζω, εἰ μηδεμίαν
προῖκα μήθ' ὁ διδοὺς μήθ' ὁ λαμβάνων διωμολογή-
σαντο ἕξειν ἐπὶ τῇ γυναικί. τοῦτο μὲν γὰρ εἴ τινα
ἐδίδου, εἰκὸς ἦν καὶ τὴν δοθεῖσαν ὑπὸ τῶν παραγενέσθαι φασκόντων μαρτυρεῖσθαι· τοῦτο δ' εἰ δι'
ἐπιθυμίαν τὴν ἐγγύην ὁ θεῖος ἡμῶν ἐποιεῖτο τῆς
τοιαύτης γυναικός, δῆλον ὅτι κἂν ἀργύριον πολλῷ
μᾶλλον [ἢ] ὁ ἐγγυῶν διωμολογήσατο ἔχειν αὐτὸν
ἐπὶ τῇ γυναικί, ἵνα μὴ ἐπ' ἐκείνῳ γένοιτο ῥᾳδίως
ἀπαλλάττεσθαι, ὁπότε βούλοιτο, τῆς γυναικός·

29 καὶ μάρτυράς γε πολλῷ πλείους ‹εἰκὸς ›[1] ἦν τὸν
ἐγγυῶντα παρακαλεῖν ἢ τὸν ἐγγυώμενον τὴν
τοιαύτην· οὐδεὶς γὰρ ὑμῶν ἀγνοεῖ ὅτι ὀλίγα δια-
μένειν εἴωθε τῶν τοιούτων. ὁ μὲν τοίνυν ἐγγυῆσαι
φάσκων μετὰ ἑνὸς μάρτυρος καὶ ἄνευ ὁμολογίας |

[41] προικὸς εἰς τὸν τριτάλαντον οἶκον ἐγγυῆσαί φησι
τὴν ἀδελφήν· οἱ δὲ θεῖοι τῷ ἀδελφιδῷ ἄπροικον τὴν
τοιαύτην ἐγγυωμένῳ μεμαρτυρήκασι παραγενέσθαι.

30 Καὶ οἱ αὐτοὶ θεῖοι οὗτοι ἐν τῇ δεκάτῃ τῆς
θυγατρὸς ἀποφανθείσης εἶναι ὑπὸ τοῦ ἀδελφιδοῦ
κληθέντες μεμαρτυρήκασι παραγενέσθαι. ἐφ' ᾧ
δὴ καὶ δεινῶς ἀγανακτῶ, ὅτι ὁ μὲν ἀνὴρ λαγχάνων ὑπὲρ τῆς γυναικὸς τῆς αὑτοῦ τοῦ κλήρου

[1] εἰκὸς add. Reiske.

---

[a] The legal contract involved by the bestowal of a dowry
constituted the most important proof of the legal character
of the union.

[b] *i.e.*, the ceremony of naming the child.

own uncles as witnesses of so outrageous an act
of folly.

Another matter which surprises me is that there
was no agreement about a dowry for the woman
on the part either of him who gave her or of him
who took her in marriage.[a] For, on the one hand,
if Nicodemus gave a dowry, it would have been only
natural that the amount of the dowry should be
mentioned in the evidence of those who allege that
they were present ; on the other hand, if our uncle,
under the influence of his passion, contracted a
marriage with a woman of this character, clearly
he who gave her in marriage would have been all
the more careful to procure an agreement from the
other party stating that he received money with her,
so that it might not be in the latter's power easily to
get rid of the woman whenever he wished. Also, it
is probable that he who gave her in marriage would
have summoned many more witnesses than the man
who was marrying such a woman ; for you all know
that such unions are very seldom permanent. The
man, then, who alleges that he gave his sister in
marriage, declares that he married her to a man
with a fortune of three talents without any agreement
about a dowry, and the uncles have given evidence
that they were present as witnesses on behalf of
their nephew when he married a woman of this
character without a dowry.

These same uncles have deposed that they were
present by invitation of their nephew at the tenth-
day ceremony [b] in honour of the child who was
declared to be his daughter. Here I note with the
utmost indignation that the husband, in claiming
her paternal inheritance on behalf of his wife, has

93

τοῦ πατρῴου Φίλην ὄνομα εἶναι ἐπεγράψατο¹ τῇ
γυναικί, οἱ δὲ τοῦ Πύρρου θεῖοι ἐν τῇ δεκάτῃ
φάσκοντες παραγενέσθαι τὸ τῆς τήθης ὄνομα
Κλειταρέτην τὸν πατέρα ἐμαρτύρησαν θέσθαι
31 αὐτῇ. θαυμάζω οὖν εἰ ὁ ἀνὴρ ὁ συνοικῶν πλείω ἢ
ὀκτὼ ἔτη ἤδη μὴ ᾔδει τοὔνομα τῆς ἑαυτοῦ γυναικός.
εἶτα οὐδὲ παρὰ τῶν αὑτοῦ μαρτύρων πρότερον
ἐδυνήθη πυθέσθαι, οὐδ' ἡ μήτηρ τῆς γυναικὸς τὸ
τῆς θυγατρὸς ὄνομα τῆς αὑτῆς ἐν χρόνῳ τοσούτῳ
32 ἔφρασεν αὐτῷ, οὐδ' ὁ θεῖος αὐτός, Νικόδημος; ἀλλ'
ἀντὶ τοῦ τῆς τήθης ὀνόματος, εἴ τις ᾔδει τοῦθ' ὑπὸ
τοῦ πατρὸς κείμενον ταύτῃ,² Φίλην ὁ ἀνὴρ ὄνομα
ἐπεγράψατο εἶναι αὐτῇ, καὶ ταῦτα λαγχάνων αὐτῇ
τοῦ κλήρου τοῦ πατρῴου. τίνος ἕνεκα; ἢ ἵνα καὶ
τοῦ τῆς τήθης ὀνόματος τοῦ ὑπὸ τοῦ πατρὸς τεθέν-
τος ἄκληρον ὁ ἀνὴρ καταστήσειεν εἶναι τὴν αὑτοῦ
33 γυναῖκα; ἆρά γε οὐχὶ δῆλον, ὦ ἄνδρες, ὅτι ἃ
πάλαι οὗτοι μαρτυροῦσι γενέσθαι, πολλῷ ὕστερον³
τῆς λήξεως τοῦ κλήρου ⟨ἕνεκα⟩⁴ σύγκειται αὐτοῖς;
οὐ γὰρ ἄν ποτε οἱ μὲν εἰς τὴν δεκάτην (ὥς φασι)
κληθέντες τῆς τοῦ Πύρρου θυγατρός, ἀδελφιδῆς
τούτου, ἐξ ἐκείνης τῆς ἡμέρας, ἥτις ἦν ποτε,
ἀκριβῶς εἰς τὸ δικαστήριον ἧκον μεμνημένοι ὅτι
34 Κλειταρέτην ὁ πατὴρ ἐν τῇ δεκάτῃ ὠνόμηνεν, οἱ δ'
οἰκειότατοι τῶν ἁπάντων, ὁ πατὴρ καὶ ὁ θεῖος καὶ
ἡ μήτηρ οὐκ ἂν ᾔδει τὸ ὄνομα τῆς θυγατρός, ὥς
φασι, τῆς αὑτοῦ. πολύ γε μάλιστ' ἄν, εἰ ἦν

---

¹ ἐπεγράψατο Dobree: ἐγράψατο.
² ταύτῃ Bekker: ταύτην.
³ ὕστερον Reiske: πλέον.
⁴ ἕνεκα add. dub. Wyse.

put down her name as Phile, while Pyrrhus's uncles, alleging that they were present, deposed that her father called her Cleitarete, after her grandmother. I am amazed that the man who had lived with her for more than eight years did not know the name of his own wife. Could he not have found it out before from his own witnesses? Did his wife's mother never in all that long period tell him her daughter's name? Did her uncle, Nicodemus himself, never do so? No, her husband, instead of giving her her grandmother's name—if it was really known that this name was given her by her father— inscribed her name as Phile, and this when he was claiming the paternal inheritance for her! What was his object? Did the husband wish to deprive his wife of any title to the name of her grandmother bestowed upon her by her father? Is it not obvious, gentlemen, that the events which they deposed to have happened long ago were invented by them much later for the purpose of claiming the estate?[a] For otherwise it would have been impossible that the uncles, who were summoned, according to their own account, to the tenth-day ceremony in honour of Pyrrhus's daughter, the defendant's niece, could ever have come into court with so accurate a recollection from that distant date, whenever it was, that her father at that ceremony named her Cleitarete, but that the nearest relatives, her father and her uncle and her mother should not know the name of the child whom they declare to be Pyrrhus's daughter. They would

---

[a] The restoration of the text here is uncertain but the meaning clear.

ἀληθὲς τὸ πρᾶγμα. ἀλλὰ περὶ μὲν τούτων καὶ ὕστερον ἐγχωρήσει εἰπεῖν.

35 Περὶ δὲ τῆς τούτου μαρτυρίας οὐ χαλεπὸν καὶ ἐξ αὐτῶν τῶν νόμων ἐστὶ γνῶναι ὅτι φαίνεται περιφανῶς τὰ ψευδῆ μεμαρτυρηκὼς οὗτος. ὅπου γάρ, ἐάν τίς τι ἀτίμητον δῷ, ἕνεκα τοῦ νόμου, ἐὰν ἀπολίπῃ ἡ γυνὴ τὸν ἄνδρα ἢ ἐὰν ὁ ἀνὴρ ἐκπέμψῃ τὴν γυναῖκα, οὐκ ἔξεστι πράξασθαι τῷ δόντι ὃ μὴ ἐν προικὶ τιμήσας ἔδωκεν, ἦ που ὅστις γέ φησιν ἄνευ ὁμολογίας προικὸς τὴν ἀδελφὴν ἐγγυῆσαι, περι-
36 φανῶς ἀναίσχυντος ὢν ἐλέγχεται. τί γὰρ ἔμελλεν ὄφελος εἶναι αὐτῷ τῆς ἐγγύης, εἰ ἐπὶ τῷ ἐγγυησαμένῳ ἐκπέμψαι ὁπότε βούλοιτο τὴν γυναῖκα ἦν; ἦν δ' ἂν ἐπ' ἐκείνῳ, ὦ ἄνδρες, δῆλον ὅτι, εἰ μηδεμίαν προῖκα διωμολογήσατο ἕξειν ἐπ' αὐτῇ. εἶτ' ἐπὶ τούτοις ἂν Νικόδημος ἠγγύησε τῷ ἡμετέρῳ θείῳ τὴν ἀδελφήν; καὶ ταῦτα εἰδὼς τὸν ἅπαντα χρόνον ἄτοκον οὖσαν αὐτήν, καὶ τῆς ὁμολογηθείσης προικὸς ἐκ τῶν νόμων γιγνομένης εἰς αὐτόν, εἴ τι ἔπαθεν ἡ γυνὴ πρὶν γενέσθαι παῖδας
37 αὐτῇ; ἆρ' οὖν δοκεῖ τῳ ὑμῶν ὀλιγώρως οὗτος ἔχειν χρημάτων Νικόδημος, ὥστε παραλιπεῖν ἄν τι τῶν τοιούτων; ἐγὼ μὲν γὰρ οὐ νομίζω. εἶτα παρὰ τούτου ὁ ἡμέτερος θεῖος ἠξίωσεν ἂν ἐγγυήσασθαι τὴν ἀδελφήν, ὃς αὐτὸς ξενίας φεύγων ὑπὸ ἑνὸς **τῶν** φρατόρων ὢν[1] φησιν αὐτοῦ εἶναι, παρὰ

---

[1] ὢν Reiske: ὄν.

most certainly have known it, if the fact had been true. But I shall have occasion to return to these uncles later.[a]

As for Nicodemus's evidence it is not difficult to decide from the actual text of the laws that he has obviously committed perjury. For seeing that, if a man gives with a woman a sum not duly assessed in a contract, and if the wife leaves her husband or the husband puts away his wife, the man who gave the money cannot, as far as the law is concerned, demand back what he gave but did not assess in a contract—the defendant when he states that he gave his sister in marriage without any contract regarding a dowry, is obviously proved to be making an impudent assertion. For what was likely to be the good to him of the marriage, if the husband could dismiss the wife whenever he wished? And this he certainly could do, if he had made no stipulation that he should receive a dowry with her. Would Nicodemus have married his sister to our uncle on these terms, and this, though he knew all the time that in the past she had produced no offspring, and though the dowry, if it had been assessed in a contract, was coming to him, if anything happened to her before she bore any children? Does any one of you really think that Nicodemus is so disinterested in money matters that he would neglect any of these considerations? For my part, I do not think it possible. Further, would our uncle have thought of marrying the sister of a man, who, when he was accused of usurping the rights of citizenship by a member of the ward to which he claimed to belong,

---

[a] §§ 63-71.

τέτταρας ψήφους μετέσχε τῆς πόλεως; καὶ ὡς
ἀληθῆ λέγω, ἀναγίγνωσκε τὴν μαρτυρίαν.

MAPTYPIA

38 Οὗτος τοίνυν τῷ ἡμετέρῳ θείῳ ἄπροικον τὴν
ἀδελφὴν τὴν ἑαυτοῦ μεμαρτύρηκεν ἐγγυῆσαι, καὶ
ταῦτα τῆς προικὸς εἰς αὐτὸν γιγνομένης, εἴ τι
ἔπαθεν ἡ γυνὴ πρὶν γενέσθαι παῖδας αὐτῇ. λαβὲ
δὴ καὶ ἀνάγνωθι τοὺς νόμους τουσδὶ αὐτοῖς.

NOMOI

39 Δοκεῖ ἂν ὑμῖν οὕτως ὀλιγώρως ἔχειν χρημάτων
Νικόδημος, ὥστε, εἰ ἦν ἀληθὲς τὸ πρᾶγμα, οὐκ ἂν
σφόδρα διακριβώσασθαι περὶ τῶν ἑαυτῷ συμφερόν-
των; ναὶ μὰ Δία, ὡς ἔγωγ' οἶμαι, ἐπεὶ καὶ οἱ
ἐπὶ παλλακίᾳ¹ διδόντες τὰς ἑαυτῶν πάντες πρότερον
διομολογοῦνται περὶ τῶν δοθησομένων ταῖς παλ-
λακαῖς· Νικόδημος δὲ ἐγγυᾶν μέλλων, ⟨ὥς⟩² φησι, |
[42] τὴν ἀδελφὴν τὴν αὐτοῦ μόνον τὸ κατὰ τοὺς νόμους
ἐγγυῆσαι διεπράξατο; ὃς ἐπ' ὀλίγῳ ἀργυρίῳ, οὗ
ἐπιθυμῶν λέγει πρὸς ὑμᾶς, σφόδρα βούλεται
πονηρὸς εἶναι;

40 Περὶ μὲν οὖν τῆς τούτου³ πονηρίας καὶ σιωπῶν-
τος ἐμοῦ οἱ πολλοὶ γιγνώσκουσιν ὑμῶν, ὥστε οὐκ
ἀπορῶ γε μαρτύρων, ὅταν τι λέγω περὶ αὐτοῦ·
βούλομαι δὲ πρῶτον ἐκ τῶν τοιῶνδε ἐξελέγξαι

---

¹ παλλακίᾳ Bekker: παλλακίδι.   ² ὥς add. Reiske.
³ τούτου Sauppe: τούτων.

ᵃ i.e., without insisting on stipulations regarding a dowry
which might eventually benefit him.

obtained those rights by a majority of only four votes? And to prove the truth of what I say, read the deposition.

DEPOSITION

The defendant then has given evidence that he gave his sister in marriage to our uncle without a dowry in spite of the fact that such a dowry was to come to him if anything happened to the woman before she had borne any children. Now take and read these laws to the judges.

LAWS

Do you think Nicodemus would be so disinterested in money matters, that, if the fact which he alleges were true, he would not have provided for his own interests with scrupulous care? By heaven, I am sure he would have done so; for even those who give their womenkind to others as mistresses make stipulations in advance as to the benefits which such women are to enjoy. And was Nicodemus, when, according to his own account, he was going to give his sister in marriage, content with simply securing the requirements of a legal marriage *a*—a man who shows himself only too anxious to be dishonest for a paltry sum which he hopes to receive for speaking in court? *b*

As for his dishonesty, most of you know all about it without any words from me, so that at any rate I have abundant witnesses when I say anything about him. But I should like in the first place to convict him in the following manner of the most

---

b *i.e.*, as a reward for his false evidence.

τοῦτον ἀναισχυντότατον τῇ μαρτυρίᾳ ὄντα ταύτῃ.
φέρε γάρ, ὦ Νικόδημε, εἰ ἦσθα ἠγγυηκὼς τῷ
Πύρρῳ τὴν ἀδελφὴν καὶ εἰ ᾔδεις ἐξ αὐτῆς θυγατέρα
41 γνησίαν καταλειπομένην, πῶς ἐπέτρεψας τῷ ἡμετέρῳ ἀδελφῷ ἐπιδικάσασθαι τοῦ κλήρου ἄνευ τῆς
γνησίας θυγατρός, ἣν φῂς τῷ ἡμετέρῳ θείῳ καταλειφθῆναι; ἢ οὐκ ᾔδεις ἐν τῇ ἐπιδικασίᾳ τοῦ
κλήρου νόθην καθισταμένην τὴν ἀδελφιδῆν τὴν
σαυτοῦ; ὁπότε γὰρ [τις] ἐπεδικάζετο τοῦ κλήρου,
νόθην τὴν θυγατέρα τοῦ καταλιπόντος τὸν κλῆρον
42 καθίστη. ἔτι δὲ πρότερον ὁ Πύρρος ὁ ποιησάμενος τὸν ἀδελφὸν τὸν ἐμὸν υἱὸν αὑτῷ· οὔτε γὰρ
διαθέσθαι οὔτε δοῦναι οὐδενὶ οὐδὲν ἔξεστι τῶν
ἑαυτοῦ ἄνευ τῶν θυγατέρων, ἐάν τις καταλιπὼν
γνησίας τελευτᾷ. γνώσεσθε δὲ αὐτῶν ἀκούσαντες
τῶν νόμων ἀναγιγνωσκομένων. ἀναγίγνωσκε
τούσδε αὐτοῖς.

ΝΟΜΟΙ

43 Δοκεῖ ἂν ὑμῖν ὁ μεμαρτυρηκὼς ἐγγυῆσαι ἐπιτρέψαι ἄν τι τούτων γίγνεσθαι, καὶ οὐκ ἂν ἐπὶ τοῦ
κλήρου τῇ λήξει, ἣν ὁ Ἔνδιος λαχὼν ἐπεδικάζετο,
ἀμφισβητῆσαι ἂν ὑπὲρ τῆς ἀδελφιδῆς τῆς ἑαυτοῦ,
καὶ οὐκ ἂν διαμαρτυρῆσαι μὴ[1] ἐπίδικον τῷ Ἐνδίῳ
τὸν ἐκείνης πατρῷον κλῆρον εἶναι; ἀλλὰ μὴν ὥς
γε ἐπεδικάσατο ὁ ἡμέτερος ἀδελφὸς τοῦ κλήρου
καὶ οὐκ ἠμφισβήτησεν οὐδεὶς ἐκείνῳ, ἀναγίγνωσκε
τὴν μαρτυρίαν.

---

[1] μὴ Schoemann: οὐκ.

---

[a] The permission of the court was necessary when the
heir was a son adopted by will and not by the deceased in
his lifetime.

impudent lying in this evidence of his. Come, tell
me this, Nicodemus : If you had given your sister
in marriage to Pyrrhus and if you knew that Pyrrhus
was leaving a legitimate daughter by her, how is it
that you allowed the inheritance to be adjudicated
to our brother *a* without the disposal of the legitimate
daughter whom you say our uncle left behind him ?
Did you not know that by the demand that the
estate should be adjudicated an attempt was being
made to bastardize your niece ? For, when he
claimed to have the estate adjudicated to him, he
thereby sought to bastardize the daughter of him
who left the estate. To go still further back, the
adoption of my brother by Pyrrhus had a similar
effect ; for no one has the right to devise or dispose
of any of his property without also disposing of any
legitimate daughters whom he may have left at his
decease. You will understand this when you hear
the text of the laws read out. Read these laws to
the judges.

LAWS

Can you suppose that the man who has declared
in evidence that he gave his sister in marriage
would have allowed any of these things to be done,
and, at the moment when Endius claimed to be
given possession and applied to the court, would
not have set up his niece's title and lodged a protestation that her paternal inheritance was not
adjudicable to Endius ? And yet that our brother
claimed to have the estate adjudicated to him and
that no one contested his claim, is proved by a
deposition. Read it.

ISAEUS

ΜΑΡΤΥΡΙΑ

44 Γενομένης τοίνυν τῆς ἐπιδικασίας ταύτης οὐκ
ἐτόλμησεν ἀμφισβητῆσαι τοῦ κλήρου Νικόδημος,
οὐδὲ διαμαρτυρῆσαι τὴν ἀδελφιδῆν τὴν ἑαυτοῦ
γνησίαν θυγατέρα Πύρρῳ καταλειφθῆναι.

45 Περὶ μὲν οὖν τῆς ἐπιδικασίας¹ ἔχοι ἄν τις ψεῦδος προφασίσασθαι πρὸς ὑμᾶς· ἢ γὰρ λαθεῖν σφᾶς²
προσποιήσαιτ᾽ ἂν οὗτος, ἢ καὶ ψεύδεσθαι αἰτιῷτ᾽
ἂν ἡμᾶς. τοῦτο μὲν οὖν παρῶμεν· ἐπειδὴ δὲ τῷ
Ξενοκλεῖ ἠγγύα ὁ Ἔνδιος τὴν ἀδελφιδῆν σου,
ἐπέτρεψας, ὦ Νικόδημε, τὴν ἐκ τῆς ἐγγυητῆς τῷ
Πύρρῳ γεγενημένην ὡς ἐξ ἑταίρας ἐκείνῳ οὖσαν

46 ἐγγυᾶσθαι; καὶ οὐκ [ἂν] εἰσήγγειλας³ πρὸς τὸν
ἄρχοντα κακοῦσθαι τὴν ἐπίκληρον ὑπὸ τοῦ εἰσ-
ποιήτου οὕτως ὑβριζομένην καὶ ἄκληρον τῶν ἑαυτῆς πατρῴων καθισταμένην, ἄλλως τε καὶ μόνων
τούτων τῶν δικῶν ἀκινδύνων τοῖς διώκουσιν οὐσῶν
καὶ ἐξὸν τῷ βουλομένῳ βοηθεῖν ταῖς ἐπικλήροις;

47 οὔτε γὰρ ἐπιτίμιον ταῖς πρὸς τὸν ἄρχοντα εἰσαγγελίαις ἔπεστιν,⁴ οὐδ᾽ ἐὰν μηδεμίαν⁵ τῶν ψήφων οἱ εἰσαγγείλαντες μεταλάβωσιν, οὔτε πρυτανεῖα οὔτε παράστασις οὐδεμιᾷ⁶ τίθεται τῶν εἰσ-
αγγελιῶν· ἀλλὰ τοῖς μὲν διώκουσιν ἀκινδύνως
εἰσαγγέλλειν ἔξεστι, [τῷ βουλομένῳ], τοῖς δ᾽ ἁλι-
σκομένοις ἔσχαται τιμωρίαι ἐπὶ ταῖς εἰσαγγελίαις

48 ἔπεισιν. ἔπειτα εἰ ἦν ἐξ ἐγγυητῆς ἡ τούτου

---

¹ ἐπιδικασίας Reiske: διαδικ-.
² σφᾶς Bekker: ἡμᾶς.
³ εἰσήγγειλας Schoemann: -γελλε.
⁴ ἔπεστιν Reiske: ἔνεστιν.
⁵ μηδεμίαν Bekker: οὐδεμίαν.
⁶ οὐδεμίᾳ Photiades: -α.

DEPOSITION

When this claim then for the adjudication of the estate was made, Nicodemus did not dare to contest the succession or put in a protestation that his niece was a legitimate daughter left by Pyrrhus.

Regarding this claim some lying explanation may be offered to you : the defendant may either pretend that they knew nothing about it or else may accuse us of lying. Let us ignore the latter suggestion. As regards the former, when Endius gave your niece in marriage to Xenocles, did you, Nicodemus, allow the daughter borne to Pyrrhus by his legitimate wife to be married in the quality of the child of a mistress ? And did you fail to bring a denunciation in the archon's court for injury to the heiress thus maltreated by the adopted son and despoiled of her paternal inheritance, especially as this is the only class of public actions which involves no risk to the party who brings it, and anyone who wishes is allowed to defend the rights of heiresses ? For no fine can be inflicted for denunciations made to the archon, even if the informants fail to receive a single vote,[a] and there are no deposits or court fees[b] paid in any impeachments ; but while the prosecutors may bring an impeachment without running any risk, extreme penalties are inflicted on those who are convicted in such impeachments. If, then, the defendant's niece had been the child of

[a] The prosecutor in other public actions was liable to a fine of 1000 drachmas if he failed to obtain one-fifth of the votes.

[b] πρυτανεῖα, deposits made by both parties in a suit and repayable to the successful litigant : παράστασις, fees payable by a prosecutor on entering upon certain suits.

ἀδελφιδῇ τῷ ἡμετέρῳ θείῳ γεγενημένη, ἐπέτρεψεν
ἂν Νικόδημος ὡς ἐξ ἑταίρας οὖσαν αὐτὴν ἐγγυᾶσθαι; καὶ γενομένων αὐτῶν οὐκ ἂν εἰσήγγειλε[1]
πρὸς τὸν ἄρχοντα ὑβρίζεσθαι τὴν ἐπίκληρον ὑπὸ
τοῦ οὕτως ἐγγυήσαντος αὐτήν; καί, εἰ ἦν ἀληθῆ
ἃ νυνὶ τετόλμηκας[2] μαρτυρῆσαι, παραχρῆμα εὐθὺς
τότε ἐτιμωρήσω ἂν τὸν ἀδικοῦντα. ἢ καὶ ταῦτα
49 λαθεῖν σεαυτὸν προσποιήσει; ἔπειτ' οὐδ' ἐκ τῆς
ἐπιδοθείσης αὐτῇ προικὸς ᾔσθου; ὥστε καὶ δι'
αὐτὸ τοῦτο ἀγανακτήσαντι δήπου σοι εἰσαγγεῖλαι
τὸν Ἔνδιον προσῆκεν, εἰ αὐτὸς μὲν τριτάλαντον
οἶκον ἔχειν ἠξίου ὡς προσῆκον αὐτῷ, τῇ δὲ
γνησίᾳ οὔσῃ ⟨θυγατρὶ⟩[3] [τρισ]χιλίας δραχμὰς
προῖκα ἐπιδοὺς ἐκδοῦναι ἠξίωσεν ἄλλῳ. εἶτ' ἐπὶ
τούτοις οὐκ ἀγανακτήσας εἰσήγγειλεν ἂν τὸν
Ἔνδιον οὗτος; ναὶ μὰ Δία, εἴ γ' ἦν ἀληθὲς τὸ
50 πρᾶγμα. οἶμαι δὲ οὐδ' ἂν τὴν ἀρχὴν ἐκεῖνον οὐδ'
ἄλλον γε[4] τῶν εἰσποιήτων οὐδένα οὕτως εὐήθη οὐδ'
[43] αὖ[5] ὀλίγωρον τῶν νόμων τῶν κειμένων | γίγνεσθαι,
ὥσθ' ὑπαρχούσης γνησίας θυγατρὸς τῷ τὸν κλῆρον
καταλιπόντι ἑτέρῳ δοῦναι ταύτην ἀνθ' ἑαυτοῦ.
ἀκριβῶς γὰρ ᾔδει διότι τοῖς γε ἐκ τῆς γνησίας
θυγατρὸς παισὶ γεγονόσιν ἁπάντων τῶν παπ-
πώων κληρονομία προσήκει. εἶτα εἰδὼς ἄν τις
ταῦτα ἑτέρῳ παραδοίη τὰ αὑτοῦ, καὶ ταῦτα τη-
51 λικαῦτα ὄντα ὅσων ἠμφισβήτησαν οὗτοι; δοκεῖ δ'

---

[1] εἰσήγγειλε Baiter: -γελλε.
[2] τετόλμηκας Reiske: τετολμήκασι.
[3] θυγατρὶ add Rauchenstein.
[4] γε Scheibe: δὲ.   [5] αὖ Bekker: ἂν.

---

[6] The ms. reading gives "3000 drachmas," which does

104

our uncle by a legitimate wife, would Nicodemus
have allowed her to be married in the quality of
the child of a mistress ? And, when this happened,
would he not have lodged a denunciation before the
archon that the heiress was being injured by him
who thus gave her in marriage ? If what you have
now dared, Nicodemus, to depose, were true, you
would then immediately have had punishment
inflicted on him who was wronging her. Or will you
pretend that you knew nothing of these circumstances
either ? Next, did not the dowry which was given
with her awake your suspicion ? This alone might
well have aroused your indignation and induced you
to denounce Endius, namely, that he himself was
claiming as his right a fortune of three talents, but
thought fit, when he was giving Pyrrhus's legitimate
daughter in marriage to another man, to bestow with
her a portion of only a thousand drachmas.[a] Would
not this have aroused the defendant's indignation
and would he not have denounced Endius ? By
heavens he would, if his story were true. I cannot
think it at all possible that Endius, or any other
adopted son, could be so foolish, so regardless of the
existing laws, as to give the legitimate daughter of
the man who left the estate in marriage to another
instead of marrying her himself ; for he knew
perfectly well that the children of a legitimate
daughter have a right to succeed to the whole
of their grandfather's estate. Knowing this, would
anyone hand over his own property to another man,
especially if it were of the value that our opponents

not accord with the statement of § 51, where the dowry
is said to be less than a tenth of Pyrrhus's estate which
amounted to three talents (18,000 drachmas).

ἄν τις ὑμῖν οὕτως ἀναιδὴς ἢ τολμηρὸς εἰσποίητος
γενέσθαι, ὥστε μηδὲ τὸ δέκατον μέρος ἐπιδοὺς ἐκδοῦναι τῇ γνησίᾳ θυγατρὶ τῶν πατρῴων; γενομένων δὲ τούτων δοκεῖ ἂν ὑμῖν ὁ θεῖος ἐπιτρέψαι,
ὁ ἐγγυῆσαι μεμαρτυρηκὼς αὐτῆς τὴν μητέρα;
ἐγὼ μὲν γὰρ οὐ νομίζω, ἀλλὰ καὶ ἠμφισβήτησεν
ἂν τοῦ κλήρου καὶ διεμαρτύρησε καὶ εἰσήγγειλεν[1]
ἂν πρὸς τὸν ἄρχοντα, καὶ ἄλλο εἴ τι ἦν ἰσχυρό-
52 τερον τούτων, ἅπαντ' ἂν διεπράξατο. ὁ μὲν τοίνυν
Ἔνδιος ὡς ἐξ ἑταίρας οὖσαν ἠγγύησεν, ἥν φησιν
ἀδελφιδῆν Νικόδημος εἶναι αὑτῷ· οὗτος δὲ οὔτε
τῷ Ἐνδίῳ τοῦ Πύρρου κλήρου ἀμφισβητῆσαι
ἠξίωσεν, οὔτ' ἐγγυήσαντα τὴν ἀδελφιδῆν <ὡς>[2]
οὖσαν ἐξ ἑταίρας εἰσαγγεῖλαι πρὸς τὸν ἄρχοντα
[ἠξίωσεν], οὔτ' ἐπὶ τῇ δοθείσῃ προικὶ αὐτῇ
ἠγανάκτησεν οὐδέν, ἀλλὰ πάντα ταῦτα εἴασε γενέσθαι. οἱ δὲ νόμοι περὶ ἁπάντων διορίζουσι τούτων.
53 ἀναγνώσεται οὖν πρῶτον ὑμῖν τὴν περὶ τῆς ἐπιδικασίας τοῦ κλήρου μαρτυρίαν πάλιν, ἔπειτα τὴν
περὶ τῆς ἐγγυήσεως τῆς γυναικός. ἀναγίγνωσκε
αὐτοῖς.

MAPTYPIA⟨I⟩

Ἀνάγνωθι δὴ καὶ τοὺς νόμους.

NOMOI

Λαβὲ δὴ καὶ τὴν τούτου μαρτυρίαν.

MAPTYPIA

54 Πῶς οὖν <ἂν>[3] τις σαφέστερον ἐξελέγχοι[4] ψευδομαρτυρίων διώκων ἢ ἔκ τε τῶν πεπραγμένων

---

[1] εἰσήγγειλεν Aldus : -ελλεν.
[2] ὡς add. Reiske.
[3] ἂν add. Dobree.
[4] ἐξελέγχοι Aldus : -ει.

claim ? Can you imagine an adopted son being so
shameless and brazen-faced as to give the legitimate
daughter in marriage with a dowry of not even a
tenth of her father's fortune ? And if he had done
so, can you imagine that her uncle, who has borne
witness that he gave her mother in marriage, would
have allowed it ? For my part I cannot believe it ;
rather would he have contested the estate and put
in a protestation and denounced him to the archon
and taken any stronger action if it were possible.
Endius then gave this woman, whom Nicodemus
alleges to be his niece, in marriage in the quality
of the daughter of a mistress ; and the defendant
did not think fit to claim the estate of Pyrrhus
from Endius, or, when Endius gave his niece in
marriage in the quality of the daughter of a mistress,
denounce him to the archon, nor did he express any
indignation at the dowry which was bestowed upon
her ; no, he took no action at all in these matters.
Yet the laws are precise on all these points. The
clerk shall read to you first of all, for the second
time, the deposition about the claim for the adjudication of the estate and then that concerning the
marriage of the woman. Read them to the court.

DEPOSITIONS

Now read the laws.

LAWS

Now take Nicodemus's deposition.

DEPOSITION

How could an accuser establish a charge of perjury
more clearly than by adducing proofs from the

αὐτοῖς τούτοις ἐπιδεικνύων καὶ ἐκ τῶν νόμων
ἁπάντων τῶν ἡμετέρων;

Περὶ μὲν οὖν τούτου σχεδὸν εἴρηται τὰ πολλά·
σκέψασθε δὲ καὶ περὶ τοῦ ἔχοντος τὴν ἀδελφιδῆν
τὴν τούτου γυναῖκα, ἐὰν ἄρα τι γένηται καὶ ἐκ
τούτου τεκμήριον ὡς ἔστι ψευδῆ τὰ μεμαρ-
55 τυρημένα Νικοδήμῳ. ὡς μὲν οὖν ἠγγυήσατο καὶ
ἔλαβεν ὡς οὖσαν ἐξ ἑταίρας τὴν γυναῖκα, ἐπιδέδεικται καὶ μεμαρτύρηται· ὡς δ' ἀληθὴς ἡ μαρτυρία ἐστὶν αὕτη, ὁ Ξενοκλῆς αὐτὸς ἔργῳ οὐκ
ὀλίγον χρόνον ἤδη [ἀληθῆ ταῦτα]· μεμαρτύρηκε.
δῆλον γὰρ ὅτι εἰ μὴ ἠγγύητο παρὰ τοῦ Ἐνδίου
ὡς ἐξ ἑταίρας οὖσαν τὴν γυναῖκα, ὄντων αὐτῷ
παίδων ἤδη τηλικούτων ἐκ τῆς γυναικός, ζῶντι
ἂν τῷ Ἐνδίῳ ἠμφισβήτησεν ὑπὲρ[1] τῆς γνησίας
56 θυγατρὸς τῶν πατρῴων, ἄλλως τε καὶ παρ-
εσκευασμένος μὴ ὁμολογεῖν τὴν τοῦ Ἐνδίου ποίησιν τῷ Πύρρῳ γενέσθαι· ὡς δὲ οὐχ ὁμολογῶν
[πῶς] ἐπεσκήπτετο[2] τοῖς μεμαρτυρηκόσιν ἐπὶ τῇ
διαθήκῃ τοῦ Πύρρου παραγενέσθαι. καὶ ὡς ἀληθῆ
λέγω, ἀναγνώσεται ὑμῖν[3] τὴν μαρτυρίαν τὴν μαρ-
τυρηθεῖσαν. ἀναγίγνωσκε αὐτοῖς.

MAPTYPIA

57 Ἀλλὰ μὴν κἀκεῖνό γε δηλοῖ,[4] ὡς οὐχ ὁμολογοῦσι τὴν τοῦ Ἐνδίου ποίησιν ὑπὸ τοῦ Πύρρου
γενέσθαι. οὐ γὰρ ἂν ὑπερβάντες τὸν τελευταῖον
τοῦ οἴκου γεγενημένον κληρονόμον ὑπὲρ τῆς
γυναικὸς τοῦ Πύρρου κλήρου λαχεῖν τὴν λῆξιν

---

[1] ἠμφισβήτησεν ὑπὲρ Bekker: -σε περί.
[2] ἐπεσκήπτετο Reiske: ἐπέσκηπτε.
[3] ὑμῖν Aldus: ἡμῖν.   [4] δηλοῖ Schoemann: δῆλον.

actual conduct of my adversaries themselves and from all the laws of our state ?

I have now said most of what I have to say about the defendant. Consider now whether the conduct of the husband of defendant's niece provides convincing argument that Nicodemus's evidence is false. That he married her and took her to be his wife as the daughter of a mistress, has been proved and attested ; and that this evidence is true, Xenocles himself has testified by his conduct over a long period. For it is evident that, if he had not received the woman in marriage from Endius as the daughter of a mistress, seeing that he had children by her who have already reached a certain age,[a] he would have claimed her patrimony on behalf of the legitimate daughter from Endius during his lifetime, especially as he was prepared to deny that the adoption of Endius by Pyrrhus ever took place ; and it was because he denied it that he denounced those who have deposed that they were present when Pyrrhus made his will. And to prove that I am speaking the truth, the clerk shall read you the deposition then made. Read it to the court.

DEPOSITION

Here is another proof that they do not admit that the adoption of Endius by Pyrrhus ever took place, namely, that they would never otherwise have thought of demanding the award of the inheritance to this woman, ignoring the long tenancy of the

---

[a] Xenocles and Phile had been married eight years (§ 31).

ἠξίωσαν οὗτοι. ὁ μὲν γὰρ Πύρρος πλείω ἢ
εἴκοσιν ἔτη τετελεύτηκεν ἤδη, ὁ δὲ Ἔνδιος τοῦ
Μεταγειτνιῶνος μηνὸς πέρυσιν, ἐν ᾧ ἔλαχον τοῦ
58 κλήρου τὴν λῆξιν τρίτῃ ἡμέρᾳ εὐθέως οὗτοι. ὁ
δὲ νόμος πέντε ἐτῶν κελεύει δικάσασθαι τοῦ
κλήρου, ἐπειδὰν τελευτήσῃ ὁ κληρονόμος. οὐκοῦν
δυοῖν τὰ ἕτερα προσῆκε τῇ γυναικί, ἢ ζῶντι τῷ
Ἐνδίῳ ἀμφισβητῆσαι τῶν πατρῴων, ἢ ἐπειδὴ
τετελευτηκὼς ἦν ὁ εἰσποίητος, τῶν τοῦ ἀδελφοῦ
τὴν ἐπιδικασίαν ἀξιοῦν ποιεῖσθαι, ἄλλως τε καὶ
εἰ, ὥς φασιν οὗτοι, ἠγγυήκει αὐτὴν τῷ Ξενοκλεῖ
59 ὡς γνησίαν ἀδελφὴν οὖσαν αὐτοῦ. ἀκριβῶς γὰρ
ἐπιστάμεθα πάντες ὅτι ἀδελφῶν μὲν κλήρων ἐπι-
δικασία πᾶσίν ἐστιν ἡμῖν, ὅτῳ δὲ γόνῳ γεγόνασι
γνήσιοι παῖδες, οὐδενὶ ἐπιδικάζεσθαι τῶν πατρῴων
προσήκει. καὶ περὶ τούτων οὐδένα λόγον λεχθῆναι
[44] δεῖ· ἅπαντες γὰρ ὑμεῖς | καὶ οἱ ἄλλοι πολῖται
ἀνεπίδικα ἔχουσι τὰ ἑαυτῶν ἕκαστοι πατρῷα.
60 οὗτοι τοίνυν εἰς τοῦτο τόλμης ἀφιγμένοι εἰσίν,
ὥστε τῷ μὲν εἰσποιήτῳ οὐκ ἔφασαν ἐπιδικάσασθαι προσήκειν τῶν δοθέντων, τῇ δὲ Φίλῃ, ἥν
φασι θυγατέρα γνησίαν τῷ Πύρρῳ καταλελεῖφθαι,
λαχεῖν τοῦ κλήρου τοῦ πατρῴου τὴν λῆξιν ἠξίωσαν.
καίτοι (ὅπερ εἶπον καὶ πρότερον) ὅσοι μὲν ⟨ἂν⟩[1]
καταλίπωσι γνησίους παῖδας ἐξ αὐτῶν, οὐ προσήκει τοῖς παισὶν ἐπιδικάσασθαι τῶν πατρῴων·
ὅσοι δὲ διαθήκαις αὐτοῖς[2] εἰσποιοῦνται, τούτοις

---

[1] ἂν add. Dobree.   [2] αὑτοῖς Dobree : αὐτοί.

---

[a] August to September.
[b] i.e., would succeed naturally without consent of the

last heir. For Pyrrhus has been dead for more than twenty years, whereas Endius died in the month of Metageitnion[a] last year, in which month they promptly claimed the inheritance only two days after his death. Now the law ordains that a petition for the adjudication of an inheritance must be presented within five years of the death of the last heir. Two courses were, therefore, open to the woman, either to claim my paternal inheritance during Endius's lifetime, or else, when the adopted son had died to claim that her brother's estate should be adjudicated to her, especially if, as our opponents allege, he had given her in marriage to Xenocles as his legitimate sister. We all know perfectly well that every one of us has the right to claim the adjudication of a brother's estate, but that, if he has left legitimate children born of his body, no child need claim to have his patrimony adjudicated to him.[b] It is quite unnecessary to labour this point, for all of you, and all other citizens as well, possess your patrimonies without any adjudication by the courts. Our opponents, then, have pushed their effrontery so far that, while they denied that the adopted son need obtain the adjudication of an estate which has been bequeathed to him, they thought fit to claim the adjudication of her father's estate to Phile, whom they allege to have been a legitimate daughter left by Pyrrhus. Yet, as I have already said, when testators leave legitimate issue, their children need not demand the adjudication of their patrimony ; but, on the contrary, when testators adopt children by will, such children must

courts, which had to be obtained by collateral and testamentary heirs.

111

61 ἐπιδικάζεσθαι προσήκει τῶν δοθέντων. τοῖς μὲν γάρ, ὅτι γόνῳ γεγόνασιν, οὐδεὶς ἂν δήπου ἀμφισβητήσειε περὶ τῶν πατρῴων· πρὸς δὲ τοὺς εἰσποιήτους ἅπαντες οἱ κατὰ γένος προσήκοντες ἀμφισβητεῖν ἀξιοῦσιν. ἵνα οὖν μὴ παρὰ τοῦ ἐντυχόντος τῶν κλήρων αἱ λήξεις [τοῖς ἀμφισβητεῖν βουλομένοις] γίγνωνται, καὶ μὴ ὡς ἐρήμων τῶν κλήρων ἐπιδικάζεσθαί τινες τολμῶσι, τούτου ἕνεκα τὰς ἐπιδικασίας οἱ εἰσποίητοι πάντες ποιοῦνται.

62 μηδεὶς οὖν ὑμῶν ἡγείσθω, εἰ ἐνόμιζε γνησίαν εἶναι τὴν ἑαυτοῦ γυναῖκα Ξενοκλῆς, λαχεῖν ἂν ὑπὲρ αὐτῆς τὴν λῆξιν τοῦ κλήρου τοῦ πατρῴου, ἀλλ' ἐβάδιζεν ἂν ἡ γνησία εἰς τὰ ἑαυτῆς πατρῷα, καὶ εἴ τις αὐτὴν ἀφῃρεῖτο ἢ ἐβιάζετο, ἐξῆγεν ἂν ἐκ τῶν πατρῴων, καὶ οὐκ ἂν ἰδίας μόνον δίκας ἔφευγεν ὁ βιαζόμενος, ἀλλὰ καὶ δημοσίᾳ εἰσαγγελθεὶς πρὸς[1] τὸν ἄρχοντα ἐκινδύνευεν ἂν περὶ τοῦ σώματος καὶ τῆς οὐσίας ἁπάσης τῆς ἑαυτοῦ.

63 Ἔτι δ' ἂν πρότερον τοῦ Ξενοκλέους οἱ τοῦ Πύρρου θεῖοι, εἰ ᾔδεσαν γνησίαν θυγατέρα τῷ ἑαυτῶν ἀδελφιδῷ καταλειπομένην καὶ ἡμῶν μηδένα λαμβάνειν ἐθέλοντα αὐτήν, οὐκ ἄν ποτε ἐπέτρεψαν Ξενοκλέα, τὸν μηδαμόθεν μηδὲν γένει προσήκοντα Πύρρῳ, λαβόντα ἔχειν τὴν κατὰ γένος προσ-
64 ήκουσαν αὐτοῖς γυναῖκα. ἢ δεινόν γ' ἂν εἴη. τὰς μὲν ὑπὸ τῶν πατέρων ἐκδοθείσας καὶ συνοικούσας ἀνδράσι γυναῖκας (περὶ ὧν τίς ἂν ἄμεινον ἢ ὁ πατὴρ βουλεύσαιτο;) καὶ τὰς οὕτω δοθείσας, ἂν

---

[1] πρὸς Reiske: εἰς.

obtain an adjudication of what is bequeathed to them. Since the former are the issue of the deceased, no one, I suppose, could dispute their possession of their patrimony ; but all blood-relations think they have the right to dispute a bequest to an adopted son. In order, therefore, that suits for such estates may not be brought by any chance claimant and that persons may not dare to demand the adjudication of them as vacant inheritances, adopted sons apply to the court for an adjudication. Let none of you, therefore, imagine that, if Xenocles had believed his wife to be a legitimate child, he would have brought a suit claiming her patrimony ; no, the legitimate daughter would have entered into possession of her father's estate, and, if anyone had tried to seize it or deprive her of it by violence, he would have been ousting her from her patrimony and would have been liable not only to a civil prosecution but also to a public denunciation to the archon and would have risked his person and all his possessions.

Even before any action on the part of Xenocles, Pyrrhus's uncles, if they had known that their nephew had left a legitimate daughter and that none of us was willing to take her in marriage, would never have allowed Xenocles, who was an entire stranger in blood to Pyrrhus, to take and marry one who belonged to them by right of kinship. Such a proceeding would have been extraordinary. The law ordains that daughters who have been given in marriage by their father and are living with their husbands—and who can judge better than a father what is to his daughter's interest ?— in spite of the fact that they are thus married,

ὁ πατὴρ αὐτῶν τελευτήσῃ μὴ καταλιπὼν αὐταῖς
γνησίους ἀδελφούς, τοῖς ἐγγύτατα γένους ἐπιδίκους ὁ νόμος εἶναι κελεύει, καὶ πολλοὶ συν-
οικοῦντες ἤδη ἀφήρηνται τὰς ἑαυτῶν γυναῖκας.
65 εἶτα τὰς μὲν ὑπὸ τῶν πατέρων ἐκδοθείσας διὰ
τὸν νόμον ἐξ ἀνάγκης ἐπιδίκους εἶναι προσήκει·
Ξενοκλεῖ δὲ ἄν τις τόδ' ἐπέτρεψε τῶν τοῦ Πύρρου
θείων, εἰ ἦν γνησία θυγάτηρ ἐκείνῳ καταλειπο-
μένη, λαβόντα ἔχειν τὴν κατὰ γένος προσήκουσαν
αὐτοῖς γυναῖκα, καὶ τοσαύτης οὐσίας τοῦτον καταστῆναι[1] κληρονόμον ἀνθ' ἑαυτῶν; μὴ νομίσητε
66 ὑμεῖς, ὦ ἄνδρες· οὐδεὶς γὰρ ἀνθρώπων μισεῖ τὸ
λυσιτελοῦν, οὐδὲ περὶ πλείονος τοὺς ἀλλοτρίους
ἑαυτοῦ ποιεῖται. ἐὰν οὖν προφασίζωνται διὰ τὴν
τοῦ Ἐνδίου ποίησιν μὴ ἐπίδικον εἶναι τὴν γυναῖκα,
καὶ διὰ ταῦτα μὴ φῶσιν ἀμφισβητῆσαι αὐτῆς,
πρῶτον μὲν ἐκεῖνα αὐτοὺς ἐρέσθαι χρή, τί[2] ὁμολογοῦντες τὴν τοῦ Ἐνδίου ποίησιν ὑπὸ τοῦ Πύρρου γενέσθαι ἐπεσκημμένοι εἰσὶ τοῖς μεμαρτυρηκόσι
67 ταῦτα, εἶτα ⟨τί⟩[3] παρελθόντες τὸν τελευταῖον τοῦ
οἴκου γεγενημένον κληρονόμον τοῦ Πύρρου κλήρου
τὴν λῆξιν λαχεῖν ἠξίωσαν παρὰ τὸν νόμον. πρὸς
δὲ τούτοις ἐκεῖνο αὐτοὺς ἔρεσθε, εἰ τις τῶν
γνησίων ⟨τῶν⟩[4] αὐτοῦ ἐπιδικάζεσθαι ἀξιοῖ. ταῦτα
πρὸς τὴν ἀναίδειαν αὐτῶν πυνθάνεσθε. ὡς δ' ἦν
ἐπίδικος ἡ γυνή, εἴ περ γνησία κατελείφθη,[5] ἐκ

---

[1] καταστῆναι Reiske : καταστῆσαι.
[2] τί Naber : εἰ.
[3] τί add. Naber.
[4] τῶν add. Reiske.
[5] κατελείφθη Aldus : καταληφθείη.

---

[a] Though the legal principle here stated is correct, it does
not apply to all cases indiscriminately. For example, if a
daughter, who was an heiress, married and had children, her
rights accrued to the children when they came of age ; no

114

shall, if their father dies without leaving them legitimate brothers, pass into the legal power of their next-of-kin ; and indeed it has frequently happened that husbands have been thus deprived of their own wives.[a] While, then, the necessary consequence of this law is that women who have been given in marriage by their fathers are thus liable to be legally claimed, would any one of Pyrrhus's uncles, if Phile were a legitimate daughter left by him, have allowed Xenocles to take and marry a woman who belonged to them by right of kinship and thus make him heir[b] to so large a fortune instead of themselves ? Do not believe it, gentlemen ; no man so hates his own advantage and prefers the interest of strangers to his own. If, therefore, they pretend that the adoption of Endius annulled their rights over this woman and allege that it is for this reason that they laid no claim to her, the following questions must be put to them : First, why have they attacked those who have borne witness to the adoption of Endius by Pyrrhus if they admit that it took place ? And, secondly, why did they think fit to claim the succession to Pyrrhus's estate illegally, ignoring him who was its last tenant ? Furthermore, you should ask them whether any legitimate child ever thinks of requesting the court to adjudicate to him what is his own. These are the questions with which you should oppose their impudence. That the woman could be legally claimed by her next-of-kin, if she was really a legitimate

doubt also, if she had no children, she could renounce her rights and remain with her husband.

[b] As a matter of fact the husband of an heiress enjoyed the usufruct of her fortune only during the minority of their son or sons.

68 τῶν νόμων σαφέστατα μαθεῖν ἔστι τοῦτο. ὁ γὰρ
νόμος διαρρήδην λέγει ἐξεῖναι διαθέσθαι ὅπως ἂν
ἐθέλῃ τις τὰ αὑτοῦ, ἐὰν μὴ παῖδας γνησίους καταλίπῃ ἄρρενας· ἂν δὲ θηλείας καταλίπῃ, σὺν ταύταις.
οὐκοῦν μετὰ τῶν θυγατέρων ἔστι δοῦναι καὶ διαθέσθαι τὰ αὑτοῦ· ἄνευ δὲ τῶν γνησίων θυγατέρων
οὐχ οἷόν τε οὔτε ποιήσασθαι οὔτε δοῦναι οὐδενὶ
69 οὐδὲν τῶν ἑαυτοῦ. οὐκοῦν εἰ μὲν ἄνευ τῆς γνησίας
θυγατρὸς τὸν Ἔνδιον Πύρρος ἐποιεῖτο ὑὸν αὑτῷ,
ἄκυρος ἂν ἦν αὐτοῦ ἡ ποίησις κατὰ τὸν νόμον·
εἰ δὲ τὴν θυγατέρα ἐδίδου καὶ ἐπὶ τούτῳ ποιη-
[45] σάμενος κατέλιπε, πῶς ἂν ὑμεῖς | ἐπετρέψατε ἐπι-
δικάζεσθαι οἱ τοῦ Πύρρου θεῖοι[1] τὸν Ἔνδιον τοῦ
Πύρρου κλήρου ἄνευ τῆς γνησίας θυγατρός, εἰ ἦν
ἐκείνῳ, ἄλλως τε εἰ καὶ ἐμαρτυρήσατε ὡς ἐπ-
έσκηψεν ὑμῖν ὁ ἀδελφιδοῦς ἐπιμελεῖσθαι τούτου
70 τοῦ παιδίου; ἀλλ' ὦ 'γαθοί,[2] τοῦτο μὲν καὶ λαθεῖν
φήσαιτ' ἂν ὑμᾶς· ὅτε δ' ἠγγύα καὶ ἐξεδίδου ὁ
Ἔνδιος τὴν γυναῖκα,[3] ἐπετρέπετε ὑμεῖς οἱ θεῖοι
τὴν τοῦ ἀδελφιδοῦ τοῦ ὑμετέρου αὐτῶν ὡς ἐξ
ἑταίρας οὖσαν ἐκείνῳ ἐγγυᾶσθαι, ἄλλως τε καὶ
παραγενέσθαι φάσκοντες, ὅτε ὁ ἀδελφιδοῦς ὑμῶν
ἠγγυᾶτο τὴν μητέρα τὴν ταύτης κατὰ ⟨τοὺς⟩[4]
νόμους ἕξειν γυναῖκα, ἔτι δὲ καὶ ἐν τῇ δεκάτῃ τῇ
71 ταύτης κληθέντες συνεστιᾶσθαι; πρὸς δὲ τούτοις
(τουτὶ γὰρ τὸ δεινόν ἐστιν) ἐπισκῆψαι φάσκοντες
ὑμῖν τὸν ἀδελφιδοῦν ἐπιμελεῖσθαι τούτου τοῦ
παιδίου, οὕτως ἐπεμελήθητε ὥστ' ἐᾶσαι ὡς ἐξ
ἑταίρας οὖσαν αὐτὴν ἐγγυᾶσθαι, ἄλλως τε καὶ

---

[1] οἱ τοῦ Πύρρου θεῖοι Buermann : τῷ τοῦ Π. θείῳ.
[2] ἀγαθοὶ Sauppe : ἀγαθέ.
[3] τὴν γυναῖκα schedae Etonenses : τῇ γυναικί.

116

daughter of the deceased, appears most evidently
from the laws. The law states explicitly that, in
the absence of legitimate male issue, a man can
dispose of his property as he pleases, but that, if
he has daughters, the legatees must take them as
well. Thus a man may bequeath and dispose of
his property with his daughters, but he may not
either adopt a son or leave any of his possessions to
anyone without also disposing of his legitimate
daughters. If, therefore, Pyrrhus adopted Endius
as his son without also disposing of his legitimate
daughter, the adoption would have been void in the
eyes of the law ; if, on the other hand, he intended to
give him his daughter and after adopting him on
these terms left her to him, how could you, the
uncles of Pyrrhus, have allowed Endius to have the
estate of Pyrrhus adjudicated to him without his
taking also his legitimate daughter, if he had one,
especially as you testified that your nephew solemnly
charged you to look after this girl ? Can you say,
my good friends, that this point escaped your notice ?
Yet when Endius betrothed the woman and gave
her in marriage, did you, his uncles, allow your own
nephew's daughter to be betrothed as his daughter
by a mistress, though you declare that you were
present when your nephew took her mother to be
his wife in due legal form, and further, that you
took part by invitation in the celebrations on the
tenth day after her child's birth ? Furthermore—
and this is the worst part of your conduct—though
you declare that your nephew solemnly charged you
to look after this girl, your mode of looking after
her was to allow her to be married as the daughter

---

⁴ τοὺς add. Schoemann.

ἔχουσαν τοὔνομα τῆς ὑμετέρας αὐτῶν ἀδελφῆς,
ὡς ἐμαρτυρεῖτε;

72 Ἐκ τοίνυν τούτων, ὦ ἄνδρες, καὶ ἐξ αὐτοῦ τοῦ
πράγματος ῥᾴδιόν ἐστι γνῶναι ὅσον ἀναισχυν-
τότατοι ἀνθρώπων εἰσὶν οὗτοι. τίνος γὰρ ἕνεκα,
εἰ ἦν γνησία θυγάτηρ τῷ ἡμετέρῳ θείῳ κατα-
λειπομένη, ποιησάμενος ὁ θεῖος κατέλιπε τὸν ἐμὸν
ἀδελφὸν ὑὸν ἑαυτῷ; πότερον ὅτι προσήκοντες
αὐτῷ ἐγγυτέρω γένους ἡμῶν ἦσαν ἄλλοι, οὓς
βουλόμενος τὴν ἐπιδικασίαν τῆς θυγατρὸς ἀποστερῆσαι ἐποιεῖτο τὸν ⟨ἐμὸν⟩[1] ἀδελφὸν ὑὸν αὐτῷ;
ἀλλ' οὔτε ἐγένετο οὔτ' ἔστι, μὴ γενομένων [δὲ]
παίδων γνησίων ἐκείνῳ, ἐγγυτέρω ἡμῶν οὐδὲ εἷς·
ἀδελφὸς μὲν γὰρ οὐκ ἦν αὐτῷ οὐδ' ἀδελφοῦ
παῖδες, ἐκ δὲ τῆς ἀδελφῆς ἡμεῖς ἦμεν αὐτῷ.

73 ἀλλὰ νὴ Δία ἄλλον τινὰ ποιησάμενος τῶν συγγενῶν ἔδωκεν ἂν ἔχειν τὸν κλῆρον καὶ τὴν θυγατέρα
τὴν ἑαυτοῦ. καὶ τί αὐτὸν ἔδει καταφανῶς καὶ
ὁτῳοῦν ἀπέχθεσθαι τῶν οἰκείων, ἐξόν, εἴπερ ἦν
ἠγγυημένος τὴν ἀδελφὴν τὴν Νικοδήμου, τὴν
θυγατέρα τὴν ἐκ ταύτης ἀποφανθεῖσαν εἶναι εἰς
τοὺς φράτορας εἰσαγαγόντι ὡς οὖσαν γνησίαν
ἑαυτῷ, ἐπὶ ἅπαντι τῷ κλήρῳ ἐπίδικον καταλιπεῖν
αὐτήν, καὶ ἐπισκῆψαι τῶν γιγνομένων ⟨ἐκ⟩[2] τῆς

74 θυγατρὸς παίδων εἰσαγαγεῖν ὑὸν ἑαυτῷ; δῆλον
[μὲν] γὰρ ὅτι ἐπίκληρον καταλιπὼν ἀκριβῶς ἂν
ᾔδει ὅτι δυοῖν θάτερον ἔμελλεν ὑπάρχειν αὐτῇ·
ἢ γὰρ ἡμῶν τινα τῶν ἐγγύτατα γένους ἐπιδικασάμενον ἕξειν γυναῖκα, ἢ εἰ μηδεὶς ἡμῶν ἐβούλετο
λαμβάνειν, τῶν θείων τινὰ τούτων τῶν μαρτυρούντων, εἰ δὲ μή, τῶν ἄλλων τινὰ συγγενῶν τὸν
αὐτὸν τρόπον ἐπὶ πάσῃ τῇ οὐσίᾳ[3] ἐπιδικασάμενον

of a mistress, although, as you testified, she bore the name of your own sister.

From all this, gentlemen, and from what actually happened, it is easy to see that these men attain the limit of human impudence. For why did our uncle, if he had a legitimate daughter who survived him, adopt and leave behind my brother as his son ? Had he nearer relatives than us whom he wished, by adopting my brother, to exclude from the right of claiming his daughter ? In the absence of legitimate sons of his own, he neither has nor ever had a single relative nearer than us ; for he had no brother or brother's sons, and we were the children of his sister. But, it may be urged, he might have adopted some other kinsman and given him the possession of his estate and his daughter. Yet what need had he openly to incur the enmity of any one of his relatives, when it was in his power, if he had really married the sister of Nicodemus, to introduce the child, who has been declared to be her offspring, to the members of his ward as his own legitimate child, and leave her sole heiress to all his estate and direct that one of her sons should be introduced as his adopted son ? For it is clear that, if he left her sole heiress, he would have been fully aware that one of two things was likely to happen to her : either one of us, the nearest relatives, would obtain an adjudication and take her as wife ; or, if none of us wished to take her, one of these uncles who just now gave evidence, or, failing them, one of the other relatives, would, on the same principle, obtain an adjudication of her together with the

---

1 ἐμὸν add. Stephanus.   2 ἐκ add. Reiske.
3 ἐπὶ πάσῃ τῇ οὐσίᾳ Wyse : περὶ πάσης τῆς οὐσίας.

119

75 κατὰ τοὺς νόμους ἕξειν[1] ταύτην γυναῖκα. οὐκοῦν
ἐκ μὲν τοῦ τὴν θυγατέρα εἰς τοὺς φράτορας εἰσαγαγεῖν καὶ μὴ ποιήσασθαι τὸν ἐμὸν ἀδελφὸν υἱὸν
αὑτῷ ταῦτ᾽ ἂν[2] διεπράξατο· ἐκ δὲ τοῦ τοῦτον μὲν
ποιήσασθαι τὴν δὲ μὴ εἰσαγαγεῖν τὴν μὲν νόθην,
ὥσπερ αὑτῷ προσῆκε, καὶ ἄκληρον κατέστησε,
76 τὸν δὲ κληρονόμον κατέλιπε τῶν ἑαυτοῦ. ἀλλὰ
μὴν ὥς γε[3] οὔτε γαμηλίαν εἰσήνεγκεν ὁ θεῖος
ἡμῶν, οὔτε τὴν θυγατέρα, ἥν φασι γνησίαν αὐτῷ
εἶναι οὗτοι, εἰσαγαγεῖν εἰς τοὺς φράτορας ἠξίωσε,
καὶ ταῦτα νόμου ὄντος αὐτοῖς, ἀναγνώσεται [δὲ]
ὑμῖν τὴν τῶν φρατόρων τῶν ἐκείνου μαρτυρίαν.
ἀναγίγνωσκε· σὺ δ᾽ ἐπίλαβε[4] τὸ ὕδωρ.

ΜΑΡΤΥΡΙΑ

Λαβὲ δὲ καὶ ὡς ἐποιήσατο τὸν ἐμὸν ἀδελφὸν υἱὸν
αὑτῷ.

ΜΑΡΤΥΡΙΑ

77 Εἶτα ὑμεῖς τὴν Νικοδήμου μαρτυρίαν τῶν αὐτοῦ
τοῦ θείου ἐκμαρτυριῶν πιστοτέραν ἡγήσεσθε εἶναι,
καὶ τὴν οὕτω κοινὴν τοῖς βουλομένοις γεγενημένην,
ταύτην ἐπιχειρήσει τις ὑμᾶς πείθειν ὅτι ἐγγυητὴν
γυναῖκα ὁ ἡμέτερος θεῖος ἔσχεν; ἀλλ᾽ ὑμεῖς, ὡς
ἔγωγ᾽ οἶμαι, οὐ πιστεύσετε,[5] ἐὰν μὴ ἀποφαίνῃ
78 ὑμῖν, ὅπερ ἀρχόμενος εἶπον τοῦ λόγου, πρῶτον μὲν
ἐπὶ τίνι προικὶ οὗτος ἐγγυῆσαι τῷ Πύρρῳ φησὶ τὴν
ἀδελφήν, ἔπειτα πρὸς ὁποῖον ἄρχοντα ἡ ἐγγυητὴ

---

[1] ἕξειν Reiske: ἔχειν.   [2] ταῦτ᾽ ἂν Aldus: ταῦτα.
[3] ὥς γε Aldus: ὥστε.
[4] ἐπίλαβε Stephanus: ἐπίβαλλε.
[5] πιστεύσετε Stephanus: πιστεύετε.

---

[a] ἐκμαρτυρία, which is strictly a technical term meaning

whole estate and take her as his wife. By presenting, then, his daughter to the members of his ward without adopting my brother as his son, he might have obtained this result; whereas, by adopting my brother without introducing his daughter to the members of his ward, he made her illegitimate, as it was right that he should, and therefore incapable of succession, and left my brother heir to his estate. Further, to prove to you that our uncle never gave a marriage-feast and never thought fit to introduce his daughter, whom our opponents declare to be his legitimate child, to the members of his ward, though their statutes demand that this should be done, the clerk shall read you the deposition of the members of Pyrrhus's ward. Read this; and you, stop the water-clock.

DEPOSITION

Now take the deposition which shows that Pyrrhus adopted my brother.

DEPOSITION

After this will you regard the testimony of Nicodemus as more worthy of credence than the evidence provided by our uncle's own acts?[a] And will anyone attempt to persuade you that our uncle made a legal marriage with this woman who was a common courtezan? No, you will never, I am sure, believe it unless Nicodemus can explain the following points, which I mentioned at the beginning of my speech; First, with what dowry does he say that he married his sister to Pyrrhus? Secondly, before what archon did this married woman give

a deposition taken in writing outside the court, is here rhetorically used for the evidence of a person's acts.

γυνὴ ἀπέλιπε τὸν ἄνδρα ἢ τὸν οἶκον [τὸν] αὐτοῦ,
εἶτα παρ' ὅτου ἐκομίσατο τὴν προῖκα αὐτῆς,
ἐπειδὴ τετελευτηκὼς ἦν ᾧ φησιν αὐτὴν ἐγγυῆσαι·
[46] ἢ εἰ ἀπαιτῶν μὴ ἐδύνατο κομίσασθαι | ἐν εἴκοσιν
ἔτεσιν, ὁποίαν δίκην σίτου ἢ τῆς προικὸς αὐτῆς
ὑπὲρ τῆς ἐγγυητῆς γυναικὸς ἐδικάσατο τῷ ἔχοντι
79 τὸν Πύρρου κλῆρον οὗτος. ἔτι δὲ πρὸς τούτοις
ἐπιδειξάτω ὅτῳ πρότερον ἢ ὕστερον ἠγγύησεν
οὗτος τὴν ἀδελφήν, ἢ εἰ ἐξ ἄλλου τινὸς γεγενημένοι
εἰσὶ παῖδες αὐτῇ. ταῦτα οὖν ἀξιοῦτε πυνθάνεσθαι
παρ' αὐτοῦ, καὶ περὶ τῆς τοῖς φράτορσι γαμηλίας
μὴ ἀμνημονεῖτε. οὐ γὰρ τῶν ἐλαχίστων πρὸς τὴν
τούτου[1] μαρτυρίαν τεκμήριόν ἐστι τοῦτο. δῆλον
γὰρ ὅτι, εἰ ἐπείσθη ἐγγυήσασθαι, ἐπείσθη ἂν καὶ
γαμηλίαν ὑπὲρ αὐτῆς τοῖς φράτερσιν εἰσενεγκεῖν
καὶ εἰσαγαγεῖν τὴν ἐκ ταύτης ἀποφανθεῖσαν θυγα-
80 τέρα ὡς γνησίαν οὖσαν αὐτῷ. καὶ ἔν τε τῷ
δήμῳ κεκτημένος τὸν τριτάλαντον οἶκον, εἰ ἦν
γεγαμηκώς, ἠναγκάζετο ἂν ὑπὲρ τῆς γαμετῆς
γυναικὸς καὶ θεσμοφόρια ἑστιᾶν τὰς γυναῖκας, καὶ
τἆλλα ὅσα προσῆκε λῃτουργεῖν ἐν τῷ δήμῳ ὑπὲρ
τῆς γυναικὸς ἀπό γε οὐσίας τηλικαύτης. οὐ
τοίνυν φανεῖται οὐδὲν τούτων γεγενημένον οὐδεπώποτε. οἱ μὲν οὖν φράτορες μεμαρτυρήκασιν
ὑμῖν· λαβὲ δὲ καὶ τὴν τῶν δημοτῶν τῶν ἐκείνου
μαρτυρίαν.

<ΜΑΡΤΥΡΙΑ>

[1] τούτου Aldus: τούτων.

---

a A festival in honour of Demeter and Persephone. The
argument is particularly effective, since women of evil life
were rigorously excluded from this festival (*cf.* vi. 49, 50).

notice of having quitted her husband or his domicile ?
Next, from whom did Nicodemus recover her dowry,
when the man had died to whom he says that he
gave her in marriage ? Or if, though he demanded
it back, he was unable to recover in the course of
twenty years, what action did he bring for alimony
or for her dowry on behalf of this married woman
against the tenant of Pyrrhus's estate ? Furthermore, in addition to all this, let him explain to whom
he married his sister at an earlier or later date
and whether she had children by another man.
These, then, are the questions which you must
make him answer, and do not forget to interrogate
him also about the marriage-feast to the members
of his ward. This is among the proofs which are
most damaging to his evidence ; for it is obvious
that if Pyrrhus was induced to marry this woman,
he would also have been induced to give a marriage-
feast for her to the members of his ward and to
introduce to them the child, who has been declared
to be this woman's daughter, as his legitimate offspring. Again in his deme, since he possessed the
fortune of three talents, he would have been obliged
on behalf of this wedded wife of his to entertain the
wives of his fellow-demesmen at the Thesmophoria,[a]
and to perform for her the other offices which the
possession of such a fortune entails. It shall therefore
be made clear to you that nothing of the kind has
ever been done. The members of his ward have
already given you their evidence ; take now and
read the deposition of Pyrrhus's fellow-demesmen.

DEPOSITION

IV. ON THE ESTATE OF NICOSTRATUS

IV. ON THE ESTATE OF NICOSTRATUS

INTRODUCTION

NICOSTRATUS,[a] a soldier of fortune, after having been absent from Athens for eleven years, died on foreign service and left a fortune of two talents. Numerous claimants came forward, but eventually only two parties persisted in their claims—two young men, the brothers Hagnon and Hagnotheus, and a certain Chariades. Chariades, who alleged that he had served as a mercenary in the same army as Nicostratus, produced a will, under the terms of which Nicostratus adopted him as his son and made him his heir. Hagnon and Hagnotheus contested the genuineness of this will, and claimed the succession on the ground that they were the next-of-kin, as sons of Thrasippus, the brother of Nicostratus's father Thrasymachus, and therefore first cousins of the deceased.

[a] STEMMA

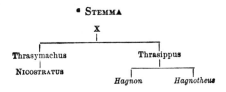

The present speech, which is a supplementary discourse (ἐπίλογος), is spoken by a family friend of the two young men, who, in view of their youth, would naturally rely on the advocacy of an older and more experienced speaker. The writer of the Argument prefixed to the Speech states that the advocate was Isaeus himself : this is hardly likely, since the personal advocacy of a professional speech-writer would have prejudiced the interests of his clients, and, further, it is more than probable that Isaeus was not an Athenian citizen, and that he would, therefore, have had no *locus standi* in the courts. The statement of the Argument is probably due to a misunderstanding of the opening words of the speech.

Chariades, who based his claim on a will, had produced witnesses in support of its genuineness ; he had also alleged that Nicostratus was the son not of Thrasymachus but of Smicrus. The two main points, therefore, which the claimants had to prove were, first, that they were really the first cousins of the deceased, and, secondly, that the will was a forgery. It is possible that the elder of the two brothers had already dealt with these topics, which are very inadequately treated in the present speech. On the question of Nicostratus's parentage each party produced evidence in support of their respective contentions ; as regards the genuineness of the will, the speaker has no better argument to urge than that the witnesses to the alleged will were friends of Chariades and therefore untrustworthy. The speech consists mainly of rhetorical commonplaces, attempts to blacken the character of Chariades and eulogies of his two opponents.

ON THE ESTATE OF NICOSTRATUS

If Valckenaer's emendation (ἐξ Ἄκης, § 7) is accepted, the date of the speech must be placed soon after 374 B.C., since Ace, the modern Acre, was the rendezvous of the army assembled by Pharnabazus for his expedition to Egypt in that year.

IV. ΠΕΡΙ ΤΟΥ ΝΙΚΟΣΤΡΑΤΟΥ ΚΛΗΡΟΥ

⟨ΕΠΙΛΟΓΟΣ⟩

ΥΠΟΘΕΣΙΣ

Νικοστράτου ἐν ὑπερορίᾳ τελευτήσαντος, Ἅγνων καὶ Ἁγνόθεος ὡς ὄντες ἀνεψιοὶ ἐκ πατραδέλφου ἀμφισβητοῦσι τοῦ κλήρου πρὸς Χαριάδην, φάσκοντα κληρονόμον αὐτοῦ εἶναι κατὰ δόσιν, ὅ ἐστι κατὰ διαθήκας. Ἰσαῖος οὖν ὁ ῥήτωρ, ὡς συγγενὴς ὢν τῶν περὶ τὸν Ἅγνωνα, λέγει συνηγορῶν αὐτοῖς. ἡ στάσις στοχασμός.

1 Ἐπιτήδειοί μοι τυγχάνουσιν, ὦ ἄνδρες, ὄντες Ἅγνων τε οὑτοσὶ καὶ Ἁγνόθεος, καὶ ὁ πατὴρ αὐτῶν ἔτι πρότερον. εἰκὸς οὖν μοι δοκεῖ εἶναι, ὡς ἂν οἷός τε ὦ, συνειπεῖν αὐτοῖς.

Περὶ μὲν οὖν τῶν ἐν τῇ ὑπερορίᾳ πραχθέντων [ὡς] οὔτε μάρτυρας ἐξευρεῖν οἷόν τε, οὔτε τοὺς ἀντιδίκους, ἐάν τι ψεύδωνται, ἐλέγχειν ῥᾴδιον, διὰ τὸ μηδέτερον τούτων ἐκεῖσε ἀφῖχθαι· τὰ δὲ ἐνθάδε [μοι] συμβεβηκότα δοκεῖ μοι ὑμῖν ἱκανὰ γενέσθαι ἂν τεκμήρια, ὅτι ἅπαντες οἱ κατὰ τὴν δόσιν τῶν Νικοστράτου ἀμφισβητοῦντες ἐξαπατῆσαι ὑμᾶς 2 βούλονται. πρῶτον μὲν οὖν, ὦ ἄνδρες, περὶ τῆς τῶν ὀνομάτων ἐπιγραφῆς ἄξιόν ἐστιν ἐξετάσαι, καὶ σκέψασθαι ὁπότεροι ἁπλούστερον καὶ κατὰ φύσιν

---

^a This statement is improbable ; see Introduction, p. 128.

IV. ON THE ESTATE OF NICOSTRATUS
SUPPLEMENTARY SPEECH

ARGUMENT

Nicostratus having died in a foreign land, Hagnon and Hagnotheus, as being his first cousins (their father having been brother to Nicostratus's father), contend for the succession to his estate against Chariades, who claims to be heir by bequest, that is to say, by will. Isaeus, the orator, being a kinsman of Hagnon and his brother, speaks as their advocate.[a] The question at issue is one of fact.

Hagnon here and Hagnotheus, gentlemen, are intimate friends of mine, as was their father before them. It seems, therefore, only natural to me to support their case to the best of my ability.

For the events which happened in a foreign land it is not possible to find witnesses or easy to convict our adversaries of any lies which they may tell, because neither of my clients has ever been to the country in question; but the events which have occurred here in Athens seem to me to provide you with sufficient proof that all those who lay claim to Nicostratus's estate on the ground of bequest are desirous of deceiving you. In the first place, gentlemen, it is proper that you should consider the different names attributed to the deceased and determine which of the two parties has laid

μᾶλλον τὰς λήξεις ἐποιήσαντο. Ἅγνων μὲν γὰρ
οὑτοσὶ καὶ Ἁγνόθεος Θρασυμάχου ἐπεγράψαντο
τὸν Νικόστρατον, καὶ ἑαυτοὺς ἐκείνῳ ἀνεψιοὺς
ἀποφαίνουσι, καὶ τούτων μάρτυρας παρέχονται·
3 Χαριάδης δὲ καὶ οἱ συνδικοῦντες αὐτῷ Σμίκρου
μὲν πατρὸς εἶναί φασι τὸν Νικόστρατον, ἀμφισβητοῦσι δὲ τοῦ Θρασυμάχου υἱοῦ κλήρου. καὶ οἵδε
μὲν οὐδὲν[1] προσποιοῦνται ἐκείνου τοῦ ὀνόματος
οὔτε γιγνώσκειν οὔτε προσήκειν αὐτοῖς· φασὶ μὲν
οὖν εἶναι Θρασυμάχου Νικόστρατον, τούτου δὲ
4 ὁμοίως τῆς οὐσίας ἀμφισβητοῦσι. καὶ εἰ μὲν τὸ
ὄνομα πατρόθεν τὸ αὐτὸ ὡμολόγουν εἶναι τοῦ
Νικοστράτου, περὶ δὲ τοῦ κλήρου μόνου διεφέροντο,
οὐδὲν ἂν ἔδει ὑμᾶς σκέψασθαι ἀλλ᾽ ⟨ἢ⟩[2] εἴ τι
διέθετο ἐκεῖνος ὁ Νικόστρατος, ὃν ἀμφότεροι
ὡμολόγουν· νῦν δὲ πῶς οἷόν τε τῷ ἀνδρὶ δύο
πατέρας ἐπιγράψασθαι; τοῦτο γὰρ Χαριάδης
πεποίηκεν· αὐτός τε γὰρ ἔλαχε ⟨τῶν⟩[3] τοῦ Σμίκρου
Νικοστράτου, τούτοις τε[4] ⟨τῶν⟩ τοῦ Θρασυμάχου
5 λαχοῦσι παρακατέβαλεν ὡς τὸν αὐτὸν ὄντα. ἔστι
μὲν οὖν ἅπαντα ταῦτα ἐπήρεια καὶ παρασκευή.
ἡγοῦνται γὰρ τούτους, ἁπλοῦ μὲν ὄντος τοῦ πράγ-
[47] ματος καὶ μηδεμιᾶς αὐτοῖς | ταραχῆς ἐγγιγνομένης,
οὐ χαλεπῶς ἐπιδείξειν ὅτι οὐδὲν Νικόστρατος
διέθετο· ἐὰν δὲ μὴ τὸν πατέρα τὸν αὐτὸν εἶναι
φῶσι, τοῦ δὲ κλήρου μηδὲν ἧττον ἀμφισβητῶσιν,
ἀκριβῶς ἴσασιν ὅτι πλείονι λόγῳ εἰπεῖν τουτουσὶ
δεήσει ὡς Νικόστρατος Θρασυμάχου ἦν ἢ ὡς οὐδὲν
6 διέθετο. ἔτι δὲ καὶ ὁμολογοῦντες Θρασυμάχου

---

[1] οὐδὲν Stephanus : οὐδέ.
[2] ἢ add. Reiske.
[3] τῶν . . . τῶν add. Hitzig.
[4] τε Fuhr : δέ.

his claim in the more straightforward and natural manner. Hagnon here and Hagnotheus described Nicostratus in their claim as the son of Thrasymachus and declare that they are his first cousins and prove these statements by witnesses. Chariades and his supporters, on the other hand, assert that Nicostratus was the son of Smicrus and yet claim the estate of the son of Thrasymachus. My clients make no pretence that they know anything of the name of Smicrus or that it has anything to do with them; they declare that Nicostratus was the son of Thrasymachus, and it is likewise his estate which they claim. If the parties were in agreement as to the name of Nicostratus's father and were disputing only about the estate, you would only have to consider whether Nicostratus, on whose identity both were agreed, did or did not leave a will. But as it is, how is it possible to assign two fathers to the man? Yet this is what Chariades has done; he himself claimed the estate of Nicostratus the son of Smicrus, and paid the deposit for a suit against my clients when they claimed the estate of the son of Thrasymachus, just as though it were a question of one and the same person. It is all an insolent plot and conspiracy. They think that my clients, if the matter is simple and nothing is introduced to confuse the issue, will have no difficulty in proving that Nicostratus made no will; whereas, if they allege that the father is not the same and likewise claim the estate, they know full well that my clients will have to employ a longer argument to prove that Nicostratus was the son of Thrasymachus than to convince you that he left no will. Further, if they admitted that Nicostratus was the

μὲν εἶναι τὸν Νικόστρατον οὐκ ἂν εἶχον ἐξελέγξαι
τούσδε ὡς οὐκ εἰσὶν ἐκείνῳ ἀνεψιοί· ἄλλον δὲ
πατέρα τῷ τεθνεῶτι κατασκευάζοντες οὐ μόνον
περὶ τῶν διαθηκῶν ἀλλὰ καὶ περὶ τοῦ γένους λόγον
ἐμβεβλήκασιν.

7 Οὐκ ἐκ τούτων δὲ μόνον γνοίητ' ἂν ὅτι ἀλλότριοί[1]
τινές εἰσιν οἱ ταῦτα ἐπὶ τουτουσὶ ἐπάγοντες, ἀλλὰ
καὶ ἐκ τῶν κατ' ἀρχὰς γεγενημένων. τίς γὰρ οὐκ
ἀπεκείρατο, ἐπειδὴ τὼ δύο ταλάντω ἐξ Ἀκῆς[2]
ἠλθέτην[3]; ἢ τίς οὐ μέλαν ἱμάτιον ἐφόρησεν,[4] ὡς[a]
διὰ τὸ πένθος κληρονομήσων τῆς οὐσίας; ἢ πόσοι
συγγενεῖς καὶ ὑεῖς κατὰ δόσιν προσεποιήσαντο τῶν
8 Νικοστράτου; Δημοσθένης μέν γε ἀδελφιδοῦς ἔφη
αὐτῷ εἶναι, ἐπειδὴ δ' ἐξηλέγχθη ὑπὸ τούτων,
ἀπέστη· Τήλεφος δὲ δοῦναι αὐτῷ Νικόστρατον
ἅπαντα τὰ ἑαυτοῦ. καὶ οὗτος οὐ πολλῷ ὕστερον
ἐπαύσατο. Ἀμεινιάδης[5] δὲ υἱὸν αὐτῷ πρὸς τὸν
ἄρχοντα ἧκεν ἄγων οὐδὲ τριετῆ γεγονότα, καὶ ταῦτ'
οὐκ ἐπιδεδημηκότος τοῦ Νικοστράτου ἕνδεκα ἐτῶν
9 Ἀθήνησι. Πύρρος δὲ ὁ Λαμπτρεὺς τῇ μὲν
Ἀθηνᾷ ἔφη τὰ χρήματα ὑπὸ Νικοστράτου καθ-
ιερῶσθαι, αὑτῷ δ' ὑπ' αὐτοῦ ἐκείνου δεδόσθαι.
Κτησίας[6] δ' ὁ Βησαιεὺς καὶ Κρανεὸς τὸ μὲν
πρῶτον δίκην ἔφασαν τοῦ Νικοστράτου ταλάντου
καταδεδικάσθαι, ἐπειδὴ δ' οὐκ εἶχον τοῦτο ἀποδεῖξαι, ἀπελεύθερον αὐτὸν ἑαυτῶν προσεποιήσαντο

---

[1] ἀλλότριοί Boekmeijer: ἄλλοι.
[2] ἐξ Ἀκῆς Valckenaer: ἐξάκις.   [3] ἠλθέτην Herwerden: -ον.
[4] ἐφόρησεν Baiter-Sauppe: ἐφόρεσεν.
[5] Ἀμεινιάδης Baiter-Sauppe: Ἀμεν-.
[6] Κτησίας Reiske: κτῆσις.

---

[a] As a sign of mourning.

son of Thrasymachus, they would be unable to prove that my clients are not his cousins ; but, by inventing another father for the deceased, they have introduced a discussion about his parentage as well as about the will.

But it is not only from these proceedings but from all that has happened from the beginning that you can be sure that those who are thus plotting against my clients are strangers to the family. For who did not cut the hair *a* when the two talents arrived from Ace *b* ? Who did not wear black, hoping by mourning to inherit the estate ? What was the number of would-be kinsmen and adopted sons who claimed Nicostratus's property ? Demosthenes declared himself to be his nephew, but renounced his claim when he was unmasked by my clients. Telephus asserted that Nicostratus had made him a gift of all his property ; he too soon desisted. Ameiniades appeared before the archon and produced as Nicostratus's son a child not yet three years old, although it was eleven years since Nicostratus had been in Athens. Pyrrhus of Lamptra declared that the property had been consecrated by Nicostratus to Athena but that it had been given him by Nicostratus himself.*c* Ctesias of Besa and Cranaus at first asserted that Nicostratus had been condemned to pay them a talent ; when they could not prove this, they pretended that he was their freedman ; *d* they were no better able to

b See Introduction, p. 129.

c The meaning is perhaps that Pyrrhus claimed a life-interest in the estate.

d If a freedman died without issue, his property could, under certain circumstances, be claimed by his former master.

10 εἶναι· καὶ οὐδ' οὗτοι ἃ ἔλεγον ἀπέδειξαν. καὶ οἱ μὲν
εὐθὺς κατὰ τὰ πρῶτα ἐπὶ τὰ Νικοστράτου ἄξαντες
οὗτοί εἰσι· Χαριάδης δὲ τότε μὲν οὐδαμοῦ ἠμφισβήτησεν, ὕστερον δὲ οὐ μόνον αὐτὸς ⟨αὑτὸν⟩[1] ἀλλὰ
καὶ τὸ ἐκ τῆς ἑταίρας παιδίον εἰσποιῶν ἦλθε.
ταὐτὸ[2] δ' ἦν αὐτῷ ὡς ἢ τῶν χρημάτων κληρο-
νομήσοντι ἢ τὸ παιδίον ἀστὸν ποιήσοντι. αἰσθο-
μενος δὲ καὶ οὗτος ὅτι περὶ τοῦ γένους ἐλεγ-
χθήσοιτο, τὴν μὲν τοῦ παιδίου ἀμφισβήτησιν παρ-
έλυσεν, ἑαυτῷ δὲ κατὰ δόσιν παρακατέβαλεν.

11 Ἐχρῆν μὲν οὖν, ὦ ἄνδρες, ὅστις κατὰ δόσιν χρημάτων ἀμφισβητῶν ἡττηθείη, μὴ κατὰ τὸ τέλος ζη-
μιοῦσθαι, ἀλλ' ἐφ' ὅσα περ ληψόμενος ᾔει,[3] τοσαῦτα
τῇ πόλει ἀποτίνειν· οὕτω γὰρ ⟨ἂν⟩[4] οὔθ' οἱ νόμοι
κατεφρονοῦντο οὔτε τὰ γένη ὑβρίζετο, πρὸ δὲ
τούτων οὐδ' ἂν τῶν τεθνεώτων οὐδεὶς κατεψεύδετο.
ἐπειδὴ δὲ ἅπασι καὶ τῶν ἀλλοτρίων ἁπάντων, καθ'
ὅ τι ἄν τις βούληται, ἀμφισβητεῖν ἔξεστιν, ὑμᾶς
χρὴ περὶ αὐτῶν ὡς οἷόν τ' ἀκριβέστατα ἐξετάζειν
12 καὶ μηδὲν εἰς ὅσον δύνασθε παραλείπειν. ἐν μόναις
δὲ ταῖς τῶν κλήρων εἰσαγωγαῖς δοκεῖ μοι προσήκειν τεκμηρίοις μᾶλλον ἢ μάρτυσι πιστεύειν. περὶ
μὲν γὰρ τῶν ἄλλων συμβολαίων οὐ πάνυ χαλεπὸν
τοὺς τὰ ψευδῆ μαρτυροῦντας ἐλέγχειν· ζῶντος γὰρ
καὶ παρόντος τοῦ πράξαντος καταμαρτυροῦσι·
περὶ δὲ τῶν διαθηκῶν πῶς ἄν τις γνοίη τοὺς μὴ
τἀληθῆ λέγοντας, εἰ μὴ πάνυ μεγάλα τὰ διαφέρον-
τα εἴη, αὐτοῦ μὲν καθ' οὗ μαρτυροῦσι τεθνεῶτος,

---

[1] αὑτὸν add. Boekmeijer.
[2] ταὐτὸ Sauppe: τοῦτο.   [3] ᾔει Bekker: ἴῃ.
[4] ἂν add. Reiske.

---

* One-tenth of the estimated value of the estate claimed.

prove their statement. These were the men who at the very beginning swooped down upon the estate of Nicostratus. Chariades at that time made no claim, but came forward later, foisting in not only himself but also his child by his mistress. It was all the same to him whether he was going to inherit the estate or have his son recognized as a citizen. He, too, perceiving that he would be defeated on the question of the child's birth, jettisoned the child's claim and paid a deposit to bring an action asserting his own right under a will.

It would be a good thing, gentlemen, that any claimant to an inheritance under a will, if he fails, should not be fined at the usual rate [a] but be made to pay into the treasury the full amount of the fortune which he set out to obtain ; thus the laws would not be despised nor would the relatives be insulted, and above all, no fictions would be invented against the dead. But, since full liberty is given to anyone according to his fancy to claim anyone else's estate, it behoves you to sift their claims with every possible care and to omit no possible precaution. It seems to me that in suits concerning inheritances, and in these alone, more credit ought to be given to circumstantial proof than to the statements of witnesses. When other legal instruments are the subject of litigation, it is not very difficult to convict those who give false evidence, for they give their evidence to the prejudice of the supposed party to the deed alive and present ; but when a will is in question, how can one recognize those who are not telling the truth, unless the divergences in the evidence are great, since the party against whom they bear witness is dead, the

τῶν δὲ συγγενῶν μηδὲν τῶν πεπραγμένων εἰδότων,
13 τοῦ δὲ ἐλέγχου μηδαμῶς ἀκριβοῦς γιγνομένου; ἔτι
δέ, ὦ ἄνδρες, καὶ τῶν διατιθεμένων οἱ πολλοὶ οὐδὲ
λέγουσι τοῖς παραγιγνομένοις ὅ τι διατίθενται, ἀλλ'
αὐτοῦ μόνου, τοῦ καταλιπεῖν διαθήκας, μάρτυρας
παρίστανται, τοῦ δὲ συμβαίνοντός ἐστι καὶ γραμματεῖον ἀλλαγῆναι καὶ τἀναντία ταῖς τοῦ τεθνεῶτος
διαθήκαις μεταγραφῆναι· οὐδὲν γὰρ μᾶλλον οἱ μάρτυρες εἴσονται, εἰ ἐφ' αἷς ἐκλήθησαν διαθήκαις,
14 αὗται ἀποφαίνονται.[1] ὁπότε δὲ καὶ τοὺς ὁμολογουμένως παραγενομένους οἷόν τ' ἐστὶν ἐξαπατῆσαι,
πῶς οὐκ ἂν ὑμᾶς γε τοὺς μηδὲν τοῦ πράγματος
εἰδότας πολὺ [μᾶλλον] ἑτοιμότερόν τις παρακρούσασθαι ἐγχειρήσειεν[2];

[48] Ἀλλὰ μὴν καὶ ὁ νόμος, ὦ | ἄνδρες, οὐκ ἐάν τις
διαθῆται μόνον, κυρίας εἶναι κελεύει τὰς διαθήκας,
ἀλλὰ ἐὰν εὖ φρονῶν. σκεπτέον δὴ[3] ὑμῖν πρῶτον
μὲν εἰ ἐποιήσατο τὰς διαθήκας, ἔπειτα εἰ μὴ
15 παρανοῶν διέθετο. ἀντιλεγόντων δ' ἡμῶν μηδὲ
τὸ παράπαν γενέσθαι τὰς διαθήκας, ἐκ τίνος ἂν
τρόπου, εἴ τις παρανοῶν διέθετο, γνοίητε, πρὶν
περὶ αὐτοῦ τοῦ διαθέσθαι πιστεῦσαι; τοὺς μὲν οὖν
κατὰ τὴν δόσιν ἀμφισβητοῦντας ὁρᾶτε ὅσον ἔργον
ἐστὶν αἰσθέσθαι εἰ ἀληθῆ λέγουσι, τοὺς δὲ κατὰ τὸ
γένος πρῶτον μὲν οὐδὲν δεῖ μάρτυρας παρασχέσθαι
ὡς αὐτῶν ἐστιν ὁ κλῆρος (παρὰ πάντων γὰρ ὡμολό-
γηται τοῖς ἐγγυτάτω γένους τὰ τοῦ τελευτήσαντος
16 γίγνεσθαι), ἔπειτα οἱ νόμοι οὐ μόνον οἱ περὶ τῶν

---

[1] ἀποφαίνονται Dobree : -οιντο.
[2] ἐγχειρήσειεν Scheibe : -ῆσαι.   [3] δὴ Reiske : δ'.

relatives know nothing of the facts, and the method of refuting the evidence is by no means clear? Further, gentlemen, most of those who make wills do not even mention to those who are present the purport of their will, but only invite them to attest the fact that they have made a will, and it is within the range of possibility that a will has been substituted or alterations made in a sense directly opposed to the wishes of the deceased; for the witnesses will have no more knowledge than anyone else whether the will produced is that which they were summoned to attest. Since, then, it is possible to deceive those who were admittedly present when the will was made, how much more easily might an attempt be made to impose upon you who know nothing of the matter?

Again, gentlemen, the law ordains that a will in order to be valid must not merely be executed but executed by a man in his right senses. You ought, therefore, to examine, first, whether the deceased made a will and, secondly, whether he was in his right mind at the time. Since, however, we deny that a will was made at all, how can you decide whether a man was insane when he made a will, until you are convinced that actually he made a will? Observe, then, how difficult it is to discover whether those who claim under a will are telling the truth; those, on the other hand, who claim by right of kinship, in the first place, need not produce witnesses to prove that the inheritance is theirs—for it is universally admitted that the property of a deceased person devolves on his next-of-kin—and, secondly, the laws, not only those which deal with consanguinity but

γενῶν ἀλλὰ καὶ οἱ περὶ τῶν δόσεων τοῖς συγγενέσι
βοηθοῦσι. δοῦναι μὲν γὰρ ὁ νόμος οὐδενὶ ἐᾷ τὰ
ἑαυτοῦ, ἐὰν ὑπὸ γήρως ἢ ὑπὸ νόσου ἢ ὑπὸ τῶν
ἄλλων ἃ καὶ ὑμεῖς ἴστε παρανοήσῃ· κατὰ δὲ τὸ
γένος καὶ τὰ τοῦ ὁπωσοῦν διακειμένου ὁ ἐγγύτατα
17 γένους ἀναμφισβητήτως λαμβάνει. χωρὶς δὲ τούτων ταῖς μὲν διαθήκαις διὰ μαρτύρων ὑμᾶς δεῖ
πιστεῦσαι, ὑφ' ὧν ἔνι καὶ ἐξαπατηθῆναι (οὐ γὰρ ἂν
ἦσαν ψευδομαρτυρίων ἐπισκήψεις), τῇ δ' ἀγχιστείᾳ
δι' ὑμῶν αὐτῶν· κατὰ γὰρ τοὺς νόμους οἱ συγγενεῖς
18 ἀμφισβητοῦσιν, οὓς ὑμεῖς ἔθεσθε. πρὸς δὲ τούτοις,
ὦ ἄνδρες, εἰ μὲν οἱ κατὰ τὰς διαθήκας ἀμφισβητοῦντες ὁμολογουμένως Νικοστράτῳ ἐπιτήδειοι
ὄντες ἐτύγχανον, τὸ μὲν ἀκριβὲς οὐδ' ἂν οὕτως,
ὅμως μέντοι μᾶλλον εἰκὸς ἦν ἀληθεῖς εἶναι δόξειν
τὰς διαθήκας· ἤδη γάρ τινες οὐκ εὖ διακείμενοι τοῖς
συγγενέσιν ὀθνείους φίλους τῶν πάνυ σφόδρα προσηκόντων περὶ πλείονος ἐποιήσαντο· νῦν δὲ οὔτε
συσσίτους οὔτε φίλους οὔτ' ἐν τάξει τῇ αὐτῇ . . .
τούτων δ' ὑμῖν μάρτυρας ἁπάντων παρεσχήμεθα.
19 ὃ δὲ μέγιστον, καὶ μάλιστα τῆς Χαριάδου ἀναιδείας
καταμαρτυρεῖ, τοῦτο σκέψασθε. ὅπου γὰρ τὸν
αὐτὸν ποιησάμενον οὔτ' ἀποθανόντα ἀνείλετο οὔτ'
ἔκαυσεν οὔτε ὠστολόγησεν, ἀλλὰ πάντα τοῖς μηδὲν
προσήκουσι παρῆκε ποιῆσαι, πῶς οὐκ ⟨ἂν⟩[1] ἀν-
οσιώτατος εἴη, ὃς τῷ τεθνεῶτι μηδὲν τῶν νομιζο-

[1] ἂν add. Bekker.

---

[a] There is a lacuna in the text at this point and the sense
is incomplete as it stands.

also those which treat of testamentary disposition, are in favour of kinsmen. For the law allows no one to dispose of his own property if his reason is impaired by old age or disease or the other causes with which you are familiar; but by right of relationship the next-of-kin has an undisputed title to the property of a deceased person, whatever was the state of the latter's faculties. Beside this, in order to believe in a will, you are obliged to rely on witnesses, by whom it is possible to be deceived—if this were not so, there would be no prosecutions for perjury—but when the claim is based on kinship, you act on your own authority, for the next-of-kin assert their right in accordance with the laws which you have laid down. In addition to this, gentlemen, if those who claim under the will were admittedly close friends of Nicostratus, even then the conclusive proof would be lacking, though there would be a greater probability that the will could be regarded as genuine; for before now testators, being ill-disposed towards their kinsmen, have preferred strangers who were their friends to their nearest relatives by blood. But in the present case Nicostratus and Chariades were neither members of the same mess nor friends nor members of the same company,[a] and on all these points we have produced witnesses before you. And consider this further point, which is of great importance and is the clearest possible proof of Chariades' impudence. Whereas he neither took up the body of his adopted father nor committed it to the flames nor collected the bones, but left all these duties to be done by complete strangers, should he not be regarded as most impious in claiming to inherit the property

μένων ποιήσας τῶν χρημάτων αὐτοῦ κληρονομεῖν
20 ἀξιοῖ; ἀλλὰ νὴ Δία ἐπειδὴ τούτων οὐδὲν ἐποίησε,
τὴν οὐσίαν τοῦ Νικοστράτου[1] διεχείρισεν; ἀλλὰ
καὶ ταῦτα μεμαρτύρηται ὑμῖν, καὶ τὰ πλεῖστα οὐδ'
αὐτὸς ἀρνεῖται. προφάσεις δὲ οἴομαι ἀναγκαίας
ἐφ' ἑκάστας τῶν πράξεων εὑρῆσθαι· τί γὰρ ὑπολείπεται τῷ διαρρήδην ὁμολογοῦντι;

21 Σαφῶς μὲν οὖν ἴστε, ὦ ἄνδρες, ὅτι οὗτοι οὐ
δικαίως τῶν Νικοστράτου[1] ἐφίενται, ἀλλὰ βούλονται μὲν ὑμᾶς ἐξαπατῆσαι, τουτουσὶ δὲ συγγενεῖς ὄντας ἐκείνου, ἃ οἱ νόμοι ἔδοσαν αὐτοῖς,
ἀποστερῆσαι. οὐ μόνος[2] δὲ Χαριάδης τοῦτο πεποίηκεν, ἀλλὰ καὶ ἄλλοι πολλοὶ ἤδη τῶν ἐν τῇ ὑπερορίᾳ ἀποθνῃσκόντων οὐδὲ γιγνώσκοντες ἐνίους τῆς
22 οὐσίας ἠμφισβήτησαν· ἐνθυμοῦνται γὰρ ὅτι κατ-
ορθώσασι μὲν ⟨ἔσται⟩[3] τὰ ἀλλότρια ἔχειν, δι-
αμαρτοῦσι δὲ μικρὸς ὁ κίνδυνος· μαρτυρεῖν δὲ καὶ
τὰ ψευδῆ τινες ἐθέλουσιν, οἱ δ' ἔλεγχοι περὶ ἀ-
φανῶν. συνελόντι πολὺ τὸ διαφέρον κατὰ γένος ἢ
κατὰ δόσιν ἀμφισβητεῖν. ἀλλ' ὑμᾶς χρή, ὦ ἄνδρες,
πρῶτον μὲν τὰς διαθήκας σκοπεῖν, εἰ δοκοῦσι
γενέσθαι· τοῦτο γὰρ οἵ τε νόμοι ⟨ὑφ⟩ηγοῦνται[4] καὶ
23 δικαιότατόν ἐστι. μὴ σαφῶς δὲ μήτ' αὐτοὺς τὴν
ἀλήθειαν εἰδότας, μήτε τῶν μαρτύρων τοῦ τελευτήσαντος ἐπιτηδείων ὄντων, ἀλλὰ Χαριάδου τοῦ

---

[1] Νικοστράτου schedae Etonenses: στρατονίκου.
[2] μόνος Papabasileiou: μόνον.
[3] ἔσται add. Scheibe.
[4] ⟨ὑφ⟩ηγοῦνται Schoemann.

---

[a] This sentence is apparently parenthetic and ironical.

of the deceased, though he never performed
any of the customary rites over him ? Shall I be
told that, after having performed none of these
duties, he administered Nicostratus's property ? [a]
Evidence of these facts, too, has been given you,
and even he himself does not deny most of them.
Makeshift excuses have, of course, been found to
explain all his acts ; for what other resource remains
to one who expressly admits the facts ?

You must now be well aware, gentlemen, that
these persons have no legal right to the property of
Nicostratus, but wish to deceive you and to deprive
my clients, who are his kinsmen, of an inheritance
which lawfully belongs to them. Chariades is not
the only person who has acted thus ; many other
claimants to the property of men who have died
abroad have arisen, sometimes even without having
been acquainted with them. For they consider that,
if they are successful, it will be possible for them to
enjoy the property of others, while, if they fail, the
risk is inconsiderable ; there are always men who are
willing to perjure themselves, and the attempted
refutations of their evidence are dealing with the
unknown. In a word, there is a vast difference
between claiming by right of kinship and claiming
under a will. But your duty, gentlemen, is first of
all to examine the will and decide whether you think
that it is genuine ; for this is what the laws enjoin
and is the justest course. But since you have no
certain personal knowledge of the truth, and since
the witnesses to the will were friends not of the
deceased but of Chariades, who wishes to seize

There is a further reference in § 26 to certain business
relations between Nicostratus and Chariades.

τἀλλότρια βουλομένου λαβεῖν, τί ἂν εἴη[1] δικαιότερον
ἢ τοῖς συγγενέσι τὰ τοῦ συγγενοῦς ψηφίζεσθαι;
καὶ γὰρ εἴ τι οἶδε ἔπαθον, οὐδενὶ ἂν ἄλλῳ ἢ
Νικοστράτῳ τὰ τούτων ἐγένετο[2]· κατὰ γὰρ τὸ αὐτὸ
γένος ἂν ἠμφισβήτει, ἀνεψιὸς ὢν αὐτοῖς ἐκ πατρ-
24 αδέλφων. μὰ Δί' ἀλλ' οὐκ ἔστιν ὁ Ἅγνων οὐδ'
ὁ Ἁγνόθεος τοῦ Νικοστράτου συγγενής,[3] ὡς οἱ
ἀντίδικοί φασιν, ἀλλ' ἕτεροι. ἔπειτα τῷ μὲν κατὰ
τὴν δόσιν τοῦ κλήρου λαχόντι μαρτυροῦσιν, αὐτοὶ
[49] δὲ κατὰ τὸ γένος οὐκ ἀμφισβητήσουσιν; | οὐ γὰρ
εἰς τοῦτό γε ἀνοίας ἥκουσιν ὥστε πιστεύσαντες
ταῖς διαθήκαις οὕτω ῥᾳδίως τοσούτων χρημάτων
ἀφίστανται. ἀλλὰ μὴν καὶ ἐξ ὧν αὐτοὶ οὗτοι
λέγουσι, τούσδε τοῖς συγγενέσιν αὐτοῖς ἐπιδικάσασθαι συμφέρει τῶν Νικοστράτου μᾶλλον ἢ
25 Χαριάδην. εἰς γὰρ τὸν λοιπὸν χρόνον, εἰ μὲν οἶδε
κατὰ τὸ γένος ἀμφισβητοῦντες λήψονται τὸν
κλῆρον, ἐξέσται καὶ τούτοις, ὁπόταν βούλωνται,
κατὰ τὸ γένος λαχοῦσιν ἐπιδεῖξαι ὑμῖν ὡς αὐτοὶ
ἐγγυτέρω ἦσαν τοῦ Νικοστράτου, καὶ ὡς Σμίκρου
ἦν καὶ οὐ Θρασυμάχου· ἐὰν δὲ Χαριάδης αὐτῶν
κληρονομήσῃ, οὐκ ἔσται οὐδενὶ συγγενεῖ ἐπὶ τὰ
Νικοστράτου ἐλθεῖν. κατὰ δόσιν γὰρ ἔχοντος τοῦ
ἐπιδεδικασμένου, τί φανοῦνται λέγοντες οἱ κατὰ
[τὸ] γένος λαγχάνοντες;

---

[1] ἂν εἴη Reiske: ἄν τι. [2] ἐγένετο M, Bekker: ἐγένοντο.
[3] συγγενής Stephanus: -εῖς.

144

property which does not belong to him, what could be juster than by your verdict to award the property of a kinsmen to his kinsmen? For, indeed, if anything had happened to my clients, their property would have passed to none other than Nicostratus; for he would have claimed it by the same right of kinship, being their first cousin, the son of their father's own brother. But, by Heaven, I am forgetting; Hagnon and Hagnotheus are not kinsmen of Nicostratus according to the allegation of our adversaries, but his kinsmen are quite different people. Are these kinsmen then bearing witness in favour of the claimant under the will rather than themselves contesting the property by right of kinship? Surely they are not so insane as to believe so easily in the will and renounce their claim to so much money! Nay, to judge from what these men themselves say, it is to the advantage of these supposed kinsmen themselves that my clients, rather than Chariades, should have the estate of Nicostratus adjudicated to them. For, if my clients, who claim by right of kinship, receive the estate, it will be always open to the supposed kinsmen whenever they like at any future date to claim the estate on the grounds of relationship, and prove to you that they are themselves more nearly related to Nicostratus, and that he was the son of Smicrus and not of Thrasymachus. On the other hand, if Chariades inherits the estate, it will never be possible for any relative to bring an action for the property of Nicostratus; for when once the property is in possession of one to whom it has been adjudicated in virtue of a will, what will those who claim by right of kinship be able reasonably to allege?

26 Ὅπερ ἂν οὖν καὶ ὑμῶν ἕκαστος ἀξιώσειε, τοῦτο
καὶ τουτοισὶ τοῖς νεανίσκοις βεβαιώσατε. παρέσχοντο δ' ὑμῖν μάρτυρας πρῶτον μὲν ὡς ἀνεψιοί
εἰσιν ἐκ πατραδέλφων Νικοστράτου, ἔπειτα δὲ ὡς
οὐδεπώποτε ἐκείνῳ[1] διάφοροι ἦσαν, ἔτι δὲ καὶ ὡς
ἔθαψαν Νικόστρατον, πρὸς δὲ τούτοις ὡς Χαριάδης
οὑτοσὶ οὐδαμῶς οὔτ'[2] ἐνθάδε οὔτ'· ἐπὶ στρατεύματι
ἐχρῆτο Νικοστράτῳ, ἔτι δὲ καὶ τὴν κοινωνίαν, ᾗ
μάλισθ' οὗτος ἰσχυρίζεται, ψευδῆ οὖσαν.

27 Καὶ ἄνευ τούτων, ὦ ἄνδρες, ἄξιον ὑμῖν ἐξετάσαι
ἑκατέρους αὐτῶν οἷοί εἰσι. Θράσιππος μὲν γὰρ ὁ
Ἁγνῶνος καὶ Ἁγνοθέου πατὴρ ἤδη τι καὶ ἐλῃτούρ-
γησεν ὑμῖν καὶ εἰσήνεγκε, καὶ ἄλλως σπουδαῖος ἦν
πολίτης· αὐτοὶ δὲ οὗτοι οὔτε ἀποδεδημήκασιν οὐδαμοῖ[3] πώποτε, ὅποι ἂν μὴ ὑμεῖς προστάξητε, οὔτ'
ἐνθάδε μένοντες ἄχρηστοί εἰσι τῇ πόλει, ἀλλὰ καὶ
στρατεύονται καὶ εἰσφέρουσι καὶ τἆλλα πάντα
ποιοῦσι τὰ προσταττόμενα καὶ αὑτούς (ὡς πάντες

28 ἴσασι) κοσμίους παρέχουσιν, ὥστε πολὺ μᾶλλον
τούτους προσήκει κατὰ δόσιν τῶν χρημάτων τῶν
Νικοστράτου ἢ Χαριάδην ἀμφισβητεῖν. οὗτος γάρ,
ὅτ' ἐπεδήμει ἐνθάδε, πρῶτον μὲν εἰς τὸ δεσμω-
τήριον ὡς κλέπτης ὢν ἐπ' αὐτοφώρῳ ἀπήχθη,
τότε δὲ ἀφεθεὶς μεθ' ἑτέρων τινῶν ὑπὸ τῶν ἕνδεκα,
οὓς δημοσίᾳ ἅπαντας ὑμεῖς ἀπεκτείνατε, πάλιν
ἀπογραφεὶς εἰς τὴν βουλὴν κακουργῶν, ὑποχωρῶν

29 ᾤχετο καὶ οὐχ ὑπήκουσεν, ἀλλ' ἀπ' ἐκείνου ἑπτα-

---

[1] ἐκείνῳ Aldus: ἐκεῖνοι.
[2] οὔτ' Bekker: οὐδ'. [3] οὐδαμοῖ Bekker: -μῆ.

---

[a] The police-magistrates of Athens.
[b] The context seems to imply that these magistrates were

Whatever each of you would consider just on his
own behalf, let that be your determination in favour
of these young men. They have produced before
you witnesses to prove, first, that they and Nicostratus are first cousins, the sons of own brothers;
secondly, that they never had any quarrel with him;
thirdly, that they carried out his burial; and further
that Chariades was never a friend of Nicostratus
either here in Athens or in the army, and, lastly, that
the supposed business association between them, on
which Chariades most relies, is a fiction.

Apart from this, gentlemen, it is only right that
you should examine the characters of the respective
claimants. Thrasippus, the father of Hagnon and
Hagnotheus, has before now supported public
burdens and paid contributions and otherwise proved
himself a worthy citizen. My clients themselves
have never quitted this country unless they have
been sent somewhere by your orders, and at home
they are not unserviceable to the state; they serve
in the army, they make contributions and in every
other respect perform what is required of them, and,
as everyone knows, they behave as law-abiding
citizens; so that it is much more fitting that they
should claim to receive the estate by gift than
Chariades. The latter, when he resided here, was
first caught in the act of theft and thrown into
prison; he was subsequently released with certain
other criminals by the Eleven,[a] all of whom you
publicly condemned to death,[b] and, having been
again denounced to the Council as a malefactor, he
absconded and did not appear to answer the charge,

tried and condemned for allowing prisoners to escape, but
nothing is known of the circumstance.

καίδεκα ἐτῶν Ἀθήναζε οὐκ ἀφίκετο, πλὴν ἐπειδὴ
Νικόστρατος ἀπέθανε. καὶ ὑπὲρ μὲν ὑμῶν οὔτε
στρατείαν οὐδεμίαν ἐστράτευται οὔτε εἰσφορὰν
οὐδεμίαν εἰσενήνοχε, πλὴν εἴ τι ἄρα ἐξ ὅτου τῶν
Νικοστράτου ἠμφισβήτησεν, οὔτ' ἄλλ' οὐδὲν ὑμῖν
λελῃτούργηκεν. ἔπειτα τοιοῦτος ὢν οὐκ ἀγαπᾷ
εἰ μὴ τῶν ἡμαρτημένων δίκην δώσει, ἀλλὰ καὶ
30 τῶν ἀλλοτρίων ἀμφισβητεῖ. εἰ μὲν οὖν οἶδε φιλο-
πράγμονες ἢ ἄλλοις ὅμοιοι πολίταις ἦσαν, ἴσως ἂν
οὐ περὶ τῶν Νικοστράτου χρημάτων ἠμφισβήτει,
ἀλλ' ὑπὲρ τοῦ σώματος ἠγωνίζετο· νῦν δ', ὦ ἄνδρες
δικασταί, τοῦτον μὲν ἄλλος, ἐάν τις βούληται,
31 τιμωρήσεται, τουτοισὶ δ' ὑμεῖς βοηθήσατε, καὶ μὴ
περὶ πλείονος ποιήσησθε τοὺς ἀδίκως τἀλλότρια
ἔχειν βουλομένους ἢ τοὺς γένει τῷ τεθνεῶτι προσήκοντας καὶ χωρὶς τούτων ἤδη τι ἐκεῖνον εὐ-
εργετηκότας, ἀλλὰ καὶ τῶν νόμων ἀναμνησθέντες
καὶ τῶν ὅρκων οὓς ὠμόσατε, πρὸς δὲ τούτοις καὶ
τῶν μαρτυριῶν ἃς ἡμεῖς παρεσχήμεθα, τὰ δίκαια
ψηφίσασθε.

and for seventeen years after this he never came near Athens, and only returned on the death of Nicostratus. He has never once served the state as a soldier nor made any contribution, except perhaps since he claimed Nicostratus's estate, nor has he performed any other public service. And now, though such is his character, so far from being content if he avoids punishment for his misdeeds, he actually claims the property of others! If my clients were fond of quarrelling or resembled so many of their fellow-citizens, he would not perhaps be claiming Nicostratus's estate but would be on trial for his life. But, as it is, gentlemen, it shall be left to someone else, if he wishes, to punish him; your care let it be to assist my clients, and not to show favour to those who wish unjustly to possess the property of others rather than to the next-of-kin of the deceased, who have besides already rendered him service. Remember the laws and the oaths which you swore and also the evidence which we have placed before you, and give your verdict in conformity with justice.

V. ON THE ESTATE OF DICAEOGENES

V. ON THE ESTATE OF DICAEOGENES

INTRODUCTION

THE chief personages concerned in this suit belonged to an important Athenian family, members of which had held high office in the state over a long period. Dicaeogenes II.,[a] whose estate is in dispute, was

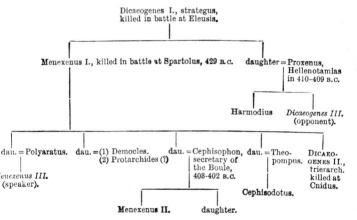

ᵃ STEMMA[1]

Dicaeogenes I., strategus, killed in battle at Eleusis.

Menexenus I., killed in battle at Spartolus, 429 B.C.   daughter = Proxenus, Hellenotamias in 410–409 B.C.

Harmodius   Dicaeogenes III. (opponent).

dau. = Polyaratus.   dau. = (1) Democles. (2) Protarchides (?)   dau. = Cephisophon, secretary of the Boule, 403–402 B.C.   dau. = Theopompus.   DICAEOGENES II., trierarch. killed at Cnidus.

Menexenus III. (speaker).

Menexenus II.   daughter.

Cephisodotus.

¹ For further details see W. Wyse, *op. cit.* p. 403, and Kirchner, *Prosopographia Attica*, i. p. 256 (No. 3773).

killed in action in a naval engagement off the island of Cnidus. He left no issue, but had four married sisters. After his death Proxenus, the husband of his father's sister and a descendant of Harmodius, one of the slayers of the tyrant Hipparchus, produced a will under which his own son Dicaeogenes III., was posthumously adopted as son of the deceased and heir to one-third of his estate. No objections were raised to this will, and Dicaeogenes III. received his share, the other two-thirds being divided between the four sisters.

Twelve years later Dicaeogenes III. produced another will, under which the whole estate was bequeathed to him. By this time one of the sisters, the wife of Cephisophon, was dead, and two other sisters, the wives of Theopompus and Democles, had lost their husbands,[a] but Polyaratus, the husband of the eldest sister, was alive, and took up the cudgels on behalf of his wife and her surviving sisters. The court, however, decided in favour of Dicaeogenes III., who thus gained possession of the whole estate. Polyaratus, who had threatened to bring an action for perjury committed in this case, died before he could carry out his intention.

For ten years Dicaeogenes III. enjoyed the whole estate. Meanwhile the children of the sisters had grown up, and one of them, Menexenus II., the son of Cephisophon, brought a successful action for perjury against Lycon, who had been one of the witnesses in support of the genuineness of the second

---

[a] It is possible that the second sister, who had married Democles, divorced her husband, since the phrase τὴν Δημοκλέους γενομένην γυναῖκα (§ 9) means simply the " former wife of Democles." If the text is correct in § 26 (where see note), she seems afterwards to have married a certain Protarchides.

will. This naturally alarmed Dicaeogenes III., who offered to restore to Menexenus II. his share of what would have come to his mother from his uncle's estate, on condition that he abstained from further action. Menexenus II. accepted the offer for himself, throwing over his cousins, who had the same rights as himself; Dicaeogenes III., however, failed to carry out his agreement. Menexenus, therefore, again made common cause with the other claimants, and they jointly demanded the restitution of the whole property as next-of-kin to an intestate estate, on the ground that both wills had been recognized by the court as invalid, the first having been annulled in favour of the second, and the second discredited by the conviction of Lycon for perjury.

This claim was met by Dicaeogenes III. by a protestation (διαμαρτυρία), which was lodged by a friend of his, Leochares, to the effect that the estate was not adjudicable to the next-of-kin, because Dicaeogenes III. had been recognized as adopted son of Dicaeogenes II. at the time of the latter's death. The claimants were thus obliged to withdraw their demand and to attack Leochares for false witness. At the trial, when the case went against Leochares, Dicaeogenes III. again offered a compromise, undertaking to surrender two-thirds of the estate. This arrangement was sanctioned by the court and accepted by the prosecutors; and two sureties, one of whom was Leochares, undertook to guarantee the fulfilment of Dicaeogenes III.'s promise.

Difficulties, however, soon arose owing to the fact that twenty-two years had elapsed since the death of the original testator and much of the property

155

had been sold or mortgaged, and quarrels arose about expenditure on building and repairs. Finding that there was practically nothing to be recovered from Dicaeogenes III., the claimants sued Leochares as surety. The cause of the nephews was this time championed by Menexenus III., the son of Polyaratus and the eldest sister of Dicaeogenes II.; it was on his behalf that Isaeus wrote the present speech. The suit, though ultimately concerned with the estate of Dicaeogenes, is strictly speaking an action to compel Leochares to discharge his liability as surety.

Only a fraction of the speech deals with the subject of the surety. It is clear that Leochares would defend himself by arguing that Dicaeogenes III. had done his best to restore the two-thirds of the estate and pointing out that the written agreement made in court (which the speaker is careful not to produce) had never stated that the property was to be handed over free of all claim and liabilities. In reply the speaker can only urge that this document was hastily drawn up and did not contain all the conditions and must be supplemented by certain verbal agreements, in support of which he offered the evidence of witnesses who had been present in court when the compromise was effected. This argument would hardly recommend itself to a court of law and constitutes a great weakness in the case. The rest of the speech is devoted to blackening the character of Dicaeogenes III., who is represented as a plunderer of widows and orphans, an unpatriotic citizen and a shirker of military service, and eulogizing the disinterestedness, generosity, and patriotism of his opponents.

156

ON THE ESTATE OF DICAEOGENES

The question of the date of the speech turns on the date of the action at Cnidus during which Dicaeogenes II. was killed, which had taken place twenty-two years earlier. The famous battle at Cnidus in 394 B.C., in which Conon defeated the Spartan fleet, cannot possibly be meant, since the suit claiming the whole estate, which was brought by Dicaeogenes III., twelve years after the death of Dicaeogenes II., was tried during the years of political disturbance which followed the close of the Peloponnesian war (δυστυχησάσης τῆς πόλεως καὶ στάσεως γενομένης, § 7). It is probable, therefore, that the action off Cnidus was the engagement near Syme in 411 B.C. (Thuc. viii. 42). The date of the speech must therefore be about 389 B.C. This theory is supported by the fact that at the date of the speech Athens was engaged in a serious war (§ 46)—no doubt the Corinthian war (394–386 B.C.)—and by the apparent allusion to the capture of Lechaeum (392 B.C.) as a recent event (§ 37).

V. ΠΕΡΙ ΤΟΥ ΔΙΚΑΙΟΓΕΝΟΥΣ ΚΛΗΡΟΥ

Δικαιογένους τελευτήσαντος ἄπαιδος ἐπὶ τέσσαρσιν ἀδελφαῖς Πρόξενος ἧκεν διαθήκην ἔχων, ἐν ᾗ Δικαιογένης ὁ τελευτήσας τὸν υἱὸν αὑτοῦ, τοῦ Προξένου, Δικαιογένην υἱὸν θετὸν ἐποιήσατο ἐπὶ τῷ τρίτῳ μέρει τῆς οὐσίας. τοῦτον δὲ τὸν τρόπον διανειμαμένων αὐτῶν τὴν ὅλην οὐσίαν, τελευταῖον ἦλθεν ὁ υἱὸς Προξένου Δικαιογένης φάσκων ἐπὶ ὅλῃ τῇ οὐσίᾳ γεγονέναι υἱός, καὶ νικήσας ἀνέλαβε καὶ τὰ δύο μέρη τῶν ἀδελφῶν τοῦ τελευτήσαντος. ὕστερον πάλιν οἱ παῖδες τῶν ἀδελφῶν δικασάμενοι πρὸς Δικαιογένην ἐνίκησαν, καὶ συνέθετο Δικαιογένης ἀποδοῦναι πάλιν τὰ δύο μέρη αὐτοῖς καθαρὰ καὶ ἀνέπαφα, ἐγγυησαμένου ταῦτα Λεωχάρους. νῦν δὲ ἀρνουμένων τὰ δόξαντα τῶν περὶ Δικαιογένην καὶ Λεωχάρην, ἐγκαλοῦσιν οἱ παῖδες τῶν ἀδελφῶν περὶ τῶν δύο μερῶν τῷ μὲν ὡς συνθεμένῳ, τῷ δὲ ὡς ἐγγυητῇ. ἡ στάσις στοχασμός· ἀρνοῦνται γάρ.

1 Ὠιόμεθα μέν, ὦ ἄνδρες, περὶ ὧν διεφερόμεθα πρὸς Δικαιογένην, τὰ ὡμολογημένα ἐπὶ τοῦ δικαστηρίου κύρια ἡμῖν ἔσεσθαι· ἀποστάντος γὰρ Δικαιογένους τοῖν δυοῖν μεροῖν τοῦ κλήρου, καὶ ἐγγυητὰς καταστήσαντος ἦ μὴν παραδώσειν ἡμῖν ταῦτα τὰ μέρη ἀναμφισβήτητα, ἀφήκαμεν ἀλλήλους τῶν ἐγκλημάτων· ἐπειδὴ δέ, ὦ ἄνδρες, οὐ ποιεῖ Δικαιο-

V. ON THE ESTATE OF DICAEOGENES

ARGUMENT

On the death of Dicaeogenes (II.), who had no children but left four sisters behind him, Proxenus came forward and produced a will by which the deceased Dicaeogenes (II.) adopted his (Proxenus's) son Dicaeogenes (III.) and left him a third of his estate. After they had distributed the whole property on this basis, Dicaeogenes (III.), the son of Proxenus, eventually came and alleged that he had been adopted as heir to the whole property ; he won his case and took possession, in addition to his own share, of the two-thirds which had been held by the sisters of the deceased. At a still later date the sons of the sisters brought a successful action against Dicaeogenes (III.), and he agreed to hand back to them the two-thirds clear and free of all charges, Leochares acting as surety for the performance of this promise. In the present suit, as Dicaeogenes (III.) and Leochares repudiate their agreement, the sons of the sisters claim the two-thirds from Dicaeogenes (III.), as having agreed to restore the property, and from Leochares as surety. The question at issue is one of fact ; for the adversaries deny their engagement.

We thought, gentlemen, that in the matter of our dispute with Dicaeogenes (III.) the agreement arrived at in court would be conclusive ; for when Dicaeogenes (III.) gave up the two-thirds of the estate and furnished sureties that he would hand over that portion to us without dispute, we reciprocally abandoned our claims. But, gentlemen, since Dicaeogenes (III.) does not perform his agreement,

159

γένης ἃ ὡμολόγησε, δικαζόμεθα Λεωχάρει ἐγγυητῇ
2 γενομένῳ Δικαιογένους, ὥσπερ ἀντωμόσαμεν. καί
μοι ἀνάγνωθι τὴν ἀντωμοσίαν.

ΑΝΤΩΜΟΣΙΑ

Ὡς τοίνυν ἀληθῆ ἀντωμόσαμεν, Κηφισόδοτος οὑτοσὶ οἶδε, καὶ μάρτυρας ὑμῖν παρεξόμεθα πρῶτον
μὲν ὡς ἀπέστη Δικαιογένης ἡμῖν τοῖν δυοῖν μεροῖν
τοῦ κλήρου, εἶτα ὡς ἠγγυήσατο Λεωχάρης. καί
μοι ἀνάγνωθι τὴν μαρτυρίαν.

ΜΑΡΤΥΡΙΑ

3 Τῶν μὲν μαρτύρων ἀκηκόατε, καὶ ὡς οὐ τἀληθῆ
μεμαρτυρήκασιν, οὐδ' ἂν αὐτὸν οἶμαι Λεωχάρην εἰ-
πεῖν· ἴσως δὲ ἐπ' ἐκεῖνον τρέψεται τὸν λόγον, ὡς
Δικαιογένης τε ἃ ἡμῖν ὡμολόγησεν ἅπαντα πεποίηκε, καὶ αὐτὸς τὴν ἐξεγγύην ὅτι ἀπέδωκεν. εἰ
οὖν ταῦτ' ἐρεῖ, ψεύσεται καὶ ῥᾳδίως ἐλεγχθήσεται.
ἀναγνώσεται γὰρ ὑμῖν ὅσα κατέλιπε Δικαιογένης ὁ
Μενεξένου ἐν τῷ κλήρῳ καὶ τὰ χρήματα ἃ ἔλαβεν.

⟨ΑΠΟΓΡΑΦΗ⟩

4 Ταῦτα εἰ μὲν μή φασι Δικαιογένην τὸν ἡμέτερον
θεῖον ζῶντα κεκτῆσθαι καὶ ἀποθνῄσκοντα ἡμῖν δοῦναι, ἀποδειξάτωσαν· εἰ δὲ καὶ ἐ⸍εῖνον καταλιπεῖν
καὶ ἡμᾶς κεκομίσθαι, μαρτυρησάτω τις αὐτοῖς.
ὅτι μὲν γὰρ Δικαιογένης ὡμολόγει παραδώσειν

ᵃ On the meaning of ἀντωμοσία see p. 80 and note.

160

we are bringing an action against Leochares, his
surety, in accordance with our affidavit.ᵃ Please
read the affidavit.

AFFIDAVIT

That the facts which we stated in the affidavit
are true, Cephisodotus here is well aware ; and we
will now produce witnesses before you to prove,
first, that Dicaeogenes (III.) gave up to us the two-
thirds of the estate, and, secondly, that Leochares
became his surety.   Please read the deposition.

DEPOSITION

You have heard what the witnesses say, and I
do not believe that even Leochares himself would
declare that their evidence has not been true.   He
will, however, perhaps have recourse to the argument
that Dicaeogenes (III.) has performed all that he
agreed to do and that he himself has fulfilled his
duties as surety.   If he says this, he will be lying
and will easily be convicted of doing so ; for the
clerk shall read you the inventory of all the property
which formed the estate left by Dicaeogenes (II.)
the son of Menexenus, and of the property received
by Dicaeogenes (III.).

INVENTORY

If they affirm that Dicaeogenes (II.), our uncle,
did not possess this property when he was alive
and did not bequeath it to us at his death, let them
prove it ; if they declare that he left it and that
we have recovered it, let them produce a witness
to support their statement.   We are producing

161

ἡμῖν ὧν κατέλιπεν ὁ Μενεξένου τὰ δύο μέρη, ἡμεῖς
μάρτυρας παρεχόμεθα,[1] καὶ ὅτι Λεωχάρης ἠγγυήσατο αὐτὸν ταῦτα ποιήσειν· καὶ γὰρ δικαζόμεθα
διὰ τοῦτο, καὶ ταῦτα ἀντωμόσαμεν. καί μοι
ἀνάγνωθι τὴν ἀντωμοσίαν.

ΑΝΤΩΜΟΣΙΑ

5 Εἰ μὲν τοίνυν, ὦ ἄνδρες, περὶ τούτων ἔμελλον
ἀπολογήσεσθαι[2] μόνον Λεωχάρης ἢ Δικαιογένης,
ἤρκει ἄν μοι τὰ εἰρημένα· ἐπειδὴ δὲ παρεσκευα-
σμένοι εἰσὶν ἐξ ἀρχῆς περὶ ⟨τοῦ⟩[3] κλήρου λέγειν,
βούλομαι ὑμᾶς καὶ παρ' ἐμοῦ τὰ πραχθέντα
πυθέσθαι, ἵνα εἰδότες τἀληθῆ, ὅ τι ἂν δοκῇ ὑμῖν,
ψηφίσησθε, ἀλλὰ μὴ ἐξηπατημένοι.

Μενεξένῳ γὰρ τῷ ἡμετέρῳ πάππῳ ἐγένετο υὸς
μὲν εἷς, Δικαιογένης, θυγατέρες δὲ τέτταρες, ὧν
ἔλαβε μίαν μὲν Πολυάρατος[4] ὁ πατὴρ ὁ ἐμός,
ἄλλην δὲ Δημοκλῆς ὁ Φρεάρριος, τὴν δὲ Κη-
φισοφῶν ὁ Παιανιεύς· ἡ δὲ ⟨τετάρτη⟩[5] Θεοπόμπῳ
6 ἐγήματο τῷ Κηφισοδότου[6] πατρί. καὶ ὁ μὲν
Δικαιογένης, τριήραρχος ἐκπλεύσας τῆς Παράλου,
ἐτελεύτησε μαχόμενος ἐν Κνίδῳ· ἀποθανόντος δ'
αὐτοῦ ἄπαιδος διαθήκην ἀπέφηνε Πρόξενος ὁ
Δικαιογένους ⟨τουδὶ⟩[7] πατήρ, ᾗ πιστεύσαντες οἱ
ἡμέτεροι πατέρες ἐνείμαντο τὸν κλῆρον. καὶ ἐπὶ

---

[1] παρεχόμεθα Baiter-Sauppe : παρεξ-.
[2] ἀπολογήσεσθαι Cobet : -ασθαι.
[3] τοῦ add. Reiske.
[4] Πολυάρατος Reiske : πολυάρατας.
[5] δ' (=τετάρτη) add. Kaibel.
[6] Κηφισοδότου Stephanus : -σιοδότου.
[7] τουδὶ add. Dobree.

witnesses to prove that Dicaeogenes (III.) agreed
to hand over to us the two-thirds of the property
which the son of Menexenus left, and that Leochares
acted as surety for his doing so ; for this is the
basis of our present action and the subject of our
affidavit. Please read me the affidavit.

AFFIDAVIT

If then, gentlemen, these were the only points
with which Leochares or Dicaeogenes (III.) were
going to deal in their defence, what I have already
said would suffice ; but since they are prepared
to treat of the question of the inheritance from the
beginning, I should like you to hear the facts from
my side also, that, knowing the truth instead of
being misled, you may give an unbiased verdict.
Our grandfather, Menexenus (I.) had an only
son, Dicaeogenes (II.), and four daughters, one of
whom was married to my father, Polyaratus, another
to Democles of Phrearrhi, the third to Cephisophon
of Paeania, while the fourth was the wife of Theopompus, the father of Cephisodotus. Dicaeogenes,
having sailed out as commander of the Paralus,[a] was
killed in action at Cnidus.[b] He died without issue,
and Proxenus, the father of Dicaeogenes (III.) here,
produced a will, in reliance on which our fathers [c]
distributed his estate. Under the will Dicaeogenes

---

[a] The Paralus, which in time of peace was one of the two
sacred vessels used for the conveyance of religious missions,
ambassadors, etc., was used in war as the flagship of the
commander of a squadron.

[b] See Introduction, p. 157.

[c] Menexenus III., the speaker, is pleading on behalf of himself and his cousins Menexenus II. and Cephisodotus, whose
fathers had married two of the sisters of Dicaeogenes II.

μὲν τῷ τρίτῳ μέρει τοῦ κλήρου Δικαιογένης ὅδε
τῷ Μενεξένου Δικαιογένει, ἡμετέρῳ δὲ θείῳ, υἱὸς
ἐγίγνετο ποιητός· τῶν δὲ λοιπῶν ἑκάστη τὸ μέ-
[51] ρος | ἐπεδικάσατο τῶν Μενεξένου θυγατέρων. ὧν
ἐγὼ τοὺς τότε παρόντας ὑμῖν μάρτυρας παρέξομαι.

<ΜΑΡΤΥΡΕΣ>

7 Ἐπειδὴ δὲ ἐνείμαντο τὸν κλῆρον, ὀμόσαντες μὴ
παραβήσεσθαι τὰ ὡμολογημένα, ἐκέκτητο ἕκαστος
δώδεκα ἔτη ἃ ἔλαχε· καὶ ἐν τοσούτῳ χρόνῳ οὐσῶν
δικῶν οὐδεὶς αὐτῶν ἠξίωσε τὰ πεπραγμένα εἰπεῖν
ἀδίκως πεπρᾶχθαι, πρὶν δυστυχησάσης τῆς πόλεως
καὶ στάσεως γενομένης Δικαιογένης οὑτοσὶ πεισθεὶς ὑπὸ Μέλανος τοῦ Αἰγυπτίου, ᾧ περ καὶ
τἆλλα ἐπείθετο, ἠμφισβήτει ἡμῖν ἅπαντος τοῦ
κλήρου, φάσκων ἐφ᾽ ὅλῃ¹ ποιηθῆναι υἱὸς ὑπὸ τοῦ
8 θείου τοῦ ἡμετέρου. ἡμεῖς μὲν οὖν μαίνεσθαι
αὐτὸν ἡγούμεθα τῇ λήξει, οὐκ ἄν ποτε οἰόμενοι
τὸν αὐτὸν ἄνδρα τοτὲ² μὲν φάσκοντα ἐπὶ τῷ τρίτῳ
μέρει ποιηθῆναι τοτὲ δ᾽ ἐφ᾽ ἅπαντι τῷ κλήρῳ
δόξαι τἀληθὲς λέγειν ὑμῖν· εἰς δὲ τὸ δικαστήριον
εἰσελθόντες καὶ πολλῷ πλείω καὶ δικαιότερα
λέγοντες ἠδικήθημεν, οὐχ ὑπὸ τῶν δικαστῶν ἀλλ᾽
ὑπὸ Μέλανος τοῦ Αἰγυπτίου καὶ τῶν ἐκείνου
φίλων, οἳ διὰ τὰς τῆς πόλεως συμφορὰς ἐξουσίαν
σφίσιν αὐτοῖς ἡγοῦντο εἶναι κεκτῆσθαί τε τἀλλότρια καὶ τὰ ψευδῆ ἀλλήλοις μαρτυρεῖν· ὑπὸ δὲ
τῶν τὰ τοιαῦτα ποιούντων ἐξηπατήθησαν οἱ δικα-

---

¹ ἐφ᾽ ὅλῃ Aldus : ἐφ᾽ ὅλον.   ² τοτὲ Aldus : ποτε.

ᵃ The reference is to the internal troubles at Athens
which followed the defeat at Aegospotami in 405 B.C.

(III.) here was to be recognized as the adopted son
of Dicaeogenes (II.), the son of Menexenus (I.)
and our uncle, and heir to a third of his estate;
of the remainder an equal share was adjudicated
to each of the daughters of Menexenus (I.). Of
these facts I will produce before you as witnesses
those who were present on that occasion.

WITNESSES

When they had thus divided up the inheritance,
having sworn not to transgress the terms agreed
upon, each remained in possession of the share
which he had received for twelve years. During
all this period, though the courts sat, no one of them
thought of claiming that there was any injustice in
what had been done, until, when the city suffered
misfortune and strife arose,[a] Dicaeogenes (III.)
here, acting at the instigation of Melas the Egyptian,
whose advice he followed in everything, claimed
from us the whole estate, alleging that he had been
adopted as sole heir by our uncle. We thought him
mad in bringing the action; for we could never
imagine that the same man could at one time state
that he had been adopted as heir to one-third and
at another time that he had been adopted as sole
heir, and be believed by you to be speaking the
truth. However, on coming into court, though we
had by far the better case, we were cheated of our
rights, not by the judges but by Melas the Egyptian
and his friends, who thought that the misfortunes
of the city gave them liberty to possess themselves
of other people's property and to bear false witness
in support of one another, and by their acting in
this manner the judges were misled. Thus we,

9 σταί. καὶ ἡμεῖς μὲν καταψευδομαρτυρηθέντες
ἀπωλέσαμεν τὰ ὄντα· καὶ γὰρ ὁ πατὴρ οὐ πολλῷ
χρόνῳ ὕστερον μετὰ τὴν δίκην ἐτελεύτησε, πρὶν
ἐπεξελθεῖν οἷς ἐπεσκήψατο τῶν μαρτύρων· Δικαιογένης δὲ πρὸς ἡμᾶς ὡς ἐβούλετο ἀγωνισάμενος
τῇ αὐτῇ ἡμέρᾳ ἐξήλασε μὲν τὴν Κηφισοφῶντος
τοῦ Παιανιέως θυγατέρα ἐκ τοῦ μέρους, ἀδελφιδῆν
οὖσαν Δικαιογένους τοῦ καταλιπόντος τὰ χρήματα,
ἀφείλετο δὲ τὴν Δημοκλέους γενομένην γυναῖκα,
ἃ¹ Δικαιογένης ἀδελφὸς ὢν ἔδωκεν, ἀφείλετο <δὲ>²
καὶ τὴν Κηφισοδότου μητέρα καὶ αὐτὸν τοῦτον
10 ἅπαντα. καὶ γὰρ τούτων [τε] ἅμα καὶ ἐπίτροπος
καὶ κύριος καὶ ἀντίδικος ἦν, καὶ οὐδὲ κατὰ τὸ
ἐλάχιστον μέρος τῆς οἰκειότητος ἐλέου παρ᾽ αὐτοῦ
ἔτυχον, ἀλλ᾽ ὀρφανοὶ καὶ ἔρημοι καὶ πένητες
γενόμενοι πάντων καὶ τῶν καθ᾽ ἡμέραν ἐπιτηδείων
ἦσαν ἐνδεεῖς. οὕτως αὐτοὺς Δικαιογένης οὑτοσὶ
ἐγγυτάτω ὢν γένους ἐπετρόπευεν· ὅς γε, ἃ μὲν
ὁ πατὴρ αὐτοῖς Θεόπομπος κατέλιπε, τοῖς τούτων
ἐχθροῖς παρέδωκεν, ἃ δὲ ὁ πρὸς μητρὸς θεῖος καὶ
ὁ πάππος αὐτοῖς ἔδωκεν, αὐτὸς ἀφείλετο πρὸ
11 δίκης. καὶ ὃ πάντων δεινότατον,³ τὴν οἰκίαν
αὐτῶν τὴν πατρῴαν, παίδων ὄντων τούτων, πριάμενος καὶ κατασκάψας [τὸν] κῆπον ἐποιήσατο
πρὸς τῇ αὐτοῦ οἰκίᾳ τῇ ἐν ἄστει. καὶ λαμβάνων
μίσθωσιν ὀγδοήκοντα μνᾶς ἐκ τῶν Δικαιογένους
τοῦ ἡμετέρου θείου χρημάτων, τὸν ἐκείνου ἀδελφιδοῦν Κηφισόδοτον τῷ ἑαυτοῦ ἀδελφῷ Ἁρμοδίῳ
συνέπεμψεν εἰς Κόρινθον ἀντ᾽ ἀκολούθου· εἰς τοῦτο
ὕβρεως καὶ μιαρίας ἀφίκετο. καὶ πρὸς τοῖς ἄλλοις

---

¹ ἃ Reiske: ᾗ.　　　　² δὲ add. Reiske.
³ ὃ π. δεινότατον Reiske: ὁ π. δεινότατος.

the victims of perjury, lost our property; for our father died not long after the case was tried and before he could prosecute those of the witnesses whom he had indicted. Dicaeogenes (III.), on obtaining against us the verdict which he desired, that very same day forcibly deprived of her share the daughter of Cephisophon of Paeania, the niece of Dicaeogenes (II.) who left the money; robbed the former wife of Democles of what Dicaeogenes (II.) had left her; and robbed the mother of Cephisodotus and Cephisodotus himself of all they possessed. For of these persons he was at the same time the guardian and legal representative and the legal adversary; yet they did not meet with the slightest degree of pity from him on account of their relationship, but, orphans and unprotected and penniless, they even lacked all the necessities of life. This is how Dicaeogenes here, their nearest kinsman, carried out his duties as their guardian; what the father Theopompus left them he handed over to their enemies, and what my maternal uncle and my grandfather gave them he himself appropriated before any judgement had been given. What was worst of all, while they were minors, he bought the house which they had inherited from their father and demolished it and used the site to make a garden adjoining his town-house. Also, though he was receiving an income of eighty minae from the property of our uncle Dicaeogenes (II.), he sent the latter's nephew Cephisodotus with his own brother Harmodius to Corinth[a] as a body servant; such was his insolence and rascality. Nay, he added

---

[a] *i.e.*, during the Corinthian war of 394–386 B.C.

κακοῖς ὀνειδίζει καὶ ἐγκαλεῖ αὐτῷ ὅτι ἐμβάδας καὶ τρίβωνα[1] φορεῖ, ὥσπερ ἀδικούμενός τι εἰ ἐμβάδας Κηφισόδοτος φορεῖ, ἀλλ' οὐκ ἀδικῶν ὅτι ἀφελόμενος αὐτὸν τὰ ὄντα πένητα πεποίηκεν.

12 Ἀλλὰ περὶ μὲν[2] τούτων τοσαῦτά μοι εἰρήσθω· πάλιν δ' ἐπάνειμι ὅθεν ἀπέλιπον. Μενέξενος γὰρ ὁ Κηφισοφῶντος υἱός, ἀνεψιὸς ὢν Κηφισοδότῳ τουτῳὶ[3] καὶ ἐμοί, καὶ προσῆκον αὐτῷ τοῦ κλήρου μέρος ὅσον περ ἐμοί, ἐπεξῄει τοῖς καταμαρτυρήσασιν ἡμῶν καὶ ἐκείνου τὰ ψευδῆ, καὶ Λύκωνα, ὅν περ εἰσήγαγε πρῶτον εἰς τὸ δικαστήριον, τοῦτον εἷλεν· ὃς ἐμαρτύρησε Δικαιογένην ποιη-θῆναι τὸν νῦν ὄντα ὑπὸ τοῦ θείου τοῦ ἡμετέρου

13 υἱὸν ἐπὶ παντὶ τῷ κλήρῳ. μαρτυρήσας δὲ ταῦτα ἑάλω ψευδομαρτυριῶν. ἐπειδὴ δὲ Δικαιογένης, ὦ ἄνδρες, οὐκέτι ὑμᾶς[4] δύναται ἐξαπατᾶν, πείθει Μενέξενον τὸν ὑπὲρ ἡμῶν τε καὶ ὑπὲρ αὐτοῦ πράττοντα, ἃ ἐγὼ αἰσχυνόμενος ἀναγκάζομαι διὰ τὴν ἐκείνου πονηρίαν λέγειν, — τί ποιῆσαι; κομι-σάμενον αὐτὸν μέρος ἐκ τοῦ κλήρου ὅ τι ἐγίγνετο, ἡμᾶς μὲν ὑπὲρ ὧν ἔπραττε προδοῦναι, τοὺς δὲ μήπω ἑαλωκότας τῶν μαρτύρων ἀφεῖναι. καὶ

[52] ἡμεῖς μὲν ταῦτα | ὑπὸ τῶν φίλων καὶ τῶν ἐχθρῶν παθόντες εἴχομεν ἡσυχίαν. τούτων δ' ὑμῖν μάρ-τυρας παρέξομαι.

ΜΑΡΤΥΡΕΣ

14 Ὁ μὲν τοίνυν Μενέξενος παθὼν ἄξια τῶν ἑαυ-τοῦ τρόπων ἠπατήθη ὑπὸ τοῦ Δικαιογένους· ἀφεὶς

---

[1] τρίβωνα Cobet: τριβώνια.
[2] περὶ μὲν Dobree: μὲν περί.
[3] τουτῳὶ Scheibe: τούτῳ.
[4] ὑμᾶς Reiske: ἡμᾶς.

168

insult to injury by reviling and upbraiding him for wearing heavy shoes and a coarse cloak, as though it was Cephisodotus who was wronging him by wearing such shoes, and not he who was wronging Cephisodotus by having reduced him to poverty by robbing him of his property.

So much must suffice on these topics ; I will now return to the point from which I digressed.[a] Menexenus (II.), the son of Cephisophon and cousin to Cephisodotus here, and to me, who had a right to the same share of the estate as I had, proceeded to prosecute those who had borne false witness against us and him, and obtained a conviction against Lycon, the first man whom he brought into court. His evidence had been that Dicaeogenes (III.) had been adopted as sole heir by our uncle ; he was convicted of perjury for giving evidence to this effect. When Dicaeogenes (III.), gentlemen, found that he could no longer deceive you, he advised Menexenus (II.), who was acting for us as well as for himself (I am ashamed to be obliged by his rascality to mention it), to do—what do you think ?—himself to take the share of the estate which was due to him and to throw over us, on whose behalf he was acting, and let off those of the witnesses who had not yet been convicted ! And we, thus treated by our friends and our enemies, kept quiet. On these points I will now produce witnesses before you.

WITNESSES

Menexenus (II.) was paid out as he deserved for his evil conduct, being deceived by Dicaeogenes

---

[a] The end of § 9.

γὰρ τοὺς μάρτυρας καὶ ἡμᾶς προδούς, ὧν ἕνεκα
ταῦτ' ἔπραξεν οὐκ ἐκομίσατο. ἀδικηθεὶς δὲ ὑπὸ
Δικαιογένους μεθ' ἡμῶν πάλιν ἔπραττεν. ἡμεῖς
δὲ καθηγούμενοι οὐκέτι προσήκειν Δικαιογένει
ἔχειν τῶν ἐκ τοῦ κλήρου μέρος οὐδέν, ἐπειδὴ οἱ
μάρτυρες ἑάλωσαν, ἀμφισβητοῦμεν αὐτῷ ἅπαντος
τοῦ οἴκου κατ' ἀγχιστείαν. καὶ ὅτι ἡμεῖς τε
ὀρθῶς ἐγνώκαμεν καὶ οὐδὲν ἔτι προσήκει Δικαιο-
15 γένει τοῦ κλήρου, ῥᾳδίως διδάξω. δύο γὰρ διαθῆκαι ⟨ἀπ⟩εφάνησαν,[1] ἡ μὲν πάλαι, ἡ δὲ πολλῷ[2]
ὕστερον· καὶ κατὰ μὲν τὴν παλαιάν, ἣν ἀπέφηνε
Πρόξενος ὁ Δικαιογένους τουτουὶ[3] πατήρ, ἐπὶ τῷ
τρίτῳ μέρει τοῦ κλήρου ἐγίγνετο τῷ θείῳ τῷ
ἡμετέρῳ υὸς ποιητός, καθ' ἣν δ' αὐτὸς ἀπέφηνε
Δικαιογένης, ἐπὶ[4] παντὶ τῷ οἴκῳ. τούτοιν δὲ
τοῖν[5] διαθήκαιν ἣν μὲν Πρόξενος ἀπέφηνε, Δικαιογένης ἔπεισε τοὺς δικαστὰς ὡς οὐκ ἀληθὴς εἴη·
ἣν δὲ Δικαιογένης ἀπέφηνεν, οἱ μαρτυρήσαντες
αὐτὴν τὸν θεῖον τὸν ἡμέτερον διαθέσθαι ἑάλω-
16 σαν ψευδομαρτυρίων. ἀμφοῖν δὲ τοῖν[6] διαθήκαιν
ἀκύροιν γιγνομέναιν, καὶ ἑτέρας μηδεμιᾶς ὁμο-
λογουμένης εἶναι, κατὰ δόσιν μὲν οὐδενὶ προσῆκε
τοῦ κλήρου, κατ' ἀγχιστείαν δὲ ταῖς Δικαιογένους
τοῦ ἀποθανόντος ἀδελφαῖς, ὧν εἰσιν αἱ ἡμέ-
τεραι μητέρες. διὰ δὲ ταῦτα ἔδοξέ τε ἡμῖν λαχεῖν
τοῦ κλήρου κατ' ἀγχιστείαν, καὶ ἐλάχομεν τοῦ
μέρους[7] ἕκαστος. μελλόντων δ' ἡμῶν ἀντόμνυσθαι
διεμαρτύρησε Λεωχάρης οὑτοσὶ μὴ ἐπίδικον εἶναι

---

[1] ⟨ἀπ⟩εφάνησαν Dobree.   [2] ἡ δὲ πολλῷ Reiske : πολλῷ ἡ δὲ.
[3] τουτουὶ Scheibe : τούτου.   [4] ἐπὶ Bekker : ἐν.
[5] τούτοιν δὲ τοῖν Naber : ταύταιν δὲ ταῖν.
[6] τοῖν Naber : ταῖν.   [7] τοῦ μέρους Buermann : τὸ μέρος.

(III.) ; he let off the accused witnesses and threw us over, but he received no reward for his services. Having been thus wronged by Dicaeogenes (III.), he made common cause with us again ; and we, judging that Dicaeogenes (III.) had no longer any right to any part of the property forming the estate, since the witnesses had been convicted, claimed from him the whole estate on the ground of affinity. That our decision to act thus has been a right one and that Dicaeogenes (III.) has no longer any right to a share in the estate, I shall easily prove to you. Two wills were produced, one made long ago, the other much more recent. Under the old will, which Proxenus, the father of Dicaeogenes (III.) here, produced, the latter was to be heir by adoption to one-third of our uncle's estate ; according to the will which Dicaeogenes (III.) himself produced, he was to be heir to the whole estate. Of these two wills Dicaeogenes (III.) persuaded the judges that the one, namely that produced by Proxenus, was not genuine ; those who bore witness that the other, namely that which Dicaeogenes (III.) produced, was our uncle's genuine will, were convicted of perjury. Both wills being thus invalidated and it being admitted that no other will existed, no one had any claim to the estate under testamentary disposition, but it could be claimed on grounds of affinity by the sisters of the deceased Dicaeogenes (II.), among whom were our mothers.[a] We therefore resolved to claim the estate on grounds of affinity, and we each claimed our share. When we were on the point of making our affidavit,[b] Leochares

[a] The mothers of Cephisodotus, Menexenus II. and his sister, and Menexenus III. [b] For ἀντωμοσία see note on iii. 6.

17 τὸν κλῆρον ἡμῖν. ἐπισκηψαμένων[1] δ' ἡμῶν ἡ μὲν
λῆξις τοῦ κλήρου διεγράφη, ἡ δὲ τῶν ψευδομαρτυρίων δίκη εἰσῄει. ἐν δὲ τῷ δικαστηρίῳ
πάντα μὲν ἡμῶν εἰπόντων ἅ περ νυνί, πολλὰ δὲ
Λεωχάρους ἀνταπολογησαμένου, ἔγνωσαν τὰ
ψευδῆ μαρτυρῆσαι Λεωχάρην οἱ δικασταί. ἐπειδὴ
δὲ τοῦτο φανερὸν ἐγένετο ἐξαιρεθεισῶν τῶν ψήφων,
ἃ μὲν τῶν δικαστῶν καὶ ἡμῶν ἐδεήθη Λεωχάρης
ἢ ὅσα ἡμῖν ἐξεγένετο διαπράξασθαι τότε, οὐκ οἶδ'
ὅ τι δεῖ λέγειν, ἃ δὲ ὡμολογήθη ἡμῖν, ταῦτα
18 ἀκούσατε. συγχωρούντων γὰρ ἡμῶν τῷ ἄρχοντι
μὴ συναριθμεῖν ἀλλὰ συγχέαι τὰς ψήφους, ἀφίστατο μὲν Δικαιογένης τοῖν δυοῖν μεροῖν τοῦ
κλήρου ταῖς Δικαιογένους ἀδελφαῖς, καὶ ὡμολόγει
ἀναμφισβήτητα[2] παραδώσειν ἡμῖν ταῦτα τὰ μέρη·
καὶ ταῦτα ἠγγυᾶτο αὐτὸν Λεωχάρης οὑτοσὶ[3] ἃ[4]
ὡμολόγει ποιήσειν, οὐ μόνος ἀλλὰ καὶ Μνησι-
πτόλεμος ὁ Πλωθειεύς.[5] καὶ τούτων ὑμῖν τοὺς
μάρτυρας παρέξομαι.

ΜΑΡΤΥΡΕΣ

19 Ἡμεῖς τοίνυν ταῦτα παθόντες ὑπὸ Λεωχάρους,
καὶ ἐγγενόμενον ἡμῖν αὐτὸν ἐπειδὴ εἵλομεν τῶν
ψευδομαρτυρίων ἀτιμῶσαι, οὐκ ἐβουλήθημεν, ἀλλ'
ἐξήρκεσε τὰ ἡμέτερα ἡμῖν κομισαμένοις ἀπ-

---

[1] ἐπισκηψαμένων Aldus: ἐπισκεψ-.
[2] ἀναμφισβήτητα Aldus: ἀναμφίβητα.
[3] οὑτοσί Scheibe: οὗτος.
[4] ἃ scripsi, cf. § 20. 9, § 22. 3: καί.
[5] Πλωθειεύς Meursius: πλωτιεύς.

---

[a] Leochares in his protestation put in evidence that
Dicaeogenes III. had been adopted under his uncle's will

172

here put in a protestation that the estate was not adjudicable to us.[a] We then indicted Leochares, with the result that the suit claiming the estate was struck off the list, and the action for perjury came on. In court, after we had brought forward all the arguments which we are presenting on the present occasion, and Leochares had made a lengthy defence, the judges decided that Leochares had committed perjury. When this result became evident after the votes had been taken out of the urns, I do not think I need dwell upon the appeals which Leochares made to the judges and to us or the penalties which we were entitled to exact on that occasion ; but I will tell you the compromise to which we came. On our agreeing with the archon not to count the votes but to mix them together, Dicaeogenes (III.) gave up two-thirds of the estate in favour of the sisters of Dicaeogenes (II.) and agreed to hand over these shares without further discussion, and Leochares here undertook to be surety that he would carry out his promise. He was not the only surety, for Mnesiptolemus of Plotheia gave a similar undertaking. Of these facts I will now produce witnesses before you.

WITNESSES

Having been thus treated by Leochares, though it was possible for us to have him deprived of civil rights since we had obtained a verdict for perjury against him, we did not wish to do so, but were satisfied to recover what belonged to us and be quit

and that therefore an adjudication by the court was unnecessary. The contention of his opponents was that the will was a forgery ; they therefore applied to the court to have the intestate estate adjudicated to them as next-of-kin.

ηλλάχθαι. τοιοῦτοι δὲ γενόμενοι περὶ Λεωχάρην
καὶ Δικαιογένην ἐξηπατήθημεν ὑπ' αὐτῶν, ὦ
ἄνδρες· οὔτε γὰρ Δικαιογένης τὰ δύο μέρη ἡμῖν
τοῦ κλήρου παρέδωκεν, ὁμολογήσας ἐπὶ τοῦ δικαστηρίου, οὔτε Λεωχάρης ὁμολογεῖ ἐγγυήσασθαι
20 αὐτὸν τότε. καίτοι εἰ μὴ ἐναντίον μὲν τῶν δικαστῶν, πεντακοσίων ὄντων, ἐναντίον δὲ τῶν περι-
εστηκότων ἠγγυᾶτο, οὐκ οἶδ' ὅ τι ἂν ἐποίησεν.
ὡς μὲν τοίνυν περιφανῶς ψεύδονται, μάρτυρας
ὑμῖν παρεχόμεθα τοὺς παρόντας, ὅτε Δικαιογένης
μὲν ἀφίστατο τοῖν δυοῖν μεροῖν τοῦ κλήρου καὶ
ὡμολόγει ἀναμφισβήτητα παραδώσειν ταῖς Δικαιογένους ἀδελφαῖς, Λεωχάρης δὲ ἠγγυᾶτο αὐτὸν ἃ
ὡμολόγησε καὶ ποιήσειν. δεόμεθα δὲ καὶ ὑμῶν,
ὦ ἄνδρες, εἴ τις ἐτύγχανε παρὼν τότε, ἀναμνησθῆ-
21 ναι εἰ λέγομεν ἀληθῆ καὶ βοηθῆσαι ἡμῖν· ἐπεί, ὦ
ἄνδρες, εἰ Δικαιογένης ἀληθῆ λέγει, τί ἡμεῖς ὠφε-
λούμεθα νικήσαντες, ἢ τί οὗτος ἐζημιώθη ἡττηθείς;
εἰ γὰρ ἀπέστη μόνον (ὥς φησι) τοῖν δυοῖν μεροῖν
[53] τοῦ κλήρου, ἀναμφισβήτητα¹ δὲ μὴ | ὡμολόγει
παραδώσειν, τί ἐζημιοῦτο ἀφιστάμενος ὧν τιμὴν
εἶχεν; οὐδὲ γὰρ πρὶν ἡττηθῆναι τὴν δίκην εἶχεν
ὧν ἡμεῖς δικαζόμεθα, ἀλλ' οἱ παρὰ τούτου πριάμενοι καὶ θέμενοι, οἷς ἔδει αὐτὸν ἀποδόντα τὴν
22 τιμὴν ἡμῖν τὰ μέρη ἀποδοῦναι. διὰ ταῦτα γὰρ
καὶ τοὺς ἐγγυητὰς παρ' αὐτοῦ ἐλάβομεν, οὐ
πιστεύοντες αὐτῷ ἃ ὡμολόγησε ποιήσειν. πλὴν

¹ ἀναμφισβήτητα Schoemann : -ον.

ᵃ *i.e.*, his becoming surety for the restoration of the
property was the only way in which he could hope to escape
punishment for his perjury.

of him. Having behaved thus towards Leochares and Dicaeogenes (III.) we were deceived by them, gentlemen; for Dicaeogenes (III.) did not hand over the two-thirds of the estate, though he had agreed in court to do so, and Leochares refuses to admit that he undertook to be surety on that occasion. Yet if he had not given surety in the presence of the judges, five hundred in number, and of those who were present in court, I don't know what he could have done.[a] To prove, therefore, that they are obviously lying, we are producing as witnesses those who were present when Dicaeogenes (III.) gave up two-thirds of the estate and promised to hand it over without further dispute to Dicaeogenes' (II.) sisters, and Leochares undertook to be surety that he would actually perform what he promised. And we beseech you, gentlemen, if any of you were present on that occasion, to recollect whether we are speaking the truth and to aid us. For, gentlemen, if Dicaeogenes (III.) is speaking the truth, what advantage was it to us to have won our case, and what disadvantage was it to my opponent to be defeated? For if he simply renounced, as he alleges, his claim to the two-thirds of the estate but did not agree to hand it over without further dispute, what did he lose by renouncing property, the value of which he was still holding? For even before he lost his case, the property which we are claiming was not in his possession but in the hands of those who bought it from him or held it on mortgage, whom he ought to have paid off and then given us our share. That is why we insisted on his providing sureties, because we had no confidence that he would carry out his agreement. Indeed except two small buildings outside

175

γὰρ δυοῖν οἰκιδίοιν ἔξω τείχους καὶ ἐν Πεδίῳ
ἑξήκοντα πλέθρων οὐδὲν κεκομίσμεθα, ἀλλ' οἱ
παρὰ τούτου θέμενοι καὶ πριάμενοι. ἡμεῖς δ' οὐκ
ἐξάγομεν· δέδιμεν[1] γὰρ μὴ ὄφλωμεν δίκας. καὶ
γὰρ Μικίωνα,[2] κελεύοντος Δικαιογένους καὶ φάσκοντος ⟨οὐ⟩[3] βεβαιώσειν, ἐξάγοντες[4] ἐκ τοῦ βαλανείου ὤφλομεν τετταράκοντα μνᾶς διὰ Δικαιο-
23 γένην, ὦ ἄνδρες. ἡγούμενοι γὰρ οὐκ ἂν αὐτὸν βεβαιῶσαι[5] οὐδὲν[6] ὧν ἡμῖν ἀπέστη ἐν τῷ δικαστηρίῳ,
διισχυριζόμεθα πρὸς Μικίωνα ἐναντίον τῶν δικαστῶν, ἐθέλοντες ὁτιοῦν πάσχειν, εἰ βεβαιώσειεν
αὐτῷ Δικαιογένης τὸ βαλανεῖον, οὐκ ἄν ποτε
οἰόμενοι αὐτὸν ἐναντία οἷς ὡμολόγησε πρᾶξαι, οὐ
δι'[7] ἀλλ' οὐδὲν ἢ διὰ τοὺς ἐγγυητάς, ὅτι καθ-
24 ειστήκεσαν ἡμῖν. ἀποστὰς δὲ Δικαιογένης ταῦτα
τὰ μέρη ὧν καὶ νῦν ὁμολογεῖ ἀφεστάναι ἡμῖν,
ἐβεβαίωσε Μικίωνι τὸ βαλανεῖον. καὶ ἐγὼ μὲν ὁ
ἄθλιος οὐχ ὅπως τι ἐκ τοῦ κλήρου εἰληφώς, ἀλλὰ
προσαπολωλεκὼς τετταράκοντα μνᾶς, ἀπῄειν ὑβρι-
σμένος ὑπὸ τοῦ Δικαιογένους. καὶ τούτων ὑμῖν
μάρτυρας παρέξομαι.

ΜΑΡΤΥΡΕΣ

25 Ταῦτα μὲν πεπόνθαμεν ὑπὸ Δικαιογένους, ὦ ἄν-
δρες· ὁ δ' ἐγγυησάμενος αὐτὸν Λεωχάρης καὶ τῶν

---

[1] δέδιμεν Cobet: δεδίαμεν.
[2] Μικίωνα Reiske: μηκίωνα.
[3] οὐ add. Wyse.   [4] ἐξάγοντες Aldus: -ος.
[5] βεβαιῶσαι Naber: -ώσειν.
[6] οὐδὲν Aldus: οὐδὲ.   [7] οὐ δι' Aldus: οὐδ'.

---

[a] About 13 acres.
[b] The upper valley of the river Cephissus.

the walls and sixty *plethra* *ᵃ* of land in the Plain *ᵇ* we
have recovered nothing : the rest is in the possession
of those to whom he sold or mortgaged it. *We* are
making no attempt to eject them, because we are
afraid of losing suits against them ; for when we
tried to eject Micion from the bath-house at the
suggestion of Dicaeogenes (III.), who said that he
would not confirm his title,*ᶜ* we were fined forty
minae, all through Dicaeogenes, gentlemen. For
thinking that he would not confirm any title to any of
the property to which he renounced his claim in our
favour in the court, we vigorously attacked Micion
before the judges, being willing to run any risk of
Dicaeogenes (III.) confirming Micion's title to the
bath-house, and never imagining that he would do the
very opposite of what he had agreed to do, our sole
reason for so acting being that the sureties had
been given. Dicaeogenes (III.), however, having
renounced the portion of the property which he still
admits that he renounced in our favour, confirmed
Micion's title to the bath-house. Thus I was in the
unfortunate position of not only having received
nothing from the estate but of having also lost forty
minae, and left the court having been fooled by
Dicaeogenes (III.). Of these things I will now produce witnesses before you.

WITNESSES

Such is the treatment, gentlemen, which we have
received from Dicaeogenes (III.). Leochares, who
became his surety and is the cause of all our troubles,

ᶜ Under Athenian law the vendor undertook to guarantee
the title of any property which he sold and assumed an
obligation if any attempt was made to evict the purchaser.

πάντων ἡμῖν κακῶν αἴτιος οὔ φησιν ἐγγυήσασθαι
ἃ καταμαρτυρεῖται αὐτοῦ, ὅτι ἐν τῷ γραμματείῳ
τῷ ἐπὶ τοῦ δικαστηρίου γραφέντι οὐκ ἔνεστι ταῦτα.
ἡμεῖς δέ, ὦ ἄνδρες, τότ᾽ ἐπὶ τοῦ βήματος σπεύδον-
τες τὰ μὲν ἐγράψαμεν, τῶν δὲ μάρτυρας ἐποιησά-
μεθα· οὗτοι δέ, ἃ μὲν αὐτοῖς συμφέρει τῶν ὁπο-
λογηθέντων τότε, κύριά φασιν εἶναι, εἰ καὶ μὴ
γέγραπται, ἃ δ᾽ οὐ συμφέρει, οὐ κύρια, εἰ μὴ γέ-
26 γραπται. ἐγὼ δ᾽, ὦ ἄνδρες, οὐ θαυμάζω ὅτι ἔξ-
αρνοί εἰσι τὰ ὡμολογημένα· οὐδὲ γὰρ τὰ γραφέντα
ἐθέλουσι ποιεῖν. ἡμεῖς δ᾽ ὡς λέγομεν[1] ἀληθῆ, καὶ
ἄλλο τι τεκμήριον παρεξόμεθα. Πρωταρχίδῃ γὰρ
τῷ Ποταμίῳ ἔδωκε Δικαιογένης τὴν ἀδελφὴν τὴν
ἑαυτοῦ ἐπὶ τετταράκοντα μναῖς, ἀντὶ δὲ τῆς
προικὸς τὴν οἰκίαν αὐτῷ τὴν ἐν Κεραμεικῷ παρέδωκε. ταύτῃ δὲ τῇ γυναικί, ἣν ὁ Πρωταρχίδης
ἔχει, προσήκει τοῦ κλήρου μέρος ὅσον περ τῇ
27 μητρὶ τῇ ἐμῇ. ἐπεὶ δ᾽ οὖν ἀπέστη Δικαιογένης
ταῖς γυναιξὶ τοῖν δυοῖν μεροῖν τοῦ κλήρου, ἠξίου
ὁ Λεωχάρης τὸν Πρωταρχίδην παραδιδόναι αὐτῷ
τὴν συνοικίαν ἣν εἶχεν ἀντὶ τῆς προικός, ὡς ὄντι
ἐγγυητῇ αὐτῷ,[2] τὸ δὲ μέρος ὑπὲρ τῆς γυναικὸς
τοῦ κλήρου παρ αὐτοῦ[3] κομίζεσθαι. παραλαβὼν
δὲ τὴν συνοικίαν τὸ μέρος οὐ παρέδωκε. καὶ

---

[1] λέγομεν Reiske : ἐλέγομεν.
[2] αὐτῷ Baiter-Sauppe : αὐτῷ.
[3] αὐτοῦ Baiter-Sauppe : αὐτοῦ.

---

[a] If the ms. reading is retained, the reference must be
to the giving in marriage of one of his sisters by Dicaeogenes
II., since a sister of Dicaeogenes III. would have no claim
to a share in the estate. The sister in question must, therefore, be the widow or divorced wife of Democles (§§ 5 and
9 τὴν Δημοκλέους γενομένην γυναῖκα).

says that he never undertook to act as surety to
the extent stated in the evidence against him, on
the ground that it is not implied in the document
drawn up before the tribunal. We, gentlemen, being
hurried at the time in court, wrote down some
of the points and obtained witnesses in support of
others; but our opponents affirm the validity of
those parts of the agreement then made which are
to their own advantage, even if they are not in writing, while they deny the validity of what is contrary
to their interests unless it exists in writing. For
myself, gentlemen, I am not surprised that they
repudiate their verbal agreements, for they are
unwilling to execute the written conditions. We
will furnish another proof of our veracity. Dicaeogenes (II.) gave his sister[a] in marriage to Protarchides of Potamos with a dowry of forty minae, but
instead of paying the dowry to her in cash he made
over to Protarchides the house which he possessed
in the Cerameicus. Now this woman, the wife of
Protarchides, has a right to just the same share of
the estate as my mother. Now when Dicaeogenes
(III.) renounced the two-thirds of the estate in
favour of the women, Leochares suggested that
Protarchides should hand over to him the building
which he possessed in lieu of the dowry, on the
ground that he was surety, and receive from him on
his wife's behalf the share of the estate which
accrued to her.[b] He took over the building, but
never paid over the share of the estate. And of

[b] If the interpretation suggested in the last note is correct,
the meaning here can only be that the dowry of the sister
of Dicaeogenes II., having originally come from him, had
to return into hotchpotch before his estate could be re-divided.

179

τούτων ὑμῖν μάρτυρα τὸν Πρωταρχίδην παρέξομαι.

ΜΑΡΤΥΣ[1]

28 Περὶ δὲ ἐπισκευῆς τοῦ βαλανείου καὶ οἰκοδομίας
καὶ πρότερον εἴρηκε Δικαιογένης καὶ νῦν ἴσως ἐρεῖ,
ὡς ὁμολογήσαντες αὐτῷ ἀποδώσειν τὰ ἀνηλωμένα
οὐκ ἀπεδώκαμεν, καὶ ὅτι διὰ τοῦτο οὐ δύναται
ἀπαλλάσσειν τοὺς χρήστας, οὐδὲ ἡμῖν παραδοῦναι
29 ἃ δεῖ αὐτόν. ἡμεῖς δέ, ὦ ἄνδρες, ἐπὶ τοῦ δικαστηρίου, ὅτε ἠναγκάζομεν αὐτὸν ἀφίστασθαι τούτων, ἀντὶ τῶν λῃτουργιῶν καὶ τῶν εἰς τὰ οἰκο-
δομήματα ἀνηλωμένων[2] ἀφεῖμεν αὐτῷ τοὺς καρπούς,
οὕτω τῶν δικαστῶν γιγνωσκόντων· ὕστερον δ' οὐκ
ἀναγκαζόμενοι ἀλλ' ἑκόντες ἔδομεν αὐτῷ τὴν ἐν
ἄστει οἰκίαν ἐξαίρετον προσθέντες[3] τῷ τρίτῳ μέρει
τοῦ κλήρου ἔχειν ἀντὶ τῶν ἐπεσκευασμένων, ἣν
οὗτος[4] ἀντὶ πεντακισχιλίων δραχμῶν παρέδωκε
30 Φιλονείκῳ. ἔδομεν[5] δὲ οὐ διὰ τὴν τοῦ Δικαιογένους χρηστότητα, ὦ ἄνδρες, ἀλλ' ἐπιδεικνύμενοι
ὅτι οὐ περὶ πλείονος χρήματα ποιούμεθα τῶν
οἰκείων, οὐδ' ἂν πάνυ πονηροὶ ὦσι. καὶ γὰρ
πρότερον ὅτ' ἐφ' ἡμῖν ἐγένετο Δικαιογένην τι-
μωρήσασθαι καὶ ἀφελέσθαι ἃ εἶχεν, οὐκ ἐβουλήθη-
[54] μεν τῶν τούτου | κτήσασθαι οὐδέν, ἀλλὰ τὰ ἡμέτερα
μόνον κομίσασθαι ἐξήρκει ἡμῖν. οὗτος δ' ὅτ' ἐκρά-
τησεν ἡμῶν, ἀπεσύλησεν ἃ ἐδύνατο, καὶ ὡς ἐχθροὺς

---

[1] μάρτυς Aldus : μάρτυρες.
[2] ἀνηλωμένων Herwerden : ἀναλ-.
[3] ἐξαίρε⟨τον προσ⟩θέντες Buermann : ἐξαιρεθέντες πρὸς.
[4] οὗτος M, Aldus : οὕτως.   [5] ἔδομεν Reiske : παρέδ-.

---

[a] Apparently during the period when Dicaeogenes III.
held the whole estate, his fortune was such that he was obliged

these facts I will now produce Protarchides as witness.

WITNESS

Regarding the repairs to the bath-house and the cost of building, Dicaeogenes (III.) has declared on a former occasion, and will now perhaps again declare, that we agreed to re-imburse him his expenses but failed to do so, and that he therefore cannot get rid of the creditors and restore what he ought to us. Now, gentlemen, we in court, when we obliged him to renounce this property, let him off the payment of the revenue he had received from it in consideration of the public services which he had performed [a] and the expenses which he had incurred on the buildings, in accordance with the decision of the judges ; and subsequently, under no compulsion but of our own free will, in consideration of the repairs which he had carried out, gave him as a special gift, in addition to his third share of the estate, the town-house which he sold to Philonicus for 5000 drachmae. We made Dicaeogenes (III.) this present not because of his honesty, but as a proof that we have more regard for our relatives, even though they may be thorough rascals, than for money. For, indeed, on an earlier occasion, when it was in our power to punish Dicaeogenes (III.) and deprive him of his property, we did not wish to possess ourselves of anything which belonged to him but were satisfied with merely obtaining what was our own. He, on the other hand, when he had us in his power, robbed us of all he could and tried to ruin us, as though we were his foes and not his

to undertake public burdens to which he otherwise would not have been liable.

181

31 ἀλλ' οὐ προσήκοντας ἀπόλλυσι. τεκμήριον δὲ καὶ
τῶν ἡμετέρων τρόπων καὶ τῆς τούτου ἀδικίας μέγα
παρεξόμεθα. μελλούσης γὰρ τῆς πρὸς Λεωχάρην
δίκης εἰσιέναι, ὦ ἄνδρες, ἐν τῷ Μαιμακτηριῶνι[1]
μηνί, ἠξίου Λεωχάρης καὶ Δικαιογένης δίαιταν
ἡμᾶς ἐπιτρέπειν[2] τὴν δίκην ἀναβαλλομένους. καὶ
ἡμεῖς ὥσπερ μικρὰ ἀδικούμενοι συνεχωρήσαμεν,
καὶ ἐπετρέψαμεν διαιτηταῖς τέτταρσιν, ὧν τοὺς
μὲν δύο ἡμεῖς ἠγάγομεν, τοὺς δὲ δύο ἐκεῖνοι. καὶ
ἐναντίον τούτων ὡμολογήσαμεν ἐμμενεῖν[3] οἷς ἂν
32 οὗτοι γνοῖεν, καὶ ὠμόσαμεν. καὶ οἱ διαιτηταὶ
ἔφασαν, εἰ μὲν ἀνώμοτοι δύναιντ' [ἂν] ἡμᾶς διαλ-
λάξαι, οὕτω ποιήσειν, εἰ δὲ μή, καὶ αὐτοὶ ὀμόσαντες
ἀποφανεῖσθαι ἃ δίκαια ἡγοῦνται εἶναι. ἀνακρίναν-
τες δὲ ἡμᾶς πολλάκις καὶ πυθόμενοι τὰ πραχθέντα
οἱ διαιτηταί, οἱ μὲν δύο οὓς ἐγὼ προὐβαλόμην,[4]
Διότιμος καὶ Μελάνωπος,[5] ἤθελον καὶ ἀνώμοτοι
καὶ ὀμόσαντες ἀποφήνασθαι ἃ ἐγίγνωσκον ἀληθέ-
στατα ἐκ τῶν λεγομένων, οὓς δὲ Λεωχάρης προὐ-
33 βάλετο, οὐκ ἔφασαν ἀποφανεῖσθαι. καίτοι Διοπείθης ὁ ἕτερος τῶν διαιτητῶν Λεωχάρει μὲν ἦν
τουτῳὶ[6] κηδεστής, ἐμὸς δ' ἐχθρὸς καὶ ἀντίδικος ἐξ
ἑτέρων συμβολαίων· Δημάρατος δὲ ὁ μετ' αὐτοῦ
Μνησιπτολέμῳ τῷ ἐγγυησαμένῳ Δικαιογένην[7] μετὰ
Λεωχάρους ἦν ἀδελφός. οὗτοι μέντοι οὐκ ἠθέλησαν ἀποφήνασθαι, ὁρκώσαντες ἡμᾶς ἦ μὴν ἐμ-

---

[1] Μαιμακτηριῶνι Aldus : μημ-.
[2] ἐπιτρέπειν Reiske : ἐπιτροπεύειν.
[3] ἐμμενεῖν Reiske hic et 33. 7 : ἐμμένειν.
[4] προύβαλόμην Reiske : προύβαλον.
[5] Μελάνωπος Aldus : -οπος.
[6] τουτωὶ Scheibe : τούτῳ.
[7] Δικαιογένην Bekker : -νει.

relatives. We will now furnish a strong proof of our own forbearance and the injustice of Dicaeogenes. When the action against Leochares was coming on, gentlemen, in the month of Maemacterion,[a] Leochares and Dicaeogenes (III.) asked us to postpone the action and submit the matter to arbitration. We, just as though we had suffered only slight injuries, agreed to this and submitted the matter to four arbitrators, two of whom were nominated by us and two by our opponents. In their presence we agreed to abide by their decision and swore an oath to this effect. The arbitrators said, that if they could effect a compromise without putting themselves under an oath, they would do so ; otherwise they would themselves also take an oath and declare what they regarded as just. The arbitrators interrogated us many times and learnt the facts. The two whom I had proposed, Diotimus and Melanopus, expressed their readiness, with or without an oath, to declare what they regarded as the truth in the statements ; but the arbitrators whom Leochares had proposed refused to do so. Yet Diopeithes, one of the two arbitrators,[b] was brother-in-law of Leochares here and a personal enemy of mine, and had been my opponent in other actions regarding contracts, while Demaratus, his colleague, was a brother of Mnesiptolemus, who acted with Leochares as surety for Dicaeogenes (III.). These men, however, refused to pronounce their opinion, although they had made us swear that we would abide by

[a] The fifth month of the Attic calendar, October to November.

[b] *i.e.*, as the context shows, one of the two arbitrators nominated by the speaker's opponents.

183

μενεῖν οἷς [ἂν] αὐτοὶ γνοῖεν. καὶ τούτων ὑμῖν μάρτυρας παρέξομαι.

34 Οὔκουν δεινὸν εἰ δεήσεται ὑμῶν, ὦ ἄνδρες, Λεωχάρης ἀποψηφίσασθαι ἃ Διοπείθης κηδεστὴς ὢν αὐτοῦ κατεψηφίσατο; ἢ ὑμῖν πῶς καλὸν ἀπογνῶναι Λεωχάρους ἅ γε οὐδ' οἱ προσήκοντες αὐτοῦ ἀπέγνωσαν[1]; δέομαι οὖν ὑμῶν καταψηφίσασθαι Λεωχάρους, ἵν' ἃ ἡμῖν οἱ πρόγονοι κατέλιπον κομισώμεθα, καὶ μὴ μόνον τὰ ὀνόματα αὐτῶν ἔχωμεν ἀλλὰ καὶ τὰ χρήματα. τῶν δὲ Λεω-
35 χάρους ἰδίων οὐκ ἐπιθυμοῦμεν.[2] Δικαιογένην γάρ, ὦ ἄνδρες, οὔτ' ἐλεεῖν ἐστε δίκαιοι ⟨ὡς⟩[3] κακῶς πράττοντα καὶ πενόμενον, οὔτ' εὖ ποιεῖν ὡς ἀγαθόν τι εἰργασμένον τὴν πόλιν· οὐδέτερα γὰρ αὐτῷ τούτων ὑπάρχει, ὡς ἐγὼ ἀποφανῶ,[4] ὦ ἄνδρες. ἅμα δὲ καὶ πλούσιον καὶ πονηρότατον αὐτὸν ὄντα ἀνθρώπων ἀποδείξω καὶ εἰς τὴν πόλιν καὶ εἰς τοὺς προσήκοντας καὶ εἰς τοὺς φίλους. οὗτος γὰρ παραλαβὼν τὸν κλῆρον παρ' ὑμῶν[5] φέροντα μίσθωσιν τοῦ ἐνιαυτοῦ ὀγδοήκοντα μνᾶς, καρπωσάμενος αὐτὸν δέκα ἔτη οὔτε ἀργύριον ὁμολογεῖ[6] κεκτῆσθαι οὔτε ὅποι ἀνήλωσεν ἔχοι ἂν ἐπιδεῖξαι,
36 ὦ ἄνδρες. ἄξιον δὲ καὶ ὑμῖν λογίσασθαι. οὗτος γὰρ τῇ μὲν φυλῇ εἰς Διονύσια χορηγήσας τέταρτος

---

[1] ἀπέγνωσαν Reiske: ἂν ἔγνωσαν.
[2] ἐπιθυμοῦμεν M, Aldus: ἐπεθ-.
[3] ὡς add. Bekker.
[4] ἀποφανῶ Reiske: ἀποφαίνω.
[5] ὑμῶν Dobree: ἡμῶν.
[6] ὁμολογεῖ Bekker: ὡμολόγει.

whatever they themselves decided. Of these facts I will now produce witnesses before you.

WITNESSES

Is it not extraordinary, gentlemen, that Leochares should ask you to absolve him where Diopeithes his brother-in-law condemned him?[a] Or how can it be right for you to acquit Leochares when even his relatives did not acquit him? I beseech you, therefore, to condemn Leochares, in order that we may recover what our forefathers left to us and possess not merely their names but their property also. The personal property of Leochares we do not covet. Dicaeogenes (III.), gentlemen, has no claim to your pity for misfortune or poverty, nor does he deserve any kindness for having done any good service to the city; he has no title to your consideration on either of these grounds, as I will prove to you, gentlemen. I will show you that he is at once rich and the meanest of men in his relations both to the city and to his kinsmen and to his friends. Having received by your verdict the property which brought in a yearly revenue of eighty minae, and having enjoyed it for ten years, he refuses to admit that he has saved money out of it nor can he show how he expended it, gentlemen. It is well worth your while to look into the matter. He acted as *choregus* for his tribe at the Dionysia and was fourth; as *choregus* in the tragic contest and Pyrrhic

---

[a] *i.e.*, by refusing to give an opinion in his favour.

ἐγένετο, τραγῳδοῖς δὲ καὶ πυρριχισταῖς[1] ὕστατος·
ταύτας δὲ μόνας ἀναγκασθεὶς ⟨τὰς ⟩[2] λῃτουργίας
λειτουργῆσαι ἀπὸ τοσαύτης προσόδου οὕτω καλῶς
ἐχορήγησεν. ἀλλὰ μὴν τριηράρχων τοσούτων κατα-
σταθέντων οὔτ' αὐτὸς ἐτριηράρχησεν οὔθ' ἑτέρῳ
συμβέβληται[3] ἐν τοιούτοις καιροῖς, ἀλλ' ἕτεροι[4]
μὲν οὐσίαν κεκτημένοι ἐλάττω ἢ οὗτος μίσθωσιν
37 λαμβάνει τριηραρχοῦσι. καίτοι, ὦ ἄνδρες, οὐχ ὁ
πατὴρ αὐτῷ τὴν πολλὴν οὐσίαν κατέλιπεν, ἀλλ'
ὑμεῖς ἔδοτε τῇ ψήφῳ· ὥστε εἰ καὶ μὴ πολίτης ἦν,
διά γε τοῦτο δίκαιος ἦν τὴν πόλιν εὖ ποιεῖν.
εἰσφορῶν τοίνυν τοσούτων γεγενημένων πᾶσι τοῖς
πολίταις εἰς τὸν πόλεμον καὶ τὴν σωτηρίαν τῆς
πόλεως Δικαιογένης οὐκ ἔστιν ἥντινα εἰσενήνοχε·
πλὴν ὅτε Λέχαιον[5] ἑάλω, κληθεὶς ὑπὸ ἑτέρου ἐπέδωκεν ἐν τῷ δήμῳ τριακοσίας δραχμάς, ἔλαττον
38 ἢ Κλεώνυμος ὁ Κρής· καὶ τοῦτο ἐπέδωκεν, οὐκ εἰσήνεγκεν, ἀλλ' ἐπ' αἰσχίστῳ ἐπιγράμματι[6] ἐξετέθη[7]
αὐτοῦ τοὔνομα ἔμπροσθεν τῶν ἐπωνύμων, ὅτι οἶδε[8]
εἰς σωτηρίαν τῆς πόλεως ὑποσχόμενοι τῷ δήμῳ
εἰσοίσειν χρήματα ἐθελονταὶ οὐκ εἰσήνεγκαν. καί-

---

[1] πυρριχισταῖς Palmer: -χυέταις.   [2] τὰς add. Reiske.
[3] συμβέβληται Fuhr: -βέβληκεν.   [4] ἕτεροι Reiske: ἕτερος.
[5] Λέχαιον Reiske: λεχίον.
[6] ἐπιγράμματι Aldus: ὑπογρ-.
[7] ἐξετέθη Schoemann: ἐξ ἑτέρου.
[8] οἶδε Bekker: εἶδεν.

---

[a] In the dithyrambic contests the competition was by
tribes, thus the chorus of which Dicaeogenes was choregus
was placed fourth out of ten competing choruses. The
tragic competition was between three choruses, not organized
on a tribal basis. The Pyrrhic or Warrior Dance was
executed at the Panathenaic festival; there is no evidence
as to the number of competing choruses.

dances he was last.*a* These were the only public services which he undertook and then only under compulsion, and this was the fine show he made as *choregus* in spite of his great wealth! Moreover, though so many trierarchs were appointed, he never acted in this capacity by himself nor has he ever been associated in it with another *b* in all those years of crisis; yet others possessing less capital than he has income, act as trierarchs. Yet, gentlemen, his large fortune was not bequeathed to him by his father but given to him by your verdict; so that, even if he were not an Athenian citizen, he was in duty bound for this reason alone to do the city good service. Though so many extraordinary contributions for the cost of the war and the safety of the city have been made by all the citizens, Dicaeogenes (III.) has never contributed anything, except that after the capture of Lechaeum,*c* at the request of another citizen, he promised in the public assembly a subscription of 300 drachmas, a smaller sum than Cleonymus the Cretan.*d* This sum he promised but did not pay, and his name was posted on a list of defaulters in front of the statues of the Eponymous Heroes,*e* which was headed : " These are they who voluntarily promised the people to contribute money for the salvation of the city and failed to pay the amounts promised."

b After the battle of Aegospotami (405 B.C.) two citizens might jointly equip a vessel of war.

c One of the harbours of Corinth which was captured by the Spartans in 392 B.C.

d *i.e.,* one who was not even an Athenian citizen.

e The statues of the heroes who gave their names to the ten tribes stood below the north side of the Areopagus and above the Metroum and Council Chamber (Paus. i. 5. 1).

τοι πῶς ἄξιον θαυμάζειν, ὦ ἄνδρες, εἰ ἐμὲ ἐξ-
ηπάτησεν ἕνα ὄντα, ὃς ὑμᾶς ἅπαντας ἅμα συν-
ειλεγμένους ἐν τῇ ἐκκλησίᾳ τοιαῦτα ἐποίησε;
καὶ τούτων ὑμῖν τοὺς μάρτυρας παρέξομαι.

ΜΑΡΤΥΡΕΣ

[55] Εἰς μὲν τὴν πόλιν οὕτω καὶ τοσαῦτα | λελητούρ-
39 γηκε Δικαιογένης ἀπὸ τοσούτων χρημάτων· περὶ
δὲ τοὺς προσήκοντας τοιοῦτός ἐστιν οἷον ὁρᾶτε,
ὥστε τοὺς μὲν ἡμῶν ἀφείλετο τὴν οὐσίαν, ὅτι
μεῖζον[1] ἐδυνήθη, τοὺς δὲ περιεώρα εἰς τοὺς
μισθωτοὺς ἰόντας δι' ἔνδειαν τῶν ἐπιτηδείων. τὴν
δὲ μητέρα [τὴν] αὑτοῦ καθημένην ἐν τῷ τῆς
Εἰλειθυίας ἱερῷ πάντες ἑώρων, καὶ τούτῳ ἐγ-
καλοῦσαν ἃ ἐγὼ αἰσχύνομαι λέγειν, οὗτος δὲ ποιῶν
40 οὐκ ᾐσχύνετο. τῶν δ' ἐπιτηδείων Μέλανα μὲν
τὸν Αἰγύπτιον, ᾧ ἐκ μειρακίου φίλος ἦν, ὅπερ
ἔλαβε παρ' αὐτοῦ ἀργύριον ἀποστερήσας, ἔχθιστός
ἐστι· τῶν δὲ ἄλλων αὐτοῦ φίλων οἱ μὲν οὐκ
ἀπέλαβον ἃ ἐδάνεισαν, οἱ δ' ἐξηπατήθησαν, καὶ
οὐκ ἔλαβον ἃ ὑπέσχετο αὐτοῖς, εἰ ἐπιδικάσαιτο
41 τοῦ κλήρου, δώσειν. καίτοι, ὦ ἄνδρες, οἱ ἡμέτεροι
πρόγονοι οἱ ταῦτα κτησάμενοι καὶ καταλιπόντες
πάσας μὲν χορηγίας ἐχορήγησαν, εἰσήνεγκαν δὲ
εἰς τὸν πόλεμον χρήματα πολλὰ ὑμῖν, καὶ τριηρ-
αρχοῦντες οὐδένα χρόνον διέλιπον. καὶ τούτων
μαρτύρια ἐν τοῖς ἱεροῖς ἀναθήματα ἐκεῖνοι ἐκ τῶν
περιόντων, μνημεῖα τῆς αὐτῶν ἀρετῆς, ἀνέθεσαν,

---

[1] μεῖζον Aldus : μεῖζων.

[a] The goddess of childbirth. Reiske conjectures that the
speaker is insinuating that Dicaeogenes committed incest
with his own mother.

188

Indeed, gentlemen, what ground is there for astonishment that he deceived me, a single citizen, when he acted in this manner towards all of you united in assembly? Of these facts I will now produce witnesses before you.

WITNESSES

Such are the manner and extent of the public services which Dicaeogenes has rendered to the city out of so large a fortune. Towards his relatives he is the sort of man that you see: some of us he robbed of our property because he was stronger than we were, others he allowed to resort to paid employment through lack of the necessities of life. Everyone saw his mother seated in the shrine of Eileithyia[a] and charging him with acts which I am ashamed to mention but which he was not ashamed to commit. Amongst his intimates he deprived Melas the Egyptian, who had been his friend from youth upwards, of money which he had received from him, and is now his bitterest enemy; of his other friends some have never received back money which they lent him, others were deceived by him and did not receive what he had promised to give them if he should have the estate adjudicated to him. And yet, gentlemen, our forefathers, who acquired and bequeathed this property, performed every kind of choregic office, contributed large sums for your expenses in war, and never ceased acting as trierarchs. As evidence of all these services they set up in the temples out of the remainder of their property,[b] as memorials of their civic worth, dedica-

[b] The expenses would be incurred in providing monuments, of which the well-known Choregic Monument of Lysicrates is a specimen, to support the tripods won as prizes.

τοῦτο μὲν ἐν Διονύσου τρίποδας, οὓς χορηγοῦντες
42 καὶ νικῶντες ἔλαβον, τοῦτο δ' ἐν Πυθίου· ἔτι δ' ἐν
ἀκροπόλει ἀπαρχὰς τῶν ὄντων ἀναθέντες πολλοῖς,
ὡς ἀπὸ ἰδίας κτήσεως, ἀγάλμασι χαλκοῖς καὶ
λιθίνοις κεκοσμήκασι τὸ ἱερόν. αὐτοὶ δ' ὑπὲρ τῆς
πατρίδος πολεμοῦντες ἀπέθανον, Δικαιογένης μὲν
ὁ Μενεξένου τοῦ ἐμοῦ πάππου πατὴρ στρατηγῶν
ὅτε ἡ ἐν Ἐλευσῖνι μάχη ἐγένετο, Μενέξενος δ' ὁ
ἐκείνου ὑὸς φυλαρχῶν τῆς Ὀλυνθίας[1] ἐν Σπαρτώλῳ,
Δικαιογένης δὲ ὁ Μενεξένου τριηραρχῶν τῆς
43 Παράλου ἐν Κνίδῳ. τὸν μὲν τούτων[2] οἶκον σύ, ὦ
Δικαιόγενες, παραλαβὼν κακῶς καὶ αἰσχρῶς δι-
ολώλεκας, καὶ ἐξαργυρισάμενος πενίαν ὀδύρῃ, ποῖ[3]
ἀναλώσας; οὔτε γὰρ εἰς τὴν πόλιν οὔτε εἰς τοὺς
φίλους φανερὸς[4] εἶ δαπανηθεὶς οὐδέν. ἀλλὰ μὴν
οὔτε[5] καθιπποτρόφηκας· οὐ γὰρ πώποτε ἐκτήσω
ἵππον πλείονος ἄξιον ἢ τριῶν μνῶν· οὔτε κατεζευγο-
τρόφηκας, ἐπεὶ οὐδὲ ζεῦγος ἐκτήσω ὀρικὸν οὐδεπώποτε ἐπὶ τοσούτοις ἀγροῖς καὶ κτήμασιν. ἀλλ'
44 οὐδ' ἐκ τῶν πολεμίων ἐλύσω οὐδένα. ἀλλ' οὐδὲ τὰ
ἀναθήματα, ἃ Μενέξενος τριῶν ταλάντων ποιησάμενος ἀπέθανε πρὶν ἀναθεῖναι, εἰς πόλιν κεκόμικας,
ἀλλ' ἐν τοῖς λιθουργείοις[6] ἔτι καλινδεῖται,[7] καὶ αὐτὸς
μὲν ἠξίους κεκτῆσθαι ἅ σοι οὐδὲν προσῆκε χρήματα,

---

[1] Ὀλυνθίας Palmer: Ὀλυσίας.   [2] τούτων Wyse: τοῦτον.
[3] ποῖ Bekker: ποῦ.   [4] φανερὸς Scaliger: φανερῶς.
[5] οὔτε scripsi: οὐδὲ.   [6] λιθουργείοις Stephanus: -γίοις.
[7] καλινδεῖται Cobet: κυλ-.

---

[a] Nothing is known of any battle at Eleusis. Dobree
reads Ἁλιεῦσι (cf. Thuc. i. 104).
[b] In 429 B.C. (cf. Thuc. ii. 79).   [c] See § 6 and note.
[d] If the text is correct, the reference must be to Menexenus
I.; but in that case it would have been the duty of Dicaeogenes II. to set up the statues after his father's death.

tions, such as tripods which they had received as prizes for choregic victories in the temple of Dionysus, or in the shrine of Pythian Apollo. Furthermore, by dedicating on the Acropolis the first-fruits of their wealth, they have adorned the shrine with bronze and marble statues, numerous, indeed, to have been provided out of a private fortune. They themselves died fighting in warfare in defence of their country; Dicaeogenes (I.), the father of my grandfather Menexenus (I.), while acting as general when the battle took place at Eleusis[a]; Menexenus (I.), his son, in command of the cavalry at Spartolus in the territory of Olynthus[b]; Dicaeogenes (II.), the son of Menexenus (I.), while in command of the Paralus[c] at Cnidus. It is the property of these men, Dicaeogenes, that you inherited and have wickedly and disgracefully squandered, and having converted it into money you now plead poverty. On what did you spend it? For you have obviously not expended anything on the city or your friends. You have certainly not ruined yourself by keeping horses—for you have never acquired a horse worth more than three minae—, nor by keeping racing teams—for you never owned even a pair of mules in spite of acquiring so many farms and estates. Nor again did you ever ransom a prisoner of war. You have never even transported to the Acropolis the dedications upon which Menexenus (I.)[d] expended three talents and which his death prevented him from setting up, but they are still knocking about in the sculptor's workshop; and thus, while you yourself claimed the possession of money to which you had no title, you

τοῖς δὲ θεοῖς οὐκ ἀπέδωκας ἃ ἐκείνων ἐγίγνετο
45 ἀγάλματα. διὰ τί οὖν ἀξιώσεις σου τοὺς δικαστὰς
ἀποψηφίσασθαι, ὦ Δικαιόγενες; πότερον ὅτι
πολλὰς λῃτουργίας λελῃτούργηκας τῇ πόλει, καὶ
πολλὰ χρήματα δαπανήσας σεμνοτέραν τὴν πόλιν
τούτοις ἐποίησας; ἢ ὡς τριηραρχῶν πολλὰ κακὰ
τοὺς πολεμίους εἰργάσω, καὶ εἰσφορὰς δεομένῃ τῇ
πατρίδι εἰς τὸν πόλεμον εἰσενεγκὼν μεγάλα ὠφέ-
46 ληκας; ἀλλ' οὐδέν σοι τούτων πέπρακται. ἀλλ'
ὡς στρατιώτης ἀγαθός; ἀλλ' οὐκ ἐστράτευσαι
τοσούτου καὶ τοιούτου γενομένου πολέμου, εἰς ὃν
Ὀλύνθιοι μὲν καὶ νησιῶται ὑπὲρ τῆσδε τῆς γῆς
ἀποθνῄσκουσι μαχόμενοι τοῖς πολεμίοις, σὺ δέ, ὦ
Δικαιόγενες, πολίτης ὢν οὐδ' ἐστράτευσαι. ἀλλ'
ἴσως διὰ τοὺς προγόνους ἀξιώσεις μου πλέον ἔχειν,
ὅτι τὸν τύραννον ἀπέκτειναν. ἐγὼ δ' ἐκείνους μὲν
ἐπαινῶ, σοὶ δὲ οὐδὲν ἡγοῦμαι τῆς ἐκείνων ἀρετῆς
47 μετεῖναι. πρῶτον μὲν γὰρ εἵλου ἀντὶ τῆς ἐκείνων
δόξης τὴν ἡμετέραν οὐσίαν κτήσασθαι, καὶ ἐβουλή-
θης μᾶλλον Δικαιογένους καλεῖσθαι ὑὸς ἢ Ἁρμο-
δίου, ὑπεριδὼν μὲν τὴν ἐν Πρυτανείῳ σίτησιν, κατα-
φρονήσας δὲ προεδριῶν[1] καὶ ἀτελειῶν, ἃ τοῖς
ἐξ ἐκείνων γεγονόσι δέδοται. ἔτι δὲ ὁ Ἀριστο-
γείτων ἐκεῖνος καὶ Ἁρμόδιος οὐ διὰ τὸ γένος
ἐτιμήθησαν ἀλλὰ διὰ τὴν ἀνδραγαθίαν, ἧς σοι οὐδὲν
μέτεστιν, ὦ Δικαιόγενες.

---

[1] προεδριῶν M, Aldus : -ρειῶν.

* Probably in the Corinthian War (394–386 B.C.).
b Hipparchus.
c i.e., was willing to be adopted into another family in
order to inherit money.
d The senior male representatives of the families of

never rendered up to the gods statues which were theirs by right. What possible reason will you give, Dicaeogenes, that the judges should acquit you? Will you allege that you have performed many public services for the city and added to the dignity of the city by lavish expenditure? Will you say that as trierarch you have inflicted heavy losses upon the enemy, or bestowed great benefits upon your country in her hour of need by contributing to the expenses of the war? No, you have done none of these things. Do you claim acquital on the ground that you have proved yourself a good soldier? But you never served at all in the whole course of the long and critical war, during which the Olynthians and the islanders are dying fighting against the foe in the defence of our land,[a] but you, Dicaeogenes, though you were an Athenian citizen, have never served at all. Perhaps you will claim an advantage over me for the sake of your forefathers, because they slew the tyrant[b]? I pay them all due homage, but I do not think that you have any share of their valour. In the first place, you preferred to possess our property rather than their glory, and wished to be called son of Dicaeogenes rather than of Harmodius,[c] despising the right of dining in the town hall and disdaining the seats of honour and the immunities granted to the descendants of those heroes.[d] Further, the great Aristogeiton and Harmodius were honoured, not because of their birth but because of their bravery, of which you, Dicaeogenes, have no share.

Harmodius and Aristogeiton enjoyed the right to dine with the prytaneis in the town hall ($\theta \acute{o} \lambda os$), seats of honour at public functions, and certain immunities from taxation.

VI. ON THE ESTATE OF PHILOCTEMON

VI. ON THE ESTATE OF PHILOCTEMON

INTRODUCTION

EUCTEMON of Cephisia,[a] a man of considerable wealth consisting mainly of real property, had three sons, Philoctemon, Ergamenes, and Hegemon, and two daughters, married respectively to Phanostratus and Chaereas. All three sons predeceased their father, the last to die being Philoctemon, who was killed in action off Chios, probably about 376 B.C. None of the sons left any issue ; but Philoctemon in his will had adopted Chaerestratus, the child of his sister, the wife of Phanostratus, as his son and heir to his estate. It appears, however, that, though the rights of a son adopted by will had to be established by an application to the courts, Chaerestratus had taken no steps, after Philoctemon's death, to have himself thus recognized—probably because Philo-

[a] STEMMA

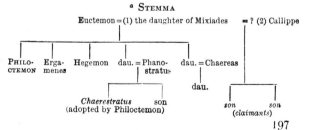

ctemon had possessed no estate separate from that of his father, and it was therefore to Chaerestratus's advantage to remain in his original family. Euctemon himself died at the advanced age of ninety-six ; whereupon Chaerestratus claimed his estate.

The claim of Chaerestratus was opposed by a kinsman of Euctemon, by name Androcles, who, after having first attempted to obtain possession of the estate by demanding the hand of Euctemon's daughter, the widow of Chaereas, on the ground that she was an heiress and he himself the next of kin, put in a protestation (διαμαρτυρία) that the estate was not liable to adjudication, because Euctemon had left two legitimate sons, the children of a certain Callippe. He also asserted that Philoctemon had made no will. Of the two youths thus put forward as heirs, the elder was not more than twenty years of age (§ 14), so that he must have been born when Euctemon was at least seventy-six years of age. There was, however, strong evidence of his legitimacy in the fact, admitted by the opposing party, that Euctemon had introduced him into his ward as his son, and that he had been accepted as such by the members of the ward, who were bound by law to exclude illegitimate sons from the rights of citizenship.

In these circumstances the only course open to Chaerestratus was to prosecute Androcles and his associate Antidorus for perjury committed in the protestation. It was in this action that the present speech was delivered by a friend of the family of Chaerestratus. He begins by calling evidence to prove that Philoctemon made a will and by quoting the laws to show that he had the right to do so. But the greater part of the speech is taken up with disproving the legitimacy of the alleged sons of Euctemon. It is asserted that during the later years of his life Euctemon fell victim to the wiles of a prostitute of servile birth, named Alce, who was the manageress of a tenement-house belonging to the old man ; visiting the house regularly to collect the rents, he at length allowed himself to be beguiled into leaving his own home and family and taking up his abode with her. The two claimants were, it is alleged, her sons by a freedman named Dion, but she persuaded Euctemon to recognize them as his children, and even to introduce one of them to the members of his ward as his legitimate son. The members of the ward at first refused to accept him ; but, after Philoctemon had been induced to withdraw his opposition on the understanding that the child should receive no property except a single farm, he was again presented and accepted by the ward. After the death of Philoctemon, Euctemon revoked the document which had recorded the arrangement between the father and son. The speaker alleged that the cause of this act was the intervention of Androcles and Antidorus, who had entered into a plot with Alce to plunder Euctemon's estate under the pretence that they were guardians of her two sons. Their plots, it is alleged, were so far successful that before Euctemon's death half his capital had been made away with and his house was actually stripped of its contents while he lay dead within it. The speaker then proceeds to point out the inconsistency of Androcles in demanding the hand of Euctemon's daughter on the ground that she was an heiress, a quality which she could not

possibly possess, if, as he further alleged, Euctemon
had left two legitimate sons. He concludes by
attacking the character of Androcles and commend-
ing the public spirit and generosity of Chaerestratus
and his family.

The case is well presented, and the speech has been
regarded by several critics as perhaps the best of the
surviving compositions of Isaeus. The weakness of
the argument lies in the facts that, as has been
pointed out, Chaerestratus had never applied for
legal recognition of his status as adopted son of
Philoctemon, and that, in any case, it was the estate
of Euctemon and not that of Philoctemon which was
really being claimed.

An interesting point, which has given rise to
various theories, is that, though the wife of Euctemon
(the daughter of Mixiades) survived her husband, her
existence is never used as an argument to disprove
the possibility of a second marriage. It has even
been employed as an argument in favour of the
theory that polygamy, or at any rate some form of
concubinage, of which the issue was regarded as
legitimate, was permitted at Athens after the Peloponnesian war. It appears from the *Andromache* of
Euripides (ll. 177 ff., 465 ff.) that such a project was
discussed, but there is no conclusive evidence that
it was ever actually carried into effect. In any
event, the present speech can hardly be employed
as evidence in favour of this theory, since it is
more than likely that Euctemon was separated from
his wife and that the speaker purposely refrained
from mentioning the circumstance, since to admit
the possibility of a second marriage would obviously
damage his case.

ON THE ESTATE OF PHILOCTEMON

The date of the speech can be fixed as 364 B.C. by the words of § 14, which state that fifty-two years had elapsed since the departure from Athens of the Sicilian expedition. It seems likely that Chaerestratus lost his case, since in an inscription (*I.G.* ii. No. 1177. 11), which is assigned by Koehler to the middle of the fourth century or a little later, he is still described as the " son of Phanostratus," whereas, if he had been successful, he would have become " the son of Philoctemon."

VI. ΠΕΡΙ ΤΟΥ ΦΙΛΟΚΤΗΜΟΝΟΣ ΚΛΗΡΟΥ

ΥΠΟΘΕΣΙΣ

[56]   Εὐκτήμονος υἱὸς Φιλοκτήμων τὸν τῆς ἑτέρας τῶν
ἀδελφῶν καὶ Φανοστράτου υἱὸν Χαιρέστρατον ποιησάμενος κατὰ διαθήκας τεθείσας παρὰ Χαιρέᾳ τῷ τῆς
ἑτέρας ἀδελφῆς ἀνδρί, ἐτελεύτησε ζῶντος ἔτι τοῦ πατρός·
ὕστερον δὲ κἀκείνου ἀποθανόντος ἔλαχεν ὁ Χαιρέστρατος
τοῦ κλήρου κατὰ τὸν νόμον. διαμαρτυρήσαντος δὲ Ἀν-
δροκλέους μὴ εἶναι ἐπίδικον ὄντος Ἀντιδώρου γνησίου
παιδὸς Εὐκτήμονι, οἱ περὶ Χαιρέστρατον ἐπεσκήψαντο τῇ
διαμαρτυρίᾳ, καὶ τοῦτον καὶ τὴν ἀδελφὴν αὐτοῦ νόθους
γεγονέναι φάσκοντες, τὸν δὲ νόμον διαγορεύειν νόθῳ καὶ
νόθῃ μὴ εἶναι ἀγχιστείαν. ἡ στάσις στοχασμός· ἄδηλον
γὰρ εἰ ἐποίησε Φιλοκτήμων Χαιρέστρατον υἱὸν ἑαυτῷ, καὶ
πάλιν ἄδηλον εἰ γνήσιοί εἰσιν οἱ περὶ Ἀντίδωρον.

1   Ὅτι μέν, ὦ ἄνδρες, πάντων οἰκειότατα <τυγ-
χάνω>[1] χρώμενος Φανοστράτῳ τε καὶ Χαιρεστράτῳ
τουτῴι,[2] τοὺς πολλοὺς οἶμαι ὑμῶν εἰδέναι, τοῖς δὲ
μὴ εἰδόσιν ἱκανὸν ἐρῶ τεκμήριον· ὅτε γὰρ εἰς

---

[1] τυγχάνω add. Blass.   [2] τουτῳί Scheibe: τούτῳ.

202

VI. ON THE ESTATE OF PHILOCTEMON

ARGUMENT

Philoctemon, a son of Euctemon, adopted Chaerestratus,
the son of one of his two sisters and of Phanostratus,
in a will which was deposited with Chaereas, the husband of
the other sister, and died during his father's lifetime. When
the latter also died, Chaerestratus claimed possession in
accordance with the law. When Androcles lodged a
protestation that the estate was not adjudicable because
Euctemon had a legitimate son, namely, Antidorus,[a]
Chaerestratus and his supporters impugned the protestation,
declaring that both Antidorus and his sister [b] were illegitimate and that the law ordains that an illegitimate son or
daughter cannot inherit as next-of-kin. The question at
issue is one of fact ; for it is uncertain whether Philoctemon
adopted Chaerestratus as his son, and, further, whether
Antidorus and the other child are legitimate.

That I am on terms of very close friendship with
Phanostratus and with Chaerestratus here, I think
most of you, gentlemen, are aware, but to those
who are not aware of it I will give a convincing
proof. When Chaerestratus [c] set sail for Sicily in

cannot have taken part in the famous Sicilian expedition
of 415–413 B.C., must have sailed to Sicily on some occasion
of which we have no historical record. The emendation
Φανόστρατος, adopted by most editors, is precluded by the
words δεομένων τούτων, which can only refer to Phanostratus and Chaerestratus ; although Phanostratus might have
taken part in the Sicilian Expedition, Chaerestratus could
not have been then alive and therefore would not have
requested the speaker to accompany his father to Sicily.

Σικελίαν ἐξέπλει τριηραρχῶν Χαιρέστρατος, διὰ
τὸ πρότερον αὐτὸς ἐκπεπλευκέναι προῄδειν πάντας
τοὺς ἐσομένους κινδύνους, ὅμως δὲ δεομένων
τούτων καὶ συνεξέπλευσα καὶ συνεδυστύχησα καὶ
2 ἑάλωμεν εἰς τοὺς πολεμίους. ἄτοπον δὴ εἰ ἐκεῖνα
μὲν προδήλων ὄντων τῶν κινδύνων ὅμως διὰ τὸ
χρῆσθαι τούτοις καὶ φίλους νομίζειν ὑπέμενον, νῦν
δὲ οὐ πειρῴμην συνειπεῖν ἐξ ὧν ὑμεῖς τε τὰ¹ εὔορκα
ψηφιεῖσθε καὶ τούτοις τὰ δίκαια γενήσεται. δέομαι
οὖν ὑμῶν συγγνώμην τε ἔχειν καὶ μετ᾽ εὐνοίας
ἀκροάσασθαι· ὁ γὰρ ἀγὼν οὐ μικρὸς αὐτοῖς, ἀλλὰ
περὶ τῶν μεγίστων.

3   Φιλοκτήμων γὰρ ὁ Κηφισιεὺς φίλος ἦν Χαιρεστράτῳ τουτῳὶ² δοὺς δὲ τὰ ἑαυτοῦ καὶ υὸν αὐτὸν
ποιησάμενος ἐτελεύτησε. λαχόντος δὲ τοῦ Χαιρε-
στράτου κατὰ τὸν νόμον τοῦ κλήρου, ἐξὸν ἀμφισβητῆσαι Ἀθηναίων τῷ βουλομένῳ καὶ εὐθυδικίᾳ
εἰσελθόντι εἰς ὑμᾶς, εἰ φαίνοιτο δικαιότερα λέγων,
4 ἔχειν τὸν κλῆρον, διεμαρτύρησεν Ἀνδροκλῆς οὑτοσὶ
μὴ ἐπίδικον εἶναι τὸν κλῆρον, ἀποστερῶν τοῦτον
τῆς ἀμφισβητήσεως καὶ ὑμᾶς τοῦ κυρίους γενέσθαι ὅντινα δεῖ κληρονόμον καταστήσασθαι³ τῶν
Φιλοκτήμονος· καὶ ἐν μιᾷ ψήφῳ καὶ ἑνὶ ἀγῶνι
οἴεται ἀδελφοὺς καταστήσειν ἐκείνῳ τοὺς οὐδὲν
προσήκοντας, καὶ τὸν κλῆρον ἀνεπίδικον ἕξειν
αὐτός, καὶ τῆς ἀδελφῆς τῆς ἐκείνου κύριος γενή-

----

¹ τε τὰ Reiske: τά τε.   ² τουτῳὶ Scheibe: τούτῳ.
³ καταστήσασθαι Aldus: -εσθαι.

----

a Being adopted posthumously he had to obtain a legal
adjudication before he could take possession. This formality

command of a trireme, although, having sailed thither myself before, I knew well all the dangers which I should encounter, yet, at the request of these friends of mine, I sailed with him and shared his misfortune, and we were both made prisoners of war. It would be strange if I endured all this in the face of evident danger because of my friendship and affection for them, and yet were not now to attempt so to plead their cause that you shall pass a sentence in accordance with your oath and that justice shall be done to my clients. I entreat you, therefore, to grant me indulgence and to listen to me with good-will ; for the suit is of no slight importance to them, but their most vital interests are at stake.

Philoctemon of Cephisia was a friend of Chaerestratus here, and died, having bequeathed to him his property and having adopted him as his son. Chaerestratus in accordance with the law *a* claimed the estate. But, since it is lawful for any Athenian who wishes to do so to dispute an inheritance by bringing a direct action before you, and if he can establish a better claim, to obtain possession of the estate, Androcles here put in a protestation declaring that the succession was not adjudicable, thus depriving my client of his right to claim the estate and you of your right to decide who ought to be declared heir to Philoctemon's property. He thus thinks by a single verdict and by a single suit to establish as brothers of the deceased men who have no sort of connexion with him, to place himself in possession of the estate without further legal procedure, to become legal representative of the sister of the

was not necessary for a son adopted in the lifetime of the testator.

5 σεσθαι, καὶ τὴν διαθήκην ἄκυρον ποιήσειν. πολλῶν δὲ καὶ δεινῶν ὄντων ἃ διαμεμαρτύρηκεν Ἀνδρο-κλῆς, τοῦτ᾽ αὐτὸ πρῶτον ἐπιδείξω ὑμῖν, ὡς διέθετο καὶ ἐποιήσατο ὑὸν τουτονὶ Χαιρέστρατον. ἐπειδὴ γὰρ τῷ Φιλοκτήμονι ἐκ μὲν τῆς γυναικὸς ᾗ συνῴκει οὐκ ἦν παιδίον οὐδέν, πολέμου δ᾽ ὄντος ἐκινδύνευε καὶ ἱππεὺς στρατευόμενος καὶ τριήρ-αρχος πολλάκις ἐκπλέων, ἔδοξεν αὐτῷ διαθέσθαι τὰ αὑτοῦ, μὴ ἔρημον καταλίπῃ τὸν οἶκον, εἴ τι
6 πάθοι. τὼ μὲν οὖν ἀδελφὼ αὐτῷ, ὥπερ[1] ἐγε-νέσθην, ἄμφω ἄπαιδε ἐτελευτησάτην· τοῖν[2] δὲ ἀδελ-φαῖν τῇ μὲν ἑτέρᾳ, ᾗ ὁ Χαιρέας συνῴκει, οὐκ ἦν ἄρρεν παιδίον οὐδὲ ἐγένετο πολλὰ ἔτη συνοικούσῃ, ἐκ δὲ τῆς ἑτέρας, ᾗ συνῴκει Φανόστρατος οὑτοσί, ἤστην ὑὼ δύο. τούτων τὸν πρεσβύτερον τουτονὶ
7 Χαιρέστρατον ἐποιήσατο ὑόν· καὶ ἔγραψεν οὕτως[3] ἐν διαθήκῃ, εἰ μὴ γένοιτο αὐτῷ παιδίον ἐκ τῆς γυναικός, τοῦτον κληρονομεῖν τῶν ἑαυτοῦ. καὶ τὴν διαθήκην κατέθετο παρὰ τῷ κηδεστῇ Χαιρέᾳ, τῷ τὴν ἑτέραν αὐτοῦ ἀδελφὴν ἔχοντι. καὶ ὑμῖν ἥ τε διαθήκη αὕτη ἀναγνωσθήσεται[4] καὶ οἱ παρα-γενόμενοι μαρτυρήσουσι. καί μοι ἀνάγνωθι.

ΔΙΑΘΗΚΗ. ⟨ΜΑΡΤΥΡΕΣ⟩

8 Ὡς μὲν διέθετο καὶ ἐφ᾽ οἷς ἐποιήσατο ὑὸν τοῦ-τον, ἀκηκόατε· ὡς δ᾽ ἐξὸν αὐτῷ ταῦτ᾽ ἔπραξεν, ὅθεν δικαιότατα ἡγοῦμαι τὰ τοιαῦτ᾽ εἶναι μαν-
[57] θάνειν, τοῦτον ὑμῖν αὐτὸν | παρέξομαι τὸν νόμον. καί μοι ἀνάγνωθι.

---

[1] ὥπερ Reiske: ὥσπερ.
[2] τοῖν Naber: ταῖν.   [3] οὕτως Aldus: οὗτος.
[4] ἀναγνωσθήσεται M, Aldus: ἀναγνώσεται.

deceased, and to annul the will. Androcles has made a number of extraordinary allegations in his protestation; I will take one point first and prove that Philoctemon made a will and adopted Chaerestratus here as his son. Seeing that Philoctemon had no issue by the woman to whom he was married, and since, as it was war-time, he was running considerable risks, serving in the cavalry and often sailing as trierarch, he resolved to dispose of his property by will, so that he might not leave his house desolate if anything happened to him. He had had two brothers, both of whom died without issue: of his two sisters one, who was the wife of Chaereas, had no son and had never had one, though she had been married for many years; the other, who was wife of Phanostratus here, had two sons. It was the elder of these, Chaerestratus here, whom Philoctemon adopted as his son. Under the terms of his will, if he should have no child by his wife, Chaerestratus inherited his estate. He deposited his will with Chaereas, his brother-in-law, the husband of his other sister. This will shall now be read to you, and those who were present at its execution shall give evidence. Please read it.

WILL. WITNESSES

You have now heard that Philoctemon made a will, and on what conditions he adopted Chaerestratus as his son. To prove that he had a right to do so, I will produce the text of the law which is in my opinion the best source of information in such matters. Please read it.

ISAEUS

9 Οὑτοσὶ ὁ νόμος, ὦ ἄνδρες, κοινὸς ἅπασι κεῖται,
ἐξεῖναι τὰ ἑαυτοῦ διαθέσθαι, ἐὰν μὴ παῖδες ὦσι
γνήσιοι ἄρρενες, ἐὰν μὴ ἄρα μανεὶς ἢ ὑπὸ γήρως ἢ
δι' ἄλλο τι τῶν ἐν τῷ νόμῳ παρανοῶν διαθῆται.
ὅτι δ' οὐδενὶ τούτων ἔνοχος ἦν Φιλοκτήμων, βραχέα
εἰπὼν δηλώσω ὑμῖν. ὅστις γὰρ καὶ ἕως ἔζη
τοιοῦτον πολίτην ἑαυτὸν παρεῖχεν, ὥστε διὰ τὸ
ὑφ' ὑμῶν τιμᾶσθαι ἄρχειν ἀξιοῦσθαι, καὶ ἐτελεύτησε μαχόμενος τοῖς πολεμίοις, πῶς ἄν τις
τοῦτον τολμήσειεν εἰπεῖν ὡς οὐκ εὖ ἐφρόνει;

10 Ὅτι μὲν οὖν διέθετο καὶ ἐποιήσατο εὖ φρονῶν,
ἐξὸν αὐτῷ, ἀποδέδεικται ὑμῖν, ὥστε κατὰ μὲν
τοῦτο ψευδῆ μεμαρτυρηκὼς Ἀνδροκλῆς ἀποδέ-
δεικται· ἐπειδὴ δὲ προσδιαμεμαρτύρηκεν [ὡς]
ὑὸν εἶναι γνήσιον Εὐκτήμονος τοῦτον, καὶ ταῦτ'
ἀποδείξω ψευδῆ ὄντα. Εὐκτήμονι γάρ, ὦ ἄνδρες,
τῷ Φιλοκτήμονος πατρί, τοὺς μὲν ὄντως γενομένους παῖδας, Φιλοκτήμονα καὶ Ἐργαμένην καὶ
Ἡγήμονα καὶ δύο θυγατέρας, καὶ τὴν μητέρα
αὐτῶν, ἣν ἔγημεν ὁ Εὐκτήμων, Μειξιάδου[1] Κηφι-
σιῶς θυγατέρα, πάντες οἱ προσήκοντες ἴσασι καὶ
οἱ φράτορες καὶ τῶν δημοτῶν οἱ πολλοί, καὶ

11 μαρτυρήσουσιν ὑμῖν· ὅτι δ' [οὐδ'] ἄλλην τινὰ
ἔγημε γυναῖκα, ἐξ ἧς τινος οἶδε αὐτῷ ἐγένοντο,
οὐδεὶς τὸ παράπαν οἶδεν οὐδ' ἤκουσε πώποτε
ζῶντος Εὐκτήμονος. καίτοι τούτους εἰκὸς πιστο-
τάτους εἶναι νομίζειν μάρτυρας· τοὺς γὰρ οἰκείους
εἰδέναι προσήκει τὰ τοιαῦτα. καί μοι τούτους
κάλει πρῶτον, καὶ τὰς μαρτυρίας ἀνάγνωθι.

---

[1] Μειξιάδου Dobree : Μηξιάδου.

LAW

This law, gentlemen, holds good for all men alike, permitting anyone to dispose of his property in default of male issue, providing that, at the time of doing so, he is not insane or mentally incapacitated by old age or any other of the causes mentioned in the law. That Philoctemon did not fall under any of these exceptions, I will prove to you in a few words. For how could anyone dare to say that a man was not in full possession of his faculties, who all his life showed himself so good a citizen, that, owing to your esteem for him, he was considered worthy to hold command, and who died fighting against the enemy ?

That he made a will and adopted a son when he was in full possession of his faculties, as he was entitled to do, has been proved to you ; it follows from this that Androcles has been proved to have committed perjury. But since he has further stated in his protestation that my opponent is a legitimate son of Euctemon, I will prove this also to be false. The real sons of Euctemon, the father of Philoctemon, namely, Philoctemon himself, Ergamenes, and Hegemon, and his two daughters and their mother, Euctemon's wife, the daughter of Meixiades of Cephisia, are well known to all their relatives and to the members of the ward and to most of the demesmen, and they shall testify to you ; but no one is aware or ever heard a word during Euctemon's lifetime of his having married any other wife who became mother by him of our opponents. Yet it is only natural that these should be thought most trustworthy witnesses ; for relatives ought to know about such matters. Please call them first and read the depositions.

MAPTYPIAI

12 Ἔτι τοίνυν καὶ τοὺς ἀντιδίκους ἐπιδείξω ἔργῳ
ὑμῖν ταῦτα μεμαρτυρηκότας. ὅτε γὰρ αἱ ἀνα-
κρίσεις ἦσαν πρὸς τῷ ἄρχοντι καὶ οὗτοι παρακατ-
έβαλον ὡς ὑπὲρ γνησίων τῶνδ' Εὐκτήμονος ὄντων,
ἐρωτώμενοι ὑφ' ἡμῶν τίς εἴη αὐτῶν μήτηρ καὶ
ὅτου θυγάτηρ οὐκ εἶχον ἀποδεῖξαι, διαμαρτυρο-
μένων ἡμῶν καὶ τοῦ ἄρχοντος κελεύοντος ἀποκρίνασθαι κατὰ τὸν νόμον. ⟨καίτοι ἄτοπον⟩,[1] ὦ
ἄνδρες, ἀμφισβητεῖν μὲν ὡς ὑπὲρ γνησίων καὶ
διαμαρτυρεῖν, μητέρα δὲ ἥτις ἦν μὴ ἔχειν ἀποδεῖξαι,

13 μηδὲ προσήκοντα αὐτοῖς μηδένα. ἀλλὰ τότε μὲν
Λημνίαν σκηψάμενοι ταύτην ἀναβολὴν ἐποιήσαντο·
τὸ δ' ὕστερον ἥκοντες εἰς τὴν ἀνάκρισιν, πρὶν καί
τινα ἐρέσθαι, εὐθὺς ἔλεγον ὅτι Καλλίππη μήτηρ,
αὕτη δ' εἴη Πιστοξένου θυγάτηρ, ὡς ἐξαρκέσον εἰ
ὄνομα μόνον πορίσαιντο τὸν Πιστόξενον. ἐρο-
μένων δ' ἡμῶν ὅστις εἴη καὶ εἰ ζῇ ἢ μή, ἐν Σικελίᾳ
ἔφασαν ἀποθανεῖν στρατευόμενον, καταλιπόντα
ταύτην θυγατέρα παρὰ τῷ Εὐκτήμονι, ἐξ ἐπι-
τροπευομένης δὲ τούτῳ γενέσθαι, πρᾶγμα πλάττοντες[2] ἀναιδείᾳ ὑπερβάλλον καὶ οὐδὲ γενόμενον,
ὡς ἐγὼ ὑμῖν ἀποφανῶ ἐκ τούτων πρῶτον ὧν αὐτοὶ

14 ἀπεκρίναντο. τῇ μὲν γὰρ στρατιᾷ, ἀφ' οὗ ἐξ-
έπλευσεν εἰς Σικελίαν, ἤδη ἐστὶ δύο καὶ πεντήκοντα
ἔτη, ἀπὸ Ἀριμνήστου ἄρχοντος, τῷ δὲ πρεσβυτέρῳ
τούτων, ὧν[3] φασιν ἐκ τῆς Καλλίππης καὶ τοῦ

[1] καίτοι ἄτοπον add. Scheibe.
[2] πλάττοντες Bekker : πράττοντες.　　[3] ὧν Reiske : ὃν.

---

[a] The Sicilian expedition set out in the summer of 415 B.C.
(Thuc. vi. 30). The date of this speech must therefore be
364 B.C.

DEPOSITIONS

Further, I will prove that our adversaries have actually given evidence in support of these facts. When the interrogations took place before the archon, and my opponents paid money into court in support of their claim that these young men were the legitimate sons of Euctemon, on being asked by us who, and whose daughter, their mother was, they could not supply the information, although we protested and the archon ordered them to reply in accordance with the law. It was surely a strange proceeding, gentlemen, to make a claim on their behalf as legitimate and to lodge a protestation, and yet not be able to state who was their mother or name any of their relatives. At the time they alleged that she was a Lemnian and so secured a delay; subsequently, when they appeared at the interrogation, without giving time for anyone to ask a question, they immediately declared that the mother was Callippe and that she was the daughter of Pistoxenus, as though it was enough for them merely to produce the name of Pistoxenus. When we asked who he was and whether he was alive or not, they said that he had died on military service in Sicily, leaving a daughter, this Callippe, in the house of Euctemon, and that these two sons were born to her while she was under his guardianship, thus inventing a story surpassing the limits of impudence and quite untrue, as I will prove to you first of all from the answers which they themselves gave. Fifty-two years have passed since the Sicilian expedition, reckoning from the date of its departure in the archonship of Arimnestus;[a] yet the elder of these two alleged sons of Callippe and

Εὐκτήμονος εἶναι, οὔπω ὑπὲρ εἴκοσιν ἔτη. ἀφ-
ελόντι οὖν ταῦτα ἀπὸ τῶν ἐν Σικελίᾳ ὑπολείπεται
πλείω ἢ τριάκοντα ἔτη· ὥστ' οὔτ'[1] ἐπιτροπεύε-
σθαι προσῆκε[2] τὴν Καλλίππην ἔτι, τριακοντοῦτίν
γε οὖσαν, οὔτε ἀνέκδοτον καὶ ἄπαιδα εἶναι, ἀλλὰ
πάνυ πάλαι συνοικεῖν, ἢ ἐγγυηθεῖσαν κατὰ νόμον
15 ἢ ἐπιδικασθεῖσαν. ἔτι δὲ καὶ γιγνώσκεσθαι αὐτὴν
ὑπὸ τῶν Εὐκτήμονος οἰκείων ἀναγκαῖον ἦν καὶ
ὑπὸ τῶν οἰκετῶν, εἴ πέρ γε συνῴκησεν ἐκείνῳ ἢ
διῃτήθη τοσοῦτον χρόνον ἐν τῇ οἰκίᾳ. τὰ γὰρ
τοιαῦτα οὐκ εἰς τὴν ἀνάκρισιν μόνον δεῖ πορίζεσθαι [ὀνόματα] ἀλλὰ τῇ ἀληθείᾳ γεγονότα φαίνεσθαι καὶ ὑπὸ τῶν προσηκόντων καταμαρτυρεῖσθαι.
16 ἀποδεῖξαι τοίνυν ἡμῶν κελευόντων ὅστις οἶδε τῶν
Εὐκτήμονος οἰκείων ἢ συνοικήσασαν ἐκείνῳ τινὰ [ἢ
τὴν] Καλλίππην ⟨ἢ⟩[3] ἐπιτροπευομένην, καὶ παρὰ
τῶν ὄντων ⟨ἡμῖν⟩[4] θεραπόντων τὸν ἔλεγχον ποιεῖσθαι, ἢ εἴ τις τῶν παρ' αὐτοῖς οἰκετῶν φάσκει
ταῦτα εἰδέναι, ἡμῖν παραδοῦναι, οὔτε λαβεῖν
[58] ἠθέλησαν οὔθ' ἡμῖν | παραδοῦναι. καί μοι λαβὲ
τήν τ' ἀπόκρισιν αὐτῶν καὶ τὰς ἡμετέρας μαρτυρίας καὶ προκλήσεις.

ΑΠΟΚΡΙΣΙΣ. ΜΑΡΤΥΡΙΑΙ. ΠΡΟΚΛΗΣΕΙΣ[5]

17 Οὗτοι μὲν τοίνυν τοιοῦτο πρᾶγμα ἔφυγον· ἐγὼ
δ' ὑμῖν ἐπιδείξω καὶ ὅθεν εἰσὶ καὶ οἵτινες, οὓς[6]

---

[1] οὔτ' Aldus: οὐδ'.　　[2] προσῆκε Sauppe: προσήκει.
[3] ἢ τὴν del., ἢ add. Reiske.
[4] ἡμῖν add. Thalheim.
[5] μαρτυρίαι. προκλήσεις Reiske: -ρία. -σις.
[6] οὓς Naber: αὐτούς.

Euctemon has not yet passed his twentieth year. If these years are deducted, more than thirty years still remain since the Sicilian expedition; so that Callippe, if she were thirty years of age,[a] ought to have been no longer under a guardian, nor unmarried and childless, but long ago married, given in marriage either by her guardian, according to the law, or else by an adjudication of the court. Furthermore, she must necessarily have been known to the relatives and to the slaves of Euctemon if she had really been married to him and lived so long in the house. It is not enough merely to produce such statements at the interrogation, but it must be proved that the alleged events really took place and they must be supported by the testimony of the relatives. When we insisted that they should indicate one of Euctemon's family who knew of anyone of the name of Callippe as having been either married to him or under his guardianship, and that they should make an inquiry from our slaves, or hand over to us for examination any of their slaves who said they had knowledge of these facts, they refused to take any of our slaves for examination or to hand over any of their own to us. Now please read their answer to the interrogation and our depositions and challenges.

ANSWER TO INTERROGATION, DEPOSITIONS, CHALLENGES

My opponents, then, avoided a mode of proof so vital to their case; but I will show you the origin and position of these men whom my opponents

---

[a] The speaker rather arbitrarily calculates the date of her marriage by the birth of her elder son.

γνησίους διεμαρτύρησαν εἶναι καὶ κληρονόμους ζη-
τοῦσι καταστῆσαι τῶν Εὐκτήμονος. ἴσως μέν ἐστιν
ἀηδὲς Φανοστράτῳ, ὦ ἄνδρες, τὰς Εὐκτήμονος συμφορὰς φανερὰς καθεστάναι· ὀλίγα δ᾽ ἀναγκαῖον ῥη-
θῆναι, ἵν᾽ ὑμεῖς τὴν ἀλήθειαν εἰδότες ῥᾷον τὰ δί-
18 καια ψηφίσησθε. Εὐκτήμων μὲν γὰρ ἐβίω ἔτη ἓξ
καὶ ἐνενήκοντα, τούτου δὲ τοῦ χρόνου τὸν μὲν πλεῖστον ἐδόκει εὐδαίμων εἶναι (καὶ γὰρ οὐσία ἦν οὐκ
ὀλίγη αὐτῷ καὶ παῖδες καὶ γυνή, καὶ τἄλλ᾽ ἐπιεικῶς
εὐτύχει), ἐπὶ γήρως δὲ αὐτῷ συμφορὰ ἐγένετο οὐ
μικρά, ἣ ἐκείνου πᾶσαν τὴν οἰκίαν ἐλυμήνατο καὶ
χρήματα πολλὰ διώλεσε καὶ αὐτὸν τοῖς οἰκειοτάτοις
19 εἰς διαφορὰν κατέστησεν. ὅθεν δὲ καὶ ὅπως ταῦτ᾽
ἐγένετο, ὡς ἂν δύνωμαι διὰ βραχυτάτων δηλώσω.
ἀπελευθέρα ἦν αὐτοῦ, ὦ ἄνδρες, ἣ ἐναυκλήρει
συνοικίαν ἐν Πειραιεῖ αὐτοῦ καὶ παιδίσκας ἔτρεφε.
τούτων μίαν ἐκτήσατο ᾗ ὄνομα ἦν Ἀλκή, ἣν καὶ
ὑμῶν οἶμαι πολλοὺς εἰδέναι. αὕτη δὲ ἡ Ἀλκὴ
ὠνηθεῖσα πολλὰ μὲν ἔτη καθῆστο ἐν οἰκήματι,[a]
ἤδη δὲ πρεσβυτέρα οὖσα ἀπὸ μὲν τοῦ οἰκήματος
20 ἀνίσταται. διαιτωμένη δὲ αὐτῇ ἐν τῇ συνοικίᾳ
συνῆν ἄνθρωπος ἀπελεύθερος, Δίων ὄνομα αὐτῷ,
ἐξ οὗ ἔφη ἐκείνη τούτους γεγονέναι· καὶ ἔθρεψεν
αὐτοὺς ὁ Δίων ὡς ὄντας ἑαυτοῦ. χρόνῳ δὲ ὕστερον
ὁ μὲν Δίων ζημίαν εἰργασμένος καὶ δείσας ὑπὲρ
αὐτοῦ ὑπεχώρησεν εἰς Σικυῶνα· τὴν δ᾽ ἄνθρωπον
ταύτην, τὴν Ἀλκήν, καθίστησιν Εὐκτήμων ἐπιμελεῖσθαι τῆς ἐν Κεραμεικῷ[b] συνοικίας, τῆς παρὰ
21 τὴν πυλίδα, οὗ ὁ οἶνος ὤνιος. κατοικισθεῖσα δ᾽

---

[a] καθῆστο ἐν οἰκήματι = in cella meretricia sedebat, a
technical term (see Wyse's note).

[b] The " Potters' Quarter " at Athens, partly inside and

testified to be legitimate and are seeking to establish
as heirs of Euctemon's property. It is perhaps
painful, gentlemen, to Phanostratus to bring to
light the misfortunes of Euctemon ; but it is essential
that a few facts should be given, so that, knowing
the truth, you may more easily give your verdict
aright. Euctemon lived for ninety-six years, and
for most of this period had the reputation of being
a fortunate man ; he possessed considerable property
and had children and a wife, and in all other respects
enjoyed a reasonable degree of prosperity. In his
old age, however, a serious misfortune befel him,
which brought ruin to his house, caused him great
financial loss, and set him at variance with his nearest
relatives. The cause and manner of it I will set
forth in the fewest possible words. He had a freed-
woman, gentlemen, who managed a tenement-
house of his at the Peiraeus and kept prostitutes.
As one of these she acquired a woman of the name
of Alce, whom I think many of you know. This
Alce, after her purchase, lived the life of a prostitute [a]
for many years but gave it up when she became too
old. While she was still living in the tenement-
house, she had relations with a freedman whose
name was Dion, whom she declared to be the father
of these young men ; and Dion did, in fact, bring
them up as his own children. Some time later
Dion, having committed a misdemeanour and being
afraid of the consequences, withdrew to Sicyon.
The woman Alce was then installed by Euctemon
to look after his tenement-house in the Cerameicus,[b]
near the postern gate, where wine is sold. Her

partly outside the walls near the Dipylon Gate (see Frazer's
note on Paus. i. 2. 4).

ἐνταυθοῖ πολλῶν καὶ κακῶν ἦρξεν, ὦ ἄνδρες.
φοιτῶν γὰρ ὁ Εὐκτήμων ἐπὶ τὸ ἐνοίκιον ἑκάστοτε
τὰ πολλὰ διέτριβεν ἐν τῇ συνοικίᾳ, ἐνίοτε δὲ καὶ
ἐσιτεῖτο μετὰ τῆς ἀνθρώπου, καταλιπὼν καὶ τὴν
γυναῖκα καὶ τοὺς παῖδας καὶ τὴν οἰκίαν ἣν ᾤκει.
χαλεπῶς δὲ φερούσης τῆς γυναικὸς καὶ τῶν ὑέων
οὐχ ὅπως ἐπαύσατο, ἀλλὰ τελευτῶν παντελῶς
διῃτᾶτο ἐκεῖ, καὶ οὕτω διετέθη εἴθ' ὑπὸ φαρμάκων εἴθ' ὑπὸ νόσου εἴθ' ὑπ' ἄλλου τινός, ὥστε
ἐπείσθη ὑπ' αὐτῆς τὸν πρεσβύτερον τοῖν παίδοιν εἰσαγαγεῖν εἰς τοὺς φράτορας ἐπὶ τῷ αὐτοῦ ὀνόματι.
22 ἐπειδὴ δὲ οὔθ' ὁ υἱὸς[1] αὐτῷ Φιλοκτήμων συνεχώρει
οὔθ' οἱ φράτορες εἰσεδέξαντο, ἀλλ' ἀπηνέχθη τὸ
κούρειον,[2] ὀργιζόμενος ὁ Εὐκτήμων τῷ ὑεῖ καὶ
ἐπηρεάζειν βουλόμενος ἐγγυᾶται γυναῖκα Δημο-
κράτους τοῦ Ἀφιδναίου[3] ἀδελφήν, ὡς ἐκ ταύτης
παῖδας ἀποφανῶν καὶ εἰσποιήσων εἰς τὸν οἶκον, εἰ
23 μὴ συγχωροίη τοῦτον ἐᾶν εἰσαχθῆναι. εἰδότες δ'
οἱ ἀναγκαῖοι ὅτι ἐξ ἐκείνου μὲν οὐκ ἂν ἔτι γένοιντο
παῖδες ταύτην τὴν ἡλικίαν ἔχοντος, φανήσοιντο δ'
ἄλλῳ τινὶ τρόπῳ, καὶ ἐκ τούτων ἔσοιντο ἔτι μείζους
διαφοραί, ἔπειθον, ὦ ἄνδρες, τὸν Φιλοκτήμονα
ἐᾶσαι εἰσαγαγεῖν τοῦτον τὸν παῖδα ἐφ' οἷς ἐζήτει
24 ὁ Εὐκτήμων, χωρίον ἓν δόντα. καὶ ὁ Φιλοκτήμων
αἰσχυνόμενος μὲν ἐπὶ τῇ τοῦ πατρὸς ἀνοίᾳ, ἀπορῶν
δ' ὅ τι χρήσαιτο τῷ παρόντι κακῷ, οὐκ ἀντ-
έλεγεν οὐδέν. ὁμολογηθέντων δὲ τούτων, καὶ εἰσ-
αχθέντος τοῦ παιδὸς ἐπὶ τούτοις, ἀπηλλάγη τῆς

---

[1] ὁ υἱὸς Bekker: οὗτος.　　[2] κούρειον Reiske: κούριον.
[3] Ἀφιδναίου Stephanus: ἀφνιδαίου.

establishment there, gentlemen, had many evil consequences. Euctemon, going there constantly to collect the rent, used to spend most of his time in the tenement-house, and sometimes took his meals with the woman, leaving his wife and children and his own home. In spite of the protests of his wife and sons, not only did he not cease to go there but eventually lived there entirely, and was reduced to such a condition by drugs or disease or some other cause, that he was persuaded by the woman to introduce the elder of the two boys to the members of his ward under his own name. When, however, his son Philoctemon refused to agree to this, and the members of the ward would not admit the boy, and the victim for the sacrifice of admission was removed from the altar,[a] Euctemon, being enraged against his son and wishing to insult him, announced his intention of marrying a sister of Democrates of Aphidna and recognizing any children who should be born to her and bringing them into the family, unless he consented to allow Alce's son to be introduced. His relatives, knowing that no more children would be born to him at his time of life but that they would be forthcoming in some other manner, and that, as a result, still more serious quarrels would arise, advised Philoctemon, gentlemen, to allow him to introduce this child on the conditions which he demanded, giving him a single farm. And Philoctemon, ashamed at his father's folly but at a loss how to deal with the embarrassment of the moment, made no objection. An agreement having been thus concluded, and the child having been intro-

---

[a] Apparently the effect of this action would be to defer the question of admission till a later meeting of the wardsmen.

γυναικὸς ὁ Εὐκτήμων, καὶ ἐπεδείξατο ὅτι οὐ
παίδων ἕνεκα ἐγάμει, ἀλλ᾽ ἵνα τοῦτον εἰσαγάγοι.
25 τί γὰρ ἔδει αὐτὸν γαμεῖν, ὦ ᾽Ανδρόκλεις, εἴ περ
οἵδε ἦσαν ἐξ αὐτοῦ[1] καὶ γυναικὸς ἀστῆς, ὡς σὺ
μεμαρτύρηκας; τίς γὰρ ἂν γνησίους ὄντας οἷός τε
ἦν κωλῦσαι εἰσαγαγεῖν; ἢ διὰ τί ἐπὶ ῥητοῖς αὐτὸν
εἰσήγαγε, τοῦ νόμου κελεύοντος ἅπαντας τοὺς
26 γνησίους ἰσομοίρους εἶναι τῶν πατρῴων; ἢ διὰ
τί τὸν μὲν πρεσβύτερον τοῖν παίδοιν ἐπὶ ῥητοῖς
εἰσήγαγε, τοῦ δὲ νεωτέρου ἤδη γεγονότος οὐδὲ
[59] λόγον ἐποιεῖτο ζῶντος | Φιλοκτήμονος οὔτε πρὸς
αὐτὸν ἐκεῖνον οὔτε πρὸς τοὺς οἰκείους; οὓς σὺ
νῦν διαρρήδην μεμαρτύρηκας γνησίους εἶναι καὶ
κληρονόμους τῶν Εὐκτήμονος. ταῦτα τοίνυν ὡς
ἀληθῆ λέγω, ἀναγίγνωσκε τὰς μαρτυρίας.

MAPTYPIAI

27 Μετὰ ταῦτα τοίνυν ὁ Φιλοκτήμων τριηραρχῶν
περὶ Χίον ἀποθνήσκει ὑπὸ τῶν πολεμίων· ὁ δ᾽ Εὐκτήμων ὕστερον χρόνῳ πρὸς τοὺς κηδεστὰς εἶπεν
ὅτι βούλοιτο τὰ πρὸς τὸν υἱόν οἱ πεπραγμένα
γράψας καταθέσθαι. καὶ ὁ μὲν Φανόστρατος ἐκπλεῖν ἔμελλε τριηραρχῶν μετὰ Τιμοθέου, καὶ ἡ
ναῦς αὐτῷ ἐξώρμει Μουνυχίασι,[2] καὶ ὁ κηδεστὴς
Χαιρέας παρὼν συναπέστελλεν αὐτόν· ὁ δ᾽ Εὐ-

---

[1] αὐτοῦ Bekker : ἀστοῦ.
[2] Μουνυχίασι Bekker : μουνυχιάει.

---

[a] See Introduction, p. 197.
[b] This expedition under Timotheus probably took place
in 375 or 373 B.C.

duced on these terms, Euctemon gave up his project of marriage, proving thereby that the object of his threatened marriage was not to procure children but to obtain the introduction of this child into the ward. For what need had he to marry, Androcles, if these children had been born to him from a marriage with an Athenian citizen, as you have affirmed them to have been in your evidence ? If they were legitimate, who could prevent him from introducing them ? And why did he introduce them on special terms, when the law ordains that all the legitimate sons have an equal right to share in their father's property ? And why did he introduce the elder of the two children on special terms, but said not a word about the younger, though already born, during the lifetime of Philoctemon either to Philoctemon or to his other relatives ? Yet you have explicitly borne witness that they are legitimate and heirs to the property of Euctemon. In proof of the truth of these assertions, read the depositions.

DEPOSITIONS

It was after this, then, that Philoctemon died by the enemy's hands while commanding a trireme off Chios.[a] Some time later Euctemon informed his sons-in-law that he wished to make a written record of his arrangement with his son and place it in safe keeping. Phanostratus was on the point of setting out with Timotheus [b] in command of a trireme, and his ship lying at anchor at Munychia,[c] and his brother-in-law Chaereas was there bidding him farewell. Euctemon, taking certain persons with

[c] A small harbour on the east of the Peiraic peninsula in which part of the Athenian navy was docked.

κτήμων παραλαβών τινας ἧκεν οὗ ἐξώρμει ἡ ναῦς,
καὶ γράψας διαθήκην, ἐφ' οἷς εἰσήγαγε τὸν παῖδα,
κατατίθεται μετὰ τούτων παρὰ Πυθοδώρῳ Κηφι-
28 σιεῖ, προσήκοντι αὐτῷ. καὶ ὅτι μέν, ὦ ἄνδρες,
οὐχ ὡς περὶ γνησίων ἔπραττεν Εὐκτήμων, ὁ[1]
Ἀνδροκλῆς μεμαρτύρηκε, καὶ αὐτὸ τοῦτο ἱκανὸν
τεκμήριον· τοῖς γὰρ φύσει ὑέσιν αὐτοῦ οὐδεὶς
οὐδενός[2] ἐν διαθήκῃ γράφει δόσιν οὐδεμίαν, διότι ὁ
νόμος αὐτὸς ἀποδίδωσι τῷ ὑεῖ τὰ τοῦ πατρὸς καὶ
οὐδὲ διαθέσθαι ἐᾷ ὅτῳ ἂν ὦσι παῖδες γνήσιοι.

29   Κειμένου δὲ τοῦ γραμματείου σχεδὸν δύ' ἔτη καὶ
τοῦ Χαιρέου τετελευτηκότος, ὑποπεπτωκότες οἵδε
τῇ ἀνθρώπῳ, καὶ ὁρῶντες ἀπολλύμενον τὸν οἶκον
καὶ τὸ γῆρας καὶ τὴν ἄνοιαν τοῦ Εὐκτήμονος, ὅτι
30 εἴη αὐτοῖς ἱκανὴ ἀφορμή, συνεπιτίθενται. καὶ
πρῶτον μὲν πείθουσι τὸν Εὐκτήμονα τὴν μὲν
διαθήκην ἀνελεῖν ὡς οὐ χρησίμην οὖσαν τοῖς
παισί· τῆς γὰρ φανερᾶς οὐσίας οὐδένα κύριον
ἔσεσθαι τελευτήσαντος Εὐκτήμονος ἄλλον ἢ τὰς
θυγατέρας καὶ τοὺς ἐκ τούτων γεγονότας· εἰ δὲ
ἀποδόμενός τι τῶν ὄντων ἀργύριον καταλίποι,
31 τοῦτο βεβαίως ἕξειν αὐτούς. ἀκούσας δ' ὁ Εὐκτήμων εὐθὺς ἀπῄτει τὸν Πυθόδωρον τὸ γραμματεῖον, καὶ προσεκαλέσατο εἰς ἐμφανῶν κατά-
στασιν. καταστάντος δὲ ἐκείνου πρὸς τὸν ἄρχοντα, ἔλεγεν ὅτι βούλοιτ' ἀνελέσθαι τὴν διαθήκην.
32 ἐπειδὴ δ' ὁ Πυθόδωρος ἐκείνῳ μὲν καὶ τῷ Φανοστράτῳ παρόντι ὡμολόγει ἀναιρεῖν, τοῦ δὲ Χαιρέου

---

[1] ὁ Bekker: ὃ.   [2] οὐδενὸς Dobree: οὐδενί.

him, came to where the ship was anchored, and
having drawn up a document detailing the conditions under which he introduced the child, deposited
it in the presence of those men with his relative
Pythodorus of Cephisia. The very fact that he
acted thus is a sufficient proof, gentlemen, that
Euctemon was not dealing with them as legitimate
children, as Androcles has declared in his evidence ;
for no one ever makes a gift by will of anything
to the sons of his own body, because the law of
itself gives his father's estate to the son and does
not even allow anyone who has legitimate children
to dispose of his property.

When the document had remained deposited for
almost two years and Chaereas had died, my
opponents, having come under the influence of Alce
and seeing that the property was going to ruin and
that the old age and imbecility of Euctemon gave
them an excellent opportunity, made a combined plan
of attack. They first urged Euctemon to cancel the
will on the ground that it was not to the boys'
advantage ; for no one would have any claim to
the real estate on Euctemon's death except the
daughters and their issue ; whereas, if he sold part
of the property and left it in cash, they would get
secure possession of it. Euctemon listened to them
and immediately demanded the document back
from Pythodorus and served upon him a summons
to produce it. When Pythodorus appeared before
the archon, Euctemon stated that he wished to
annul the will. Pythodorus was prepared to agree
with Euctemon and Phanostratus, who was present,
that the document should be destroyed ; but, as
Chaereas, who had been a party to its deposition,

τοῦ συγκαταθεμένου θυγάτηρ ἦν μία, ἧς ἐπειδὴ
κύριος κατασταίη, τότε ἠξίου ἀνελεῖν, καὶ ὁ ἄρχων
οὕτως ἐγίγνωσκε, διομολογησάμενος ὁ Εὐκτήμων
ἐναντίον τοῦ ἄρχοντος καὶ τῶν παρέδρων καὶ
ποιησάμενος πολλοὺς μάρτυρας ὡς οὐκέτ' αὐτῷ
33 κέοιτο ἡ διαθήκη, ᾤχετο ἀπιών. καὶ ἐν πάνυ
ὀλίγῳ χρόνῳ, οὗπερ ἕνεκα οὗτοι λῦσαι αὐτὸν
ἔπεισαν, ἀποδίδοται[1] ἀγρὸν μὲν Ἀθμονοῖ πέντε
καὶ ἑβδομήκοντα μνῶν Ἀντιφάνει, τὸ δ' ἐν Σηραγ-
γίῳ βαλανεῖον τρισχιλίων Ἀριστολόχῳ· οἰκίαν δὲ ἐν
ἄστει τεττάρων καὶ τεσσαράκοντα μνῶν ὑποκειμέ-
νην ἀπέλυσε τῷ ἱεροφάντῃ. ἔτι δὲ αἶγας ἀπέδοτο
σὺν τῷ αἰπόλῳ τριῶν καὶ δέκα μνῶν, καὶ ζεύγη
δύο ὁρικά, τὸ μὲν ὀκτὼ μνῶν τὸ δὲ πεντήκοντα
καὶ πεντακοσίων δραχμῶν, καὶ δημιουργοὺς ὅσοι
34 ἦσαν αὐτῷ. σύμπαντα δὲ πλείονος ἢ τριῶν ταλάντων, ἃ ἐπράθη διὰ ταχέων πάνυ τελευτήσαντος
Φιλοκτήμονος. καὶ ταῦθ' ὅτι ἀληθῆ λέγω, καθ'
ἕκαστον ὑμῖν τῶν εἰρημένων πρῶτον καλῶ τοὺς
μάρτυρας.

⟨ΜΑΡΤΥΡΕΣ⟩

35 Ταῦτα μὲν δὴ τοῦτον τὸν τρόπον εἶχε· περὶ δὲ
τῶν ὑπολοίπων εὐθὺς ἐπεβούλευον, καὶ πάντων
δεινότατον πρᾶγμα κατεσκεύασαν, ᾧ ἄξιόν ἐστι
προσέχειν τὸν νοῦν. ὁρῶντες γὰρ τὸν Εὐκτήμονα

---

[1] ἀποδίδοται Stephanus : -ονται.

---

[a] The site of this place was near the modern *Marusi*,
about seven miles north-east of Athens (see Frazer on Paus.
i. 31. 4).

[b] The site of these baths has been discovered below the
eastern end of the hill on Munychia on the Peiraic peninsula.

had left an only daughter, he suggested that it should be destroyed only after appointment of her legal representative, and the archon decided in favour of this course. Euctemon, after agreeing to this in the presence of the archon and his assessors, called many persons to witness that the will deposited by him no longer existed and then went his way. In a very short time—and this was the object of their advice to Euctemon to annul the will—he sold a farm at Athmonon *a* to Antiphanes for seventy-five minas and the bath-house at Serangion *b* to Aristolochus for 3000 drachmas ; and he realized a mortgage of forty-four minas on a house in Athens from the hierophant.*c* Further, he sold some goats with their goat-herd for thirteen minas, and two pairs of mules, one for eight minas and the other for five hundred and fifty drachmas, and all the slaves he had that were craftsmen. In all, the value of the property which he hurriedly sold after Philoctemon's death, was more than three talents. And to prove that I am speaking the truth, I will first call witnesses in support of each of my statements.

WITNESSES

So much for these transactions. They then immediately began scheming to obtain the rest of the property and planned the most outrageous plot of all, which merits your careful attention. Seeing

They consisted of a subterranean chamber with openings in different directions through the cliff (see Frazer's *Paus.* v. p. 477).
c The official who displayed the sacred emblems at the Eleusinian mysteries ; he was a member of the house of the Eumolpidae.

κομιδῇ ἀπειρηκότα ὑπὸ γήρως καὶ οὐδ᾽ ⟨ἐκ⟩[1] τῆς
κλίνης ἀνίστασθαι δυνάμενον, ἐσκόπουν ὅπως καὶ
τελευτήσαντος ἐκείνου δι᾽ αὐτῶν[2] ἔσοιτο ἡ οὐσία.
36 καὶ τί ποιοῦσιν; ἀπογράφουσι τὼ παῖδε τούτω
πρὸς τὸν ἄρχοντα ὡς εἰσποιήτω τοῖς τοῦ Εὐκτήμονος υἱέσι τοῖς τετελευτηκόσιν, ἐπιγράψαντες
σφᾶς αὐτοὺς ἐπιτρόπους, καὶ μισθοῦν ἐκέλευον τὸν
ἄρχοντα τοὺς οἴκους ὡς ὀρφανῶν ὄντων, ὅπως
ἐπὶ τοῖς τούτων ὀνόμασι τὰ μὲν μισθωθείη τῆς
οὐσίας, τὰ δὲ ἀποτιμήματα κατασταθείη καὶ ὅροι
[60] | τεθεῖεν ζῶντος ἔτι τοῦ Εὐκτήμονος, μισθωταὶ
δὲ αὐτοὶ[3] γενόμενοι τὰς προσόδους λαμβάνοιεν.
37 καὶ ἐπειδὴ πρῶτον τὰ δικαστήρια ἐπληρώθη, ὁ
μὲν ἄρχων προεκήρυττεν, οἱ δ᾽ ἐμισθοῦντο. παρα-
γενόμενοι δέ τινες ἐξαγγέλλουσι τοῖς οἰκείοις τὴν
ἐπιβουλήν, καὶ ἐλθόντες ἐδήλωσαν τὸ πρᾶγμα τοῖς
δικασταῖς, καὶ οὕτως ἀπεχειροτόνησαν οἱ δικασταὶ
μὴ μισθοῦν τοὺς οἴκους· εἰ δ᾽ ἔλαθεν, ἀπωλώλει[4]
ἂν ἅπασα ἡ οὐσία. καί μοι κάλει τοὺς παραγενομένους μάρτυρας.

ΜΑΡΤΥΡΕΣ

38 Πρὶν μὲν τοίνυν τούτους γνωρίσαι τὴν ἄνθρωπον καὶ μετ᾽ ἐκείνης ἐπιβουλεῦσαι Εὐκτήμονι,
οὕτω πολλὴν οὐσίαν ἐκέκτητο Εὐκτήμων μετὰ
τοῦ υἱέος Φιλοκτήμονος, ὥστε ἅμα τά τε[5] μέγιστα
ὑμῖν λῃτουργεῖν ἀμφοτέρους τῶν τε ἀρχαίων μηδὲν
πραθῆναι τῶν τε προσόδων περιποιεῖν, ὥστε ἀεί

---

[1] οὐδ᾽ ἐκ Dobree: οὐδέ.
[2] αὐτῶν Baiter-Sauppe: αὑτῶν.
[3] δὲ αὐτοὶ Meutzner: δι᾽ αὐτοῦ.
[4] ἀπωλώλει Scheibe: ἀπο-.   [5] τά τε Fuhr: τε τὰ.

that Euctemon was completely incapacitated by old age and could not even leave his bed, they began to look about for a means whereby all his property should be under their control after his death. And what did they do? They inscribed these two boys before the archon as adopted children of the sons of Euctemon who had died,[a] inscribing themselves as guardians, and requested the archon to grant a lease of the house-property as being the property of orphans, in order that part of the property might be leased and part might be used as a security, and mortgage notices adfixed to it in the children's names during the lifetime of Euctemon, and they themselves might become lessees and receive the income. On the first day that the courts met, the archon put the lease up for auction and they offered to lease the property. Certain persons, however, who were present, denounced the plot to the relatives, and they came and informed the judges of the real state of affairs. The result was that the judges voted against allowing the houses to be leased. If the plot had not been detected, the whole property would have been lost. Please call as witnesses those who were present.

WITNESSES

Before my opponents had made the woman's acquaintance and plotted with her against Euctemon, he and his son Philoctemon possessed so large a fortune that both of them were able to undertake the most costly public offices without realizing any of their capital, and at the same time to save out of their income, so that they continually grew richer.

---

[a] Philoctemon and Ergamenes (cf. § 44).

τι προσκτᾶσθαι· ἐπειδὴ δ' ἐτελεύτησε Φιλοκτήμων,
οὕτω διετέθη ἡ οὐσία, ὥστε τῶν ἀρχαίων μηδὲ τὰ
ἡμίσεα εἶναι λοιπὰ καὶ τὰς προσόδους ἁπάσας
39 ἠφανίσθαι. καὶ οὐδὲ ταῦτα ἐξήρκεσεν αὐτοῖς δια-
φορῆσαι, ὦ ἄνδρες, ἀλλ' ἐπειδὴ καὶ ἐτελεύτησεν
ὁ Εὐκτήμων, εἰς τοῦτο ἦλθον τόλμης ὥστ' ἐκείνου
κειμένου ἔνδον τοὺς μὲν οἰκέτας ἐφύλαττον, ὅπως
μηδεὶς ἐξαγγείλειε μήτε τοῖν¹ θυγατέροιν μήτε τῇ
γυναικὶ αὐτοῦ μήτε τῶν οἰκείων μηδενί, τὰ δὲ
χρήματα ἔνδοθεν ἐξεφορήσαντο μετὰ τῆς ἀνθρώπου
εἰς τὴν ὁμότοιχον οἰκίαν, ἣν ᾤκει μεμισθωμένος
40 εἰς τούτων, Ἀντίδωρος ἐκεῖνος. καὶ οὐδ' ἐπειδὴ
ἑτέρων πυθόμεναι ἦλθον αἱ θυγατέρες αὐτοῦ καὶ
ἡ γυνή, οὐδὲ τότε εἴων² εἰσιέναι, ἀλλ' ἀπέκλεισαν
τῇ θύρᾳ,³ φάσκοντες οὐ προσήκειν αὐταῖς θάπτειν
Εὐκτήμονα· καὶ οὐδ' εἰσελθεῖν ἐδύναντο, εἰ μὴ
41 μόλις καὶ περὶ ἡλίου δυσμάς. εἰσελθοῦσαι δὲ
κατέλαβον ἐκεῖνον μὲν ἔνδον κείμενον δευτεραῖον,
ὡς ἔφασαν οἱ οἰκέται, τὰ δ' ἐκ τῆς οἰκίας ἅπαντα
ἐκπεφορημένα ὑπὸ τούτων. αἱ μὲν οὖν γυναῖκες,
οἷον εἰκός, περὶ τὸν τετελευτηκότα ἦσαν· οὗτοι
δὲ τοῖς ἀκολουθήσασι παραχρῆμα ἐπεδείκνυσαν τὰ
ἔνδον ὡς εἶχε, καὶ τοὺς οἰκέτας πρῶτον ἠρώτων
ἐναντίον τούτων ὅποι⁴ τετραμμένα εἴη τὰ χρήματα.
42 λεγόντων δὲ ἐκείνων ὅτι οὗτοι ἐξενηνοχότες εἶεν
εἰς τὴν πλησίον οἰκίαν, καὶ ἀξιούντων παραχρῆμα
τῶνδε φωρᾶν⁵ κατὰ τὸν νόμον καὶ τοὺς οἰκέτας
ἐξαιτούντων τοὺς ἐκφορήσαντας, οὐκ ἠθέλησαν

---

¹ τοῖν M, Naber: ταῖν.
² εἴων Hirschig: ἠφ(ε)ίων, ε eraso.
³ τῇ θύρᾳ Dobree: τὴν θύραν.   ⁴ ὅποι Aldus: ὅπῃ (sic).
⁵ τῶνδε φωρᾶν Scaliger: τῶν δ' ἐφορᾶν.

After the death of Philoctemon, on the other hand, the property was reduced to such a condition that less than half the capital remains and all the revenues have disappeared. And they were not even content, sirs, with this misappropriation; but, when Euctemon also died, they had the impudence, while he was lying dead in the house, to shut up the slaves, so that none of them might take the news to his two daughters or to his wife or to any of his relatives. Meanwhile, with the aid of the woman they conveyed the furniture from within to the adjoining house, which was leased and occupied by one of their gang, the infamous Antidorus. When Euctemon's daughters and wife arrived, having learnt the news from others, even then they refused them admittance and shut the door in their faces, declaring that it was not their business to bury Euctemon. They only obtained admittance with difficulty about sunset. When they entered, they found that he had been dead in the house for two days, as the slaves declared, and that everything in the house had been carried off by these people. While the women, as was right, were attending to the deceased, my clients here immediately called the attention of those who had accompanied them to the state of affairs in the house, and began by asking the slaves in their presence to what place the furniture had been removed. When they replied that our opponents had conveyed it away to the next house, and my clients immediately claimed the right to search the house in the proper legal manner, and requested that the slaves who had removed it should be produced, our opponents refused to accede to any of

τῶν δικαίων οὐδὲν ποιῆσαι. καὶ ὅτι ἀληθῆ λέγω,
λαβὲ ταυτὶ καὶ ἀνάγνωθι.

⟨ΜΑΡΤΥΡΙΑΙ⟩

43 Τοσαῦτα μὲν τοίνυν χρήματα ἐκ τῆς οἰκίας ἐκ-
φορήσαντες, τοσαύτης δ' οὐσίας πεπραμένης τὴν
τιμὴν ἔχοντες, ἔτι δὲ τὰς προσόδους τὰς ἐν ἐκείνῳ
τῷ χρόνῳ γενομένας διαφορήσαντες, οἴονται καὶ
τῶν λοιπῶν κύριοι γενήσεσθαι· καὶ εἰς τοῦτο
ἀναιδείας ἥκουσιν, ὥστ' εὐθυδικίᾳ μὲν οὐκ ἐτόλμησαν εἰσελθεῖν, ἀλλὰ διεμαρτύρουν ὡς ὑπὲρ γνησίων ἅμα μὲν τὰ ψευδῆ ἅμα δὲ τἀναντία οἷς
44 αὐτοὶ ἔπραξαν· οἵτινες πρὸς μὲν τὸν ἄρχοντα ἀπ-
έγραψαν αὐτοὺς ὡς ὄντας τὸν μὲν Φιλοκτήμονος
τὸν δ' Ἐργαμένους, νῦν δὲ διαμεμαρτυρήκασιν
Εὐκτήμονος εἶναι. καίτοι οὐδ' εἰ γνήσιοι ἦσαν, εἰσποίητοι δέ, ὡς οὗτοι ἔφασαν, οὐδ' οὕτω προσήκει[1]
αὐτοὺς Εὐκτήμονος εἶναι· ὁ γὰρ νόμος οὐκ ἐᾷ
ἐπανιέναι, ἐὰν μὴ ὑὸν καταλίπῃ γνήσιον. ὥστε
καὶ ἐξ ὧν αὐτοὶ ἔπραξαν ἀνάγκη τὴν μαρτυ-
45 ρίαν ψευδῆ εἶναι. καὶ εἰ μὲν τότε διεπράξαντο[2]
μισθωθῆναι τοὺς οἴκους, οὐκ ἂν ἔτι ἦν τοῖσδε
ἀμφισβητῆσαι· νῦν δὲ ἀποχειροτονησάντων τῶν
δικαστῶν ὡς οὐδὲν αὐτοῖς προσῆκον,[3] οὐδὲ ἀμφισβητῆσαι τετολμήκασιν, ἀλλὰ πρὸς ὑπερβολὴν ἀναισχυντίας προσμεμαρτυρήκασι τουτους εἶναι κληρονόμους, οὓς ὑμεῖς ἀπεχειροτονήσατε.

46 Ἔτι δὲ καὶ τοῦ μάρτυρος αὐτοῦ σκέψασθε τὴν

---

[1] προσήκει scripsi: -ῆκεν.
[2] διεπράξαντο Reiske: -ατο.
[3] προσῆκον Dobree: -ῆκεν.

---

[a] i.e., by Philoctemon and Ergamenes.

their just demands. And to prove that I am speaking the truth, take and read these documents.

DEPOSITIONS

Having removed all this furniture from the house, and sold so much property and kept the proceeds, and having further made away with the revenue which accrued during that period, they yet expect to obtain possession of what remains ; and their impudence is such that, not daring to bring a direct action, they lodged a protestation—as though it were a question of legitimate children—which is at once false and in contradiction to their own previous action. For, whereas they had inscribed the children before the archon, one as the son of Philoctemon and the other as the son of Ergamenes, they have now stated in their protestation that they are the sons of Euctemon. Yet if they were Euctemon's legitimate sons and had afterwards been adopted,[a] as our opponent states, even so they cannot be described as the sons of Euctemon : for the law does not allow the return of an adopted son to his original family, unless he leaves a legitimate son in the family which he quits. So that in view even of their own acts their evidence is necessarily untrue. If our opponents had then so contrived that the houses were leased, my clients would no longer have been able to claim them ; but, as it is, since the judges decided against them as having no right, they have not dared to put in a claim, but, to put the finishing touch to their impudence, they have submitted additional evidence to the effect that these young men, whom you excluded by your verdict, are heirs.

Further, mark the effrontery and impudence of

τόλμαν καὶ ἀναίδειαν, ὅστις εἴληχε μὲν αὐτῷ τῆς
θυγατρὸς τῆς Εὐκτήμονος ὡς οὔσης ἐπικλήρου,
καὶ αὐτοῦ τοῦ κλήρου τοῦ Εὐκτήμονος πέμπτου |
[61] μέρους ὡς ἐπιδίκου ὄντος, μεμαρτύρηκε δ' Εὐκτήμονος υἱὸν εἶναι γνήσιον. καίτοι πῶς οὗτος
οὐ σαφῶς ἐξελέγχει αὐτὸς αὑτὸν τὰ ψευδῆ μεμαρτυρηκότα; οὐ γὰρ δήπου γνησίου ὄντος υἱέος
Εὐκτήμονι ἐπίκληρος ἂν ἦν ἡ θυγάτηρ αὐτοῦ,
οὐδὲ ὁ κλῆρος ἐπίδικος. ὡς τοίνυν ἔλαχε ταύτας
τὰς λήξεις, ἀναγνώσεται ὑμῖν τὰς μαρτυρίας.

<MAPTTPIAI>

47 Τοὐναντίον τοίνυν συμβέβηκεν ἢ ὡς ὁ νόμος γέ-
γραπται· ἐκεῖ μὲν γάρ ἐστι νόθῳ μηδὲ νόθῃ <μὴ>[1]
εἶναι ἀγχιστείαν μήθ' ἱερῶν μήθ' ὁσίων ἀπ' Εὐ-
κλείδου ἄρχοντος, Ἀνδροκλῆς[2] δὲ καὶ Ἀντίδωρος
οἴονται δεῖν, ἀφελόμενοι τὰς Εὐκτήμονος θυγατέρας τὰς γνησίας καὶ τοὺς ἐκ τούτων γεγονότας,
τόν τε Εὐκτήμονος οἶκον καὶ τὸν Φιλοκτήμονος
48 ἔχειν. καὶ ἡ διαφθείρασα τὴν Εὐκτήμονος γνώμην
καὶ πολλῶν ἐγκρατὴς γενομένη οὕτως ὑβρίζει
σφόδρα πιστεύουσα τούτοις, ὥστε οὐ μόνον τῶν
Εὐκτήμονος οἰκείων καταφρονεῖ, ἀλλὰ καὶ τῆς
πόλεως ἁπάσης. ἀκούσαντες δὲ ἓν μόνον σημεῖον
ῥᾳδίως γνώσεσθε τὴν ἐκείνης παρανομίαν. καί
μοι λαβὲ τοῦτον τὸν νόμον.

<NOMOΣ>

[1] μὴ add. Sauppe.   [2] Ἀνδροκλῆς Schoemann : -κλείδης.

[a] Namely, the widow of Chaeres, cf. § 51.
[b] The words πέμπτου μέρους are certainly corrupt : there
is no reason in law why a fifth part should have been claimed.
No satisfactory emendation has been proposed.

230

the witness himself, who has claimed for himself
Euctemon's daughter [a] as being an heiress and a
fifth [b] of Euctemon's estate itself as being adjudicable,
while he has given evidence that Euctemon has a
legitimate son. In doing so does he not clearly
convict himself of having given false evidence?
For obviously, if Euctemon had a legitimate son,
his daughter could not be heiress or the estate
adjudicable. To prove, then, that he made these
claims, the clerk shall read you the depositions.

DEPOSITIONS

Thus the contrary has been done of that which
the law has prescribed; for according to the law
no male or female bastard has any right, based on
kinship, to participate in the cults or property of
a family since the archonship of Eucleides [c]; yet
Androcles and Antidorus consider themselves entitled
to rob the legitimate daughters of Euctemon and
their issue, and to possess the property both of
Euctemon and of Philoctemon. And the woman
who destroyed Euctemon's reason and laid hold of
so much property is so insolent, that relying on the
help of our opponents, she shows her contempt not
only for the members of Euctemon's family but for
the whole city. When you have heard a single
instance, you will easily realize the lawlessness of
her conduct. Please take and read this law.

LAW [d]

[c] 403–402 B.C.
[d] The law here cited must have been that which excluded
slaves and women of immoral life from participating in the
festival of the Thesmophoria celebrated in honour of Demeter
and Persephone (cf. iii. 80).

49 Ταυτὶ τὰ γράμματα, ὦ ἄνδρες, ὑμεῖς οὕτω
σεμνὰ καὶ εὐσεβῆ ἐνομοθετήσατε, περὶ πολλοῦ
ποιούμενοι καὶ πρὸς ταύτας[1] καὶ πρὸς τοὺς ἄλλους
θεοὺς εὐσεβεῖν· ἡ δὲ τούτων μήτηρ, οὕτως ὁμολογουμένως[2] οὖσα δούλη καὶ ἅπαντα τὸν χρόνον
50 αἰσχρῶς βιοῦσα, ἣν οὔτε[3] παρελθεῖν εἴσω τοῦ
ἱεροῦ ἔδει οὔτ᾽[4] ἰδεῖν τῶν ἔνδον οὐδέν, οὔσης τῆς
θυσίας ταύταις ταῖς θεαῖς ἐτόλμησε συμπέμψαι
τὴν πομπὴν καὶ εἰσελθεῖν εἰς τὸ ἱερὸν καὶ ἰδεῖν ἃ
οὐκ ἐξῆν[5] αὐτῇ. ὡς δὲ ἀληθῆ λέγω, ἐκ τῶν
ψηφισμάτων γνώσεσθε ἃ ἐψηφίσατο ἡ βουλὴ περὶ
αὐτῆς. λαβὲ τὸ ψήφισμα.

ΨΗΦΙΣΜΑ

51 Ἐνθυμεῖσθαι τοίνυν χρή, ὦ ἄνδρες, πότερον δεῖ
τὸν ἐκ ταύτης τῶν Φιλοκτήμονος εἶναι κληρονόμον
καὶ ἐπὶ τὰ μνήματα ἰέναι χεόμενον καὶ ἐναγιοῦντα,
ἢ τὸν ἐκ τῆς ἀδελφῆς τούτον, ὃν ὑὸν αὐτὸς ἐποιή-
σατο· καὶ πότερον δεῖ τὴν ἀδελφὴν Φιλοκτήμονος,
ἢ Χαιρέᾳ συνῴκησε, νῦν δὲ χηρεύει, ἐπὶ τούτοις
γενέσθαι ἢ ἐκδοῦναι ὅτῳ βούλονται ἢ ἐᾶν κατα-
γηράσκειν, ἢ γνησίαν οὖσαν ὑφ᾽ ὑμῶν ἐπι-
52 δικασθεῖσαν συνοικεῖν ὅτῳ ἂν ὑμῖν δοκῇ. ἡ γὰρ
ψῆφός ἐστι περὶ τούτων νυνί. τουτὶ γὰρ αὐτοῖς ἡ
διαμαρτυρία δύναται, ἵν᾽ ὁ κίνδυνος τοῖσδε μὲν ᾖ
περὶ πάντων,[6] οὗτοι δὲ κἂν νῦν διαμάρτωσι τοῦ
ἀγῶνος, δόξῃ δὲ ὁ κλῆρος ἐπίδικος εἶναι, ἀντι-
γραψάμενοι δὶς περὶ τῶν αὐτῶν ἀγωνίζωνται.

---

[1] ταύτας Reiske: ταῦτα.
[2] ὁμολογουμένως Dobree: -η.
[3] οὔτε Bekker: οὐδέ.
[4] οὔτ᾽ Bekker: οὐδ᾽.
[5] ἐξῆν Bekker: ἐξὸν.
[6] πάντων Naber: τούτων.

Such are the solemn and pious terms in which you gave legal expression to the importance which you attach to piety towards these goddesses and all the other deities. Yet the mother of these young men, being admittedly a slave, and having always lived a scandalous life, who ought never to have entered the temple and seen any of the rites performed there, had the effrontery to join in the procession when a sacrifice was being made in honour of these goddesses and to enter the temple and see what she had no right to see. That I am speaking the truth you will learn from the decrees which the Council passed concerning her. Take this decree.

DECREE

You have, therefore, gentlemen, to consider whether this woman's son ought to be heir to Philoctemon's property and go to the family tombs to offer libations and sacrifices, or my client, Philoctemon's sister's son, whom he himself adopted ; and whether Philoctemon's sister, formerly the wife of Chaereas and now a widow, ought to pass into the power of our opponents and be married to anyone they choose or else be allowed to grow old in widowhood, or whether, as a legitimate daughter, she ought to be subject to your decision as to whom she ought to marry. These are the points which you have now to decide by your verdict ; for the purpose of their protestation is to throw all the risk upon my clients, and that our opponents, even if they lose their case on this occasion and the estate is held to be adjudicable, may, by bringing forward a competing claim, fight a second action about the

καίτοι εἰ μὲν διέθετο Φιλοκτήμων μὴ ἐξὸν αὐτῷ, τοῦτ' αὐτὸ ἐχρῆν διαμαρτυρεῖν, ὡς οὐ κύριος ἦν ὑὸν τόνδε ποιήσασθαι· εἰ δ' ἔξεστι μὲν διαθέσθαι, ἀμφισβητεῖ δὲ ὡς οὐ δόντος οὐδὲ διαθεμένου, μὴ 53 διαμαρτυρίᾳ κωλύειν ἀλλ' εὐθυδικίᾳ εἰσιέναι. νῦν δὲ πῶς ἂν [τις] περιφανέστερον ἐξελεγχθείη τὰ ψευδῆ μεμαρτυρηκὼς ἢ εἴ τις αὐτὸν ἔροιτο '' Ἀνδρόκλεις, πῶς οἶσθα Φιλοκτήμον'[1] ὅτι οὔτε διέθετο οὔτε ὑὸν Χαιρέστρατον ἐποιήσατο; '' οἷς μὲν γάρ τις παρεγένετο, δίκαιον, ὦ ἄνδρες, μαρτυρεῖν, οἷς δὲ μὴ παρεγένετο ἀλλ' ἤκουσέ τινος, ἀκοὴν μαρτυ-54 ρεῖν· σὺ δ' οὐ παραγενόμενος διαρρήδην μεμαρτύρηκας ὡς οὐ διέθετο Φιλοκτήμων, ἀλλ' ἄπαις ἐτελεύτησε. καίτοι πῶς οἷόν τε εἰδέναι, ὦ ἄνδρες; ὅμοιον γὰρ ὥσπερ ἂν εἰ φαίη εἰδέναι, καὶ μὴ παραγενόμενος, ὅσα ὑμεῖς πάντες πράττετε. οὐ γὰρ δὴ τοῦτό γε ἐρεῖ, καίπερ ἀναίσχυντος ὤν, ὡς ἅπασι παρεγένετο καὶ πάντ' οἶδεν ὅσα Φιλοκτήμων 55 ἐν τῷ βίῳ διεπράξατο. πάντων γὰρ αὐτὸν ἐκεῖνος ἔχθιστον ἐνόμιζε διά ⟨τε⟩[2] τὴν ἄλλην πονηρίαν, καὶ διότι τῶν συγγενῶν μόνος μετὰ τῆς Ἀλκῆς ἐκείνης τούτῳ καὶ τοῖς ἄλλοις συνεπιβουλεύσας τοῖς τοῦ Εὐκτήμονος χρήμασι τοιαῦτα διεπράξατο, οἷά περ ὑμῖν ἀπέδειξα.

56 Πάντων δὲ μάλιστα ἀγανακτῆσαί ἐστιν ἄξιον, ὅταν οὗτοι καταχρῶνται τῷ Εὐκτήμονος ὀνόματι

---

[1] Φιλοκτήμον' Dobree: -μων. [2] τε add. Aldus.

---

[a] i.e., Antidorus.

234

same property. Yet if Philoctemon disposed of his property by will when he was not entitled to do so, the point against which they ought to have protested is that he was not legally capable of adopting my client as his son ; but if is lawful to make a will, and our opponent claims on the ground that Philoctemon made no donation or will, he ought not to have hindered proceedings by a protestation, but to have proceeded by means of a direct action. As it is, what clearer method is there of convicting him of perjury than by putting the following question to him : " How do you know, Androcles, that Philoctemon neither made a will nor adopted Chaerestratus as his son ? " For when a man has been present, gentlemen, it is just that he should give evidence of what he has seen, and when he has not been present but has heard someone else describe what happened, he can give evidence by hearsay ; but you, though you were not present, have given explicit evidence that Philoctemon made no will and died childless. How, gentlemen, can he possibly know this ? It is as though he were to say, not having been present, that he knows about all the acts of you all. Impudent as he is, he will scarcely assert that he was present at and is acquainted with all the acts of Philoctemon's life ; for Philoctemon regarded him as his bitterest enemy, both because of his general bad character, and because he was the only one of his kinsmen who, in league with the infamous Alce, plotted with this friend of his *a* and his other accomplices against the property of Euctemon, and committed the acts which I have described to you.

But what calls for the greatest indignation is the wicked use which our opponents make of the name

τοῦ τουδὶ πάππου.[1] εἰ γάρ, ὡς οὗτοι λέγουσι,
τῷ μὲν Φιλοκτήμονι μὴ ἐξῆν διαθέσθαι, τοῦ δ᾽
Εὐκτήμονός ἐστιν ὁ κλῆρος, πότερον δικαιότερον
τῶν Εὐκτήμονος κληρονομεῖν τὰς ἐκείνου θυγατέ-
[62] ρας, ὁμολογουμένως οὔσας γνησίας, | καὶ ἡμᾶς τοὺς
ἐκ τούτων γεγονότας, ἢ τοὺς οὐδὲν προσήκοντας,
57 οἳ οὐ μόνον ὑφ᾽[2] ἡμῶν ἐλέγχονται, ἀλλὰ καὶ ἐξ
ὧν αὐτοὶ ἐπίτροποι διαπεπραγμένοι εἰσί; τοῦτο
γὰρ ὑμῶν δέομαι καὶ ἱκετεύω σφόδρα μεμνῆσθαι,
ὦ ἄνδρες, ὅπερ ὀλίγῳ πρότερον ἀπέδειξα ὑμῖν,
ὅτι Ἀνδροκλῆς οὑτοσὶ φησὶ[3] μὲν εἶναι ἐπίτροπος
αὐτῶν ὡς ὄντων γνησίων Εὐκτήμονος, εἴληχε δ᾽
αὐτός[4] [ἐφ᾽] ἑαυτῷ τοῦ Εὐκτήμονος κλήρου καὶ
τῆς θυγατρὸς αὐτοῦ ὡς οὔσης ἐπικλήρου· καὶ
58 ταῦτα μεμαρτύρηται ὑμῖν. καίτοι πῶς οὐ δεινόν,
ὦ ἄνδρες, πρὸς θεῶν Ὀλυμπίων, εἰ μὲν οἱ παῖδές
εἰσι γνήσιοι, τὸν ἐπίτροπον ἑαυτῷ λαγχάνειν τοῦ
Εὐκτήμονος κλήρου καὶ τῆς θυγατρὸς αὐτοῦ ὡς
οὔσης ἐπιδίκου, εἰ δὲ μή εἰσι γνήσιοι, νῦν δια-
μεμαρτυρηκέναι ὡς εἰσὶ γνήσιοι; ταῦτα γὰρ αὐτὰ
ἑαυτοῖς ἐναντία ἐστίν.[5] ὥστ᾽ οὐ μόνον ὑφ᾽ ἡμῶν
ἐλέγχεται τὰ ψευδῆ διαμεμαρτυρηκώς, ἀλλὰ καὶ
59 ἐξ ὧν αὐτὸς πράττει. καὶ τούτῳ μὲν οὐδεὶς
διαμαρτυρεῖ μὴ ἐπίδικον εἶναι τὸν κλῆρον, ἀλλ᾽
εὐθυδικίᾳ εἰσιέναι ⟨ἐξῆν⟩,[6] οὗτος δ᾽ ἅπαντας ἀπο-
στερεῖ τῆς ἀμφισβητήσεως. καὶ διαρρήδην μαρτυρήσας γνησίους τοὺς παῖδας εἶναι, οἴεται ἐξ-
αρκέσειν ὑμῖν παρεκβάσεις, ἐὰν δὲ τοῦτο μὲν μηδ᾽

---

[1] τοῦ τουδὶ πάππου Reiske: τῷ τουδὶ πάππῳ.
[2] ὑφ᾽ Bekker: ἐξ. [3] φησὶ Aldus: φήσει.
[4] αὐτὸς Reiske: αὐτοῖς.
[5] ἐστίν M, Bekker: εἰσὶν. [6] ἐξῆν add. Thalheim.

of Euctemon, my client's grandfather. For if, as they assert, Philoctemon had no right to make a will, and the estate was Euctemon's, who have a better right to inherit Euctemon's property? His daughters, who are admittedly legitimate, and we [a] who are their sons? Or men who bear no relation to him, and whose claims are refuted not only by us but also by the acts which they have themselves committed as guardians? For I beg and earnestly beseech you, gentlemen, to remember the point which I put before you a short while ago, that Androcles here declares that he is guardian of the claimants as being the legitimate sons of Euctemon, and has also himself claimed for himself the estate of Euctemon and his daughter as heiress; and evidence of this has been placed before you. By the gods of Olympus, is it not extraordinary, gentlemen, that, if the children are legitimate, their guardian should claim for himself the estate of Euctemon and his daughter as an heiress, and, if they are not legitimate, that he should have given evidence now in support of their legitimacy? For these acts are the very contrary of one another; so that he is convicted of perjury not only by us but by his own acts. No one is putting in a protestation that the estate is not adjudicable, and Androcles was at liberty to proceed by means of a direct action; now he is depriving everyone else of their right to claim. Having explicitly stated in his evidence that the children are legitimate, he thinks that you will be satisfied with rhetorical digressions, and that if he does not attempt to

[a] The speaker here associates himself with his clients.

237

ἐγχειρήσῃ ἐπιδεικνύναι ἢ καὶ κατὰ μικρόν τι
ἐπιμνησθῇ, ἡμῖν δὲ λοιδορήσηται[1] μεγάλῃ τῇ φωνῇ
καὶ λέγῃ[2] ὡς εἰσὶν οἵδε μὲν πλούσιοι αὐτὸς δὲ
πένης, διὰ δὲ ταῦτα δόξειν τοὺς παῖδας εἶναι
60 γνησίους. τῆς δὲ τούτων οὐσίας, ὦ ἄνδρες, εἰς
τὴν πόλιν πλείω ἀναλίσκεται ἢ εἰς αὐτοὺς τούτους.
καὶ Φανόστρατος μὲν τετριηράρχηκεν ἑπτάκις ἤδη,
τὰς δὲ λῃτουργίας ἁπάσας λελῃτούργηκε καὶ τὰς
πλείστας νίκας νενίκηκεν· οὑτοσὶ δὲ Χαιρέστρατος
τηλικοῦτος ὢν τετριηράρχηκε, κεχορήγηκε δὲ
τραγῳδοῖς, γεγυμνασιάρχηκε δὲ λαμπάδι· καὶ τὰς
εἰσφορὰς εἰσενηνόχασιν[3] ἀμφότεροι πάσας ἐν τοῖς
τριακοσίοις. καὶ τέως μὲν δύ᾽ ὄντες, νῦν δὲ καὶ
ὁ νεώτερος οὑτοσὶ χορηγεῖ μὲν τραγῳδοῖς, εἰς δὲ
τοὺς τριακοσίους ἐγγέγραπται καὶ εἰσφέρει τὰς
61 εἰσφοράς. ὥστ᾽ οὐ φθονεῖσθαί εἰσιν ἄξιοι, ἀλλὰ
πολὺ μᾶλλον νὴ Δία καὶ τὸν Ἀπόλλω οὗτοι, εἰ
λήψονται ἃ μὴ προσήκει αὐτοῖς. τοῦ γὰρ Φιλοκτήμονος κλήρου ἂν μὲν ἐπιδικάσηται ὅδε, ὑμῖν
αὐτὸν ταμιεύσει, τὰ προσταττόμενα λῃτουργῶν
ὥσπερ καὶ νῦν καὶ ἔτι μᾶλλον· ἐὰν δ᾽ οὗτοι λάβωσι,
διαφορήσαντες ἑτέροις ἐπιβουλεύσουσι.
62 Δέομαι οὖν ὑμῶν, ὦ ἄνδρες, ἵνα μὴ ἐξαπατηθῆτε, τῇ διαμαρτυρίᾳ τὸν νοῦν προσέχειν περὶ ἧς
τὴν ψῆφον οἴσετε· καὶ πρὸς ταύτην αὐτὸν κελεύετε
τὴν ἀπολογίαν ποιεῖσθαι, ὥσπερ καὶ ἡμεῖς κατηγο-
ρήσαμεν. γέγραπται ὡς οὐκ ἔδωκεν οὐδὲ διέθετο

---

[1] λοιδορήσηται Aldus : -εται.
[2] λέγῃ Aldus : λέγει.
[3] εἰσενηνόχασιν Reiske : -ήνοχαν.

---

[a] i.e., the richest class.

prove his point or dwells only very lightly upon it, but rails against us in a loud voice and says that my clients are rich, while he is poor—all this will make it appear that the children are legitimate. Now the fortune of my clients, sirs, is being spent rather upon the city than upon these clients themselves. Phanostratus has already been trierarch seven times, and he has performed all the public services and has generally been victorious. Chaerestratus here, young as he is, has been trierarch ; he has been *choregus* in the tragic competitions ; he has been gymnasiarch at the torch-races. Both of them have paid all the special war-taxes, being numbered among the three hundred.ᵃ Formerly only these two members of the family contributed, but now the younger son here is *choregus* in the tragic competitions and has been enrolled among the three hundred and pays the war-tax. No grudge ought, therefore, to be felt against them, but rather, by Zeus and Apollo, against our opponents, if they obtain what does not belong to them. If the estate of Philoctemon is adjudicated to my client, he will hold it in trust for you, performing all the public services which you lay upon him, as he has done hitherto, and with even greater generosity. If, on the other hand, our opponents receive it, they will squander it and then seek other victims.

I beseech you, therefore, gentlemen, in order that you may not be misled, to give your careful attention to the protestation about which you are going to give your verdict. Instruct him to make that the subject of his defence, just as it has been the subject of our accusation. The text of the pro-

Φιλοκτήμων· τοῦτο ἐπιδέδεικται ψεῦδος ὄν· καὶ γὰρ [ὁ δοὺς καὶ ὁ διαθέμενος καὶ] μαρτυροῦσιν οἱ
63 παραγενόμενοι. τί ἔτι; τελευτῆσαι ἄπαιδα Φιλοκτήμονα. πῶς οὖν ἄπαις ἦν ὅστις[1] τὸν ἑαυτοῦ ἀδελφιδοῦν ὑὸν ποιησάμενος κατέλιπεν, ᾧ ὁμοίως ὁ νόμος τὴν κληρονομίαν ἀποδίδωσι καὶ τοῖς ἐξ αὑτοῦ γενομένοις; καὶ διαρρήδην ἐν τῷ νόμῳ γέγραπται, ἐὰν ποιησαμένῳ παῖδες ἐπιγένωνται, τὸ μέρος ἑκάτερον ἔχειν τῆς οὐσίας καὶ κληρο
64 νομεῖν ὁμοίως ἀμφοτέρους. ὡς οὖν εἰσὶ γνήσιοι οἱ παῖδες οἵδε, τοῦτ' αὐτὸ ἐπιδεικνύτω, ὥσπερ ἂν ὑμῶν ἕκαστος. οὐ γὰρ ἂν εἴπῃ μητρὸς ὄνομα, γνήσιοί εἰσιν,[2] ἀλλ' ἐὰν ἐπιδεικνύῃ ὡς ἀληθῆ λέγει, τοὺς συγγενεῖς παρεχόμενος τοὺς εἰδότας συνοικοῦσαν τῷ Εὐκτήμονι <καὶ>[3] τοὺς δημότας καὶ τοὺς φράτορας, εἴ τι ἀκηκόασι πώποτε ἢ ἴσασιν ὑπὲρ αὐτῆς Εὐκτήμονα λῃτουργήσαντα, ἔτι δὲ ποῦ
65 τέθαπται, ἐν ποίοις μνήμασι, <καὶ>[4] τίς εἶδε τὰ νομιζόμενα ποιοῦντα Εὐκτήμονα· ποῖ δ' ἔτ' ἰόντες οἱ παῖδες ἐναγίζουσι καὶ χέονται, καὶ τίς εἶδε ταῦτα τῶν πολιτῶν ἢ τῶν οἰκετῶν <τῶν>[5] Εὐκτήμονος. ταῦτα γάρ ἐστιν ἔλεγχος[6] ἅπαντα, καὶ οὐ λοιδορία. καὶ ἐὰν περὶ αὐτοῦ τούτου κελεύητε ἐπιδεικνύναι ὥσπερ καὶ διεμαρτύρησεν, ὑμεῖς τε τὴν ψῆφον ὁσίαν καὶ κατὰ τοὺς νόμους θήσεσθε, τοῖσδέ τε τὰ δίκαια γενήσεται.

---

[1] ἄπαις ἦν ὅστις Reiske: ἂν αἴσιμός τις.
[2] γνήσιοι εἰσιν Bekker: γνήσιός ἐστιν.
[3] καὶ add. Sauppe.   [4] καὶ add. Buermann.
[5] τῶν add. Dobree.   [6] ἔλεγχος Aldus: ἔνοχος.

testation has stated that Philoctemon made no gift of property or will; this has been proved to be false, for those who were present are witnesses that he did so. What further do they say? That Philoctemon died childless. How could he be childless, when he adopted and was survived by his own nephew, to whom the law gives the right of inheritance just as much as to children of his own body? Indeed, it is expressly stated in the law that, if children are born subsequently to one who has adopted a son, each child takes his share of the estate and both classes of children alike inherit. Let Androcles, therefore, prove that the children are legitimate, as any one of you would have to do in similar circumstances. His mere mention of a mother's name does not suffice to make them legitimate, but he must prove that he is speaking the truth by producing the relatives who know that she was married to Euctemon, and the members of the deme and of the ward, if they have ever heard or have any knowledge that Euctemon performed any public services on her behalf. We must know where she is buried and in what sort of tomb, and who has ever seen Euctemon performing the customary rights over her, and whither her sons still go to offer sacrifices and libations, and who of the citizens or of the slaves of Euctemon has ever seen these rites being performed. It is all these details, and not mere invective, which constitute a proof. If you bid him prove the actual contention which is the subject of his protestation, you will give a verdict which accords with your oath and with the laws, and justice will be done to my clients.

VII. ON THE ESTATE OF
APOLLODORUS

VII. ON THE ESTATE OF APOLLODORUS

INTRODUCTION

THREE brothers, Eupolis, Mneson, and Thrasyllus I.,[a] had inherited a substantial fortune from their father. Mneson died without issue ; and Thrasyllus was killed during the Sicilian expedition (415–413 B.C.), leaving a young son Apollodorus I., of whom the surviving brother, Eupolis, became guardian. The widow of Thrasyllus I. married a certain Archedamus, who, finding that his stepson Apollodorus I. was being defrauded by his guardian, helped him to obtain redress in the law-courts. Apollodorus, being on terms of close friendship with his stepfather, and having lost his only son, determined to adopt

[a] STEMMA

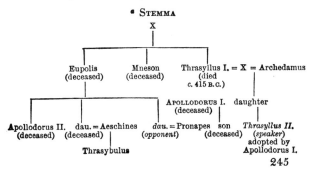

245

the grandchild of Archedamus, the son of his half-sister, who took the name of Thrasyllus and delivered the present speech. Unfortunately, Apollodorus died before the formalities of the adoption had been completed. Though registered with the heads of families and in the ward, Thrasyllus II. had not been inscribed as a member of the deme ; he was, however, admitted to the deme after his adopted father's death. In spite of this, the estate was claimed by the wife of Pronapes, a daughter of Eupolis and therefore the first cousin of Apollodorus. Her sister's son, Thrasybulus, who had an equal claim in law, refused to press it, because, according to Thrasyllus, he was satisfied that the adoption was valid.

That Apollodorus had intended to complete the formalities of the adoption does not seem to have been disputed ; the fact remains, however, that he had not done so, and thus on his death the estate had become vacant, and claimable by law, before Thrasyllus II. had been duly registered in the deme. This point is skilfully treated by the speaker, who dwells at length upon the formalities actually carried out before Apollodorus's death, and only casually slips in, as the confirmation of a later argument, the fact that he was afterwards registered in the deme. He is at pains to show the close bonds of material benefits and of affection which subsisted between Apollodorus and himself, his mother and his grandfather, and the enmity between them all and Eupolis ; and he enlarges on the public spirit shown by Thrasyllus I., Apollodorus, and himself, and the meanness of Pronapes, who, he says, has failed to declare his full fortune so as to avoid performing public

services, and who, though his wife had inherited
half the fortune of her brother Apollodorus II., has
allowed his house to become extinct. Apollodorus's
quarrel with Eupolis and the mean behaviour of
his daughters towards their deceased brother were,
he urges, a strong motive for leaving his property
elsewhere ; in addition to this he desired a son to
take the place of his dead child and naturally sought
one in the family of his half-sister.

Though legally the non-completion of the formalities of adoption raises a difficulty, there can be little
doubt that in equity the claim of Thrasyllus was a
strong one.

The speech must have been delivered at a date
subsequent to 357–356 B.C., the earliest date at which
there is any evidence of the system of joint contribution for the trierarchy (§ 38). It has been argued
from § 27 that the speech was delivered in the year
of the Pythian Festival, which fell in the third year
of the Olympiad, and that, therefore, the speech
was delivered in 354–353 B.C. or 350–349 B.C. This
argument, however, rests on the substitution of
Πυθιάδος for the ms. reading Πυθαΐδος. The latter
is supported by Delphic inscriptions and has reference
to a festival which was celebrated by the Athenians
at Delphi in May or June and had no connexion
with the pan-Hellenic Pythian festival.[a] H. L.
Parke (*J.H.S.* vol. ix. (1939), pp. 79-83) argues on
historical grounds that the speech was delivered
in 355 B.C.

[a] This festival has been the subject of a treatise by A.
Boëthius, *Die Pythaïs : Studien zur Geschichte der Ver-
bindungen zwischen Athen und Delphi* (Upsala, 1918), who
is of opinion that its celebration only took place at
rare intervals.

VII. ΠΕΡΙ ΤΟΥ ΑΠΟΛΛΟΔΩΡΟΥ ΚΛΗΡΟΥ

ΥΠΟΘΕΣΙΣ

Εὔπολις καὶ Θράσυλλος καὶ Μνήσων ἀδελφοὶ γεγόνασι. τούτων ὁ μὲν Μνήσων ἄπαις ἐτελεύτησεν, ὁ δὲ
Θράσυλλος παῖδα καταλιπὼν Ἀπολλόδωρον· μόνος δ'
Εὔπολις καταλειφθεὶς πολλὰ τὸν Ἀπολλόδωρον ἠδίκη-
σεν. ὅθεν Ἀρχέδαμος, πάππος τοῦ λέγοντος τὸν λόγον,
τῇ τοῦ Ἀπολλοδώρου μητρὶ συνοικῶν μετὰ τὸν Θρασύλλου τοῦ ἀνδρὸς αὐτῆς θάνατον, καὶ τὸν Ἀπολλόδωρον
ὡς ὀρφανὸν ἐλεῶν, πολλὰ τὸν Εὔπολιν ἀπήτησε χρήματα
ὑπὲρ ὧν Ἀπολλόδωρον ἠδίκησε. τούτων μεμνημένος
Ἀπολλόδωρος εἰσήγαγεν εἰς τοὺς φράτορας θετὸν υἱὸν
ἑαυτῷ Θράσυλλον τοῦτον, υἱὸν ὄντα τῆς [τε] ὁμομητρίας
αὐτοῦ ἀδελφῆς καὶ ⟨θυγατριδοῦν⟩[1] Ἀρχεδάμου. τοῦ δὲ
Θρασύλλου ἤδη μὲν εἰς τοὺς γεννήτας καὶ φράτορας
ἐγγεγραμμένου, οὔπω δ' εἰς τὸ ληξιαρχικὸν γραμματεῖον,
ἐτελεύτησεν Ἀπολλόδωρος. καὶ μετὰ τὴν αὐτοῦ τελευτὴν
ἐγγέγραπται μὲν ὁ Θράσυλλος εἰς τὸ ληξιαρχικὸν γραμματεῖον, οὐδὲν δ' ἧττον Εὐπόλιδος θυγάτηρ, τοῦ θείου
Ἀπολλοδώρου, ἀμφισβητεῖ πρὸς Θράσυλλον, λέγουσα
μηδ' ὅλως ἐγγεγράφθαι τὸν Θράσυλλον εἰς τοὺς φράτορας
καὶ γεννήτας κατὰ γνώμην τοῦ Ἀππολλοδώρου, ἀλλὰ
πεπλασμένην εἶναι τὴν ποίησιν. καὶ ἡ μὲν ὑπόθεσις
αὕτη, ἡ δὲ στάσις στοχασμός· διὸ καλῶς πάνυ καὶ
τεχνικῶς τὸν λόγον οἰκονομῶν τὴν ἔχθραν[2] διεξέρχεται
τὴν Ἀπολλοδώρου πρὸς Εὔπολιν, ὅπερ μέγα σημεῖον

VII. ON THE ESTATE OF APOLLODORUS

ARGUMENT

Eupolis, Thrasyllus (I.), and Mneson were brothers. Mneson died without issue; Thrasyllus (I.) died leaving a son, Apollodorus; Eupolis, the sole survivor of the three, acted with great injustice towards Apollodorus. Archedamus, therefore, the grandfather of the man who makes the speech, being married to Apollodorus's mother after her first husband's death, pitying Apollodorus because he was an orphan, claimed a large sum of money from Eupolis on account of the wrongs committed by the latter against Apollodorus. Mindful of this kindness Apollodorus introduced Thrasyllus, the son of his half-sister and grandson of Archedamus, to his fellow-wardsmen as his adopted son. Thrasyllus (II.) had already been inscribed among the members of the families and of the ward, but had not yet been placed on the official register of the deme, when Apollodorus died. After Apollodorus's death Thrasyllus (II.) was inscribed on the register; nevertheless the daughter of Eupolis, the uncle of Apollodorus, contested the succession against Thrasyllus (II.), alleging that it was not by any means in accordance with the wishes of Apollodorus that Thrasyllus had been inscribed among the wardsmen and kindred, and that the adoption was fictitious. Such is the subject of the trial; the discussion turns on a question of fact, and so, with great skill and ingenuity, the speaker explains the enmity of Apollodorus towards Eupolis, which

---

[1] θυγατριδοῦν add. Schoemann.
[2] ἔχθραν Reiske: ἐλευθέραν.

γίγνεται τοῦ μὴ θέλειν αὐτὴν ὑπὸ τῆς Εὐπόλιδος θυγατρὸς κληρονομηθῆναι.

1 Ὤιμην μέν, ὦ ἄνδρες, προσήκειν οὐ τὰς τοιαύτας ἀμφισβητεῖσθαι ποιήσεις, εἴ τις αὐτὸς ζῶν καὶ εὖ φρονῶν ἐποιήσατο καὶ ἐπὶ τὰ ἱερὰ ἀγαγὼν εἰς τοὺς συγγενεῖς ἀπέδειξε καὶ εἰς τὰ κοινὰ γραμματεῖα ἐνέγραψεν, ἅπανθ᾽ ὅσα προσῆκεν αὐτὸς ποιήσας, ἀλλ᾽ εἴ τις τελευτήσειν μέλλων διέθετο, εἴ τι πάθοι, τὴν οὐσίαν ἑτέρῳ, καὶ ταῦτ᾽ ἐν[1] γράμ-
2 μασι κατέθετο παρά τισι σημηνάμενος. ἐκεῖνον μὲν γὰρ τὸν τρόπον ποιησάμενος φανερὰς κατέστησε τὰς αὑτοῦ βουλήσεις, ὅλον τὸ πρᾶγμα ἐπικυρώσας, δόντων αὐτῷ τῶν νόμων· ὁ δ᾽ ἐν διαθήκαις σημηνάμενος ἀδήλους ἐποίησε, διὸ πολλοὶ πεπλάσθαι φάσκοντες αὐτὰς ἀμφισβητεῖν ἀξιοῦσι πρὸς τοὺς ποιηθέντας. ἔοικε δ᾽ οὐδὲν προὔργου τοῦτο εἶναι· καὶ γὰρ οὕτως αὐτῶν φανερῶς πεπραγμένων ὅμως ὑπὲρ τῆς θυγατρὸς τῆς Εὐπόλιδος ἥκουσι περὶ τῶν Ἀπολλοδώρου χρημά-
3 των πρὸς ἐμὲ ἀμφισβητήσοντες. ἐγὼ δ᾽ εἰ μὲν ἑώρων ὑμᾶς μᾶλλον ἀποδεχομένους τὰς διαμαρτυρίας ἢ τὰς εὐθυδικίας, κἂν μάρτυρας προὐβαλόμην μὴ ἐπίδικον εἶναι τὸν κλῆρον ὡς ποιησαμένου με υἱὸν Ἀπολλοδώρου κατὰ τοὺς νόμους. ἐπειδὴ δ᾽ οὐ διαφεύγει τὰ δίκαια μὴ οὐ κατὰ τοῦτον γιγνώσκεσθαι τὸν τρόπον [καὶ] παρ᾽ ὑμῖν, αὐτὸς[2]

---

[1] ταῦτ᾽ ἐν Reiske: ταύτην. [2] αὐτὸς Dobree: αὐτοῖς.

⁶ See p. 37.

supplies a strong presumption that he did not wish that his property should be inherited by Eupolis's daughter.

I should have thought, gentlemen, that there was one class of adoptions which could not be disputed, namely, those which are made by the adopter personally in his lifetime and in full possession of his faculties, after he has led his adopted son to the domestic shrines and presented him to his kindred and inscribed him in the official registers, and himself carried out all the proper formalities. On the other hand, a dispute might well arise, when a man, feeling that his end is near, has disposed of his property in favour of another, if anything should happen to him, and putting his wishes in a written document has sealed it up and deposited it in the custody of others. By the former method the adopter sets forth his wishes with perfect clearness, making the whole transaction valid in the manner permitted by the laws ; whereas the man who commits his wishes to a sealed-up will makes them secret, with the result that claimants often think fit to contest the succession against adopted sons, alleging that the will is a forgery. It appears, however, that this distinction is of little practical value ; for though my adoption was quite openly carried out, yet representatives of Eupolis's daughter have come forward to contest my right to Apollodorus's estate. If I observed that you prefer a protestation [a] to a direct action, I should have brought forward witnesses to show that the estate is not liable to adjudication, seeing that Apollodorus adopted me in the proper legal form ; but since I am sensible that by the former method the rights of the case cannot fully be made known to you, I

ἥκω διαλεξόμενος περὶ τῶν πεπραγμένων, ἵνα μηδεμίαν ἡμῖν[1] αἰτίαν περὶ τοῦ μὴ βούλεσθαι
4 δοῦναι δίκην τοιαύτην ἐπιφέρωσιν. ἀποδείξω δὲ ὡς οὐ μόνον ἐπὶ τοῖς ἐγγυτάτω γένους τὸν κλῆρον Ἀπολλόδωρος οὐ καταλέλοιπε, πολλὰ καὶ δεινὰ ὑπὸ τούτων ἀδικηθείς, ἀλλὰ καὶ ὡς ἐμὲ ἐποιήσατο δικαίως, ὄντα ἀδελφιδοῦν, καὶ μεγάλα[2] εὐεργετημένος ὑφ' ἡμῶν. δέομαι δὲ ὑμῶν, ὦ ἄνδρες, πάντων ὁμοίως εὔνοιάν τέ μοι παρασχεῖν, κἂν ἐπὶ τὸν κλῆρον ἀναιδῶς αὐτοὺς ἰόντας ἐξελέγχω, βοηθεῖν μοι τὰ δίκαια. ποιήσομαι δ' ὡς ἂν κἀγὼ δύνωμαι[3] διὰ βραχυτάτων τοὺς λόγους, ἐξ ἀρχῆς ὡς ἔχει τὰ γενόμενα διδάσκων ὑμᾶς.

5 Εὔπολις γάρ, ὦ ἄνδρες, καὶ Θράσυλλος καὶ Μνήσων ἀδελφοὶ ἦσαν ὁμομήτριοι καὶ ὁμοπάτριοι. τούτοις οὐσίαν ὁ πατὴρ κατέλιπε πολλήν, ὥστε καὶ λῃτουργεῖν ἕκαστον ἀξιοῦσθαι παρ' ὑμῖν. ταύτην ἐκεῖνοι τρεῖς ὄντες ἐνείμοντο πρὸς ἀλλήλους. τούτων τὼ δύο ἐτελευτησάτην[4] περὶ τὸν αὐτὸν χρόνον, ὁ μὲν Μνήσων ἐνθάδε ἄγαμος καὶ ἄπαις, ὁ δὲ Θράσυλλος τῶν ἐν Σικελίᾳ καταλεγεὶς τριηράρχων, καταλιπὼν υόν[5] Ἀπολλόδωρον τὸν
6 ἐμὲ νῦν ποιησάμενον. Εὔπολις οὖν μόνος αὐτῶν
[64] λειφθεὶς οὐ μικρὰ | ἀπολαῦσαι τῶν χρημάτων ἠξίωσεν, ἀλλὰ τὸν μὲν Μνήσονος κλῆρον, οὗ καὶ Ἀπολλοδώρῳ προσῆκε τὸ ἡμικλήριον, πάντα εἰς αὑτὸν περιεποίησε, φάσκων αὐτῷ δοῦναι τὸν ἀδελφόν, αὐτὸν δ' ἐκεῖνον οὕτω διῴκησεν ἐπιτροπεύων ὥστε τριῶν αὐτῷ ταλάντων δίκην ὀφλεῖν.[6]

---

[1] ἡμῖν Reiske: ὑμῖν.   [2] μεγάλα Dobree: μέγα.
[3] δύνωμαι Aldus: δύναμαι.
[4] τὼ δύο ἐτελευτησάτην Bekker: τῶν δύο ** τελευτησάντων.

have myself come forward to explain the facts, so
that they may bring no charge against us of being
unwilling to submit to such a trial. I shall prove
to you, not only that Apollodorus was prevented
from leaving his estate to his nearest relatives by
the many injuries which he had sustained at their
hands, but also that he legally adopted me, his
nephew, after having received great benefits from
my family. I beg you all, gentlemen, to accord
me your goodwill, and, if I can prove that my
opponents are laying impudent claim to the estate,
to help me to obtain my just rights. I will speak
as briefly as I can, relating to you all that has
happened from the beginning.

Eupolis, Thrasyllus, and Mneson were brothers,
children of the same father and mother. Their
father left them a large property, so that each of
them was considered able to perform public offices
in the city. This fortune the three brothers divided
amongst themselves. Two of them died about the
same time, Mneson here in Athens, unmarried and
without issue, Thrasyllus in Sicily,[a] having been
chosen as one of the trierarchs, leaving a son Apollodorus, who afterwards adopted me. Eupolis, the
sole survivor of the three brothers, was not content
to enjoy only a part of the family fortune, but
seized for himself the whole of Mneson's estate, half
of which belonged to Apollodorus, alleging that his
brother had given it to him, and, as guardian,
so administered the affairs of Apollodorus that he
was condemned to restore three talents to him.

---

[a] During the Sicilian expedition of 415–413 B.C.

7 Ἀρχέδαμος γὰρ ὁ πάππος οὑμός, ἐξ οὗ τὴν
μητέρα ἔσχε¹ τὴν Ἀπολλοδώρου, τήθην δὲ ἐμήν,²
ὁρῶν αὐτὸν πάντων ἀποστερούμενον τῶν χρημάτων, ἔτρεφέ τε αὐτὸν παῖδα ὄνθ', ὡς ἑαυτὸν³
καὶ τὴν μητέρα κομισάμενος, ἀνδρί τε γενομένῳ
συνηγωνίσατο καὶ εἰσέπραξε τὸ ἡμικλήριον ὧν
Μνήσων κατέλιπεν ὅσα τε ἐκ τῆς ἐπιτροπῆς ἀπ-
εστέρησε, δίκας δύο ἑλών, καὶ τὴν οὐσίαν ἐποίησε
8 κομίσασθαι τὴν αὐτοῦ πᾶσαν. καὶ διὰ ταῦτα
Εὔπολις μὲν καὶ Ἀπολλόδωρος ἐχθρῶς ἔχοντες
τὸν πάντα χρόνον διετέλεσαν πρὸς ἀλλήλους, ὁ δὲ
πάππος οὑμὸς καὶ Ἀπολλόδωρος φιλικῶς, ὥσπερ
προσῆκε. τοῖς δ' ἔργοις ἄν τις τεκμήραιτο μάλιστα
ὅτι Ἀπολλόδωρος πέπονθεν ὃ ἀντευποιεῖν ἠξίου
τοὺς ἑαυτὸν εὐεργετήσαντας. συμφορᾷ γὰρ τοῦ
πάππου χρησαμένου καὶ ληφθέντος εἰς τοὺς πολεμίους, καὶ χρήματα εἰσενεγκεῖν εἰς λύτρα καὶ
ὁμηρεῦσαι ὑπὲρ αὐτοῦ ἠθέλησεν, ἕως [οὗ] εὐ-
9 πορήσειεν ἐκεῖνος τἀργύριον. ἐξ εὐπόρου τε ἀ-
πορωτέρῳ γεγενημένῳ συνδιώκει τὰ ἐκείνου, μεταδιδοὺς ὧν εἶχεν. εἰς Κόρινθόν τε στρατεύεσθαι
μέλλων, εἴ τι πάθοι, διέθετο τὴν οὐσίαν καὶ ἔδωκε
τῇ ἐκείνου μὲν θυγατρί, ἐμῇ δὲ μητρί, αὐτοῦ δὲ
ἀδελφῇ, διδοὺς αὐτὴν Λακρατίδῃ τῷ νῦν ἱεροφάντῃ
γεγενημένῳ. τοιοῦτος ἦν ἐκεῖνος περὶ ἡμᾶς τοὺς
10 ἐξ ἀρχῆς αὐτὸν σώσαντας. ὡς δ' ἀληθῆ λέγω,
καὶ δίκας εἷλεν Εὔπολιν δύο, τὴν μὲν ἐπιτροπῆς

---

¹ ἔσχε Sauppe: ἔχων.   ² ἐμήν M, Bekker: ἐμοί.
³ ἑαυτὸν Schoemann: -οῦ.

ᵃ Athenian troops were engaged in the region of Corinth
from 394 to 390 B.C.
ᵇ See note on vi. 33.

For my grandfather Archedamus, from the time
that he married Apollodorus's mother, my grandmother, seeing that he was deprived of all his fortune,
took him to his own house and to his mother and
brought him up while he was a boy, and, when he
came to man's estate, assisted him to bring an action
and secured the restitution of the half-share of the
estate left by Mneson and all that Eupolis embezzled
in his capacity as guardian, winning two law-suits,
and so enabled Apollodorus to recover all his fortune.
As a result Eupolis and Apollodorus were always
at enmity with one another, while my grandfather
and Apollodorus were naturally close friends. The
acts of Apollodorus supply the best evidence that
he has received kind treatment for which he thought
fit to make return to his benefactors. For, when
my grandfather met with misfortune and was taken
a prisoner of war, Apollodorus consented to contribute money for his ransom and act as a hostage
for him until he could raise the necessary sum of
money. When Archedamus had been reduced from
affluence to embarrassment, Apollodorus helped him
to look after his affairs, sharing his own money with
him. Again, when he was on the point of starting for
Corinth on military service,[a] he made a will in case
anything happened to him and devised his property
to Archedamus's daughter, his own sister and my
mother, providing for her marriage with Lacratides,
who has now become hierophant.[b] Such was his
conduct towards us who had originally saved him
from ruin. To prove the truth of my statements
that Apollodorus won two actions against Eupolis,
one in respect of his guardianship and the other
concerning the half-share of Mneson's estate, my

τὴν δὲ ἡμικληρίου, τοῦ πάππου συνηγωνισμένου
καὶ λέγοντος, τά τε χρήματα ἐκομίσατο δι' ἡμᾶς
καὶ ταύτας τὰς χάριτας ἡμῖν ἀνταπέδωκε, τούτων
πρῶτον βούλομαι παρασχέσθαι τοὺς μάρτυρας.
καί μοι κάλει δεῦρο αὐτούς.

ΜΑΡΤΥΡΕΣ

11 Αἱ μὲν οὖν παρ' ἡμῶν εὐεργεσίαι τοιαῦται καὶ
τηλικαῦται τὸ μέγεθός εἰσιν· αἱ δὲ πρὸς ἐκεῖνον
ἔχθραι περὶ τοσούτων χρημάτων ἦσαν, ἃς οὐχ
οἷόν τ' εἰπεῖν ὡς διελύσαντο καὶ φίλοι ἐγένοντο.
μεγάλα γὰρ τεκμήρια αὐτῶν ἐστιν· Εὔπολις γὰρ
αὐτῷ δυοῖν θυγατέρων οὐσῶν καὶ ἐκ τῶν αὐτῶν
αὐτῷ γεγονὼς καὶ χρήμαθ' ὁρῶν κεκτημένον,
12 οὐδετέραν αὐτῷ τούτων ἔδωκε. καίτοι δοκοῦσιν
ἐπιγαμίαι καὶ μὴ συγγενεῖς ἄνδρας ἀλλὰ καὶ τοὺς
τυχόντας ἀπαλλάττειν μεγάλης διαφορᾶς, ὅταν ἃ
περὶ πλείστου ποιοῦνται, ταῦτ' ἀλλήλοις ἐγχειρί-
ζωσιν. εἶτ' οὖν Εὔπολις γεγένηται αἴτιος ⟨δοῦ-
ναι⟩[1] μὴ βουληθείς, εἴτ' Ἀπολλόδωρος λαβεῖν μὴ
ἐθελήσας, τὰς ἔχθρας, ὅτι διέμειναν, τὸ ἔργον
δεδήλωκε.

13 Καὶ περὶ μὲν τῆς ἐκείνων διαφορᾶς ἱκανοὺς εἶναι
νομίζω καὶ τοὺς εἰρημένους λόγους· οἶδα γὰρ ὅτι
καὶ ὑμῶν ὅσοι πρεσβύτεροι μνημονεύουσιν ὅτι ἐγένοντο ἀντίδικοι· τό τε γὰρ μέγεθος τῶν δικῶν, καὶ
διότι πολὺ αὐτὸν Ἀρχέδαμος εἷλεν, ἐπιφάνειάν
τινα ἐποίησεν. ὡς δὲ ἐμὲ ἐποιήσατο υἱὸν ζῶν
αὐτὸς καὶ κύριον τῶν αὐτοῦ κατέστησε καὶ εἰς

---

[1] δοῦναι add. Hirschig.

grandfather having supported his case and speaking on his behalf, and that it was thanks to us that he recovered his fortune, and that he requited these good services of ours—on all these points I wish first to produce the witnesses. Please summon them hither.

WITNESSES

Such is the nature and importance of the benefits which Apollodorus received from us ; on the other hand, his feelings of enmity towards Eupolis had their origin in disputes about such large sums of money that it is impossible to pretend that they could ever make up their quarrel and become friends. A convincing proof of their enmity is the fact that, though Eupolis had two daughters and was descended from the same ancestors and saw that Apollodorus was possessed of money, yet he gave neither of them to him in marriage. Yet it is generally held that marriages reconcile serious animosities not only between relatives but also between ordinary acquaintances, when they entrust one another with what they value most. Whether Eupolis has been to blame in not wishing to give his daughter or Apollodorus in being unwilling to accept her, the fact has proved that their enmity continued.

What has been said about their quarrel is, I think, sufficient ; for I know that the older men among you remember that they were opponents in the law-courts, for the importance of the cases and the fact that heavy damages were obtained by Archidamus gave publicity to their quarrel. I must now ask you, gentlemen, to give your kind attention to the proofs, that Apollodorus himself adopted me during his lifetime and gave me power over his

τοὺς γεννήτας καὶ εἰς τοὺς φράτορας ἐνέγραψε,
τούτοις ἤδη μοι τὸν νοῦν προσέχετε, ὦ ἄνδρες.
14 Ἀπολλοδώρῳ γὰρ ἦν ὑός, ὃν ἐκεῖνος καὶ ἤσκει
καὶ δι' ἐπιμελείας εἶχεν, ὥσπερ καὶ προσῆκον ἦν.
ἕως μὲν οὖν ἐκεῖνος ἔζη, διάδοχον τῆς οὐσίας
ἤλπιζεν αὐτὸν καταστήσειν τῆς ἑαυτοῦ· ἐπειδὴ δὲ
ἐτελεύτησε νοσήσας τοῦ ἐξελθόντος ἐνιαυτοῦ μηνὸς
Μαιμακτηριῶνος, ἐπὶ τοῖς παροῦσιν ἀθυμήσας καὶ
τὴν ἡλικίαν τὴν ἑαυτοῦ καταμεμψάμενος οὐκ
ἐπελάθετο ὑφ' ὧν καὶ ἐξ ἀρχῆς εὖ πεπονθὼς ἦν,
ἀλλ' ἐλθὼν ὡς[1] τὴν ἐμὴν μητέρα ἑαυτοῦ δὲ ἀδελφήν,
ἣν περὶ πλείστου πάντων ἐποιεῖτο, λαβεῖν ἠξίωσέ
15 με ὑὸν καὶ ᾔτησε καὶ ἔτυχεν. οὕτω δ' ἐπείσθη
ταῦτα ποιῆσαι διὰ ταχέων, ὥστ' εὐθέως με λαβὼν
ᾤχετ' ἔχων πρὸς αὐτὸν καὶ πάντα τὰ αὐτοῦ
[65] διοικεῖν παρέδωκεν, ὡς αὐτὸς μὲν | οὐδὲν ἂν ἔτι
πρᾶξαι τούτων δυνηθείς, ἐμοῦ δὲ ταῦτα πάντα
οἵου τε ἐσομένου ποιεῖν. καὶ ἐπειδὴ Θαργήλια[2]
ἦν, ἤγαγέ με ἐπὶ τοὺς βωμοὺς εἰς τοὺς γεννήτας
16 τε καὶ φράτορας. ἔστι δ' αὐτοῖς νόμος ὁ αὐτός,
ἐάν τέ τινα φύσει γεγονότα εἰσάγῃ τις ἐάν τε
ποιητόν, ἐπιτιθέναι πίστιν κατὰ τῶν ἱερῶν ἦ μὴν
ἐξ ἀστῆς εἰσάγειν καὶ γεγονότα ὀρθῶς καὶ τὸν
ὑπάρχοντα φύσει καὶ τὸν ποιητόν· ποιήσαντος δὲ
τοῦ εἰσάγοντος ταῦτα μηδὲν ἧττον διαψηφίζεσθαι
καὶ τοὺς ἄλλους, κἂν δόξῃ, τότ' εἰς τὸ κοινὸν γραμματεῖον ἐγγράφειν, πρότερον δὲ μή· τοιαύτας ἀκρι-
17 βείας ἔχει τὰ δίκαια τὰ παρ' αὐτοῖς. τοῦ νόμου

---

[1] ὡς Reiske : εἰς.   [2] Θαργήλια Aldus : Θαλγηλ*ια.

---

[a] October to November.

property and inscribed me in the registers of the members of the families and of the ward. Now Apollodorus had a son whom he brought up and dearly cherished, as indeed was only natural. As long as this child lived, he hoped to make him heir to his property ; but when he fell ill and died in the month of Maemacterion *a* of last year, Apollodorus, depressed by his misfortunes and viewing his advanced age with regret, did not fail to bethink him of the family at whose hands he had in earlier years received kindness ; so he came to my mother, his own sister, for whom he had a greater regard than for anyone else, and expressed a wish to adopt me and asked her permission, which was granted. He was so determined to act with all possible haste that he straightway took me to his own house and entrusted me with the direction of all his affairs, regarding himself as no longer capable of managing anything himself, and thinking that I should be able to do everything. When the Thargelia *b* came round, he conducted me to the altars and to the members of the families and ward. Now these bodies have a uniform rule, that when a man introduces his own son or an adopted son, he must swear with his hand upon the victims that the child whom he is introducing, whether his own or an adopted son, is the offspring of an Athenian mother and born in wedlock ; and, even after the introducer has done this, the other members still have to pass a vote, and, if their vote is favourable, they then, and not till then, inscribe him on the official register ; such is the exactitude with which their formalities are

b A festival celebrated on the 6th and 7th of the month of Thargelion (May to June).

δὴ[1] οὕτως ἔχοντος, καὶ τῶν φρατόρων τε καὶ γεννητῶν ἐκείνῳ οὐκ ἀπιστούντων ἐμέ τε οὐκ ἀγνοούντων, ὅτι ἦν ἐξ ἀδελφῆς αὐτῷ γεγονώς, ἐγγράφουσί με εἰς τὸ κοινὸν γραμματεῖον ψηφισάμενοι πάντες, ἐπιθέντος ἐκείνου τὴν πίστιν καθ᾽ ἱερῶν. καὶ οὕτω μὲν ὑπὸ ζῶντος ἐποιήθην, καὶ εἰς τὸ κοινὸν γραμματεῖον ἐνεγράφην Θράσυλλος Ἀπολλοδώρου, ποιησαμένου με ἐκείνου τοῦτον τὸν τρόπον, τῶν νόμων αὐτῷ δεδωκότων. ὡς δ᾽ ἀληθῆ λέγω, λαβέ μοι τὰς μαρτυρίας.

ΜΑΡΤΥΡΙΑΙ

18 Οἶμαι τοίνυν, ὦ ἄνδρες, μᾶλλον ἂν ὑμᾶς τοῖς μεμαρτυρηκόσι πιστεύειν, εἰ καί τινες[2] τῶν ὁμοίως προσηκόντων ἔργοις φανερῶς μεμαρτυρήκασιν ὡς ἐκεῖνος ταῦτα ὀρθῶς καὶ κατὰ τοὺς νόμους ἔπραξε. κατέλιπε γὰρ Εὔπολις θυγατέρας δύο, ταύτην τε ἣ νῦν ἀμφισβητεῖ καὶ Προνάπει συνοικεῖ, καὶ ἄλλην ἣν ἔσχεν Αἰσχίνης ὁ Λουσιεύς, ἣ τετελεύτηκεν υἱὸν
19 ἄνδρα ἤδη καταλιποῦσα, Θρασύβουλον. ἔστι δὲ νόμος ⟨ὃς⟩,[3] ἐὰν ἀδελφὸς ὁμοπάτωρ ἄπαις τελευτήσῃ καὶ μὴ διαθέμενος, τήν τε ἀδελφὴν ὁμοίως, κἂν ἐξ ἑτέρας ἀδελφιδοῦς ᾖ γεγονώς, ἰσομοίρους τῶν χρημάτων καθίστησι. καὶ τοῦτο οὐκ ἀγνοούμενόν ἐστιν οὐδὲ παρ᾽ αὐτοῖς τούτοις. ἔργῳ γὰρ οὗτοι φανερὸν τοῦτο πεποιήκασι· τοῦ γὰρ Εὐπόλιδος υἱέος ἄπαιδος Ἀπολλοδώρου τελευτήσαντος τὰ ἡμίσεα Θρασύβουλος εἴληφεν, οὐσίας καὶ
20 πεντεταλάντου καταλειφθείσης ῥᾳδίως. πατρῴων μὲν οὖν καὶ ἀδελφοῦ χρημάτων τὸ ἴσον αὐτοῖς ὁ

---

[1] δὴ Bekker: διό.   [2] εἰ καί τινες Bekker: καὶ οἵτινες.
[3] ὅς add. Aldus.

carried out. Such being the rule, the members of the families and of the ward having full confidence in Apollodorus and being well aware that I was his sister's son, passed an unanimous vote and inscribed my name in the public register, after Apollodorus had sworn with his hand upon the victims. Thus I was adopted by him in his lifetime and my name inscribed in the public register as Thrasyllus the son of Apollodorus, after he had adopted me in this manner, as the laws have given him the power to do. To prove that I am speaking the truth, please take the depositions.

DEPOSITIONS

I imagine, gentlemen, that you would more readily believe those who have given evidence, if certain of the relatives of the same degree as my opponent have obviously attested by their conduct that Apollodorus carried out the adoption in a correct and legal manner. Now Eupolis left two daughters, one who is the present claimant and the wife of Pronapes, and another whom Aeschines of Lusia married and who is dead, but left a son Thrasybulus, who is now of full age. There is a law which provides that, if a brother by the same father dies without issue and intestate, his property shall be divided equally between his surviving sister and any nephew who has been born from another sister. My opponents themselves are well aware of this, as their actual conduct has proved; for, Eupolis's son, Apollodorus (II.), having died without issue, Thrasybulus has received half his estate, which may fairly be estimated at five talents. Thus the law gives the sister and the sister's son an equal

νόμος μετασχεῖν δίδωσιν· ἀνεψιοῦ δέ, καὶ εἴ τις
ἔξω ταύτης τῆς συγγενείας ἐστίν, οὐκ ἴσον, ἀλλὰ
προτέροις τοῖς ἄρρεσι τῶν θηλειῶν τὴν ἀγχιστείαν
πεποίηκε. λέγει γάρ " κρατεῖν δὲ τοὺς ἄρρενας
καὶ τοὺς ἐκ τῶν ἀρρένων, οἳ ἂν ἐκ τῶν αὐτῶν ὦσι,
κἂν γένει ἀπωτέρω τυγχάνωσιν ὄντες." ταύτῃ μὲν
οὖν οὐδὲ[1] μέρους λαχεῖν προσῆκε, Θρασυβούλῳ
δὲ ἁπάντων, εἰ μὴ κυρίαν ἡγεῖτο εἶναι τὴν ἐμὴν
21 εἰσποίησιν. ἐκεῖνος τοίνυν οὔτε ἐξ ἀρχῆς ἠμφισ-
βήτηκε πρὸς ἐμὲ οὐδὲν οὔτε νῦν δίκην εἴληχε
περὶ αὐτῶν, ἀλλὰ ταῦτα πάντα καλῶς ἔχειν ὡμο-
λόγηκεν· οἱ δ' ὑπὲρ ταύτης πάντων ἀμφισβητεῖν
τετολμήκασιν· εἰς τοῦτο ἀναιδείας ἐληλύθασι.
λαβὲ δὴ αὐτοῖς τοὺς νόμους, παρ' οὓς ταῦτα
πεποιήκασι, καὶ ἀνάγνωθι.

ΝΟΜΟΣ[2]

22 Ἐνταῦθα μὲν ὁμοίως καὶ ἀδελφὴ καὶ ἀδελφιδοῦς
ἰσόμοιροι κατὰ τὸν νόμον εἰσί. λαβὲ δὴ καὶ
τοῦτον, καὶ ἀναγίγνωσκε αὐτοῖς.

⟨ΝΟΜΟΣ⟩

Ἐὰν μὴ ὦσιν ἀνεψιοὶ μηδὲ ἀνεψιῶν παῖδες, μηδὲ
τοῦ πρὸς πατρὸς γένους[3] ᾖ προσήκων μηδείς, τότε
ἀπέδωκε τοῖς πρὸς μητρός, διορίσας οὓς δεῖ
κρατεῖν. λαβὲ δὲ αὐτοῖς καὶ τοῦτον τὸν νόμον
καὶ ἀνάγνωθι.

ΝΟΜΟΣ

---

[1] οὐδὲ Aldus: οὐδὲν.   [2] νόμος Aldus: νόμοι.
[3] γένους Dobree: γενομένου.

---

a The law is given *in extenso* in [Dem.] *In Macartatum*
(Or. xliii.) § 51.

share of their father's and their brother's estate ; but when a first cousin, or any other kinsman in a remoter degree, dies, it no longer grants such equality, but gives the male relatives the right of succession as next-of-kin in preference to the female. For it declares that " the males and the issue of the males, who are descended from the same stock, shall be preferred, even though their relationship to the deceased is more remote." The wife of Pronapes, therefore, had no right to claim a share at all, and Thrasybulus ought to have claimed the whole if he regarded my adoption as invalid. Yet from the first he has never disputed my title nor has he now made any claim at law to the estate, but has admitted that everything is in order. On the other hand, those who are acting for this woman have dared—such is their impudence—to claim the whole estate. Take the clauses of the law [a] which they have violated and read them to the court.

CLAUSE OF THE LAW

Under this clause the sister and the nephew share and share alike. Now take this clause and read it to the court.

CLAUSE OF THE LAW

If there are no first cousins or their children or other relatives on the father's side, then the law gives the right of inheritance to the relatives on the mother's side, specifying the order of succession. Now take this clause and read it to the court.

CLAUSE OF THE LAW

23 Ταῦτα τῶν νόμων κελευόντων ὁ μὲν ἀνὴρ ὢν
οὐδὲ μέρους[1] εἴληχεν, οἱ δ' ὑπὲρ ταύτης, τῆς
γυναικός, ἁπάντων· οὕτω τὴν ἀναίδειαν οὐδεμίαν
ζημίαν εἶναι νομίζουσι. καὶ ὑπὲρ τούτων τολ-
μήσουσι καὶ τοῖς λόγοις χρῆσθαι[2] τοιούτοις, ὡς
αὐτοῖς ὅλου τοῦ κλήρου ληκτέον, ὅτι Θρασύβουλος
ἐκποίητος εἰς τὸν οἶκον τὸν Ἱππολοχίδου γέγονε,
λέγοντες τοῦτο μὲν ἀληθές, ἐκεῖνο δ' οὐ προσῆκον·
24 τί γὰρ ἧττον αὐτῷ τῆς συγγενείας ταύτης προσῆκεν; οὐ γὰρ κατὰ τὸν πατέρα ἀλλὰ κατὰ τὴν
μητέρα καὶ τῶν Ἀπολλοδώρου τοῦ Εὐπόλιδος
[66] ὑέος τὸ μέρος εἴληφε· καὶ τῶνδε ἐξῆν | αὐτῷ κατὰ
ταύτην τὴν συγγένειαν λαγχάνειν, ὄντι προτέρῳ
ταύτης, εἴπερ τὰ πεπραγμένα μὴ κυρίως ἔχειν
25 ἐνόμιζεν. ἀλλ' οὐκ ἔστιν ἀναίσχυντος. μητρὸς
δ' οὐδείς ἐστιν ἐκποίητος, ἀλλ' ὁμοίως ὑπάρχει
τὴν αὐτὴν εἶναι μητέρα, κἂν ἐν τῷ πατρῴῳ μένῃ
τις οἴκῳ κἂν ἐκποιηθῇ.[3] διὸ τῶν Ἀπολλοδώρου
χρημάτων οὐκ ἀπεστερήθη τοῦ μέρους, ἀλλὰ μετ-
ειλήφει τὸ ἡμικλήριον, πρὸς ταύτην νειμάμενος.
ὡς δ' ἀληθῆ λέγω, κάλει μοι τούτων τοὺς μάρτυρας.

ΜΑΡΤΥΡΕΣ

26 Οὕτω μὲν οὐχ οἱ γεννῆται μόνον καὶ φράτορες
γεγόνασι μάρτυρες τῆς ἐμῆς ποιήσεως, ἀλλὰ καὶ
Θρασύβουλος οὐκ ἀμφισβητῶν αὐτὸς[4] ἔργῳ δε-

---

[1] μέρους Dobree: τὸ μέρος.
[2] χρῆσθαι scripsi: χρῶνται.
[3] ἐκποιηθῇ Bekker: -θείη.
[4] αὐτὸς Buermann: αὑτῷ.

264

Such being the provisions of the law, Thrasybulus, a male relative, has not claimed even a portion of the estate, but those who are acting for this woman, a female relative, have claimed the whole of it; so persuaded are they that loss of honour is no loss. With this object, to prove that the whole estate ought to be awarded to them, they will have the impudence to use the argument that Thrasybulus has been adopted out of his own family into that of Hippolochides. While the fact is true, the conclusion drawn from it does not apply. For what detriment was caused by this adoption to the bond of kinship which is in question? For it was not in the right of his father but in that of his mother that he has received half the estate of Apollodorus (II.), the son of Eupolis; and by this right of kinship he might have claimed the estate now in dispute, since he has a claim prior to that of this woman, if he thought that the act of adoption was not valid; he is not, however, so devoid of honour. Now the act of adoption into another family does not detach a son from his mother; she is his mother just the same, whether he remains in his father's house or is adopted out of it. That is why Thrasybulus was not deprived of his share of the fortune of Apollodorus (II.), but has received half of it, sharing it with this woman. And to prove that I am speaking the truth, please call the witnesses to these facts.

WITNESSES

Thus not only have the members of the families and of the ward borne testimony to my adoption, but also Thrasybulus has made it clear, by his conduct in not himself claiming the estate, that he considers

δήλωκεν ὅτι τὰ πεπραγμένα ᾿Απολλοδώρῳ κυρίως
ἔχειν νομίζει καὶ κατὰ τοὺς νόμους· οὐ γὰρ ἂν
ποτε τοσούτων χρημάτων οὐκ ἐλάγχανε. γεγόνασι
27 δὲ ὅμως καὶ ἄλλοι μάρτυρες αὐτῶν.[1] πρὶν γὰρ ἐμὲ
ἥκειν ἐκ τῆς Πυθαΐδος, ἔλεγε πρὸς τοὺς δημότας
᾿Απολλόδωρος ὅτι πεποιημένος εἴη με ὑὸν καὶ
ἐγγεγραφὼς εἰς τοὺς συγγενεῖς καὶ φράτορας, καὶ
παραδεδώκοι τὴν οὐσίαν, καὶ διεκελεύεθ᾿ ὅπως, ἄν
τι πάθῃ[2] πρότερον, ἐγγράψουσι[3] με εἰς τὸ ληξιαρχικὸν γραμματεῖον Θράσυλλον ᾿Απολλοδώρου καὶ
28 μὴ ὡς ἄλλως ποιήσουσι.[4] κἀκεῖνοι ταῦτα ἀκούσαντες, τούτων ἐν ἀρχαιρεσίαις κατηγορούντων
καὶ λεγόντων ὡς οὐκ ἐποιήσατό με ὑόν, καὶ ἐξ ὧν
ἤκουσαν καὶ ἐξ ὧν ᾔδεσαν, ὀμόσαντες καθ᾿ ἱερῶν
ἐνέγραψάν με, καθάπερ ἐκεῖνος ἐκέλευε· τοσαύτη
περιφάνεια τῆς ἐμῆς ποιήσεως ἐγένετο παρ᾿
αὐτοῖς. ὡς δ᾿ ἀληθῆ λέγω, κάλει μοι τούτων τοὺς
μάρτυρας.

ΜΑΡΤΥΡΕΣ

29 ᾿Επὶ μὲν τοσούτων μαρτύρων, ὦ ἄνδρες, γέγονεν ἡ ποίησις, ἔχθρας μὲν παλαιᾶς αὐτῷ πρὸς τούτους οὔσης, φιλίας δὲ πρὸς ἡμᾶς καὶ συγγενείας
οὐ μικρᾶς ὑπαρχούσης. ὡς δ᾿ οὐδ᾿ εἰ μηδέτερον
τούτων ὑπῆρχε, μήτε ἔχθρα πρὸς τούτους μήτε
φιλία πρὸς ἡμᾶς, οὐκ ἄν ποτε ᾿Απολλόδωρος ἐπὶ

---

[1] αὐτῶν Scheibe: αὐτῷ. [2] πάθη Schaefer: -οι.
[3] ἐγγράψουσι Dobree: -φουσι. [4] ποιήσουσι Dobree: -ωσι.

---

[a] i.e., his adoption of the speaker.
[b] See Introduction, p. 247.

the acts of Apollodorus [a] to be valid and in conformity with the laws ; for otherwise he would not
fail now to claim so large a fortune. But there
have been other witnesses to these facts. For
before my return from the Pythaid festival,[b] Apollodorus informed his fellow demesmen that he had
adopted me as his son and had registered me with
the members of the families and of the ward and had
committed his property to my care, and he begged
them, if anything should happen to him before my
return, to enrol me on the public register as Thrasyllus the son of Apollodorus and not to fail him in
the matter. Having heard this expression of his
wishes, although our opponents complained at the
electoral meeting of the deme and declared that
Apollodorus had not adopted me, the members,
as a result of what they had heard and from their
own knowledge of the facts, took the oath over the
victims and registered my name in accordance with
Apollodorus's injunctions ; so notorious among them
was the fact of my adoption. And to prove the
truth of my statements, please call the witnesses
to these facts.

WITNESSES

It was before all these witnesses, gentlemen, that
my adoption took place, at a time when an inveterate
enmity existed between Apollodorus and my
opponent, and a close friendship as well as kinship
between Apollodorus and us. But it is, I think,
quite easy to prove to you, that, even if he had had
neither of these sentiments—enmity towards my
opponents and affection towards us—Apollodorus
would never have left his estate to them. All men,

τούτοις τὸν κλῆρον τοῦτον κατέλιπεν, οἶμαι καὶ
30 ταῦθ' ὑμῖν ῥᾳδίως ἐπιδείξειν. πάντες γὰρ οἱ
τελευτήσειν μέλλοντες πρόνοιαν ποιοῦνται σφῶν
αὐτῶν, ὅπως μὴ ἐξερημώσουσι τοὺς σφετέρους
αὐτῶν οἴκους, ἀλλ' ἔσται τις [καὶ] ὁ ἐναγιῶν
καὶ πάντα τὰ νομιζόμενα αὐτοῖς ποιήσων· διὸ
κἂν ἄπαιδες τελευτήσωσιν, ἀλλ' οὖν ποιησάμενοι καταλείπουσι. καὶ οὐ μόνον ἰδίᾳ ταῦτα
γιγνώσκουσιν, ἀλλὰ καὶ δημοσίᾳ τὸ κοινὸν τῆς
πόλεως οὕτω ταῦτ' ἔγνωκε· νόμῳ γὰρ τῷ ἄρχοντι
τῶν οἴκων, ὅπως ἂν μὴ ἐξερημῶνται, προστάττει
31 τὴν ἐπιμέλειαν. ἐκείνῳ δὲ πρόδηλον ἦν ὅτι εἰ
καταλείψει τὸν κλῆρον ἐπὶ τούτοις, ἔρημον ποιήσει
τὸν οἶκον, τί προορῶντι; ταύτας τὰς ἀδελφὰς τὸν
μὲν Ἀπολλοδώρου τοῦ ἀδελφοῦ κλῆρον ἐχούσας,
ἐκείνῳ δ' οὐκ εἰσποιούσας ὄντων αὐταῖς παίδων,
καὶ τοὺς μὲν ἄνδρας αὐτῶν τὴν γῆν, ἣν ἐκεῖνος
κατέλιπε, καὶ τὰ κτήματα πέντε ταλάντων πεπρα-
κότας καὶ τὸ ἀργύριον διανειμαμένους, τὸν δὲ
οἶκον αἰσχρῶς οὕτω καὶ δεινῶς ἐξηρημωμένον.
32 ὃς δὴ ταῦτ' ᾔδει τὸν τούτων ἀδελφὸν πεπονθότα,
πῶς ἂν προσεδόκησεν αὐτός, εἰ καὶ φίλος ἦν,
τυχεῖν τῶν νομιζομένων ὑπ' αὐτῶν, ἀνεψιὸς ὢν
ἀλλ' οὐκ ἀδελφὸς αὐταῖς; οὐκ ἐνῆν ἐλπίσαι
δήπουθεν. ἀλλὰ μὴν ὅτι ἄπαιδα ἐκεῖνον περι-
εωράκασι καὶ τὰ χρήματα ἔχουσι καὶ οἶκον ἐκ τοῦ
φανεροῦ τριηραρχοῦντα ἀνῃρήκασι, κάλει μοι καὶ
τούτων τοὺς μάρτυρας.

when they are near their end, take measures of precaution on their own behalf to prevent their families from becoming extinct and to secure that there shall be someone to perform sacrifices and carry out the customary rites over them. And so, even if they die without issue, they at any rate adopt children and leave them behind. And there is not merely a personal feeling in favour of this course, but the state has taken public measures to secure that it shall be followed, since by law it entrusts the archon with the duty of preventing families from being extinguished. Now it was quite clear to Apollodorus that, if he left his estate in the hands of my opponents, he would be securing the extinction of his house. For what did he see before his eyes? He saw that these sisters of Apollodorus (II.) inherited their brother's estate, but never gave him a son by adoption, though they had sons of their own, and that their husbands had sold the landed property which he left behind him and his possessions for five talents and divided up the proceeds, but that his house had been left shamefully and deplorably desolate. Knowing that their brother had been treated thus, could he himself have ever expected, even if there had been friendship between him and them, to receive the customary rites from them, being only their cousin and not their brother? Surely he could have no such expectation. And now please summon the witnesses to show that my opponents have viewed with indifference their brother's childlessness, and are in possession of his fortune, and have allowed a family to die out which was obviously capable of supporting the expense of a trierarchy.

ISAEUS

33 Εἰ τοίνυν καὶ τοιοῦτοι τὰς φύσεις περὶ ἀλλήλους
εἰσὶ καὶ ἔχθραι πρὸς Ἀπολλόδωρον τὸν ἐμὲ ποιησάμενον ὑπῆρχον αὐτοῖς[1] τηλικαῦται τὸ μέγεθος, τί
βέλτιον ἂν ἔπραξεν ἢ ταῦτα βουλευσάμενος ἅπερ
ἐποίησεν; εἰ νὴ Δία παιδίον ἐποιήσατο λαβὼν
παρά του τῶν[2] φίλων ὄντων, καὶ τούτῳ τὴν
οὐσίαν ἔδωκεν; ἀλλὰ [καὶ] τοῦτ᾽ ἦν ἄδηλον καὶ
τοῖς γεννήσασιν, εἴτε σπουδαῖον εἴτε μηδενὸς ἄξιον
34 ἔμελλεν ἔσεσθαι, διὰ τὴν ἡλικίαν. ἐμοῦ δὲ πεῖραν
εἰλήφει, δοκιμασίαν ἱκανὴν λαβών. εἴς τε γὰρ
[67] τὸν πατέρα καὶ τὴν μητέρα | οἷος ἦν ἀκριβῶς
ᾔδει, τῶν τ᾽ οἰκείων ἐπιμελῆ καὶ τἀμαυτοῦ πράττειν ἐπιστάμενον· ἐν ἀρχῇ τε, θεσμοθετήσας, ὡς
ἐγενόμην οὐκ ἄδικος οὐδὲ πλεονέκτης, ἠπίστατο
σαφῶς. ὥστ᾽ οὐκ ἀγνοῶν ἀλλὰ σαφῶς εἰδὼς
35 ἐποίει με τῶν αὑτοῦ κύριον. καὶ μὴν οὐδὲ ἀλλότριον ἀλλ᾽ ὄντα ἀδελφιδοῦν, οὐδ᾽ αὖ μικρὰ πεπονθὼς ἀλλὰ μεγάλα ἀγαθὰ ὑφ᾽ ἡμῶν, οὐδ᾽ αὖ ἀφιλό-
τιμον, ὃς τὰ ὄντα ἀφανιεῖν[3] ἔμελλον ὥσπερ οὗτοι
τὰ τοῦ κλήρου πεποιήκασιν, ἀλλὰ βουλησόμενον
καὶ τριηραρχεῖν καὶ πολεμεῖν καὶ χορηγεῖν καὶ
πάνθ᾽ ὑμῖν τὰ προσταττόμενα ποιεῖν, ὥσπερ
36 κἀκεῖνος. καίτοι εἰ καὶ συγγενὴς καὶ φίλος καὶ
εὐεργέτης καὶ φιλότιμος καὶ δεδοκιμασμένος ὑπῆρχον τοιοῦτος εἶναι, τίς ⟨ἂν⟩[4] ἀμφισβητήσειε μὴ

---

[1] αὐτοῖς Reiske: αὐταῖς.
[2] παρά του τῶν Reiske: παρὰ τούτων.
[3] ἀφανιεῖν Cobet: ἀφιέναι.   [4] ἂν add. Bekker.

---

[a] This title was given to the six junior archons, who

270

WITNESSES

Since such was the disposition of the cousins towards one another and so grave the resentment towards Apollodorus who adopted me, how could he have done better than follow the course which he did? Would he, in Heaven's name, have done better if he had chosen a child from the family of one of his friends and adopted him and given him his property? But even such a child's own parents would not have known, owing to his youth, whether he would turn out a good man or worthless. On the other hand, he had had experience of me, having sufficiently tested me; he well knew what had been my behaviour towards my father and mother, my care for my relatives and my capacity for managing my own affairs. He was well aware that in my official capacity as thesmothete *a* I have been neither unjust nor rapacious. It was then not in ignorance, but with full knowledge, that he was making me master of his property. Further, I was no stranger but his own nephew; the services which I had rendered him were not unimportant but very considerable; he knew that I was not a man devoid of public spirit, who would be likely to squander his possessions, as my opponents have squandered the property which composes the estate, but that I should be anxious to act as a trierarch and go on service and act as choregus and do everything else that the state requires, as he himself had done. Since I was his kinsman, his friend, his benefactor, and a man of public spirit, and had been approved as such, who could maintain that my adoption was

presided at the allotment of the magistrates and were responsible for revising the laws.

οὐκ ἀνδρὸς εὖ φρονοῦντος εἶναι ταύτην τὴν ποίησιν; ἐγὼ τοίνυν ἔν γε τῶν ὑπ᾽ ἐκείνου δοκιμα-
σθέντων ἤδη πεποίηκα· γεγυμνασιάρχηκα γὰρ εἰς
Προμήθεια[1] τοῦδε τοῦ ἐνιαυτοῦ φιλοτίμως, ὡς οἱ
φυλέται πάντες ἴσασιν. ὡς δ᾽ ἀληθῆ λέγω, κάλει
μοι τούτων τοὺς μάρτυρας.

MAPTYPEΣ

37 Τὰ μὲν ἡμέτερα δίκαια, καθ᾽ ἃ προσηκόντως
ἔχειν φαμὲν τὸν κλῆρον, ταῦτ᾽ ἐστίν, ὦ ἄνδρες·
δεόμεθα δ᾽ ὑμῶν βοηθεῖν ἡμῖν καὶ ἕνεκα Ἀπολλοδώρου καὶ ἕνεκα τοῦ ἐκείνου πατρός· οὐ γὰρ
ἀχρήστους αὐτοὺς εὑρήσετε πολίτας, ἀλλ᾽ ὡς οἷόν
38 τ᾽ εἰς τὰ ὑμέτερα προθυμοτάτους.[2] ὁ μὲν γὰρ
πατὴρ αὐτοῦ τάς τε ἄλλας ἁπάσας λητουργίας
λελητούργηκε, καὶ τριηραρχῶν τὸν πάντα χρόνον
διετέλεσεν, οὐκ ἐκ συμμορίας [τὴν ναῦν ποιησά-
μενος] ὥσπερ οἱ νῦν, ἀλλ᾽ ἐκ τῶν αὑτοῦ δαπανῶν,
οὐδὲ δεύτερος αὐτὸς ὢν ἀλλὰ κατὰ μόνας, οὐδὲ
δύο ἔτη διαλιπὼν ἀλλὰ συνεχῶς, οὐδ᾽ ἀφοσιού-
μενος ἀλλ᾽ ὡς οἷόν τ᾽ ἄριστα παρασκευαζόμενος.
ἀνθ᾽ ὧν ὑμεῖς κἀκεῖνον ἐτιμᾶτε, μεμνημένοι τούτων τῶν ἔργων, καὶ τὸν υἱὸν αὐτοῦ τῶν χρημάτων
ἀποστερούμενον ἐσώσατε, τοὺς ἔχοντας ἀποδοῦναι
39 τὰ ὄντ᾽ αὐτῷ καταναγκάσαντες. καὶ μὴν καὶ
αὐτὸς Ἀπολλόδωρος οὐχ ὥσπερ Προνάπης ἀπ-
εγράψατο μὲν τίμημα μικρόν, ὡς ἱππάδα δὲ τελῶν

---

[1] Προμήθεια Meursius: προμήθειαν.
[2] προθυμοτάτους Stephanus: -τέρους.

---

[a] The duty of a gymnasiarch at the festival of Prometheus
was to provide a team to compete in the inter-tribal torch-
race.

not the act of a man of sound judgement ? Indeed,
I have already performed one of those acts, the
promise of which had won his approval ; for I have
acted as gymnasiarch [a] at the festival of Prometheus
in the present year with a liberality which all my
fellow-tribesmen acknowledge. Please call the
witnesses to prove that these statements are true.

WITNESSES

These, gentlemen, are the just grounds on which
we claim that we are entitled to keep the estate ;
and we beseech you to help us for the sake of Apollodorus and his father, for you will find that they were
useful citizens and as zealous as possible for your
interests. His father not only performed all the
other state services but also acted continuously as
a trierarch, not contributing jointly with several
others,[b] as is the practice nowadays, but bearing
the expenses out of his own fortune, and not jointly
with one other but by himself alone ; nor did he
intermit his duties for two years [c] but served continuously, not performing his duties in a perfunctory
manner but providing the most perfect equipment.
Wherefore, mindful of these services you honoured
him and saved his son when he was being robbed
of his fortune, forcing those who were in possession
of his property to restore it. Again, Apollodorus
himself did not, like Pronapes, assess his property
below its value, but, paying taxes as a knight, aspired

[b] The system under which several citizens could jointly
contribute to provide a trireme for the service of the state
appears to have come into force about 357 B.C.; see Introduction, p. 247.

[c] *i.e.*, he did not avail himself of the period of exemption
allowed by law.

ἄρχειν ἠξίου τὰς ἀρχάς, οὐδὲ βίᾳ μὲν ἐζήτει τὰ
ἀλλότρι' ἔχειν, ὑμᾶς δ' ᾤετο δεῖν μηδὲν ὠφελεῖν,
ἀλλὰ φανερὰ τὰ ὄντα καταστήσας ὑμῖν, ὅσα προσ-
τάττοιτε, πάνθ' ὑπηρέτει [φιλοτίμως] οὐδέν τ'
ἀδικῶν ἐκ τῶν ἑαυτοῦ φιλοτίμως ἐπειρᾶτο ζῆν,
εἰς αὑτὸν μὲν τὰ μέτρια ἀναλίσκειν οἰόμενος δεῖν,
τὰ δ' ἄλλα τῇ πόλει περιποιεῖν, ἵνα ἐξαρκοίη πρὸς
40 τὰς δαπάνας. κἀκ τούτων τίνα λῃτουργίαν οὐκ
ἐξελῃτούργησεν; ἢ τίνα εἰσφορὰν οὐκ ἐν πρώτοις
εἰσήνεγκεν; ἢ τί παραλέλοιπεν ὧν προσῆκεν; ὅς
γε καὶ παιδικῷ χορῷ χορηγῶν ἐνίκησεν, ὧν
μνημεῖα τῆς ἐκείνου φιλοτιμίας ὁ τρίπους ἐκεῖνος
ἔστηκε. καίτοι τί χρὴ τὸν μέτριον πολίτην; οὐχ
οὗ μὲν ἕτεροι τὰ μὴ προσήκοντ' ἐβιάζοντο λαμβάνειν, τούτων μηδὲν ποιεῖν, τὰ δ' ἑαυτοῦ πειρᾶσθαι σῴζειν; οὗ δ' ἡ πόλις δεῖται χρημάτων, ἐν
πρώτοις εἰσφέρειν καὶ μηδὲν ἀποκρύπτεσθαι τῶν
41 ὄντων; ἐκεῖνος τοίνυν τοιοῦτος ἦν· ἀνθ' ὧν δικαίως ἂν αὐτῷ ταύτην τὴν χάριν ἀποδοίητε, τὴν
ἐκείνου γνώμην περὶ τῶν αὑτοῦ κυρίαν εἶναι ποιήσαντες. καὶ μὴν καὶ ἐμέ γε, ὅσα κατὰ τὴν ἐμὴν
ἡλικίαν, εὑρήσετε οὐ κακὸν οὐδὲ ἄχρηστον. ἐστράτευμαι τὰς στρατείας[1] τῇ πόλει, τὰ προσταττόμενα ποιῶ· τοῦτο γὰρ τῶν τηλικούτων ἔργον ἐστί.
42 καὶ ἐκείνων οὖν ἕνεκα καὶ ἡμῶν εἰκότως ἂν

---

[1] τὰς στρατείας Scaliger: ταῖς στρατείαις.

to hold the offices open to that rank, nor did he seek
to possess himself by violence of the property of
others and think that you ought to have no advantage
from his wealth, but he openly declared the amount
of his fortune and met whatever demands for service
you made upon him, and wronging no man he tried
to live honourably on his own fortune, considering
that he ought to be moderate in his personal expenditure and dedicate the surplus to the service of the
state, so that it might meet its expenses. As a
result of these principles, what public service did
he fail perfectly to discharge ? To what war-tax
was he not among the first to contribute ? What
duty has he ever failed to perform ? When he
undertook the provision of a choir of boys, he was
victorious in the competition, and the well-known
tripod still stands as a memorial of his honourable
ambition. And what is the duty of a respectable
citizen ? Was it not his duty, while others were trying
to take by force what did not belong to them, to do
no such thing himself but to try and preserve what
was his own ? Is it not his duty, when the state
needs money, to be among the first to contribute
and not to conceal any part of his fortune ? Such
then was Apollodorus ; and you would make a just
return for his services if you ratified his intentions
as to the disposal of his own property. As for myself,
you will find me, as far as my youth allows, neither
a bad nor a useless citizen. I have served on your
military expeditions, I perform all the duties which
are laid upon me ; for this is the function of men of
my age. For the sake, then, of Apollodorus and
his father and for the sake of me and my family
you would be justified in considering our case with

275

ποιήσαισθε[1] πρόνοιαν, ἄλλως τε καὶ τούτων τριηραρχοῦντα οἶκον πεντετάλαντον ἀνῃρηκότων καὶ πε-
πρακότων καὶ ἔρημον πεποιηκότων, ἡμῶν δὲ καὶ
λελῃτουργηκότων ἤδη καὶ λῃτουργησόντων, ἂν
ὑμεῖς ἐπικυρώσητε τὴν Ἀπολλοδώρου γνώμην ἀπο-
δόντες ἡμῖν τοῦτον τὸν κλῆρον.

43 Ἵνα δὲ μὴ δοκῶ διατρίβειν περὶ ταῦτα ποιούμενος τοὺς λόγους, βούλομαι διὰ βραχέων ὑμᾶς
ὑπομνήσας οὕτω καταβαίνειν, τί ἑκάτερος ἡμῶν
ἀξιοῖ, δηλώσας. ἐγὼ μὲν ἀδελφῆς οὔσης τῆς ἐμῆς
[68] | μητρὸς Ἀπολλοδώρῳ, φιλίας αὐτοῖς πολλῆς ὑπ-
αρχούσης, ἔχθρας δ᾽ οὐδεμιᾶς πώποτε γενομένης,
ἀδελφιδοῦς ὢν καὶ ποιηθεὶς υἱὸς ὑπ᾽ ἐκείνου ζῶντος
καὶ εὖ φρονοῦντος, καὶ εἰς τοὺς γεννήτας καὶ
φράτορας ἐγγραφείς, ἔχειν τὰ δοθέντα, καὶ μὴ
ἐπὶ τούτοις ⟨εἶναι⟩[2] ἐξερημῶσαι τὸν οἶκον τὸν
ἐκείνου· Προνάπης δὲ τί ὑπὲρ τῆς ἀμφισβητούσης;

44 ἔχειν μὲν τοῦ τῆς γυναικὸς ἀδελφοῦ τιμὴν τοῦ
ἡμικληρίου πένθ᾽ ἡμιτάλαντα, λαβεῖν δὲ καὶ τόνδε
τὸν κλῆρον ἑτέρων ταῖς ἀγχιστείαις προτέρων
αὐτοῦ τῆς γυναικὸς ὄντων, οὔτ᾽ ἐκείνῳ παῖδα
εἰσπεποιηκὼς ἀλλὰ τὸν οἶκον ἐξηρημωκώς, οὔτε[3]
τούτῳ ἂν εἰσποιήσας, ἀλλ᾽ ὁμοίως ἂν καὶ τοῦτον
ἐξερημώσας, καὶ ἔχθρας μὲν τηλικαύτης ὑπαρχούσης αὐτοῖς, διαλλαγῆς δὲ οὐδεμιᾶς πώποτε

45 ὕστερον γενομένης. ταῦτα χρὴ σκοπεῖν, ὦ ἄνδρες,
κἀκεῖνο ἐνθυμεῖσθαι, ὅτι ἐγὼ μὲν ἀδελφιδοῦς αὐτῷ,

---

[1] ποιήσαισθε Bekker: -ησθε.
[2] εἶναι add. Reiske. [3] οὔτε Bekker: οὐδὲ.

benevolence, especially since our adversaries have made away with and sold an estate of five talents that supported the trierarchy and reduced it to desolation, whereas we have already supported public burdens and will continue to do so in the future, if you ratify the intentions of Apollodorus by restoring to us this estate.

But, in order that I may not seem tedious by dwelling any longer on these facts, I should like, before I step down, to lay before you, by way of brief reminder, the points on which each party bases its claim. My mother was Apollodorus's sister, and a close affection, never interrupted by any quarrel, existed between them ; being his nephew and having been adopted by him as his son during his lifetime and when he was in full possession of his faculties, and having been registered with the members of the families and of the ward, I claim to possess the estate which he gave me and demand that my opponents should not be in a position to make his house desolate. What does Pronapes claim on behalf of the plaintiff ? He claims to keep half of the estate of his wife's brother, valued at two-and-a-half talents, and also to receive this estate, although there are others more nearly related to the deceased than his wife ; yet he has not given him a son by posthumous adoption but has left his house desolate, and he would similarly fail to give Apollodorus a son by adoption and would leave his house likewise desolate ; and he makes this claim although such enmity existed between them and no subsequent reconciliation took place. You must take these facts into consideration, gentlemen, and remember that I am the nephew of the deceased,

ἡ δὲ ἀνεψιὰ τοῦ τελευτήσαντος, καὶ ὅτι ἡ μὲν δύ᾽
ἔχειν ἀξιοῖ κλήρους, ἐγὼ δὲ τοῦτον μόνον εἰς
ὅνπερ εἰσεποιήθην, καὶ ὅτι αὕτη μὲν οὐκ εὔνους
τῷ καταλιπόντι τὸν κλῆρον, ἐγὼ δὲ καὶ ὁ ἐμὸς
πάππος εὐεργέται γεγόναμεν αὐτοῦ. ταῦτα πάντα
σκεψάμενοι καὶ διαλογιζόμενοι πρὸς ὑμᾶς αὐτοὺς
τίθεσθε τὴν ψῆφον ᾗ δίκαιόν ἐστι.

Οὐκ οἶδ᾽ ὅτι δεῖ πλείω λέγειν· οἶμαι γὰρ ὑμᾶς
οὐδὲν ἀγνοεῖν τῶν εἰρημένων.

while the plaintiff is only his cousin ; that she claims two estates, I claim only one, to which I have a right by adoption ; that she was not on good terms with him who left the property, whereas I and my grandfather have been his benefactors. Having considered all these points and weighing them in your own minds, give your verdict in accordance with justice.

I do not know of anything more that I need say ; for I think that no part of my argument has escaped your attention.

VIII ON THE ESTATE OF CIRON

VIII. ON THE ESTATE OF CIRON

INTRODUCTION

Ciron having died without leaving a son, two claimants contested his estate. One was the son of his brother; the other claimed to be the son of his daughter, and is the speaker of the present oration.[a] Ciron had been twice married. By his first wife, who was also his first cousin, he had, according to the speaker, a daughter, who married, firstly, Nausimenes, by whom she had no issue,

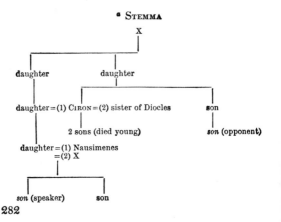

[a] STEMMA

X
├── daughter
└── daughter
    ├── daughter = (1) CIRON = (2) sister of Diocles
    │   │   2 sons (died young)
    │   └── daughter = (1) Nausimenes
    │   = (2) X
    │   ├── son (speaker)
    │   └── son
    └── son
        son (opponent)

and after his death a second husband, whose name is not given, by whom she had two sons, the present speaker and his brother. Secondly, Ciron had married the sister of Diocles of Phlya, by whom he had two sons, who died in infancy. Both claimants had presented themselves at the house of the deceased as soon as he had died, eager to carry out the funeral rites and so establish a claim to be the heir; and an unseemly wrangle seems to have occurred at the grave-side.

It is clear from the speech that the opposing party, whose speech was delivered first, had based his claim on the grounds, first, that the speaker's mother was not a legitimate daughter of Ciron, and, secondly, that even if she were legitimate, a brother's son has a better claim in law than a daughter's son.

On the first point the speaker finds it difficult to produce any convincing arguments. He can only furnish hearsay evidence of Ciron's first marriage, which must have taken place some forty years earlier, and the birth of a daughter. He relies, therefore, in the main on the conduct of Ciron towards his daughter, showing that he formally betrothed her to both her husbands, giving a marriage feast and entertaining the members of his ward, and on the fact that he and his brother were duly enrolled in their father's ward without any objection being raised. He further states that his grandfather Ciron had frequently taken himself and his brother with him to public festivals and had invited them to his domestic sacrifices. He seeks support for such evidence as he can produce by pointing out that his opponents have refused to allow the slaves of Ciron, who might be supposed to know the facts better than anyone else, to be examined under torture, and draws the conclusion that his opponents feared that the evidence of the slaves would be unfavourable to their case.

The speaker next deals with the second argument of his opponents and contends that descendants have a stronger claim to an intestate estate than collaterals. He takes the case of the nearest collateral, namely, a brother, and argues that a daughter's child has a better claim to his grandfather's estate than the grandfather's brother, and therefore, *a fortiori*, a better claim than a nephew. He supports his argument by citing the law under which descendants are obliged to support their indigent parents and grandparents, an obligation which does not apply to collaterals; if, he argues, a man is legally bound to support his grandfather, he has a corresponding right to inherit his intestate estate.

The last division of the speech is devoted to detailing the misdeeds of Diocles, who is alleged to be the real instigator of the counter-claim, the nominal opponent being merely a man of straw. He is represented as having defrauded his sister and his nephew, as having murdered one brother-in-law and having caused the other to be deprived of his civic rights, and as a man of notoriously evil life. He is alleged to have obtained possession by fraud of Ciron's estate during his lifetime, and now, being afraid of having to give it up, to have stated that Ciron left nothing at all, though at the same time he was instigating his nephew to claim the estate. He promises further revelations in a prosecution which is still pending against Diocles.[a]

The date of the present speech, which is one of the best arranged and best argued of the extant orations of Isaeus, can be fixed within rather wide limits. Since Ciron's grandsons were born after the archonship of Eucleides in 403 B.C. (§ 43), and were certainly more than twenty years of age at the time of the speech, the date cannot be earlier than 383 B.C.: on the other hand, it cannot be later than 363 B.C., since certain passages in it are borrowed by his pupil Demosthenes in his speeches against guardians, Aphobus and Onetor, which were delivered in that and the following year.[b]

[a] We should know more about Diocles if we possessed the two speeches known to have been written against him by Isaeus, of which only insignificant fragments have survived, for which see pp. 449-50.

[b] See Introduction, p. ix.

VIII. ΠΕΡΙ ΤΟΥ ΚΙΡΩΝΟΣ ΚΛΗΡΟΥ

ΥΠΟΘΕΣΙΣ

Κίρωνος ἄπαιδος γνησίων τελευτήσαντος παίδων ἀδελφιδοῦς τις αὐτοῦ κατὰ πατέρα ἀντιποιηθεὶς τοῦ κλήρου
παρέλαβε τὴν οὐσίαν αὐτοῦ παρὰ τῆς γυναικός· καὶ
μετὰ ταῦτα ὁ λέγων τὸν λόγον γράφεται τὸν ἀδελφιδοῦν,
φάσκων θυγατριδοῦς εἶναι Κίρωνος, καὶ ὅτι ἡ γυνὴ τοῦ
τετελευτηκότος ἑκοῦσα προέδωκε τὸν κλῆρον τῷ ἀδελφιδῷ, ἵνα μέρος δοῦσα αὐτῷ τὰ λοιπὰ κερδάνῃ. καὶ ἡ μὲν
ὑπόθεσις αὕτη, ἡ στάσις δὲ στοχασμός· ζητεῖται γὰρ
εἴτε θυγατριδοῦς ἐστιν οὗτος τοῦ Κίρωνος γνήσιος εἴτε
οὔ. ἐπιπλέκεται δ' αὐτῷ καὶ ἡ κατὰ ποιότητα ζήτησις.
ὁ γὰρ ἀδελφιδοῦς ἠγωνίζετο, λέγων ὅτι εἰ καὶ δῶμεν
ἐκείνην γνησίαν εἶναι θυγατέρα Κίρωνος, ἐπειδὴ ἐτελεύτησεν ἐκείνη, ὁ δ' υἱὸς αὐτῆς ἀμφισβητεῖ νῦν, προ-
τιμητέος ἐστὶν ὁ κατὰ πατέρα ἀδελφιδοῦς τοῦ ἀπὸ θυγατρὸς ἐκγόνου, κατὰ τὸν νόμον ἐκεῖνον, τὸν κελεύοντα
προτιμᾶσθαι τοὺς ἀπὸ τῶν ἀρρένων τῶν ἀπὸ τῶν θηλειῶν. οὗτος γὰρ τεχνικώτατα πάνυ σιωπήσας τοῦτον
τὸν νόμον, ἐκ τῆς τῶν τεκόντων διαφορᾶς ἀγωνίζεται,
δεικνὺς ὅτι ὅσον θυγάτηρ ἀδελφοῦ οἰκειοτέρα τοῖς τε-
λευτῶσι, τοσοῦτον ἔκγονος ἀδελφιδοῦ διαφέρει. ἔρρωται
οὖν ἐνταῦθα τῷ δικαίῳ καὶ ἀσθενεῖ τῷ νομίμῳ· τὴν
δὲ ἐργασίαν τῶν κεφαλαίων κατὰ τὴν οἰκείαν πάλιν
ἐργάζεται δύναμιν.

1 Ἐπὶ τοῖς τοιούτοις, ὦ ἄνδρες, ἀνάγκη ἐστὶ χαλε-

286

VIII. ON THE ESTATE OF CIRON

ARGUMENT

Ciron having died without legitimate offspring, his nephew, the son of his brother, claimed his estate and took over the property from the widow. After this the speaker of the present oration indicts the nephew, alleging that he himself is a son of Ciron's daughter and that the wife of the deceased designedly handed over the estate to the nephew with the intention of giving him a part and appropriating the remainder. Such is the subject; the discussion turns on a question of fact, the point at issue being whether the claimant is a legitimate grandson of Ciron or not. A further question is also involved, namely, one of qualification: for the nephew argued that, even if we grant that his opponent's mother is a legitimate daughter of Ciron, since she is dead and it is her son who now claims, the nephew, the son of a brother, ought to have preference over a daughter's issue under the law which ordains that the descendants of males have precedence over those of females. The speaker with great skill completely ignores this law and bases his case upon the different qualifications of the parents, showing that, in as much as a daughter is nearer in kin to the deceased than a brother, so her son has a stronger claim than a brother's son. It is a strong case in equity but a weak case in law. The working out of the various topics is carried out with Isaeus's usual skill.

It is impossible, gentlemen, not to feel indignation

πῶς φέρειν, ὅταν τινὲς μὴ μόνον τῶν ἀλλοτρίων
ἀμφισβητεῖν τολμῶσιν, ἀλλὰ καὶ τὰ ἐκ τῶν νόμων
δίκαια τοῖς σφετέροις αὐτῶν λόγοις ἀφανιεῖν[1] ἐλπί-
ζωσιν· ὅπερ καὶ νῦν οὗτοι ποιεῖν ἐγχειροῦσι. τοῦ
γὰρ ἡμετέρου πάππου Κίρωνος οὐκ ἄπαιδος τελευτήσαντος, ἀλλ' ἡμᾶς ἐκ θυγατρὸς αὐτοῦ γνησίας
παῖδας αὐτῷ καταλελοιπότος, οὗτοί τοῦ τε[2] κλήρου
λαγχάνουσιν ὡς ἐγγυτάτω γένους ὄντες, ἡμᾶς τε
ὑβρίζουσιν ὡς οὐκ ἐξ ἐκείνου θυγατρὸς ὄντας, οὐδὲ[3]
2 γενομένης αὐτῷ πώποτε τὸ παράπαν. αἴτιον δὲ
τοῦ ταῦτα ποιεῖν αὐτούς ἐστιν ἡ τούτων πλεον-
εξία <καὶ>[4] τὸ πλῆθος τῶν χρημάτων ὧν Κίρων
μὲν καταλέλοιπεν, οὗτοι δ' ἔχουσι βιασάμενοι καὶ
κρατοῦσι· καὶ τολμῶσιν ἅμα μὲν λέγειν ὡς οὐδὲν
καταλέλοιπεν ἐκεῖνος, ἅμα δὲ ποιεῖσθαι τοῦ κλή-
3 ρου τὴν ἀμφισβήτησιν. τὴν μὲν οὖν κρίσιν οὐ δεῖ
μοι νομίζειν εἶναι ταύτην πρὸς τὸν εἰληχότα τοῦ
κλήρου τὴν δίκην, ἀλλὰ πρὸς Διοκλέα τὸν Φλυέα,
[69] τὸν Ὀρέστην ἐπικαλούμενον· οὗτος γάρ ἐστιν | ὁ
τοῦτον παρασκευάσας πράγμαθ' ἡμῖν παρέχειν,
ἀποστερῶν τὰ χρήματα ἃ Κίρων ὁ πάππος ἀπο-
θνῄσκων κατέλιπεν, ἡμῖν δὲ τούτους τοὺς κινδύνους ἐπάγων, ἵνα μηδὲν ἀποδιδῷ τούτων, ἐὰν
ὑμεῖς ἐξαπατηθῆτε πεισθέντες ὑπὸ τῶν τούτου
4 λόγων. δεῖ δὴ τούτων τοιαῦτα μηχανωμένων
πάνθ' ὑμᾶς τὰ πεπραγμένα μαθεῖν, ἵνα μηδὲν
ἀγνοήσαντες τῶν γεγενημένων ἀλλὰ σαφῶς εἰδότες
περὶ αὐτῶν, οὕτως ἐνέγκητε[5] τὴν ψῆφον. εἴ τινι
οὖν καὶ ἄλλῃ πώποτε δίκῃ προσέσχετε[6] ἀκριβῶς

---

[1] ἀφανιεῖν Baiter : ἀφανίζειν.
[2] τοῦ τε Reiske : τε τοῦ.
[3] οὐδὲ Reiske : οὔτε.
[4] καὶ add. Reiske.
[5] ἐνέγκητε Aldus : -οιτε.
[6] προσέσχετε Aldus : -έχετε.

against men who not only have the impudence to claim the property of others but also hope by their arguments to abolish the rights which the laws confer ; and this is what our opponents are now trying to do. For, though our grandfather Ciron did not die childless but has left us behind him, the sons of his legitimate daughter, yet our opponents claim the estate as next-of-kin and insult us by alleging that we are not the issue of his daughter, and indeed that he never had a daughter at all. The reason of their acting thus is their avarice, and the high value of the estate which he has left behind him and which they have taken by force and still hold ; and they have the impudence both to assert that he has left nothing and at the same time to lay claim to the estate. Now you must not imagine that my real opponent in this case is the man who has brought the suit claiming the estate ; no, it is Diocles of Phlya, surnamed Orestes.[a] He it is who has suborned our opponent to cause us trouble by trying to deprive us of the fortune which our grandfather left us at his death and exposing us to these dangers, in order that he may not have to give back any of it, if you listen to him and are misled by his words. Such being their machinations, you must be informed of all the facts, in order that, being well aware of all that has happened, you may give your verdict with perfect knowledge of them. If, therefore, you have ever listened with

---

[a] An Orestes, son of Timocrates, is said to have been a notorious footpad ; hence the name is applied to any violent character. *Cf.* Aristoph. *Acharnians*, 1166.

τὸν νοῦν, δέομαι ὑμῶν καὶ ταύτῃ προσέχειν ὁμοίως,
ὥσπερ καὶ τὸ δίκαιόν ἐστι. πολλῶν δὲ δικῶν ἐν
τῇ πόλει γενομένων, οὐδένες ἀναιδέστερον τούτων
οὐδὲ καταφανέστερον ἀντιποιησάμενοι φανήσονται
5 τῶν ἀλλοτρίων. ἔστι μὲν οὖν χαλεπόν, ὦ ἄνδρες,
πρὸς παρασκευὰς λόγων καὶ μάρτυρας οὐ τἀληθῆ
μαρτυροῦντας εἰς ἀγῶνα καθίστασθαι περὶ τηλικούτων, παντάπασιν ἀπείρως ἔχοντα δικαστηρίων·
οὐ μὴν ἀλλὰ πολλὰς ἐλπίδας ἔχω καὶ παρ' ὑμῶν
τεύξεσθαι τῶν δικαίων καὶ μέχρι γε τοῦ τὰ δίκαια
εἰπεῖν καὶ αὐτὸς ἀρκούντως ἐρεῖν, ἂν μή τι συμβῇ
τοιοῦτον ὃ νῦν ὑπ' ἐμοῦ τυγχάνει προσδοκώμενον.
δέομαι οὖν ὑμῶν, ὦ ἄνδρες, μετ' εὐνοίας τέ μου
ἀκοῦσαι, κἂν ἠδικῆσθαι δοκῶ, βοηθῆσαί μοι τὰ
δίκαια.

6 Πρῶτον μὲν οὖν, ὡς ἦν ἡ μήτηρ ἡ 'μὴ Κίρωνος
θυγάτηρ γνησία, ἐπιδείξω τοῦτο ὑμῖν, τὰ μὲν πάλαι[1]
γεγενημένα λόγων ἀκοῇ καὶ μαρτύρων, τὰ δ' ὥστε
καὶ μνημονεύεσθαι, τοῖς εἰδόσι χρώμενος μάρτυσιν,
ἔτι δὲ τεκμηρίοις ἃ κρείττω τῶν μαρτυριῶν ἐστιν·
ἐπειδὰν δὲ ταῦτα φανερὰ καταστήσω, τόθ' ὡς καὶ
κληρονομεῖν μᾶλλον ἡμῖν ἢ τούτοις[2] προσήκει τῶν
Κίρωνος χρημάτων. ὅθεν οὖν ἤρξαντο περὶ αὐτῶν,
ἐντεῦθεν ὑμᾶς κἀγὼ πειράσομαι διδάσκειν.

7 Ὁ γὰρ πάππος ὁ ἐμός, ὦ ἄνδρες, Κίρων ἔγημε
τὴν ἐμὴν τήθην οὖσαν ἀνεψιάν, ἐξ ἀδελφῆς τῆς
αὑτοῦ μητρὸς αὐτὴν γεγενημένην. ἐκείνη μὲν οὖν
συνοικήσασα οὐ πολὺν χρόνον, τεκοῦσα αὐτῷ τὴν
ἐμὴν μητέρα, μετὰ ἐνιαυτοὺς τέτταρας[3] τὸν βίον

---

[1] πάλαι Stephanus : παλαιά.
[2] τούτοις Scheibe : τοῦτον.
[3] τέτταρας (i.e. δ') Dobree : τριάκοντα (i.e. λ').

scrupulous attention to any other case, I beg you to give like attention to this case, as indeed justice demands. Though lawsuits abound in our city, yet it will be shown that no parties have ever claimed the property of others with greater impudence and effrontery than my opponents. It is a difficult task therefore, gentlemen, for one who is wholly without experience of litigation, when such important interests are at stake, to contend against fabricated stories and witnesses whose evidence is false ; yet I have great hopes that I shall obtain my rights from you, and that I shall myself speak sufficiently well at least to state what those rights are, unless some such chance should befall me as it is now my lot to anticipate.[a] I beg you, therefore, gentlemen, to listen to me with goodwill, and, if I seem to have been wronged, to aid me to obtain my rights.

First, then, I shall prove to you that my mother was Ciron's legitimate daughter ; for events which have happened long ago I shall rely on report and statements which have been heard by witnesses, while for events within living memory I shall employ witnesses who know the facts, and proofs which are better than any evidence. When I have established this, I shall then show that we have a better claim to Ciron's estate than our opponents. Starting, therefore, from the point at which they began their narrative of the events, I, too, shall try and put my version before you.

My grandfather Ciron, gentlemen, married my grandmother, his first cousin, herself the daughter of his own mother's sister. She did not live long with him ; she bore my mother, and died after four

---

[a] The allusion is obscure.

ἐτελεύτησεν· ὁ δὲ πάππος μιᾶς μόνης οὔσης αὐτῷ
θυγατρὸς λαμβάνει πάλιν τὴν Διοκλέους ἀδελφήν,
ἐξ ἧς αὐτῷ ἐγιγνέσθην[1] ὑεῖς δύο. καὶ ἐκείνην τε
ἔτρεφε παρὰ τῇ γυναικὶ καὶ μετὰ τῶν ἐξ ἐκείνης
8 παίδων, ἐκείνων τε ἔτι ζώντων, ἐπεὶ συνοικεῖν εἶχεν
ἡλικίαν, ἐκδίδωσιν αὐτὴν Ναυσιμένει Χολαργεῖ,
σὺν ἱματίοις καὶ χρυσίοις πέντε καὶ εἴκοσι μνᾶς
ἐπιδούς. κἀκεῖνος μὲν τρισὶν ἢ τέτταρσιν ἔτεσι
μετὰ ταῦτα καμὼν[2] ἀποθνῄσκει, πρὶν αὐτῷ γενέσθαι παῖδας ἐκ τῆς ἡμετέρας μητρός· ὁ δὲ πάππος
κομισάμενος αὐτήν, καὶ τὴν προῖκα οὐκ ἀπολαβὼν
ὅσην ἔδωκε διὰ τὴν Ναυσιμένους ἀπορίαν τῶν
πραγμάτων, πάλιν ἐκδίδωσι τῷ ἐμῷ πατρὶ καὶ
9 χιλίας δραχμὰς προῖκ' ἐπιδίδωσι.[3] ταυτὶ δὴ πάντα
πρὸς τὰς αἰτίας, ἃς νῦν οὗτοι λέγουσι, πῶς ἄν τις
δείξειε γεγενημένα φανερῶς; ἐγὼ ζητῶν ἐξεῦρον.
ἀνάγκη τὴν ἐμὴν μητέρα, εἴτε θυγάτηρ ἦν Κίρωνος
εἴτε μή, καὶ εἰ παρ' ἐκείνῳ διῃτᾶτο ἢ οὔ, καὶ
γάμους εἰ διττοὺς ὑπὲρ ταύτης εἱστίασεν ἢ μή,
καὶ προῖκα ἥντινα ἑκάτερος ἐπ' αὐτῇ τῶν γημάν-
των ἔλαβε, πάντα ταῦτα εἰδέναι τοὺς οἰκέτας καὶ
10 τὰς θεραπαίνας ἃς ἐκεῖνος ἐκέκτητο. βουλόμενος
οὖν πρὸς τοῖς ὑπάρχουσι μάρτυσιν ἔλεγχον ἐκ
βασάνων ποιήσασθαι περὶ αὐτῶν, ἵνα μᾶλλον
αὐτοῖς πιστεύητε μὴ μέλλουσι δώσειν ἔλεγχον ἀλλ'
ἤδη δεδωκόσι περὶ ὧν μαρτυροῦσι, τούτους ἠξίουν
ἐκδοῦναι τὰς θεραπαίνας καὶ τοὺς οἰκέτας περί τε

---

[1] ἐγιγνέσθην M, Scheibe: γιγνέσθην.
[2] καμὼν Boekmeijer: κάμνων.   [3] ἐπιδίδωσι Reiske: ἀποδ-.

---

[a] Slaves could give evidence only under torture.
[b] If the slaves confirmed the evidence of his witnesses,
the latter would come forward to give evidence in court

years. My grandfather, being left with an only daughter, married the sister of Diocles as his second wife, who bore him two sons. He brought up his daughter in the house with his wife and her children, and while the latter were still alive, he gave her in marriage, when she reached the proper age, to Nausimenes of Cholargus, giving her a dowry of twenty-five minae including raiment and jewelry. Three or four years later Nausimenes fell ill and died without leaving any issue by our mother. My grandfather received her back again—without, however, recovering the dowry which he had given, owing to the embarrassed condition of Nausimenes' affairs—and gave her in a second marriage to my father with a dowry of one thousand drachmae. How is one to prove clearly that all these events occurred in face of the imputations which our opponents are now uttering? I sought and discovered a way. Whether my mother was or was not the daughter of Ciron, whether she lived in his house or not, whether he did or did not on two occasions give a feast in honour of her marriage, and what dowry each of her husbands received with her—all these things must necessarily be known to the male and female slaves who belonged to Ciron. Wishing, therefore, in addition to the witnesses which I already had, to obtain proof of these facts by evidence given under torture [a]—in order that the veracity of my witnesses might be tested before, and not after, they gave their evidence, and so your belief in them might be confirmed [b]—I demanded that our opponents should surrender the male and

with a presumption already established that the evidence which they were going to give was true.

τούτων καὶ περὶ τῶν ἄλλων ἁπάντων ὅσα τυγ-
11 χάνουσι συνειδότες. οὗτος δ' ὁ νῦν ὑμᾶς ἀξιώσων
τοῖς αὑτοῦ μάρτυσι πιστεύειν ἔφυγε τὴν βάσανον.
καίτοι εἰ φανήσεται ταῦτα ποιῆσαι μὴ θελήσας, τί
ὑπολείπεται τοῖς ἐκείνου μάρτυσιν ἢ δοκεῖν νυνὶ
τὰ ψευδῆ μαρτυρεῖν, τούτου τηλικοῦτον ἔλεγχον πε-
φευγότος; ἐγὼ μὲν οἶμαι οὐδέν. ἀλλὰ μὴν ὡς
[70] ἀληθῆ λέγω, λαβέ μοι πρῶτον | ταύτην τὴν μαρ-
τυρίαν καὶ ἀνάγνωθι.

ΜΑΡΤΥΡΙΑ

12 Ὑμεῖς μὲν τοίνυν καὶ ἰδίᾳ καὶ δημοσίᾳ βάσανον
ἀκριβέστατον ἔλεγχον νομίζετε· καὶ ὁπόταν δοῦλοι
καὶ ἐλεύθεροι παραγένωνται καὶ δέῃ εὑρεθῆναί τι
τῶν ζητουμένων, οὐ χρῆσθε ταῖς τῶν ἐλευθέρων
μαρτυρίαις, ἀλλὰ τοὺς δούλους βασανίζοντες, οὕτω
ζητεῖτε εὑρεῖν τὴν ἀλήθειαν τῶν γεγενημένων.
εἰκότως, ὦ ἄνδρες· σύνιστε γὰρ ὅτι τῶν μὲν μαρτυρησάντων ἤδη τινὲς ἔδοξαν οὐ τἀληθῆ μαρτυρῆσαι, τῶν δὲ βασανισθέντων οὐδένες πώποτε
ἐξηλέγχθησαν ὡς οὐκ ἀληθῆ ἐκ τῶν βασάνων
13 εἰπόντες. οὗτος δ' ὁ πάντων ἀναισχυντότατος
ἀνθρώπων λόγοις πεπλασμένοις καὶ μάρτυσιν οὐ
τἀληθῆ μαρτυροῦσιν ἀξιώσει πιστεύειν ὑμᾶς, φεύγων οὕτως ἀκριβεῖς ἐλέγχους; ἀλλ' οὐχ ἡμεῖς,
ἀλλὰ πρότερον ὑπὲρ τῶν μαρτυρηθήσεσθαι μελλόντων ἀξιώσαντες εἰς βασάνους ἐλθεῖν, τούτου
294

female slaves to be put to the question on these points and any others of which they had cognizance. My adversary, however, who will presently demand that you shall believe *his* witnesses, refused the examination under torture. Yet, if he shall be shown to have refused my request, what remains to be thought of his witnesses except that they are giving false evidence, since he has refused so decisive a method of testing them? In my opinion no other conclusion is possible. But to prove that what I am saying is true, please first take and read this deposition.

DEPOSITION

You Athenians hold the opinion that both in public and in private matters examination under torture is the most searching test; and so, when you have slaves and free men before you and it is necessary that some contested point should be cleared up, you do not employ the evidence of free men but seek to establish the truth about the facts by putting the slaves to torture. This is a perfectly reasonable course; for you are well aware that before now witnesses have appeared not to be giving true evidence, whereas no one who has been examined under torture has ever been convicted of giving false evidence as the result of being tortured. And will my opponent, the most impudent of men, demand that you shall believe his fictitious stories and lying witnesses, while he thus declines so sure a method of proof? Our conduct has been quite different. Seeing that we first demanded that recourse should be had to examination under torture on the points about which evidence was to be given, and my opponent refuses to allow this, under these

δὲ φεύγοντος,[1] οὕτως οἰησόμεθα δεῖν ὑμᾶς τοῖς ἡμετέροις μάρτυσι πιστεύειν. λαβὲ οὖν αὐτοῖς ταυτασὶ τὰς μαρτυρίας καὶ ἀνάγνωθι.

ΜΑΡΤΥΡΙΑΙ

14 Τίνας εἰκὸς εἰδέναι τὰ παλαιά; δῆλον ὅτι τοὺς χρωμένους τῷ πάππῳ. μεμαρτυρήκασι τοίνυν ἀκοὴν οὗτοι. τίνας εἰδέναι τὰ περὶ τὴν ἔκδοσιν τῆς μητρὸς ἀνάγκη; τοὺς ἐγγυησαμένους καὶ τοὺς ἐκείνοις παρόντας ὅτε ἠγγυῶντο. μεμαρτυρήκασι τοίνυν οἵ τε Ναυσιμένους προσήκοντες καὶ οἱ τοῦ ἐμοῦ πατρός. τίνες δὲ οἱ τρεφομένην ἔνδον[2] καὶ θυγατέρα οὖσαν εἰδότες γνησίαν Κίρωνος; οἱ νῦν ἀμφισβητοῦντες ἔργῳ φανερῶς μαρτυροῦσιν ὅτι ταῦτ' ἐστὶν ἀληθῆ, φεύγοντες τὴν βάσανον. ὥστε οὐ δήπου τοῖς ἡμετέροις ἂν ἀπιστήσαιτε[3] εἰκότως, ἀλλὰ πολὺ μᾶλλον τοῖς τούτων μάρτυσιν.

15 Ἡμεῖς τοίνυν καὶ ἄλλα τεκμήρια πρὸς τούτοις ἔχομεν εἰπεῖν, [ἵνα γνώσεσθε] ὅτι ἐκ θυγατρὸς ἡμεῖς Κίρωνός ἐσμεν. οἷα γὰρ εἰκὸς παίδων ὄντων[4] ἐξ ἑαυτοῦ θυγατρός, οὐδεπώποτε θυσίαν ἄνευ ἡμῶν οὐδεμίαν ἐποίησεν, ἀλλ' εἴ τε μικρὰ εἴ τε μεγάλα θύοι, πανταχοῦ παρῆμεν ἡμεῖς καὶ συνεθύομεν. καὶ οὐ μόνον εἰς τὰ τοιαῦτα παρεκαλούμεθα, ἀλλὰ καὶ εἰς Διονύσια εἰς ἀγρὸν ἦγεν

16 ἀεὶ ἡμᾶς, καὶ μετ' ἐκείνου τε ἐθεωροῦμεν καθήμενοι παρ' αὐτόν, καὶ τὰς ἑορτὰς ἤγομεν παρ' ἐκεῖνον πάσας· τῷ Διί τε θύων τῷ Κτησίῳ, περὶ ἣν

---

[1] τούτου δὲ φεύγοντος Voightlaender: τούτους δὲ φεύγοντας.
[2] ἔνδον Reiske: εἶδον.
[3] ἀπιστήσαιτε Reiske: -ητε.
[4] ὄντων Sauppe: υἱέων.

conditions we shall consider that you ought to believe our witnesses. Take, therefore, these depositions and read them to the court.

DEPOSITIONS

Who are likely to be best acquainted with the events of the distant past? Obviously those who were intimate with my grandfather; they, then, have given evidence of what was told them. Who must necessarily know the facts about the giving of my mother in marriage? Those who betrothed her and those who were present when they betrothed her; the relatives, then, of Nausimenes and of my father have given their evidence. Who know best that my mother was brought up in Ciron's house and was his legitimate daughter? The present claimants clearly give evidence of the truth of these facts by their action in declining to put the slaves to torture. Thus, I think, you have much better reason for disbelieving their witnesses than mine.

Now there are other proofs, besides these, which we can state to show we are the children of Ciron's daughter. For, as was natural, seeing that we were the sons of his own daughter, Ciron never offered a sacrifice without our presence; whether he was performing a great or small sacrifice, we were always there and took part in the ceremony. And not only were we invited to such rites but he also always took us into the country for the Dionysia, and we always went with him to public spectacles and sat at his side, and we went to his house to keep all the festivals; and when he sacrificed to Zeus Ctesius [a]—

---

[a] Zeus as the guardian of family possessions.

μάλιστ' ἐκεῖνος θυσίαν ἐσπούδαζε καὶ οὔτε δούλους προσῆγεν οὔτε ἐλευθέρους ὀθνείους, ἀλλ'
αὐτὸς δι' ἑαυτοῦ πάντ' ἐποίει, ταύτης ἡμεῖς ἐκοι-
νωνοῦμεν καὶ τὰ ἱερὰ συνεχειρουργοῦμεν καὶ συνεπετίθεμεν[1] καὶ τἆλλα συνεποιοῦμεν, καὶ ηὔχετο
ἡμῖν ὑγίειαν διδόναι καὶ κτῆσιν ἀγαθήν, ὥσπερ
17 εἰκὸς ὄντα πάππον. καίτοι εἰ μὴ θυγατριδοῦς
ἡμᾶς ἐνόμιζεν εἶναι καὶ μόνους ἐκγόνους ἑώρα
λοιποὺς καταλελειμμένους αὑτῷ, οὐκ ἄν ποτε
ἐποίει τούτων οὐδέν, ἀλλὰ τόνδ' ἂν αὑτῷ παρ-
ίστατο, ὃς ἀδελφιδοῦς αὑτοῦ νῦν εἶναι φησί. καὶ
ταῦθ' ὅτι ἀληθῆ πάντ' ἐστίν, ἀκριβέστατα μὲν οἱ
τοῦ πάππου θεράποντες ἴσασιν, οὓς οὗτος[2] παραδοῦναι εἰς βάσανον οὐκ ἠθέλησεν, ἴσασι δὲ περι-
φανέστατα καὶ τῶν ἐκείνῳ χρωμένων τινές, οὓς
παρέξομαι μάρτυρας. καί μοι λαβὲ τὰς μαρτυρίας
καὶ ἀνάγνωθι.

ΜΑΡΤΥΡΙΑΙ

18 Οὐ τοίνυν ἐκ τούτων δῆλόν ἐστι μόνον ὅτι ἦν
ἡμῶν ἡ μήτηρ θυγάτηρ γνησία Κίρωνος, ἀλλὰ καὶ
ἐξ ὧν ὁ πατὴρ ἡμῶν ἔπραξε καὶ ἐξ ὧν αἱ γυναῖκες
αἱ τῶν δημοτῶν περὶ αὐτῆς ἐγίγνωσκον. ὅτε γὰρ
ὁ πατὴρ αὐτὴν ἐλάμβανε, γάμους εἱστίασε καὶ
ἐκάλεσε τρεῖς αὑτοῦ φίλους μετὰ τῶν αὑτοῦ προσηκόντων, τοῖς τε φράτορσι γαμηλίαν εἰσήνεγκε
19 κατὰ τοὺς ἐκείνων νόμους. αἵ τε γυναῖκες αἱ
τῶν δημοτῶν μετὰ ταῦτα προὔκριναν αὐτὴν μετὰ
τῆς Διοκλέους γυναικὸς τοῦ Πιθέως[3] ἄρχειν εἰς
τὰ Θεσμοφόρια καὶ ποιεῖν τὰ νομιζόμενα μετ'

---

[1] συνεπετίθεμεν Scheibe : συνετ-.
[2] οὗτος Dobree : αὐτὸς.
[3] Πιθέως Meursius : πίτεως.

a festival to which he attached a special importance, to which he admitted neither slaves nor free men outside his own family, at which he personally performed all the rites — we participated in this celebration and laid our hands with his upon the victims and placed our offerings side by side with his, and took part in all the other rites, and he prayed for our health and wealth, as he naturally would, being our grandfather. Yet if he had not regarded us as his daughter's children and seen in us his only surviving lineal descendants, he would have done none of these things but would have placed at his side my opponent, who now claims to be his nephew. And that I am telling the truth on all these points is well known to my grandfather's attendants, whom my opponent refused to give up to be questioned; the same facts are perfectly well known to some of his intimate friends also, whose evidence I will produce. Please take and read the depositions.

DEPOSITIONS

Now it is not only from these proofs that our mother is clearly shown to be the legitimate daughter of Ciron; but there is also the evidence of our father's conduct and the attitude adopted by the wives of his fellow-demesmen towards her. When our father took her in marriage, he gave a wedding-feast and invited three of his friends as well as his relatives, and he gave a marriage-banquet to the members of his ward according to their statutes. Also the wives of the demesmen afterwards chose our mother, together with the wife of Diocles of Pithus, to preside at the Thesmophoria [a] and to carry out the

● *Cf.* iii. 80 ; vi. 49.

ἐκείνης. ὅ τε πατὴρ ἡμῶν, ἐπειδὴ ἐγενόμεθα, εἰς
τοὺς φράτορας ἡμᾶς εἰσήγαγεν, ὀμόσας κατὰ τοὺς
νόμους τοὺς κειμένους ἦ μὴν ἐξ ἀστῆς καὶ ἐγγυητῆς
[71] γυναικὸς εἰσάγειν· τῶν δὲ | φρατόρων οὐδεὶς ἀντ-
εἶπεν οὐδ' ἠμφισβήτησε μὴ οὐκ ἀληθῆ ταῦτ'
εἶναι, πολλῶν ὄντων καὶ ἀκριβῶς τὰ τοιαῦτα
20 σκοπουμένων. καίτοι μὴ οἴεσθ' ἄν, εἰ τοιαύτη
τις ἦν ἡ μήτηρ ἡμῶν οἵαν οὗτοί φασι, μήτ' ἂν
τὸν πατέρα ἡμῶν γάμους ἑστιᾶν καὶ γαμηλίαν
εἰσενεγκεῖν, ἀλλὰ ἀποκρύψασθαι ταῦτα πάντα,
μήτε τὰς τῶν ἄλλων δημοτῶν γυναῖκας αἱρεῖσθαι
ἂν αὐτὴν συνιεροποιεῖν τῇ Διοκλέους γυναικὶ καὶ
κυρίαν ποιεῖν ἱερῶν, ἀλλ' ἑτέρᾳ ἄν τινι περὶ τούτων ἐπιτρέπειν, μήτε τοὺς φράτορας εἰσδέχεσθαι
ἡμᾶς, ἀλλὰ κατηγορεῖν καὶ ἐξελέγχειν, εἰ μὴ
πάντοθεν ἦν ὁμολογούμενον τὴν μητέρα ἡμῶν
εἶναι θυγατέρα γνησίαν Κίρωνος. νῦν δὲ τῇ περι-
φανείᾳ τοῦ πράγματος καὶ τῷ συνειδέναι ταῦτα
πολλοὺς οὐδαμόθεν ἠμφισβητήθη τοιοῦτον οὐδέν.
καὶ ταῦθ' ὡς ἀληθῆ λέγω, κάλει τούτων τοὺς
μάρτυρας.

MΑΡΤΥΡΕΣ

21 Ἔτι τοίνυν, ὦ ἄνδρες, καὶ ἐξ ὧν ὁ Διοκλῆς
ἔπραξεν ὅτε ἡμῶν ὁ πάππος ἐτελεύτησε, γνῶναι
ῥᾴδιον ὅτι ὡμολογούμεθα εἶναι θυγατριδοῖ Κίρωνος.
ἧκον γὰρ ἐγὼ κομιούμενος αὐτὸν ὡς θάψων ἐκ
τῆς οἰκίας τῆς ἐμαυτοῦ, τῶν ἐμαυτοῦ οἰκείων τινὰ
ἔχων, ἀνεψιὸν τοῦ πατρός· καὶ Διοκλέα μὲν οὐ
κατέλαβον ἔνδον, εἰσελθὼν δὲ εἴσω κομίζειν οἷος

ceremonies jointly with her. Again, our father at our birth introduced us to the members of his ward, having declared on oath, in accordance with the established laws, that he was introducing the children of an Athenian mother duly married ; and none of the wardsmen made any objection or disputed the truth of his statements, though they were present in large numbers and always look carefully into such matters. Yet do not for a moment suppose, that, if our mother had been such as our opponents allege, our father would have either given a wedding-feast or provided a marriage-banquet and not rather hushed up the whole matter ; or that the wives of the other demesmen would have chosen her to celebrate the festival with the wife of Diocles and given the sacred objects into her hands and not rather entrusted this office to some other woman ; or that the wardsmen would have admitted us and not rather objected and justified their objection, if it had not been universally admitted that our mother was a legitimate daughter of Ciron. As it was, owing to the notoriety of the fact and its recognition by so many persons, no such question was raised from any quarter. Now call the witnesses to prove the truth of these statements.

WITNESSES

Furthermore, gentlemen, the conduct of Diocles on the occasion of our grandfather's death clearly shows that we were acknowledged as the grandchildren of Ciron. I presented myself, accompanied by one of my relatives, a cousin of my father, to convey away the body with the intention of conducting the funeral from my own house. I did not find Diocles in the house, and I entered and was

22 ἦν, ἔχων τοὺς οἴσοντας. δεομένης δὲ τῆς τοῦ
πάππου γυναικὸς ἐκ τῆς οἰκίας αὐτὸν ἐκείνης
θάπτειν, καὶ λεγούσης ὅτι βούλοιτ' ἂν αὐτὴ τὸ
σῶμα τὸ ἐκείνου συμμεταχειρίζεσθαι μεθ' ἡμῶν
καὶ κοσμῆσαι, καὶ ταῦτα ἱκετευούσης καὶ κλαι-
ούσης, ἐπείσθην, ὦ ἄνδρες, καὶ τούτῳ προσελθὼν
μαρτύρων ἐναντίον εἶπον ὅτι ἐντεῦθεν ποιήσομαι
τὴν ταφήν· δεδεημένη γὰρ εἴη[1] ταῦτα ποιεῖν ἡ
23 τούτου ἀδελφή. καὶ ταῦτα Διοκλῆς ἀκούσας οὐδὲν
ἀντεῖπεν, ἀλλὰ καὶ ἐωνῆσθαί τι τῶν εἰς τὴν ταφήν,
τῶν δὲ[2] ἀρραβῶνα δεδωκέναι αὐτὸς[3] φάσκων, ταῦτα
ἠξίου παρ' ἐμοῦ λαβεῖν, καὶ διωμολογήσατο τῶν
μὲν ἠγορασμένων τιμὴν ἀπολαβεῖν, ὧν δὲ ἀρραβῶνα ἔφασκε δεδωκέναι, συστῆσαι τοὺς λαβόντας.
εὐθὺς οὖν τοῦτο παρεφθέγγετο, ὡς οὐδ' ὁτιοῦν εἴη
Κίρων καταλελοιπώς, οὐδένα λόγον ἐμοῦ πω
24 ποιουμένου περὶ τῶν ἐκείνου χρημάτων. καίτοι
εἰ μὴ ἦν θυγατριδοῦς Κίρωνος, οὐκ ἂν ταῦτα
διωμολογεῖτο, ἀλλ' ἐκείνους ἂν τοὺς λόγους ἔλεγε
" σὺ δὲ τίς εἶ; σοὶ δὲ τί προσήκει θάπτειν; οὐ
γιγνώσκω σε· οὐ μὴ εἴσει εἰς[4] τὴν οἰκίαν." ταῦτ'
εἰπεῖν προσῆκεν, ἅ περ νῦν ἑτέρους πέπεικε λέγειν.
νῦν δὲ τοιοῦτον μὲν οὐδὲν εἶπεν, εἰς ἕω δὲ τἀργύριον ἐκέλευεν εἰσενεγκεῖν. καὶ ταῦτα ὡς ἀληθῆ
λέγω, κάλει μοι τούτων τοὺς μάρτυρας.

ΜΑΡΤΥΡΕΣ

25 Οὐ τοίνυν ἐκεῖνος μόνος, ἀλλ' οὐδὲ ὁ νῦν ἀμφι-

---

[1] εἴη Reiske: ἔνι.   [2] τῶν δὲ Bekker: τὸν δὲ.
[3] αὐτὸς Reiske: οὗτος.   [4] εἴσει εἰς Bekker: εἰσίης.

prepared to remove the body, having bearers with me for this purpose. When, however, my grandfather's widow requested that the funeral should take place from that house, and declared that she would like herself to help us to lay out and deck the corpse, and entreated me and wept, I acceded to her request and went to my opponent and told him in the presence of witnesses that I would conduct the funeral from the house of the deceased, since Diocles' sister had begged me to do so. Diocles, on hearing this, made no objection, but asserting that he had actually bought some of the requisites for the funeral and had himself paid a deposit for the rest, demanded that I should pay him for these, and arranged to recover from me the cost of the objects which he had purchased and to produce those who had received the deposit for the objects for which he alleged that he had paid a deposit. Immediately afterwards he casually remarked that Ciron had left nothing at all, although I had not said a single word about his money. Yet had I not been Ciron's grandson, he would never have made these arrangements with me, but would rather have said, " Who are you ? What right have you to carry out the burial ? I do not know you : you shall not set foot in the house." This is what he ought to have said, and what he has now instigated others to say. As it was, he said nothing of the kind, but only told me to bring the money next morning. And to prove the truth of these statements, please summon the witnesses.

WITNESSES

Diocles was not the only person who made no such objections at the time ; the present claimant to

σβητῶν τοῦ κλήρου τοιοῦτον εἶπεν οὐδέν, ἀλλ᾽
ὑπὸ τούτου παρασκευασθεὶς ἀμφισβητεῖ. κἀκείνου τὸ μὲν παρ᾽ ἐμοῦ κομισθὲν ἀργύριον οὐκ
ἐθελήσαντος ἀπολαβεῖν, παρὰ τούτου δ᾽ ἀπειληφέναι τῇ ὑστεραίᾳ φάσκοντος, οὐκ ἐκωλυόμην
συνθάπτειν ἀλλὰ πάντα συνεποίουν· οὐχ ὅπως
τοῦδε ἀναλίσκοντος οὐδὲ Διοκλέους, ἀλλ᾽ ἐξ ὧν
ἐκεῖνος κατέλιπε γιγνομένων τῶν εἰς αὐτὸν ἀνα-
26 λωμάτων. καίτοι καὶ τούτῳ προσῆκεν, εἰ μὴ
πάππος ἦν μοι Κίρων, ὠθεῖν ⟨καὶ⟩[1] ἐκβάλλειν καὶ
κωλύειν συνθάπτειν. οὐδὲν γὰρ ὅμοιον ἦν μοι
πρὸς τοῦτον· ἐγὼ μὲν γὰρ εἴων αὐτὸν ἀδελφιδοῦν
ὄντα τοῦ πάππου ταῦτα πάντα συμποιεῖν, τούτῳ
δ᾽ ἔμ᾽ οὐ προσῆκεν ἐᾶν, εἴπερ ἀληθῆ ταῦτα ἦν
27 ἅπερ νῦν λέγειν τολμῶσιν. ἀλλ᾽ οὕτω τῇ τοῦ
πράγματος ἀληθείᾳ κατεπέπληκτο,[2] ὥστ᾽ οὐδ᾽ ἐπὶ
τοῦ σήματος[3] ἐμοῦ ποιουμένου λόγους, καὶ κατ-
ηγοροῦντος Διοκλέους ὅτι τὰ χρήματα ἀποστερῶν
τοῦτόν μοι πέπεικεν ἀμφισβητεῖν, οὐκ ἐτόλμησε
γρύξαι[4] τὸ παράπαν οὐδὲν οὐδ᾽[5] εἰπεῖν ἃ νῦν
τολμᾷ λέγειν. καὶ ταῦθ᾽ ὅτι ἀληθῆ λέγω, κάλει
μοι τούτων τοὺς μάρτυρας.

ΜΑΡΤΥΡΕΣ

28 Πόθεν χρὴ πιστεύεσθαι τὰ εἰρημένα; οὐκ ἐκ
τῶν μαρτυριῶν; οἶμαί γε. πόθεν δὲ τοὺς μάρ-
τυρας; οὐκ ἐκ τῶν βασάνων; εἰκός γε. πόθεν |
[72] δ᾽ ἀπιστεῖν τοῖς τούτων λόγοις; οὐκ ἐκ τοῦ

---

[1] καὶ add. Scheibe.   [2] κατεπέπληκτο M, Aldus: κατα-.
[3] σήματος Photiades: βήματος.
[4] γρύξαι Scaliger: ἐρύξαι.   [5] οὐδ᾽ Bekker: οὔτ᾽.
304

the estate was also silent and is now making his claim because he has been suborned by Diocles. Though Diocles refused to accept the money which I brought and alleged next day that he had received payment from my opponent, yet I was not prevented from attending the burial but joined in all the ceremonies, the expenses of the funeral, so far from being paid by my opponent or Diocles, being defrayed from the property left by the deceased. Yet if Ciron had not really been my grandfather, it was the duty of my opponent to repulse me and reject me and prevent me from taking part in the burial. My position with regard to him was quite a different one : for I allowed him, as my grandfather's nephew, to share in all the rites, but he ought never to have allowed me to do so, if what they now have the audacity to say were true. But he was so overawed by his knowledge of the true facts, that at the tomb, when I spoke and accused Diocles of detaining the property and of having suborned him to dispute the inheritance, he did not venture to utter a sound or say a word of what he now has the impudence to assert. And to prove that I am telling the truth, please call the witnesses to these events.

WITNESSES

What ought to induce you to believe the statements which you have heard ? Ought not the evidence of witnesses to induce you to do so ? I certainly think so. But what entitles you to believe the witnesses ? Is it not the confirmation of their evidence under torture ? It seems only reasonable. But what entitles you to disbelieve the statements of my opponents ? Is it not their refusal to put

φεύγειν τοὺς ἐλέγχους; ἀνάγκη μεγάλη. πῶς
οὖν ἄν τις σαφέστερον ἐπιδείξειε γνησίαν οὖσαν
θυγατέρα Κίρωνος τὴν μητέρα τὴν ἐμὴν ἢ τοῦτον
29 τὸν τρόπον ἐπιδεικνύς; τῶν μὲν παλαιῶν ἀκοὴν
μαρτυρούντων παρεχόμενος, τῶν δὲ ἔτι ζώντων
τοὺς εἰδότας ἕκαστα τούτων, οἳ συνῄδεσαν παρ'
ἐκείνῳ τρεφομένην, θυγατέρα νομιζομένην, δὶς
ἐκδοθεῖσαν, δὶς ἐγγυηθεῖσαν, ἔτι δὲ περὶ πάντων
τούτους[1] βάσανον ἐξ οἰκετῶν πεφευγότας, οἳ ταῦτα
πάντα ᾔδεσαν. ἔγωγε[2] μὰ τοὺς θεοὺς τοὺς Ὀλυμ-
πίους οὐκ ἂν ἔχοιμι πίστεις μείζους τούτων εἰπεῖν,
ἀλλ' ἱκανὰς εἶναι νομίζω τὰς εἰρημένας.

30 Φέρε δή, καὶ ὡς προσήκει ἐμοὶ μᾶλλον ἢ τούτῳ
τῶν Κίρωνος χρημάτων, νῦν ἤδη τοῦτο ἐπιδείξω.
καὶ νομίζω μὲν ἁπλῶς καὶ ὑμῖν ἤδη εἶναι φανερὸν
ὅτι οὐκ ἐγγυτέρω ταῖς ἀγχιστείαις[3] εἰσὶν οἱ μετ'
ἐκείνου φύντες ἢ οἱ ἐξ ἐκείνου γεγονότες (πῶς
γάρ; οἱ μὲν γὰρ ὀνομάζονται συγγενεῖς, οἱ δ'
ἔκγονοι τοῦ τελευτήσαντος)· οὐ μὴν ἀλλ' ἐπειδὴ
καὶ οὕτως ἐχόντων τολμῶσιν ἀμφισβητεῖν, καὶ
31 ἐξ αὐτῶν τῶν νόμων ἀκριβέστερον διδάξομεν. εἰ
γὰρ ἔζη μὲν ἡ ἐμὴ μήτηρ, θυγάτηρ δὲ Κίρωνος,
μηδὲν δὲ ἐκεῖνος διαθέμενος ἐτελεύτησεν, ἦν δὲ
ἀδελφὸς οὗτος αὐτῷ, μὴ ἀδελφιδοῦς, συνοικῆσαι
μὲν ἂν τῇ γυναικὶ κύριος ἦν, τῶν δὲ χρημάτων
οὐκ ἄν, ἀλλ' οἱ γενόμενοι παῖδες ἐκ τούτου καὶ

---

[1] τούτους Aldus: τούτων.   [2] ἔγωγε Dobree: ἐγὼ δέ.
[3] ταῖς ἀγχιστείαις Emper: τῆς ἀγχιστείας.

the matter to the test? This is an absolutely necessary conclusion. How then could anyone prove that my mother is a legitimate daughter of Ciron more clearly than by the method which I am adopting? For events in the distant past I furnished hearsay evidence vouched for by witnesses; where living witnesses are available, I produced those who are familiar with the facts, who knew perfectly well that my mother was brought up in Ciron's house, that she was regarded as his daughter, and that she was twice betrothed and twice married; I further showed that on all these points my opponents have refused to allow the evidence of slaves under torture, who knew all the facts. By the gods of Olympus, I could not possibly give stronger proofs than these, and I think that those which I have produced are sufficient.

But to continue; let me next prove to you that I have a better right than my opponent to Ciron's fortune. I suppose that you admit in principle as a self-evident fact that those who are descended from the same stock as Ciron are not nearer in right of succession than those who are descended from him. (How, indeed, could they be, since the former are called collateral kinsmen, the latter lineal descendants of the deceased?) Since, however, even though this is so, they have the impudence to dispute my right, we will explain the point in greater detail from the actual laws. Supposing that my mother, Ciron's daughter, were still alive and that her father had died intestate and that my opponent were his brother and not his nephew, he would have the right to claim the daughter in marriage, but he could not claim the estate, which would go to the children born of their marriage when they had

ἐξ ἐκείνης, ὁπότε ἐπὶ διετὲς ἥβησαν· οὕτω γὰρ
οἱ νόμοι κελεύουσιν. εἰ τοίνυν καὶ ζώσης κύριος
αὐτὸς μὴ ἐγένετο τῶν τῆς γυναικός, ἀλλ' οἱ
παῖδες, δῆλον ὅτι καὶ τετελευτηκυίας, ἐπεὶ παῖδας
ἡμᾶς καταλέλοιπεν, οὐ τούτοις ἀλλ' ἡμῖν προσήκει
κληρονομεῖν τῶν χρημάτων.

32 Οὐ τοίνυν ἐκ τούτου μόνον, ἀλλὰ καὶ ἐκ τοῦ
περὶ τῆς κακώσεως νόμου δῆλόν ἐστιν. εἰ γὰρ
ἔζη μὲν ὁ πάππος, ἐνδεὴς δὲ ἦν τῶν ἐπιτηδείων,
οὐκ ἂν οὗτος ὑπόδικος[1] ἦν τῆς κακώσεως ἀλλ'
ἡμεῖς. κελεύει γὰρ τρέφειν τοὺς γονέας· γονεῖς
δ' εἰσὶ μήτηρ καὶ πατὴρ καὶ πάππος καὶ τήθη καὶ
τούτων μήτηρ καὶ πατήρ, ἐὰν ἔτι ζῶσιν· ἐκεῖνοι
γὰρ ἀρχὴ τοῦ γένους εἰσί, καὶ τὰ ἐκείνων παρα-
δίδοται τοῖς ἐκγόνοις[2]· διόπερ ἀνάγκη τρέφειν
αὐτούς ἐστι, κἂν μηδὲν καταλίπωσι. πῶς οὖν
δίκαιόν ἐστιν, ἐὰν μὲν μηδὲν καταλίπωσιν, ἡμᾶς
ὑποδίκους εἶναι τῆς κακώσεως, ἢν μὴ τρέφωμεν,
εἰ δέ τι καταλελοίπασι, τόνδ' εἶναι κληρονόμον
ἀλλὰ μὴ ἡμᾶς; οὐδαμῶς δήπουθεν.

33 Πρὸς ἕνα δὲ τὸν πρῶτον τῶν συγγενῶν προσάξω,
καὶ τοῦ γένους καθ' ἕκαστον ὑμᾶς ἐρωτήσω·
ῥᾷστα γὰρ οὕτω μάθοιτ' ἄν. Κίρωνος πότερον
θυγάτηρ ἢ ἀδελφὸς ἐγγυτέρω τοῦ γένους ἐστί;
δῆλον γὰρ ὅτι θυγάτηρ· ἡ μὲν γὰρ ἐξ ἐκείνου
γέγονεν, ὁ δὲ μετ' ἐκείνου. θυγατρὸς δὲ παῖδες
ἢ ἀδελφός; παῖδες δήπουθεν· γένος γὰρ ἀλλ' οὐχὶ

---

[1] ὑπόδικος Scaliger: ἐπίδικος.
[2] ἐκγόνοις Baiter-Sauppe: ἐγγόνοις.

completed two years after puberty ; for this is what the laws ordain. Since, then, the children, and not my opponent himself, would have become masters of her property if she were alive, it is obvious, since she is dead and has left children, namely, my brother and myself, that we, and not our opponents, have the right to succeed to the estate.

This is the clear intention not only of this law but also of that dealing with the neglect of parents. For if my grandfather were alive and in want of the necessities of life, we, and not our opponent, would be liable to prosecution for neglect. For the law enjoins us to support our parents, meaning by " parents " father, mother, grandfather, and grandmother, and their father and mother, if they are still alive ; for they are the source of the family, and their property is transmitted to their descendants, and so the latter are bound to support them even if they have nothing to bequeath to them. How then can it be right that, if they have nothing to leave, we should be liable to prosecution for neglecting them, yet that, if they have something to leave, our opponent should be the heir and not we ? Surely it cannot be right.

I will now institute a comparison with the nearest collateral relative and question you on the various degrees of relationship ; [a] for this is the easier way of making the matter clear to you. Is Ciron's daughter or his brother the nearer of kin to him ? Clearly his daughter ; for she is his issue, while the brother is only born of the same stock. Next, is the brother nearer of kin or the daughter's children ? Certainly the daughter's children ; for they are

* The text is doubtful here, but the general sense is clear.

συγγένεια τοῦτ' ἐστίν. εἰ δὴ προέχομεν ἀδελφοῦ
τοσοῦτον, ἦ που τοῦδέ γ' ὄντος[1] ἀδελφιδοῦ πάμ-
34 πολυ πρότεροί ἐσμεν. δέδοικα δὲ μὴ λίαν ὁμολογούμενα λέγων ἐνοχλεῖν ὑμῖν δόξω· πάντες γὰρ
ὑμεῖς τῶν πατρῴων, τῶν παππῴων, τῶν ἔτι
περαιτέρω κληρονομεῖτε ἐκ γένους παρειληφότες
τὴν ἀγχιστείαν ἀνεπίδικον,[2] καὶ οὐκ οἶδ' εἴ τινι
πρὸ τοῦ[3] πώποτε τοιοῦτος ἀγὼν συμβέβηκεν.
ἀναγνοὺς οὖν τὸν τῆς κακώσεως νόμον, ὧν ἕνεκα
πάντα[4] γίγνεται, καὶ ταῦτ' ἤδη πειράσομαι
διδάσκειν.

ΝΟΜΟΣ

35 Κίρων γὰρ ἐκέκτητο οὐσίαν, ὦ ἄνδρες, ἀγρὸν
μὲν Φλυῆσι, καὶ ταλάντου ῥᾳδίως ἄξιον, οἰκίας δ'
ἐν ἄστει δύο, τὴν μὲν μίαν μισθοφοροῦσαν, παρὰ
τὸ ἐν Λίμναις Διονύσιον, δισχιλίας εὑρίσκουσαν,
τὴν δ' ἑτέραν, ἐν ᾗ αὐτὸς ᾤκει, τριῶν καὶ δέκα
μνῶν· ἔτι δὲ ἀνδράποδα μισθοφοροῦντα καὶ δύο
θεραπαίνας καὶ παιδίσκην, καὶ ἔπιπλα δι' ὧν ᾤκει
τὴν οἰκίαν, σχεδὸν σὺν τοῖς ἀνδραπόδοις ἄξια
τριῶν καὶ δέκα[5] μνῶν· σύμπαντα δὲ ὅσα φανερὰ
ἦν, πλέον ἢ ἐνενήκοντα μνῶν· χωρὶς δὲ τούτων
δανείσματα οὐκ ὀλίγα, ἀφ' ὧν ἐκεῖνος τόκους
36 ἐλάμβανε. τούτοις Διοκλῆς μετὰ τῆς ἀδελφῆς |
[73] πάλαι ἐπεβούλευεν, ἐπειδὴ τάχιστα οἱ παῖδες οἱ
Κίρωνος ἐτελεύτησαν. ἐκείνην μὲν γὰρ οὐκ ἐξεδίδου δυναμένην ἔτι τεκεῖν παῖδας ἐξ ἑτέρου

---

[1] τοῦδέ γ' ὄντος Reiske: τοῦ λέγοντος.
[2] ἀνεπίδικον Reiske: ἐπίδικον.
[3] πρὸ τοῦ sched. Eton., Bekker: πρώτω.
[4] πάντα Scheibe: τἄλλα.
[5] τριῶν καὶ δέκα Blass: τρισκαίδεκα.

lineal descendants and not mere collaterals. If then our rights are so far superior to those of a brother, *a fortiori* we are still more to be preferred to our opponent, who is only a nephew. But I am afraid of seeming tiresome in repeating truths so universally recognized; for you all inherit the property of your fathers, grandfathers, and remoter ancestors by the incontrovertible title of lineal descent, and I do not know that such a case as the present has ever been brought against anyone before. I shall therefore read the law about the neglect of parents and then try and show you the motives which led to the whole affair.

LAW

The property of Ciron, gentlemen, consisted of an estate at Phlya, easily worth a talent, two houses in the city, one near the sanctuary of Dionysus in the Marshes,[a] let to a tenant and worth 2000 drachmae, the other, in which he himself used to live, worth thirteen minae; he also had [b] slaves earning wages, two female slaves and a young girl, and the fittings of his private residence, worth, including the slaves, about thirteen minae. The total value of his real property was thus more than ninety minae; but besides this he had considerable sums lent out, of which he received the interest. It was to obtain this property that Diocles, together with his sister, carried on his plots for a long time, ever since the death of Ciron's sons. For he did not try to find another husband for her, although she was still capable of bearing children to another

---

[a] On the probable position of this shrine S. of the Areopagus see Jane Harrison, *Primitive Athens*, pp. 83 ff.

[b] A number has fallen out here probably.

ἀνδρός, ἵνα μὴ χωρισθείσης περὶ τῶν αὑτοῦ βουλεύσαιτο καθάπερ προσῆκεν, ἔπειθε δὲ μένειν
φάσκουσαν ἐξ αὐτοῦ κυεῖν οἴεσθαι, προσποιου-
μένην δὲ διαφθείρειν ἄκουσαν, ἵν' ἐλπίζων ἀεὶ
γενήσεσθαι παῖδας αὑτῷ μηδέτερον ἡμῶν εἰσποιή-
σαιτο υἱόν· καὶ τὸν πατέρα διέβαλλεν ἀεί, φάσκων
37 αὐτὸν ἐπιβουλεύειν τοῖς ἐκείνου. τά τε οὖν χρέα
πάντα, ὅσα ὠφείλετο αὐτῷ, καὶ ⟨τοὺς⟩[1] τόκους
ἔπειθε ⟨πράξασθαι⟩[2] τά τε φανερὰ δι' αὑτοῦ ποιεῖσθαι,
παράγων ἄνδρα πρεσβύτερον θεραπείαις καὶ κολα-
κείαις, ἕως ἅπαντα τὰ ἐκείνου περιέλαβεν. εἰδὼς δὲ
ὅτι πάντων ἐγὼ τούτων κατὰ τὸ προσῆκον εἶναι
κύριος ζητήσω, ὁπότε ὁ πάππος τελευτήσειεν,[3]
εἰσιέναι μέν με καὶ θεραπεύειν ἐκεῖνον καὶ συν-
διατρίβειν οὐκ ἐκώλυε, δεδιὼς μὴ τραχυνθεὶς εἰς
ὀργὴν κατασταίη[4] πρὸς αὐτόν, παρεσκεύαζε δέ
μοι τὸν ἀμφισβητήσοντα τῆς οὐσίας, μέρος πολλο-
στὸν τούτῳ μεταδιδοὺς εἰ κατορθώσειεν, αὑτῷ δὲ
ταῦτα πάντα περιποιῶν, καὶ οὐδὲ πρὸς τοῦτον ὁμολογῶν τὸν πάππον χρήματα καταλείπειν,[5] ἀλλ'
38 εἶναι φάσκων οὐδέν. καὶ ἐπειδὴ τάχιστα ἐτελεύτησεν, ἐντάφια προπαρασκευασάμενος τὸ μὲν ἀργύριον ἐμὲ ἐκέλευεν ἐνεγκεῖν, ὡς τῶν μαρτύρων
ἠκούσατε μαρτυρησάντων, ἀπειληφέναι δὲ παρὰ
τοῦδε προσεποιεῖτο, παρ' ἐμοῦ δὲ οὐκέτι ἤθελεν

---

[1] τοὺς add. Herwerden.
[2] πράξασθαι add. Buermann.
[3] τελευτήσειεν Scaliger: ἐτελεύτησεν.
[4] κατασταίη schedae Etonenses, Reiske: -αίην.
[5] καταλείπειν scripsi: -λιπεῖν.

man; for he feared that, if she were separated from Ciron, the latter would resolve to dispose of his estate in the proper manner; [a] but he kept on urging her to remain with him, and to allege that she thought she was with child by him and then pretend that she had an accidental miscarriage, in order that he might be always hoping that a child would be born to him, and might not, therefore, adopt myself or my brother. Diocles also continually calumniated my father, alleging that he was intriguing against Ciron's property. So he gradually persuaded Ciron to let him handle all the sums owing to him, and the interest upon them, and to manage his real property, cajoling the old man by his attentions and flattery until he had all his estate in his grasp. But, although he knew that in accordance with my rights I should seek to be master of this property when my grandfather was dead, yet he did not try to prevent me from visiting him and paying him attentions and conversing with him (for he was afraid that Ciron might become exasperated and be angry with him); but he was all the time preparing a claimant to dispute my right to the property, promising him a small share, if he were successful, and securing the whole estate for himself, and not admitting even to his accomplice that my grandfather had any money to leave, but pretending that there was nothing. Immediately after Ciron's death he lost no time in making preparations for the funeral, the expenses of which he required me to pay, as you have heard the witnesses testifying; but he afterwards pretended that he had received the money from my opponent and refused any longer

[a] *i.e.*, by leaving it to the speaker and his brother.

ἀπολαβεῖν, ὑποπαρωθῶν, ὅπως ἐκεῖνος δοκοίη
θάπτειν ἀλλὰ μὴ ἐγὼ τὸν πάππον. ἀμφισβητοῦν-
τος δὲ τούτου καὶ τῆς οἰκίας ταύτης καὶ τῶν
ἄλλων ὧν ἐκεῖνος κατέλιπε, καὶ οὐδὲν φάσκοντος
καταλελοιπέναι, βιάσασθαι μὲν καὶ τὸν πάππον
μεταφέρειν ἐν ταῖς τοιαύταις ἀκαιρίαις οὐκ ᾤμην
δεῖν, τῶν φίλων μοι ταῦτα συγγιγνωσκόντων,
συνεποίουν δὲ καὶ συνέθαπτον, ἐξ ὧν ὁ πάππος
39 κατέλιπε τῶν ἀναλωμάτων γιγνομένων. καὶ ταῦτα
μὲν οὕτως ἀναγκασθεὶς ἔπραξα τοῦτον τὸν τρό-
πον· ὅπως δὲ μηδέν μου ταύτῃ πλεονεκτοῖεν, παρ'
ὑμῖν φάσκοντες οὐδέν με εἰς τὴν ταφὴν ἀνηλωκέναι, τὸν ἐξηγητὴν ἐρόμενος ἐκείνου κελεύσαντος
ἀνήλωσα παρ' ἐμαυτοῦ καὶ τὰ ἔνατα ἐπήνεγκα, ὡς
οἷόν τε κάλλιστα παρασκευάσας, ἵνα αὐτῶν ἐκ-
κόψαιμι ταύτην τὴν ἱεροσυλίαν, καὶ ἵνα μὴ δοκοῖεν
οὗτοι μὲν ἀνηλωκέναι πάντα, ἐγὼ δὲ μηδέν,[1] ἀλλ'
ὁμοίως κἀγώ.

40 Καὶ τὰ μὲν γεγενημένα, καὶ δι' ἃ τὰ πράγματα
ταῦτ' ἔχομεν, σχεδόν τι ταῦτ' ἐστίν, ὦ ἄνδρες· εἰ
δὲ εἰδείητε τὴν Διοκλέους ἀναισχυντίαν, καὶ περὶ
τὰ ἄλλα οἷός ἐστιν, οὐκ ἂν ἀπιστήσαιτε[2] τῶν
εἰρημένων οὐδενί. οὗτος μὲν γὰρ ἔχει[3] τὴν οὐσίαν,
ἀφ' ἧς νῦν ἐστι λαμπρός, ἀλλοτρίαν, ἀδελφῶν
τριῶν ὁμομητρίων ἐπικλήρων καταλειφθεισῶν αὐτὸν
τῷ πατρὶ αὐτῶν εἰσποιήσας, οὐδεμίαν ἐκείνου περὶ
41 τούτων ποιησαμένου διαθήκην. τοῖν δ' ἀδελφαῖν
τοῖν[4] δυοῖν ἐπειδὴ τὰ χρήματα εἰσεπράττετο ὑπὸ

---

[1] μηδέν Herwerden : οὐδέν.
[2] ἀπιστήσαιτε Reiske : ἀπιστῆσαί τις.
[3] ἔχει Baiter : εἶχε.
[4] τοῖν . . . τοῖν Naber : ταῖν . . . ταῖν.

to accept payment from me, stealthily thrusting me aside, in order that it might appear that my opponent, and not I, was burying my grandfather. And when my opponent claimed this house and everything else that Ciron left behind him, although he said that he had left nothing, I did not think (and my friends agreed with me) that in these painful circumstances I ought to use violence and carry off my grandfather's body, but I took part in the rites and was present at the burial, the expenses of which were defrayed out of my grandfather's estate. Thus I acted in this manner under compulsion; but in order that they might gain no advantage over me by alleging to you that I bore no part of the funeral expenses, I consulted the interpreter of the sacred law and by his advice I paid for at my own expense and offered the ninth-day offerings in the most sumptuous manner possible, in order that I might confound their sacrilegious tricks, and that it might not seem that they had paid for everything and I for nothing, but that I might be thought to have done my share.

Such in substance, gentlemen, are the events which have occurred and the causes of all this trouble. If you understood the impudence of Diocles and his behaviour on all other occasions, you would have no difficulty in believing anything in my story. For the fortune which he now possesses, and with which he makes such a brave show, is not really his; for when his three half-sisters, the children of his mother, were left heiresses, he represented himself as the adopted son of their father, though the latter left no will to this effect. When the husbands of two of the sisters tried to obtain possession of their

τῶν ἐκείναις συνοικούντων, τὸν μὲν τὴν πρεσβυτέραν ἔχοντα κατοικοδομήσας καὶ ἐπιβουλεύσας
ἠτίμωσε, καὶ γραφὴν ὕβρεως γραφεὶς οὐδέπω
τούτων δίκην δέδωκε,[1] τῆς δὲ μετ' ἐκείνην γενομένης τὸν ἄνδρα ἀποκτεῖναι κελεύσας οἰκέτην
ἐκεῖνον μὲν ἐξέπεμψε, τὴν δ' αἰτίαν εἰς τὴν ἀδελ-
42 φὴν ἔτρεψε, καταπλήξας δὲ ταῖς αὑτοῦ βδελυρίαις
προσαφῄρηται τὸν υἱὸν αὐτῆς[2] τὴν οὐσίαν ἐπι-
τροπεύσας, καὶ κατέχει τὸν ἀγρόν, φελλέα [χωρία
ἄττα] δὲ ἐκείνῳ δέδωκε. καὶ ταῦτα ὅτι ἀληθῆ
λέγω, δεδίασι μὲν αὐτόν, ἴσως δ' ἄν μοι καὶ
μαρτυρῆσαι ἐθελήσειαν· εἰ δὲ μή, τοὺς εἰδότας
παρέξομαι μάρτυρας. καί μοι κάλει δεῦρο αὐτοὺς
πρῶτον.

MΑΡΤΥΡΕΣ

43 Οὕτω τοίνυν ἀσελγὴς ὢν καὶ βίαιος καὶ τὴν τῶν
ἀδελφῶν οὐσίαν ἀπεστερηκὼς οὐκ ἀγαπᾷ τὰ
ἐκείνων ἔχων, ἀλλ' ὅτι δίκην οὐδεμίαν αὐτῶν
δέδωκεν, ἥκει καὶ τὰ τοῦ πάππου χρήματα ἡμᾶς
ἀποστερήσων, καὶ τούτῳ δύο μνᾶς (ὡς ἀκούομεν) |
[74] μόνας δεδωκὼς οὐ μόνον περὶ χρημάτων ἡμᾶς
ἀλλὰ καὶ περὶ τῆς πατρίδος εἰς κινδύνους καθίστησιν. ἐὰν γὰρ ἐξαπατηθῆτε ὑμεῖς πεισθέντες
ὡς ἡ μήτηρ ἡμῶν οὐκ ἦν πολῖτις, οὐδ' ἡμεῖς
ἐσμεν· μετ' Εὐκλείδην γὰρ ἄρχοντα γεγόναμεν.
ἆρα περὶ μικρῶν τινῶν ἡμῖν τὸν ἀγῶνα κατ-

---

[1] δέδωκε Sauppe: ἔδωκε.
[2] αὐτῆς Rauchenstein: -οῦ.

---

[a] The reading οἰκοδομήσας is supported by Harpocration,
s.v. (i.q. κατακλεῖν εἰς οἴκημα), but the meaning is uncertain.
Possibly Diocles forcibly detained his brother-in-law from

fortune, he imprisoned the husband of the elder of them by walling him up [a] and by a plot deprived him of his civic rights, and though he was indicted for outrage he has not yet been punished. As for the husband of the next sister, he ordered a slave to kill him and smuggled away the murderer, and then threw the guilt upon his sister, and having terrified her by his abominable conduct he has robbed her son, whose guardian he became, of his property, and is still in possession of his land and has only given him some stony ground. To prove that what I say is true, his victims, though they are afraid of him, yet may perhaps be willing to support me by their evidence ; otherwise, I will produce as witnesses those who know the facts. Please call them first.

WITNESSES

This man, then, having shown himself so brutal and violent and having robbed his sisters of their fortune, is not content with the possession of their property, but, since he has not been punished, has now come forward to rob us of our grandfather's fortune ; and having given our opponent—so we are informed—the paltry sum of two minae is exposing us to the risk of losing not only our property but also our fatherland. For if you are misled into the belief that our mother was not an Athenian citizen, neither are we citizens ; for we were born after the archonship of Eucleides.[b] Can it be said, therefore, that the suit which he has trumped up

performing some duty to the state and thus caused his disenfranchisement.

[b] The children of mothers who were not citizens, born after 403 B.C., did not enjoy civic rights.

317

ἐσκεύακε; καὶ ζῶντος μὲν τοῦ πάππου καὶ τοῦ
πατρὸς οὐδεμίαν αἰτίαν εἴχομεν, ἀλλ' ἀναμφισβή-
44 τητοι τὸν ἅπαντα χρόνον διετελέσαμεν· ἐπειδὴ δ'
ἐκεῖνοι τετελευτήκασι, κἂν νῦν νικήσωμεν, ὄνειδος
ἕξομεν, διότι ἠμφισβητήθημεν, διὰ τὸν Ὀρέστην
τοῦτον τὸν κακῶς ἀπολούμενον, ὃς μοιχὸς ληφθεὶς
καὶ παθὼν ὅ τι προσήκει τοὺς τὰ τοιαῦτα ποιοῦντας
οὐδ' ὡς ἀπαλλάττεται τοῦ πράγματος, ὡς οἱ συνειδότες καταμαρτυροῦσι. τοῦτον μὲν οὖν, οἷός ἐστι,
καὶ νῦν ἀκούετε καὶ αὖθις ἀκριβέστερον πεύσεσθε,
45 ὅταν κατ' αὐτοῦ τὴν δίκην ἡμεῖς εἰσίωμεν· ὑμῶν
δ' ἐγὼ δέομαι καὶ ἱκετεύω, μή με περιίδητε περὶ
τούτων ὑβρισθέντα τῶν χρημάτων ὧν ὁ πάππος
κατέλιπε, μηδ' ἀποστερηθέντα, ἀλλὰ βοηθήσατε
καθ' ὅσον ὑμῶν ἕκαστος τυγχάνει δυνάμενος.
ἔχετε δὲ πίστεις ἱκανὰς ἐκ μαρτυριῶν, ἐκ βασάνων,
ἐξ αὐτῶν τῶν νόμων, ὅτι τ' ἐσμὲν ⟨ἐκ⟩¹ θυγατρὸς
γνησίας Κίρωνος, καὶ ὅτι προσήκει ἡμῖν μᾶλλον
ἢ τούτοις κληρονομεῖν τῶν ἐκείνου χρημάτων,
46 ἐκγόνοις οὖσι τοῦ πάππου. μνησθέντες οὖν καὶ
τῶν ὅρκων οὓς ὀμόσαντες δικάζετε, καὶ τῶν
λόγων οὓς εἰρήκαμεν, καὶ τῶν νόμων, ᾗ δίκαιόν
ἐστι, ταύτῃ τὴν ψῆφον τίθεσθε.

Οὐκ οἶδ' ὅ τι δεῖ πλείω λέγειν· οἶμαι γὰρ ὑμᾶς
οὐδὲν ἀγνοεῖν τῶν εἰρημένων. λαβὲ δ' αὐτοῖς τὴν
μαρτυρίαν τὴν λοιπήν, ὡς ἐλήφθη μοιχός, καὶ
ἀνάγνωθι.

⟨ΜΑΡΤΥΡΙΑ⟩

¹ ἐκ add. Dobree.

ᵃ Cf. § 3 and note.
ᵇ Cf. Aristoph. Clouds, 1083 ; and Suidas, s.v. ῥαφανίς.
ᶜ Probably an allusion to the indictment for ὕβρις men-

against us is of only trifling importance? While our grandfather and our father were alive, no charge was ever brought against us and our rights were never impeached; but now that they are dead, even if we win our case, we shall always bear the stigma of having had our rights disputed, thanks to this accursed Orestes,[a] who, taken in adultery and having suffered the treatment which befits such evil-doers,[b] has not even so abandoned the practice, as those who know the facts can testify. You know now the character of this fellow, and you will learn about it in still greater detail, when our suit against him comes on.[c] But do not, I beg and implore you, allow me to be insulted and robbed in the matter of this money which my grandfather left, but help me as far as each of you is able. Ample proof is before you from depositions, evidence given under torture, and the laws themselves that we are the children of a legitimate daughter of Ciron and that we have a better right than our opponents to inherit our grandfather's property as his lineal descendants. Remember, therefore, the oaths under which you sit in judgement, the arguments which we have presented, and the laws, and give your verdict as justice demands.

I do not know of anything which I ought to add; for I think that nothing which I have said has escaped your attention. Now take the only remaining deposition, proving that Diocles was taken in adultery, and read it to the court.

DEPOSITION

tioned in § 41; see p. 449 for the evidence of the speech composed by Isaeus for delivery in this suit.

IX. ON THE ESTATE OF ASTYPHILUS

IX. ON THE ESTATE OF ASTYPHILUS

INTRODUCTION

ASTYPHILUS, the son of Euthycrates,[a] after having fought in several campaigns, died while serving at Mytilene. When the news of his death reached Athens, his first cousin Cleon seized possession of his estate in the name of his own son, whom he alleged to have been adopted by Astyphilus in a will which was deposited with Hierocles. The sister of this Hierocles had been married twice, first, to Euthycrates, by whom she was mother of Astyphilus and an unnamed daughter, and, secondly, to Theophrastus, whose son is the speaker of this oration. The deceased was, therefore, the half-brother of the speaker and the first cousin of Cleon, his opponent.

[a] STEMMA

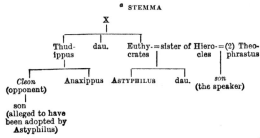

The main contentions of the speaker are that
the will produced by Cleon and Hierocles is a forgery
and that he himself has a better legal and moral
claim to the estate. To prove the first point he
has to rely on circumstantial evidence. Why, he
asks, should Astyphilus have made a will before
setting out for Mytilene, though he had never done
so before his other campaigns, and why did he choose
for adoption the son of his bitterest enemy? The
real instigator of the claim is, he alleges, not his
nominal opponent Cleon but Hierocles, who had
gone round offering to produce a will in favour of
anyone who would agree to share the spoils with
him.

The speaker bases his moral right to inherit the
estate of his half-brother on the grounds that the
deceased had experienced many benefits from himself and his family and had lived on terms of the
closest affection with them. Astyphilus, when his
mother remarried, was still a young child and had
accompanied her to the house of her second husband
Theophrastus, who had brought him up with his own
son, the speaker; on the other hand, he had never
in his life even addressed a word to Cleon, who, the
speaker alleges, had been the cause of the death
of Astyphilus's father, Euthycrates. As for the
legal claim, it is admitted as a general principle of
Attic law that, if a man dies intestate, his relatives
on the paternal side as far as the children of first
cousins have preference over all the relatives on
the maternal side; in the present case, however,
the half-brother claims that he has a better right
to the estate than the cousin, in view of the fact
that Cleon had been adopted into another family

and had thus renounced all claim to inherit from a relative in the family out of which he had been adopted.

The case is well argued and the material skilfully arranged, but it is hardly one which would recommend itself to a modern jury. In particular, no convincing proof is adduced for setting aside the will and no objection is raised to any of the circumstances connected with it ; for example, none of the usual allegations are made against those who had witnessed it. Moreover, Hierocles, if we disregard the vague assertions made against him by the speaker, would seem *prima facie* a suitable depositary for the will, since he was a relative and did not benefit under it.

Seeing that Astyphilus died during an expedition to Mytilene, it would be easy to fix the date of the speech if we had any conclusive evidence of such an expedition. We are informed that Astyphilus had previously served in the Theban war (378–371 B.C.), so that the speech cannot be earlier than some little time after 371 B.C. The years immediately following 371 B.C. were not apparently marked by any military activity on the part of Athens, and no operations are known to have been undertaken until 366 B.C., when Timotheus commanded an Athenian force in the eastern Aegean ; it is possible that Athenian troops were landed at Mytilene in the course of these operations. The names of Cleon and various other members of the family occur in inscriptions, without, however, throwing any light on the question of the date of the speech.

IX. ΠΕΡΙ ΤΟΥ ΑΣΤΥΦΙΛΟΥ ΚΛΗΡΟΥ

ΥΠΟΘΕΣΙΣ

Ἀστύφιλος καὶ ὁ λέγων τὸν λόγον ἀδελφοὶ ὁμο-
μήτριοι· τελευτήσαντος δὲ τοῦ Ἀστυφίλου διαθήκας
προήνεγκε Κλέων τις, ἀνεψιὸς ὢν αὐτοῦ, φάσκων αὐτὰς
γενέσθαι εἰς τὸν υἱὸν ἑαυτοῦ. ὁ δὲ ἀδελφὸς τοῦ
Ἀστυφίλου κατηγορεῖ τῶν διαθηκῶν ὡς πλαστῶν. ἡ
στάσις στοχασμός.

1 Ἀδελφός μοι ἦν ὁμομήτριος, ὦ ἄνδρες, Ἀστύφιλος, οὗ ἐστιν ὁ κλῆρος· ἀποδημήσας οὖν μετὰ
τῶν εἰς Μυτιλήνην στρατιωτῶν ἐτελεύτησε. πειρά-
ράσομαι δ᾽ ὑμῖν ἐπιδεῖξαι ὅπερ ἀντώμοσα, ὡς οὔτε
ἐποιήσατο ἐκεῖνος υὸν ἑαυτῷ, οὔτ᾽ ἔδωκε τὰ
ἑαυτοῦ, οὔτε διαθήκας κατέλιπεν, οὔτε προσήκει
2 ἔχειν τὰ Ἀστυφίλου οὐδενὶ ἄλλῳ ἢ ἐμοί. ἔστι
γὰρ [ὁ] Κλέων οὑτοσὶ ἀνεψιὸς Ἀστυφίλῳ πρὸς
πατρός, ὁ δὲ υὸς ὁ τούτου, ὃν εἰσποιεῖ ἐκείνῳ,
ἀνεψιαδοῦς. εἰσποίητος δ᾽ ἦν ὁ πατὴρ ὁ Κλέωνος
εἰς ἄλλον οἶκον, καὶ οὗτοι ἔτι εἰσὶν ἐν ἐκείνῳ τῷ
οἴκῳ, ὥστε γένει μὲν διὰ τὸν νόμον οὐδὲν προσ-
ήκουσιν Ἀστυφίλῳ. ἐπειδὴ δὲ κατὰ ταῦτα οὐκ ἦν
ἀμφισβήτησις, διαθήκας, ὦ ἄνδρες, ψευδεῖς (ὡς
ἐγὼ οἶμαι ἐπιδείξειν) κατεσκεύασαν καὶ ζητοῦσιν

IX. ON THE ESTATE OF ASTYPHILUS

ARGUMENT

Astyphilus and the speaker of this oration were half-brothers, children of the same mother. On the death of Astyphilus a certain Cleon, his first cousin, produced a will, alleging that it had been made in favour of his own son. The brother of Astyphilus attacks the will as being a forgery. The question at issue is one of fact.

Astyphilus, the owner of the estate, was my half-brother, gentlemen, the son of my mother. He went abroad with the force which sailed to Mytilene, and died there. I shall try and prove to you what I stated in my affidavit, namely, that the deceased did not adopt a son, that he did not bequeath his property, that he left no will, and that no one except myself has a right to the estate of Astyphilus. Cleon, my adversary, is first cousin to Astyphilus on his father's side, and his son, whom he pretends that Astyphilus adopted, is his first cousin once removed. Cleon's father, however, passed by adoption into another family, and they still belong to that family, so that in law they have no sort of relationship with Astyphilus. Seeing that they had no claim on these grounds, gentlemen, they concocted a will, which, as I think I shall be able to prove, is a forgery, and

327

3 ἀποστερῆσαί με τῶν τἀδελφοῦ.[1] καὶ οὕτω σφόδρα
Κλέων οὑτοσὶ καὶ πρότερον καὶ νῦν οὐδένα ἄλλον
τὸν κλῆρον ἡγεῖται ἕξειν ἢ αὑτόν, ὥστ' ἐπειδὴ
τάχιστα ἠγγέλθη Ἀστύφιλος τετελευτηκώς, τοῦ
μὲν πατρὸς τοῦ ἐμοῦ ἀσθενοῦντος, ἐμοῦ δὲ οὐκ
ἐπιδημοῦντος ἀλλὰ στρατευομένου, εἰς τὸ χωρίον
ἐνεβάτευσε, καὶ εἴ τι ἄλλο ἐκεῖνος κατέλιπεν,
ἅπαντα ἔφη τοῦ υἱοῦ τοῦ ἑαυτοῦ εἶναι, πρίν τι
4 ὑμᾶς ψηφίσασθαι. ἐπεὶ δ' ἐκομίσθη τὰ ὀστᾶ τοῦ
ἀδελφοῦ, ὁ μὲν προσποιούμενος πάλαι υὸς εἰσ-
[75] πεποιῆσθαι οὐ προὔθετο οὐδ' ἔθαψεν, | οἱ δὲ φίλοι
Ἀστυφίλου καὶ οἱ συστρατιῶται, ὁρῶντες τὸν
πατέρα τὸν ἐμὸν ἀρρωστοῦντα, ἐμὲ δὲ οὐκ ἐπιδημοῦντα, αὐτοὶ καὶ προὔθεντο καὶ τἆλλα πάντα τὰ
νομιζόμενα ἐποίησαν καὶ τὸν ἐμὸν πατέρα ἀσθε-
νοῦντα ἐπὶ τὸ μνῆμα ἤγαγον, εὖ εἰδότες ὅτι ἀσπά-
ζοιτο αὐτὸν Ἀστύφιλος. τούτου δ' ὑμῖν αὐτοὺς
τοὺς ἐπιτηδείους τοὺς ἐκείνου μάρτυρας παρέξομαι
τῶν παρόντων.

ΜΑΡΤΥΡΕΣ

5 Ὅτι μὲν οὐκ ἔθαψε Κλέων Ἀστύφιλον, οὐδ'
⟨ἂν⟩[2] αὐτὸς ἔξαρνος γένοιτο μεμαρτύρηταί τε ὑμῖν·
ἐπειδὴ δ' ἐπεδήμησα ἐγὼ καὶ ᾐσθόμην καρπου-
μένους τούτους τὰ ἐκείνου, . . . ὁ [δὲ] υὸς αὐτοῦ
ποιηθείη ὑπὸ Ἀστυφίλου, καὶ τούτων διαθήκας
καταλίποι παρὰ Ἱεροκλεῖ Ἰφιστιάδῃ.[3] ἀκούσας

---

[1] τῶν τἀδελφοῦ Reiske : τοῦ (τῶν A[1]) ἀδελφοῦ.
[2] ἂν add. Bekker.
[3] Ἰφιστιάδῃ Thalheim : ἡφαιστίδῃ.

---

* There is a lacuna in the text at this point. " Post τὰ
ἐκείνου est lacuna. [Adii Cleonem, qui dixit] suum filium
ab Astyphilo adoptatum esse" (Dobree, Adversaria, i. p. 305).

are trying to deprive me of my brother's estate. So confident, indeed, has Cleon here always been, and still is, that no one but himself is to have the estate, that, as soon as the news of Astyphilus's death was reported—my father being ill at the time and I abroad on military service—he entered into possession of the landed estate and declared that anything else which Astyphilus left belonged to his own son, without ever giving you the opportunity to decide the matter. When, however, my brother's remains were brought home, the person who claims to have been long ago adopted as his son did not lay them out or bury them, but Astyphilus's friends and companions-in-arms, seeing that my father was ill and I was abroad, themselves laid out the remains and carried out all the other customary rites, and conducted my father, ill though he was, to the tomb, well knowing the affection in which Astyphilus held him. I will produce before you the friends of the deceased, who were amongst those who were present, as witnesses of this.

WITNESSES

That Cleon did not bury Astyphilus, even he himself would not deny, and evidence of the fact has been given you. On my return home I found my opponents in enjoyment of the property of the deceased; [I, therefore, sought out Cleon, who informed me that] [a] his son had been adopted by Astyphilus, and that the latter had left a will to this effect in the keeping of Hierocles of Iphistiadae.[b]

---

[b] A deme of the tribe of Acamantis, situated on the left bank of the Cephissus.

δ' ἐγὼ λέγοντος αὐτοῦ ταῦτα ἐπορευόμην παρὰ
τὸν Ἱεροκλέα, εὖ μὲν εἰδὼς ὅτι ὡς οἷόν τε μάλιστα
6 ἐπιτήδειος εἴη Κλέωνι, οὐχ ἡγούμενος δ' ἂν αὐτὸν
τολμῆσαί τι ψεύσασθαι κατὰ Ἀστυφίλου τετελευτηκότος, καὶ ταῦτα θεῖον ὄντα καὶ ἐμοῦ καὶ
ἐκείνου. ὅμως δέ, ὦ ἄνδρες, οὐδὲν τούτων ὑπο-
λογισάμενος ὁ Ἱεροκλῆς ἐρωτώμενος ὑπ' ἐμοῦ
ἀπεκρινατό μοι ὅτι ἔχοι τὰς διαθήκας· λαβεῖν δὲ
ἔφη αὐτὰς παρὰ Ἀστυφίλου, ὅτε εἰς Μυτιλήνην
ἔμελλεν ἐκεῖνος ἐκπλεῖν. ὡς δὲ ταῦτ' ἔλεγεν,
ἀνάγνωθί μοι ταύτην τὴν μαρτυρίαν [ὅτι Ἱεροκλῆς ἀπεκρίνατο].

MAPTTPIA

7 Ἐπειδὴ τοίνυν, ὦ ἄνδρες, οὔτε παραγενόμενος
οὐδεὶς ἔτυχε τῶν οἰκείων ὅτε ὁ ἀδελφὸς ἐτελεύτησεν, οὔτε ἐγὼ ἐπεδήμουν ὅτε τὰ ὀστᾶ αὐτοῦ
δεῦρο ἐκομίσθη, ἀναγκαῖόν μοί ἐστιν ἐξ αὐτῶν
ὧν οὗτοι λέγουσιν ἐλέγχειν ψευδεῖς οὔσας τὰς
διαθήκας [ἃς ἐποιήσαντο]. εἰκὸς γὰρ ἐκεῖνον
οὐ μόνον ἐπιθυμεῖν ὑὸν ποιησάμενον καταλιπεῖν,
ἀλλὰ καὶ σκοπεῖσθαι ὅπως κυριώτατα ἔσται ἃ
ἂν διαθῆται, καὶ τήν τε οὐσίαν, ὃν ἂν ἐκεῖνος
εἰσποιήσηται, οὗτος ἕξει, καὶ ἐπὶ τοὺς βωμοὺς
τοὺς πατρῴους οὗτος βαδιεῖται, καὶ τελευτήσαντι
αὐτῷ καὶ τοῖς ἐκείνου προγόνοις τὰ νομιζόμενα
8 ποιήσει· ἅπαντα δὲ ταῦτα μάλιστ' ἂν εἰδέναι ὅτι
γένοιτο,[1] εἰ μὴ ἄνευ τῶν οἰκείων τῶν ἑαυτοῦ τὰς
διαθήκας ποιοῖτο, ἀλλὰ πρῶτον μὲν συγγενεῖς
παρακαλέσας, ἔπειτα δὲ φράτορας καὶ δημότας,
ἔπειτα τῶν ἄλλων ἐπιτηδείων ὅσους δύναιτο πλεί-

---

[1] γένοιτο Dobree : γένοιντο.

On hearing this from him I proceeded to the house of Hierocles, knowing full well that he was on terms of the closest possible intimacy with Cleon, though I never thought that he would dare to lie against the wishes of Astyphilus now that he was dead, especially as he was his uncle as well as mine.[a] Nevertheless, gentlemen, regardless of these considerations, Hierocles in reply to my questions stated that the will was in his possession and said that he had received it from Astyphilus when he was on the point of sailing to Mytilene. And to prove that he made these statements, please read this deposition.

DEPOSITION

Since, then, gentlemen, no one of my brother's relatives was present when he died and I was abroad when his remains were brought hither, I am obliged to use the actual statements of my adversaries to prove that the will is a forgery. It is only reasonable to suppose that Astyphilus did not merely feel a desire to adopt a son, but also provided that whatever dispositions he made should be as effectual as possible, and that, whomsoever he adopted, that person should both possess his estate and have access to his ancestral altars and perform all the customary rites for himself after his death and for his forefathers. He would be assured that all these intentions would be best effected, not if he made his will without the attestation of his relatives, but if he summoned first his kinsmen, then the members of his ward and deme, and finally as many as possible of his other acquaintances ; for then

---

[a] The sister of Hierocles was mother of Astyphilus and of the speaker, cf. §§ 23, 27.

στους· οὕτω γὰρ εἴτε κατὰ γένος εἴτε κατὰ δόσιν
ἀμφισβητοίη τις, ῥᾳδίως ἂν ἐλέγχοιτο ψευδόμενος.
9 ὁ τοίνυν Ἀστύφιλος οὐδὲν φαίνεται τοιοῦτον
ποιήσας, οὐδὲ παραστησάμενος οὐδένα τούτων ὅτε
διέθετο ἃ οὗτοί φασιν, εἰ μή τις ἄρα ὑπὸ τούτων
πέπεισται ὁμολογεῖν παρεῖναι. αὐτὸς δ᾽ ὑμῖν
πάντας τούτους μαρτυροῦντας παρέξομαι.

ΜΑΡΤΥΡΕΣ

10 Ἴσως τοίνυν Κλέων οὑτοσὶ φήσει[1] οὐκ εἰκὸς
εἶναι τεκμηρίοις ὑμᾶς χρήσασθαι τούτοις τοῖς
μάρτυσιν, ὅτι μαρτυροῦσι μὴ εἰδέναι Ἀστύφιλον
ταῦτα διατιθέμενον. ἐγὼ δ᾽ οἶμαι, περί γε διαθηκῶν οὔσης τῆς ἀμφισβητήσεως καὶ περὶ τοῦ
ποιηθῆναί τινα υἱὸν Ἀστυφίλῳ, ἡμῖν πολὺ βεβαιοτέραν εἶναι μαρτυρίαν ἣν οἱ ἀναγκαῖοι <οἳ>[2] ἐκείνου
περὶ τῶν μεγίστων μὴ φασι παραγενέσθαι, μᾶλλον
ἢ ἣν οἱ μηδὲν προσήκοντες μαρτυροῦσι παρεῖναι.
11 καὶ ἐχρῆν δ᾽, ὦ ἄνδρες, καὶ αὐτὸν Κλέωνα, μὴ
δοκοῦντα εἶναι ἠλίθιον, ὅτε τὸν υἱὸν τὸν τούτου
ἐποιεῖτο Ἀστύφιλος καὶ τὰς διαθήκας κατέλειπε,
παρακαλέσαι εἴ τέ[3] τινα συγγενῆ ἐπιδημοῦντα
ἐγίγνωσκε, καὶ τοὺς ἄλλους, ὅτῳ περ ἔμβραχυ[4]
ᾔδει Ἀστύφιλον χρώμενον. κωλῦσαι μὲν γὰρ
οὐδεὶς ἂν αὐτὸν ἐδύνατο, ὅτῳ ἐβούλετο, δοῦναι
τὰ ἑαυτοῦ· τούτῳ δ᾽ ἂν μεγάλη μαρτυρία ἦν, ὅτι
12 οὐ λάθρα ταῦτα διέθετο. ἔτι δ᾽, ὦ ἄνδρες, εἰ μὲν
ὁ Ἀστύφιλος μηδένα ἐβούλετο εἰδέναι ὅτι τὸν
Κλέωνος υἱὸν ἐποιεῖτο μηδ᾽ ὅτι διαθήκας καταλίποι,

---

[1] φήσει Naber: φησιν. [2] οἳ add. Sauppe. [3] τέ Dobree: γέ.
[4] περ ἔμβραχυ Cobet: ἐπιβραχύ περ.

anyone who might claim the estate either as next-of-kin or as legatee could be easily convicted of false pretences. Astyphilus is shown to have taken none of these precautions, and not to have summoned any of the persons whom I have mentioned when he made the will which my opponents allege that he made—unless, indeed, anyone has been suborned by them to state that he was present. I will myself produce all these persons before you as witnesses.

WITNESSES

Cleon will perhaps contend that you ought not to draw any conclusions from the evidence of these witnesses, because they merely depose that they have no knowledge of the making of this will by Astyphilus. But in my opinion, since the controversy is about a will and about the adoption of a son by Astyphilus, more weight should be attached by you to the evidence of the intimate friends of the deceased, when they declare that they were not present on so important an occasion, than to the evidence of those who have no connexion with him, to the effect that they were present. Also Cleon himself, sirs, being apparently no fool, when Astyphilus was adopting his son and making the will, ought to have summoned any relatives whom he knew to be in the city and any other person with whom he knew Astyphilus to be at all intimate. For no one could have prevented Astyphilus from devising his property to whomsoever he wished ; but the fact that the will was not made in secret, would have been strong evidence in Cleon's favour. Furthermore, gentlemen, if Astyphilus wished that no one should know that he was adopting Cleon's

εἰκὸς ἦν μηδὲ ἄλλον μηδένα ἐγγεγράφθαι ἐν τῷ
γραμματείῳ μάρτυρα· εἰ δ' ἐναντίον μαρτύρων
φαίνεται διαθέμενος, τούτων δὲ μὴ τῶν μάλιστα
χρωμένων ἀλλὰ τῶν ἐντυχόντων, πῶς εἰκός ἐστιν
13 ἀληθεῖς εἶναι τὰς διαθήκας; οὐ γὰρ ⟨ἂν⟩[1] ἡγοῦμαι
ἔγωγε οὐδένα, υἱὸν ἑαυτῷ ποιούμενον, τολμῆσαι
[76] ἄλλους τινὰς παρακαλέσαι ἢ | τούτους, οἷς[2] περ
καὶ ἱερῶν καὶ ὁσίων κοινωνὸν[3] ἀνθ' αὑτοῦ εἰς τὸν
ἔπειτα χρόνον ἔμελλε καταλιπεῖν. ἀλλὰ μὴν οὐδ'
αἰσχυνθῆναι οὐδενὶ προσήκει ἐπὶ τοιαύταις διαθήκαις ὡς πλείστους μάρτυρας παρίστασθαι, νόμου
γε ὄντος ἐξεῖναι ὅτῳ βούλοιτο δοῦναι τὰ ἑαυτοῦ.

14 Σκέψασθε δέ, ὦ ἄνδρες, καὶ ἐκ τοῦ χρόνου ὃν
οὗτοι λέγουσι περὶ τῶν διαθηκῶν. ὅτε γὰρ εἰς
Μυτιλήνην ἐξέπλει στρατευόμενος, τότε φασὶν
αὐτὸν ταῦτα διαθέσθαι· φαίνεται δὲ ὁ Ἀστύφιλος
τῷ τούτων λόγῳ τὰ μέλλοντα ἅπαντα ἔσεσθαι
προειδώς. πρῶτον μὲν γὰρ ἐστρατεύσατο εἰς
Κόρινθον, ἔπειτα εἰς Θετταλίαν, ἔτι δὲ τὸν Θη-
βαϊκὸν πόλεμον ἅπαντα, καὶ ἄλλοσε ὅπου περ
αἰσθάνοιτο στράτευμα συλλεγόμενον, ἁπανταχοῖ[4]
ἀπεδήμει λοχαγῶν· καὶ οὐδ' ἐν μιᾷ τούτων τῶν
ἐξόδων διαθήκας κατέλιπεν. ἡ δὲ εἰς τὴν Μυτιλήνην στρατεία τελευταία αὐτῷ ἐγένετο, ἐν ᾗ καὶ
15 ἀπέθανε. τῷ οὖν ἂν ὑμῶν φανείη πιστόν, πρότερον ἄλλας στρατείας τοῦ Ἀστυφίλου στρατευομένου καὶ εὖ εἰδότος ὅτι ἐν ἁπάσαις μέλλοι

[1] ἂν add. Scheibe.
[2] οἷς Dobree: οὕς.
[3] κοινωνὸν Dobree: κοινωνούς.
[4] ἁπανταχοῖ Reiske: -ῆ.

[a] See Introduction, p. 325.

son or that he had left a will, no one else's name ought to have been inscribed in the document as witness ; but if it appears that he made a will in the presence of witnesses, and those witnesses were not taken from among those who were most intimate with him but were chance persons, is there any probability that the will is genuine ? For my part I cannot believe that anyone, when he was adopting a son, would have ventured to summon as witnesses any other persons except those with whom he was about to leave that son, to take his own place as an associate for the future in their religious and civic acts. Moreover, no one ought to be ashamed of summoning the largest possible number of witnesses to the execution of such a will, when there is a law which permits a man to bequeath his property to whomsoever he wishes.

Now consider the matter, gentlemen, from the point of view of the date which my opponents assign to the will. They say that he made these dispositions when he was sailing for Mytilene on military service ; it is clear then from their account that he knew beforehand all that fate had in store for him ! For he served first at Corinth, then in Thessaly and again throughout the Theban war,[a] and wherever else he heard of an army being collected, he went abroad holding a command ; yet never on his departure for any one of these campaigns did he leave a will behind him. The expedition to Mytilene was his last, for in it he perished. Who among you can believe it possible that the decrees of fate should correspond so exactly with Astyphilus's conduct, that when he was preparing for other campaigns and was well aware that he was going to run risks on

κινδυνεύειν, οὕτως ἀκριβῶς τὰ παρὰ τῆς τύχης
συμβῆναι, ὥστ᾽ ἐν μὲν τῷ πρόσθεν χρόνῳ μηδὲ
περὶ ἑνὸς αὐτὸν τῶν αὑτοῦ διαθέσθαι, ὅτε δὲ τὸ
τελευταῖον ἔμελλε στρατεύεσθαι, ἐθελοντήν τε
ἐκπλέοντα[1] καὶ μάλιστα ἐκ ταύτης τῆς στρατείας
ἐλπίζοντα σωθήσεσθαι (πῶς τοῦτον πιστὸν ἤδη[2];)
τὰς διαθήκας τότε καταλιπεῖν καὶ ἐκπλεύσαντα
τελευτῆσαι;

16 Χωρὶς δὲ τούτων, ὦ ἄνδρες δικασταί, ἔτι μείζω
τεκμήρια παρέξομαι ὡς οὐδὲν ἀληθὲς λέγουσιν
οὗτοι. ἐπιδείξω γὰρ ὑμῖν ἔχθιστον ἁπάντων ὄντα
Ἀστύφιλον Κλέωνι, καὶ οὕτω σφόδρα καὶ δικαίως μισοῦντα τοῦτον, ὥστε πολὺ ἂν[3] θᾶττον διαθέμενον μηδένα ποτὲ τῶν ἑαυτοῦ οἰκείων δια-
λεχθῆναι Κλέωνι, μᾶλλον ἢ τὸν τούτου ὑὸν ποιη-
17 σάμενον.[4] Εὐθυκράτει γάρ, ὦ ἄνδρες, τῷ πατρὶ
τῷ Ἀστυφίλου αἴτιος γενέσθαι λέγεται τοῦ θανάτου Θούδιππος ὁ Κλέωνος τουτουὶ[5] πατήρ, αἰκι-
σάμενος ἐκεῖνον διαφορᾶς τινος αὐτοῖς γενομένης
ἐν τῇ νεμήσει τοῦ χωρίου, καὶ οὕτως αὐτὸν δια-
τεθῆναι, ὥστε ἐκ τῶν πληγῶν αὐτὸν ἀσθενήσαντα
18 οὐ πολλαῖς ἡμέραις ὕστερον ἀποθανεῖν. ὡς δὲ
ταῦτ᾽ ἐστὶν ἀληθῆ, ἴσως μὲν καὶ Ἀραφηνίων[6] καὶ
πολλοὶ τῶν τότε συγγεωργούντων μαρτυρήσειαν[7]
ἄν μοι, διαρρήδην δὲ περὶ τηλικούτου πράγματος
οὐκ ἂν ἔχοιμι ὅπως ὑμῖν παρασχοίμην. καὶ γὰρ
αὐτὸν τυπτόμενον ἰδὼν Ἱεροκλῆς, ὁ τὸ γραμματεῖον φάσκων παρ᾽ ἑαυτῷ τεθῆναι, οἶδ᾽ ὅτι οὐκ ἂν

---

[1] ἐκπλέοντα Dobree: ἐκπλεῖν τῷ.
[2] ἤδη Aldus: ἤδει.   [3] ἂν Dobree: δή.
[4] ποιησάμενον Reiske: -όμενον.
[5] τουτουὶ Scheibe: τούτου.

all of them, on no previous occasion did he make any disposition of his property, yet when he was about to set out on his last expedition, going out as a volunteer with every prospect of returning safe and sound from this campaign, on this occasion only did he make a will and then sail away and lose his life ? How can you credit such a coincidence ?

But besides this, judges, I will produce still stronger indications that there is no truth in what my opponents say. I will prove to you that Astyphilus had no such bitter enemy as Cleon, and hated him so much and with such good cause, that he would have been much more likely to have arranged that no one of his family should ever speak to Cleon than to have adopted his son. For the death of Euthycrates, the father of Astyphilus, is said to have been caused by an assault made upon him by Thudippus, the father of Cleon here, in the course of a quarrel which arose between them over the division of their land, and he is said to have received such treatment that he fell ill as a result of the blows and died not many days later. That this story is true, many of the Araphenians,[a] who were tilling their land at the time, would probably testify for me, but I could not find anyone to give positive evidence in so grave a matter. Hierocles, the man who alleges that the will was deposited in his custody, saw Euthycrates struck, but I am sure that he

---

[a] Members of the deme of Araphen in Eastern Attica, to which both the brothers belonged.

[6] Ἀραφηνίων Palmer: ῥάφηνίων (sic).
[7] μαρτυρήσειαν Scheibe: -αιεν.

ἐθελήσειε[1] μαρτυρῆσαι ἐναντία ταῖς διαθήκαις αἷς
αὐτὸς ἀποφαίνει. ὅμως μέντοι καὶ κάλει Ἱεροκλέα,
ἵνα ἐναντίον τούτων μαρτυρήσῃ ἢ ἐξομόσηται.

ΕΞΩΜΟΣΙΑ[2]

19 Ἀκριβῶς μὲν ᾔδειν· τοῦ γὰρ αὐτοῦ ἀνδρός ἐστιν,
ἃ μὲν οἶδεν, ἐξόμνυσθαι, τῶν δὲ μὴ γενομένων
πίστιν ἐθέλειν ἐπιθεῖναι ἦ μὴν εἰδέναι γενόμενα·
ὡς δέ, ὅτε ἀπέθνησκεν [ὁ] Εὐθυκράτης ὁ πατὴρ
Ἀστυφίλου, ἐπέσκηψε τοῖς οἰκείοις μηδένα ποτὲ
ἐᾶσαι[3] ἐλθεῖν τῶν Θουδίππου ἐπὶ τὸ μνῆμα τὸ
ἑαυτοῦ, τούτων ὑμῖν τὸν[4] ἔχοντα τὴν τηθίδα τοῦ
Ἀστυφίλου μάρτυρα[5] παρέξομαι.

ΜΑΡΤΥΡΙΑ

20 Ἀκούων τοίνυν ταῦτα ὁ Ἀστύφιλος καὶ τούτου
καὶ τῶν ἄλλων προσηκόντων εὐθέως ἐκ παιδίου,[6]
ἐπειδὴ τάχιστα ἤρχετο φρονεῖν, οὐδὲ πώποτε δι-
ελέχθη Κλέωνι, ἀλλὰ πρότερον ἐτελεύτησεν, οὐχ
ἡγούμενος ὅσιον εἶναι, τοιαύτην αἰτίαν ἔχοντος
Θουδίππου περὶ τὸν αὑτοῦ πατέρα, τῷ ἐκείνου
ὑεῖ διαλέγεσθαι. ὡς οὖν τὸν ἅπαντα χρόνον διάφορος ἦν Κλέωνι, τούτων ὑμῖν τοὺς συνειδότας
μάρτυρας παρέξομαι.

ΜΑΡΤΥΡΕΣ

21 Εἰς τὰς θυσίας τοίνυν, ἐν αἷσπερ οἱ ἄλλοι Ἀθηναῖοι ἑστιῶνται, πρῶτον μὲν δημότην ὄντα, ἔπειτα

---

[1] ἐθελήσειε Dobree: -ση.
[2] ἐξωμοσία Baiter-Sauppe: μαρτυρία.
[3] ἐᾶσαι Baiter: ἐάσειν.   [4] τὸν Buermann: τὴν.
[5] μάρτυρα Stephanus: μαρτυρίαν.
[6] παιδίου Dobree: παίδων.

would not be willing to give evidence to the detriment of the will which he is himself producing. But for all that, summon Hierocles that he may give his evidence before the court or else swear to his ignorance of the fact.

OATH OF IGNORANCE

I was quite sure he would say this; for it is quite in the same character for a man to swear that he is ignorant of facts which he really knows and to be willing to pledge his oath to the truth of what has never really happened. However, to prove that Euthycrates, the father of Astyphilus, on his deathbed charged his relatives never to allow any of Thudippus's family to come near his tomb, I will produce as witness before you the husband of Astyphilus's aunt.

EVIDENCE

Astyphilus, then, hearing of this in childhood from his uncle and his other relatives, as soon as he reached the age of reason, would never speak to Cleon, and maintained this attitude up to his death, holding the opinion that it was impious to speak to the son of Thudippus, when the latter was charged with so grave a crime against his father. To prove that he remained throughout his life at variance with Cleon, I will produce as witnesses before you those who know the facts.

WITNESSES

It would have been only natural, I suppose, for Astyphilus, whenever he was at home, to attend the sacrifices, at which all the Athenians entertain one

ἀνεψιόν, ἔτι δὲ τὸν υἱὸν τὸν τούτου μέλλοντα ποιεῖσθαι, εἰκὸς δήπου ἦν, ὁπότε περ ἐπιδημοίη,[1] μηδὲ μεθ' ἑνὸς ἄλλου ἰέναι[2] τὸν Ἀστύφιλον ἢ μετὰ Κλέωνος. ὡς τοίνυν οὐδέποτ' ἦλθε μετ' αὐτοῦ, [77] ὑμῖν τῶν δημοτῶν μαρτυρίαν | ἀναγνώσεται.

ΜΑΡΤΥΡΙΑ

22 Οὕτως τοίνυν διακείμενος τῷ τετελευτηκότι Κλέων ἀξιοῖ τὸν υἱὸν τὸν ἑαυτοῦ τὰ ἐκείνου ἔχειν. καὶ τί δεῖ τοῦτον λέγειν; ἀλλ' Ἱεροκλῆς, θεῖος ὢν καὶ <ἐκείνῳ καὶ>[3] ἐμοί, οὕτως ἐστὶ τολμηρὸς ὥστε οὐ γενομένας διαθήκας ἥκει φέρων, καί φησι παρ' 23 ἑαυτῷ Ἀστύφιλον ταύτας καταλιπεῖν. καίτοι, Ἱερόκλεις, πολλὰ κἀγαθὰ παθὼν ὑπὸ Θεοφράστου τοῦ πατρὸς τοῦ ἐμοῦ, ὅτε χεῖρον ἔπραττες ἢ νυνί, καὶ ὑπὸ Ἀστυφίλου, οὐδετέρῳ αὐτοῖν τὴν ἀξίαν χάριν ἀποδίδως· ἐμὲ μὲν γὰρ υἱὸν ὄντα Θεοφράστου, σαυτῷ δὲ ἀδελφιδοῦν, ἀποστερεῖς ἅ μοι οἱ νόμοι ἔδοσαν, Ἀστυφίλου δὲ τεθνεῶτος καταψεύδῃ, καὶ τὸ κατὰ σαυτὸν μέρος τοὺς ἐχθίστους 24 καθίστης τῶν ἐκείνου κληρονόμους. καὶ πρὶν μὲν ληχθῆναι τοῦ κλήρου, ὦ ἄνδρες, εὖ εἰδὼς ὁ Ἱεροκλῆς ὅτι οὐδενὶ ἄλλῳ γίγνοιτο τὰ Ἀστυφίλου ἢ ἐμοί, ἐν μέρει ἑκάστῳ τῶν ἐκείνου ἐπιτηδείων προσῄει πωλῶν τὸ πρᾶγμα καὶ τοὺς οὐδὲν προσήκοντας πείθων ἀμφισβητεῖν, λέγων ὅτι θεῖος εἴη Ἀστυφίλῳ καὶ ἀποφανοίη[4] διαθήκας ἐκεῖνον καταλελοιπότα, εἴ τις αὐτῷ κοινώσοιτο· ἐπειδὴ δὲ πρὸς Κλέωνα διωμολογήσατο καὶ τῶν τοῦ ἀδελφοῦ

---

[1] ἐπιδημοίη Reiske: ἀπο-
[2] ἰέναι Reiske: εἶναι.
[3] ἐκείνῳ καὶ add. Dobree.
[4] ἀποφανοίη Scheibe: -φάνοι.

another, accompanied by Cleon rather than by anyone else, since he was of the same deme and his cousin and, moreover, intended to adopt his son. The clerk shall, therefore, read you the deposition of the demesmen to prove that on no occasion was he accompanied by him.

DEPOSITION

Such then being the relations between Cleon and the deceased, he now demands that his son should inherit his property. Yet why should I speak of Cleon? It is rather Hierocles, the uncle of the deceased and of me, who has had the audacity to come here with a forged will and declare that Astyphilus left it in his keeping. And yet, Hierocles, though you received many kindnesses from my father Theophrastus, when you were less prosperous than you are now, and from Astyphilus, you are paying to neither of them the return which is their due; for you are robbing me, the son of Theophrastus and your own nephew, of property which the laws awarded to me, and you are slandering the memory of the dead Astyphilus and doing your best to put his bitterest enemies in possession of his property. Nay, before any formal claim was laid to the estate, sirs, Hierocles, well aware that it was coming by rights to me and to no one else, went round in turn to all the friends of the deceased, hawking his scheme and trying to persuade men who had no title to it to claim the estate, saying that he was Astyphilus's uncle and would declare that he had left a will, if anyone would go shares with him; and now that he has made a bargain with Cleon and divided up my brother's property,

ἐμερίσατο, νυνὶ ὡς ἀληθῆ λέγων ἀξιώσει πιστεύεσθαι. δοκεῖ δέ μοι κἂν ὀμόσαι ἄσμενος, εἴ τις
25 αὐτῷ ὅρκον διδοίη. καὶ ἐμοὶ μὲν συγγενὴς ὢν
οὐδὲ τὰ γενόμενα ἐθέλει μαρτυρεῖν, ᾧ δ' οὐδὲν
προσήκει, τούτῳ τὰ ψευδῆ συλλαμβάνει καὶ τῶν
οὐ πραχθέντων γραμματεῖον ἥκει φέρων· πολὺ
γὰρ προὐργιαίτερον ἡγεῖται εἶναι τὸ χρημα-
τίζεσθαι ἢ τὴν ἐμὴν συγγένειαν. ὡς δὲ ἐπηγγέλ-
λετο περιιὼν διαθήκας ἀποφανεῖν,[1] εἴ τις αὐτῷ
κοινώσαιτο, αὐτοὺς ὑμῖν οἷς προσῆλθε μάρτυρας[2]
παρέξομαι.[3]

ΜΑΡΤΤΡΕΣ[4]

26 Τί οὖν χρή, ὦ ἄνδρες, ὄνομα θέσθαι τούτῳ τῷ
ἀνδρί, ὅστις ἐθέλει οὕτω ῥᾳδίως διὰ τὸ ἑαυτοῦ κέρ-
δος τῶν τεθνεώτων τινὸς καταψεύδεσθαι; ὡς δὲ
οὐδὲ Κλέωνι προῖκα τὰς διαθήκας ἀποφαίνει, ἀλλὰ
μισθὸν εἴληφεν, αὕτη ὑμῖν ἡ μαρτυρία οὐ μικρὸν
τεκμήριον ἔσται. τοιαῦτα μέντοι κοινῇ ἐπ' ἐμοὶ
τεχνάζουσιν· ἡγεῖται γὰρ αὐτῶν ἑκάτερος εὕρημα
ἔχειν ὅ τι ἂν τῶν Ἀστυφίλου λάβῃ.

27 Ὡς μὲν οὖν οὐκ εἰσὶν ἀληθεῖς αἱ διαθῆκαι, ἀλλὰ
Κλέων καὶ Ἱεροκλῆς βούλονται ὑμᾶς ἐξαπατῆσαι,
καθ' ὅσον ἐδυνάμην ἀπέδειξα· ὡς δ' εἰ καὶ μηδὲν
προσήκων ἔτυχον Ἀστυφίλῳ, δικαιότερός εἰμι
ἔχειν τὰ ἐκείνου ἢ οὗτοι, διδάξω ὑμᾶς. ὅτε γὰρ
ἐλάμβανε Θεόφραστος ὁ ἐμὸς πατὴρ τὴν ἐμὴν
μητέρα καὶ Ἀστυφίλου παρὰ Ἱεροκλέους, ἦλθε
καὶ αὐτὸν ἐκεῖνον ἔχουσα μικρὸν ὄντα, καὶ διῃτᾶτο

[1] ἀποφανεῖν Dobree: -φαίνειν.
[2] αὐτοὺς ὑμῖν οἷς προσῆλθε μάρτυρας Scheibe: αὐτοῦ ὑμῖν ὡς
προσῆλθε μαρτυρίας.   [3] παρέξομαι Dobree: παρέχ-.
[4] μάρτυρες Scheibe: μαρτυρίαι.

342

he will demand to be believed on the ground that he is speaking the truth. He would, I believe, be delighted even to take an oath, if anyone were to propose it to him. For me, though he is my kinsman, he refuses to testify even to events which have actually happened, but with my opponent, who is no relative of his, he co-operates in telling lies and has brought a document in his favour to prove events which have never occurred; for he considers that to make money is much more important than his kinship with me. To prove that he went round and promised to produce a will in favour of anyone who would share the estate with him, I will produce as witnesses the actual persons to whom he addressed himself.

WITNESSES

What name ought to be given, gentlemen, to this man, who is willing so lightly for his own profit to slander one who is dead? This evidence will furnish you with a strong presumption that he is not producing this will in favour of Cleon for nothing, but has received a recompense. Such, however, are the artifices which they are concerting against me; for each regards as clear gain anything that he can filch from the property of Astyphilus.

I have proved to you to the best of my ability that the will is not genuine, and that Cleon and Hierocles are seeking to mislead you; I will now proceed to show that, even if I had borne no relationship to Astyphilus, I have a better right to his property than my opponents. For when my father Theophrastus received my mother—who was also the mother of Astyphilus—in marriage from Hierocles, she brought with her Astyphilus, then a

343

παρ' ἡμῖν τὸν ἅπαντα χρόνον ὁ Ἀστύφιλος, καὶ
28 ἐπαιδεύθη ὑπὸ τοῦ πατρὸς τοῦ ἐμοῦ. καὶ ἐπειδὴ
ἐγὼ ἐγενόμην καὶ ὥραν εἶχον παιδεύεσθαι, μετ'
ἐκείνου συνεπαιδευόμην. λαβὲ δέ μοι ταύτην τὴν
μαρτυρίαν, εἶτα τῶν διδασκάλων ὅποι ἐφοιτῶμεν.

ΜΑΡΤΥΡΙΑΙ[1]

Τὸ τοίνυν χωρίον τὸ ἐκείνου πατρῷον, ὦ ἄνδρες,
ὁ πατὴρ ὁ ἐμὸς ἐφύτευσε καὶ ἐγεώργει καὶ ἐποίει
διπλασίου ἄξιον. ἀνάβητέ μοι καὶ τούτων μάρτυρες.

ΜΑΡΤΥΡΕΣ

29 Ἐπεὶ τοίνυν ἐδοκιμάσθη ὁ ἀδελφός, ἀπέλαβε
πάντα ὀρθῶς καὶ δικαίως, ὥστε ἐκεῖνον μηδὲ
πώποτε μηδὲν ἐγκαλέσαι τῷ ἐμῷ πατρί. μετὰ δὲ
ταῦτα τὴν ἀδελφὴν τὴν ἐκείνου ὁμοπατρίαν ἠγγύησεν ὁ ἐμὸς πατὴρ ὅτῳ ἐδόκει αὐτῷ, καὶ τἆλλα
διῴκει, καὶ ταῦτα τῷ Ἀστυφίλῳ ἐξήρκει· ἱκανὴν
γὰρ ἡγήσατο βάσανον εἰληφέναι ἀπὸ τοῦ πατρὸς
τοῦ ἐμοῦ τῆς εἰς αὐτὸν εὐνοίας, ἐκ μικροῦ παιδίου
τεθραμμένος παρ' αὐτῷ. μαρτυροῦσι δὲ ὑμῖν[2] καὶ
περὶ τῆς ἐγγύης οἱ εἰδότες.

ΜΑΡΤΥΡΕΣ

30 Εἰς τοίνυν τὰ ἱερὰ ὁ πατὴρ ὁ ἐμὸς τὸν Ἀστύφιλον ⟨ὄντα⟩[3] παῖδα ἦγε μεθ' ἑαυτοῦ ὥσπερ καὶ ἐμὲ
πανταχῇ καὶ εἰς τοὺς θιάσους τοὺς Ἡρακλέους

---

[1] μαρτυρίαι Reiske: -ία.   [2] ὑμῖν Sauppe: ἡμῖν.
[3] ὄντα add. Dobree.

young child, and he lived continuously in our house, and was brought up by my father. When I was born and was of an age to be instructed, I was educated with him. Please take this deposition, and after it that of the masters whose classes we attended.

DEPOSITIONS

My father, gentlemen, planted the paternal estate of Astyphilus and continued to cultivate it and doubled its value. Let the witnesses of this also, please, come up.

WITNESSES

When my brother came of age, he received all his possessions in so correct and regular a manner that he never had any complaint to make against my father. After this my father gave Astyphilus's sister in marriage [a] to a man of his choice and managed everything else to Astyphilus's complete satisfaction; for the latter thought that he had received an ample proof from my father of his goodwill towards him, in the fact that he had been brought up by him from early childhood. Those who know the facts are my witnesses before you about his sister's betrothal.

WITNESSES

My father took Astyphilus with him when he was a child, as also he took me, to the religious ceremonies on every occasion; he also introduced him to the

---

[a] This duty would naturally fall to the brother when he came of age; but Astyphilus preferred that his stepfather should act for him.

ἐκεῖνον [αὐτὸν] εἰσήγαγεν, ἵνα μετέχοι τῆς κοινωνίας. αὐτοὶ ὑμῖν οἱ θιασῶται μαρτυρήσουσιν.

ΜΑΡΤΥΡΕΣ[1]

[78] Ἐγὼ δέ, | ὦ ἄνδρες, ὡς διεκείμην πρὸς τὸν ἀδελφόν, σκέψασθε. πρῶτον μὲν γὰρ συνετράφην ἐκείνῳ ἐκ παιδίου, ἔπειτα οὐδέποτε διάφορος ἐγενόμην, ἀλλ' ἠσπάζετό με, ὡς ἴσασιν οἱ οἰκεῖοι πάντες οἱ ἡμέτεροι καὶ οἱ φίλοι· οὓς βούλομαι ὑμῖν μάρτυρας ἀναβιβάσαι.

ΜΑΡΤΥΡΕΣ

31 Δοκεῖ ἂν οὖν ὑμῖν Ἀστύφιλος, ὦ ἄνδρες, οὕτω μὲν μισῶν Κλέωνα, τοσαῦτα δ' ἀγαθὰ ὑπὸ τοῦ πατρὸς τοῦ ἐμοῦ πεπονθώς, αὐτὸς τῶν ἐχθρῶν ἄν τινος υἱὸν ποιήσασθαι ἢ τὰ ἑαυτοῦ δοῦναι, τοὺς εὐεργέτας καὶ τοὺς συγγενεῖς ἀποστερήσας; ἐγὼ μὲν οὐκ ἂν οἴομαι, εἰ καὶ δεκάκις ὁ Ἱεροκλῆς διαθήκας ψευδεῖς ἀποδεικνύει, ἀλλὰ καὶ διὰ τὸ ἀδελφὸν εἶναι καὶ διὰ τὴν ἄλλην οἰκειότητα πολὺ 32 μᾶλλον προσήκειν ἐμοὶ ἢ τῷ Κλέωνος υἱεῖ, ἐπεὶ[2] τούτοις γε οὐδὲ προσποιήσασθαι καλὸν ἦν τῶν Ἀστυφίλου, οἵτινες οὕτω διέκειντο πρὸς αὐτόν, τὰ δὲ ὀστᾶ οὐκ ἔθαψαν, ἀλλὰ πρότερον ἐπὶ τὴν οὐσίαν ἦλθον πρὶν ἐκείνῳ τὰ νομιζόμενα ποιῆσαι. ἔπειτα νῦν ἀξιώσουσι κληρονομεῖν τῶν Ἀστυφίλου οὐ μόνον τὰς διαθήκας λέγοντες, ἀλλὰ καὶ τὸ γένος παρατιθέντες, ὅτι ἀνεψιὸς ἦν Κλέων πρὸς πατρός.

---

[1] μάρτυρες Aldus: μαρτυρία.
[2] ἐπεὶ sched. Eton., Reiske: ἐπί.

confraternity of Heracles in order that he might become a member of this association. The other members will themselves bear witness to this.

WITNESSES

Next consider, gentlemen, my own relations with my brother. In the first place, I was brought up with him from infancy ; secondly, I never had a quarrel with him, but he had a great affection for me, as all the members of our family and our friends know. I should like them to come forward and testify to you.

WITNESSES

Can you imagine, gentlemen, that Astyphilus, detesting Cleon so heartily and having experienced so many kindnesses at the hands of my father, would himself have adopted a son of one of his enemies or bequeathed his property to him, to the detriment of his benefactors and relatives ? Personally, I regard it as impossible, even though Hierocles produces forged wills ten times over : no, I am convinced that, because I am his brother and we were united by every other family-tie, I have a much stronger claim than the son of Cleon ; for it was positively indecent in them to put forward pretensions to the estate of Astyphilus, when they were on the terms with him that I have described and never buried his remains, but entered into possession before performing the customary rites over him. Further, they intend now to demand the succession to Astyphilus's property not only because of the will which they allege to exist, but also by a comparison of their relationship and mine, on the ground that Cleon was a first cousin of the deceased on his father's

33 ὑμᾶς δέ, ὦ ἄνδρες, οὐκ εἰκός ἐστι τῷ τούτου
γένει προσέχειν τὸν νοῦν· οὐδεὶς γὰρ πώποτε
ἐκποίητος γενόμενος ἐκληρονόμησε τοῦ οἴκου ὅθεν
ἐξεποιήθη, ἐὰν μὴ ἐπανέλθῃ κατὰ τὸν νόμον. . . .
οὗτοι μέντοι ἀκριβῶς εἰδότες ὅτι οὐκ ἐποιήσατο
'Αστύφιλος τὸν Κλέωνος ὑόν, πολλάκις ἐληλυθότι
αὐτῷ οὐδεπώποτε κεκρεανομήκασι. λαβέ μοι καὶ
ταύτην τὴν μαρτυρίαν.

ΜΑΡΤΥΡΙΑ

34 'Εκατέρῳ οὖν ἡμῶν, ἐξ ὧν ἀντωμόσαμεν σκεψάμενοι, ψηφίσασθε. Κλέων μὲν γάρ φησι τὸν
ὑὸν τὸν ἑαυτοῦ 'Αστυφίλῳ εἰσποιηθῆναι, καὶ ταῦτ'
ἐκεῖνον διαθέσθαι· ἐγὼ δ' οὔ φημι, ἀλλ' ἐμὰ εἶναι
πάντα τὰ 'Αστυφίλου, ἀδελφὸς ὢν ἐκείνου, ὡς καὶ
αὐτοὶ οὗτοι[1] ἴσασι. μὴ τοίνυν, ὦ ἄνδρες, εἰσποιήσητε[2] ὑὸν 'Αστυφίλῳ ὃν οὐδ' αὐτὸς ζῶν ἐκεῖνος
ἐποιήσατο, ἀλλὰ τοὺς νόμους οὓς ὑμεῖς ἔθεσθε βε-
βαιώσατέ μοι· κατὰ τούτους γὰρ ἀμφισβητῶ, ὁσιω-
τάτην δέησιν δεόμενος, ὦ ἄνδρες, τῆς τοῦ ἀδελφοῦ
35 οὐσίας κληρονόμον με καταστῆσαι. ἀπέδειξα δ'
ὑμῖν ὡς οὐδενὶ ἐκεῖνος δέδωκε τὰ ἑαυτοῦ, καὶ μάρτυρας ἁπάντων ὧν εἶπον παρεσχόμην. βοηθήσατε
οὖν μοι, καὶ εἰ λέγειν ἐμοῦ δύναται Κλέων μᾶλλον,
τοῦτο αὐτῷ ἄνευ τοῦ νόμου καὶ τοῦ δικαίου μηδὲν
ἰσχυσάτω, ἀλλ' ὑμᾶς αὐτοὺς βραβευτὰς ἁπάντων
καταστήσατε. διὰ τοῦτο γὰρ συλλέγεσθε, ἵνα τοῖς

---

[1] οὗτοι Dobree: τούτο.
[2] εἰσποιήσητε Sauppe: -σησθε.

ᵃ There is obviously a lacuna in the text at this point,
which must have contained a reference to the devices
whereby Cleon attempted to obtain the recognition of his son by the
members of Astyphilus's ward.

side. There is little likelihood, however, gentlemen, of your paying any attention to his claim of kinship ; for no one, after passing by adoption into another family, has ever inherited from the family out of which he was adopted, unless he re-entered it in the proper legal manner.[a] . . . These men,[b] however, well knowing that Astyphilus never adopted Cleon's son, though he has often presented himself, have never given him any share in the victims. Please take this deposition also.

DEPOSITION

I call upon you, therefore, to decide between us after considering our declarations under oath. Cleon declares that his son was adopted by Astyphilus and that the latter made dispositions to this effect ; this I deny and declare that all Astyphilus's possessions belong to me, because I am his brother, as my opponents are themselves well aware. Do not, therefore, gentlemen, give Astyphilus an adopted son whom he himself never in his life adopted, but confirm in my favour the laws which you yourselves enacted ; for it is in conformity with them that I make my claim, addressing to you a most pious prayer, that you should establish me as heir of my brother's property. I have shown that he never devised his estate to anyone, and I have produced witnesses in support of all my statements. Assist me, therefore, and, if Cleon is a more clever speaker than I am, let not his talent avail him unsupported by law and justice, but constitute yourselves arbitrators on the whole case. You are gathered here that the impudent may gain no

---

[b] *i.e.*, the fellow-wardsmen of Astyphilus.

μὲν ἀναισχυντοῦσι μηδὲν πλέον ᾖ, οἱ δὲ ἀδυνατώ-
τεροι τολμῶσι περὶ τῶν δικαίων ἀμφισβητεῖν, εὖ
εἰδότες ὅτι ὑμεῖς οὐδενὶ ἄλλῳ τὸν νοῦν προσέχετε.
36 ἅπαντες οὖν, ὦ ἄνδρες, μετ᾽ ἐμοῦ γένεσθε· ὡς
ἐάν τι ἄλλο ψηφίσησθε Κλέωνι πειθόμενοι, σκέψασθε ὁπόσων αἴτιοι γενήσεσθε. πρῶτον μὲν τοὺς
ἐχθίστους Ἀστυφίλου ἐπί τε τὰ μνήματα ἰέναι καὶ
ἐπὶ τὰ ἱερὰ <τὰ>[1] ἐκείνου ποιήσετε· ἔπειτα τὰς
Εὐθυκράτους ἐπισκήψεις, τοῦ πατρὸς τοῦ Ἀστυφίλου, ἀκύρους ποιήσετε, ἃς αὐτὸς πρότερον
ἀπέθανεν ἢ[2] παραβῆναι· ἔπειτα τετελευτηκότα
37 Ἀστύφιλον παρανοίας αἱρήσετε· εἰ γὰρ τοῦτον
ἐποιήσατο υἱὸν οὗ[3] τῷ πατρὶ πολεμιώτατος ἦν,
πῶς οὐ δόξει τοῖς ἀκούσασι παρανοεῖν ἢ ὑπὸ
φαρμάκων διεφθάρθαι; ἔτι δ᾽ ἐμέ, ὦ ἄνδρες δικασταί, ἐκτραφέντα ἐν τῷ αὐτῷ καὶ συμπαι-
δευθέντα Ἀστυφίλῳ καὶ ἀδελφὸν ὄντα, περιόψεσθε
ὑπὸ Κλέωνος ἀποστερηθέντα τῶν ἐκείνου. ἀντιβολῶ ὑμᾶς καὶ ἱκετεύω ἐκ παντὸς τρόπου ψηφί-
σασθαί μοι· οὕτω γὰρ ἂν μάλιστα Ἀστυφίλῳ τε
χαρίσαισθε κἀμὲ οὐκ ἂν ἀδικήσαιτε.[4]

---

[1] τὰ add. Sauppe. [2] ἀπέθανεν ἢ Bekker: ἢ ἀπέθανεν.
[3] οὗ Sauppe: ὃς. [4] ἀδικήσαιτε Bekker: -σητε.

advantage and the weaker may venture to assert their righteous claims, knowing full well that you are intent upon justice and upon nothing else. Take, therefore, my part, all of you, gentlemen; for if you allow yourselves, under the persuasion of Cleon, to give any other verdict, consider the responsibility which you will assume. First, you will send the bitterest enemies of Astyphilus to his tomb to celebrate the rites over him; secondly, you will make of none effect the injunctions of Euthycrates, the father of Astyphilus, which he himself never transgressed up to the end of his life; lastly, you will convict Astyphilus after his death of consummate folly. For if he adopted this man as his son with whose father he was on terms of the bitterest enmity, will not those who hear of it imagine that he was mad or that his senses had been impaired by drugs? Further, judges, you will be allowing me, after having been brought up under the same roof and educated with Astyphilus, being also his brother, to be deprived of his estate by Cleon. I beg and beseech you by every means in my power to give your verdict in my favour; for then you would best gratify the wishes of Astyphilus and save me from injustice.

X. AGAINST XENAENETUS
ON THE ESTATE OF ARISTARCHUS

X. AGAINST XENAENETUS
ON THE ESTATE OF ARISTARCHUS

INTRODUCTION

ARISTARCHUS I.[a] had two sons, Cyronides and Demochares, and two daughters. Cyronides, having been adopted by his maternal grandfather Xenaenetus I., passed out of the family, and Demochares became heir to his father's estate.

On the death of Aristarchus I., his brother Aristomenes became guardian of his children. When Demochares died as a minor and one of the sisters also predeceased her father, the succession became vested in the surviving daughter and would pass by law to her son when he came of age. According to Attic law, since the surviving daughter was still unmarried, her hand together with the estate might

[a] STEMMA

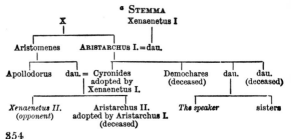

have been claimed by Aristomenes as next-of-kin or his son Apollodorus. Neither of them claimed her, and she married a husband who had no connexion with the family. Aristomenes, however, gave his own daughter in marriage to Cyronides, to whom he handed over the estate of Aristarchus I. in spite of the fact that he had forfeited his position as his father's heir on his adoption by his grandfather. Cyronides had two sons, Xenaenetus II. and Aristarchus II., of whom the latter was (according to the speaker of the present speech, illegally) introduced by posthumous adoption as son of Aristarchus I. and enjoyed the estate for his lifetime. He fell in battle, leaving no issue, and bequeathed the property to his brother Xenaenetus II.

Such is the case presented in the present speech. At first sight it appears simple and the claim a reasonable one ; but a closer examination reveals considerable complications. In the first place, the fact is revealed that the archon had obliged the speaker to declare in his claim to the estate that his mother was the sister of Aristarchus II., that is to say, to recognize the posthumous adoption of Aristarchus II. as the son of Aristarchus I.—the very point which the speaker is seeking to disprove. This ruling of the archon seems to show that the speaker had no standing as grandson of Aristarchus I. and was only allowed to claim at all as nephew of Aristarchus II. Secondly, if his claim was good, why had it not been made earlier ? According to the speaker, his mother had been shamelessly defrauded by her guardian and her brother, who are now dead and cannot defend themselves ; but why had her husband and her son taken no steps

before to recover the estate ? The speaker antici-
pates this objection by stating that his father after
his marriage had, at the suggestion of his wife, put
in such a claim but had been silenced by the threat
that, if he persisted in it, the next-of-kin would
claim his wife and the estate with her, and he preferred
to keep silence rather than lose his wife. Later,
the speaker alleges, both he and his father had been
absent on military service, and on his return he had
been detained from pleading because he was a state-
debtor. These excuses do not appear to possess
much force.

That Cyronides had, by his adoption out of the
family, forfeited his right to the estate seems in-
contestible ; and the posthumous adoption of
Aristarchus II. as son of Aristarchus I. would have
been an audacious proceeding if its object had been
to deprive the rightful heir of a large fortune. But
the adoption had been officially recognized by the
archon, and for a reason which the speaker incident-
ally divulges in an attempted anticipation of an
argument which his opponents are likely to use
(§ 15). He says that Xenaenetus II. will allege
that his father Cyronides had paid a debt on behalf
of the estate and will use this as an argument in
support of his claim. The speaker makes no attempt
to disprove the statement that the property was
encumbered, but contents himself with saying that
no one is such a fool as to discharge debts on someone else's insolvent estate. It may well be, however,
that Cyronides, whose strong family feeling is
indicated by his bestowal of family names on both
his sons, was inspired by a desire to clear the memory
of his father by paying the debts which he left

behind him and to give him, by posthumous adoption, a son who would carry on his family and perform those rites at his tomb on which every Athenian set so much store. If this is so, his act was one of piety and generosity, not of fraud and rapacity.

The speech, which does not rank high among the orations of Isaeus from the point of view either of style or argument, can be dated within a few years. The speaker had fought in the Corinthian war of 394–386 B.C. (§ 20); Aristarchus II. fell in a war which was still in progress (§ 22) and can only have been the Theban war of 378–371 B.C. The speech must, therefore, fall within the latter period.

X. ΠΡΟΣ ΞΕΝΑΙΝΕΤΟΝ
ΠΕΡΙ ΤΟΥ ΑΡΙΣΤΑΡΧΟΥ ΚΛΗΡΟΥ

ΥΠΟΘΕΣΙΣ

Ἀρίσταρχός τις τεσσάρων πατὴρ γενόμενος παίδων, Κυρωνίδου καὶ Δημοχάρους καὶ τῆς μητρὸς τοῦ λέγοντος τὸν λόγον καὶ ἄλλης κόρης, τούτων[1] μὲν τὸν Κυρωνίδην ἔτι περίων εἰσεποίησεν εἰς τὸν Ξεναινέτου τοῦ κατὰ μητέρα πάππου κλῆρον, αὐτὸς δὲ κληρονόμους τοὺς λοιποὺς ἑαυτῷ κατέλειψε παῖδας. μετὰ ταῦτα τελευτᾷ μὲν Δημοχάρης ἄπαις, καὶ ἡ μία θυγάτηρ [αὐτοῦ] καὶ αὐτὴ ἄπαις, ὁ δὲ κλῆρος ὅλος ἔρχεται δικαίως εἰς τὴν μητέρα τοῦ λέγοντος τὸν λόγον. καὶ ταῦτα μὲν οὕτω· μετὰ δὲ τὴν τελευτὴν Ἀριστάρχου Ἀριστομένης ἀδελφὸς ὢν αὐτοῦ καὶ κατὰ νόμον ἐπίτροπος τῶν τοῦ ἀδελφοῦ γινόμενος παίδων, ἐκδέδωκε Κυρωνίδῃ τῷ ἐκποιήτῳ υἱῷ Ἀριστάρχου τὴν θυγατέρα ἑαυτοῦ, ἐπαγγειλάμενος περιποιῆσαι αὐτῷ τὸν Ἀριστάρχου κλῆρον. ὃ δὴ καὶ πεποίηκε· γενομένου γὰρ υἱοῦ τῷ Κυρωνίδῃ πρῶτον μὲν ὄνομα τῷ παιδὶ τὸ τοῦ πάππου δεδώκασιν, Ἀρίσταρχον ὀνομάσαντες, εἶτα εἰσεποίησαν αὐτὸν εἰς τὸν ⟨τοῦ⟩[2] πάππου οἶκον ὡς δὴ τοῦτο ἐκείνου προστάξαντος, καὶ παραδέδωκεν Ἀριστομένης αὐτῷ τὸν ὅλον τοῦ πάππου κλῆρον. ἔτι δὲ ἄπαις[3] ὢν ἐκεῖνος [καὶ] τελευτῶν κληρονόμον κατὰ διαθήκας ἐνεστήσατο τὸν ἴδιον ἀδελφὸν Ξεναίνετον. τούτων οὕτω γενομένων, καὶ κρατοῦντος Ξεναινέτου τὴν Ἀριστάρχου τοῦ παλαιοῦ οὐσίαν, ἀμφι-

358

X. AGAINST XENAENETUS
ON THE ESTATE OF ARISTARCHUS

ARGUMENT

A certain Aristarchus was the father of four children,
Cyronides, Demochares, the mother of the speaker of this
oration, and another daughter. During his lifetime he
gave Cyronides in adoption to be heir of the estate of his
maternal grandfather Xenaenetus, and left his other children
as his own heirs. Subsequently Demochares died without
issue, as also did one of the daughters, and the whole estate
passed by law to the mother of the speaker. Such was the
position of affairs; but, after the death of Aristarchus,
Aristomenes, his brother and now the legal representative
of his brother's children, gave his own daughter in marriage
to Cyronides, the son of Aristarchus, who had been adopted
out of the family, having promised to obtain for him the
estate of Aristarchus. This he succeeded in doing; for,
when a son was born to Cyronides, they first gave him his
grandfather's name, calling him Aristarchus (II.), and then
had him adopted into his grandfather's family, on the ground
that the latter had given instructions to this effect, and
Aristomenes handed over to him all his other grandfather's
estate. Aristarchus (II.), dying without issue, constituted
his own brother Xenaenetus (II.) by will as his heir. This
being so and Xenaenetus being in possession of the property
of Aristarchus the elder, the son of the latter's daughter

---

¹ τούτων Bekker : τοῦτον.
² τοῦ add. Bekker.   ³ ἄπαις Graux : παῖς.

σβητεῖ πρὸς αὐτὸν ὁ υἱὸς τῆς θυγατρὸς Ἀριστάρχου τοῦ παλαιοῦ, λέγων ἑαυτὸν μόνον εἶναι κληρονόμον δικαίως τῶν Ἀριστάρχου τοῦ παλαιοῦ χρημάτων. ὁ μὲν γὰρ Κυρωνίδης (φησίν) ἐκποίητος ἐγένετο· ὁ δὲ πατὴρ υἱὸν ἔχων γνήσιον τὸν Δημοχάρην, οὐκ ἐδύνατο θετὸν ἑαυτῷ ποιῆσαι παῖδα· ὁ δὲ Δημοχάρης ἀτελὴς ὢν οὐδὲ αὐτὸς ἐδύνατο εἰσποιῆσαι τῷ πατρὶ θετὸν υἱόν· ἀλλ' οὐδ' ἡ ἄλλη θυγάτηρ αὐτοῦ ἡ προτελευτήσασα. ὥστε οὐ κατὰ τὸν νόμον (φησί) τῆς εἰσποιήσεως γενομένης τοῦ μικροῦ Ἀριστάρχου, οὐκέτι συνίστατο ἡ διαθήκη αὐτοῦ, τοῦ νέου Ἀριστάρχου· ἃ γὰρ μὴ δικαίως ἐκτήσατο, πῶς ἄλλῳ παραπέμπειν ἐδύνατο; ἀναιρουμένης δὲ τῆς διαθήκης εἰκότως ὁ κλῆρος εἰς τὸν λέγοντα τὸν λόγον ἐφέρετο, υἱὸν ὄντα τῆς γνησίας θυγατρὸς Ἀριστάρχου τοῦ παλαιοῦ. καὶ ἡ μὲν ὑπόθεσις αὕτη, ἡ στάσις δὲ πραγματικὴ ἔγγραφος· ζητεῖ⟨ται⟩[1] γὰρ εἰ δεῖ τὰς τοιαύτας συνεστάναι διαθήκας, καὶ τίς δικαιότερα λέγει.

1 Ἐβουλόμην ⟨μέν⟩,[2] ὦ ἄνδρες, ὥσπερ Ξεναίνετος οὑτοσὶ δύναται ψευδῆ λέγειν θαρραλέως, οὕτω κἀγὼ τἀληθῆ πρὸς ὑμᾶς περὶ ὧν ἀμφισβητοῦμεν εἰπεῖν δυνηθῆναι· οἶμαι γὰρ ἂν ὑμῖν εὐθέως δῆλον γενέσθαι εἴθ' ἡμεῖς ἀδίκως ἐπὶ τὸν κλῆρον ἥκομεν, εἴθ' οὗτοι μὴ προσηκόντως πάλαι τὰ χρήματα ταῦτα εἰλήφασι. νῦν δὲ οὐκ ἐξ ἴσου διακείμεθα, ὦ ἄνδρες. οἱ μὲν γὰρ καὶ λέγειν δεινοὶ καὶ παρασκευάσασθαι ἱκανοί, ὥστε καὶ ὑπὲρ ἑτέρων πολλάκις ἐν ὑμῖν ἠγωνίσθαι· ἐγὼ δὲ μὴ ὅτι ὑπὲρ ἄλλου ἀλλ' οὐδὲ ὑπὲρ ἐμαυτοῦ πώποτε δίκην ἰδίαν εἴρηκα, ὥστε πολλῆς δεῖ με συγγνώμης τυχεῖν παρ' ὑμῶν.

2 Ἠνάγκασμαι μὲν οὖν, ὦ ἄνδρες, διὰ τὸ μὴ δύνασθαι δίκην παρ' αὐτῶν λαβεῖν, τὴν μητέρα τὴν

[1] ζητεῖ⟨ται⟩ Wyse.　　　　[2] μέν add. Bekker.

360

claims the estate from him, asserting that he is himself by law the sole heir to the fortune of Aristarchus the elder. For, he declares, Cyronides passed out of the family by adoption, and his father, having a legitimate son, namely, Demochares, could not adopt a child; nor were Demochares, being under age, and the other sister who predeceased him in a position to adopt a son into their father's family. Therefore, he argues, since the adoption of Aristarchus the younger was not good in law, his will could not stand either; for how could he pass on to another property which he acquired without right? The will being thus annulled, the estate ought naturally to pass to the speaker as son of the legitimate daughter of Aristarchus the elder. Such is the subject; the discussion is concerned with validity, namely, that of a written document; for the questions are whether such a will ought to stand and which party has the better claim.

I could wish, gentlemen, that, as Xenaenetus here finds it easy to lie with boldness, so I with like confidence could speak the truth to you in presenting my claim; for then, I think, it would immediately become clear to you whether we have unjustly come forward to claim the inheritance and whether our opponents have been for a long time in wrongful possession of this fortune. But, as it is, sirs, we are not on equal terms; for they are both able speakers and clever plotters, so that they have often pleaded before you on behalf of others, whereas I, so far from speaking on behalf of another, have never before pleaded on my own behalf in a private suit, and therefore deserve great indulgence at your hands.

I was obliged, it is true, judges, because I could not obtain justice against my opponents, to add

ἐμὴν ἐν[1] τῇ ἀνακρίσει Ἀριστάρχου εἶναι ἀδελφὴν
προσγράψασθαι· οὐ μὴν διὰ τοῦτο ὑμῖν ἡ διάγνωσις[2] ἧττον περὶ αὐτῶν εὐκρινὴς γενήσεται,
[ἀλλ'] ἐκ τῶν νόμων σκοποῦσιν εἰ τὰ ἑαυτοῦ δέδωκε τούτῳ Ἀρίσταρχος ἢ τὰ μηδὲν προσήκοντα.
ἔστι δὲ δίκαιον τοῦτο, ὦ ἄνδρες· ὁ γὰρ νόμος κελεύει τὰ μὲν ἑαυτοῦ διαθέσθαι ὅτῳ ἂν ἐθέλῃ, τῶν
3 δὲ ἀλλοτρίων οὐδένα κύριον πεποίηκε. τοῦτο οὖν
ὑμᾶς πειράσομαι πρῶτον διδάσκειν, ἐάν μου μετ'
εὐνοίας ἀκοῦσαι ἐθέλητε. εἴσεσθε γὰρ ὡς ὁ
κλῆρος οὗτος οὐ τούτων ἦν ἐξ ἀρχῆς, ἀλλὰ τῆς
ἐμῆς μητρὸς πατρῷος, ἔπειτα καὶ ὡς Ἀρίσταρχος
οὐδὲ καθ' ἕνα νόμον αὐτὸν εἴληφεν, ἀλλὰ παρὰ
πάντας τοὺς νόμους ἀδικεῖ μετὰ τῶν οἰκείων τὴν
ἐμὴν μητέρα. ὅθεν οὖν σαφέστατα μαθήσεσθε ὡς
ἔχει ταῦτα, ἐντεῦθεν ὑμᾶς πρῶτον πειράσομαι
διδάσκειν.

4 Ἀρίσταρχος γὰρ ἦν, ὦ ἄνδρες, Συπαλήττιος.[3]
οὗτος ἔλαβε Ξεναινέτου Ἀχαρνέως θυγατέρα, ἐξ
ἧς γίγνεται Κυρωνίδης καὶ Δημοχάρης καὶ ἡ
μήτηρ ἡ ἐμὴ καὶ ἄλλη τούτων ἀδελφή. Κυρωνίδης μὲν οὖν ὁ τοῦδε πατὴρ καὶ θατέρου τοῦ
τόνδε τὸν κλῆρον ἀδίκως ἔχοντος ἐξεποιήθη εἰς
ἕτερον οἶκον, ὥστε αὐτῷ τῶν χρημάτων οὐδὲν ἔτι
προσῆκεν· Ἀριστάρχου δὲ τοῦ πατρὸς ⟨τοῦ⟩[4]
[80] τούτων | τελευτήσαντος Δημοχάρης ⟨ὁ⟩[5] υἱὸς κληρο-
νόμος τῶν ἐκείνου κατέστη. τούτου δὲ παιδὸς
ἀποθανόντος καὶ τῆς ἑτέρας ἀδελφῆς, ἡ μήτηρ ἡ

[1] ἐν Dobree: πρὸς.   [2] ἡ διάγνωσις Scheibe: ἥδε ἡ γνῶσις.
[3] Συπαλήττιος Baiter-Sauppe: συπαλλήτιος.
[4] τοῦ add. Dobree.   [5] ὁ add. Sauppe.

[a] See Introduction, p. 355.   [b] i.e., Aristarchus II.

to my petition at the preliminary inquiry that my
mother was sister of Aristarchus (II.).[a] This will
not, however, make your decision any the less easy, if
you ask yourselves the question in the light of the
laws whether the estate which Aristarchus (II.) has
bequeathed to my opponent was his own or whether
it was property to which he had no right. This
question, judges, is legal ; for the law ordains
that a man can dispose of what is his own to anyone
he likes, but it has never given anyone power over
the possessions of another. This, then, is the first
point which I shall try to make clear to you, if
you will give me your kind attention ; for you will
recognize that this estate belonged from the first,
not to my opponents but to my mother, who inherited it from her father, and, secondly, that
Aristarchus (II.) seized it without the sanction of any
law, and that he and the members of his family
are wronging my mother in violation of every law.
I will try to put the matter before you, going back
to a point which will enable you to form the clearest
conception of the facts.

Aristarchus (I.), gentlemen, belonged to the
deme of Sypalettus. He married the daughter of
Xenaenetus (I.) of Acharnae, by whom he had two
sons, Cyronides and Demochares, and two daughters,
one of whom was my mother. Cyronides, the father
of my opponent and of the other party [b] who illegally
kept possession of this estate, was adopted into
another family, so that he had no further claim to
the property. On the death of Aristarchus (I.),
the father of these two sons, Demochares his son
became his heir ; but, when he died in his minority
and the other sister also died, my mother became

ISAEUS

5 ἐμὴ ἐπὶ[1] παντὶ τῷ οἴκῳ ἐπίκληρος ἐγένετο. καὶ
οὕτω μὲν ἐξ ἀρχῆς ἅπαντα ταυτὶ τῆς ἐμῆς μητρὸς
ἐγένετο· προσῆκον δ' αὐτῇ μετὰ τῶν χρημάτων τῷ
ἐγγύτατα γένους συνοικεῖν, πάσχει δεινότατα, ὦ
ἄνδρες. Ἀριστομένης γὰρ ἀδελφὸς ὢν ἐκείνου
τοῦ Ἀριστάρχου, ὄντος αὐτῷ ὑέος καὶ θυγατρός,
ἀμελήσας ἢ αὐτὸς αὐτὴν ἔχειν ἢ τῷ ὑεῖ μετὰ τοῦ
κλήρου ἐπιδικάσασθαι, τούτων μὲν οὐδὲν ἐποίησε,
τὴν δὲ ἑαυτοῦ θυγατέρα ἐπὶ τοῖς τῆς ἐμῆς μητρὸς
χρήμασι Κυρωνίδῃ ἐξέδωκεν, ἐξ ἧς ὁ Ξεναίνετος
6 οὗτος καὶ Ἀρίσταρχος ὁ τελευτήσας ἐγένετο. τὸ
μὲν οὖν ἀδίκημα, καὶ ὃν τρόπον τῶν χρημάτων
ἀπεστερήθη,[2] τοῦτ' ἐστίν, ὦ ἄνδρες· μετὰ δὲ
ταῦτα τὴν ἐμὴν μητέρα ἐκδίδωσι τῷ ἐμῷ πατρί.
Κυρωνίδου δὲ τελευτήσαντος τὸν τοῦ Ξεναινέτου
ἀδελφὸν εἰσάγουσιν Ἀριστάρχῳ ὑόν, οὐδὲ καθ'
ἕνα νόμον, ὦ ἄνδρες, ὡς ἐγὼ ἐκ πολλῶν τεκ-
μηρίων ὑμῖν ἐπιδείξω.

7 Πρῶτον μὲν οὖν μάρτυρας ὑμῖν παρέξομαι ὡς
Κυρωνίδης ἐκποίητος εἰς τὸν Ξεναινέτου οἶκον ἐγένετο καὶ ἐν ἐκείνῳ ἐτελεύτησεν, ἔπειθ' ὡς Ἀρίσταρχος, οὗ ἦν οὗτος ὁ κλῆρος, πρότερος τοῦ ὑέος
Δημοχάρους ἐτελεύτησε, Δημοχάρης δὲ παῖς ὢν
ἀπέθανε καὶ ἡ ἑτέρα ἀδελφή, ὥστε τὸν κλῆρον ἐπὶ
τῇ ἐμῇ μητρὶ γενέσθαι. καί μοι κάλει τούτων
τοὺς μάρτυρας.

<ΜΑΡΤΥΡΕΣ>

8 Οὕτω μὲν ἐξ ἀρχῆς <τῆς μητρὸς τῆς ἐμῆς>[3] ἦν,

---

[1] ἐπὶ Valckenaer: ἐν.
[2] ἀπεστερήθη Schoemann: -θην.
[3] τῆς μητρὸς τῆς ἐμῆς add. Buermann.

---

[a] i.e., Aristarchus II.

heiress to the whole of the family estate. Thus from the beginning all this fortune really belonged to my mother; but, although she ought to have passed by marriage, together with her fortune, into the hands of her nearest relative, she is being abominably treated. For Aristomenes, the brother of Aristarchus the elder, having a son and a daughter of his own, neglected to make her his own wife or to have her married to his own son by an adjudication of the court; refusing both these alternatives, he gave his own daughter in marriage to Cyronides, endowing her with the fortune which belonged to my mother. Xenaenetus here and Aristarchus (II.), now deceased, were the issue of this marriage. This is the injury, this the manner, gentlemen, in which my mother was deprived of her fortune. Subsequently Aristomenes gave my mother in marriage to my father. On the death of Cyronides, they introduced Xenaenetus's brother [a] as the adopted son of Aristarchus (I.), a proceeding which cannot be justified by any law, as I will demonstrate to you by many proofs.

I will produce witnesses to testify, in the first place, that Cyronides entered by adoption into the family of Xenaenetus (I.) and belonged to that family at the time of his death; secondly, that Aristarchus (I.), to whom this estate belonged, predeceased his son Demochares, and that Demochares died while yet a minor, as did also the other sister, with the result that the estate devolved on to my mother. Please summon the witnesses to these facts.

WITNESSES

Thus, gentlemen, the estate now in question

ὦ ἄνδρες, ὁ κλῆρος, περὶ οὗ νῦν ὁ λόγος ἐστί,
Κυρωνίδου μὲν ἐκποιήτου γενομένου εἰς τὸν
Ξεναινέτου οἶκον, τοῦ δὲ πατρὸς Ἀριστάρχου τῷ
ὑεῖ Δημοχάρει καταλιπόντος, ἐκείνου δὲ τῇ ἀδελφῇ
τῇ ἑαυτοῦ ταύτῃ, μητρὶ δὲ ἐμῇ.[1] δεῖ δέ, ἐπειδὴ
λίαν ἀναισχυντοῦσιν, ὦ ἄνδρες, καὶ τὰ χρήματα
παρὰ τὸ δίκαιον ἔχειν ἀξιοῦσι, μαθεῖν ὑμᾶς ὡς
οὐδὲ καθ᾿ ἕνα νόμον Ἀρίσταρχος εἰς τοὺς φράτορας
τοὺς ἐκείνου εἰσῆκται· ἐὰν γὰρ τοῦτο μάθητε,
σαφῶς εἴσεσθε ὅτι τῷ μὴ δικαίως ἔχοντι οὐδὲ
9 διατίθεσθαι περὶ αὐτῶν προσῆκεν. οἶμαι τοίνυν
πάντας ὑμᾶς εἰδέναι, ὦ ἄνδρες, ὅτι κατὰ διαθήκας
αἱ εἰσαγωγαὶ τῶν εἰσποιήτων γίγνονται, διδόντων
τὰ ἑαυτῶν[2] καὶ ὑεῖς ποιουμένων, ἄλλως δὲ οὐκ ἔξεστιν. εἴτε οὖν Ἀρίσταρχον φήσει τις αὐτὸν διαθέσθαι, οὐκ ἀληθῆ λέξει· γνησίου γὰρ ὄντος αὐτῷ
Δημοχάρους ὑέος οὔτ᾿ ἂν ἐβούλετο ταῦτα [δια-]
πρᾶξαι, οὔτε ἐξῆν δοῦναι τὰ ἑαυτοῦ ἑτέρῳ· εἴτε
Ἀριστάρχου τελευτήσαντος Δημοχάρην αὐτὸν ποιή-
10 σασθαι, καὶ ταῦτα ψεύσονται. παιδὸς γὰρ οὐκ ἔξεστι διαθήκην γενέσθαι· ὁ γὰρ νόμος διαρρήδην
κωλύει παιδὶ μὴ ἐξεῖναι συμβάλλειν μηδὲ γυναικὶ
πέρα μεδίμνου κριθῶν. μεμαρτύρηται δὲ Ἀρίσταρχον μὲν πρότερον Δημοχάρους τοῦ ὑέος τελευτῆσαι, ἐκεῖνον δὲ ὕστερον τοῦ πατρός· ὥστε κατά
γε διαθήκην ἐκείνων, οὐδ᾿ εἰ διέθεντο προσῆκεν
αὐτῷ τούτων τῶν χρημάτων κληρονομῆσαι. ἀνά-

---

[1] ἐμῇ Aldus: ἐμοί.   [2] τὰ ἑαυτῶν Sauppe: τε αὐτῶν.

[a] Which would be invalid because Aristarchus (I.) could
not make a will in favour of anyone except Demochares,
and predeceased Demochares, who, having died under age,
was incapable of making a will.

belonged to my mother from the beginning, since Cyronides was adopted out of the family into that of Xenaenetus (I.), and his father, Aristarchus (I.), left his property to his son Demochares, who left it to his own sister, my mother. But since they are so exceedingly impudent and claim this fortune against all right, you must see, gentlemen, that no law whatever authorized the introduction of Aristarchus (the younger) into the ward of Aristarchus (the elder); if you see this, you will clearly apprehend that the illegal detainer of the property had no right to dispose of it either. I think that you are all aware, gentlemen, that the introduction of adopted children is always carried out by a will, the testator simultaneously devising his estate and adopting the son, and that this is the only legal method. If, therefore, anyone shall assert that Aristarchus (I.) himself made a will, he will be saying what is not true; for, while he possessed a legitimate son, Demochares, he could not have wished to do so and he was not permitted to devise his property to anyone else. Again, if they declare that Demochares adopted Aristarchus (II.) after the death of Aristarchus (I.), they will likewise be lying. For a minor is not allowed to make a will; for the law expressly forbids any child—or woman—to contract for the disposal of more than a bushel of barley. Now evidence has been given you that Aristarchus (I.) predeceased his son Demochares and that the latter died after his father; and so, even supposing they had made wills, Aristarchus (II.) could never have inherited this property under their wills.[a] Now read the laws

γνῶθι δὴ καὶ τοὺς νόμους, καθ᾽ οὓς οὐδετέρῳ
αὐτῶν ἐξῆν διαθήκας ποιήσασθαι.

ΝΟΜΟΙ

11 Οὐ τοίνυν, ὦ ἄνδρες, οὐδὲ Κυρωνίδην οἷόν τε
ἦν ὑὸν Ἀριστάρχῳ εἰσποιῆσαι, ἀλλ᾽ αὐτῷ μὲν
ἐπανελθεῖν εἰς τὸν πατρῷον οἶκον ἐξῆν, ὑὸν ἐγ-
καταλιπόντα ἐν τῷ Ξεναινέτου οἴκῳ, ἐξ αὐτοῦ
δὲ ἀντεισαγαγεῖν[1] οὐκ ἔστι νόμος· ἢ ἐὰν φῶσι,
ψεύσονται. ὥστε οὐδ᾽ ἂν φάσκωσιν ὑπ᾽ ἐκείνου
⟨εἰσ⟩ποιηθῆναι,[2] νόμον ἔξουσι δεῖξαι καθ᾽ ὃν ἐξῆν
αὐτῷ ταῦτα πρᾶξαι, ἀλλ᾽ ἐξ ὧν αὐτοὶ λέγουσιν ἔτι
φανερώτερον ὑμῖν γενήσεται τοῦτο, ὅτι παρανόμως
12 καὶ ἀσελγῶς ἔχουσι τὰ τῆς μητρὸς χρήματα. καὶ
μὲν δή, ὦ ἄνδρες, οὐδὲ Ἀριστομένει γε οὐδὲ
Ἀπολλοδώρῳ, οἷς προσῆκε[3] τῆς ἐμῆς μητρὸς ἐπιδικάσασθαι, οὐδὲ τούτοις ἐξῆν. θαυμαστὸν γὰρ
ἂν ἦν, εἰ τὴν ἐμὴν μητέρα ἔχοντι Ἀπολλοδώρῳ ἢ
Ἀριστομένει οὐκ ἂν οἷόν τε ἦν τῶν ἐκείνης κυρίῳ
γενέσθαι, κατὰ τὸν νόμον ὃς οὐκ ἐᾷ τῶν τῆς ἐπικλήρου κύριον εἶναι, ἀλλ᾽ ἢ τοὺς παῖδας ἐπὶ δίετες
[81] ἡβήσαντας | κρατεῖν τῶν χρημάτων, ἀλλ᾽ ἑτέρῳ
αὐτὴν ἐκδόντι ἐξέσται εἰς τὰ ταύτης χρήματα ὑὸν
13 εἰσποιῆσαι. δεινὰ μέντ᾽ ἂν γίγνοιτο. καὶ τῷ μὲν
πατρὶ αὐτῆς, εἰ παῖδες ἄρρενες μὴ ἐγένοντο, οὐκ
ἂν ἐξῆν ἄνευ ταύτης διαθέσθαι· κελεύει γὰρ ὁ
νόμος σὺν ταύταις κύριον εἶναι δοῦναι, ἐάν τῳ
βούληται,[4] τὰ ἑαυτοῦ· τῷ δὲ μήτε λαβεῖν αὐτὴν

---

[1] ἀντεισαγαγεῖν Dobree: ἄν τις ἀναγαγεῖν.
[2] ⟨εἰσ⟩ποιηθῆναι Aldbrecht.
[3] προσῆκε Reiske: -ήκει. [4] βούληται Dobree: -οιτο.

which show that neither of them had the right to make a will.

LAWS

Nor again, gentlemen, could Cyronides give Aristarchus (I.) a son by adoption ; he could, it is true, have returned to his father's family, if he had left a son in the family of Xenaenetus (I.), but there is no law which permits him to introduce a son of his own to take his place. If they assert the existence of such a law they will be lying. So, not even if they assert that the adoption was carried out by Cyronides, will they be able to point to any law which authorized him to do so ; but from their own assertions it will become still more evident to you that they are illegally and impudently detaining my mother's property. Furthermore, gentlemen, though Aristomenes or Apollodorus might have had my mother adjudicated to them in marriage, yet they had no right to her estate. Seeing that neither Apollodorus nor Aristomenes, if either of them had married my mother, could possibly have had the disposal of her property—in accordance with the law which does not allow anyone to have the disposal of the property of an heiress except her sons, who obtain possession of it on reaching the second year after puberty—it would be strange if Aristarchus is going to be allowed, after giving her in marriage to another, to introduce a son to inherit her fortune. It would indeed be an extraordinary state of affairs. Again, her own father, in default of male heirs, could not have disposed of his estate without disposing of her with it ; for the law ordains that he may dispose of his property to whomsoever he wishes, if he disposes of his daughters with it. But

ἀξιώσαντι μήτε πατρὶ ὄντι, ἀλλ' ἀνεψιῷ, παρὰ
πάντας τοὺς νόμους εἰσαγαγόντι ἔσται κυρίως
ταῦτα πεπραγμένα; καὶ τίς ὑμῶν ταῦτα πεισθή-
14 σεται; ἐγὼ μέν, ὦ ἄνδρες, σαφῶς ἐπίσταμαι ὅτι
οὔτε Ξεναίνετος οὔτε ἄλλος οὐδεὶς ἀνθρώπων ἕξει
ἀποδεῖξαι ὡς οὐ τῆς ἐμῆς μητρὸς οὗτος <ὁ>[1]
κλῆρός ἐστι, τοῦ ἀδελφοῦ αὐτῇ τοῦ Δημοχάρους
καταλιπόντος· ἐὰν δ' ἄρα τολμῶσι περὶ αὐτῶν
λέγειν, νόμον κελεύετε δεῖξαι καθ' ὃν γεγένηται ἡ
εἰσποίησις Ἀριστάρχῳ, καὶ τίς ὁ εἰσποιήσας·
τοῦτο γὰρ δίκαιόν ἐστιν. ἀλλ' οἶδ' ὅτι οὐχ ἕξουσιν
ἐπιδεῖξαι.

15 Περὶ μὲν οὖν τοῦ τὸν κλῆρον εἶναι τῆς μητρὸς
ἐξ ἀρχῆς καὶ ἀδίκως αὐτὴν ὑπὸ τούτων ἀπεστερῆ-
σθαι, ἔκ τε τῶν εἰρημένων καὶ μεμαρτυρημένων
καὶ ἐξ αὐτῶν τῶν νόμων ἱκανῶς ἡγοῦμαι ἀπο-
δεδεῖχθαι. οὕτω δὲ καὶ τούτοις φανερόν ἐστιν ὅτι
οὐ προσηκόντως ἔχουσι ταῦτα τὰ χρήματα, ὥστε
οὐκ ἐπὶ τῷ δικαίως Ἀρίσταρχον εἰσαχθῆναι εἰς
τοὺς φράτορας τὸν λόγον ποιοῦνται μόνον ἀλλὰ
καὶ δίκην φασὶν ὑπὲρ τούτων τῶν χρημάτων τὸν
πατέρα τὸν ἑαυτῶν ἐκτετικέναι, ἵνα, ἂν μὴ κατ'
ἐκεῖνον δικαίως δοκῶσιν ἔχειν, κατά γε ταῦτα
16 εἰκότως προσῆκον αὐτοῖς φαίνηται. ἐγὼ δ', ὦ
ἄνδρες, ὅτι οὐκ ἀληθῆ λέγουσι, μεγάλοις ὑμᾶς
τεκμηρίοις διδάξω. εἰ γὰρ ἦν, ὡς οὗτοι λέγουσιν,
ὑπόχρεως οὗτος ὁ κλῆρος, οὔτ' ἂν χρήματα οὗτοι

---

[1] ὁ add. Sauppe.

[a] Wyse suggests that Aristarchus I. died in debt to the
state and therefore without civic rights, and that Cyronides
settled his liabilities to save the estate from confiscation and
the heir from the disabilities which he would inherit.

when one who has refused to take the heiress in marriage and is not her father but her cousin, introduces an heir to her fortune in violation of every law, is this to be recognized as a valid act? Who of you can possibly believe it to be so? For myself, gentlemen, I am perfectly certain that neither Xenaenetus nor anyone else can prove that this estate does not belong to my mother, having come to her through her brother Demochares. But, if, after all, they venture to deal with the question, order them to indicate the law under which the adoption has been carried out in favour of Aristarchus (II.) and to declare who carried it out. This is a perfectly just demand. But I know that they will not be able to indicate any such law.

That the estate, then, belonged to my mother from the beginning and that she has been unjustly deprived of it by my opponents, has, I think, been sufficiently demonstrated by my arguments, by the evidence which has been produced, and by the citation of the actual laws. Indeed, these men are so perfectly well aware that they are wrongfully in possession of this fortune that they do not rest their argument solely upon the legality of the introduction of Aristarchus (II.) to the members of the ward, but also allege that Xenaenetus's father has paid a judgement-debt on behalf of the estate,[a] in order that, if their claim on the former ground should not seem just, it may appear that they have a good claim to the estate on the second ground. I shall show you, gentlemen, by convincing proofs that there is no truth in what they say. For if, as they allege, this estate had been insolvent, they would never have expended any money upon it—

ὑπὲρ αὐτῶν ἐξέτινον (οὐ γὰρ προσῆκεν[1] αὐτοῖς,
ἀλλ' οἷς ἐγένετο ἡ ἐμὴ μήτηρ ἐπίδικος, τούτοις
ἀναγκαῖον ἦν ὑπὲρ αὐτῶν βουλεύσασθαι), οὔτε ἂν
εἰσεποίουν[2] εἰς τοῦτον τὸν κλῆρον υἱὸν Ἀριστάρχῳ,
μέλλοντες ὠφεληθήσεσθαι μὲν μηδέν, ζημιωθήσε-
17 σθαι δὲ μεγάλα. ἢ ἕτεροι μέν, ὅταν περὶ χρημάτων δυστυχῶσι, τοὺς σφετέρους αὐτῶν παῖδας
εἰς ἑτέρους οἴκους εἰσποιοῦσιν, ἵνα μὴ μετάσχωσι
τῆς τοῦ πατρὸς ἀτιμίας· οὗτοι δὲ ἄρα εἰς ὑπόχρεων
οὐσίαν καὶ οἶκον[3] εἰσεποίουν σφᾶς αὐτούς, ἵνα καὶ
τὰ ὑπάρχοντα προσαπολέσειαν; οὐκ ἔστι ταῦτα,
ἀλλ' ὁ μὲν κλῆρος ἐλεύθερος ἦν καὶ τῆς ἐμῆς
μητρὸς ἐγένετο, οὗτοι δὲ φιλοχρηματοῦντες καὶ
ἐκείνην ἀποστεροῦντες ταῦτα πάντα ἐμηχανήσαντο.
18 Ἴσως οὖν ⟨ἄν⟩[4] τις, ὦ ἄνδρες, τὸν χρόνον ὑμῶν
θαυμάσειε, πῶς ποτε πολὺν οὕτως εἰάσαμεν καὶ
ἀποστερούμενοι οὐκ ἦμεν ἐπ' αὐτά, ἀλλὰ νυνὶ περὶ
αὐτῶν τοὺς λόγους ποιούμεθα. ἐγὼ δὲ οἶμαι μὲν
οὐ δίκαιον εἶναι διὰ τοῦτο ἔλαττον ἔχειν, εἴ τις
μὴ ἐδυνήθη ἢ κατημέλησεν (οὐ γὰρ τοῦτό ἐστι
σκεπτέον, ἀλλὰ τὸ πρᾶγμα εἰ δίκαιον ἢ μή)· ὅμως
μέντοι καὶ περὶ τούτων αἴτιον εἰπεῖν ἔχομεν, ὦ
19 ἄνδρες. ὁ γὰρ πατὴρ οὑμὸς ἐπὶ προικὶ ἐγγυησάμενος τὴν ἐμὴν μητέρα συνῴκει, τὸν δὲ κλῆρον
τούτων καρπουμένων οὐκ εἶχεν ὅπως εἰσπράξαιτο·
ὅτε γὰρ περὶ αὐτοῦ λόγους ἐποιήσατο τῆς μητρὸς
κελευούσης, οὗτοι ταῦτα αὐτῷ ἠπείλησαν, αὐτοὶ
ἐπιδικασάμενοι αὐτὴν ἕξειν, εἰ μὴ βούλοιτο αὐτὸς

---

[1] προσῆκεν Reiske: -ον. [2] εἰσεποίουν Aldus: εἰσποιεῖν.
[3] οἶκον Scheibe: οἴκοθεν. [4] ἄν add. Baiter-Sauppe.

for it was not their business to do so, but those who had the right to claim my mother's hand ought to have concerned themselves with the matter—nor would they have introduced a son as the adopted child of Aristarchus (I.) to inherit his estate, if they were not going to get any advantage but only suffer considerable loss. Other people indeed, when they have had monetary losses, introduce their children into other families in order that they may not share in their parents' loss of civic rights ; and did my opponents adopt themselves into a succession and family which was insolvent, in order that they might lose in addition what they already possessed ? Nay, it is impossible ; the estate was unencumbered and descended to my mother, and these men, in their greed for money and their anxiety to rob her, devised all this story.

Some among you, gentlemen, may be surprised at the delay, and ask how it is that we allowed so long an interval to elapse, and, being defrauded, took no steps in the matter, and are only now putting in our claim. Now, although I think it unjust that anyone should have less than his due rights through inability or neglect to assert them— for such a consideration should not be taken into account, but only the justice or injustice of his plea— yet even for this delay, gentlemen, we can furnish an explanation. My father received a dowry when he engaged himself to my mother and married her, but, while these men were enjoying the estate, he had no means of obtaining its restitution ; for when, at my mother's instance, he raised the question, they threatened that they themselves would obtain the adjudication of her hand and marry her, if he were

ἐπὶ προικὶ ἔχειν. ὁ δὲ πατήρ, ὥστε τῆς μητρὸς
μὴ στερηθῆναι, καὶ δὶς τοσαῦτα χρήματα εἴασεν
20 ἂν αὐτοὺς καρποῦσθαι. καὶ τοῦ μὲν τὸν πατέρα
μὴ ἐπεξελθεῖν ὑπὲρ τούτων τοῦτό ἐστι τὸ αἴτιον·
μετὰ δὲ ταῦτα ὁ Κορινθιακὸς πόλεμος ἐγένετο,
ἐν ᾧ ἐγὼ κἀκεῖνος στρατεύεσθαι ἠναγκαζόμεθα,
ὥστε οὐδετέρῳ ἂν ἡμῶν δίκην ἐξεγένετο λαβεῖν.
εἰρήνης τ᾽ αὖ γενομένης ἐμοί τι ἀτύχημα πρὸς τὸ
δημόσιον συνέβη, ὥστε μὴ ῥᾴδιον εἶναι πρὸς τούτους διαφέρεσθαι. ὥστε οὐ μικρὰς ἔχομεν αἰτίας
21 περὶ τοῦ πράγματος. ἀλλὰ νυνὶ δίκαιον εἰπεῖν ἐστιν,
ὦ ἄνδρες, τίνος δόντος [ἔχει] τὸν κλῆρον, κατὰ
ποίους νόμους εἰς τοὺς φράτορας εἰσῆκται, καὶ
[82] πῶς | οὐκ ἐπίκληρος ἦν ἐπὶ τούτοις τοῖς χρήμασιν
ἡ ἐμὴ μήτηρ. ταῦτα γάρ ἐστι περὶ ὧν ὑμᾶς δεῖ
τὴν ψῆφον ἐνεγκεῖν, οὐκ εἰ χρόνῳ τι ὕστερον
ἡμεῖς τῶν ἡμετέρων εἰσπραττόμεθα. μὴ δυνη-
θέντων δὲ ἐπιδεῖξαι, δικαίως ἂν ἐμὸν αὐτὸν
εἶναι ψηφίσαισθε.

22 Τοῦτο μὲν οἶδ᾽ ὅτι ποιεῖν οὐχ οἷοί τ᾽ ἔσονται·
χαλεπὸν γὰρ πρὸς νόμους καὶ δίκαιον πρᾶγμα ἀντι-
λέγειν ἐστί· περὶ δὲ τοῦ τεθνεῶτος λέξουσιν,
ἐλεοῦντες ὡς ἀνὴρ ὢν ἀγαθὸς ἐν τῷ πολέμῳ
τέθνηκε, καὶ ὅτι οὐ δίκαιόν ἐστι τὰς ἐκείνου διαθήκας ἀκύρους καθιστάναι. ἐγὼ δὲ καὶ αὐτός, ὦ
ἄνδρες, οἶμαι δεῖν κυρίας εἶναι τὰς διαθήκας, ἃς
⟨ἂν⟩¹ ἕκαστος διαθῆται περὶ τῶν ἑαυτοῦ, περὶ
μέντοι τῶν ἀλλοτρίων οὐ κυρίας εἶναι τὰς διαθήκας,
ὥσπερ ἃς ἂν ἕκαστος περὶ τῶν αὑτῶν διαθῆται.

¹ ἂν add. Baiter-Sauppe.

not satisfied to keep her with only a dowry. Now my father would have allowed them to enjoy an estate of even double the value so as not to be deprived of her. That is why my father never brought a suit for the estate. Then came the Corinthian war,[a] in which my father and I were obliged to serve, so that neither of us could have obtained justice. When peace was restored, I had unfortunate difficulties with the public treasury,[b] so that it was not easy for me to contend with my opponents. Thus we have good reasons for our conduct in the matter. But the time has come, sirs, when it is only right that my opponent should declare who it was that gave him the estate, and what laws justify his introduction in the ward, and why it is that my mother was not heiress to this fortune. These are the points on which you must give your verdict, not as to whether we are late in demanding what is our own. If they cannot explain these points, you would be justified in deciding that the estate is mine.

I am sure they will not be able to do so; for it is difficult to argue against law and justice. But they will talk about the deceased, saying how sad it is that so brave a man has fallen in battle and declaring that it is unjust to set aside his will. I myself, gentlemen, am of opinion that any will which a man may make about his own property ought to be valid, but that wills which concern other people's property ought not to have the same validity as those in which a man disposes of what is his own.

---

[a] 394–386 B.C.
[b] Debtors to the public treasury were temporarily deprived of their rights as citizens and therefore could not engage in litigation.

23 ταῦτα δὲ οὐ τούτων ὄντα ἀλλ᾽ ἡμέτερα φαίνεται. ὥστε ἂν ἐπὶ τοῦτον τὸν λόγον καταφεύγῃ καὶ μάρτυρας παρέχηται ὡς διέθετο ἐκεῖνος, ἐπιδεικνύναι κελεύετε καὶ ὡς[1] τὰ ἑαυτοῦ. τοῦτο γὰρ δίκαιόν ἐστι. δεινότατα γὰρ ⟨ἂν⟩[2] πάντων γένοιτο, εἰ Κυρωνίδης μὲν καὶ οὗτοι, ὄντες ἐξ ἐκείνου, μὴ μόνον τὸν Ξεναινέτου οἶκον πλέον ἢ τεττάρων ταλάντων ἕξουσιν, ἀλλὰ καὶ τόνδε προσλήψονται, ἐγὼ δὲ τῆς μητρὸς οὔσης κυρίας καὶ ἐκ τῶν αὐτῶν Κυρωνίδῃ γεγενημένος εἰ μηδὲ τὸν τῆς μητρὸς κλῆρον λήψομαι, καὶ ταῦτα μηδὲ ἐχόντων τού-
24 των ἐπενεγκεῖν παρ᾽ ὅτου ποτ᾽ εἰλήφασι. καίτοι δίκαιον, ὦ ἄνδρες, ὥσπερ τῶν ἀμφισβητησίμων[3] χωρίων δεῖ τὸν ἔχοντα ἢ θέτην ἢ πρατῆρα[4] παρέχεσθαι ἢ καταδεδικασμένον φαίνεσθαι, οὕτω καὶ τούτους καθ᾽ ἕν τι τούτων ἀποφήναντας αὐτοῦ[5] ἀξιοῦν ἐπιδικάζεσθαι, μὴ πρὸ δίκης τὴν Ἀριστάρχου θυγατέρα, ἐμὴν δὲ μητέρα, ἐκ τῶν πατρῴων
25 ἐκβάλλειν. ἀλλὰ γάρ, ὦ ἄνδρες, οὐχ ἱκανόν ἐστι Ξεναινέτῳ τὸν Ἀριστομένους οἶκον καταπεπαιδεραστηκέναι, ἀλλὰ καὶ τοῦτον οἴεται δεῖν τὸν αὐτὸν τρόπον διαθεῖναι. ἐγὼ δ᾽, ὦ ἄνδρες δικασταί, βραχείας οὐσίας ὑπαρξάσης ἀδελφὰς μὲν ἐξέδωκα, ὅσα ἐδυνάμην ἐπιδούς, κόσμιον δ᾽[6] ἐμαυτὸν παρέχων καὶ ποιῶν τὰ προσταττόμενα καὶ τὰς στρατείας στρατευόμενος ἀξιῶ τῶν τῆς
26 μητρὸς πατρῴων μὴ ἀποστερηθῆναι. ἀπέδειξα δ᾽ ὑμῖν Κυρωνίδην μὲν τὸν τούτων πατέρα ἐκποίητον

---

[1] καὶ ὡς Sauppe: δικαίως. [2] ἂν add. Bekker.
[3] ἀμφισβητησίμων Aldus: -τήσεων.
[4] πρατῆρα Stephanus: πρακτῆρα.
[5] αὐτοῦ Schoemann: αὐτὸν.
[6] κόσμιον δ᾽ Reiske: κόσμιόν τ᾽.

Now this property is clearly not theirs but ours; and so, if he takes refuge in this argument and produces witnesses to testify that Aristarchus (I.) made a will, you must order him to prove also that what he devised was his own. This is only just, for it would be a most terrible state of affairs if Cyronides and my opponents, his children, are not only to possess the fortune of Xenaenetus (I.) of the value of more than four talents, but are also to receive this estate, while I, though my mother was the rightful owner and I am descended from the same ancestors as Cyronides, am not to receive even my mother's estate, especially as these men cannot indicate the person through whom it has been transmitted to them. Yet in all justice, just as the holder of a disputed piece of land must produce the mortgagee or vendor, or else prove that he has had it adjudicated to him by the court, so ought these men to set forth their titles in detail and claim to have the estate adjudicated to them, instead of ejecting my mother, the daughter of Aristarchus (I.), from her paternal inheritance before any suit has been heard. But no doubt, gentlemen, it is not enough for Xenaenetus (II.) to have dissipated the fortune of Aristomenes in unnatural debauchery; he thinks that he ought to dispose of this estate also in like manner. I, on the other hand, jurymen, though my means are slender, bestowed my sisters in marriage, giving them what dowry I could; and as one who leads an orderly life and performs the duties assigned to him and serves in the army, I demand not to be deprived of my mother's paternal estate. I have proved to you that Cyronides, the father of my opponents,

γενόμενον καὶ οὐκ ἐπανελθόντα εἰς τὸν πατρῷον
οἶκον, τὸν δὲ πατέρα τὸν Κυρωνίδου καὶ τῆς ἐμῆς
μητρὸς Δημοχάρει τῷ ὑῷ τοῦτον τὸν κλῆρον
καταλιπόντα, ἐκεῖνον δὲ παῖδα[1] ὄντα τελευτήσαντα
καὶ εἰς τὴν ἐμὴν μητέρα τοῦτον τὸν κλῆρον ἐπι-
γιγνόμενον.

[1] παῖδα Meutzner: ἄπαιδα.

was adopted into another family and did not return to his father's house ; that the father of Cyronides and of my mother left this estate to Demochares ; that Demochares died in his minority, and that it was upon my mother that this estate then devolved.

XI. ON THE ESTATE OF HAGNIAS

XI. ON THE ESTATE OF HAGNIAS

INTRODUCTION

THE parties in this case belonged to a large family, of which a complete pedigree *a* can be constructed, thanks to the additional material provided by the Pseudo - Demosthenic speech *Against Macartatus* ([Dem.] xliii.).

Hagnias II. on his way to Persia on an embassy in the year 396 B.C. was captured by the Spartan commander, Pharax, and handed over to the Spartans, by whom he was put to death.*b* By his will he adopted his niece and left her his property ; if she died, the property was to pass to his half-brother, Glaucon, the son of his mother and of Glaucetes of Aeum ([Dem.] xliii. 4). The daughter having died at an early age, the claims of Glaucon were attacked by Eubulides II., who stood in a double relation to Hagnias II., being a second cousin on his father's side and a first cousin through his mother. Eubulides died before the case could be tried, but his claims were taken up on behalf of his daughter Phylomache II., with the result that the will was annulled and the estate awarded to her. The effect of this judge-

---

a For Stemma see opposite page.

b *Hellenica Oxyrhynchia*, ii. 1, gives an account of this incident. The date 396 B.C. is deduced from the mention of other events in the same passage.

ON THE ESTATE OF HAGNIAS

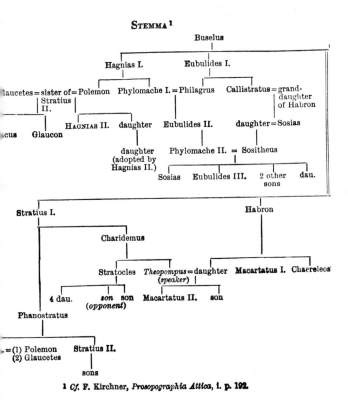

STEMMA [1]

ment was to encourage other second cousins of Hagnias to put in a claim, namely, Stratius II., Stratocles, and Theopompus. Stratius and Stratocles, however, died before the case came on, and Theopompus fought the case by himself. According to Isaeus, the three parties were Theopompus, Phylomache II., and the mother of Hagnias, who was also a second cousin of her own son. According to the Pseudo-Demosthenes, however, there were five claimants, Phylomache II., Theopompus, Glaucon, and his brother Glaucus, and Eupolemus, of whom nothing else is known. The discrepancy between the two accounts is remarkable, especially the omission by Isaeus of the names of Glaucon and Glaucus. The estate was awarded to Theopompus, whose claim appears to have had sound basis, since, though a second cousin, he was not outside the right of succession to an intestate estate. There can be little doubt that the claims of Glaucon and Glaucus were stronger, since, in default of relatives within the requisite degree on the male side, the estate should have passed to the nearest relative on the maternal side, and they were half-brothers of Hagnias. The omission of their names by Isaeus in his references to this case was probably deliberate.

Theopompus was not allowed to assume possession of the estate without further opposition. This took the form of a prosecution for the maltreatment of an orphan, namely, the son of his brother Stratocles, whose guardian he was, brought by a fellow-guardian of the child, who accused Theopompus of having defrauded his nephew of half Hagnias's estate.

ON THE ESTATE OF HAGNIAS

It was in answer to this charge that Isaeus was employed to write the present speech.

The speech opens abruptly with the citation of the law regulating the succession of collateral relatives to an intestate estate. Under this law, in the absence of a brother or sister by the same father as the deceased, an estate passed to first or second cousins on the father's side and their children ; if these failed, the title reverted to the relatives on the mother's side in the same order. Theopompus had no difficulty in showing that his ward was outside the requisite degree of kinship, being a second cousin once removed. His opponent had asserted that Theopompus had bargained with Stratocles before his death, and afterwards with his nephew, to share the estate. This, Theopompus says, is absurd ; for it was unnecessary to make such an arrangement with Stratocles, since their claims were identical, and he would never have compromised with his nephew, who had no shadow of a title to the estate. Again, if the orphan had justice on his side, why had not his representative brought a civil action for damages instead of employing the indirect method of a criminal prosecution ? The attempt of the other side to prove that Theopompus is rich and miserly, while the orphan is poor, is met by a detailed statement of their respective fortunes with the object of showing that the speaker is poor, and that, by his careful management, the orphan's estate has been largely increased. The conclusion of the speech is lost. He enjoyed the estate for the rest of his life in spite of a further prosecution for perjury of one or more of the witnesses who had given evidence on his behalf in the earlier suit against Phylomache II.

On his death the estate passed to his son **Macartatus**, whose title was attacked by Sositheus, the husband of Phylomache II., acting on behalf of his second son, Eubulides III., whom he had enrolled as the adopted son of Eubulides II., his maternal grandfather, thus bringing him within the requisite degree of relationship as the son of a first cousin of the original tenant of the estate, Hagnias II. The Pseudo-Demosthenic speech *Against Macartatus* was delivered in this suit. It is wordy and ill-arranged, and its perusal makes the reader appreciate still more highly the extraordinary skill attained by Isaeus in the representation of a case of this kind.

A deposition inserted in the Pseudo-Demosthenic speech (§ 31) states that the earlier trial, as a result of which the will was annulled and the estate awarded to Phylomache II., took place in the archonship of Nicophemus (361–360 B.C.). If this deposition is genuine, the present speech would have to be dated a few years later; Jebb suggests 359 B.C. There can be little doubt that this is too late a date. It has already been seen that, thanks to the *Hellenica Oxyrhynchia*, the death of Hagnias can be dated at 396 B.C.; it is scarcely possible that thirty-five years can have elapsed between that event and the present speech. An incident mentioned in the speech, the adventure of Macartatus I. in Crete (§ 48), which appears to have made a stir at the time and to have endangered the relations between Athens and Sparta, might have provided a clue, but there is no reference to it elsewhere. A privateering enterprise of this kind is, however, more likely to have occurred during the period when the Spartans were masters at sea as well as on land, that is to say, before the Athenians recovered their naval power in 378 B.C. Thus, while we have not the necessary material for fixing the exact date of this speech, it appears to be considerably earlier than that indicated by the deposition in the Pseudo-Demosthenic oration, which, like many similar documents, is probably a fabrication.

In this speech the word ἀνεψιός is translated as " cousin ". But it covers not only " first cousin " but also " first cousin once removed " and "second cousin ". It does not however cover " second cousin once removed ". Theopompus was a second cousin, and as such had a claim to the estate. But his nephew (ward) had not.

XI. ΠΕΡΙ ΤΟΥ ΑΓΝΙΟΥ ΚΛΗΡΟΥ

Ἀγνίας τις εἶχεν ἀνεψιοὺς πολλούς, Θεόπομπον καὶ τὸν ἀδελφὸν αὐτοῦ Στρατοκλέα καὶ Στρατίον[1] καὶ Εὐβουλίδην. οὗτος μέλλων τελευτᾶν ἐποιήσατο θετὴν ἑαυτῷ[2] θυγατέρα, κελεύσας ἐν ταῖς διαθήκαις, εἴ τι πάθοι ἡ θυγάτηρ, ἔρχεσθαι τὸν κλῆρον εἰς Γλαύκωνα, ἀδελφὸν αὐτοῦ τυγχάνοντα ὁμομήτριον. ἐπὶ τούτοις αὐτοῦ τελευτήσαντος ἡ θυγάτηρ λαβοῦσα τὸν κλῆρον ἐτελεύτησεν. ἀποθανόντος δὲ καὶ Εὐβουλίδου ἡ θυγάτηρ αὐτοῦ, τοῦ Εὐβουλίδου, δικασαμένη πρὸς Γλαύκωνα ἔλαβε τὴν οὐσίαν. μετὰ ταῦτα τελευτησάντων καὶ τῶν περὶ τὸν Στρατοκλέα καὶ Στρατίον Θεόπομπος μόνος ἐδικάσατο πρὸς αὐτήν, καὶ ἔλαβε τὸν κλῆρον. πρὸς τούτου ὁ υἱὸς τοῦ ἀδελφοῦ αὐτοῦ, Στρατοκλέους, δικάζεται [πρὸς αὐτὸν] δι[3] ἐπιτρόπου τινὸς [υἱός], φάσκων ἐξ ἴσου τὰ τῆς κληρονομίας ἁρμόζειν τῷ τε Θεοπόμπῳ καὶ τῷ παιδὶ τοῦ ἀδελφοῦ αὐτοῦ. ἡ στάσις πραγματική.

<ΝΟΜΟΙ>

1 Διὰ ταῦθ' ὑμῖν ἀνέγνων τοὺς νόμους, ὅτι κατὰ τὸν πρῶτον αὐτῶν ἰσχυρίζεται τῷ παιδὶ τοῦ ἡμικληρίου προσήκειν, οὐκ ἀληθῆ λέγων. οὐ γὰρ ἦν ἡμῖν Ἀγνίας ἀδελφός, ὁ δὲ νόμος περὶ ἀδελφοῦ χρημάτων πρῶτον ἀδελφοῖς τε καὶ ἀδελφιδοῖς πεποίηκε
388

XI. ON THE ESTATE OF HAGNIAS

ARGUMENT

A certain Hagnias had several cousins, namely, Theopompus, his brother Stratocles, Stratius, and Eubulides. When he was at the point of death he adopted a daughter, stipulating in his will that, if anything should happen to her, the estate should pass to Glaucon, who was his half-brother, his mother's son. After making these arrangements he died; and the daughter received the inheritance and then herself died. Eubulides having also died, his daughter brought an action against Glaucon and was awarded the estate. After this, Stratocles and Stratius having died, Theopompus, acting alone, brought a suit against her and was awarded the estate. It is against him that the son of his brother Stratocles brings an action through a guardian, alleging that the inheritance belongs in equal shares to Theopompus and to his brother's son. The discussion turns on a point of fact.

LAWS

I have read you the laws because my opponent bases on the first of them the claim of the child to half the estate—a claim which is false. Hagnias, it is true, was not our brother; but in the matter of a brother's property the law *a* has given the right

---

a The text of the law is given in [Dem.] xliii. (Πρὸς Μακάρ-τατον) § 51.

---

¹ Στρατίον Scheibe: -τίαν.

² ἑαυτῷ Buermann: -τοῦ.   ³ δι' Schoemann: δὲ.

τὴν κληρονομίαν, ἂν ὦσιν ὁμοπάτορες· τοῦτο γὰρ
ἐγγυτάτω τοῦ τελευτήσαντος ⟨τὸ⟩[1] γένος ἐστίν.
2 ἐὰν δ' οὗτοι μὴ ὦσι, δεύτερον ἀδελφὰς ὁμοπατρίας
καλεῖ καὶ παῖδας τοὺς ἐκ τούτων. ἐὰν δὲ μὴ ὦσι,
τρίτῳ γένει δίδωσι τὴν ἀγχιστείαν, ἀνεψιοῖς πρὸς
πατρὸς μέχρι ἀνεψιῶν παίδων. ἐὰν δὲ καὶ τοῦτ'
ἐκλείπῃ [εἰς] τὸ γένος, πάλιν ἐπανέρχεται καὶ
ποιεῖ τοὺς πρὸς μητρὸς τοῦ τελευτήσαντος κυρίους
αὐτῶν, κατὰ ταὐτὰ[2] καθάπερ τοῖς πρὸς πατρὸς ἐξ
3 ἀρχῆς ἐδίδου τὴν κληρονομίαν. ταύτας ποιεῖ
τὰς ἀγχιστείας ὁ νομοθέτης μόνας, συντομωτέρως[3]
τοῖς ῥήμασιν ἢ ἐγὼ φράζω· τὴν μέντοι διάνοιαν
ὧν βούλεται ταύτῃ δείκνυσιν. ὁ δὲ παῖς οὗτος
οὐδὲ καθ' ἓν τούτων τῶν ὀνομάτων Ἁγνίᾳ προσήκει τῇ ἀγχιστείᾳ, ἀλλ' ἔξω τῆς συγγενείας
ἐστίν. ἵνα δ' ἀκριβῶς μάθητε περὶ ὧν ψηφιεῖσθε,
τοὺς πολλοὺς λόγους ἐάσας οὗτος εἰπάτω ὅ τι ὁ
παῖς προσήκει τουτωνὶ τῶν εἰρημένων τῷ τὸν
κλῆρον καταλιπόντι· κἂν φανῇ κατά τι προσήκων,
ἑκὼν ἐγὼ συγχωρῶ τὸ ἡμικλήριον εἶναι τοῦ
4 παιδός. εἰ δέ τοι μηδὲν τούτων ἕξει εἰπεῖν, πῶς
οὐκ ἐλεγχθήσεται φανερῶς ἐμὲ μὲν συκοφαντῶν,
ὑμᾶς δ' ἐξαπατῆσαι παρὰ τοὺς νόμους ζητῶν;
ἀναβιβασάμενος οὖν αὐτὸν ἐναντίον ὑμῶν ἐρωτήσω
τὰ ἐν τοῖς νόμοις ὑπαναγιγνώσκων· οὕτω γὰρ
εἴσεσθε εἰ προσήκει τῷ παιδὶ τῶν Ἁγνίου χρη-

---

[1] τὸ add. Sauppe.   [2] ταὐτὰ Taylor: ταῦτα.
[3] συντομωτέρως Reiske: -ας.

of inheritance first to brothers and nephews provided they are on the father's side ; for they are related to the deceased in the nearest degree. In default of these, the law next names sisters by the same father and their issue. If these fail, it gives the right of succession as next-of-kin to the third degree, namely, the cousins on the father's side including their children. If this degree is also lacking, the law goes back and gives the succession to the relatives of the deceased on his mother's side on the same principles as originally regulated the rights of inheritance by the relatives on the father's side. These are the only rights of next-of-kin which the framer of the law recognizes ; the wording which he employs is briefer than my paraphrase, but he shows his intention quite clearly in the text of the law. This child does not possess a single one of these titles as next-of-kin to Hagnias, but is outside all relationship. In order that you may know exactly upon what points you are going to give your verdict, I challenge my opponent to state, without superfluous words, in which of the above-mentioned degrees of relationship this child stands to the former tenant of the estate. If he can be shown to be in any way related, I willingly concede that half the estate is his. If, on the other hand, he cannot prove the existence of any such relationship, surely he will be clearly convicted of bringing a vexatious suit against me and of trying to deceive you in contravention of the laws. I intend, therefore, to make him stand up before you and to interrogate him, reading out the text of the law. You will thus learn whether, or no, the child has any right to the fortune of Hagnias. (*To the Clerk*)

μάτων ἢ μή. λαβὲ οὖν αὐτοῖς τοὺς νόμους· σὺ δ'
ἀνάβηθι δεῦρο, ἐπειδὴ δεινὸς εἶ διαβάλλειν καὶ
τοὺς νόμους διαστρέφειν. σὺ δ' ἀναγίγνωσκε.

NOMOI

5 Ἐπίσχες. ἐρωτήσω σέ. ἀδελφός ἐσθ' ὁ παῖς
Ἁγνίου ⟨ἢ⟩[1] ἀδελφιδοῦς ἐξ ἀδελφοῦ ἢ ἐξ ἀδελφῆς
γεγονώς, ἢ ἀνεψιός, ἢ ἐξ ἀνεψιοῦ πρὸς μητρὸς ἢ
πρὸς πατρός; τί τούτων τῶν ὀνομάτων, οἷς ὁ
νόμος τὴν ἀγχιστείαν δίδωσι; καὶ ὅπως μὴ
ἐκεῖνο ἐρεῖς, ὅτι ἐμὸς ἀδελφιδοῦς. οὐ γὰρ περὶ
τοῦ ἐμοῦ κλήρου νῦν ὁ λόγος ἐστί· ζῶ γάρ. εἰ
δ' ἦν ἄπαις ἐγὼ τετελευτηκὼς καὶ ἠμφισβήτει
τῶν ἐμῶν, τοῦτο ἂν προσῆκεν[2] ἀποκρίνασθαι
ἐρωτωμένῳ. νῦν δὲ φῂς τῶν Ἁγνίου χρημάτων
τὸ ἡμικλήριον εἶναι τοῦ παιδός· δεῖ δή σε τῆς
ἀγχιστείας, ὅ τι ὁ παῖς Ἁγνίᾳ προσήκει, τὸ γένος
εἰπεῖν. φράσον οὖν τουτοισί.

6 Αἰσθάνεσθε ὅτι οὐκ ἔχει τὴν συγγένειαν εἰπεῖν,
ἀλλ' ἀποκρίνεται πάντα μᾶλλον ἢ ὃ δεῖ μαθεῖν
ὑμᾶς. καίτοι τόν γε πράττοντά τι δίκαιον οὐ
προσῆκεν ἀπορεῖν ἀλλ' εὐθὺς λέγειν, καὶ μὴ μόνον
τοῦτο ποιεῖν, ἀλλὰ καὶ διόμνυσθαι καὶ τοῦ γένους
παρέχεσθαι μάρτυρας,[3] ἵνα μᾶλλον [ἂν] ἐπι-
στεύετο ὑφ' ὑμῶν. νῦν δ' ἐφ' οἷς ἀπόκρισιν οὐ
δέδωκεν, οὐ μάρτυρας παρέσχετο, οὐχ ὅρκον
[84] ὤμοσεν, οὐ νόμον | ἀνέγνωκεν, οἴεται δεῖν ὑμᾶς,
ὀμωμοκότας ψηφιεῖσθαι κατὰ τοὺς νόμους, αὐτῷ
πειθομένους ἐμοῦ καταγνῶναι ταύτην τὴν εἰσ-

---

[1] ἢ add. Taylor.   [2] προσῆκεν Schoemann : -ήκη.
[3] μάρτυρας Cobet : μαρτυρίας.

Please take these laws ; and (*to his opponent*) you, come up here, since you are so clever at misrepresentation and at distorting the laws. Read on.

LAWS

Stop. I wish to question you. Is the child a brother of Hagnias, or a nephew, the son of a brother or sister, or a cousin, or the child of a cousin on his mother's or his father's side ? Which of these titles, which are regarded by the law as constituting kinship, does he possess ? And beware of saying that he is *my* nephew ; for it is not a question now of my estate, for I am still alive. If I had died without issue and he were claiming my property, it would be quite fitting that he should give this reply to one who interrogated him. On the present occasion, however, it is the half of Hagnias's estate that you say belongs to the child ; you must, therefore, define the degree of relationship which unites him to Hagnias. Tell these gentlemen, therefore, what it is.

You observe that he cannot define the relationship, but gives any sort of answer rather than the information which you require. Yet one who is acting in good faith ought not to be embarrassed, but ought to be able to answer immediately, and not only so but also swear an oath and produce witnesses about the degree of relationship, so that you might have attached greater credence to what he said. As it is, regarding matters about which he has given no answer, produced no witnesses, sworn no oath and quoted no law, he thinks that you, who have sworn to give your verdict according to the laws, ought to believe him and illegally con-

ἀγγελίαν παρὰ τοὺς νόμους· οὕτω σχέτλιος καὶ
7 ἀναιδὴς ἄνθρωπός ἐστιν. ἀλλ' οὐκ ἐγὼ ποιήσω
τούτων οὐδέν, ἀλλὰ καὶ τὸ γένος ἐρῶ τοὐμὸν καὶ
ὅθεν μοι προσήκει τῆς κληρονομίας, καὶ τὸν παῖδα
ἐπιδείξω καὶ τοὺς πρότερον ἀμφισβητήσαντας ἐμοὶ
τοῦ κλήρου πάντας ἔξω τῆς ἀγχιστείας ὄντας, ὥσθ'
ὑμᾶς ὁμολογεῖν. ἀνάγκη δ' ἐστὶν ἐξ ἀρχῆς τὰ
συμβεβηκότα εἰπεῖν· ἐκ τούτων γὰρ γνώσεσθε τήν
τε ἐμὴν ἀγχιστείαν καὶ ὅτι τούτοις οὐδὲν προσήκει
τῆς κληρονομίας.

8 Ἐγὼ γὰρ καὶ Ἁγνίας, ὦ ἄνδρες, καὶ Εὐβουλίδης καὶ Στρατοκλῆς καὶ Στράτιος ὁ τῆς Ἁγνίου
μητρὸς ἀδελφὸς ἐξ ἀνεψιῶν ἐσμεν γεγονότες· καὶ
γὰρ οἱ πατέρες ἡμῶν ἦσαν ἀνεψιοὶ ἐκ πατραδέλφων. Ἁγνίας οὖν, ὅτε ἐκπλεῖν παρεσκευάζετο
πρεσβεύσων ἐπὶ ταύτας τὰς πράξεις αἳ τῇ πόλει
συμφερόντως εἶχον, οὐκ ἐφ' ἡμῖν τοῖς ἐγγύτατα
γένους, εἴ τι πάθοι, τὰ ὄντα κατέλιπεν, ἀλλ'
ἐποιήσατο θυγατέρα αὑτοῦ ἀδελφιδῆν· εἰ δέ τι καὶ
αὐτὴ πάθοι, Γλαύκωνι τὰ ὄντα ἐδίδου, ἀδελφῷ
ὄντι ὁμομητρίῳ· καὶ ταῦτ' ἐν διαθήκαις ἐνέγραψε.

9 χρόνων δὲ διαγενομένων μετὰ ταῦτα τελευτᾷ μὲν
Εὐβουλίδης, τελευτᾷ δ' ἡ θυγάτηρ ἣν ἐποιήσατο
Ἁγνίας, λαμβάνει δὲ τὸν κλῆρον Γλαύκων κατὰ
τὴν διαθήκην. ἡμεῖς δ' οὐ πώποτ' ἠξιώσαμεν
ἀμφισβητῆσαι πρὸς τὰς ἐκείνου διαθήκας, ἀλλ'
ᾠόμεθα δεῖν περὶ τῶν αὑτοῦ τὴν ἐκείνου γνώμην
εἶναι κυρίαν, καὶ τούτοις ἐνεμένομεν. ἡ δ' Εὐβουλίδου θυγάτηρ μετὰ τῶν αὐτῇ συμπραττόντων
λαγχάνει τοῦ κλήρου καὶ λαμβάνει νικήσασα τοὺς
κατὰ τὴν διαθήκην ἀμφισβητήσαντας, ἔξω μὲν

demn me in this criminal suit. This is the wicked
and shameless sort of scoundrel that he is. I have
no intention of following his example ; instead, I
shall state my degree of relationship and the basis
of my claim to the estate, and I shall prove, in such
a manner as to win your assent, that the child and
the former claimants against me for the estate are
all outside the limits of kinship. I must state the
facts from the beginning ; for you will thus recognize
my claim as next-of-kin and see that my opponent
has no title to the succession.

Hagnias, Eubulides, Stratocles, Stratius, the
brother of Hagnias's mother, and I, gentlemen, are
all the children of cousins, our fathers having been
cousins, the children of brothers by the same father.
When Hagnias was preparing to set out as ambassador
on that mission [a] which had such favourable results
for the city, he did not leave his possessions, in case
anything happened to him, to us, his nearest relatives,
but adopted a niece ; and if anything happened
to her, he devised his property to Glaucon, his half-
brother on his mother's side. These dispositions
he embodied in a will. After some interval of time
Eubulides died. The daughter whom Hagnias had
adopted also died, and Glaucon received the estate
in accordance with the will. We never for a moment
thought of contesting Hagnias's will, but considered
that his intentions regarding his own property ought
to be carried into effect, and by these we abode.
But the daughter of Eubulides, with the assistance
of her confederates, laid claim to the estate and
obtained it, having gained an action against those
who based their rights on the will. She was outside

---

[a] See Introduction, p. 382.

οὖσα τῆς ἀγχιστείας, ἐλπίσασα δ' (ὡς ἔοικεν)
ἡμᾶς πρὸς αὐτὴν οὐκ ἀντιδικήσειν, ὅτι οὐδὲ πρὸς
10 τὰς διαθήκας ἡμφισβητήσαμεν. ἡμεῖς δέ, ἐγὼ καὶ
Στράτιος καὶ Στρατοκλῆς, ἐπειδὴ τοῖς ἐγγύτατα
γένους ἐγεγένητο ἐπίδικος ὁ κλῆρος, παρεσκευαζόμεθα[1] ἅπαντες λαγχάνειν· πρὶν δὲ γενέσθαι τὰς
λήξεις τῶν δικῶν ἡμῖν τελευτᾷ μὲν ὁ Στράτιος,
τελευτᾷ δ' ὁ Στρατοκλῆς, λείπομαι δ' ἐγὼ μόνος
τῶν[2] πρὸς πατρὸς ὢν ἀνεψιοῦ παῖς, ᾧ μόνῳ κατὰ
τοὺς νόμους ἐγίγνετο ἡ κληρονομία, πάντων ἤδη
τῶν ἄλλων ἐκλελοιπότων, οἳ ταὐτὸν ἐμοί[3] τῇ
11 συγγενείᾳ προσήκοντες ἐτύγχανον. τῷ δὲ γνώσεσθε τοῦθ', ὅτι ἐμοὶ μὲν ἀγχιστεύειν, τοῖς δ' ἐξ
ἐκείνων γεγονόσιν οὐκ ἦν, ἐν οἷς οὗτος ὁ παῖς ἦν·
αὐτὸς ὁ νόμος δηλώσει. τὸ μὲν γὰρ εἶναι τὴν ἀγχιστείαν ἀνεψιοῖς πρὸς πατρὸς μέχρι ἀνεψιῶν παίδων
ὁμολογεῖται παρὰ πάντων. εἰ δὲ μεθ' ἡμᾶς
δίδωσι τοῖς ἡμετέροις παισί, τοῦτ' ἤδη σκεπτέον
ἐστί. λαβὲ οὖν αὐτοῖς τὸν νόμον καὶ ἀναγίγνωσκε.

ΝΟΜΟΣ. Ἐὰν δὲ μηδεὶς ᾖ πρὸς πατρὸς μέχρι ἀνεψιῶν παίδων, τοὺς πρὸς μητρὸς κυρίους εἶναι κατὰ
τὰ αὐτά.

12 Ἀκούετε, ὦ ἄνδρες, ὅτι ὁ νομοθέτης οὐκ εἶπεν,
ἐὰν μηδεὶς ᾖ πρὸς πατρὸς μέχρι ἀνεψιῶν παίδων,
τοὺς τῶν ἀνεψιαδῶν εἶναι κυρίους, ἀλλὰ ἀπέδωκε

---

[1] παρεσκευαζόμεθα Reiske: -άζοντο.
[2] τῶν Dobree: τοῦ.   [3] ταὐτὸν ἐμοὶ Bekker: ταύτῃ μοι.

[a] The will having been set aside, the next-of-kin would
have to prove his title to the intestate estate.
[b] This is the only law which is quoted in the MSS. of
Isaeus; it has probably been invented on the basis of
the following section.

396

the prescribed degree of kinship, but hoped, it seems, that we should not bring an action against her, because we had not contested the will either. But we—that is to say, Stratius, Stratocles, and myself—since the estate had now become adjudicable to the next-of-kin,[a] all prepared to bring a suit. However, before the hearing of the case, Stratius and Stratocles both died ; and thus I am the only surviving relative on the father's side, being the son of a cousin and the only person to whom, according to the law, the estate could pass, all the other relatives having died who possessed the same degree of kinship as myself. But, it may be asked, how are you to know that I possess the rights of a next-of-kin, while the children of the other cousins, including this child, did not possess them ? The law itself will make this clear. It is universally admitted that the rights as next-of-kin belong to cousins on the father's side, including their children, but the point which we have now to examine is whether the law grants these rights to our children also. Take, therefore, the law and read it to the court.

LAW.—[If there is no relative on the father's side as far as the degree of the children of cousins, then the right of inheritance passes to the mother's side in the same order of succession.][b]

Mark you, gentlemen, the legislator did not say that, in default of heirs on the father's side up to the degree of cousin's children, the rights descend to the latter's children ; no, in default of us,[c] he

[c] *i.e.*, on the failure of the children of cousins on the male side. For ἀνεψιὸς as used in this speech see p. 387.

τοῖς πρὸς μητρὸς τοῦ τελευτήσαντος, ἂν ἡμεῖς μὴ
ὦμεν, τὴν κληρονομίαν ἤδη, ἀδελφοῖς καὶ ἀδελφαῖς
καὶ παισὶ τοῖς τούτων καὶ τοῖς ἄλλοις, κατὰ ταὐτὰ[1]
καθάπερ καὶ ἐξ ἀρχῆς ἦν ὑπειρημένον· τοὺς δὲ
ἡμετέρους παῖδας ἔξω τῆς ἀγχιστείας ἐποίησεν.
οἷς δὲ μηδ᾽ ἐὰν τετελευτηκὼς ἦν ἐγώ,[2] δίδωσιν ὁ
νόμος τὴν Ἁγνίου κληρονομίαν, πῶς ἐμοῦ τε
ζῶντος καὶ κατὰ τοὺς νόμους ἔχοντος οἴονται
αὐτοῖς εἶναι τὴν ἀγχιστείαν; οὐδαμῶς δήπουθεν.
13 ἀλλὰ μὴν εἰ τούτοις μὴ μέτεστιν, ὧν οἱ πατέρες
ταὐτὸν ἐμοὶ προσῆκον, οὐδὲ τούτῳ τῷ παιδὶ
γίγνεται· καὶ γὰρ ὁ τούτου πατὴρ ὁμοίως ἦν
ἐκείνοις συγγενής. οὔκουν δεινὸν ἐμοὶ μὲν
διαρρήδην οὕτω τῶν νόμων δεδωκότων τὴν
κληρονομίαν, τούτους δ᾽ ἔξω τῆς ἀγχιστείας πεποιηκότων, τολμᾶν τουτονὶ συκοφαντεῖν, καὶ δι-
αγωνίσασθαι μέν, ἡνίκ᾽ ἐγὼ τοῦ κλήρου τὴν δίκην
[85] ἐλάγχανον, | μὴ οἴεσθαι δεῖν, μηδὲ παρακατα-
βάλλειν, οὗ περὶ τῶν τοιούτων εἴ τι δίκαιον εἶχεν
εἰπεῖν διαγνωσθῆναι προσῆκεν, ἐπὶ δὲ ⟨τῷ⟩[3] τοῦ
παιδὸς ὀνόματι πράγματ᾽ ἐμοὶ παρέχειν καὶ περὶ
14 τῶν μεγίστων εἰς κίνδυνον καθιστάναι; καὶ περὶ
μὲν τῶν ὁμολογουμένων εἶναι τοῦ παιδὸς χρημάτων μηδ᾽ αἰτιᾶσθαί με, μηδ᾽ ὥς τι εἴληφα ἔχειν
εἰπεῖν (ἐφ᾽ οἷς, εἴ τι αὐτῶν κακῶς διώκουν ὥσπερ
οὗτος, κρίνεσθαί μοι προσῆκεν), ἃ δ᾽ ὑμεῖς[4] ἐμὰ
εἶναι ἐψηφίσασθε, τῷ βουλομένῳ δόντες ἐξουσίαν

---

[1] ταὐτὰ Reiske : ταῦτα.
[2] τετελευτηκὼς ἦν ἐγώ Dobree : -ηκότες ὦσιν ὡς ἐγώ.
[3] τῷ add. Schoemann.　　[4] ὑμεῖς Aldus : ἡμεῖς.

gives the inheritance to the relatives of the deceased on his mother's side, namely, to brothers and sisters and their children, and so on, in the same order as was laid down before. But he has placed our children outside the right of succession. How, then, can those to whom, even if I were dead, the law does not award Hagnias's estate, imagine that, while I am alive and have a legal right to the property, they themselves can have any title as next-of-kin? Their claim is quite preposterous. Indeed, if the right of succession is not possessed by those whose fathers stood in the same degree of relationship as myself, neither is it possessed by this child; for his father stood in the same degree as they. Is it not, therefore, outrageous, that, whereas the laws have thus explicitly given me the right of inheritance and have placed my opponents outside the requisite degree of kinship, this fellow should dare to play these pettifogging tricks and, at the moment when I was laying claim to the estate, should think fit, not to bring an action against me and pay the necessary deposit—this being the proper moment to have the question settled, if his claims were well-founded—but to annoy me in the name of this child and make me run the most serious risks? His charge is not concerned[a] with money which admittedly belongs to the child, nor can he say that I have received any such money—if I had administered any property in the manner in which he has done, I should deserve to be prosecuted; no, in bringing this kind of suit he has designs upon property which you, after permitting anyone who

---

[a] Grammatically the whole of this sentence depends on οὔκουν δεινόν (13. 4).

ἀμφισβητεῖν αὐτῶν, ἐπὶ τούτοις ἐμοὶ τοιούτους
ἀγῶνας παρασκευάζειν καὶ εἰς τοῦτο ἀναισχυντίας
ἥκειν;

15 Οἶμαι μὲν οὖν καὶ ἐκ τῶν ἤδη εἰρημένων γιγνώσκεσθαι ὑμῖν ὅτι οὔτ' ἀδικῶ τὸν παῖδα οὐδὲν οὔτ'
ἔνοχός εἰμι ταύταις ταῖς αἰτίαις οὐδὲ κατὰ μικρόν·
ἔτι δὲ ἀκριβέστερον ἡγοῦμαι καὶ ἐκ τῶν ἄλλων
ὑμᾶς μαθήσεσθαι, καὶ τὴν ἐμὴν ἐπιδικασίαν, ὡς
γέγονεν, ἀκούσαντας περὶ αὐτῶν. ἐμοὶ γάρ, ὦ
ἄνδρες, λαχόντι τοῦ κλήρου τὴν δίκην οὔτε οὗτος
ὁ νῦν ἐμὲ εἰσαγγέλλων ᾠήθη δεῖν παρακαταβάλλειν ὑπὲρ τοῦ παιδός, οὔτε οἱ Στρατίου παῖδες
οἱ ταὐτὸ[1] τῷ παιδὶ προσήκοντες . . . οὔτε δι'
ἄλλο οὐδὲν αὐτοῖς ἐνόμιζον προσήκειν τούτων τῶν
16 χρημάτων· ἐπεὶ οὐδ' ἂν οὗτος νῦν ἐμοὶ πράγματα
παρεῖχεν, εἰ τὰ τοῦ παιδὸς εἴων ἁρπάζειν καὶ μὴ
ἠναντιούμην αὐτῷ. οὗτοι μὲν οὖν, ὥσπερ εἶπον,
εἰδότες ὅτι ἔξω ἦσαν τῆς ἀγχιστείας, οὐκ ἠμφισβήτουν ἀλλ' ἡσυχίαν εἶχον· οἱ δ' ὑπὲρ τῆς Εὐβουλίδου θυγατρὸς πράττοντες, τῆς τὸ αὐτὸ τῷ
παιδὶ καὶ τοῖς Στρατίου παισὶ[2] προσηκούσης, καὶ
οἱ κύριοι τῆς Ἁγνίου μητρὸς ἦσαν οἷοί [τε] πρὸς
17 ἐμὲ ἀντιδικεῖν. εἰς τοσαύτας δ' ἀπορίας κατ-
έστησαν ὅ τι ἀντιγράψωνται περὶ τῆς ἀγχιστείας,
ὥστε ἡ μὲν τὸν κλῆρον ἔχουσα καὶ οἱ λέγοντες τὸ
περὶ αὐτῆς γένος, ἐπειδὴ κατεψεύσαντο, ῥᾳδίως
ὑπ' ἐμοῦ τότε ἐξηλέγχθησαν οὐκ ἀληθές τι γράψαι
τολμήσαντες, οἱ δ' ὑπὲρ τῆς Ἁγνίου μητρὸς γένει

---

[1] ταὐτὸ Bekker : τούτῳ.
[2] τὸ αὐτὸ τῷ παιδὶ καὶ τοῖς Στρατίου παισὶ Buermann : τὸ
αὐτὸ ** δικαίως τοῦ Στρατίου παιδί.

wished to dispute my claim to it, assigned by your verdict to me. Such is the extent of his impudence.

From what I have already said I think that you fully recognize that I am doing no wrong to the child and that I am not in the least degree guilty of these charges; but you will, I think, understand this still more exactly from the rest of my story, and, in particular, when you have heard how the adjudication to me of the inheritance took place. When I brought the action claiming the inheritance, neither did my opponent, who is now bringing an impeachment against me, think fit to make the necessary deposit on behalf of the child, nor did the sons of Stratius, who stand in the same relationship as the child, ⟨either for this⟩ [a] or for any other reason think that they had any right to the money; for my opponent would not be troubling me now, if I had allowed him to dissipate the child's property and had not opposed him. These men, then, as I have said, knowing that they were outside the requisite degree of relationship, kept quiet; but those who were acting on behalf of the daughter of Eubulides, who stands in the same degree of relationship as the child and the sons of Stratius, and the legal representatives of Hagnias's mother, were disposed to contest my claim. They found it so difficult to know what to say in their written counter-claim about the degree of relationship, that the woman who was in possession of the estate and those who were seeking to explain her kinship, when they lied, were easily convicted by me of daring to put in writing what was not true; and those who were supporting Hagnias's mother, who

[a] There is a lacuna in the text at this point.

μὲν ἐμοὶ ταὐτὸ προσηκούσης (ἀδελφὴ **γὰρ ἦν**
τοῦ Στρατίου) νόμῳ δὲ ἀποκλειομένης, ὃς **κελεύει**
κρατεῖν τοὺς ἄρρενας, τοῦτο μὲν εἴασαν, οἰόμενοι
δ' ἐμοῦ πλεονεκτήσειν μητέρα εἶναι τοῦ τελευτήσαντος ἔγραψαν· ὃ συγγενέστατον μὲν ἦν τῇ φύσει
πάντων, ἐν δὲ ταῖς ἀγχιστείαις ὁμολογουμένως
18 οὐκ ἔστιν. εἶτα γράψας ἀνεψιοῦ παῖς[1] εἶναι
κἀκείνας ἐξελέγξας[2] οὐκ οὔσας ἐν ταῖς ἀγχιστείαις, οὕτως ἐπεδικασάμην παρ' ὑμῖν, καὶ αὐτῶν
οὐκ ἴσχυσέ τι[3] οὔτε τῇ τὸν κλῆρον ἐχούσῃ τὸ προ-
νενικηκέναι τοὺς κατὰ διαθήκην ἀμφισβητήσαντας,
οὔτε τῇ ἑτέρᾳ τὸ μητέρα εἶναι τοῦ τὸν κλῆρον
καταλιπόντος, ἀλλ' οὕτως οἱ τότε δικάζοντες καὶ
τὸ δίκαιον καὶ τοὺς ὅρκους περὶ πολλοῦ ἐποιήσαντο,
ὥστ' ἐμοὶ τῷ κατὰ τοὺς νόμους ἀμφισβητοῦντι
19 τὴν ψῆφον ἤνεγκαν. καίτοι εἰ τὰς μὲν νενίκηκα
τοῦτον τὸν τρόπον, ἐπιδείξας μηδὲν Ἁγνίᾳ κατ'
ἀγχιστείαν προσηκούσας, οὗτος δὲ μὴ ἐτόλμησεν
ἀντιδικῆσαι τῷ παιδὶ τοῦ ἡμικληρίου πρὸς ἡμᾶς,[4]
οἱ δὲ Στρατίου παῖδες οἱ ταὐτὸν τούτῳ προσήκοντες μηδὲ νῦν ἀξιοῦσιν ἀντιδικῆσαι πρὸς ἐμὲ
περὶ αὐτῶν, ἔχω δ' ἐγὼ τὸν κλῆρον ἐπιδικασάμενος παρ' ὑμῖν, ἐξελέγχω δὲ τοῦτον μηδέπω καὶ
τήμερον ἔχοντ' εἰπεῖν ὅ τι ὁ παῖς Ἁγνίᾳ προσήκει κατ' ἀγχιστείαν, τί ἔτι δεῖ μαθεῖν ὑμᾶς
ἢ <τί>[5] ποθεῖτε ἀκοῦσαι περὶ τούτων; ἐγὼ

---

[1] παῖς Emper: παῖδας.   [2] ἐξελέγξας Reiske: ἐξελέγξα.
[3] τι Reiske: τις.   [4] ἡμᾶς Reiske: ὑμᾶς.
[5] τί add. Reiske.

stands in the same degree of relationship as I do (being sister of Stratius) but who is excluded by the law which ordains that the males shall have the preference, omitted all reference to this point, and, thinking to gain an advantage over me, described her as the mother of the deceased—the nearest possible relationship by blood, but admittedly conferring no rights as next-of-kin. Having thus described myself as the son of a cousin and having proved that these women were not within the requisite degree of kinship, I thus had the estate adjudicated to me by you ; and her former success against those who claimed on the basis of the will was of no avail to the woman who was in possession of the inheritance, nor did it avail the other woman that she was mother of the deceased who left the estate, but those who were trying the case attached so much importance to justice and their oaths that they gave their verdict in favour of me, whose claim was in conformity with the law. Yet since I thus triumphed over these women by proving that they were not within the requisite degree of kinship to Hagnias ; and since my present opponent did not venture to go to law with me, claiming half the estate for the child ; and since the sons of Stratius, who stand in the same degree of kinship as this child, do not even now think of bringing a suit against me for the estate ; and since I am in possession of the estate by your adjudication ; and since I can prove that my opponent even at the present time cannot state what relationship the child possesses which confers rights as next-of-kin to Hagnias— what further information do you require, and what more do you wish to hear on the subject ? Since I

μὲν γὰρ ὡς εὖ φρονοῦσιν ὑμῖν ἱκανὰ τὰ εἰρημένα νομίζω.

20 Οὗτος τοίνυν ῥᾳδίως ὅ τι ἂν τύχῃ ψευδόμενος, καὶ τὴν αὑτοῦ πονηρίαν οὐδεμίαν ζημίαν εἶναι νομίζων, τολμᾷ με διαβάλλειν ἄλλα τε πολλά, περὶ ὧν ποιήσομαι τοὺς λόγους τάχα, καὶ νυνὶ λέγει ὡς ἐκοινωσάμεθα ἐγώ τε καὶ Στρατοκλῆς, τὸν ἀγῶνα εἰσιέναι περὶ τοῦ κλήρου μέλλοντες. ὃ μόνοις ἡμῖν τῶν ἀμφισβητεῖν παρεσκευασμένων 21 οὐκ ἐνῆν, διομολογήσασθαι πρὸς ἀλλήλους. τῇ μὲν γὰρ Εὐβουλίδου θυγατρὶ καὶ τῇ Ἁγνίου μητρὶ πρὸς ἡμᾶς ἀγωνιζομέναις, μὴ κατὰ ταὐτὸ ἀμφισβητούσαις, ἐνῆν ποιήσασθαι συνθήκας, ἂν ἡ ἑτέρα νικᾷ, μετεῖναί τι καὶ τῇ ἡττηθείσῃ· κάδισκος [86] γὰρ ἔμελλεν | ἑκατέρᾳ τεθήσεσθαι. τὸ δ' ἡμέτερον οὐ τοιοῦτον ἦν, ἀλλ' ἓν τὸ γένος, δύο δὲ λήξεις, ἡμικληρίου ἑκατέρῳ· τοῖς δὲ κατὰ ταὐτὰ ἀμφισβητοῦσιν εἷς τίθεται κάδισκος, οὗ οὐκ ἂν ἦν τὸν μὲν ἡττᾶσθαι τὸν δὲ νικᾶν,[1] ἀλλ' ὁμοίως ἀμφοτέροις ἦν ὁ αὐτὸς κίνδυνος, ὥστ' οὐκ ἐνῆν κοινωνίαν οὐδὲ διομολογίαν ποιήσασθαι περὶ αὐτῶν. 22 ἀλλ' οὗτος, ἐπειδὴ Στρατοκλῆς ἐτελεύτησε πρὶν γενέσθαι τοῦ ἡμικληρίου τὰς λήξεις ἡμῶν ἑκατέρῳ, καὶ οὐκέτ' ἦν μετουσία τῷ Στρατοκλεῖ τούτων οὐδὲ τῷ παιδὶ τῷδε διὰ τὸν νόμον, ἀλλ' ἐγίγνετο εἰς ἐμὲ ἡ κληρονομία κατ' ἀγχιστείαν πάντων, εἰ νικήσαιμι τοὺς ἔχοντας, τότ' ἤδη πλάττει ταῦτα

[1] ἡττᾶσθαι τὸν δὲ νικᾶν Valckenaer: νικᾶσθαι τὸν δὲ ἡττᾶν.

regard you as men of good sense, I think that what I have said is sufficient.

My opponent, thinking nothing of telling any lie whatever and considering that his own rascality does him no harm, dares to utter many calumnies against me, with which I will deal presently. In particular, he now alleges that Stratocles and I made a compact, when we were about to engage in the suit about the inheritance, though of those who had prepared to put in a claim we were the only persons for whom such a mutual agreement was impossible. The daughter of Eubulides and the mother of Hagnias, in an action against me, since they were not claiming on the same grounds, might have made an agreement, that if one of them were successful, she should give a share to the defeated claimant; for the votes accorded to each of them would be placed in different urns. But with us it was quite otherwise; we stood in the same relationship and were making two separate claims, each to have half the estate; and when two claimants found their claims on the same grounds, only one voting urn is employed, so that it would be impossible for one to be unsuccessful and the other successful, but we both ran the same risk, so we could not possibly have made any compact or agreement about the inheritance. But when Stratocles died before the actions claiming half the estate, which we were each bringing, could come on, and so there was no further question of his participating in the estate, nor had this child of his any title owing to the law, but the whole inheritance devolved upon me as next-of-kin, if I could defeat those who are now in possession, then and not till then does my

καὶ μηχανᾶται, προσδοκῶν τούτοις τοῖς λόγοις
ῥᾳδίως ὑμᾶς ἐξαπατῆσαι. ὅτι δ' οὐχ οἷόν τ' ἦν
τούτων γίγνεσθαι οὐδέν, ἀλλὰ διείρηται[1] καθ'
ἕκαστον περὶ αὐτῶν, ἐκ τοῦ νόμου γνῶναι ῥᾴδιον.
λαβὲ δ' αὐτοῖς καὶ ἀναγίγνωσκε.

ΝΟΜΟΣ

23 Ἆρ' ὑμῖν ὁ νόμος δοκεῖ ποιεῖν ἐξουσίαν κοινωνίας, ἀλλ' οὐκ ἄντικρυς οὑτωσὶ πᾶν τοὐναντίον, εἰ
καὶ τὸ πρότερον ὑπῆρχε κοινωνία, προστάττει,
διαρρήδην κελεύων τοῦ μέρους ἕκαστον λαγχάνειν
καὶ τοῖς κατὰ ταὐτὸ ἀμφισβητοῦσι τιθεὶς ἕνα
καδίσκον καὶ τὰς ἐπιδικασίας τοῦτον τὸν τρόπον
ποιῶν; ὁ δέ, ταῦτα τῶν νόμων λεγόντων καὶ οὐκ
ἐνούσης γενέσθαι διομολογίας, οὕτως ἀλόγως
24 πρᾶγμα τηλικοῦτον ψεύσασθαι τετόλμηκεν. οὐ
μόνον δὲ τοῦτο πεποίηκεν, ἀλλὰ καὶ τὸ πάντων
ἐναντιώτατον πρᾶγμα εἴρηκεν, ᾧ προσέχετε τὸν
νοῦν, ὦ ἄνδρες. φησὶ γὰρ ὁμολογῆσαί με τοῦ
κλήρου τῷ παιδὶ τὸ ἡμικλήριον μεταδώσειν, εἰ
νικήσαιμι τοὺς ἔχοντας αὐτόν. καίτοι εἰ μέν τι
καὶ αὐτῷ μετῆν κατὰ τὸ γένος, ὡς οὗτος λέγει, τί
ἔδει γενέσθαι ταύτην αὐτοῖς παρ' ἐμοῦ τὴν ὁμο-
λογίαν; ἦν γὰρ ὁμοίως καὶ τούτοις ἐπίδικον τὸ
25 ἡμικλήριον, εἴ περ ἀληθῆ λέγουσιν. εἰ δὲ μὴ
προσῆκεν αὐτοῖς τῆς ἀγχιστείας μηδέν, διὰ τί ἂν
μεταδώσειν ὡμολόγουν, τῶν νόμων ἐμοὶ πάντων
αὐτῶν δεδωκότων τὴν κληρονομίαν; πότερα δ'

[1] διείρηται Reiske: διῄρηται.

opponent devise and invent these fictions, expecting
easily to mislead you by these stories. That no
such compact was possible but that all the details
of procedure are already provided for, can easily
be seen from the law. Please take and read it to
the court.

LAW

Does it appear to you that the law gives any
liberty for a concerted arrangement? Or are not
its provisions in an exactly contrary sense, since,
even if a previous arrangement existed, it expressly
ordains that each party shall bring an action for his
own share, and prescribes a single voting-urn, when
the two parties base their claims on the same ground,
and makes this the system of adjudication? But
my opponent, in spite of these legal provisions and
the impossibility of a preconcerted arrangement,
has had the impudence to invent this lie against all
common sense. But he has not stopped there;
he has also invented the most inconsistent story
possible, to which, gentlemen, please give your close
attention. He declares that I agreed, if I won my
case against the present possessors of the estate,
to give the child a half-share of the inheritance. Yet
if the child had any right to a share in virtue of his
relationship, as my opponent declares, what need
was there for this agreement between me and them?
For the half of the estate was adjudicable to them
just as much as to me, if what they say is true. If,
on the other hand, they had no claim by right of
kinship, why should I have agreed to give them a
share, when the laws have given me the right of
succession to the whole estate? Was it then

οὐκ ἦν μοι λαχεῖν, εἰ μὴ πείσαιμι τούτους; ἀλλ'
ὁ νόμος τῷ βουλομένῳ δίδωσι τὴν ἐξουσίαν, ὥστε
τοῦτο οὐκ ἦν αὐτοῖς εἰπεῖν. ἀλλ' εἶχόν τινά μοι
μαρτυρίαν τοῦ πράγματος, ἣν εἰ μὴ ἐμαρτύρουν,
οὐκ ἔμελλον ἐπιδικάσασθαι τούτων; ἀλλὰ κατὰ
γένος ἠμφισβήτουν, οὐ κατὰ δόσιν, ὥστ' οὐδὲν
26 ἔδει μαρτύρων. ἀλλὰ μὴν εἰ μήτε κοινώσασθαι
τὸ πρᾶγμα ἐνῆν, ὅτ' ἔζη Στρατοκλῆς, μήτε ὁ
πατὴρ αὐτῷ κατέλιπεν ἐπιδικασάμενος τούτων
μηδέν,[1] μήτε εἰκὸς ἦν μεταδώσειν ἐμὲ τὸ ἡμικλήριον ὁμολογῆσαι αὐτῷ, ἀπέδοτε[2] ⟨δ'⟩[3] ὑμεῖς
ἐπιδικάσαντές μοι τοῦτον τὸν κλῆρον, οἱ[4] δὲ μήτε
ἔλαχον τότε[5] αὐτῶν μήτ' ἀμφισβητῆσαι πώποτ'
ἠξίωσαν, πῶς χρὴ πιστοὺς εἶναι νομίζειν τοὺς
τούτων λόγους; ἐγὼ μὲν οἶμαι οὐδαμῶς.

27 Προσποιεῖται τοίνυν οὗτος (ἐπειδὴ τοῦτ' εἰκότως
ἂν θαυμάζοιτε, ὅτι τοῦ ἡμικληρίου τότε τὴν δίκην
οὐκ ἐλάγχανον) τοῦ μὲν μὴ λαχεῖν πρὸς ἐκείνους
ἐμὲ εἶναι αἴτιον ὡς ὁμολογήσαντα μεταδώσειν,
ὥστε διὰ τοῦτ' οὐ[6] παρακαταβάλλειν αὐτούς,[7] τῆς
δὲ πρὸς ἐμὲ λήξεως ἐμποδὼν εἶναι τοὺς νόμους
(οὐ γὰρ εἶναι τοῖς ὀρφανοῖς κατὰ τῶν ἐπιτρόπων),
28 οὐδέτερ' ἀληθῆ λέγων. οὔτε γὰρ ἂν νόμον δείξειεν
ὃς κωλύει τοῦτον ὑπὲρ τοῦ παιδὸς δίκην παρ'
ἐμοῦ λαμβάνειν· οὐ γάρ ἐστιν ἐναντιούμενος οὐδείς,
ἀλλ' ὥσπερ καὶ γραφὰς κατ' ἐμοῦ δέδωκεν, οὕτω

---

[1] μηδέν Bekker: οὐδέν.   [2] ἀπέδοτε Schoemann: ἀπόδοτε.
[3] δ' add. Schoemann.   [4] οἱ Schoemann: εἰ.
[5] τότε Münscher: τῶν.   [6] τοῦτ' οὐ Reiske: τούτου.
[7] αὐτούς Dobree: αὐτοῖς.

408

mpossible for me to make my claim without their consent ? But the law gives full liberty to anyone who likes to make a claim, so that they could not possibly make this allegation. Did they then have some evidence material for my case, in default of which I was unlikely to secure the adjudication of the estate ? No, I was claiming by right of kinship, not of testamentary disposition, so that I had no need of witnesses. And indeed, if it was impossible for me to have made an arrangement with Stratocles in his lifetime ; if his father did not bequeath the estate to him, since he never had any of t adjudicated to him ; if it was unlikely that I should have agreed to give the child half the inheritance ; and since you awarded me the estate by your adjudication and my opponents brought no action at the time and have never yet thought of disputing the estate—how can you believe their allegations to be true ? In my opinion you cannot possibly do so.

Seeing that you might reasonably be astonished that they did not at the time bring a suit claiming half the estate, my opponent pretends that I was the cause of their not bringing a suit against the other parties, because I had agreed to give them a share and so they did not make the necessary deposit, while he alleges that the laws forbade them to bring a suit against me on the ground that orphans may not bring actions against their guardians. Both these statements are untrue. For my opponent could not point to any law which forbids him to bring a private action against me on behalf of the child ; for no law exists which is opposed to such a proceeding, but, just as the law has granted the

καὶ δίκας ἐμοὶ εἶναι καὶ τῷ παιδὶ πεποίηκεν· οὔτ
αὖ διὰ ταῦτα ἐκείνοις τοῖς ἔχουσι¹ τοῦ κλήρου οὐκ
ἐλάγχανον, ὡς ἐμοῦ μεταδώσειν ὁμολογήσαντος
ἀλλ' ὅτι οὐδ' ὁτιοῦν αὐτοῖς τούτων τῶν χρημάτων
29 προσῆκεν. εὖ δ' οἶδ' ὅτι <οὐδ'>² εἰ συνεχώρουν
τῷ παιδὶ λαβεῖν ἐπιδικασαμένῳ παρ' ἐμοῦ τὸ ἡμι
κλήριον, οὐκ ἄν ποτε ταῦτ' ἐποίησαν οὐδ' ἐπεχείρη
σαν, εἰδότες <ὅτι>,³ ὁπότ' ἐν τῇ ἀγχιστείᾳ μὴ
ὄντες εἶχόν τι τῶν μὴ προσηκόντων, τοῦτ' ἂν ὑπὸ
τῶν ἐγγύτατα γένους ῥᾳδίως ἀφῃρέθησαν. ὅπερ
γὰρ καὶ πρότερον εἶπον, οὐ δίδωσι μεθ' ἡμᾶς τοῖς
[87] ἡμετέροις παισὶ τὸ παράπαν τὴν ἀγχιστείαν |
νόμος, ἀλλὰ τοῖς πρὸς μητρὸς τοῦ τελευτήσαντος
30 ἧκεν ἂν οὖν ἐπ' αὐτὰ τοῦτο μὲν ὁ Γλαύκων ὁ τοῦ
Ἁγνίου ἀδελφός, πρὸς ὃν μὴ ὅτι γένος εἶχον
ἄμεινον εἰπεῖν, ἀλλὰ καὶ ἔξω τῆς ἀγχιστείας
ἐφαίνοντ' ἂν ὄντες, τοῦτο δ', εἰ μὴ ἐβούλετο οὗτος
ἡ Ἁγνίου κἀκείνου μήτηρ, προσῆκον καὶ αὐτῇ
τῆς ἀγχιστείας τοῦ αὑτῆς ὑέος, ὥσθ' ὁπότ
ἠγωνίζετο πρὸς τοὺς μηδὲν γένει προσήκοντας,
φανερῶς ἂν ἔλαβε τὸ ἡμικλήριον παρ' ὑμῶν, τούτο
τοῦ δικαίου καὶ τῶν νόμων αὐτῇ δεδωκότων
31 οὐκοῦν διὰ ταῦτ' οὐκ ἐλάγχανεν, οὐχ ὡς δι' ἐμὲ
ἢ τοὺς νόμους κωλυόμενος, ἀλλὰ ταύτας [τὰς]

¹ ἔχουσι Dobree : προσήκουσι.   ² οὐδ' add. Scaliger.
³ ὅτι add. Stephanus.

ᵃ Not as his mother but as her son's cousin; see Stemma,
p. 383.
410

right to bring a public indictment against me, so it has created the opportunity either for me or the child to bring a private suit. Again, it was not because I agreed to give them a share that they failed to bring an action against the other parties who were in possession of the estate, but because they had absolutely no right to this money. I am convinced that even had I agreed to let the child receive from me by the adjudication of the court a half of the inheritance, they would never have carried out this bargain or attempted to do so ; they know perfectly well, that if, being outside the requisite degree of kinship, they had been in possession of anything which did not belong to them, they would have been easily deprived of it by the next-of-kin. For, as I said before, the law does not give any rights at all as next-of-kin to our children after us, but transfers them to the relatives of the deceased on his mother's side. In the first place, then, Glaucon, the brother of Hagnias, would have come forward, against whom they could not urge a claim of closer relationship ; on the contrary, they would have been clearly shown to be outside the requisite degree of kinship. Next, if Glaucon had been unwilling to come forward, the mother of Hagnias and Glaucon would have done so, since she possessed a claim of kinship to her son,[a] and so, if she had engaged in a suit against those who possessed no title as next-of-kin, she would clearly have been awarded half the estate by you, since justice and the laws have given her a right to it. These, then, are the reasons why he did not bring an action, and it was not because he was prevented from doing so by me or by the laws ; and these are the pretexts which

προφάσεις ποιούμενος ἐπὶ ταύτας τὰς συκοφαντίας
ἐλήλυθεν, ἐξ ὧν γραφὴν γραψάμενος καὶ ἐμὲ
διαβάλλων ἐλπίζει χρήματα λήψεσθαι καὶ ἐμὲ τῆς
ἐπιτροπῆς ἀπαλλάξειν. καὶ οἴεται δεινοῦ τινος
ἀνδρὸς ἔργον διαπράττεσθαι ταύταις ταῖς παρασκευαῖς, ὅτι μὴ κατορθώσας μὲν οὐδὲν ἀπολεῖ τῶν
αὑτοῦ, διαπραξάμενος δ' ἃ βούλεται καὶ τὰ τοῦ
παιδὸς ἀδεῶς ἤδη διαφορήσει.

32 Οὐκοῦν οὐ δεῖ προσέχειν ὑμᾶς τοῖς τούτου λόγοις τὸν νοῦν, οὐδ' ἐπιτρέπειν, οὐδ' ἐθίζειν εἶναι
γραφὰς περὶ ὧν ἰδίας δίκας οἱ νόμοι πεποιήκασιν.
ἁπλᾶ γὰρ τὰ δίκαια παντάπασίν ἐστι καὶ γνώριμα
μαθεῖν· ἃ ἐγὼ διὰ βραχέων εἰπὼν καὶ παρακατα-
θέμενος ὑμῖν μνημονεύειν, ἐπὶ τὴν ἄλλην ἀπολογίαν
33 ἤδη τρέψομαι τῶν κατηγορηθέντων. τί οὖν ἔστι
ταῦτα, καὶ τί διορίζομαι; εἰ μὲν κατ' ἀγχιστείαν
τῶν Ἁγνίου μετεῖναί φησι τῷ παιδί, τοῦ ἡμικληρίου λαχέτω πρὸς τὸν ἄρχοντα, κἂν ὑμεῖς ψηφίσησθε, λαβέτω· ταῦτα γὰρ οἱ νόμοι κελεύουσιν. εἰ
δὲ μὴ κατὰ τοῦτο ἀμφισβητεῖ, φησὶ δὲ ὁμολογῆσαί
με τῷ παιδὶ μεταδώσειν, φάσκοντος ἐμοῦ τούτων
εἶναι μηδέν, δικασάσθω, κἂν ἐξελέγξῃ με ὡς ὡμο-
λόγησα, τότ' ἤδη πραξάσθω· δίκαιον γὰρ οὕτως
34 ἐστίν. εἰ δὲ μήτε πρὸς ἐμὲ μήτε κατ' ἐμοῦ δίκην
εἶναί φησι τῷ παιδί, τὸν κωλύοντα νόμον εἰπάτω,

ᵃ An action claiming property was described as πρός τινα,
an action for breach of contract as κατά τινος.

he has invented for resorting to these vexatious proceedings against me, and it is upon the basis of them, that having brought a public indictment against me and slandering me, he hopes to obtain money and to deprive me of my guardianship. He thinks that he is managing very cleverly in employing these devices, because, if he is unsuccessful, he will lose nothing of his own, whereas, if he can carry out his wishes, he will henceforward be able to squander the child's property as well with impunity.

You must, therefore, not listen to his arguments nor tolerate his utterance of them, nor allow the custom to grow up of bringing public actions about matters for which the laws have prescribed private suits. For the rights of the case are perfectly simple and easy to understand. After dealing briefly with them and leaving them stored in your memory, I will then turn to the rest of my defence against the charges brought against me. What then are the rights of the case and how do I define them? If my opponent declares that part of Hagnias's estate belongs to the child by right of kinship, let him bring an action before the archon claiming the half, and, if you decide in his favour, let him take it; for thus the laws ordain. But if he does not claim on these grounds but alleges that I agreed to give the child a share—though I declare that there is not a word of truth in his allegation—let him bring an action and, if he can prove that I made such an agreement, let him secure the execution of it; for that is only right. But if he declares that the child cannot either claim a share from me at law or sue me for breach of contract,[a] let him name the

κἂν ἔχῃ δεῖξαι, λαβέτω καὶ οὕτω τὸ μέρος τῶν
χρημάτων. εἰ δ᾽ αὖ μήτ᾽ ἐπιδικάσασθαί φησι δεῖν
τοῦ ἡμικληρίου μήτ᾽ ἐμοί¹ δικάσασθαι, ἀλλ᾽ ἤδη
εἶναι ταῦτα τοῦ παιδός, ἀπογραψάσθω πρὸς τὸν
ἄρχοντα εἰς τὴν μίσθωσιν τῶν ἐκείνου χρημάτων,
ἣν ὁ μισθωσάμενος εἰσπράξει με ταῦτα ὡς ὄντα
35 τοῦ παιδός. ταῦτα μεγάλα δίκαιά ἐστι. ταῦτα
καὶ οἱ νόμοι κελεύουσιν, οὐ μὰ Δία οὐ γραφὰς ἐμὲ
φεύγειν περὶ ὧν δίκας ἰδίας εἶναι πεποιήκασιν,
οὐδὲ κινδυνεύειν περὶ τοῦ σώματος, ὅτι οὐ μετα-
δίδωμι τῷ παιδὶ τούτων, ἃ ψήφῳ κρατήσας ἐγὼ
τοὺς ἔχοντας οὕτω παρ᾽ ὑμῶν ἔλαβον· ἀλλ᾽ εἴ τι
τῶν ὁμολογουμένων εἶναι τοῦ παιδὸς εἶχον καὶ κακῶς διέθηκα ὥστ᾽ ἐκεῖνον κακοῦσθαι, τότε ἄν μοι
κατὰ ταύτην προσῆκε κρίνεσθαι τὴν γραφήν, οὐ
μὰ Δί᾽ οὐκ ἐπὶ τοῖς ἐμοῖς.

36 Ὅτι μὲν οὖν οὔτε περὶ τούτων οὐδὲν δίκαιον πεποίηκεν οὔτε περὶ τῶν ἄλλων ἀληθὲς οὐδὲν εἴρηκεν,
ἅπαντα δὲ δεινῶς πλεονεξίᾳ μεμηχάνηται διαβάλλων καὶ τοὺς νόμους παράγων καὶ ὑμῶν καὶ
ἐμοῦ παρὰ τὸ δίκαιον περιγενέσθαι ζητῶν, οἶμαι
μὰ τοὺς θεοὺς οὐδ᾽ ὑμᾶς ἀγνοεῖν ἀλλ᾽ ὁμοίως εἰδέναι πάντας, ὥστ᾽ οὐκ οἶδ᾽ ὅ τι δεῖ πλείω περὶ
τούτων λέγειν.

37 Ὁρῶ δέ, ὦ ἄνδρες, τὴν πλείστην διατριβὴν τῶν
λόγων ποιούμενον περὶ τὴν τοῦ παιδὸς οὐσίαν καὶ
περὶ τὴν ἐμήν, καὶ τὰ μὲν ἐκείνου παντάπασιν ὡς

¹ μητ ἐμοὶ Blass: μήτε μὴ.

law which prohibits this, and, if he can indicate it, let the child in these circumstances, too, receive the share of the estate. If, again, he contends that there is no need to have the half-share adjudicated or to go to law with me at all, but that this share already belongs to the child, let him make an application to the archon for its inclusion in the lease of the orphan's estate and let the lessee exact from me this portion as belonging to the child. Such are the essential rights of the case, and such the provisions of the laws, which do not, thank heaven, oblige me to submit to criminal trials in matters about which they have instituted private suits nor to run any personal risk because I refuse to share with the child this estate, which I received by your verdict when I won my case against those who were in possession. If I were holding any property which admittedly belonged to the child and had maladministered it to his detriment, then he would be justified in bringing this criminal charge against me, but not, by heaven, when it is a question of my own property.

That my adversary has in this matter acted entirely unjustly, and that otherwise he has never spoken a word of truth, but has cleverly devised the whole plot from motives of self-interest, uttering calumnies, misinterpreting the laws and seeking to get the better both of you and of me contrary to justice—of all this, by heaven, you are, I think, well aware and all alike understand; and so I do not know what more I need say.

I notice, gentlemen, that most of his speech is taken up with a discussion of my fortune and of that of the child; he represents the circumstances

ἄπορα διεξιόντα,[1] περὶ δ' ἐμὲ πλοῦτόν τινα τῷ
λόγῳ κατασκευάσαντα, καί τινα κακίαν κατηγοροῦντα[2] ὡς ἐγὼ τεττάρων οὐσῶν Στρατοκλέους
θυγατέρων οὐδεμιᾷ τολμῶ συνευπορῆσαι προικός,
καὶ ταῦτ' ἔχων (ὡς οὗτός φησι) τὰ τοῦ παιδίου.
38 βούλομαι δὴ καὶ περὶ τούτων εἰπεῖν· ἐλπίζει γὰρ
διὰ τῶν λόγων ἐμοὶ μέν τινα φθόνον γενήσεσθαι
παρ' ὑμῶν περὶ τῶν προσγεγενημένων χρημάτων,
τοῖς δὲ παισὶν ἔλεον, ἂν ἄποροι παρ' ὑμῖν εἶναι
δόξωσιν. οὔκουν ἀγνοῆσαι δεῖ περὶ αὐτῶν ὑμᾶς
οὐδέν, ἀλλ' ἀκριβῶς καὶ ταῦτα μαθεῖν, ἵν' εἰδῆθ'
[88] ὅτι ψεύδεται, ὥσπερ καὶ περὶ τῶν ἄλλων | ἁπάν-
των. ἐγὼ γάρ, ὦ ἄνδρες, πάντων ⟨ἂν⟩[3] ὁμολογή-
σαιμι εἶναι κάκιστος, εἰ Στρατοκλέους ἄπορα τὰ
πράγματα καταλιπόντος αὐτὸς εὔπορος ὢν [καὶ]
μηδεμίαν ἐπιμέλειαν ποιούμενος φαινοίμην τῶν
39 ἐκείνου παίδων. εἰ δὲ πλείονα κατέλιπεν αὐτοῖς
τὰ ὄντα τῶν ἐμῶν καὶ βεβαιότερα, καὶ ταῦτα
τοσαῦτ' ἐστὶν ὥστε καὶ τὰς θυγατέρας ἐξ αὐτῶν
διαθεῖναι καλῶς καὶ τὸν παῖδα ἐκ τῶν λοιπῶν
μηδὲν ἧττον εἶναι πλούσιον, ἐπιμελοῦμαί τε
τοῦτον τὸν τρόπον αὐτῶν ὥστε καὶ πολλῷ πλείω
γενέσθαι τὴν οὐσίαν, εἰκότως μὲν οὐκ ἂν ἔχοιμι
μέμψιν, εἰ μὴ τἀμαυτοῦ προστίθημι τούτοις,
σώζων δὲ τὰ τούτων καὶ πλείω ποιῶν δικαίως ἂν
ἐπαινοίμην. ὅτι δὲ ταῦτα οὕτως ἔχει, ῥᾳδίως ἐπι-
40 δείξω. πρῶτον μὲν οὖν τὰ τῆς οὐσίας διέξειμι,
μετὰ δὲ ταῦτα ὡς καὶ διοικεῖν ἀξιῶ τὰ τοῦ παιδός.

Στρατοκλεῖ γὰρ κἀμοὶ τὰ μὲν ὑπάρξαντα πατρῷα

---

[1] διεξιόντα Aldus: -ντος.
[2] κατηγοροῦντα Stephanus: -ντος.
[3] ἂν add. Schoemann.

of the child as embarrassed, while he attributes to
me a position of wealth and accuses me of baseness
on the ground that I cannot bring myself to provide
any of the four daughters of Stratocles with a dowry,
although, according to his account, I am in possession
of the child's property. I should like to deal with
this too; for he hopes by his arguments to arouse
in your minds a prejudice against me regarding the
fortune which has accrued to me, and a feeling of
pity in favour of the children, if they can be represented to you as reduced to poverty. You must not,
therefore, be left in any ignorance on these points
but must have an exact idea of them, so that you
may understand that here, too, my opponent is lying,
as he has lied about everything else. For, gentlemen, I would admit myself to be the basest of all
men, if it could be shown that the affairs of Stratocles
were left in a state of embarrassment at his death
and that I, being myself in easy circumstances, gave
not a thought to his children. But if he left them a
fortune more considerable and better secured than
my own and sufficient to endow his daughters fittingly
without sensibly diminishing his son's wealth, and if
I am so managing the property as greatly to increase
it, surely I cannot reasonably be blamed for not
giving them my own money as well; I rather deserve to be praised for preserving and increasing
their fortune. That these statements are true, I
shall easily prove to you. First, therefore, I will
give you details about the property, and after that
state the principles on which I think fit to administer
the child's affairs.[a]

Stratocles and I had a patrimony sufficient to

[a] This part of the speech is lost.

τοσαῦτα ἦν, ὥστε εἶναι μὲν [οὐχ] ἱκανά, λητουρ-
γεῖν δὲ μὴ ἄξια. τεκμήριον δέ· εἴκοσι μνᾶς
ἑκάτερος ἡμῶν ἐπὶ τῇ γυναικὶ προῖκα ἔλαβε,
τοσαύτη δὲ προῖξ οὐκ ἂν εἰς πολλήν τινα οὐσίαν
41 δοθείη. συνέβη δὲ Στρατοκλεῖ πρὸς τοῖς ὑπάρχουσι πλέον ἢ πένθ' ἡμιταλάντων οὐσίαν λαβεῖν·
Θεοφῶν[1] γὰρ ὁ τῆς γυναικὸς αὐτοῦ ἀδελφὸς ἀπο-
θνῄσκων ἐποιήσατο τῶν θυγατέρων αὐτοῦ μίαν,
καὶ τὰ ὄνθ'[2] αὐτοῦ ἔδωκεν, ἀγρὸν τὸν Ἐλευσῖνι
δυοῖν ταλάντοιν, πρόβατα ἑξήκοντα, αἶγας ἑκατόν,
ἔπιπλα, ἵππον λαμπρὸν ἐφ' οὗ ἐφυλάρχησε, καὶ
42 τὴν ἄλλην κατασκευὴν ἅπασαν, ἧς κύριος ἐκεῖνος
γενόμενος ἐννέα ἔτη ὅλα κατέλιπε πέντε ταλάντων οὐσίαν καὶ τρισχιλίων δραχμῶν σὺν τοῖς
ἑαυτοῦ πατρῴοις, χωρὶς ἐκείνης ἧς Θεοφῶν τῇ
θυγατρὶ αὐτοῦ ἔδωκεν, ἀγρὸν μὲν Θριᾶσι πένθ'
ἡμιτάλαντα εὑρίσκοντα, οἰκίαν δὲ Μελίτῃ τρισχιλίων ἐωνημένην,[3] ἄλλην δὲ Ἐλευσῖνι πεντακοσίων. ἐδάφη μὲν ταῦτα, ἀφ' ὧν ἡ μίσθωσις τοῦ
μὲν ἀγροῦ δώδεκα μναῖ, τῶν δὲ οἰκιῶν τρεῖς,
αἱ πεντεκαίδεκα μναῖ συναμφότερα γίγνονται· χρέα
δ' ἐπὶ τόκοις ὀφειλόμενα περὶ τετρακισχιλίας, ὧν
τὸ ἔργον ἐπ' ἐννέα ὀβολοῖς ἑπτακόσιαι καὶ εἴκοσι
43 δραχμαὶ γίγνονται τοῦ ἐνιαυτοῦ ἑκάστου. πρόσ-
οδος μὲν αὕτη δύο καὶ εἴκοσι μναῖ καὶ πρός·
χωρὶς δὲ τούτων κατέλιπεν ἔπιπλα, πρόβατα,
κριθάς, οἶνον, ὀπώρας, ἐξ ὧν ἐνεπόλησαν[4] τετρακισχιλίας ἐννακοσίας· ἔτι δὲ ἔνδον ἐννακοσίας
δραχμάς. πρὸς δὲ τούτοις ἐξ ἐράνων ὀφλήματα
εἰσπεπραγμένα, μικροῦ δεούσας χιλίας δραχμάς,

[1] Θεοφῶν Aldus: -φρων.   [2] τὰ ὄνθ' Blass: τὸν θ'.
[3] ἐωνημένην Reiske: ὠν-.   [4] ἐνεπόλησαν Scaliger: ἐνεπώλ-.

supply our needs but not large enough to defray
the cost of public services. An indication of this
is that each of us received a dowry of only 20 minae
with his wife, and so small a dowry would not be
given to a husband with a large fortune. Stratocles,
however, happened to receive an addition of more
than two and a half talents to his fortune; for
Theophon, his wife's brother, at his death adopted
one of his daughters and left her his property, consisting of land at Eleusis worth two talents, 60
sheep, 100 goats, furniture, a fine horse which he
rode when he was a cavalry commander, and all the
rest of his goods and chattels. Having had complete
control of this property for nine whole years, he
left a fortune of 5 talents 3000 drachmae, including his patrimony but excluding the fortune left
to his daughter by Theophon. His property com-
prised land at Thria [a] worth two and a half talents,
a house at Melite [b] bringing 3000 drachmae, and
another at Eleusis bringing 500 drachmae. These
made up his real property, the land being let at
12 minae and the houses at 3, a total of 15 minae;
but he had also about 4000 drachmae lent out at
interest, the yearly income of which, at a monthly
rate of 9 obols, amounts to 720 drachmae. He thus
had a total income of rather more than 20 minae.
Besides this he left furniture, sheep, barley, wine,
and fruits, the sale of which brought in 4900 drachmae;
also 900 drachmae were found in the house. In
addition his—that is the child's—mother included
in the inventory made in the presence of witnesses
sums lent without interest, which were recovered,

[a] North-west of Eleusis.
[b] A quarter of Athens west of the Areopagus.

μαρτύρων ἐναντίον ἡ μήτηρ αὐτοῦ, τοῦ παιδός, ἀπ-
εγράψατο. καὶ οὔπω λέγω περὶ τῶν ἄλλων, ἃ
κατελείφθη μὲν οὗτοι δ' οὐκ ἀποφαίνουσιν, ἀλλὰ τὰ
φανερὰ καὶ τὰ ὑπὸ τούτων ὁμολογούμενα. κάλει
δέ μοι τῶν εἰρημένων τοὺς μάρτυρας.

ΜΑΡΤΥΡΕΣ

44 Ἡ μὲν τοίνυν Στρατοκλέους οὐσία καὶ πλείων
ταύτης ἐστίν· ἀλλ' ὕστερον περὶ τῶν παρακλεπτο-
μένων ὑπὸ τούτων ποιήσομαι τοὺς λόγους· ἡ δ'
ἐμὴ πόση τις; χωρίον ἐν Οἰνόῃ πεντακισχιλίων
καὶ Προσπαλτοῖ τρισχιλίων, καὶ οἰκία ἐν ἄστει
δισχιλίων, πρὸς δὲ τούτοις ⟨ὁ⟩[1] κλῆρος ὃν Ἁγνίας
κατέλιπε, περὶ δύο τάλαντα· οὐ γὰρ ἂν οἶδ' ὅτι
πλέον εὕροι[2] τούτου. ταῦτ' ἐστὶ τρία τάλαντα καὶ
τετρακισχίλιαι μόνον, δέκα καὶ ἑκατὸν μναῖς
45 ἐλάττω τῶν τοῦ παιδός. κἀγὼ μὲν ἐγκαταλογί-
ζομαι καὶ τὰ τοῦ ὑέος τοῦ ἐκποιηθέντος εἰς ταῦτα,
τοῖς τοῦ παιδὸς δὲ οὐ προσέθηκα τὴν Θεοφῶντος
οὐσίαν, πένθ' ἡμιταλάντων οὖσαν, ἐφ' ᾗ[3] ἐποιήσατο
τὴν ἀδελφὴν αὐτοῦ· ῥᾳδίως γὰρ ἂν εὑρεθείη καὶ
ὀκτὼ ταλάντων ὁ τούτων οἶκος· ἀλλ' ἐκεῖνα
ἀφῄρηται χωρίς. κἀμοὶ μὲν ὁ κλῆρος ὃν Ἁγνίας
κατέλιπεν, οὗτος οὔπω βέβαιός ἐστι· δίκαι γὰρ
46 ἐνεστήκασι ψευδομαρτυριῶν, κελεύει δ' ὁ νόμος,
ἐὰν ἁλῷ τις τῶν ψευδομαρτυριῶν, πάλιν ἐξ ἀρχῆς
εἶναι περὶ αὐτῶν τὰς λήξεις· τὰ δὲ τοῦ παιδὸς
ὡμολογημένα καὶ ἀναμφισβήτητα καταλέλοιπε
Στρατοκλῆς. ὅτι δὲ τοσαῦτά ἐστι τἀμὰ σὺν

---

[1] ὁ add. Schoemann. [2] εὕροι Bekker: εὕρη.
[3] ᾗ Schoemann: ἤν.

amounting to nearly 1000 drachmae. I make no mention now of the other property which was left, but which my opponents refuse to disclose ; I only include what was declared and admitted by them. Please call the witnesses in support of the above statements.

WITNESSES

Stratocles' fortune amounts to even more than this ; but I will deal later with my opponents' embezzlements. Now to what does my fortune amount ? I have a property at Oenoë worth 5000 drachmae and another at Prospalta worth 3000 drachmae and a house in Athens worth 2000 drachmae ; to this must be added the estate left by Hagnias, worth about two talents ; for I am sure that it would not fetch more than this. This gives a total of only three talents 4000 drachmae—110 minae less than the fortune of the child. I include in the reckoning the fortune of my son, who was adopted into another family, while I excluded from the child's fortune the property of Theophon, $2\frac{1}{2}$ talents, which he left to the boy's sister when he adopted her ; for their family property could be easily reckoned at eight talents, but the money which came from Theophon has been reckoned separately. On my side, the estate left by Hagnias is not yet secured to me ; for trials for perjury are still pending, and the law ordains that, if there is any conviction for perjury, the action claiming an estate must be heard over again. On the other hand, the child's fortune bequeathed to him by Stratocles is admitted and not contested. To prove that this is the amount of my property, including that of my son who has been adopted into another

421

τοῖς τοῦ ἐκποιήτου ὑέος, καὶ ψευδομαρτυριῶν
ἐνεστᾶσι δίκαι περὶ τῶν Ἁγνίου, λαβὲ τὰς μαρτυρίας καὶ ἀνάγνωθι.

MAPTΥΡΙAI

[89]
47 Ἆρα μικρὰ τὰ διάφορα | ἑκατέροις τῆς οὐσίας
ἡμῶν ἐστιν, ἀλλ᾽ οὐ τηλικαῦτα ὥστε <ἐμοὶ>[1]
μηδεμίαν γενέσθαι παρὰ[2] τοὺς Στρατοκλέους παῖδας; <οὐκοῦν>[3] οὐκ ἄξιον τοῖς τούτου[4] λόγοις
πιστεύειν, ὃς τοσαύτης οὐσίας καταλελειμμένης
ἐτόλμησεν ἐπὶ διαβολῇ ψεύσασθαι κατ᾽ ἐμοῦ
τηλικαῦτα[5] τὸ μέγεθος. καταλογίζεται τοίνυν ὡς
ἐγὼ τρεῖς κλήρους εἰληφὼς καὶ πολλῶν χρημάτων
εὐπορῶν ἀφανίζω τὴν οὐσίαν, ἵν᾽ ὡς ἐλάχισθ᾽
ὑμεῖς αὐτῶν ἀπολαύητε.[6] τοῖς γὰρ μηδὲν δίκαιον ἔχουσι περὶ τῶν πραγμάτων λέγειν ἀνάγκη
πορίζεσθαι τοιούτους λόγους, ἐξ ὧν [ἂν] δια-
βάλλοντες πλέον ἔχειν δυνήσονται τῶν ἀντιδίκων.
48 ἐμοὶ δὲ μάρτυρές ἐστε πάντες ὅτι οἱ τῆς ἐμῆς
γυναικὸς ἀδελφοί, Χαιρέλεως καὶ Μακάρτατος, οὐ
τῶν λῃτουργούντων ἦσαν ἀλλὰ τῶν βραχεῖαν
κεκτημένων οὐσίαν. Μακάρτατον γὰρ ἴστε ὅτι
τὸ χωρίον ἀποδόμενος καὶ τριήρη πριάμενος καὶ
ταύτην πληρωσάμενος εἰς Κρήτην ἐξέπλευσεν· οὐ
γὰρ τὸ ἔργον ἀφανὲς ἐγένετο, ἀλλὰ καὶ λόγον
ἐν τῷ δήμῳ παρέσχε, μὴ πόλεμον ἡμῖν ἀντ᾽
εἰρήνης ἐκεῖνος πρὸς Λακεδαιμονίους ποιήσειε.
49 Χαιρέλεως δὲ τὸ Προσπαλτοῖ χωρίον κατέλιπεν, ὃ

---

[1] ἐμοὶ add. Schoemann.   [2] παρὰ sched. Eton.: περὶ.
[3] οὐκοῦν add. Buermann.
[4] τοῖς τούτου Reiske: τούτοις τοῖς.
[5] τηλικαῦτα Aldus: -αύτη.   [6] ἀπολαύητε Aldus: -οιτε.

family, and that suits for perjury in connexion with Hagnias's estate are still pending, take and read the depositions.

DEPOSITIONS

Is the difference, then, trifling between our respective fortunes? Or rather, is it not so great that mine is nothing in comparison with that of the children of Stratocles? No credence must therefore be attached to the statements of my opponent, who, though so large a fortune has been left to the children, has dared to utter such lies with the object of discrediting me. According to his reckoning I have received three inheritances and am in enjoyment of a large fortune, but I hide my wealth in order that you may derive as little advantage from it as possible.[a] Those who have no just claims to urge on the matters at issue must bring forward such arguments as will give them an advantage over their adversaries by calumniating them. But you all are my witnesses that my wife's brothers, Chaereleos and Macartatus, were not among those who supported public burdens but among those who possessed only slender fortunes. You know that Macartatus sold his land and bought a trireme which he manned and sailed away in it to Crete. The affair was no secret but even gave rise to a discussion in the Assembly,[b] since it was feared that he might bring about a state of war instead of peace between us and the Lacedaemonians. Chaereleos left the estate at Prospalta, which would not fetch more

---

[a] *i.e.*, in order to avoid the performance of public services.
[b] See Introduction, pp. 386, 387.

πλέον οὐκ ἂν εὕροι[1] τριάκοντα μνῶν. συνέβη δὲ
τὸν μὲν ταῦτα καταλιπόντα τελευτῆσαι πρότερον
ἢ Μακάρτατον, ἐκεῖνον δὲ μετὰ ταύτης τῆς οὐσίας,
ἣν ἔχων ἐξέπλευσεν· ἅπαντα γὰρ καὶ τὴν τριήρη
καὶ αὐτὸν κατὰ τὸν πόλεμον ἀπώλεσε. κατα-
λειφθέντος δὲ τοῦ Προσπαλτοῖ χωρίου καὶ γιγνομένου τῆς ἐκείνων ἀδελφῆς, ἐμῆς δὲ γυναικός,
ἐπείσθην ὑπ' ἐκείνης εἰσποιῆσαι Μακαρτάτῳ τὸν
ἕτερον τῶν παίδων· οὐχ ἵνα ⟨μὴ⟩[2] λῃτουργοίην,
50 εἰ[3] προσγένοιτό μοι τοῦτο τὸ χωρίον. ὁμοίως γὰρ
καὶ [μὴ] εἰσποιήσαντος τοῦτό γ' ὑπῆρχεν· οὐδὲ
γὰρ ἐλῃτούργουν διὰ τοῦτό γ' ἧττον οὐδέν, ἀλλὰ
καὶ τῶν εἰσφερόντων ἦν καὶ τῶν τὰ προσταττόμενα ὑμῖν ἅπαντα ποιούντων. ὁ δὲ ὡς περὶ
ἀχρήστου μὲν πλουσίου δὲ ἐπὶ διαβολῇ ποιεῖται
τούτους τοὺς λόγους.

Ἐγὼ δ' ἐν κεφάλαιον ἐρῶ πάντων μέγιστον, ὃ
καὶ ὑμῖν οἶδ' ὅτι δόξει δίκαιον. κοινώσασθαι γὰρ
ἐθέλω τὴν οὐσίαν τὴν ἐμὴν τῇ τοῦ παιδός, καὶ εἴτε
πολλὰ εἴτ' ὀλίγα ἐστίν, ἐν κοινῷ γενομένης λάβω-
μεν τὰ ἡμίσεα ἑκάτερος, ἵνα μηδὲν πλέον ἔχῃ
ἅτερος τοῦ ἑτέρου τοῦ προσήκοντος· ἀλλ' οὐκ
ἐθελήσει.

ΛΕΙΠΕΙ

---

[1] εὕροι Reiske: εὕρητε.
[2] μὴ add. Bekker.   [3] εἰ Aldus: εἰς.

[a] This child is the Macartatus attacked in the pseudo-
Demosthenic speech, [Dem.] xliii.
[b] Theopompus has already stated that his fortune did
not render him liable to perform any λειτουργία (e.g., the

424

than 30 minae. The brother who left this estate happened to die before Macartatus, who in his turn perished with all the property which he took with him when he sailed away ; for he lost the trireme and everything else in the war as well as his own life. The estate at Prospalta was left and passed to their sister, who is my wife, and I was persuaded by her to allow one of our two sons to be adopted into the family of Macartatus.[a] My object was not to avoid the performance of public services which the addition of this estate would involve ; for my having allowed my son to be adopted made no difference, for indeed I performed public services [b] no less than before, but was among those who paid war contributions and carried out all the duties imposed by the state. My opponent, however, in representing me as a wealthy but unprofitable citizen is using these terms to calumniate me.

As the strongest argument of all, I will sum the matter up in a single proposal, which, I am sure, will appear to you to be just. I am willing to bring my whole estate into hotchpotch with that of the child, and let us each take half of the aggregate amount, whether it be large or small, so that neither party may have more than is fitting ; but my opponent will never consent to this.

[*The rest of the speech is lacking.*]

τριηραρχία or χορηγία)**:** he is, therefore, here using the term in the wider sense of the duties of a citizen (*e.g.*, the payment of the war-tax and service in the army).

XII. ON BEHALF OF EUPHILETUS

XII. ON BEHALF OF EUPHILETUS

INTRODUCTION

These chapters, which have been preserved to us by Dionysius of Halicarnassus (*De Isaeo*, 17), are now usually numbered by the editors as the 12th Oration instead of being placed, as formerly, among the fragments. The subject differs from that of all the other speakers, being concerned with a question not of inheritance but of civic rights. Euphiletus, the son of Hegesippus, had been struck off the roll of the deme of Erchia by the decision of his fellow-demesmen, on whom a law had conferred the right of revising their lists. Anyone so rejected had the right of appeal to the courts, but the failure of the appeal involved the sale of the appellant into slavery and the confiscation of his property. The case had already been twice heard before arbitrators, who had given their decision in favour of Euphiletus ; nevertheless a majority of the demesmen seem to have persisted in their exclusion of him. The grounds of their action are not stated, except that the speaker alleges a private grudge. Thus no other course was left to Euphiletus, if he believed in the justice of his claims, except to bring the case into court.

The speech was delivered not by Euphiletus

himself but by his elder half-brother, the son of
Hegesippus by a former marriage, acting as his
advocate. As Dionysius explains in his argument,
the facts of the case have already been stated and
the various relatives have given their evidence ; the
speaker in the passage before us then proceeds to
confirm the evidence by showing that the witnesses
had no motive for foisting an alien into the deme ;
on the contrary, such witnesses as the speaker's
maternal uncle or his brothers-in-law, who stood in
no sort of relationship to Euphiletus, would have
every motive for giving evidence against his claim,
since the establishment of his rights as a citizen
would mean that he would share in the paternal
estate to the detriment of the speaker and his
sisters. Dionysius seems justified in the admiration
which he expresses for the argumentative skill
displayed by Isaeus in this passage.

As we have seen, the argument prefixed to the
passage by Dionysius states that the occasion of
the speech was the passing of a law ordering the
revision by the demes of their lists of members.
Our authorities ascribe the proposal for this revision
to Demophilus and place it in the archonship of
Archias (346–345 B.C.). The law seems to have given
rise to considerable commotion and to have been
the cause of much litigation. We know the title
of another speech of a similar character to the
present, composed by Isaeus, *Against Boeotus, on his
appeal against the demesmen* (Πρὸς Βοιωτὸν ἐκ δημοτῶν
ἔφεσις), and the speech of Demosthenes *Against
Eubulides* (Or. lvii.) deals with the same topic. If
this date is accepted, we must place the present
speech in the year 344–343 B.C., two years having

ON BEHALF OF EUPHILETUS

elapsed while the case was before the arbitrators. This seems a very late date for Isaeus to be still writing speeches, but the only alternative is to suppose an earlier decree to the same effect as that of Demophilus, for which we have no evidence and which is in itself improbable.

THE TEXT.—The treatise by Dionysius of Halicarnassus Περὶ τῶν ἀρχαίων ῥητόρων, which deals with Isaeus and includes this and other fragments, is preserved in MSS. which belong to two main families, which are best represented by a Florentine codex (F) in the Library of San Lorenzo (No. LIX., 15) and a Milan MS. (M) in the Ambrosian Library (No. D 119, Sup.). An account of the MSS. and a full *apparatus criticus* are to be found in *Dionysii Halicarnasei opuscula*, ediderunt H. Usener et L. Radermacher, vol. i. (Leipzig, Teubner, 1899). It has been considered sufficient in the present edition to note the emendations introduced into the text which have no MS. authority.

XII. ΥΠΕΡ ΕΥΦΙΛΗΤΟΥ

ΥΠΟΘΕΣΙΣ

Τὸν Ἐρχιέων δῆμον εἰς τὸ δικαστήριον προσκαλεῖταί[1] τις τῶν ἀποψηφισθέντων ὡς ἀδίκως τῆς πολιτείας ἀπελαυνόμενος. ἐγράφη γὰρ δή τις ὑπὸ τῶν Ἀθηναίων νόμος, ἐξέτασιν γενέσθαι τῶν πολιτῶν κατὰ δήμους, τὸν δὲ ἀποψηφισθέντα ὑπὸ τῶν δημοτῶν τῆς πολιτείας μὴ μετέχειν, τοῖς δὲ ἀδίκως ἀποψηφισθεῖσιν ἔφεσιν εἰς τὸ δικαστήριον εἶναι προσκαλεσαμένοις[1] τοὺς δημότας, καὶ ἐὰν τὸ δεύτερον ἐξελεγχθῶσι, πεπρᾶσθαι αὐτοὺς καὶ τὰ χρήματα εἶναι δημόσια. κατὰ τοῦτον τὸν νόμον ὁ Εὐφίλητος, προσκαλεσάμενος[1] τοὺς Ἐρχιέας ὡς ἀδίκως καταψηφισαμένους αὐτοῦ, τὸν ἀγῶνα τόνδε διατίθεται. προείρηται μὲν δὴ τὰ πράγματα ταῦτ' ἀκριβῶς καὶ πεπίστωται διὰ τῶν μαρτύρων· οἷς δὲ βεβαίως βούλεται ποιῆσαι τὰς μαρτυρίας, τάδ' ἐστίν, ὡς μὲν ἐγὼ δόξης ἔχω, πάντ' ἀκριβῶς ἐξειργασμένα, κρινέτω δὲ ὁ βουλόμενος εἰ τὰ προσήκοντα ἔγνωκα περὶ αὐτῶν.

1   Ὅτι μὲν τοίνυν, ὦ ἄνδρες δικασταί, ἀδελφὸς ἡμῖν ἐστιν οὑτοσὶ Εὐφίλητος, οὐ μόνον ἡμῶν ἀλλὰ καὶ τῶν συγγενῶν ἁπάντων ἀκηκόατε μαρτυρούντων. σκέψασθε δὲ πρῶτον τὸν πατέρα ἡμῶν, τίνος ἕνεκεν ἂν ψεύδοιτο καὶ τοῦτον μὴ ὄντα αὐτοῦ υἱὸν

---

[1] προσκαλεῖταί, προσκαλεσαμένοις, προσκαλεσάμενος Reiske : FM προκ-.

XII. ON BEHALF OF EUPHILETUS

ARGUMENT

(By Dionysius of Halicarnassus)

The Deme of Erchia is summoned before the court by one of its members who has been rejected by its vote and who pleads that he is being unjustly disfranchised. A law had been passed by the Athenians ordering that a revision should be made of the lists of citizens according to demes, and that anyone who was rejected by the votes of his fellow-demesmen should no longer enjoy the rights of citizenship ; those, however, who were unjustly rejected had the right to appeal to the court by summoning the members of the deme, and, if they were again excluded, they were to be sold as slaves and their property confiscated. It is under this law that Euphiletus, having summoned the demesmen of Erchia on the ground that they had unjustly rejected him, instituted the present case. The facts have been already skilfully set forth and confirmed by witnesses. The following passage, in which the orator seeks to confirm the evidence, is composed, in my opinion, with consummate skill, but the reader must decide for himself whether my judgement of it is correct.

Gentlemen, you have heard not only us but also all our kinsmen give evidence that Euphiletus here is our brother. Next consider, in the first place, what motive our father could have for lying and for having adopted Euphiletus as his son, if he

2 εἰσεποιεῖτο. πάντας γὰρ εὑρήσετε τοὺς τὰ τοιαῦτα πράττοντας ἢ οὐκ ὄντων αὐτοῖς γνησίων παίδων ἢ διὰ πενίαν ἀναγκαζομένους ξένους ἀνθρώπους εἰσποιεῖσθαι, ὅπως ὠφελῶνταί τι ἀπ' αὐτῶν δι' αὑτοὺς Ἀθηναίων γεγονότων. τῷ τοίνυν πατρὶ τούτων οὐδέτερον ὑπάρχει· γνήσιοι μὲν γὰρ αὐτῷ ἡμεῖς δύο υἱεῖς ἐσμεν, ὥστε οὐκ ἄν γε δι' ἐρημίαν **3** τοῦτον εἰσεποιεῖτο. ἀλλὰ μὴν οὐδὲ τροφῆς τε καὶ εὐπορίας τῆς παρὰ τούτου δεόμενος· ἔστι γὰρ αὐτῷ ⟨βίος⟩[1] ἱκανός, καὶ χωρὶς τούτου μεμαρτύρηται ὑμῖν τοῦτον ἐκ παιδίου[2] τρέφων καὶ ἀσκῶν καὶ εἰς ⟨τοὺς⟩[3] φράτορας εἰσάγων,[4] καὶ ταῦτα οὐ μικρὰ δαπανήματά ἐστιν. ὥστε τόν γε[5] πατέρα ἡμῶν οὐκ εἰκός ἐστιν, ὦ ἄνδρες δικασταί, μηδὲν ὠφελούμενον οὕτως ἀδίκῳ πράγματι ἐπιχειρῆσαι. **4** ἀλλὰ μὴν οὐδ' ἐμέ γε οὐδεὶς ἀνθρώπων οὕτω τελέως ἂν ἄφρονα ὑπολάβοι, ὥστε τούτῳ μαρτυρεῖν τὰ ψευδῆ, ὅπως τὰ πατρῷα διὰ πλειόνων διανείμωμαι. καὶ γὰρ οὐδ' ἀμφισβητῆσαί μοι ἐξουσία γένοιτ' ἂν ὕστερον ὡς οὐκ ἔστιν ἀδελφὸς οὗτος ἐμοῦ· οὐδεὶς γὰρ ἂν ὑμῶν τὴν ⟨ἐμὴν⟩[6] φωνὴν ἀνάσχοιτ' ἂν ἀκούων, ⟨εἰ⟩[7] νῦν μὲν ὑπόδικον ἐμαυτὸν καθιστὰς μαρτυρῶ ὡς ἔστιν ἀδελφὸς ἡμέτερος, ὕστερον δὲ φαινοίμην τούτοις ἀντιλέγων. **5** οὐ μόνον τοίνυν ἡμᾶς, ὦ ἄνδρες δικασταί, εἰκός ἐστι τἀληθῆ μεμαρτυρηκέναι, ἀλλὰ καὶ τοὺς ἄλλους συγγενεῖς. ἐνθυμήθητε γὰρ πρῶτον μὲν ὅτι οἱ τὰς ἀδελφὰς ἡμῶν ἔχοντες οὐκ ἄν ποτε ἐμαρ-

---

[1] βίος add. Reiske. [2] παιδίου Scheibe: παίδων FM.
[3] τοὺς add. Schoemann. [4] εἰσαγαγὼν Scheibe: εἰσάγων FM.
[5] γε Bekker: τε M, om. F, add. F[2].
[6] ἐμὴν add. Sauppe. [7] εἰ add. Sylburgh.

were not really so. You will find that all those
who do such things either have no legitimate children
of their own or else are constrained by poverty
to adopt aliens in order that they may receive
some assistance from them, because they are
indebted to them for their Athenian citizenship.
Our father had neither of these motives, for in us
he has two legitimate sons, so that he would never
have adopted Euphiletus because he lacked an heir.
Nor again is he in need of any material support or
comfort which Euphiletus could give him ; for he
is possessed of sufficient resources, and further
evidence has been given you that he brought up
Euphiletus and educated him from childhood and
introduced him to the members of his ward—all of
which represents a considerable outlay. So that it is
unlikely, judges, that my father committed so wicked
a crime from which he derived no advantage. Again,
as for myself, no one could imagine me to be so completely insane as to bear false witness in favour of
Euphiletus with the result that I should have to
share my patrimony with a larger number of heirs.
For I should never hereafter be at liberty to plead
that Euphiletus is not my brother ; for none of you
would listen to me for a moment, if, after now
bearing witness that he is my brother and making
myself liable to the penalties of the law,[a] I should
hereafter openly contradict this assertion. Thus,
gentlemen, the probabilities are in favour of my
having given true evidence, and the same is true
of the other relatives. For observe, in the first
place, that the husbands of our sisters would never
have given false evidence in favour of Euphiletus ;

---

[a] *i.e.*, as a perjurer.

τύροιν περὶ τούτου τὰ ψευδῆ· μητρυιὰ γὰρ ἡ
τούτου μήτηρ ἐγεγένητο ταῖς ἡμετέραις ἀδελφαῖς,
εἰώθασι δέ πως ὡς ἐπὶ τὸ πολὺ διαφέρεσθαι ἀλλή-
λαις αἵ τε μητρυιαὶ καὶ αἱ[1] πρόγονοι· ὥστε εἰ
οὗτος ἐξ ἄλλου τινὸς ἀνδρὸς ἦν τῇ μητρυιᾷ καὶ
οὐκ ἐκ τοῦ ἡμετέρου πατρός, οὐκ ἂν ποτε, ὦ
ἄνδρες δικασταί, τοὺς ἑαυτῶν ἄνδρας αἱ ἀδελφαὶ
6 μαρτυρεῖν [εἴασαν καὶ] ἐπέτρεψαν. καὶ μὴν οὐδ᾽[2]
ἂν ὁ θεῖος πρὸς μητρὸς ἡμῖν ὤν, τούτῳ δὲ οὐδὲν
προσήκων δήπου τῇ τούτου μητρὶ ἠθέλησεν ἄν, ὦ
ἄνδρες δικασταί, μαρτυρῆσαι ψευδῆ μαρτυρίαν, δι᾽
ἣν ἡμῖν γίγνεται βλάβη περιφανής, εἴ περ ξένον
ὄντα τοῦτον εἰσποιοῦμεν ἀδελφὸν ἡμῖν αὐτοῖς.
ἔτι τοίνυν, ὦ ἄνδρες δικασταί, πρὸς τούτοις ⟨πῶς⟩[3]
ἄν τις ὑμῶν[4] καταγνοίη ψευδομαρτυριῶν[5] Δημ-
αράτου τουτουὶ καὶ Ἡγήμονος καὶ Νικοστράτου,
οἳ πρῶτον μὲν οὐδὲν αἰσχρὸν οὐδέποτε φανήσονται
ἐπιτηδεύσαντες, εἶτα δ᾽ οἰκεῖοι ὄντες ἡμῖν καὶ εἰδότες ἡμᾶς ἅπαντας[6] μεμαρτυρήκασιν Εὐφιλήτῳ
7 τουτῳὶ τὴν αὑτοῦ συγγένειαν ἕκαστος; ὥστε
ἡδέως κἂν τῶν ἀντιδικούντων ἡμῖν τοῦ σεμνοτά-
του πυθοίμην, εἰ ἄλλοθέν ποθεν ἔχοι ἄν[7] ἐπιδεῖξαι
αὐτὸν Ἀθηναῖον ἢ ἐκ τούτων ὧν καὶ ἡμεῖς Εὐφίλητον ἐπιδείκνυμεν. ἐγὼ μὲν γὰρ οὐκ οἶμαι ἄλλο
τι ἂν αὐτὸν ⟨εἰπεῖν⟩[8] ἢ ὅτι ἡ μήτηρ ἀστή τέ ἐστι
καὶ ⟨γαμετὴ καὶ ἀστὸς⟩[9] ὁ πατήρ, καὶ ὡς ταῦτ᾽
ἀληθῆ λέγει, παρέχοιτ᾽ ἂν αὐτῷ τοὺς συγγενεῖς
8 μάρτυρας. εἶτα, ὦ ἄνδρες δικασταί, εἰ μὲν οὗτοι

[1] αἱ Reiske: οἱ FM.   [2] οὐδ᾽ Bekker: οὐκ FM.
[3] πῶς add. Savile.   [4] ὑμῶν Sylburg: ἡμῶν FM.
436

for his mother had become stepmother to our sisters, and it is customary for differences to exist between stepmothers and the daughters of a former marriage ; so that, if their stepmother had borne Euphiletus to any man other than our father, our sisters would never have allowed their husbands to give evidence in his favour. Again, our uncle, a relative on our mother's side and no kinsman of Euphiletus, would never have consented, judges, to give in favour of Euphiletus's mother evidence which was manifestly against our interests, if Euphiletus were an alien whom we are attempting to introduce into the family as our own brother. Furthermore, judges, how could any of you convict of perjury Demaratus here and Hegemon and Nicostratus, who, in the first place, will never be shown to have lent themselves to any base action, and who, secondly, being our kinsmen and knowing us all, have each borne witness to his own relationship to Euphiletus ? I should like, then, to hear from the most respectable of our opponents, whether he can produce any other sources of evidence to prove his own Athenian citizenship than those which we are employing in support of Euphiletus. I do not think he could urge any plea except that his mother was a citizen and a married woman and his father a citizen, and he would produce his kinsmen to bear witness that he was speaking the truth. Next, judges, if it were our opponents who were

---

⁵ ψευδομαρτυρίων Wyse: -ίαν FM.
⁶ ἅπαντας Reiske: -τα FM.
⁷ ἔχοι ἂν Holwell: ἔχοιεν FM.
⁸ εἰπεῖν add. Sauppe.
⁹ γαμετὴ καὶ ἀστὸς add. Radermacher.

ἐκινδύνευον, ἠξίουν ἂν τοῖς αὑτῶν οἰκείοις ὑμᾶς[1]
πιστεύειν μαρτυροῦσι μᾶλλον ἢ τοῖς κατηγόροις·
νυνὶ δὲ ἡμῶν πάντα ταῦτα παρεχομένων ἀξιώσουσιν
ὑμᾶς τοῖς αὑτῶν πείθεσθαι λόγοις μᾶλλον ἢ τῷ
πατρὶ τῷ Εὐφιλήτου καὶ ἐμοὶ καὶ τῷ ἀδελφῷ καὶ
τοῖς φράτορσι καὶ πάσῃ τῇ ἡμετέρᾳ συγγενείᾳ;
καὶ μὴν οὗτοι μὲν οὐδ᾽ ἐν ἑνὶ[2] κινδυνεύοντες ἰδίας
ἔχθρας ἕνεκα ποιοῦσιν, ἡμεῖς δὲ πάντας ὑποδίκους
9 ἡμᾶς[3] αὐτοὺς καθιστάντες μαρτυροῦμεν. καὶ πρὸς
ταῖς μαρτυρίαις, ὦ ἄνδρες δικασταί, πρῶτον μὲν ἡ
τοῦ Εὐφιλήτου μήτηρ, ἣν οὗτοι ὁμολογοῦσιν ἀστὴν
εἶναι, ὅρκον ὀμόσαι ἐπὶ τοῦ διαιτητοῦ ἐβούλετο ἐπὶ
Δελφινίῳ ἦ μὴν τουτονὶ Εὐφίλητον εἶναι ἐξ αὑτῆς καὶ
τοῦ ἡμετέρου πατρός. καίτοι τίνα προσῆκε μᾶλλον
αὐτῆς ἐκείνης τοῦτο εἰδέναι; ἔπειτα, ὦ ἄνδρες
δικασταί, ὁ πατὴρ ὁ ἡμέτερος, ὃν εἰκός ἐστι μετὰ
τὴν τούτου μητέρα ἄριστα τὸν[4] αὑτοῦ υἱὸν γιγνώσκειν,[5] οὗτος καὶ τότε καὶ νυνὶ βούλεται ὀμόσαι ἦ
μὴν[6] Εὐφίλητον τουτονὶ υἱὸν εἶναι αὑτοῦ ἐξ ἀστῆς
10 καὶ γαμετῆς γυναικός. πρὸς τούτοις τοίνυν, ὦ
ἄνδρες δικασταί, ἐγὼ ἐτύγχανον μὲν τρισκαι-
δεκαέτης ὤν, ὥσπερ καὶ πρότερον εἶπον, ὅτε
οὗτος ἐγένετο, ἕτοιμος δ᾽ εἰμὶ ὀμόσαι ἦ μὴν[7]
Εὐφίλητον τουτονὶ ἀδελφὸν εἶναι ἐμαυτοῦ ὁμο-
πάτριον. ὥστε, ὦ ἄνδρες δικασταί, δικαίως ἂν καὶ
τοὺς ἡμετέρους ὅρκους πιστοτέρους νομίζοιτε ἢ
τοὺς τούτων λόγους· ἡμεῖς μὲν γὰρ ἀκριβῶς
εἰδότες ὀμόσαι περὶ αὐτοῦ θέλομεν, οὗτοι δὲ

---

[1] ὑμᾶς Savile : ἡμᾶς FM.
[2] οὐδ᾽ ἐν ἑνὶ Scheibe : οὐδὲν οὐδενὶ FM.
[3] ὑποδίκους ἡμᾶς Victorius : ὑποδημᾶς F, ὑποδίκους F[2]M.
[4] ἄριστα τὸν Reiske : ἄριστον FM.

438

on their trial, they would demand that you should believe the evidence of their kinsmen rather than their accusers ; and now, when we produce all these proofs, are they going to demand that you should believe what they say, rather than Euphiletus's father and me and my brother and the members of the ward and all our kindred ? Furthermore, our opponents are acting out of personal spite without exposing themselves to any risk, while we are all rendering ourselves liable to the penalties of the law in giving evidence. And in addition to the depositions, judges, in the first place, the mother of Euphiletus, who is admitted by our opponents to be a citizen, expressed before the arbitrators her willingness to swear an oath in the sanctuary of Delphinian Apollo that Euphiletus here was the issue of herself and our father ; and who had better means of knowing than she ? Secondly, judges, our father, who naturally is better able to recognize his own son than anyone else except his mother, was ready on the former occasion, and is ready now, to swear that Euphiletus here is his son by a mother who is a citizen and legally married. In addition to this, judges, I was thirteen years old, as I have already said, when he was born, and I am ready to swear that Euphiletus here is my brother by the same father. You would be justified then, judges, in regarding our oaths as more worthy of credence than the statements of our opponents ; for we, knowing all the facts, are willing to swear oaths concerning him, while they are repeating state-

---

5 γιγνώσκειν Sylburg: ἐγίνωσκεν FM.
6 ἦ μὴν Sylburg: ἡμῖν FM.
7 ἦ μὴν Sylburg: ὑμῖν FM.

439

ταῦτα ἀκηκοότες παρὰ τῶν τούτου διαφόρων ἢ
11 αὐτοὶ πλάττοντες λέγουσι. πρὸς δὲ τούτοις, ὦ
ἄνδρες δικασταί, ἡμεῖς μὲν τοὺς συγγενεῖς μάρτυρας καὶ ἐπὶ τῶν διαιτητῶν καὶ ἐφ' ὑμῶν παρεχόμεθα, οἷς οὐκ ἄξιον ἀπιστεῖν· οὗτοι δέ, ἐπειδὴ
ἔλαχεν ὁ Εὐφίλητος τὴν δίκην τὴν προτέραν τῷ
κοινῷ τῶν δημοτῶν καὶ τῷ τότε δημαρχοῦντι, ὃς
νῦν τετελεύτηκε, δύο ἔτη τοῦ διαιτητοῦ τὴν
δίαιταν ἔχοντος οὐκ ἐδυνήθησαν οὐδεμίαν μαρτυρίαν εὑρεῖν ὡς οὑτοσὶ ἄλλου τινὸς πατρός ἐστιν
ἢ τοῦ ἡμετέρου. τοῖς δὲ διαιτῶσι μέγιστα ⟨ταῦτα⟩[1]
σημεῖα ἦν τοῦ ψεύδεσθαι τούτους, καὶ κατ-
εδιῄτησαν αὐτῶν ἀμφότεροι. καί μοι λαβὲ[2] τῆς
προτέρας διαίτης τὴν μαρτυρίαν.

ΜΑΡΤΥΡΙΑ

12 Ὡς μὲν τοίνυν καὶ τότε ὦφλον[3] τὴν δίαιταν, ἀκηκόατε. ἀξιῶ δέ, ὦ ἄνδρες δικασταί, ὥσπερ οὗτοι
μέγα[4] τοῦτ' ἂν[5] ἔφησαν εἶναι σημεῖον ὡς οὐκ ἔστιν
Ἡγησίππου, εἰ οἱ διαιτηταὶ αὐτῶν ἀπεδιῄτησαν,
οὕτω τὸ νῦν ἡμῖν τοὐναντίον εἶναι μαρτύριον, ὅτι
ἀληθῆ λέγομεν, ἐπεὶ ἔδοξαν αὐτοῖς[6] ἀδικεῖν τοῦτον
Ἀθηναῖον ὄντα καὶ κυρίως πρῶτον ἐγγραφέντα
ὕστερον ἐξαλείψαντες. ὅτι μὲν οὖν ἀδελφὸς ἡμῶν
ἐστιν οὑτοσὶ Εὐφίλητος καὶ πολίτης ὑμέτερος, καὶ
ἀδίκως ὑβρίσθη ὑπὸ τῶν ἐν τῷ δήμῳ συστάντων,
ἱκανῶς οἶμαι ὑμᾶς, ὦ ἄνδρες δικασταί, ἀκηκοέναι.

---

[1] ταῦτα add. Reiske. [2] λαβὲ Reiske: λάβετε FM.
[3] ὦφλον Holwell: ὤφειλον. [4] μέγα Reiske: μετὰ FM.
[5] τοῦτ' ἂν Schoemann: ταῦτα FM.
[6] αὐτοῖς Radermacher: αὐτοὶ FM.

nents which they have heard from his enemies
or uttering their own fabrications. Furthermore,
judges, we are producing before you our kinsmen,
as we produced them before the arbitrators, as
witnesses whom there is no reason for you to disbelieve ; whereas our opponents, when Euphiletus
brought his former case against the community of
the deme and the demarch then in office, who has
since died, though the case was before the arbitrator
for two years, could never find a single piece of
evidence to show that Euphiletus was the son of
any father other than our father. In the opinion
of the arbitrators this was the strongest indication
that our opponents were lying, and they both gave
their award against them. Please take the deposition about the former arbitration.

DEPOSITION

You have now heard that my opponents lost
their case before the arbitrators. I claim, judges,
that, just as they would have declared, if the
arbitrators had decided in their favour, that this
was a strong proof that Euphiletus is not the son
of Hegesippus, so now you should regard as equally
strong evidence of the truth of our contention the fact
that they were considered by the arbitrators to be
doing Euphiletus an injury in having subsequently
deleted his name, though he was a citizen and had
before been legally enrolled. You have, I think,
now heard enough, judges, to convince you that
Euphiletus here is our brother and your fellow-
citizen, and that he has been unjustly insulted by
those who have conspired against him in the deme.

THE LOST SPEECHES AND
FRAGMENTS OF ISAEUS

THE LOST SPEECHES AND FRAGMENTS
OF ISAEUS

BESIDES the fragment of the *Speech for Euphiletus* (Or. xii.), passages from several lost speeches of Isaeus are quoted by Dionysius of Halicarnassus, who also indicates the subject matter of several of them. Numerous short sentences and still more numerous single words are quoted by the lexicographers. It is thus possible to compile a list of some forty-three orations of Isaeus which are lost to us. These are given below in alphabetical order with a short account of their subject, when anything is known about them, and the text and translation of all the existing fragments, except single words, have been added.

I. Πρὸς Ἁγνόθεον.

Against Hagnotheus.

(Harpocration, *s.v.* ἐπισημαίνεσθαι : Dion. Hal. *De Isaeo*, § 8, pp. 598-599 ; § 12, pp. 607-608 [FRS. 1 and 2].)

The editors are in agreement in referring both the passages from Dionysius of Halicarnassus cited above to the same speech. That this speech is that *Against Hagnotheus* has been generally accepted, since Cobet's restoration of the name of Hagnotheus in the second line of the first passage.

A difficult point in connexion with the title of this speech is raised by the fact that Harpocration (*l.c.*) calls it ἡ ἐξούλης Καλυδῶνι πρὸς Ἀγνόθεον ἀπολογία. Now there are several mentions (see below, No. xxiv.) of a speech πρὸς Καλυδῶνα or πρὸς Καλυδῶνα ἐπιτροπῆς. Blass (*Att. Ber.* ii.² 573) is probably right in holding that the title given by Harpocration is a confusion of two titles and that there is no connexion between Hagnotheus and Calydon. The two passages given by Dionysius of Halicarnassus certainly seem to have nothing to do with an ἐξούλης δίκη (action for ejectment) being concerned with a guardianship.

Dionysius prefaces the first passage which he quotes with the following words : " Isaeus in the defence which he composed for a guardian accused by his own nephew,[a] begins as follows."

II. Πρὸς Ἀπολλόδωρον ἀποστασίου ἀπολογία.

Against Apollodorus, a defence against a charge of contumacious conduct.

(Harpocration, *s.vv.* ἀπεργασάμενος, πολέμαρχος, etc.)

This speech, as its title indicates, was the defence of a resident alien, whose patron, Apollodorus, had summoned him for deserting or insulting him. Such cases were tried before the Polemarch (Aristot. *Ath. Pol.* 58 ; [Dem.] xxxv. p. 940).

[a] There is little doubt that ὑπὸ τοῦ ἰδίου ἀδελφιδοῦ, "by his own nephew," should be read for ὑπὸ τῶν ἰδίων ἀδελφῶν, " by his own brothers."

III. Περὶ τῶν ἀποφάσεων.

On the decisions (?).

(Photius, *s.v.* φαῦλον.)

Of this speech nothing is known.

IV. Πρὸς ᾿Αριστογείτονα καὶ ῎Αρχιππον περὶ τοῦ ᾿Αρχεπόλιδος κλήρου.

Against Aristogeiton and Archippus, concerning the estate of Archepolis.

(Dion. Hal. *De Isaeo*, § 15, pp. 613-614; Suidas, *s.v.* διάθεσις [Fr. 3]; Pollux, x. 15 [Fr. 4]; Harpocration, *s.v.* ἐνεσκευασμένην.)

The argument of this speech is recorded by Dionysius of Halicarnassus (*l.c.*) and is as follows : " In the suit against Aristogeiton and Archippus a person claiming an estate, being brother of the deceased, summons the detainer of the personal property to produce it in court.[a] The possessor of the estate enters a special plea against the summons, alleging that the property has been left to him by will. Two points are in dispute, first, whether a will was made or not, secondly, if the will is controverted, which party ought then to have the estate. The speaker, having first dealt with the legal question and having shown from this point of view that the estate which is the subject of litigation ought not to be in the possession of one of the parties before a legal decision has been given, then goes on to his narrative, whereby he shows that the will was never made by the deceased."

• *Cf.* Or. vi. 31.

V. Κατ' Ἀριστοκλέους.

Against Aristocles.

(Harpocration, *s.v.* ὑπερήμεροι, who, however, throws doubt on the genuineness of this speech.)

VI. Κατὰ Ἀριστομάχου.

Against Aristomachus.

(Pollux, ii. 61, *s.v.* ἀνάπηρος [Fʀ. 5] ; ii. 8, *s.v.* νεογιλόν.)

VII. Πρὸς Βοιωτὸν ἐκ δημοτῶν ἔφεσις.

Against Boeotus, in an appeal against the decision of the demesmen.

(Harpocration, *s.vv.* Κειριάδης, λῆξις.)

The occasion of this speech was the passage of a law calling upon the members of the demes to revise their lists ; the date and the effect of this law have been discussed in connexion with Or. xii. (see p. 430), which was delivered under the same circumstances. In Or. xii. Isaeus is supporting the claims of Euphiletus to be included on the roll of the deme ; here he is arguing for the exclusion of Boeotus from the deme of Ceiriadae. The Demosthenic speech *Against Boeotus about the name* (Or. xxxix.) was written against the same person, who was then claiming the name of Mantitheus against his half-brother. In that speech it is maintained that Boeotus was an illegitimate son of Mantias, by whom he had been adopted before his father's death, while Mantitheus was a legitimate son ; no doubt the same argument was used by Isaeus in support of his exclusion from the rights of citizenship.

VIII. Πρὸς τοὺς δημότας περὶ χωρίου.

Against the demesmen concerning an estate.

(Dion. Hal. *De Isaeo*, § 10, p. 603 [Fʀ. 6]; Harpocration, *s.v.* Σφηττός.)

The opening passage of this speech is preserved by Dionysius of Halicarnassus, who states that it was delivered in support of a claim to an estate detained by the members of a deme who had received it as a pledge. It may be concluded from the citation by Harpocration that the deme was that of Sphettus belonging to the tribe Acamantis.

IX. Κατὰ Διοκλέους ὕβρεως.

Against Diocles for violence.

(Harpocration, *s.vv.* καταδικασάμενος, etc.; Pollux, vii. 151; Bekker, *Anecd.* i. p. 173. 26 [Fʀ. 7].)

Fragments of two speeches against Diocles, who also figures in Or. viii. as the instigator of the claimant to the estate of Ciron, who had married Diocles' sister as his second wife. One of these was a prosecution for violence no doubt in connexion with Diocles' treatment of the husband of one of his half-sisters referred to in Or. viii. 41, where it is said that " he imprisoned him by walling him up [a] and by a plot deprived him of his civic rights, and though he was indicted for outrage he has not yet been punished."

[a] The words ἐκπλινθεύσας and κατῳκοδόμησεν quoted by Harpocration from this speech no doubt refer to this incident.

449

X. Πρὸς Διοκλέα περὶ χωρίου.

Against Diocles in the matter of an estate.

(Suidas, *s.v.* πατρῴων [Fr. 8]; Harpocration, *s.v.* 'Αμαζόνιον; Pollux, x. 11.)

Diocles' treatment of another half-sister is the subject of this speech. According to Or. viii. 41, "As for the husband of the next sister, he ordered a slave to kill him and smuggled away the murderer, and then threw the guilt upon his sister, and having terrified her by his abominable conduct he has robbed her son, whose guardian he became, of all his property, and is still in possession of his land and has only given him some stony ground." We learn from a fragment that the present speech was composed for delivery on behalf of Menecrates, and that his father, who had married a half-sister of Diocles, was named Lysimenes.

XI. Πρὸς Διοφάνην ἐπιτροπῆς ἀπολογία.

Against Diophanes, a defence in an action about a guardianship.

(Harpocration, *s.vv.* παρηγγύησεν καὶ παρεγγυηθέντος [Frs. 9 and 10] and ἱερὰ ὁδός.)

XII. Πρὸς Δωρόθεον ἐξούλης.

Against Dorotheus, in an action for forcible ejectment.

(Suidas, *s.vv.* ὁμοῦ [Fr. 11], and ἐπιτήθη; Harpocration, *s.v.* οἰσίας δίκη.)

XIII. Κατ' Ἐλπαγόρου καὶ Δημοφάνους.

Against Elpagoras and Demophanes.

(Harpocration, *s.vv.* σύνδικοι (*cf. Etym. Magn.* p. 734. 57) [Fr. 12], ἀλουργοπωλική, 'Αραφήνιος, etc.)

An oratorical fragment preserved in a papyrus (*Oxyrh. Pap*. iii. 415) has been conjecturally attributed to this speech by the restoration of the names [Elpagor]as and De[mophanes]. Though the restoration of the names is possible, there does not seem sufficient evidence for the inclusion of the passage among the fragments of Isaeus.

XIV. Πρὸς ᾿Επικράτην.

Against Epicrates.

(Lexicon ed. Sakkelion, *B.C.H.* i. (1877) p. 151 [Fr. 13].)

This speech was unknown until the publication of a Demosthenic Lexicon from a manuscript discovered in the island of Patmos.

XV. Πρὸς ῞Ερμωνα περὶ ἐγγύης.

Against Hermon, in the matter of a surety.

(Suidas, *s.v.* ἀνακαῖον (*sic*) [Fr. 14] ; Harpocration, *s.vv.* ἀναγκαῖον, ἀφοσιῶ, Βόθυνος, etc.)

XVI. Πρὸς Εὐκλείδην περὶ τῆς τοῦ χωρίου λύσεως.

Against Eucleides, regarding the release of a plot of land.

(Dion. Hal. *De Isaeo*, § 14, p. 612 ; Harpocration, *s.vv.* Τρικέφαλος [Fr. 15], ᾿Αγνάας, etc. ; Pollux, viii. 48 ; Priscian, *Inst. Gram.* xvii. 18 (p. 70), [Fr. 16].)

This case was no doubt concerned with the release of a piece of land from mortgage.

XVII. Πρὸς Εὐκλείδην τὸν Σωκρατικόν.

Against Eucleides the Socratic.

(Harpocration, *s.v.* ὅτι [Fʀ. 17].)

It is uncertain whether this is a separate speech or identical with No. xv. Eucleides of Megara was present at the death of Socrates (Plato, *Phaedo*, 59 c) and is represented in the *Theaetetus* as devoted to the memory of Socrates ; but it is difficult to see how he could have become involved in a lawsuit at Athens, unless he had become a resident alien at Athens, which is unlikely as he was head of a school of philosophy at Megara.

XVIII. Ὑπὲρ Εὐμάθους, εἰς ἐλευθερίαν ἀφαίρεσις.

On behalf of Eumathes, for the assertion of the liberty of a freedman.

(Dion. Hal. *De Isaeo*, § 5, p. 592 [Fʀ. 18]; Harpocration, *s.v.* ἄγει [Fʀ. 19] ; Suidas, *s.v.* ἐμποδών [Fʀ. 20].)

Dionysius of Halicarnassus introduces his quotation with the following words : " There is a speech of Isaeus in defence of a resident alien Eumathes, who was among those who carried on the business of banking at Athens. When the heir of the man who had given him his liberty tried to seize him as a slave, one of the citizens asserted his right to freedom and pleaded in his defence. His speech opens as follows."

We learn from the fragment preserved by Dionysius of Halicarnassus that the original owner of Eumathes was Epigenes and that the name of his

heir was Dionysius. The citizen who opposed the
enslavement of Eumathes was Xenocles. The result
of his interposition was that Eumathes was set at
liberty but had to appear before the Polemarch
and provide three sureties ; Dionysius then brought
an action claiming his person (δίκη ἀφαιρέσεως).
The passage quoted by Dionysius shows that the
date of the speech is subsequent to 358–357 B.C.
(the archonship of Cephisodotus).

XIX. Κατὰ Θουτίμου.

Against Thutimus.

(Harpocration, *s.v.* Περγασῆθεν.)

XX. Πρὸς Ἰσχόμαχον.

Against Ischomachus.

(Harpocration, *s.v.* χίλιοι διακόσιοι [Fr. 21].)

XXI. Πρὸς Καλλικράτην.

Against Callicrates.

(Suidas, *s.v.* ὁμοῦ [Fr. 22] ; Harpocration, *s.vv.* διασκευά-
σασθαι, ἐνδικάσασθαι.)

XXII. Πρὸς Καλλιππίδην.

Against Callippides.

(Harpocration, *s.v.* ἀντεπιτίθησιν.)

XXIII. Κατὰ Καλλιφῶντος.

Against Calliphon.

(Harpocration, *s.v.* ἐπιτρίταις [Fr. 23].)

XXIV. Πρὸς Καλυδῶνα.

Against Calydon.

(Harpocration, *s.vv.* Ἀνθεμόκριτος [Fʀ. 24], Κεφαλῆθεν, χρῆσται, etc.)

XXV. Κατὰ Κλεομέδοντος.

Against Cleomedon.

(Harpocration, *s.v.* κλητῆρες.)

XXVI. Πρὸς Λυσίβιον περὶ ἐπικλήρου.

Against Lysibius, in the matter of an heiress.

(Pollux, x. 15 [Fʀ. 25]; Suidas, *s.v.* τέως [Fʀ. 26]; Harpocration, *s.vv.* ἐπίδικος, νοθεῖα.)

XXVII. Περὶ τῶν ἐν Μακεδονίᾳ ῥηθέντων.

On the speeches made in Macedonia.

(Harpocration, *s.vv.* Ἀλκέτας, Ἐπικράτης, πέπλος.)

The occasion of this embassy to Macedonia is uncertain. Alcetas, whose name is quoted by Harpocration, was king of the Molossians.

XXVIII. Κατὰ Μεγάρεων.

Against the Megarians.

(Harpocration, *s.v.* Σφοδρίας.)

Harpocration throws doubt on the genuineness of this speech.

XXIX. Πρὸς Μέδοντα περὶ χωρίου.
Against Medon, regarding a plot of ground.
(Harpocration, *s.vv.* πανδαισία, ψευδεγγραφή, etc.)

XXX. Πρὸς Μενεκράτην.
Against Menecrates.
(Harpocration, *s.v.* περιοίκιον [FR. 27].)

XXXI. Μετοικικός.
On the status of a resident alien.
(Harpocration, *s.v.* συλλογῆς.)

XXXII. Ὑπὲρ τῆς Μνησιθέου θυγατρός.
On behalf of the daughter of Mnesitheus.
(Harpocration, *s.v.* ἀπορώτατος [Bekker, *Anecd.* i. 434].)

XXXIII. Ὑπὲρ Νικίου.
On behalf of Nicias.
(Harpocration, *s.vv.* ἀπορρέξαντες, χίλιοι διακόσιοι.)

XXXIV. Πρὸς Νικοκλέα (*sive* Νεοκλέα) περὶ χωρίου.
Against Nicocles (or Neocles) regarding a plot of ground.
(Harpocration, *s.vv.* Θυργωνίδαι, κλητῆρες, etc.)

XXXV. Πρὸς ὀργεῶνας.

Against the members of a religious confraternity.

(Harpocration, *s.vv.* παλίνσκιον [Fr. 28], ἀποφοράν [Fr. 29], ὀργεῶνας, etc.)

The suit in which this speech was delivered appears to have been concerned with the possession of a piece of land.

XXXVI. Περὶ τῆς ποιήσεως.

On the adoption.

(Harpocration, *s.v.* Οἶον.)

XXXVII. Κατὰ Ποσειδίππου.

Against Poseidippus.

(Harpocration, *s.v.* Θορικός.)

XXXVIII. Πρὸς Πύθωνα ἀποστασίου.

Against Python, on an accusation of contumacious conduct.

(Harpocration, *s.vv.* διαμαρτυρία, κλητῆρες.)

Compare Πρὸς Ἀπολλόδωρον ἀποστασίου ἀπολογία (p. 446).

XXXIX. Πρὸς Σάτυρον ὑπὲρ ἐπικλήρου.

Against Satyrus, on behalf of an heiress.

(Harpocration, *s.v.* ἐπίδικος.)

XL. Κατὰ Στρατοκλέουν.
Against Stratocles.
(Harpocration, *s.v.* ὀθνεῖος.)

This is perhaps identical with No. xli.

XLI. Πρὸς Στρατοκλέα.
Against Stratocles.
(Harpocration, *s.vv.* διωλύγιον [Fr. 30], μεῖον [Fr. 31].)

XLII. Τεμενικός.
On a sacred enclosure.
(Harpocration, *s.vv.* ἄμιπποι, Λύκος ἥρωs.)

XLIII. Πρὸς Τιμωνίδην περὶ χωρίου.
Against Timonides, concerning a plot of ground.
(Harpocration, *s.v.* οὐσίας δίκη.)

XLIV. Πρὸς Τληπόλεμον ἀντωμοσία.
Against Tlepolemus, on a special plea.

(Ptolemaeus, Περὶ διαφορᾶς λέξεων, *Hermes*, xxii. (1887) p. 410 [Fr. 32]; Harpocration, *s.v.* ἐπώνια.)

ΑΠΟΣΠΑΣΜΑΤΑ

I. Πρὸς Ἁγνόθεον

1

(Dion. Hal. *De Isaeo*, § 8, pp. 598-599.)[1]

[Th. 22] Ἐβουλόμην μέν, ὦ ἄνδρες δικασταί, μὴ λίαν
οὕτως Ἁγνόθεον[2] πρὸς χρήματ᾽[3] ἔχειν αἰσχρῶς
ὥστε τοῖς ἀλλοτρίοις ἐπιβουλεύειν καὶ δίκας
τοιαύτας λαγχάνειν, ἀλλ᾽ ὄντα γε[4] οὖν ἀδελφιδοῦν
ἐμὸν καὶ κύριον τῆς πατρῴας οὐσίας, οὐ μικρᾶς
ἀλλ᾽ ἱκανῆς ὥστε καὶ λῃτουργεῖν, ὑφ᾽ ἡμῶν αὐτῷ[5]
παραδοθείσης, ταύτης ἐπιμελεῖσθαι, τῶν δ᾽ ἐμῶν
μὴ ἐπιθυμεῖν, ἵνα βελτίων τ᾽ ἐδόκει[6] πᾶσιν εἶναι
σῴζων αὐτὴν καὶ πλείω ποιῶν χρησιμώτερον ὑμῖν
πολίτην παρεῖχεν ἑαυτόν. ἐπεὶ δὲ τὴν μὲν ἀνῄρηκε
καὶ πέπρακε καὶ αἰσχρῶς καὶ κακῶς διολώλεκεν,
ὡς οὐκ ἂν ἐβουλόμην, πιστεύων δ᾽ ἑταιρείαις καὶ
λόγων παρασκευαῖς ἐπὶ τὴν ἐμὴν ἐλήλυθεν,
ἀνάγκη, ὡς ἔοικε, συμφορὰν μὲν εἶναι νομίζειν

---

[1] For the mss. of Dion. Hal. see p. 431.
[2] Ἁγνόθεον Cobet: ἀγνοηθέντα FM.
[3] πρὸς χρήματ᾽ Bekker: προσσχήματ᾽ F, προσχήματ᾽ M.
[4] ἀλλ᾽ ὄντα γε Dobree: ἀλλ᾽ οὐ τό γε FM.
[5] αὐτῷ Reiske: αὐτῶν FM.
[6] τ᾽ ἐδόκει Reiske: τε δοκῇ M, -κῃ F.

---

[a] The speaker had been guardian to Hagnotheus during his minority.

458

FRAGMENTS

I. *Against Hagnotheus*

1

I could have wished, judges, that Hagnotheus were not possessed by so discreditable a passion where money is concerned as to intrigue against the property of others and institute lawsuits such as the present. Since he is my nephew and master of a considerable property, ample enough for the discharge of public services, and handed over to him by us,[a] I would that he took due care of his own estate instead of coveting mine, so that by conserving his wealth he might have enjoyed a better reputation and by increasing it might have shown himself a more profitable member of your community. But since he has squandered, alienated, and disgracefully and wickedly made away with it —conduct which no one deplores more than I do— and now, trusting to the support of his political associates[b] and to methods of chicanery, has attacked my property, no course, it seems, is open to me but to regard it as a misfortune that I have such a man

---

[b] Thucydides (viii. 54) refers to the increasing activity, even in his day, of the political clubs in support of their members who engaged in litigation.

ὅτι τοιοῦτός ἐστιν οἰκεῖος ὤν, ἀπολογεῖσθαι δὲ περὶ ὧν ἐγκέκληκε καὶ ἔξω με τοῦ πράγματος διαβέβληκεν, ὡς ἂν οὖν δυνώμεθα προθυμότατα πρὸς ὑμᾶς.

2

(*Ib.* § 12, pp. 607-608.)

[Th. 23] Πόθεν χρὴ πιστεύεσθαι τὰ εἰρημένα πρὸς θεῶν; οὐκ ἐκ τῶν μαρτύρων; οἴομαί γε. πόθεν δὲ τοὺς μάρτυρας; οὐκ ἐκ τῶν βασάνων; εἰκός γε. πόθεν δέ γε ἀπιστεῖσθαι τοὺς λόγους τοὺς τούτων; οὐκ ἐκ τοῦ φεύγειν τοὺς ἐλέγχους; ἀνάγκη μεγάλη. φαίνομαι τοίνυν ἐγὼ μὲν διώκων ταῦτα καὶ τὰ πράγματα εἰς βασάνους ἄγων, οὗτος δὲ ἐπὶ διαβολὰς καὶ λόγους καθιστάς, ὅπερ ἄν τις πλεονεκτεῖν βουλόμενος ποιήσειεν.[1] ἐχρῆν δὲ αὐτόν, εἴ πέρ τι δίκαιον ἐφρόνει[2] καὶ μὴ παρακρούσασθαι[3] τὰς ὑμετέρας γνώμας ἐζήτει,[4] μὴ μὰ Δία ταῦτα ποιεῖν, ἀλλ᾽ ἐπὶ τὸν λογισμὸν μετὰ μαρτύρων ἐλθεῖν καὶ ἐξετάζειν ἕκαστα τῶν ἐν τῷ λόγῳ, τοῦτον τὸν τρόπον παρ᾽ ἐμοῦ πυνθανόμενον. εἰσφορὰς λογίζῃ πόσας;[5]—τόσας.—κατὰ[6] πόσον ἀργύριον εἰσενηνεγμένας;[7]—κατὰ τόσον καὶ τόσον. —κατὰ ποῖα[8] ψηφίσματα; —ταυτί.—ταύτας εἰλήφασι τίνες;—οἴδε.—καὶ[9] ταῦτα μαρτυρόμενον[10] σκέ-

---

[1] ποιήσειεν Schoemann: ἐποίησε FM.
[2] ἐφρόνει Reiske: φρονεῖ FM.
[3] παρακρούσασθαι Sylburg: -εσθαι FM.
[4] ἐζήτει Reiske: ζητεῖ FM.
[5] πόσας Reiske: πρὸς FM.   [6] κατὰ Reiske: καὶ FM.
[7] εἰσενηνεγμένας Sylburg: -νης FM.
[8] ποῖα Reiske: πόσα FM.
[9] οἴδε. καὶ Buermann: οἱ καὶ FM.
[10] μαρτυρόμενον Buermann: -νοι FM.

460

as a relative, and to make my defence before you against the charges which he has brought, and his entirely irrelevant calumnies, with all the energy of which I am capable.

2

Why, in heaven's name, ought you to believe what I have said ? Ought you not to do so because of the witnesses ? I certainly think so. But why should you believe the witnesses ? Should you not do so, because of the examinations under torture ? It is only reasonable. And why should you disbelieve the story of my opponents ? Should you not do so because they refuse the usual tests ? This is an absolutely necessary consequence.[a] It is quite obvious, then, that I am pursuing this course [b] and bringing the case to the test of examination under torture, while my opponent makes it an occasion for calumnies and argument, as a man would do whose sole object is to win his case. If he had any thoughts of justice and were not seeking to mislead your judgement, he ought not, by heaven, to be acting like this but ought to proceed to an exact reckoning supported by witnesses and examine every item in the accounts, interrogating me in the following manner : " How much do you reckon for taxes ? " " So much." " On what basis were they paid ? " " On such and such a basis." " In accordance with what decrees ? " " These." " Who have received the contributions ? " " So and so." And

---

[a] Cf. Or. viii. 28, where the same commonplace is found.
[b] The words διώκων ταῦτα are perhaps corrupt : Rauchenstein suggests διακριβῶν πάντα, " particularizing every detail."

ψασθαι, τὰ ψηφίσματα, τὸ πλῆθος τῶν εἰσφορῶν, τὰ εἰσενηνεγμένα, τοὺς λαβόντας, καὶ εἰ μὲν εὖ τε <καὶ καλῶς εἶχε>,[1] τῷ λόγῳ πιστεύειν, εἰ δὲ μή, νῦν παρασχέσθαι μάρτυρας, εἴ τι ψεῦδος ἦν ὧν ἐλογισάμην αὐτῷ.[2]

[1] καὶ καλῶς εἶχε add. Sauppe.
[2] αὐτῷ Buermann: -τῆς FM.

[Th. 1] IV. Πρὸς Ἀριστογείτονα καὶ Ἄρχιππον περὶ τοῦ Ἀρχεπόλιδος κλήρου

3

(Suidas, s.v. διάθεσις.)

Μετὰ ταύτην τοίνυν τὴν ἀπόκρισιν ἑτέραν δια-θήκην ἐκόμισαν, ἣν ἔφασαν Ἀρχέπολιν ἐν Λήμνῳ διαθέσθαι.

4

(Pollux, x. 15.)

[Th. 2] Διαθηκῶν δὲ τεσσάρων ὑπ' αὐτῶν ἐσκευασμέ-νων. . . .

VI. Κατὰ Ἀριστομάχου

5

(Pollux, ii. 61.)

[Th. 3] Κατέλιπεν ἐν τῷ χωρίῳ γέροντας καὶ ἀναπήρους.

VIII. Πρὸς τοὺς δημότας περὶ χωρίου

6

(Dion. Hal. De Isaeo, § 10, p. 603.)

[Th. 4] Μάλιστα μὲν ἐβουλόμην, ὦ ἄνδρες δικασταί, μηδ' ὑφ' ἑνὸς ἀδικεῖσθαι τῶν πολιτῶν, εἰ δὲ μή, τοιού-

he ought to scrutinize my evidence on these points—
the decrees, the number of contributions, the sums
paid, and the receivers of them—and if everything
were exact and in order, he ought to trust my reckoning; if not, he ought now to produce witnesses
regarding any misstatements in the accounts which
I submitted to him.

IV. *Against Aristogeiton and Archippus, in the matter
of the estate of Archepolis*

3

After this reply they produced another will
which they alleged Archepolis had made in Lemnos.

4

Four wills having been forged by them.

VI. *Against Aristomachus*

5

He left on the estate old men and cripples.

VIII. *Against the demesmen, concerning an estate*

6

My desire, judges, would have been never to
suffer injustice at the hands of any one of my fellow-
citizens; or, if that were impossible, to find adver-

τῶν ἀντιδίκων τυχεῖν πρὸς οὓς. ἂν οὐδὲν ἐφρόντιζον
διαφερόμενος. νῦν δέ μοι πάντων πραγμάτων
λυπηρότατον συμβέβηκεν· ἀδικοῦμαι γὰρ ὑπὸ τῶν
δημοτῶν, οὓς περιορᾶν μὲν ἀποστεροῦντας οὐ
ῥᾴδιον, ἀπέχθεσθαι δὲ ἀηδές,[1] μεθ᾽ ὧν ἀνάγκη ‹καὶ
θύειν›[2] καὶ συνουσίας κοινὰς ποιεῖσθαι. πρὸς μὲν
οὖν πολλοὺς χαλεπὸν ἀντιδικεῖν· μέγα γὰρ μέρος
συμβάλλεται ‹τὸ›[3] πλῆθος αὐτοῖς πρὸς τὸ δοκεῖν
ἀληθῆ λέγειν· ὅμως δὲ διὰ τὸ πιστεύειν τοῖς
πράγμασι, πολλῶν μοι καὶ δυσκόλων συμπιπτόν-
των, οὐχ ἡγούμην δεῖν κατοκνῆσαι δι᾽ ὑμῶν πειρᾶσθαι τυγχάνειν τῶν δικαίων. δέομαι οὖν ὑμῶν
συγγνώμην ἔχειν, εἰ καὶ νεώτερος ὢν λέγειν ἐπὶ
δικαστηρίου τετόλμηκα· διὰ γὰρ τοὺς ἀδικοῦντας
ἀναγκάζομαι παρὰ τὸν ἐμαυτοῦ τρόπον τοιοῦτόν τι
ποιεῖν. πειράσομαι δ᾽ ὑμῖν ἐξ ἀρχῆς ὡς ἂν δύνωμαι
διὰ βραχυτάτων εἰπεῖν περὶ τοῦ πράγματος.

---

[1] ἀηδές Sylburg: ἡδέως FM.
[2] καὶ θύειν add. Sauppe.   [3] τὸ add. Sylburg.

IX. Κατὰ Διοκλέους ὕβρεως

7

(Bekker, *Anecd.* p. 173. 26.)

[Th. 5] Ὁ δὲ ἀδελφὸς ὁ ἐμὸς καὶ Κτήσων, οἰκεῖος ὢν
ἡμῖν, συντυγχάνουσι τῷ Ἕρμωνι εἰς Βόθυνον
ἀπιόντι.

X. Πρὸς Διοκλέα περὶ χωρίου

8

(Suidas, *s.v.* πατρῴων.)

[Th. 6] Ἀποφανῶ γὰρ ὑμῖν, ὡς οὐκ ἔστι τῆς ἐπι-

saries, to quarrel with whom would cause me little concern. As it is, the most grievous thing possible has happened to me; I am the victim of injustice at the hands of my fellow-demesmen, whose robbery I cannot easily pass over in silence, yet with whom it is unpleasant to be at enmity, since I am obliged to share their sacrifices and attend their common gatherings. It is difficult to defend oneself at law against a large body of adversaries; for their mere number contributes in no small degree to give their statements an appearance of truth. Nevertheless, since I have confidence in the facts, though many difficulties beset me, I think I ought not to shrink from trying to obtain justice at your hands. I beg you, therefore, to excuse me, if at my early age I have ventured to address a court of law; it is those who are wronging me who constrain me to act thus in a manner alien to my natural character. I will try to put my story before you from the beginning in the briefest possible words.

IX. *Against Diocles for violence*

7

My brother and Cteson, a relative of ours, met Hermon as he was starting for Bothynus.[a]

X. *Against Diocles, in the matter of an estate*

8

I will prove to you that this estate does not belong,

[a] Harpocration (*s.v.*) states that Bothynus was on the Sacred Way leading from Athens to Eleusis.

κλήρου τὸ χωρίον τοῦτο οὐδ' ἐγένετο πώποτε,
ἀλλ' ὡς ἦν πατρῷον Λυσιμένει τῷ πατρὶ Μενε-
κράτους· ὁ δὲ Λυσιμένης ἔσχε τὰ πατρῷα πάντα.

XI. Πρὸς Διοφάνην ἐπιτροπῆς ἀπολογία

9

(Harpocration, s.v. παρηγγύησεν καὶ παρεγγυηθέντος.)

[Th. 7] Τὸ μὲν παρών,[1] τὸ δὲ παρ' ἑτέρων μεταλαβεῖν
παρηγγύησεν.

[1] παρών Sauppe : παρόν.

10

(Harpocration, ib.)

[Th. 8] Τὰ μὲν ἐμοῦ διαλύσαντος, β' τάλαντα καὶ λ'
μνᾶς, τὰ δὲ τοῦ γεωργοῦ παρεγγυηθέντος. . . .

XII. Πρὸς Δωρόθεον ἐξούλης

11

(Suidas, s.v. ὁμοῦ.)

[Th. 9] Εἰς τοσοῦτον πονηρίας ὁμοῦ καὶ τόλμης ἐλήλυθεν.

XIII. Κατ' Ἐλπαγόρου καὶ Δημοφάνους

12

(Harpocration, s.v. σύνδικοι (cf. Etym. Magn. p. 734. 57).)

[Th. 10] Οἱ μετὰ τὰ ἐκ Πειραιῶς, ⟨ὡς⟩[1] ἐγὼ ἀκούω,
σύνδικοι ἦσαν, πρὸς οὓς τὰ δημευόμενα ἀπεφέρετο.[2]

[1] ὡς add. Bekker.
[2] ἀπεφέρετο Baiter-Sauppe : ἀπεφέροντο Etym. Magn. :
ἐπεφέρετο Harpocration.

466

and never has belonged to the heiress, but formed part of the patrimony of Lysimenes, the father of Menecrates, and Lysimenes received the whole of his father's estate.

XI. *Against Diophanes, a defence in an action about a guardianship*

9

Part of the money ⟨he paid⟩ on the spot ; he instructed them to receive payment of the rest from others.

10

Having myself paid part, namely, two talents and thirty minae, and instructions having been given to the farmer to pay the rest. . . .

XII. *Against Dorotheus, in an action for forcible ejectment*

11

To such baseness and at the same time to such impudence has he resorted.

XIII. *Against Elpagoras and Demophanes*

12

Those who after the return from the Peiraeus,[a] as I am told, acted as Syndics,[b] to whom questions of confiscated goods were referred.

[a] *i.e.*, after the expulsion of the Thirty Tyrants and the restoration of the democracy in 403 B.C.
[b] *Cf.* Lysias xvi. 7 (p. 146).

ISAEUS

XIV. Πρὸς Ἐπικράτην

13

(Lexicon ed. Sakkeliou, *B.C.H.* i. (1877) p. 151.)

[Th. 10ᵃ] Οὐ τοίνυν μόνον, ὦ ἄνδρες δικασταί, ταύτην τὴν μαρτυρίαν παρέξομαι, ἀλλὰ καὶ ἐκμαρτυρίαν ἑτέραν Μυρωνίδου, ὃς ἦν τῶν δημοτῶν πρεσβύτατος.

XV. Πρὸς Ἕρμωνα περὶ ἐγγύης

14

(Suidas, *s.v.* ἀνακαῖον (*sic*).)

[Th. 11] Ἑρμοκράτην δὲ εἰς τὸ ἀναγκαῖον ἐνέβαλε φάσκων ἀπελεύθερον εἶναι, καὶ οὐ πρότερον ἀφῆκε πρὶν τριάκοντα δραχμὰς ἐπράξατο.

XVI. Πρὸς Εὐκλείδην περὶ τῆς τοῦ χωρίου λύσεως

15

(Harpocration, *s.v.* Τρικέφαλος.)

[Th. 12] Μικρὸν δ' ἄνω τοῦ Τρικεφάλου παρὰ τὴν ⟨ἐς⟩ Ἑστιαῖαν[1] ὁδόν.

[1] ἐς Ἑστιαῖαν Ross : Ἑστίαν.

16

(Priscian, *Inst. Gram.* xvii. 18 (p. 70).)

[Th. 13] Οὐκ ἂν τὰ ἴδια τὰ ἐμαυτοῦ.

XVII. Πρὸς Εὐκλείδην τὸν Σωκρατικόν

17

(Harpocration, *s.v.* ὅτι.)

[Th. 14] Ὅτι τὰ ἐπικηρυττόμενά τισι χρήματα ἐπὶ τῶν βωμῶν ἐτίθετο.

468

XIV. *Against Epicrates*

13

I will produce, judges, not only this evidence but also a written deposition[a] made by Myronides, who was the senior among the demesmen.

XV. *Against Hermon, in the matter of a surety*

14

He cast Hermocrates into prison, alleging that he was a freedman, and did not release him until he had extracted thirty drachmae from him.

XVI. *Against Eucleides, regarding the release of a plot of land*

15

A little above the Three-headed statue[b] by the road leading to Hestiaea.

16

My private possessions would not be my own.

XVII. *Against Eucleides the Socratic*

17

That sums offered for the apprehension of persons were placed upon the altars.

[a] *Cf.* iii. 18 and note.
[b] According to Harpocration a Hermes, *i.e.* a triple bust mounted on a pillar.

XVIII. Ὑπὲρ Εὐμάθους, εἰς ἐλευθερίαν ἀφαίρεσις

18

(Dion. Hal. *De Isaeo*, § 5, p. 592.)

Th. 15] Ἄνδρες δικασταί, ἐγὼ καὶ πρότερον Εὐμάθει
τουτωὶ[1] ἐγενόμην χρήσιμος, [καὶ] δικαίως, καὶ νῦν,
εἴ τι ἔστιν ἐν ἐμοί, πειράσομαι συσσῴζειν αὐτὸν
μεθ' ὑμῶν· μικρὰ δέ μου ἀκούσατε, ἵνα μηδεὶς
ὑπολάβῃ ὑμῶν ὡς ἐγὼ προπετείᾳ ἢ ἄλλῃ τινὶ
ἀδικίᾳ πρὸς τὰ Εὐμάθους πράγματα προσῆλθον.
τριηραρχοῦντος γάρ μου ἐπὶ Κηφισοδότου ἄρχοντος, καὶ λόγου ἀπαγγελθέντος πρὸς τοὺς
οἰκείους ὡς ἄρα τετελευτηκὼς εἴην ἐν τῇ ναυμαχίᾳ,
οὔσης μοι παρακαταθήκης παρ' Εὐμάθει τουτωί,
μεταπεμψάμενος τοὺς οἰκείους τε καὶ φίλους τοὺς
ἐμοὺς Εὐμάθης ἐνεφάνισε τὰ χρήματα ἃ ἦν μοι
παρ' αὐτῷ, καὶ ἀπέδωκε πάντα ὀρθῶς καὶ δικαίως.
ἀνθ' ὧν ἐγὼ σωθεὶς ἐχρώμην τε αὐτῷ ἔτι μᾶλλον,
καὶ κατασκευαζομένῳ τὴν τράπεζαν προσεισευ-
πόρησα ἀργυρίου, καὶ μετὰ ταῦτα ἄγοντος αὐτὸν
Διονυσίου ἐξειλόμην εἰς ἐλευθερίαν, εἰδὼς ἀφ-
ειμένον ἐν τῷ δικαστηρίῳ ὑπὸ Ἐπιγένους. ἀλλὰ
περὶ μὲν τούτων ἐπισχήσω.[2]

[1] τουτωὶ Scheibe: τούτῳ FM.
[2] ἐπισχήσω Sylburg: ὑποσχήσω FM.

19

(Harpocration, *s.v.* ἄγει.)

[Th. 16] Ἔβλαψέ με Ξενοκλῆς ἀφελόμενος Εὐμάθην εἰς
ἐλευθερίαν, ἄγοντος ἐμοῦ εἰς δουλείαν κατὰ τὸ
ἐμὸν μέρος.

470

XVIII. *On behalf of Eumathes, for the assertion of the liberty of a freedman*

18

On a former occasion, judges, I rendered a service to Eumathes here, as was only right, and on the present occasion I intend to try, to the best of my ability, and save him with your assistance. I beg you to hear a short explanation from me, so that no one of you may imagine that I have interfered in his affairs in a spirit of petulance or from any other wrong motive. When I was trierarch in the archonship of Cephisodotus and news was brought to my relations that I had fallen in the sea-fight,[a] Eumathes here, with whom I had deposited some funds, sent for my relatives and friends and declared the money belonging to me which was in his hands and handed over the whole amount with scrupulous correctness and honesty. As a result of this conduct, when I returned safe home, I became still more intimate with him, and, when he established his bank, I provided him with capital, and afterwards, when Dionysius tried to enslave him, I asserted his liberty, being well aware that he had been liberated by Epigenes in open court. But of this I will say no more.

19

Xenocles wronged me in asserting the liberty of Eumathes when I claimed him for a slave as part of my inheritance.[b]

[a] The naval battle fought off Chios in 358 B.C. at the outbreak of the Social War.
[b] This appears to be a quotation from the adversary's speech.

ISAEUS

20

(Suidas, *s.v.* ἐμποδών.)

[Th. 17] Ἀλλὰ τὸ πρωιζόν, ὦ ἄνδρες δικασταί[1]· τουτὶ γὰρ παντελῶς ἐμποδών ἐστι.

[1] δικασταί Scheibe: Ἀθηναῖοι libri.

XX. Πρὸς Ἰσχόμαχον

21

(Harpocration, s.v. χίλιοι διακόσιοι.)

[Th. 18] Οὐδεὶς Λυσίδης ἐστὶ τῶν διακοσίων καὶ χιλίων.

XXI. Πρὸς Καλλικράτην

22

(Suidas, s.v. ὁμοῦ.)

[Th. 19] Οὐ μὴν ἀλλὰ τούτου πάντα ὁμοῦ ταῦτα ἐπιτάξαντος

XXIII. Κατὰ Καλλιφῶντος

23

(Harpocration, s.v. ἐπιτρίταις.)

[Th. 20] Ἑξακοσίαις δραχμαῖς ἐπιτρίταις

XXIV. Πρὸς Καλυδῶνα

24

(Harpocration, s.v. Ἀνθεμόκριτος.)

[Th. 21] Τό τε βαλανεῖον τὸ παρ' Ἀνθεμοκρίτου ἀνδριάντα

472

20

But consider the recent past, judges ; for this is before your very eyes.

XX *Against Ischomachus*

21

There is no one of the name of Lysides among the Twelve Hundred.[a]

XXI. *Against Callicrates*

22

However since he gave all these instructions at the same time . . .

XXIII. *Against Calliphon*

23

Six hundred drachmae at $33\frac{1}{3}$ per cent interest . . .

XXIV. *Against Calydon*

24

And the bath-house near the statue of Anthemocritus . . .

[a] *i.e.*, the richest class of citizens who were liable to undertake the state services.

XXVI. Πρὸς Λυσίβιον περὶ ἐπικλήρου

25

(Pollux, x. 15.)

[Th. 24] Τοιαῦτα μέντοι οὗτοι ἐπὶ τῷ τεθνεῶτι σκευο-
ποιοῦντες

26

(Suidas, *s.v.* τέως.)

[Th. 25] Ἡγούμεθα γὰρ ἐκείνῃ μὲν τὸν ἐγγυτάτω γένους
δεῖν συνοικεῖν, τὰ δὲ χρήματα τέως μὲν τῆς
ἐπικλήρου εἶναι, ἐπειδὰν δὲ παῖδες ἐπὶ δίετες
ἡβήσωσιν, ἐκείνους αὐτῶν κρατεῖν.

XXX. Πρὸς Μενεκράτην

27

(Harpocration, *s.v.* περιοίκιον.)

[Th. 25a] Καὶ τὸ περιοίκιον καὶ τὴν οἰκίαν

XXXV. Πρὸς Ὀργεῶνας

28

(Harpocration, *s.v.* παλίνσκιον.)

[Th. 26] Μήτε παλίνσκιον γίγνεσθαι τὸ χωρίον

29

(Harpocration, *s.v.* ἀποφοράν.)

[Th. 27] Εἴπερ γοῦν ὥριζον ταῖς ἀποφοραῖς ταύταις τῶν
ποδῶν ἀλλότριον εἶναι τὸ χωρίον
474

XXVI. *Against Lysibius, in the matter of an heiress*

25

My opponents, however, forging documents such as these in the name of the deceased . . .

26

For we consider that the next-of-kin ought to marry this woman, and that the property ought for the present to belong to the heiress, but that, when there are sons who have completed their second year after puberty, they should have possession of it.[a]

XXX. *Against Menecrates*

27

The ground round the house and the house itself . . .

XXXV. *Against the members of a religious confraternity*

28

And that the plot of ground should not become overshadowed . . .

29

Since by these removals of the landmarks they indicated that the plot of ground belonged to someone else . . .

[a] *Cf.* Or. viii. 31.

XLI. Πρὸς Στρατοκλέα

30

(Harpocration, *s.v.* διωλύγιον.)

[Th. 27ª] Πράγματα διωλύγια

31

(Harpocration, *s.v.* μεῖον.)

[Th. 27ᵇ] Παρέστησε μεῖον.

XLIV. Πρὸς Τληπόλεμον ἀντωμοσία

32

(Ptolemaeus, Περὶ διαφορᾶς λέξεων (*Hermes*, xxii. (1887) p. 410).)

[Th. 27ᶜ] Ἐπειδὴ γοῦν οὐκ ἐδόκει χρῆναι πλέον δανεί ζεσθαι

ΑΠΑΡΑΣΗΜΑ

33

(Dion. Hal. *De Isaeo*, § 13, p. 609.)

[Th. 28] Καὶ οὗτος ὁ πάντων ἀνθρώπων σχετλιώτατος οὐ παρεχομένων[1] αὐτῶν μάρτυρας [δοῦναι], ὧι ἐναντίον ἡμῖν ἀποδοῦναί φασιν, [ὧν] ἐκείνοις πιστεύειν προσποιεῖται μᾶλλον ὡς ἀποδεδώκασιν ἡμῖν, ἢ ⟨ἡμῖν⟩[2] ὡς οὐκ ἀπειλήφαμεν. καίτοι πᾶσι φανερόν, [ὡς] οἵ γε[3] τὸν τούτου πατέρα ἀπεστέρουν

---

[1] παρεχομένων Schoemann : -όμενος FM.
[2] ἡμῖν add. Reiske.　　[3] οἵ γε Bekker : ἔοικε FM.

XLI. *Against Stratocles*

30

Important matters[a] . . .

31

He offered a victim for sacrifice smaller than was prescribed.[b]

XLIV. *Against Tlepolemus, on a special plea*

32

Since it did not seem that he ought to borrow more . . .

UNIDENTIFIED FRAGMENTS

33

And my opponent, of all men the most wicked, though they do not produce any witnesses in whose presence they allege that they paid us, claims that you should believe their statement that they have paid us rather than our statement that we have received no payment. Yet it is obvious to all that men who defrauded my client's father when he was in full possession of civic rights, would not have

---

[a] διωλύγια ἀντὶ τοῦ μεγάλα (Harpocration).
[b] The meaning is explained by Harpocration.

ὄντα ἐπίτιμον, ὅτι ἡμῖν ἑκόντες οὐκ ἂν ἀπέδοσαν
εἰσπράξασθαι ⟨δ᾽⟩[1] οὕτως ἔχοντες· οὐκ ἂν ἐδυνή-
θημεν.

[1] δ᾽ add. Sauppe.

34

(Dion. Hal. *De Isaeo*, § 13, p. 610.)

[Th. 29] Ὧι γὰρ ἃ μὲν ὑπῆρχεν ἔξω τῶν ἀποτιμηθέντων
κατελελητούργητο,[1] δανειζομένῳ δ᾽ οὐδεὶς ἂν ἔδωκεν ἐπ᾽ αὐτοῖς ἔτι πλέον οὐδὲν ἀποδεδωκότι τὰς
μισθώσεις, ἔχειν ἐμοὶ προσῆκον ἀναμφισβητήτως,
οὗτοι τηλικαύτην δίκην λαχόντες καὶ σφέτερα
αὐτῶν εἶναι φάσκοντες ἐκώλυσάν με ἐξ αὐτῶν
ποιήσασθαι τὴν ἐπισκευήν.

[1] κατελελητούργητο Buermann : καταλελειτουργηκότα M,
καταλειτουργηκότα F.

35

(Stobaeus, *Florileg.* v. 54.)

[Th. 30] Ἡγοῦμαι μεγίστην εἶναι τῶν λῃτουργιῶν τὸν
καθ᾽ ἡμέραν βίον κόσμιον καὶ σώφρονα παρέχειν.

36

(Stobaeus, *Florileg.* xlvi. 25.)

[Th. 32] Ὅσοι τοὺς ἀδικοῦντας κολάζουσιν, οὗτοι τοὺς
ἄλλους ἀδικεῖσθαι κωλύουσιν.

37

(Stobaeus, *Florileg.* xlviii. 25.)

[Th. 31] Χρὴ τοὺς νόμους μὲν τίθεσθαι σφοδρούς,[1] πραο-
τέρως δὲ κολάζειν ἢ ὡς ἐκεῖνοι κελεύουσιν.

[1] σφοδρούς H. P. Richards : -ῶς FM.

478

paid us voluntarily, and that our situation[a] would not have allowed us to obtain recovery of it.

34

For since all I possessed, except property which had been mortgaged, had been spent on state services, and if I had tried to borrow on it, no one would have lent me any more, as I had alienated the revenue from it, though I have an undoubted right to . . .,[b] my opponents, by bringing so serious a suit against me and alleging that the property is theirs, prevented me from using the money to carry out repairs.

35

I consider that the best state-service one can render to the state is orderly and sober conduct in everyday life.

36

They who punish those who wrong them prevent the rest of the citizens from being wronged.

37

The laws which are passed ought to be rigorous, but the punishment which is inflicted ought to be milder than they prescribe.

[a] *i.e.*, because they had lost their civic rights.
[b] The object of ἔχειν appears to have fallen out.

479

38

(Suidas, *s.v.* αἰσθέσθαι.)

[Th. 33] Τί¹ δ᾽ ⟨ἐπὶ⟩² τοιούτων δεῖ³ μαρτυριῶν, ⟨ὧν⟩⁴ οἱ δικάζοντες τὰ μὲν αὐτοί εἰσιν εἰδότες,⁵ ὅτι ὑγίαινεν ὁ παῖς, ⟨τὰ δὲ⟩⁶ τῶν ἑωρακότων αἰσθανόμενοι μαρτυρούντων, τὰ δὲ ἀκοῇ πυνθανόμενοι;

¹ τί Schoemann: τὰ libri.   ² ἐπὶ add. Sauppe.
³ δεῖ Schoemann: δὴ libri.   ⁴ ὧν add. Bernadakis.
⁵ εἰσιν εἰδότες Sauppe: συνειδότες libri.
⁶ τὰ δὲ add. Schoemann.

39

(Priscian, xviii. 25, p. 230.)

[Th. 34] Ὅταν ἔλθῃ, εἰώθει παρ᾽ ἐμοὶ κατάγεσθαι. Et iterum: ὅταν ἔλθω, παρ᾽ ἐκείνῳ κατηγόμην.

40

(Pollux, iii. 6.)

[Th. 35] Ἐκ τῆς Ἀναξίωνος γέννας καὶ Πολυαράτου ὄντα

41

(Pollux, viii. 33.)

[Th. 36] Εἰς Ἄρειον πάγον αὐτῷ ἐπέσκημμαι.

38

What need is there for depositions in such circumstances, when those who are trying the case themselves know part of the truth, namely, that the child was in good health, and can learn the other facts from eyewitnesses or from hearsay?

39

Whenever he came, he used to stay at my house. Whenever I came, I used to stay at his house.

40

Of the family of Anaxion and Polyaratus

41

I denounced him before the Areopagus.

INDEX

483

INDEX

INDEX

485

INDEX

486

INDEX

Printed in Great Britain by
CLARK CONSTABLE (1982) LIMITED, *Edinburgh*

THE LOEB CLASSICAL LIBRARY

VOLUMES ALREADY PUBLISHED

LATIN AUTHORS

AMMIANUS MARCELLINUS. J. C. Rolfe. 3 Vols.

APULEIUS: THE GOLDEN ASS (METAMORPHOSES). W. Adlington (1566). Revised by S. Gaselee.

ST. AUGUSTINE: CITY OF GOD. 7 Vols. Vol. I. G. E. McCracken. Vol. II. W. M. Green. Vol. III. D. Wiesen. Vol. IV. P. Levine. Vol. V. E. M. Sanford and W. M. Green. Vol. VI. W. C. Greene. Vol. VII. W. M. Green.

ST. AUGUSTINE, CONFESSIONS OF. W. Watts (1631). 2 Vols.

ST. AUGUSTINE: SELECT LETTERS. J. H. Baxter.

AUSONIUS. H. G. Evelyn White. 2 Vols.

BEDE. J. E. King. 2 Vols.

BOETHIUS: TRACTS AND DE CONSOLATIONE PHILOSOPHIAE. Rev. H. F. Stewart and E. K. Rand. Revised by S. J. Tester.

CAESAR: ALEXANDRIAN, AFRICAN AND SPANISH WARS. A. G. Way.

CAESAR: CIVIL WARS. A. G. Peskett.

CAESAR: GALLIC WAR. H. J. Edwards.

CATO AND VARRO: DE RE RUSTICA. H. B. Ash and W. D. Hooper.

CATULLUS. F. W. Cornish; TIBULLUS. J. B. Postgate; and PERVIGILIUM VENERIS. J. W. Mackail.

CELSUS: DE MEDICINA. W. G. Spencer. 3 Vols.

CICERO: BRUTUS AND ORATOR. G. L. Hendrickson and H. M. Hubbell.

CICERO: DE FINIBUS. H. Rackham.

CICERO: DE INVENTIONE, etc. H. M. Hubbell.

CICERO: DE NATURA DEORUM AND ACADEMICA. H. Rackham.

CICERO: DE OFFICIIS. Walter Miller.

CICERO: DE ORATORE, etc. 2 Vols. Vol. I: DE ORATORE, Books I and II. E. W. Sutton and H. Rackham. Vol. II: DE ORATORE, Book III; DE FATO; PARADOXA STOICORUM; DE PARTITIONE ORATORIA. H. Rackham.

CICERO: DE REPUBLICA, DE LEGIBUS. Clinton W. Keyes.

THE LOEB CLASSICAL LIBRARY

NEMESIANUS, AVIANUS, with "Aetna," "Phoenix" and other poems. J. Wight Duff and Arnold M. Duff. 2 Vols.

MINUCIUS FELIX. *Cf.* TERTULLIAN.

OVID : THE ART OF LOVE AND OTHER POEMS. J. H. Mozley. Revised by G. P. Goold.

OVID : FASTI. Sir James G. Frazer. [by G. P. Goold.

OVID : HEROIDES AND AMORES. Grant Showerman. Revised

OVID : METAMORPHOSES. F. J. Miller. 2 Vols. Vol. I revised by G. P. Goold.

OVID : TRISTIA AND EX PONTO. A. L. Wheeler.

PERVIGILIUM VENERIS. *Cf.* CATULLUS.

PETRONIUS. M. Heseltine ; SENECA : APOCOLOCYNTOSIS. W. H. D. Rouse. Revised by E. H. Warmington.

PHAEDRUS AND BABRIUS (Greek). B. E. Perry.

PLAUTUS. Paul Nixon. 5 Vols.

PLINY : LETTERS, PANEGYRICUS. B. Radice. 2 Vols.

PLINY : NATURAL HISTORY. 10 Vols. Vols. I-V. H. Rackham. Vols. VI-VIII. W. H. S. Jones. Vol. IX. H. Rackham. Vol. X. D. E. Eichholz.

PROPERTIUS. H. E. Butler.

PRUDENTIUS. H. J. Thomson. 2 Vols.

QUINTILIAN. H. E. Butler. 4 Vols.

REMAINS OF OLD LATIN. E. H. Warmington. 4 Vols. Vol. I (Ennius and Caecilius). Vol. II (Livius, Naevius, Pacuvius, Accius). Vol. III (Lucilius, Laws of the XII Tables). Vol. IV (Archaic Inscriptions).

RES GESTAE DIVI AUGUSTI. *Cf.* VELLEIUS PATERCULUS.

SALLUST. J. C. Rolfe.

SCRIPTORES HISTORIAE AUGUSTAE. D. Magie. 3 Vols.

SENECA : APOCOLOCYNTOSIS. *Cf.* PETRONIUS.

SENECA : EPISTULAE MORALES. R. M. Gummere. 3 Vols.

SENECA : MORAL ESSAYS. J. W. Basore. 3 Vols.

SENECA : NATURALES QUAESTIONES. T. H. Corcoran. 2 Vols.

SENECA : TRAGEDIES. F. J. Miller. 2 Vols.

SENECA THE ELDER. M. Winterbottom. 2 Vols.

SIDONIUS : POEMS AND LETTERS. W. B. Anderson. 2 Vols.

SILIUS ITALICUS. J. D. Duff. 2 Vols.

STATIUS. J. H. Mozley. 2 Vols.

SUETONIUS. J. C. Rolfe. 2 Vols.

TACITUS : AGRICOLA AND GERMANIA. M. Hutton ; DIALOGUS. Sir Wm. Peterson. Revised by R. M. Ogilvie, E. H. Warmington, M. Winterbottom.

TACITUS : HISTORIES AND ANNALS. C. H. Moore and J. Jackson. 4 Vols.

THE LOEB CLASSICAL LIBRARY

TERENCE. John Sargeaunt. 2 Vols.
TERTULLIAN: APOLOGIA AND DE SPECTACULIS. T. R. Glover;
MINUCIUS FELIX. G. H. Rendall.
TIBULLUS. *Cf.* CATULLUS.
VALERIUS FLACCUS. J. H. Mozley.
VARRO: DE LINGUA LATINA. R. G. Kent. 2 Vols.
VELLEIUS PATERCULUS AND RES GESTAE DIVI AUGUSTI.
F. W. Shipley.
VIRGIL. H. R. Fairclough. 2 Vols.
VITRUVIUS: DE ARCHITECTURA. F. Granger. 2 Vols.

GREEK AUTHORS

ACHILLES TATIUS. S. Gaselee.
AELIAN: ON THE NATURE OF ANIMALS. A. F. Scholfield.
3 Vols.
AENEAS TACTICUS, ASCLEPIODOTUS AND ONASANDER. The
Illinois Greek Club.
AESCHINES. C. D. Adams.
AESCHYLUS. H. Weir Smyth. 2 Vols.
ALCIPHRON, AELIAN AND PHILOSTRATUS: LETTERS. A. R.
Benner and F. H. Fobes.
APOLLODORUS. Sir James G. Frazer. 2 Vols.
APOLLONIUS RHODIUS. R. C. Seaton.
THE APOSTOLIC FATHERS. Kirsopp Lake. 2 Vols.
APPIAN: ROMAN HISTORY. Horace White. 4 Vols.
ARATUS. *Cf.* CALLIMACHUS: HYMNS AND EPIGRAMS.
ARISTIDES. C. A. Behr. Vol. I.
ARISTOPHANES. Benjamin Bickley Rogers. 3 Vols. Verse
trans.
ARISTOTLE: ART OF RHETORIC. J. H. Freese.
ARISTOTLE: ATHENIAN CONSTITUTION, EUDEMIAN ETHICS.
VIRTUES AND VICES. H. Rackham.
ARISTOTLE: THE CATEGORIES. ON INTERPRETATION. H. P.
Cooke; PRIOR ANALYTICS. H. Tredennick.
ARISTOTLE: GENERATION OF ANIMALS. A. L. Peck.
ARISTOTLE: HISTORIA ANIMALIUM. A. L. Peck. 3 Vols.
Vols. I and II.
ARISTOTLE: METAPHYSICS. H. Tredennick. 2 Vols.
ARISTOTLE: METEOROLOGICA. H. D. P. Lee.
ARISTOTLE: MINOR WORKS. W. S. Hett. " On Colours,"
" On Things Heard," " Physiognomics," " On Plants,"
" On Marvellous Things Heard," " Mechanical Prob-
lems," " On Invisible Lines," " Situations and Names of
Winds," " On Melissus, Xenophanes, and Gorgias."

THE LOEB CLASSICAL LIBRARY

ARISTOTLE: NICOMACHEAN ETHICS. H. Rackham.
ARISTOTLE: OECONOMICA AND MAGNA MORALIA. G. C. Armstrong. (With METAPHYSICS, Vol. II.)
ARISTOTLE: ON THE HEAVENS. W. K. C. Guthrie.
ARISTOTLE: ON THE SOUL, PARVA NATURALIA, ON BREATH. W. S. Hett.
ARISTOTLE: PARTS OF ANIMALS. A. L. Peck: MOVEMENT AND PROGRESSION OF ANIMALS. E. S. Forster.
ARISTOTLE: PHYSICS. Rev. P. Wicksteed and F. M. Cornford. 2 Vols.
ARISTOTLE: POETICS; LONGINUS ON THE SUBLIME. W. Hamilton Fyfe; DEMETRIUS ON STYLE. W. Rhys Roberts.
ARISTOTLE: POLITICS. H. Rackham.
ARISTOTLE: POSTERIOR ANALYTICS. H. Tredennick; TOPICS. E. S. Forster.
ARISTOTLE: PROBLEMS. W. S. Hett. 2 Vols.
ARISTOTLE: RHETORICA AD ALEXANDRUM. H. Rackham. (With PROBLEMS, Vol. II.)
ARISTOTLE: SOPHISTICAL REFUTATIONS. COMING-TO-BE AND PASSING-AWAY. E. S. Forster; ON THE COSMOS. D. J. Furley.
ARRIAN: HISTORY OF ALEXANDER AND INDICA. 2 Vols. P. Brunt.
ATHENAEUS: DEIPNOSOPHISTAE. C. B. Gulick. 7 Vols.
BABRIUS AND PHAEDRUS (Latin). B. E. Perry.
ST. BASIL: LETTERS. R. J. Deferrari. 4 Vols.
CALLIMACHUS: FRAGMENTS. C. A. Trypanis; MUSAEUS: HERO AND LEANDER. T. Gelzer and C. Whitman.
CALLIMACHUS: HYMNS AND EPIGRAMS, AND LYCOPHRON. A. W. Mair; ARATUS. G. R. Mair.
CLEMENT OF ALEXANDRIA. Rev. G. W. Butterworth.
COLLUTHUS. Cf. OPPIAN.
DAPHNIS AND CHLOE. Cf. LONGUS.
DEMOSTHENES I: OLYNTHIACS, PHILIPPICS AND MINOR ORATIONS: I-XVII AND XX. J. H. Vince.
DEMOSTHENES II: DE CORONA AND DE FALSA LEGATIONE. C. A. and J. H. Vince.
DEMOSTHENES III: MEIDIAS, ANDROTION, ARISTOCRATES, TIMOCRATES, ARISTOGEITON. J. H. Vince.
DEMOSTHENES IV-VI: PRIVATE ORATIONS AND IN NEAERAM. A. T. Murray.
DEMOSTHENES VII: FUNERAL SPEECH, EROTIC ESSAY, EXORDIA AND LETTERS. N. W. and N. J. DeWitt.
DIO CASSIUS: ROMAN HISTORY. E. Cary. 9 Vols.
DIO CHRYSOSTOM. 5 Vols. Vols. I and II. J. W. Cohoon.

THE LOEB CLASSICAL LIBRARY

Vol. III. J. W. Cohoon and H. Lamar Crosby. Vols. IV and V. H. Lamar Crosby.

DIODORUS SICULUS. 12 Vols. Vols. I-VI. C. H. Oldfather. Vol. VII. C. L. Sherman. Vol. VIII. C. B. Welles. Vols. IX and X. Russel M. Geer. Vols. XI and XII. F. R. Walton. General Index. Russel M. Geer.

DIOGENES LAERTIUS. R. D. Hicks. 2 Vols. New Introduction by H. S. Long.

DIONYSIUS OF HALICARNASSUS : CRITICAL ESSAYS. S. Usher. 2 Vols. Vol. I.

DIONYSIUS OF HALICARNASSUS : ROMAN ANTIQUITIES. Spelman's translation revised by E. Cary. 7 Vols.

EPICTETUS. W. A. Oldfather. 2 Vols.

EURIPIDES. A. S. Way. 4 Vols. Verse trans.

EUSEBIUS : ECCLESIASTICAL HISTORY. Kirsopp Lake and J. E. L. Oulton. 2 Vols.

GALEN : ON THE NATURAL FACULTIES. A. J. Brock.

THE GREEK ANTHOLOGY. W. R. Paton. 5 Vols.

THE GREEK BUCOLIC POETS (THEOCRITUS, BION, MOSCHUS). J. M. Edmonds.

GREEK ELEGY AND IAMBUS WITH THE ANACREONTEA. J. M. Edmonds. 2 Vols.

GREEK LYRIC. D. A. Campbell. 4 Vols. Vol. I.

GREEK MATHEMATICAL WORKS. Ivor Thomas. 2 Vols.

HERODES. *Cf.* THEOPHRASTUS : CHARACTERS.

HERODIAN. C. R. Whittaker. 2 Vols.

HERODOTUS. A. D. Godley. 4 Vols.

HESIOD AND THE HOMERIC HYMNS. H. G. Evelyn White.

HIPPOCRATES AND THE FRAGMENTS OF HERACLEITUS. W. H. S. Jones and E. T. Withington. 4 Vols.

HOMER : ILIAD. A. T. Murray. 2 Vols.

HOMER : ODYSSEY. A. T. Murray. 2 Vols.

ISAEUS. E. S. Forster.

ISOCRATES. George Norlin and LaRue Van Hook. 3 Vols.

[ST. JOHN DAMASCENE]: BARLAAM AND IOASAPH. Rev. G. R. Woodward, Harold Mattingly and D. M. Lang.

JOSEPHUS. 10 Vols. Vols. I-IV. H. St. J. Thackeray. Vol. V. H. St. J. Thackeray and Ralph Marcus. Vols. VI and VII. Ralph Marcus. Vol. VIII. Ralph Marcus and Allen Wikgren. Vols. IX-X. L. H. Feldman.

JULIAN. Wilmer Cave Wright. 3 Vols.

LIBANIUS : SELECTED WORKS. A. F. Norman. 3 Vols. Vols. I and II.

LONGUS : DAPHNIS AND CHLOE. Thornley's translation revised by J. M. Edmonds ; and PARTHENIUS. S. Gaselee.

THE LOEB CLASSICAL LIBRARY

LUCIAN. 8 Vols. Vols. I–V. A. M. Harmon. Vol. VI. K. Kilburn. Vols. VII and VIII. M. D. Macleod.

LYCOPHRON. *Cf.* CALLIMACHUS : HYMNS AND EPIGRAMS.

LYRA GRAECA. J. M. Edmonds. 2 Vols.

LYSIAS. W. R. M. Lamb.

MANETHO. W. G. Waddell

MARCUS AURELIUS. C. R. Haines.

MENANDER I. New edition by W. G. Arnott.

MINOR ATTIC ORATORS. 2 Vols. K. J. Maidment and J. O. Burtt.

MUSAEUS : HERO AND LEANDER. *Cf.* CALLIMACHUS : FRAGMENTS.

NONNOS : DIONYSIACA. W. H. D. Rouse. 3 Vols.

OPPIAN, COLLUTHUS, TRYPHIODORUS. A. W. Mair.

PAPYRI. NON-LITERARY SELECTIONS. A. S. Hunt and C. C. Edgar. 2 Vols. LITERARY SELECTIONS (Poetry). D. L. Page.

PARTHENIUS. *Cf.* LONGUS.

PAUSANIAS : DESCRIPTION OF GREECE. W. H. S. Jones. 4 Vols. and Companion Vol. arranged by R. E. Wycherley.

PHILO. 10 Vols. Vols. I–V. F. H. Colson and Rev. G. H. Whitaker. Vols. VI–X. F. H. Colson. General Index. Rev. J. W. Earp.
Two Supplementary Vols. Translation only from an Armenian Text. Ralph Marcus.

PHILOSTRATUS : THE LIFE OF APOLLONIUS OF TYANA. F. C. Conybeare. 2 Vols.

PHILOSTRATUS : IMAGINES ; CALLISTRATUS : DESCRIPTIONS. A. Fairbanks.

PHILOSTRATUS AND EUNAPIUS : LIVES OF THE SOPHISTS. Wilmer Cave Wright.

PINDAR. Sir J. E. Sandys.

PLATO : CHARMIDES, ALCIBIADES, HIPPARCHUS, THE LOVERS, THEAGES, MINOS AND EPINOMIS. W. R. M. Lamb.

PLATO : CRATYLUS, PARMENIDES, GREATER HIPPIAS, LESSER HIPPIAS. H. N. Fowler.

PLATO : EUTHYPHRO, APOLOGY, CRITO, PHAEDO, PHAEDRUS. H. N. Fowler.

PLATO : LACHES, PROTAGORAS, MENO, EUTHYDEMUS. W. R. M. Lamb.

PLATO : LAWS. Rev. R. G. Bury. 2 Vols.

PLATO : LYSIS, SYMPOSIUM, GORGIAS. W. R. M. Lamb.

PLATO : REPUBLIC. Paul Shorey. 2 Vols.

PLATO : STATESMAN, PHILEBUS. H. N. Fowler ; ION. W. R. M. Lamb.

THE LOEB CLASSICAL LIBRARY

PLATO : THEAETETUS AND SOPHIST. H. N. Fowler.
PLATO : TIMAEUS, CRITIAS, CLITOPHO, MENEXENUS, EPISTU-
LAE. Rev. R. G. Bury.
PLOTINUS. A. H. Armstrong. 7 Vols. Vols. I-III.
PLUTARCH : MORALIA. 16 Vols. Vols. I-V. F. C. Babbitt.
Vol. VI. W. C. Helmbold. Vol. VII. P. H. De Lacy and
B. Einarson. Vol. VIII. P. A. Clement, H. B. Hoffleit.
Vol. IX. E. L. Minar, Jr., F. H. Sandbach, W. C.
Helmbold. Vol. X. H. N. Fowler. Vol. XI. L. Pearson,
F. H. Sandbach. Vol. XII. H. Cherniss, W. C. Helmbold.
Vol. XIII, Parts 1 and 2. H. Cherniss. Vol. XIV. P. H.
De Lacy and B. Einarson. Vol. XV. F. H. Sandbach.
PLUTARCH : THE PARALLEL LIVES. B. Perrin. 11 Vols.
POLYBIUS. W. R. Paton. 6 Vols.
PROCOPIUS : HISTORY OF THE WARS. H. B. Dewing. 7 Vols.
PTOLEMY : TETRABIBLOS. F. E. Robbins.
QUINTUS SMYRNAEUS. A. S. Way. Verse trans.
SEXTUS EMPIRICUS. Rev. R. G. Bury. 4 Vols.
SOPHOCLES. F. Storr. 2 Vols. Verse trans.
STRABO : GEOGRAPHY. Horace L. Jones. 8 Vols.
THEOCRITUS. Cf. GREEK BUCOLIC POETS.
THEOPHRASTUS : CHARACTERS. J. M. Edmonds ; HERODES,
etc. A. D. Knox.
THEOPHRASTUS : DE CAUSIS PLANTARUM. G. K. K. Link and
B. Einarson. 3 Vols. Vol. I.
THEOPHRASTUS : ENQUIRY INTO PLANTS. Sir Arthur Hort.
2 Vols.
THUCYDIDES. C. F. Smith. 4 Vols.
TRYPHIODORUS. Cf. OPPIAN.
XENOPHON : ANABASIS. C. L. Brownson.
XENOPHON : CYROPAEDIA. Walter Miller. 2 Vols.
XENOPHON : HELLENICA. C. L. Brownson.
XENOPHON : MEMORABILIA AND OECONOMICUS. E. C. Mar-
chant ; SYMPOSIUM AND APOLOGY. O. J. Todd.
XENOPHON : SCRIPTA MINORA. E. C. Marchant and G. W.
Bowersock.

DESCRIPTIVE PROSPECTUS ON APPLICATION

CAMBRIDGE, MASS.   LONDON
HARVARD UNIV. PRESS   WILLIAM HEINEMANN LTD

Two men have
women v

Made for Love

**First there's North.
He knows he should resist Melody.
They've been through this before.
But she's just so…tempting.**

**And then there's Rafe.
He doesn't need a woman in
his life. Except Molly keeps
popping up at the most
convenient moments…**

Dear Reader,

Welcome to Desire.

We start this month of fabulous Desire stories, with the final books in the ROYALLY WED series featuring the Stanford dynasty. **To Wed a Royal** has stories from reader favourites Valerie Parv – *Code Name: Prince* – and Carla Cassidy – *An Officer and a Princess*. Look out for more royal stories later in the year…

Another dose of opulent settings and sexy, wealthy men comes in the form of **Millionaire Bachelors**, which finishes THE MILLIONAIRE'S CLUB series with Sheri WhiteFeather's *Tycoon Warrior* and continues the Leanne Banks trilogy MILLION DOLLAR MEN with *Millionaire Husband*. (The final story in Leanne's MILLION DOLLAR MEN is in next month's **Millionaire Marriages**.)

Finally, **Made For Love** is wild and tempestuous reading; it pairs *Cowboy Fantasy* by the always marvellous Ann Major with Dixie Browning's moving *More to Love*—two more popular writers would be hard to find!

Enjoy!

The Editors

Made For Love

ANN MAJOR
DIXIE BROWNING

SILHOUETTE® DESIRE™

*Silhouette, Silhouette Desire and Colophon
are registered trademarks of Harlequin Books S.A.,
used under licence.*

*First published in Great Britain 2002
Silhouette Books, Eton House, 18-24 Paradise Road,
Richmond, Surrey TW9 1SR*

MADE FOR LOVE © Harlequin Books S.A. 2002

The publisher acknowledges the copyright holders of the
individual works as follows:

Cowboy Fantasy © Ann Major 2001
More to Love © Dixie Browning 2001

ISBN 0 373 04742 8

51-0302

*Printed and bound in Spain
by Litografía Rosés S.A., Barcelona*

COWBOY FANTASY

by
Ann Major

ANN MAJOR

loves writing romance novels as much as she loves reading them. She is the proud mother of three grown children. She lists hiking in the Colorado mountains with her husband, playing tennis, sailing, enjoying her cats and playing the piano among her favourite activities.

I dedicate this story to my darling mother, the 'real' ANN MAJOR. Nobody ever had a sweeter mother.

Prologue

———

South Texas
The borderlands

Black feathers spun lazily above in a cloudless, azure sky.

Teo's head hurt as he lay on the hard earth watching the big black birds. His stomach throbbed queasily.

He didn't know where he was, only that he was somewhere north of the border, somewhere in *Tejas*. Somewhere on a huge ranch the *coyote* had called El Dorado.

Teofilo Perez was ten years old and he was dying.

"Mamacíta!"

Teofilo's hands clawed sand. Then he remembered.

She'd sent him off to scavenge another part of *el dompe* with Chaco and his gang. Then she and Papacíto had run away.

When Teo had stayed up all night waiting for them, Chaco had laughed.

"They aren't coming back. It happens all the time. *Todo el tiempo.*" Chaco had stared indifferently toward the north. "There are many orphans in *el dompe*. Left behind when their families disappear over the wire. My father...too."

Now Chaco was gone as well.

Sweat stung Teo's eyes like hot tears. Where was he?

Burrs and thorns bit into his back. Here there were snakes and spiders in the high grasses; wild animals, too. If Teo didn't get up and go on, he'd die.

Then it would all be for nothing.

He was burning up, from the inside out; starving, too. He felt as thirsty for water as a bone-dry sponge. Then the coyotes started howling again, and he tasted the coppery flavor of his own panic.

He had to get up and catch Chaco. He had to keep walking north through the endless sandy pastures choked with mesquite and huisache that led to *el norte.*

To Houston. To Tiá Irma.

Chaco had warned him to stay out of the open, so *La Migra* couldn't spot him from their helicopters.

Teo felt too weak to stand, so he lay on the hard, packed ground, his swollen, sunburned lids blinking, his eyes blurring every time he opened them. Through the screen of his dense lashes a too-bright sun spun above the stunted oak trees, shooting diamond-patterned pricks through the branches. The orange orb grew bigger and bigger until it exploded in a blinding brilliance that flooded the white-heat of that harsh, unforgiving sky.

His last meal had been breakfast two days ago—two boiled eggs and three tortillas that had been gritty and stale. His hands fisted again; he tried to swallow, but his tongue was too swollen and his throat too raw and gritty.

Fat black flies buzzed. Some mysterious creature grunted and snorted in the thicket. Teo shivered as he imagined the claws of a puma or the teeth of a coyote.

"*Ayudame, Dios.*"

He wanted to go home, not to *Cartolandia,* which was *pocho* for Cardboard Land, the barrio where they'd lived near *el dompe* in Nuevo Laredo. No, he wanted to go back home to his mountainous village, Tepóztlan. But there were no jobs there for Papacíto, no future for any of them. Nothing.

Nada, nada, mi hijo.

Papacíto had said those same words a week ago after government tractors and bulldozers had crushed their shack and bedraggled garden along with thousands of others and left them homeless again.

The next day, Papacíto had run away. Probably to look for work in *el norte.*

Teo couldn't remember the last time he'd been in school or even his last bath. He felt like a slab of meat drying in the sun, a worn-out corpse.

Papacíto had promised him a house in *el norte* with a flush toilet, toys, a garden where he could play.

Swish. Black feathers were falling out of the sky, crash-landing clumsily, settling themselves in the branches of the thorny thicket.

Vultures.

Teo stared stupidly at the big black bird folding his wings. Another bird hopped out of a tree and scuttled closer.

Teo had to get up, but when he struggled to his knees, he reeled dizzily. Once he had crawled on bleeding knees to pray to the Virgin in Mexico City. That memory was followed by a sweeter one. He was home in the cool shade of his porch, lying on his hammock, and his mother and grandmother were singing him a lullaby. He began whispering his Hail Marys.

When he opened his eyes again, he was on the ground, and the buzzards were circling lazily against the pale blue. Through swirls of dust, a lone rider on a big black horse moved toward him. The tall man, whose low-crowned sombrero was the color of dust, wore a strange costume of weathered rawhide. He was as filthy as Teo, yet he sat on his horse with a world-weary cockiness that said he was somebody, more than border trash from *el dompe*.

Although the man's coppery face was hard and lean, his teeth were as white as the *chicles* Teo had sold to the fat gringo *turistas*. He had a golden mustache.

Terrified, Teo grabbed at his plastic bag of tortillas that Chaco had tied to his belt. In his other hand he gripped the bottle that held the remains of Chaco's red soft drink. Swaying weakly, drowning in the blinding sunlight, Teo struggled to his feet.

The man called down to him gently in his native tongue, more gently than Papacíto ever spoke. *"Cuidado, manito."*

Was he a phantom? A trick, like the trick the *coyote* had played when he'd dumped Chaco and the other toughs from *el dompe* here, in the middle of nowhere, swearing that a truck would be waiting for them a little farther where the pasture hit the road past the immigration checkpoint.

The stranger's manner and the fact that he spoke a lilting, peculiarly accented Spanish was more terrifying than anything.

Then he saw her.

The trees began to whirl, and Teo was on the ground again, his dirty white shirt covered in blood. Only it wasn't blood. It was the sugary soft drink. He'd spilled the last of Chaco's precious drink.

Chaco would beat him for sure. Sobbing, he begged God to tell Chaco he was sorry, to tell his mother he was sorry he hadn't minded when she'd told him to sweep the street or bring her a bucket of water.

When the tall dusty rider got off his horse, Teo screamed and screamed.

Until he saw a girl running lightly beside the huge man. Her hair was straight and reddish gold, with deep shifting highlights glinting in the hot blaze of light that flowed all around her.

She was an angel.

His very own angel.

Teo closed his eyes, and a great peace stole over him. He wasn't afraid to die anymore.

"Angelita!" he whispered.

He opened his eyes. The girl wasn't an angel. It was his mother, and her voice was as sweet as those songs she used to sing before he went to sleep.

"Don't be afraid. You are safe, little one."

With the last of his strength, Teo stretched his thin hand toward her, but she vanished.

There was only the mysterious rider.

Only terror.

Only death in a strange, wild land.

One

South Texas
El Dorado Ranch

A bad woman can ruin the best man alive, same as a bad man can destroy a good woman.

El Dorado Ranch, set as it was right square in the borderlands cactus country of the biggest state in the continental union, might seem too rough a place for sob-sister tales to get a firm hold. But there's nothing more fascinating than love gone wrong; nothing more fun to talk about, either—especially if it's the boss's love life gone wrong.

North Black, for all that his daddy had been a local legend, for all that North had inherited his own natural arrogance and aura of cowboy majesty, for all that he sat that high-steppin', champion quarter horse, which had set him back a cool half million, for all that his carved leather saddle was trimmed in sterling, for all that he'd been billed by the state's most popular magazine as the most eligible bachelor in Texas—for all *that,* this cowboy king was damned near done for.

Nothing is more disagreeable or more difficult to stop than gossip, especially when it's true. It was common knowledge at El Dorado Ranch—better known, at least in these parts, as North Black's private kingdom—that the king was on the verge of collapse. And not only because the worst drought in living memory plagued his vast ranch in south Texas. But because an impossible little spitfire had gotten a grip on his heart and then done him wrong.

North was killing himself with overwork, his loyal crew said, doing way more than his share of the real cowboying. Why, the king was up before dawn and working cattle long after dark. Even when his hands quit, he never took a break. His lunch was a sandwich in the saddle topped off with a swig out of his canteen. Evenings, when no serious rustling or poaching mischief was afoot, were spent in his office poring over ledgers or talking on the phone.

Wherever there was trouble—illegals, bulls loose, broken pipes, cut fences, dry water holes, cows lost, a horse that needed to be broken, or more of the Midnight Bandit's mischief, North took the job on himself. Then there was Gran, who stole his best cowboys to work her garden every time he turned his back.

Nobody blamed North for wanting to work himself to death. Not after what that little witch, Melody Woods, had done to him—time and again.

First, she'd jilted him at the altar like he was a nobody—right there, in front of God, his crew, his friends, his family; hell, in front of the entire damned ranching aristocracy of Texas. She'd made a fool of him, the king, a man known to be too arrogant and too proud.

"She did worse than hurt his pride," said Sissy, his wild sister, who was worrying about him more than usual. "She broke his heart." And Sissy knew a thing or two about broken hearts.

"His father would never have lost it over a woman,"
Libby Black, his grandmother asserted at every possible
occasion. "The ranch came first."

"You always make El Dorado sound like a religion,
Gran," Sissy said.

"It was till I got some sense and took up gardening."

"It's not a religion," Sissy said. "Not for me."

"Which is why I put North in charge."

Not that North ever talked about the impossible Miss
Woods. Not even after he'd fallen for her sister, Claire, on
the rebound. Fortunately he and Claire had come to their
senses, realizing they should be friends rather than lovers.

Gossip had it that Miss Melody Woods had had a hand
in the breakup of that romance. That very same night, first
chance she got, she'd gone and made a fool of him again.

Yes, sirree. She'd turned the king into a jealousy-crazed
maniac in a run-down bar in Rockport, Texas. Hell, that
shrimpers' dive better known as Shorty's, was so bad, the
king would never have set the scuffed toe of his handmade,
black boot inside it, if Melody hadn't lured him there on
purpose. For reasons known only to her, she'd danced and
gotten those rough, dangerous fishermen in such a rowdy
stir, they would've given her more than she'd bargained
for, if the king hadn't rushed her and carried her off over
his shoulders like he was a caveman and she was his
woman.

Only she wasn't his woman or ever going to be—according to him. The hands knew that because the very next
day a couple of greenhorns at El Dorado were stupid
enough to make crude bets as to exactly what the king
must've done to punish Miss Woods in bed later that night.
When Lester Rivers got himself liquored up enough to ask
the king, who was even taller and broader-shouldered than
Lester, for details about their little romp, it had taken Jeff
Gentry, his burly foreman and best friend, and W.T., the
laziest cowboy on El Dorado, to hold North long enough
for Lester to hightail it to Laredo.

Later, the king had thanked everybody, even W.T., for saving him from strangling Lester with his bare hands. Then North had said, very softly, very calmly, but in *that* voice, everybody in his kingdom, even Gran, understood.

"What happened *that* night is nobody's business but mine! Nobody, none of you, is to ever even think about what Melody Woods does in or out of my bed or ever say her name at El Dorado Ranch again! As far as I'm concerned, she no longer exists. Understand? *Comprende?*"

Nobody had spoken of her, in Spanish or English—at least, not directly and not within the king's earshot. But the forbidden holds a mighty powerful appeal. Especially for comrades in a cow camp lonely for female companionship, especially when that forbidden female is willowy and sexy and full of surprises as a brand-new kitten.

It was plain to see by the stubborn set of North's strong, jutting jaw, he wasn't over *that* night. Plain to see by his stern silences and his inability to even crack a smile at his men's dirty banter, that the king hadn't forgotten the young lady or that night any more than they had.

No, sirree. The king wasn't through with Miss Melody Woods.

Any more than that little firecracker was through with him.

It was just a matter of time before that pair got into a tussle again.

What would that sexy little gal dream up for an encore?

His men's yelps along with that damn cow's stomping and grunting and snorting inside the jug at the far end of the huge barn would have set a sane man's nerves on edge. North was hardly sane.

He hadn't been himself since that night when Melody had danced for the world and then refused to dance with him in private. To make matters worse, Dee Dee Woods, Melody's socially ambitious mom, had him on the phone and was unraveling the fraying ends of his frazzled psyche with her shrill demands.

"I said supper!"

He held the phone away from his ear. How could such a pretty woman have such a grating voice? "Tonight? Your house? I don't think that's a good—"

"But Melody's safe and sound in Austin."

He knew better than to argue.

"Sam and I miss you. That's why when your accountant said you were coming to town, I decided to call."

He missed them, too. "Just a second, Dee Dee. We've got a cow in labor, and Jeff's yelling so loud—"

On a shudder, North pressed the cordless telephone tighter against his ear and bolted himself inside the stall with his pet llamas. Camels, he called them when he was feeling affectionate or worried, which was all the time, ever since Little Camel had been born so puny.

Not that it was any quieter inside their stall. Not with that distressed cow in labor, bawling and fit to be tied again.

"What was that you said, Dee Dee?" North demanded.

He liked Dee Dee Woods even if she'd set her sights on him as a future son-in-law for all the wrong reasons.

"I heard you'd be in town," Dee Dee shrieked. "So, I called to invite you to supper."

The cow started kicking so loud North could barely hear her.

"It'll just be Sam and me…I promise!"

"All right."

"Seven-thirty sharp."

He said bye and hung up.

"Boys," he shouted. "I was on the phone. Y'all were hollering so loud, I couldn't hear myself think. I just did a very stupid thing."

"W.T. let go, and she kicked me—two hooves, square in the chest!" Jeff yelled back at him. "Get down here, King!"

North was so mad he stayed put.

Damn it. It was Jeff's fault he'd said yes to Dee Dee Woods. Gentry deserved to sweat. Hell, droplets of the stuff were trickling from North's wet black hair, soaking his denim shirt and blue surgical overalls as he considered sitting down to dinner in the Woodses' house again.

He'd said yes.

Not to worry. You have a date with Maria on Saturday. You're through with Melody.

Just talking to *her* mother had brought everything back, especially *that* night.

North stood alone in a stall, occupied not by a cow or horse, but by that unlikely pair of camels and wondered if he should call Dee Dee back and send his regrets.

He began to frown in earnest as he stroked the mama llama. Then he eyed her gangly newborn more worriedly. The mother was dark brown with black patches on her face and rump. Her milk wouldn't come, and the baby—an impossibly skinny runt who was all ribs and neck and matchstick legs—couldn't suckle.

For some foolish reason, even after nights spent chasing the Midnight Bandit, North had been getting to the barn at 4:00 a.m. to play nursemaid to the shy baby llama, warming bottles, cradling him, feeding him. Even so, Little Camel wasn't putting on weight.

Jeff yelled, "Time to play vet, King."

"See you later, Little Camel," North whispered with more affection than he wanted to feel.

The shy, scared baby reminded him of...

He saw a little girl on the ground, her skirts hiked, her skinny knees torn and bloody; worse, her smoky-blue eyes dark with fear. Abruptly the king stopped that memory.

His defiant boot heels echoing all the way to the rafters, North stalked across the concrete floor of his barn toward the scuffle of his men and the cow in that distant stall.

It was late August and 113 degrees in the shade outside if it was a degree. Inside the barn felt like a sauna. He could almost feel the beige dust that coated his wavy hair and dark skin turn to mud and ooze under his collar.

North was exhausted, on edge, but he forced himself to concentrate on the job ahead instead of on...on Melody.

Damn her hide...or rather her silky, golden skin. And she was soft—he'd never forget how good she'd felt the first time he'd accidentally touched her and she'd jumped as if she'd been shot. Not that every nerve in his body hadn't popped like sparklers, too.

Why the hell had Dee Dee called? He didn't want Melody on his mind. For months he'd refused to think about her.

He didn't still want her, still dream about her. He didn't. Not after what she'd done. Not after what she hadn't done.

But if some idiotic part of him still did want her, that was the part he was trying damned hard to kill by working himself so hard. His misplaced affection for the wrong woman had jeopardized not only his pride and his heart, but also his family and their ranch.

He had a position to uphold. When he married, if he married after what she'd put him through, it would be to a mature, sensible woman who understood ranching, who could contribute something of value to El Dorado, who would lend sanity to his hard life instead of chaos, who could make commitments and stick to them. He wanted a harmonious marriage to a woman, who could show a man she loved him in a warm womanly way, to a woman like Maria Langly, who had been born and bred to ranch life, just as he had.

North was fighting for his ranch, his legacy and his world. His back was against the wall. He had no time to waste on a woman who'd never known for sure whether she wanted him, a woman who would never be anything but trouble.

Unbidden came the vision of a long, cool slip of a girl in skintight jeans and a halter top. Melody did have the cutest and most mischievous smile and the softest honey-red, straight hair. She smelled good, too. And, boy, when that little exhibitionist hadn't been driving him crazy, or turning him on, she sure had made him laugh. Nobody had ever been able to make him forget, at least for a little while, the ranch and the heavy responsibilities he'd assumed too young.

She was cute. Trouble was, she knew it. She'd reveled in making him forget that he was supposed to be stern and tough, that as the largest landowner in south Texas, he was supposed to set an example for his men, for the whole damn ranching community in these parts.

Hell, his granddaddy had taken him up on his saddle when he was five. They'd worked cattle together, and all the while the old man had been whispering that when he was a man, all this—meaning the cattle, the vast acreage— would be his responsibility. His father, Rand Black, had been a legend. North was determined to carry on his daddy's legacy and support the people whose families had lived here for generations, who depended on him for their very livelihoods.

Melody never bowed down and worshiped him like everybody else around here. So, why the hell had he loved this defiant brat since she'd been a young girl? She wasn't even any good in bed. She was too uptight and skittish to be sexy in private. At least with him. No, she preferred public displays of wanton affection that drove him and every other guy who caught her performance wild. Always, she left him hot and hard and frustrated, and jealous as all get out. When they were alone, and he made a move, she got as scared and shy as his baby camel. He loathed everybody thinking she was hot and easy when that's the last thing she was.

Except for that last night.

You're not supposed to think about her or what happened, ever again. You're supposed to work—till you forget her.

So, how come you accepted a dinner invitation tonight in Corpus Christi from her mother?

Because Dee Dee swore Melody's in Austin and you won't see her. Or talk about her. Because it was so hot and loud in the barn you hadn't been able to think.

Liar.

You want to see Dee Dee's most recent pictures of *her* on the fridge. You want Dee Dee to drop those annoying little hints…

Forget her!

North was trying. He'd all but imprisoned himself on his ranch. He had 800,000 acres of baking shin oak and prickly pear and thousands of head of cattle to protect him from that clueless she-devil, who had a lot of growing up to do up in Austin.

North could hear his stressed cattle outside squalling as his men cut them from the herd and drove them into pens and chutes, some to be kept and fed, some to be vaccinated and tagged, some to be loaded onto the cattle trucks that were discreetly hidden in mesquite thickets.

Tough times made for brutal decisions.

No matter how much land or money a rancher had, he was powerless against the weather and the hard realities of market prices. Due to the drought, he'd run out of grass. The beef market was flooded. The cost of feed was too high to keep the herd. Then last night the Midnight Bandit had cut his fence and tried to rustle a truckload of cows again.

Outside the barn, horses neighed and sputtered. The cattle roared, and his men shouted. These were the familiar, beloved sounds of home to North. And of doom.

For more than a hundred years this ranch had been owned and run by Blacks. The pictures of his ancestors hung inside the ranch house, their grim expressions setting standards and demanding impossibilities of him in these modern times.

Inside the stall now, North was still sweating profusely

as he picked up a scalpel, still in its wrapper. He picked up the irritated, very pregnant cow's tail, then let it drop. She didn't react.

"Looks like the spinal's okay, King," Jeff said behind him.

"Good."

Jeff was wide as a beam and nearly as tall as North; he was red-haired, bowlegged, narrow-eyed, and bullheaded. But a lady's man nonetheless. His daddy had been the ranch foreman before him, and his daddy before him. Jeff had grown up on the ranch just like North had. They were closer than most brothers. El Dorado was that kind of place.

"So, let's get to work—fast," Jeff urged.

North inspected the shaved area and the black lines Jeff had drawn along the reddish brown hide. When he was satisfied, he injected a topical anesthetic along every inch of the line. After he sliced through the hide with the scalpel, Jeff injected more anesthetic inside the incision. North began to cut deeper.

There were a lot of bleeders, but North deftly stopped them. Within a minute he was popping hooves out of the cow's belly and Jeff was pulling the rest of the calf free. They worked together, in harmony, as they always did, smiling at each other after it was over because it was a helluva rush to look into those wet brown eyes and witness the beginning of a new life.

Another life saved.

But for what? North wondered silently as he knew Jeff did. If it didn't rain? For an early death in a slaughterhouse…his short life bartered for a few peanuts? Worse, he might get himself rustled and hauled south to Mexico.

Again, North thought of Melody who'd become a vegetarian just to spite him after her first and only visit to the ranch.

North frowned as he dropped antibiotics into the uterus and then began to sew up the cow, barking questions at

Jeff to distract himself from Melody. "Calf breathing okay?"

North remembered Melody saying after he'd finished a long day at the squeeze chute, "I won't ever eat a hamburger again. I keep seeing a cute little brown-eyed calf peeping its head out of my hamburger bun and pleading for help."

He stared at the cute new calf. It galled him that Melody thought he didn't care about his animals.

"He's a cute little cuss, ain't he, King?"

Forget Melody Woods.

"Get him tagged and shot!"

Within minutes, North was done and striding out of the barn in shotgun chaps made of scarred leather. He made his way toward the cloud of dust that muted the harsh sun somewhere up above in that bluish white sky.

He pulled his bandanna up and took Mr. Jim's reins. As he rode toward the herd, Jeff and the other cowboys seemed to float in a golden haze of dust.

When North got closer, Mr. Jim shook his long red mane and neighed. His vaqueros nodded in deference, and Mr. Jim reared.

"Easy, champ," North whispered to Mr. Jim.

He flicked the reins and began shouting orders to his men in fluent Spanish right before he galloped into the herd. Then, and only then, as he cut cattle alongside his day-labor cowboys, was he able to forget the impossible Melody Woods.

Because he had to drive in to Corpus Christi, he quit earlier than he had in weeks. Before going to the house, he returned to the barn.

The calf he'd delivered was doing fine, so he made a final stop at that stall occupied by the mama llama and her pitifully skinny baby.

"Jeff," he shouted.

Jeff came running. Hell, everybody came running when the king yelled.

Everybody except...*her.*

When the baby llama forgot his shyness for the first time and moved toward him trustingly on shaky legs, North melted. He remembered a skinny little girl on the ground, drying her tears with the back of her hand before throwing herself into his arms.

"How long since my baby camel here ate?" North demanded in an oddly rough voice.

"Three hours. Want me to feed her again?"

"*Him.* No," North said, surprising himself as he strode toward the refrigerator and grabbed a bottle of fresh milk. "Warm this. I'll do it."

"You're wasting a lot of time on that runt," Jeff said as North squatted near the fragile newborn.

"I guess I'm a sucker for lost causes."

Melody had said he had no heart.

The barn phone began to ring as North cradled the llama across his knees and offered him the bottle. As the camel nibbled tentatively, W.T. banged inside the stall with the cordless. The llama shivered and stopped suckling. If anybody had the look of a dimestore cowboy, it was W.T. Scuffed high-heeled boots, wide hat, the shiftless fraud carried himself with more style than anybody on El Dorado.

"Take it easy when you come in here," North whispered testily.

"Border Patrol. Delfino's at the gate in his Dodge Ramcharger demandin' access—"

North grabbed the phone. "Delfino, you'd better be here to tell me you've got a lead on the Midnight Bandit. He damn near made off with a truck—"

"No. Some half-starved illegals. Kids. Not ten miles south of your headquarters. From our helicopter. Brush too dense to land."

"Damn," North muttered.

Tough as it was in Texas, it was tougher in Mexico. And getting tougher. *Ejidos,* small Mexican settlements, sprang up along the southern edge of El Dorado almost weekly.

The people who lived in them were unemployed. They didn't have a damned thing to do but watch the goings-on at El Dorado.

North had started wearing his Colt when he worked remote pastures of his ranch. He never knew anymore who or what he might run into on his own land. Anytime he spotted illegals, he called the Border Patrol.

Melody's voice piped up in his mind. "Americans spend more than four billion dollars a year on pet food. You know what else, Bertie? We don't spend a fourth of that on food to feed starving people in third world countries."

Bertie. That was Melody's special name for the king. If ever there was a sissy nickname—

More and more, intense, desperate men seemed to be making border crossings. Not just men these days. Women and children, who were pitifully unprepared to attack the desert.

Delfino repeated that single word, "Kids."

Ten miles. Illegals never carried much food or more than a gallon of water. In this heat, on foot, they'd be dead before they reached his headquarters.

North nodded glumly. "Keep an eye out for my bandit, you hear?"

After North hung up, the llama suckled indifferently. Still, North fed the baby camel with a vengeance till the bottle was completely empty. When he was done, he touched his brow to the furry ear. "You're not going to starve on me, Little Camel. Not if I can help it!"

When North was done, he found Jeff in the tack room. "You gonna take care of Little Camel, here, while I'm gone to Corpus?"

"Corpus?" Jeff shot him a look. "What about Saturday and Maria and me and Tina?"

"Right. Saturday. Maria." North took his sweat-stained Stetson off, raked brown fingers through his black hair, set his hat back on. "Wouldn't miss it for the world." His deep voice lacked enthusiasm.

"We'll cook 'em steaks, take 'em ridin' around on the ranch, show off the spread, impress 'em and bed 'em," Jeff reminded him. "Just like old times...before *her*."

"Right. Just like old times."

Jeff resented Melody more than anybody else on the ranch. North and he had gone to college together, double-dated together. They'd been inseparable until Melody.

"Don't you worry none about Little Camel, King."

North showered and changed into a pair of faded jeans with razor-sharp creases, a long-sleeved white shirt and his best boots—his uniform, Melody used to say. Then he stomped out to his white pickup. First thing he saw was his Colt in its holster on the seat.

He was licensed to carry. Quickly wrapping the belt around the holster, he got inside and jammed it into his glove compartment.

Once he left the ranch, the flat, familiar highway was clogged with speeding NAFTA trucks all the way to Robstown where he turned off for Corpus Christi.

The drive through flat, unremarkable countryside was so familiar it soon grew boring. Maybe that's why he noticed the bumper stickers peeling off the eighteen-wheeler in front of him. One was about beautifying Texas and the need to put a Yankee on a bus.

The other was about Humpty Dumpty being pushed.

North grinned. Melody loved bumper stickers.

Melody. He'd been thinking about her way too much. He should have canceled dinner at the Woodses'.

Too late. Dee Dee was a superb cook. Sam knew everything there was to know about football. North's own father had died young. Too young. Not that North let himself dwell on that.

Hell, his own mother certainly didn't dwell on it. She was in Europe blowing her fortune on the immense schloss of a Bavarian count she'd met in Paris.

The Woodses had always made a helluva fuss over North, a helluva lot more of a fuss than Melody or his own mother or even Gran ever had. Besides, he did have appointments with his accountant and cattle buyer in Corpus Christi. A frozen dinner in his bachelor apartment there held no appeal.

But the Woodses were *her* parents, and he was dating Maria now.

Only one date so far.

Not counting next Saturday.

An hour later, he was knocking briskly on the front door of the Woodses' two-story home, fighting to pretend he felt cool and was in control. When nobody answered, he jammed his fist on the doorbell. He turned to go when he heard lightly racing footsteps.

The door was thrown open by a slim hand with glossily white fingernails that had ridiculous little silver moons etched into them.

Little silver moons.

They sparkled, winking at him. Even before he saw the rest of *her,* the jolt of male-female awareness that shuddered down his spinal column told him to bolt.

Instead he drawled lazily, ''Hello there, Melody.''

Two

"Smile, Bertie boy. It's the second best thing you can do with your lips."

Something about Melody's low, Southern voice, something in the images she conjured was so damn sexy, so damn blatant. He began to dream about how good it could be if she put those lips to work.

"Naughty, naughty," she whispered, reading his mind.

"What the hell…"

"Relax. I didn't mean anything. I got that line off some bumper sticker when I was driving home today."

So, she'd been reading bumper stickers, too.

He moved closer. Big mistake. She smelled too good.

"I've got one for you, too, darlin'. Humpty Dumpty was pushed."

She laughed.

To keep from grinning back, he bit his tongue till he tasted blood.

Peeking from behind the door, Melody batted her long,

burnished lashes at him, just as she had *that* night when
she'd come looking for him at his apartment. When the
lash work got no visible reaction, her impish smile bright-
ened, and she began to tease him in earnest.

His palms dampened. The smile was overkill. Her lash
work had done the trick. So had the comment about what
he could do with his lips.

No wonder the ambitious Dee Dee had called this morning. A mother knew when her daughter was in the mood
to start something. In Dee Dee's mind he was a prize catch
and a big enough dope to fall for her little girl all over
again.

"What the hell are you doing home?" he demanded.

"Hi there to you, too—Bertie."

His mouth thinned. "Don't call me that unless…"

"Then, hi there, Rancher Black," she said sassily.

"North will do just fine."

"Aye. Aye." Instead of saluting, she touched her lip
with a fluttery white fingertip and blew him a kiss.

Little moons sparked.

His lips actually got hot.

Hell, it *was* August.

His sneer was slow and deliberate, "So, you've come
back—" Then he added, "What the hell for?"

She flinched at those secret code words, just as he did.
Her beauty upset him even more. Her long, straight, reddish-gold hair framed the slender oval of her flushed face.
Her golden skin was damp as if she'd just stepped from the
shower. And those half-scared, flirty, smoky-blue eyes ate
him alive. Why, oh why, did she have to smell of soap and
perfumed bath oils?

Even without makeup, she was naturally, heart-
wrenchingly beautiful, more beautiful and innocent looking
and yet voluptuous than he remembered. She'd come looking for him after her little dance in Shorty's, after their wild
kisses in the parking lot. No sooner had he pulled her inside

his place *that* night, the night he'd wanted her so damn much, he'd felt as if he'd die if he couldn't have her.

She'd let him take her to bed. But first, she'd actually stripped for him.

"You say I only want to perform in public. Not tonight. Tonight I want to dance just for you. Do you want to dance with me?"

"I'm not the exhibitionist. I'll watch."

"You're gonna have fun. I promise." Her eyes had gleamed, teasing him, luring him.

She'd put a CD in his player, turned his lights way down and had begun to move in the velvet shadows. For a long time all she'd done was sway back and forth to the heavy beat and run her hands over her body. When he'd joined her, she'd let him grasp her by the waist, pull her close, let him put his hands wherever he wanted, let him strip her ever so slowly. She hadn't even fought him when he'd undone the buttons of her blouse, one by one. She'd danced and smiled and lured them both to their doom.

The ground rocked under him as he stood on her porch. His heart thudded.

"You look too damn good, darlin'," he whispered.

"So do you," she said in a sad, lost tone that matched his own.

Just those words, and he wanted to touch her so bad he hurt. But he remembered the dangerous place that desire had led them to so many times before, so he knotted his callused hands, slipped them into his hip pockets. He took a deep breath and a long step backward.

Instead of her usual grunge attire, she wore some sort of silky, scarlet sarong that clung to her curves so tightly, he saw nipples. And that there was no panty line. It wasn't hard to imagine her body since he knew exactly what she looked like with nothing on. Show but don't let him touch, being her motto.

"How the hell could you answer the door in that? I could've been anyone."

"It would have been a whole lot less dangerous if you had been," she teased before she realized what she was doing. "I was expecting you."

Her pupils darkened with alarm, but not before her husky voice had rippled over every raw nerve ending, making his skin sting as if he was on fire the way it had *that* night.

"But you have no right, no claim on me or what I wear...or don't wear—ever again, Rancher Black." She lifted her chin, challenging him to more verbal dueling.

"You're right, of course—Miss Woods!"

No doubt she'd purchased the improbable garment somewhere in the Orient when she'd run away from him on that freighter and driven him mad with jealousy, rage and fear. When she'd finally turned up safe and sound, she'd thrown his life into turmoil all over again when she'd almost seduced him. Then she'd gone off to India.

"I was in the shower," she said demurely without lifting her gaze to his. "My muscles were stiff after the long drive."

All of a sudden he had a stiff muscle problem and a mighty keen need for a cold shower, too.

"Would you prefer it if I'd answered the door stark naked?" she teased.

The vision of her naked in a shower stall brought a rush of heat and made the muscle in question pull even tighter. Just for an instant he remembered her in a black lace bra and matching panties and a black velvet hat after he'd removed her blouse and jeans. For no reason at all, he was tugging at his collar.

"Don't worry...Bertie. If I'd known you were going to be in such a bad mood, I wouldn't have answered the door at all."

"Why aren't you in Austin where you belong?" His voice was as cold as ice.

"Why did you say yes to my mother? This is my parents' house. It's your own fault if you're not where you belong—

out on your big ole ranch. Playing king, doing your big man things. Ordering everybody in your kingdom around.''

That wasn't how it was. Not that he let on.

''Is that what you think of me and my business?''

''Isn't that what you want everybody to think?''

''I have responsibilities.''

''And they came before me.''

His family hadn't thought so. ''They're a part of who I am.''

''And I don't know who I am. Is that what you're saying?''

In bed or out of it, he almost shouted. Instead he flushed darkly. ''My ranch wasn't the problem.''

''You give everything of yourself to that ranch.''

''Because I have to.''

''Why?''

''Because my father died that's why!'' North remembered the fire. He remembered running. He remembered screaming for help.

''Why you, Bertie?''

''Just…just…'' An emotion built and burst inside him, so he waited. ''Just because,'' he finished darkly, remembering his father's funeral. ''I'm his son. That's all.''

Her eyes seemed to see inside him, into that shadowy secret place.

She smiled. ''You can tell me.''

He glared. ''Can I? If you were me, would you trust you…after…''

They'd hardly said hi, and already they were at it.

Yet he preferred arguing and probably so did she—to remembering *that* night and what had happened in his apartment and what hadn't.

She was pale and yet breathing hard, every bit as agitated as he was. Those fingers with the little silver moons were tugging at her silken sash. ''How can we be discussing this…like it still matters? When nothing about us matters…anymore.''

He watched that rhythmic tugging of those little half

moons at her sash as if hypnotized. "My thoughts exactly, darlin'."

So why was there a painful lump in his throat? Why that painful thickening lower down that stretched his jeans and made him too conscious of her easy power? Why were the memories of his childhood all mixed up with the crazy sexual frustration of that last night? Why this insane desire to yank that infernal sash loose, slide his hands inside that silk robe and pull her against his body when he knew why wanting her was so impossible?

Why couldn't she be *normal*? Why did she have to be the sexiest woman alive and not sexy at all?

Those moving fingertips with the little moons that twinkled slid along red silk. He felt his collar tighten like it was really choking him. "Stop playing with that damned sash!"

"Sorry."

"Do I come in or go?" he growled when her slim hands were still at last. "It's been a long day."

"Oh, do come in, Rancher Black," she teased, pushing the door wider.

"Quit calling me that!"

When she didn't move out of his way, he was forced to sidle so close to her he almost brushed against her. Which was what she must have wanted because when he was almost past her, she reached out and laid her hand on his shoulder.

"North, I…" Even before the panic flared in her eyes, she chopped off the end of her sentence.

Instantly his muscles contracted beneath the liquid heat of her slim hand. His black head jerked, startling her, and for a long moment they both stared at those fingertips with the tiny silver moons. She'd scarcely touched him, but the effect on his senses was electrifying.

He remembered that last night when her hands had been all over him. She'd been eager, as eager as he. And then suddenly, she'd gotten scared.

"North..." Her little girl voice died in her throat as she splayed her fingers, causing the tiny little moons to twinkle.

He felt her, remembered her in every pore. They'd lain in his bed that night, his body pressed firmly against hers, her lips against his throat, her breast against his chest, the rest of their bodies touching all the way down. She'd felt so right. She always did.

He'd held her for a long time, stroking her hair, trying to gentle her as he might a frightened colt. But she'd gotten frightened again and gone back to the wild on him anyway.

"Don't start in on me again, darlin'...unless you intend to finish what you start...this time."

Her hand tightened and then fell away slowly, and still he couldn't move past her any more than she seemed able to escape him.

"I want to forget you," he said, but his gaze was on her pink lips.

"That does seem like the sensible solution to our problem."

"*Your* problem," he said in a flat tone.

"And yet—"

"There is not going to be a yet—damn you."

She blushed. Her eyes remained downcast. "What if I can't be as sensible or as rational as you? What if I—"

"Not if you crawled—"

She went white at that code word.

"You broke up with me, remember?" he said in a softer tone.

"And you'll never be able to forgive—" Her husky voice had dropped, too—to something that sounded close to shame or regret.

"That's right."

Leave her alone. Cool off. Talk football outside with Sam.

But she looked so small and vulnerable. Suddenly he couldn't stop staring at her lips and wondering how long since anybody had kissed their wet, pink fullness. Wondering who else knew how they tasted. These thoughts got him so riled, North pushed his way inside, grabbed her, backed her against the red flowers on the foyer wallpaper and pressed his body firmly against hers.

She swallowed. Her eyes shone nervously; her cheeks blazed a brighter hue, but for once, she didn't try to run.

Suddenly his breathing was fast and irregular. "Why? Why do you always goad me? Why do you always have to push?"

"I—I don't know. I-it's just the way I am with you. I don't like it that I do it, either. North—"

"Shut up," he said silkily.

Then he touched her cheek with the back of his hand, ran it along her throat. Her skin was smooth and soft. Womanly soft. And hot. So hot. She was burning up just like he was.

"Let me go," she whispered.

He stroked her hair. "Not just yet. You touched me. You led me on."

"You're too easy."

He grinned. "If only you were as easy."

She shut her eyes as if to shut him out.

"Your desires are every bit as deep and dark as mine," he murmured. "Have you found someone else to satisfy them?" Just asking her drove him crazy.

Her lashes fluttered. Her smoky eyes darkened. "No…"

"How long…since you've been held? Kissed?"

"Not since…that night." She turned deep red.

"Me, either."

Why the hell had he admitted that? Unwanted desire for her wound him tighter. When she tried to run, he seized her arm again. "Not yet, darlin'. You're not going anywhere. Not just yet. Not till I've had a final taste."

Melody was tall, but he dwarfed her. Easily he scooped her closer. When he snugged her hips against his, she quivered, and even the slight response on her part that warred with the wild panic in her eyes made him explosively needy. Always, always she drove him past the limits of his careful control.

"Why do you always bully me?" she whispered.

"Sometimes I think because you want me to."

"Don't say that."

"What do you want, Melody? What's so wrong—"

An electric silence hummed between them. She was nervy, yet secretly thrilled and eager, too.

"You scare me," she said breathily.

"You scare you. You ought to know by now I would never hurt you. Or force you—"

"That's exactly what you're doing."

"I just want to touch you." He wanted to slide his fingers inside her again, to know she was wet as she'd been that night, despite all her puritanical and hung-up assertions to the contrary.

She shut her eyes, half opened her mouth and sank back against the wall. "If only—"

God, it had been so long. Six months since that wonderful, awful night. He had told himself, never, ever again—not with her. Then the minute he set eyes on her, the minute she touched him, she had him again. More than anything he craved to kiss her, to run his hands through her long, soft hair, to do all the things she'd forbidden him to do.

What would she do this time if he tried? What would she say? What would he do if she ever let him? He'd wanted her so damn much. He'd waited so long.

Maybe he would have held himself in check if Melody hadn't reached up and brushed her fingertips against the crisp black hair above his white collar. Maybe. But even though her touch was light and tentative, he felt her feverish response behind it, and that alone set him off.

He seized her shoulders to pull her toward him, wondering if this time she'd—

His head came down. Her lips pursed eagerly as she lifted them. In the fraction of a second before their mouths touched, he thought she whispered, ''I'm sorry, North. So, sorry.''

But before he could deepen their kiss, he heard the brisk patter of Dee Dee's footsteps. Quickly he straightened, and Melody twisted her crimson face away, so her mother couldn't read her.

''Is that you, North!'' Dee Dee shrieked from the other end of the hall as she rushed down the hall that was papered to look like a voluptuous garden gone wild in spring.

He froze.

Melody jumped free and began smoothing her hair.

''North...Melody...''

Dee Dee, who was golden and gorgeous and looked years younger than she was, smiled as they hastily backed away from each other and began to fidget—Melody with her sash after she'd finished on her hair and he with his tight collar.

''It's so good to see you, dear.'' Dee Dee smiled knowingly as she came forward and stretched on tiptoes as if to peck his dark cheek. All he felt when her glossy lips hovered close was the stir of her warm breath against his skin. ''I'm the chairman of the charity ball, so I was on the phone and couldn't get the door.''

''You said Melody was in Austin.''

''Did I?'' Dee Dee smiled up at him artlessly. ''You know Melody. She's as fickle as Texas weather, and I suppose we're about due for a norther.''

''After this hellish summer, something a little cool...and frosty might be a welcome change,'' he agreed thickly, his eyes on Melody.

''Sam's out back,'' Dee Dee said. When an alarm buzzed in her kitchen, she started. ''Why don't you join him, dear? And while you're outside, make sure he doesn't burn up my rib eyes. Meanwhile, I'll go get you a beer out of the fridge.'' Then she flew to the kitchen to check on whatever she had in the oven.

''It's only one evening together,'' North muttered in a hoarse whisper to Melody. ''Surely we can be civil and behave ourselves in front of your parents for a few hours— for their sake. For ours, too.''

''Only one night?'' Melody looked a little strained as she smiled up at him. ''Oh, no, North. I quit my job. I'm home to stay. Or at least I'll be at Nana's. You and I could see each other anytime—that is, if we wanted to.''

''Which we don't.''

''Speak for yourself. The last thing I intend to do where you're concerned—is behave myself.''

Nana was her grandmother.

''I thought south Texas bored you.''

''I was wrong…about a lot of things.''

He remembered her apology right before their kiss. ''What things? What do you mean?''

''I'll be around. That's all.''

''You said you loved Austin because it was wild. That south Texas and I bored—''

Her parting shots had cut him to the quick. At one point she'd said he was so ultraconservative that she felt stifled and dead anytime she was anywhere near him.

''Well—'' She paused. ''I'm here for a while. Not because of you, but because I'm going back to school. To get a masters and a teaching certificate.''

''Teaching? You said you didn't want to settle for any sort of traditional roles like wife or teacher that women used to be forced into by macho men.''

''I was a child. Naturally I wanted to be glamorous and special.'' She paused. ''I guess I figured out I like kids. I figured out some other stuff…that I like, too.''

Like men? Like sex? *Like me?*

As if she read his mind, Melody notched her chin upward a bit defiantly, and he found himself drinking in the beauty of her long slender neck and wondering if she really might be referring to sex.

"With this degree and certificate," Melody continued, "I can work anywhere in the world. I'll be independent."

So that was it! She hadn't come back because of him. This was about her infernal determination to be independent of him. To stay single.

Not that he cared.

"So you still want to travel?" he whispered, making his voice both insolent and admiring. "To see the world?"

"To be free," she agreed, but her tone was low and urgent as if this really was important to her, as if making him understand mattered.

"Sexually free?"

She turned red again. "Is that all you ever think about?"

"That does seem to be a burning issue when you're around."

"Which is why I wanted to get as far away from you as I possibly could!"

"To have more of your little adventures?"

Her eyes blazed. "You don't get me at all. I should've known better than to try to talk to you. You wouldn't understand."

He understood, all right. She teased him. Did she want real adventures with other, wilder men, who weren't so predictable, who didn't bore her—as he did?

"You might get into trouble. I worry about you."

"Well, don't." Her eyes smoldered. "This isn't about you, North."

Something cold coiled around his heart, and then he saw that she was trembling.

"You're right, of course," he forced himself to agree. "We broke up. Or rather, you broke up with me. You said we're—"

"Finished. And you said—" Her voice was tight and sad, and he realized his parting shots had hurt her, too.

He'd said she was doing him a favor.

She was right. They were finished. It was what she'd wanted, what he wanted, too. He was a rancher, born and bred—traditional to the core. He couldn't change that. He couldn't—not for her, not after everything she'd done.

Even so, the thought of other men touching her...of her touching them...

That shouldn't have bothered him. But his stomach twisted, and a bleak, lonely wave of despair washed over him as he considered working his ranch, dating other women, even Maria—while Melody had romantic adventures.

"I—I guess I'll go and get dressed," she said after an awkward spell.

When she left him, North's gaze followed her. Her waist was slim, the flare of her hips and thighs enticingly sweet. That short red silk thing made her look leggy and coltish. He couldn't seem to move till she disappeared from his view.

Then he adjusted his collar and raked his hand through his hair. So what if he had to endure one miserable night with her?

They'd catch up on old times. Then he really would forget her. He'd see Maria on Saturday, and maybe he'd find a bad girl on the side to sleep with. From now on, he'd drown himself in other women instead of work.

The only reason Miss Melody Woods was getting to him tonight was that she'd burned him so bad, he'd avoided all women since her.

Until Maria, he reminded himself. Maria was perfect for him. At least Jeff said so.

Could he help it if Melody looked good enough to eat, and that he was starved?

One night with her.

What could possibly go wrong?

Smile. It's the second best thing you can do with your lips.

Why did those infernal words keep repeating themselves

like a broken record? Why did he keep imagining her mouth on his body?

He didn't like the heat those images brought.

One night.

That was all.

Three

Vegetarian alert: Take a flying leap!
—The Plants

The bumper sticker tacked to her mirror was the first thing Melody saw when she raced into her room. North had given it to her as a joke after she'd become a vegetarian. She'd kept it, even when he'd dated Claire. Just like she'd kept all her pictures of him, those framed and those not, at the bottom of her underwear drawer.

She was shaking as she studied the skimpy red, one-piece bathing suit she'd grabbed from her mother's drawer, shaking when she thought of wearing it outside with North there.

She shut her bedroom door and sank against it. For a second the wood felt cool against her hot skin after her steamy backyard.

After North.

Uncertain, conflicted, she threw the suit on the floor. She hated red, more than any color in the world, hated the sexy style cut high over the thigh her mother had chosen. And yet...

Mother had said it was so hot, that they should swim before supper. When Melody had mentioned she hadn't unpacked and didn't know where her suit was, Dee Dee had said, "I have a brand-new one in my top drawer you can borrow."

Stripping off her T-shirt and shorts, Melody moved past the piles of suitcases and boxes toward her flamboyantly red flowered bed, only to be upset not by her mother's gaudy decorating, but by her own reflection in the long mirror beneath the bumper sticker.

The frightened girl with those rosy cheeks in the push-up black bra and thong panties reminded her of that other queasy girl she'd seen in North's apartment mirror six months ago when she'd been trapped between boundless love and desire and sexual despair.

She'd called him an animal.

His hand had been inside her when he'd muttered, "An animal? I love you, Melody. This is what men and women who love each other do together—in private. Someday, you're going to grow up. You'll come running home, for this, darlin', but I won't be here waiting. I'm sick and tired of waiting."

Then he'd let her go and had lain on the bed beside her for a while, staring up at his ceiling fan that had spun lazily above them. Finally, when they'd both recovered a little, he'd balled her black lace panties and bra in his brown fist and thrown them at her, saying she'd come back, begging for more of the same. Saying that even if she crawled, he'd tell her he was done with a tease like her for good.

"I'm sorry," he'd said after he'd dressed, apologizing for what he'd done to her in bed and for some of what he'd said.

"I'm sorry, too."

From the door he'd lashed her with rough words that had smashed her heart. "I'm sorry I ever met you." He hadn't slammed the door. It had clicked so softly; she'd barely heard him leave. Still, a cold chill had run down her spine at the utter finality of his retreating footsteps.

Desolation had overpowered her just as fear had gotten a grip on her when he'd started making love to her, and she'd just felt so scared and helpless and had wanted to get away.

She hadn't been able to face her true feelings that night much less try to tell him. But over time, when he hadn't called, she'd begun to miss him terribly. Some inner resilience had lessened her sense of shame and intensified all the other inexplicable needs that had made her unable to forget North.

He'd been so wonderful to her in so many ways. So kind and patient, especially in those early years. But he was a man, and he needed a woman.

"I want a grown-up woman, a real woman, who knows how to love."

"You mean you want sex."

"Now that you mention it—yes. That would be a great start."

And here she was, home again, and more confused than ever about everything, including North.

North hadn't said, "I told you so," tonight.

Not in so many words. But he'd made her feel it—in every cell of her being. Every time he'd looked at her so coldly, and she'd flamed to life again, she'd remembered that night when she'd enflamed him, enticed him, and then gotten terrified, and hurt him all over again.

Melody opened her closet to search her built-in drawers for another suit. In the second drawer she found a stack of videocassette tapes. Blushing, remembering where she'd found them and what they were of, she fisted her hands like a defiant child. Then she slammed the drawer.

How could her parents watch those things? Sex? Why was it so important to everybody except her?

She'd made her choices. Why, oh why, did they have to be so hard to live with? Why, oh why, did she have to be the only modern girl in all of the United States who had hang-ups about sex?

"Get over it," Cathy, her best friend would say. "You know what they say, practice makes perfect."

North's cockiness and blatant sexiness along with Melody's natural wariness weren't going to get her down tonight. Neither was his cool, calculated indifference. Tonight would be short and sweet, like they'd agreed. Then they'd go their separate ways.

Tonight wasn't going to be about sex!

She picked up the red suit and pulled it on. When she saw herself, she gasped at how much of her backside was hanging out.

Through her gauzy curtains, she could see North and her father talking amiably, more amiably than when she'd been out there with them. She was too far away to hear the rumble of his deep drawl, too far for it to send shivers through her, but it was all too obvious, North was much more relaxed when she wasn't around.

Likewise.

He lounged against the garage, his arms crossed, his long legs sprawled apart, laughing at something her father said. When she'd been out there, too, he'd stood stiffly by her father's side, his eyes on the shrimp appetizers sizzling on the grill, his answers to her father's questions brief and uninformative when Sam had done his best to ask intelligent questions about the ranch or roundup and the drought.

Sam had watched them both as he'd taken a lengthy pull of his imported beer. "Long, hot summer?"

"Yes."

"Bad for ranching?"

North had nodded.

For the first time Melody had noticed the dark circles

under his eyes, the weariness behind his smiles. He'd been working too hard she could tell.

"Any chance of rain?" her father had asked.

"Not unless we get a hurricane."

"It rained out west last night."

Then Melody had asked, "What do you hear from your mother, North?"

"Not much."

"Do you miss her?"

"What the hell kind of question is that?" he'd snapped.

North, who had been so dark and intense in the foyer, hadn't even looked up from the grill when she'd joined them there or when she'd spoken. Not even when he'd burst out at her so angrily. His refusal to do so had gotten her even more dizzily nervous than she'd been in the foyer when he'd pinned her against the wall.

First, he'd been all over her in the foyer. Then in the backyard, not only hadn't she existed, she'd been the last person he intended to confide in.

But he'd come over, and he made her feel alive, as she hadn't in months. More alive than in India or any other exotic locale.

In the six months since *that* night, she'd gone to India and Manhattan and Boston and then back to Texas. She'd moved into a tiny cottage with an older woman named Elizabeth, who was a musician in the Austin music scene. Elizabeth did gigs almost every night. Home alone, Melody had realized she was lonelier than she ever had been in her whole life. Even so, after North she hadn't wanted to date.

She'd gotten up every morning, flossed and brushed her teeth, washed her hair and gone out to her menial job at the park. Her parents hadn't understood her not getting a "real" job, not using her education. But she'd preferred wandering through the park, being out with nature, even picking up garbage, to a real adult job.

Nights, she'd showered and gotten into bed—alone again. Her life had been a dull routine until that day Randy

Hunter, a guy she intensely disliked from school in Corpus Christi, had shown up at the park.

He'd leaned against the door of her tiny tollbooth, trapping her inside. "You look awful good in those short shorts, sugar." His hot eyes had lingered on her legs long after she'd handed him his receipt and change.

"What is that getup, a little rangerette costume?"

"I'm a park tech."

"Aren't you the girl that used to wear red panties in elementary school?"

She hadn't answered.

"What color are you wearing under—"

Shaking, she'd closed her eyes in mute panic. "Why don't you go enjoy the park."

"You still like sexy underwear?"

Randy had come to the park too often after that. But what had really bothered her was the package somebody had sent her later the same week. When she'd opened it and a pair of red thong panties had spilled out of it, she'd quit on the spot.

And come running home.

To North.

No. No. But, when Melody lifted her gauzy curtain and caught another glimpse of North, her heart started hammering. He did make her feel, make her feel she was real, make her know that she wanted more than she had.

And North wanted her, too.

Which was why she'd run from him.

Yet what she felt for him was profoundly different than anything she'd ever felt for another man. Suddenly she realized that she'd thought about him for months and months even when she hadn't admitted it to herself.

When her mother had sent her applications for an internship in Paris, Melody hadn't bothered to fill the papers out. Paris had suddenly seemed too far away. Why had she turned down so many wonderful opportunities?

She told North she wanted adventures with other less

controlling men, men who didn't press her to give what she couldn't give. The truth was she had zero interest in other men. Zero interest in being so far away.

Still, North was all wrong for her. Maybe he was only twenty-nine, maybe he was only seven years older than she was; still, because he'd assumed massive responsibilities at such a young age, he seemed a lifetime ahead of her. He'd managed a difficult family, employees, land, animals and lots of money. As a result, he seemed so sure of himself, he made her feel even younger and less certain than she did with other people.

He'd had no choice about choosing his career. She was trying to discover who she was and what she wanted to do with the rest of her life. Not that she really wanted to grow up. Childhood had seemed such a simple time. She'd been popular and loved until…

Until that long-ago afternoon when she'd been a sixth-grader, when a group of boys had followed her home from school. Their singsong taunts had set her heart to pounding like a drum. She'd run, but they'd been faster. It hadn't been long before one of them had tripped her, toppling her onto a shell driveway under the purple shade of a chinaberry tree. Like a pack, they'd jumped her, their hands tugging at her skirt.

Her fingers clawed the gauzy curtains, and she forced her attention to her daddy, who was swinging his can of lighter fluid with a great flourish over the grate.

Mother would flip if she saw him do that.

Then Daddy struck a match, and flames whooshed four feet high. He jumped back. So did Melody.

On a deep shuddering breath, she opened her patio door and ran outside just as her mother tore out of the kitchen and began to shout about her precious rib eyes. North dashed out of the pool house and went straight to her father.

As North worked to get the fire back under control, Melody stood beneath the lush red bougainvillea that dripped from the balcony and watched the ripple of muscles in his broad brown shoulders and strong, wide chest. Long hours of brutal work in the sun had him leaner and tougher than ever.

Her mouth curved with amusement when she saw the thick gathers of the overlarge bathing suit he must've borrowed from Daddy bunching at his narrow waist.

Mother had a thing about staying slim. Maybe she had a point about putting Daddy on a diet.

When the fire was tamer, North stared across the yard at her, too. A different kind of panic lit his eyes when he saw her hiding from him amidst the purple-red blossoms in her mother's tight scarlet swimsuit with way too much of her bare bottom showing.

His beautiful mouth twisted.

She froze in that breathless instant before he tore his deep, dark gaze away and began poking at the fire again.

She jumped back inside. To find her mother's sarong, she told herself. After all, she needed a cover-up.

The next hour was filled with more little awkward moments when she joined North at the pool. When she removed the sarong, his black eyebrows slammed together. Then he dived into the pool.

Her parents were bickering good-humoredly beside the grill, but she was barely aware of them. A pang of regret tugged at her heart as she sank down on a chaise longue near a bed of ferns on the far side of the terrace.

North began swimming laps. Usually he worked so hard all day and was too tired for such vigorous exercise. She wondered if the only reason he was swimming like that was to avoid her.

He probably wanted to get through tonight and be done with her.

The same as she did.

Not so long ago, he would've knelt beside her and teased her. He would've wanted her attention, her smiles. Not so long ago, he'd loved her fiercely.

What made love like that stop? Had he simply willed it to stop?

Glumly she pasted on a smile and forced her gaze to slide past the translucent ferns toward her parents. Her father was tossing bits of rib eye down to Baby, the family's pedigreed Himalayan.

"Why does she meow if she doesn't want it?" Sam threw another chunk of meat down. "See—she's just sniffing and pawing at it."

"You have to cut Baby's steak into itsy-bitsy pieces," Dee Dee said, stealing his knife.

"What kind of sissy, no-good, snaggle-toothed cat—"

Baby had one crooked tooth that curled upward toward her nose like a miniature fang, making her look both darling and ridiculous.

"If you're mad at me," Dee Dee said, "don't attack my precious Baby. Give me that knife—"

"Ha! Don't think I'm going to use that knife after you use it on that cat's meat."

Geography. Suddenly it felt good to be home, good to have North here even if he didn't love her, Melody thought. The heavy air was warm and wet, pleasantly tropical. Wind rustled though the thick ferns and trees. Wind chimes tinkled. Her parents' jibes blended into the sounds of traffic from Ocean Drive, the scenic boulevard a block away that curved around the bay.

Almost she was a little girl again, safe and sound—here. Or a young woman in love for the first time. She remembered other suppers cooked outside, hamburgers made marvelous because North had been there. After dinner sometimes they'd put on music and had danced out by the pool. Sometimes he'd taken her for a spin in his pickup along the bay. Often they'd stopped at a seaside park and run, hand in hand, down to the beach as a full bright moon lit a golden path across black waves. Sometimes he'd stayed so late, he'd fallen asleep on the couch in the day and been there the next day when Sam got up.

Never looking her way, North swam furiously.

Turning her back to him, Melody revealed way too much hip and thigh.

Did she only imagine that North lowered his black head and swam even faster? The sun was low, but she rubbed lotion onto her legs anyway.

When he still wouldn't look, she got up and grabbed her mother's yellow air mattress and dragged it to the shallow end. Lying down on it carefully, she kicked herself toward the middle of the pool, straight into North's path.

Without looking up, he veered and swam even faster. She closed her eyes and just drifted, pretending she was enjoying the evening sounds and the way the water sloshed against her skin every time North swam by.

In reality she was remembering that terrible time when he'd dated her sister, Claire—the perfect, gorgeous Claire. Melody had pretended she hadn't cared about that, too. But all the time she'd felt so betrayed that he'd turned to Claire so soon after she'd jilted him. If he'd really loved her—

"Tell North it's nearly time for supper," her mother called.

Melody did a flutter kick and paddled with her hands until she got herself right in front of his path. As she waited for North there, her heart began to race absurdly.

He would have veered away from her again, only she thunked a knuckle on his wet black head. Instantly his big body slid to halt, his head stopping within inches of her parted legs.

"Supper," she said a little shyly.

"What's left of it," Dee Dee shouted at them. "Your father burned the rib eyes—as usual."

A heavy silence descended over the foursome. Sam, who was extremely sensitive about his cooking skills, wore a wounded frown as he flung the blackened steaks from the grill onto Dee Dee's platter. Abruptly North stood up and stomped toward the concrete stairs, dripping water. Melody raced after him and handed him her towel.

"Don't tell me how to cook, woman!" Sam thundered.

"Oh, dear," Melody whispered shyly to North.

North smiled. "I was wondering when he'd blow. A guy like your dad can only swallow so much."

"If you'd let me cook inside," Dee Dee countered.

"I'm retired, so I have time to barbecue."

"Who asked you to retire? I like to cook."

"Dee—"

Dee Dee raced toward the house in a huff. Sam grabbed the platter of steaks and followed her. "She's nicer to that damned cat than she ever is to me!"

"Alone at last," Melody said. "Just what you've been so scared of."

"I'm not scared."

"You look about as happy as Daddy did before he blew."

"That bad, huh?"

"Now that we're alone—you just might have to talk to me. A smile would be nice, too."

In spite of himself, North actually grinned at her.

"Ignoring you is as hard as talking to you."

"I wonder why?"

"I don't even want to know."

"Maybe because we loved each other for years and years," she whispered.

"You jilted me!"

"You turned to Claire fast enough!"

"So—how is the new bride?" he asked.

"Madly in love. Pregnant. Living in New Orleans."

They fell silent.

"We certainly made a mess of things," he said.

"I usually do...even when I try not to. You know that, North. You're so much older and more competent, you show me up...more than a less experienced kind of guy would."

As always when she even mentioned other guys, he scowled. When he lapsed into one of his moody silences, she could tell she was going to have to help him. Sometimes he couldn't get two words out of his mouth.

"What have you been doing...since—" she asked.

"Since *that* night?"

"I really want to know."

"Same as always. Just working."

"You're so brown," she said, her gaze drifting over his body.

"I'm outside a lot. You know that."

"And the big muscles?"

"From mucking stalls. Bailing hay. Fixing trucks. Working cows. Repairing fences."

"Don't you have cowboys?"

"I am a cowboy."

"Mr. Macho—always out to prove—"

"You don't know anything."

"Or maybe I do."

"Sometimes it's harder crunching numbers...thinking...than doing the actual work itself. Then there's this little camel...really he's a llama. He's a newborn and having a tough time. I get up every morning to feed him. He's not putting on weight."

"Why not?"

"He needs his mama's milk straight out of his mama, I guess."

"I can see you're worried about him."

"He was real shy at first. He's getting used to me." He looked at her. "He climbed into my lap once.... It's ridiculous."

"No, being tenderhearted is never ridiculous," she said softly. "I'd like to meet your llama."

"Little Camel."

"Little Camel," she repeated.

"What about you?"

"After India...Manhattan...Boston...then home to Austin.... The big cities weren't as exciting as I thought they'd be, so I didn't stay long. So, mostly, it's just been the same old stuff for me, too.''

"The same park job?"

"I just quit. Two weeks ago."

"For good, I hope. I never liked you working..."

When she frowned, he stopped.

"You didn't like that one park because of its clothing optional beach."

"Men go there. They take off their clothes."

"I worked the ticket booth. Besides, it wasn't like I worked there every day."

"Why didn't it bother you that those guys strutted around with nothing when you wouldn't let me..."

"Maybe if you'd been content just to strut." She giggled. "Maybe you should be glad I was trying to get over my...er...hang-up and get used to the idea of naked men and..."

"Usually a virgin gets comfortable about that with the man she loves."

"There aren't rules for life—Bertie."

"You taught me that. That's for damn sure. You wear the sexiest underwear in the universe...and can't stand sex."

"Other people's rules don't work for me."

"So, you're making up a set of your own as you go?"

As he stared at her, she lowered her gaze to the ripple of hard teak flesh that laced his chest and shoulders. All of a sudden she imagined that sleek, bronzed body on one of those limestone shelves at the park's clothing optional beach. How glorious he'd be out there—naked.

Why didn't he put his shirt on? Why did he have to be so virile and dark, so honed with muscle—so male.

She flushed, and that made her angry. "Maybe I can't work my problems out—the usual way."

"Keep staring, darlin'." He grinned. "Dirty thoughts?"

"Of course not."

"Hope springs eternal."

"All you ever think about is sex."

When his white grin broadened, she felt wild for him. Which made her even more uncomfortable. She knew that if he'd touched her or tried to kiss her, she would have died from the thrill of it even though it would have scared her.

She hadn't dated since him. All of a sudden she knew why. She wanted him even though she was scared of sex. She licked her lips and then rubbed her brow.

"It's okay...what you did," he said, "your wanting to break up. It was for the best. I see that now. Like I told you, I need a woman."

She frowned.

"We're too different," he persisted. "What we want is too different."

"Really?" She swallowed hard.

"I wanted you in bed."

"And now you don't?" She flushed, feeling strange and hurt, which was ridiculous.

"Now I just want you to be happy," he murmured.

For a second she felt so shy and awkward, she couldn't think of anything else to say, so she said the first thing that popped into her mind. Which was stupid.

"I'm sorry I ruined your relaxing evening with my parents."

"I guess we'd better go in and get to relaxing. I'll get dressed."

"You look good."

"Dirty thoughts again?" The warmth in his teasing voice was sweet and familiar.

"I do have dirty thoughts," she admitted. "Oh, Bertie, I'm all mixed up."

"I won't argue that point." But he smiled down at her with genuine affection.

"We used to be such good friends," she said. "I've missed that."

"Me, too." He tensed. "But we can't be friends. Not when I still feel—"

"You do?"

A quick heat washed and ebbed in her cheeks.

Before he could answer, Dee Dee opened the door and called out to them, "Y'all coming?"

"What do you feel?"

"It doesn't matter." His voice was colder. "It can't matter."

He was right, of course. So why did she feel curiously deflated?

"I'm hungry. That's all," he said. "Starved." His eyes lingered on her. "Let's go eat. At least that's something we can still do together without getting into trouble."

"Maybe I want to get into trouble."

"You always say that. You always back down."

"What if I didn't?"

"It's too late. I've got a new girl—Maria. Everybody says she's perfect for me."

Her heart slammed painfully. Her stomach knotted. "Oh, North, I—I'm so happy for you."

Four

North felt so tired. The den was icy cold, refreshingly so after the long hot day. The Woodses' couch was way too comfortable all of a sudden. North was glad dinner was over and the Woodses and their impossible sexy daughter were all out of the dining room. Even sprawled out on their extra-long sofa, his legs felt cramped from sitting still so long underneath that antique table.

Voices were talking in North's head, but he was too drowsy to be turned-on by *her* to heed them.

Say goodbye and leave.

In a minute.

You shouldn't have trailed so dutifully after Melody down that flowery hall when Dee Dee and Sam came in here.

If you don't git, you'll be trapped for sure, pardner.

Obstinately he pillowed his hands behind his black head and tried to ignore Melody so he could make sense out of the Woodses' conversation that was getting more rambling and less coherent with every drink.

Melody had gotten really quiet when he'd told her about Maria. All through the interminable dinner she'd just sat still and alert, barely picking at her spinach salad, not daring even to look at him. Maybe because he and Melody had been so strained, Dee Dee and Sam had drunk too much and taken over.

Say goodbye. Maria's perfect for you.

Dee Dee's voice was shrill; Sam's speech was slurred but was going strong.

Smile. It's the second best thing you can do with your lips.

All of a sudden, North couldn't take his eyes off Melody. In the shadowy light, she seemed so young and vulnerable and yet utterly delectable. So lost and needy.

Like him.

So kissable.

His physical reaction to her bothered him. Maybe he was too bone-weary to fight it. He'd worked too hard and long in the sun. He'd swum too vigorously and eaten too much as well. Suddenly he felt incredibly at home on the Woodses' couch.

At least he knew where Melody was for a change.

Not that he cared. Maria was going to be his girl. As he'd said, she was perfect.

When Dee Dee and Sam suddenly stopped talking, North felt he had to say something to get them going again, so he could stay.

"So, how do you like retirement, Sam?"

They both bristled, feathers straight up, like two cocks in a ring.

North was soon so sleepy he caught only fragments of their tense answers.

"—great…great—"

"—I wish Sam still had some hobbies—"

"—you have enough for both of us, spending money—"

"—bet you're working hard, too hard, on that big ranch—"

"—from before sunup to after sundown, sir. Day after day—"

"—those long hot days finally catching up to you—"

Their voices blurred. All he saw was Melody, sitting stiffly at the other end of the couch in that sexy red one-piece suit that fit her pert breasts like a glove and left too much of her legs exposed. More than anything he wanted to hold her.

If he fell asleep, he could stay.

The Woodses' voices softened, and North's chest began to feel very heavy. Then it began to rise and fall more rhythmically. Vaguely he was aware of Dee Dee and Sam whispering and then tiptoeing silently past him. Of Melody staying.

He wanted to pull her closer, to feel the heat of her body next to his as they lay there together. But when he finally murmured her name, she was gone, and there was only the hum of the deliciously cold air conditioner.

The den got colder and darker. When he opened his eyes a long while later, Melody was back, kneeling beside him, looking more gorgeous than ever in a red knit blouse with spaghetti straps, white short skirt edged with red rickrack, and strappy red sandals. Her reddish gold hair was piled high, caught in a scarlet ribbon, loose tendrils of the silky stuff spilling over her shoulders. Was she wearing black lace underneath?

"Why red tonight? You hate red," he muttered thickly running a fingertip beneath her chin even as he wondered about her underwear.

She shivered.

"Yes."

"How come?"

Her smoky-blue eyes darkened.

When he kept stroking her, she swallowed. "The suit was Mother's." She swallowed. "The blouse is hers, too. I haven't unpacked yet."

"And you'll probably let a year go by before you do,"

he teased, remembering how she had a bad habit of putting things off. "Is it morning? How long did I sleep, darlin'?"

"A couple of hours."

"What?" He jumped up. Sitting forward, he raked his hands through his hair.

"You must be awful tired, North."

"Long days," he admitted. "Long nights, too." Long lonely nights. Then there were those strange, surreal, wild nights chasing the Midnight Bandit.

"Maria?"

"Work."

"So, you're neglecting your perfect girlfriend, too?"

"We just started dating." Why the hell had he admitted that?

"Hey, I don't want to talk about her."

Struck anew by Melody's beauty, he reached out and touched her lips with his fingertip. She looked like an angel with that halo of hair glowing around her face.

Smile. It's the second best thing you can do with your lips.

He jerked his hand from that luscious, swollen mouth.

"I came to see if you're all right," she said gently. "To tell you goodbye. I'm going out."

He stole a peek at his watch under his white cuff. It was past midnight. "At this hour? Alone?"

"Not alone."

That made him fiercer.

"You could come with us." She hesitated as if her invitation had been accidental, impulsive. "I mean…only if you wanted to."

"*Us?* Where? Who?"

"Us. Cathy and me. Out dancing."

Damn. "Just Cathy?" He didn't much like Cathy Murano. He didn't consider her a good influence. She had sex on the brain and considered herself a fount of wisdom in that department. But she and Melody had been friends since preschool, and Melody had a soft spot for old friends.

At least they didn't have dates. Not that he cared.

Then it hit him. Maybe they were going out to look for guys.

"You're going to a bar, aren't you?" he asked.

Melody shrugged, causing a thin red strap to fall off her shoulder. "You know Cathy."

"And you know what I think of her, too."

"Don't start. You're not my boyfriend anymore. You've got Maria."

Smile. It's the second... He blocked that refrain.

"Right." Why was that always so hard to remember when Melody was anywhere near?

A minute ago he'd been dead tired. He'd given her the impression he intended to get serious about Maria, who really was perfect for him if only... The last thing he needed was to go dancing with Melody at some pickup place.

"Yes," he growled.

"Yes?"

"Yes, I'll go."

"Oh, dear."

"What?"

When she burst out laughing, she looked so beautiful he forgot to wonder why he'd worried that she'd seemed so alarmed at first.

He found out soon enough once they parked in front of a squatty, windowless, black building downtown and saw the huge hot pink letters throbbing as if they'd come to life. The Liquid Poodle's marquee was advertising a drag show at 1:00 a.m.

"A drag show? Tell me we aren't going to a gay bar," he muttered.

"We aren't going to a gay bar," Melody teased.

"We sure as hell are," he growled.

"So—you told me to lie."

He got out and went around the car and opened her door. "How come you two chose a gay bar?"

"Guys in gay bars don't hit on girls."

"Oh, wise up, Mel," Cathy said from the back seat, smacking her chewing gum as she pushed her own door open. She paused to blow a big pink bubble which Melody popped with a white polished fingernail. "Sometimes they do."

North lifted an eyebrow.

On that cheery note, Cathy, who was tall and dark with spiky, red-tipped black hair and a tiny silver ring through her left eyebrow, slid out of the car. While North locked the car, Cathy breezed ahead of them to try to talk the bouncer into lowering her cover charge.

"You go to these places with her often?" North asked.

"She called me. We both felt like dancing tonight."

"I forgot—you're the extrovert."

"You're getting nicer. Usually you call me the exhibitionist, the show-off."

"You're that, too."

"Maybe someday, I'll put on a private show just for you."

"Been there. Done that. Please just swear you won't do it in public again."

"I swear."

"Why don't I feel the least bit reassured?"

"'Cause you're a worrywart, Rancher Black! Cheer up. I mean that in a good way."

"What if somebody sees me here?" he said.

"You're with me. So, you're safe."

"You have a funny definition of safe."

Inside the bar, the beat of the music was all powerful. North liked rock, but this industrial hip-hop had no melody and was blasting so loud he had to jam bits of paper napkin into his ears. Not that the lyrics were worth listening to anyway.

Other than the loud music, the bar seemed dead.

"Not many people tonight," he said to Melody as he eyed the empty tables and the men sitting alone at the bar.

"We're here," she said brightly.

North cast a suspicious eye on the other patrons, who were mostly men. Guys with earrings. Guys in sleeveless T-shirts that showed off sculpted brown arms and a few creative tattoos. Guys with lean waists and hips in low-slung, flared jeans prowled the edges of the room. They were watching him, too.

Dark lights made everybody's earrings and white shirts glow, including his. The weird effect made him feel exposed.

He was glad he didn't see anybody he knew.

"Now don't panic, Bertie."

"Who the hell's panicking?" He rubbed his collar.

She put a fingertip on his brown nose. "I know that look."

"You ought to. You can get kinda panicky yourself."

They stared at each other's lips, and he wondered if she was remembering lying in his bed, snuggled close, his hands all over her. He took her arm and led her upstairs, so he could keep an eye on the action. Cathy followed them.

The men sat on their stools drinking and smoking, not talking. Nobody danced.

Then a waiter with stark white hair and intense light eyes swaggered up to their table. "What'll you have?"

North quickly ordered three beers. "Straight out of the bottle. No glasses."

The man's laser blue-white eyes burned into North's. The boy grinned. "Gotcha."

Cathy excused herself to go to the ladies' room.

"Brave lady," North murmured in an undertone as he glared at the sign above the men's room.

Melody threaded her fingers around his. "Let's dance."

The empty dance floor was ringed by silent men, their shirts eerily aglow.

"You've got to be out of your mind."

"Then I'll dance by myself."

"Don't you dare—"

"Bertie-boy, your earplugs are glowing."

"Bertie was bad enough, little darlin'...."

"Bertie's cute," she breathed. "So are you." Her eyes glinted with mischief as she rested her hand lightly on his forearm.

He forgot where they were. He forgot everything but her. His heart pulsed from her light touch. Overhead spots started to flash.

Before he could grab her wrist and hold on to her, the brat was gone. Almost instantly, the impertinent exhibitionist was in the middle of the dance floor. When somebody aimed a spotlight on her, she winked at North.

When he scowled down at her, she closed her eyes, extended both hands toward him and began undulating to the wild jungle beat.

All by herself.

In front of all those guys.

North's blood ran cold as he stared at her. It turned to ice when he realized the guys weren't watching her.

They were watching him.

The black walls seemed to close in on him as everybody's white shirts seemed to brighten with an otherworldly brilliance. Nose rings and earrings flamed blue.

When a blond fellow in a radiant tank top with light eyes and an eyebrow ring smiled and then swaggered toward him, North shoved back his stool and raced toward Melody.

Three long strides had North in the middle of that dance floor with Melody who beamed at him playfully.

"It was only the waiter," she giggled.

He grabbed her by the waist and pulled her to him.

Big mistake—even here, even with guys gawking at him, he was instantly more aware of Melody than of anything else in the room. Through his jeans, he felt the heat of her pelvis, the heat of her legs.

She put her mouth against his ear. "What about your new, perfect girl?"

"Who?"

"Maria."

"Oh—her. Forget I ever mentioned her." He pulled her close.

For an instant Melody's smoky-blue eyes darkened as she caught the rhythm and swayed into him. Hips molded to his, their bodies writhing in perfect harmony, she felt better and better to him. The throbbing beat played havoc with his other senses.

He'd wanted a woman. She'd been a shy girl.

Something told him the rules of the game they'd always played together were about to change.

Too late. She'd done him wrong.

Then he felt her lips against his collar. Her body was sleek and warm. His body didn't care what she'd done.

Smile. It's the second best thing you can do with your lips.

The jukebox changed. Somebody played their song, and he forgot where they were and what she'd done. He closed his eyes and forgot everything but Melody.

Dancing, the music, the woman, his own longing stripped him of the last of his logical sense. He responded against his will.

"Oh, Bertie. Bertie…Bertie…Bertie…"

Her hands caressed his neck. Her breath was warm against his throat.

Here we go again.

She was putting on one of her performances. Getting him all worked up—for nothing. He was twenty-nine. He knew better. He wanted more.

He'd loved her. For as long as he could remember, he'd loved her. But his love hadn't been enough. She hadn't wanted him enough. She'd wanted adventures, an exciting life, not some rancher tied to his land, his family, to his duty. And not sex.

His brain screamed at him to take her home, but his flesh

was weak. She tantalized him with her sweet promises. And as always, he was a sucker for lost causes.

So, he swirled her into a dark corner where they danced alone, where he got hotter and hotter whether the songs were slow or fast. Only vaguely was he aware of Cathy coming up to them and whispering through the shadows that she was going to another bar with a friend.

"Why don't we go somewhere, too, Bertie?" Melody whispered.

"Where?"

"Wherever you want."

"All right." His voice was soft even though his body throbbed to have her.

He grabbed her by the hand and led her outside. The warm, salt-laden breeze felt heavy and yet fresh after the smoky bar. Glad to be outside, he inhaled deeply. So did she.

He wanted to kiss her so badly he hurt, to push for more as he always had in the past.

Instead he walked her to her car in silence. After he helped her inside, he got behind the wheel. When he drove her to her parents' home, she seemed surprised.

"But I thought you wanted—"

"Not anymore," he lied even as he felt he was dying inside because he wanted her so much.

"Because of your new, perfect girl—"

"Don't bring anybody else into this."

"I didn't. You did."

"Be fair." He brushed his hand against her velvet soft cheek for the last time and felt its dampness wetting his finger. Tears. God, she was killing him.

"Good night, Melody," he rasped. "Have a nice life."

"You, too." Her glassy blue eyes caught the night light and reflected pain as intense with torment as his own. "And y-you take good care of that baby llama, you hear," she murmured.

"I will. I swear it."

"Goodbye then…" The sheen of tears glazing her eyes cut through him like a knife.

"Mel, don't cry—"

"Don't go to Maria. Not…not tonight."

"What?"

"I had fun tonight…with you," she said. "Like always."

He nodded and swallowed the hard lump in his throat. He didn't speak as she opened her door and got out and ran up the walk.

At the door she turned as if willing him to weaken and change his mind.

Clenching the steering wheel, he waited until the foyer lights were snuffed out before he opened the car door. Only then did he get out and walk ever so slowly toward his own truck.

It was over.

At last.

Five

"**Y**ou don't understand, Cathy. I'm not like you. I'm still a…a…" Melody's heart pounded as she lay on her bed, pressing the receiver against her ear as she toyed with the cord, which wound between her legs. "Well," she whispered. "You know, the V-word."

The wind had picked up. Outside the palm fronds clattered. Her parents' two-story, wooden house was talking to her, too. Melody held her breath as she waited, but Cathy was silent.

"Say something!"

"I knew you were hung-up, Mel. But…but…this is too much! This is the twenty-first century! You can't still be a—!"

Melody put her hand over the mouthpiece. "Shh! What if my dad picks up the phone?"

"What about North? I thought you went to his place *that* night—"

"But I didn't sleep with him," she whispered.

"But you let me think— He broke up with Claire for you."

"It's why we broke up in the first place. Why we never really got back together after Claire."

Cathy snickered. "You're twenty-two. You've got to be joking!"

Melody closed her eyes. "Don't laugh at me…please."

Cathy smacked her gum. "I'm not. This is serious. This is not normal. You know that, don't you? Have you considered therapy?"

Melody swallowed. "You sound like Mother! I can't talk about this to some stranger! It's hard enough telling you!"

"You've gotta do something about this, babe. Right away."

"Like what?"

"Like face the fact North wants you. Real bad. The way he was dancing… The way he couldn't take his eyes off you, not for a second… God, you two got *me* hot. Just watching you— He's on testosterone overload. He's hurting, babe."

"He drove me straight home."

"So? You two have a history."

"He dated my sister. My perfect sister."

"Because you jilted him."

"Because… Oh, I don't know what's wrong with me. He and I don't communicate."

"That's the best reason I know to have sex! You've gotta go for it."

"Believe me, I've tried."

"So—don't quit. I've got a feeling you're on a roll tonight."

"But—"

"Just go over there."

"To North's? What would I say to him? Do?"

"Just go! Then play it by ear. Put on some music. Guys like…"

"They like what?"

"Sexual favors. You know. Show him how much you care."

"I don't know how. I always get scared when he tries something."

"So you try something! It's not like you need lessons. You were born knowing how. Besides, North knows how."

"But I don't know anything but stuff other girls talk about or stuff I see in movies. And when it happens it always makes me feel sick. This is easy for you. It's hard for me. I—I don't know why."

"You think too much." Cathy paused. "It gets easier. You've just gotta practice. You'll like it."

"I—I don't know where to start."

"From first base. Kiss him. Go now."

"I can't."

More gum smacking and bubble blowing. "You mentioned movies. And that got me thinking about those videos you stole out of your parents' closet when you were sifting through their stuff."

"That was years ago!"

"Not all that long really. We watched that one about that girl named Ala over and over two months ago!"

"I didn't! You did!"

"You watched it through your fingers!"

"It was so disgusting. What they did. What she did."

"Guys don't think so. Go now!"

"I don't think—"

"Do you want that Maria, whoever she is, to get him?"

"Maria?" Did the whole world know about Maria?

A gum bubble popped. "Jeff's telling everybody about Miss Perfection—especially your friends."

"He's never liked me."

"Well, he likes Maria, and she's gorgeous. He says she's been after North since forever. She's got a great big ranch right next to his, and it's almost as big as El Dorado. Besides being impressed with her land, Jeff says she's real sexy. Big at the top. If you don't do something to knock

North's socks off and fast, she's gonna get him, babe! A smart woman knows how to hook a lonely man with sex and then reel him in real slow."

"But I can't!"

"I'll tell you what to do. If other people can do it, you can, too. Drink a glass of wine. Watch the video. Let it spark some creativity. Then imagine yourself and North doing—"

"Cathy, you really are disgusting."

"Maybe so, but I'm not frigid. My guys like me."

Melody gasped. "Guys? The only man I've ever really wanted is—"

"Go over there. Put on some music. Start dancing. It'll happen. You can't stay eleven years old forever."

"Eleven years old—" Melody's voice trailed off. "Why did you pick that age?"

"I gotta go," Cathy said. "Just remember sex is the hook that is the main weapon in a fishergirl's box of lures. Use it or lose him. And you don't have to tell him you're still a…a…the V-word."

Cathy hung up.

Eleven.

Melody had been eleven that day she'd worn those red cotton panties to school and Randy Hunter had glimpsed bright ruffles under her skirt when she'd been jumping rope. He'd told some other guys, and they'd all wanted to see her panties, too.

So, they'd followed her home and scared her so bad she still couldn't—

Maybe if she had just one glass of wine…

A little dazed, Melody lay still on the den couch, her hands covering her eyes, staring into blackness, instead of at those awful images flickering on the television screen.

Why was sex such a big deal?

A low moan broke the silence when she finally managed

to part her fingers and stare through them at the wiggling couple.

Tongues. Hands. Lips.

She couldn't watch the odious pair.

Forcing her fingers wider, she stared at a seedy-looking black-haired man unzipping his jeans while a brassy redhead unbuttoned her blouse. Their eyes were dead, their complexions waxen. But they tongued their lips, straining to give the illusion of sexual ecstasy to their viewers.

Melody tensed. She shut her eyes.

They were faking it. She couldn't watch them smile when their hearts weren't in it. Oh, they knew what to do, what part to put where. But it was all so mechanical, so contrived and spiritless. Where was love, tenderness?

What did love and tenderness have to do with sex?

Cathy had said to imagine other people she knew doing this. Melody tightened her fingers over her eyes and resisted that advice.

Instead of the woman on her television screen, Melody saw a little girl running down a tree-lined street as fast as she could. She heard cruel, jeering voices behind her. Four bigger boys wearing mirrored sunglasses. She felt hunted, terrified. Then they were on top of her.

North had come, and the boys had run. They hadn't really done anything but look at her red panties and laugh. Just the same, she'd felt violated. She hadn't been sure exactly what they'd even intended. But that hadn't stopped her from filling in all the empty blanks in her imagination with terror and shame.

She'd pushed her skirt down and gotten herself more or less together before North had seen her. He'd wanted to know why they'd chased her and what they'd done to her. She hadn't told him. After all, it was her fault for wearing the pretty new red panties to school. Her behavior had been even every bit as shameful as theirs.

"Your heart's racing like a rabbit's," North had whispered as he helped her up.

"I'm fine."

"Did they hurt you?"

She'd shaken her head.

"These yours?" In his hand he'd held a pair of mirrored sunglasses.

She'd screamed and thrown herself into his arms and sobbed. Then she'd pushed him away. "Don't tell Mother."

"But—"

"You know how she is. She'll come up to the school. Then everybody'll know—"

"Know what?"

About my red panties.

She'd taken the sunglasses and thrown them down. Then she'd stomped on them until nothing was left but glittering bits. "I just don't want people to know. That's all."

When Melody opened her eyes, the man on the television was pushing the woman down, nestling her face against his waist. When she licked her lips, he forced her to—

She shut her eyes. When she peered through her fingers again, he no longer looked like he was having to fake ecstasy.

In a single fluid movement Melody got up and yanked the obscene tape from the tape player. She set it down slowly and buried her face in her hands again.

The wind continued drumming through the palms. The house creaked. But more than that she felt the mad thumping of her own heart.

North was in town tonight, in his apartment. He'd be gone in a day or two.

She knew she should get undressed for bed, but if she did, she wouldn't be able to sleep. She would think of North, of the way he'd looked at her so hungrily when she'd answered the front door, of the way he'd shoved her against the wall, of the way he hadn't looked at her when she'd lain beside the pool and he'd swum.

Confusing images bombarded her.

North hurtling his huge body at her on the dance floor; North holding her close.

North in her car, his big brown hand gentle on her cheek, his look of profound pain when he'd seen her tears.

She imagined him alone now, lying in his bed fast asleep.

Was he dreaming of Maria? Dreaming of Maria doing all those things that man in the video had had the cheap-looking actress do?

Picking up the bottle of wine, Melody carried it to her bedroom. There she poured herself another glass. Then she opened the drawer that contained all North's old pictures. She had ones from every stage of his life.

When he'd been six, his ears had stuck out through his thick black hair. He'd told her he'd been a brat back then. When he'd been ten, his daddy's big cowboy hat had swallowed him. When he'd been twelve, a darkly slim boy with a solemn face stood stiffly holding on to his daddy's big deer rifle.

In all his older pictures his expression was grave. It was as if he'd lost some vital spark. His college pictures were of a stern young man. Melody reshuffled. She preferred his laughing baby pictures. What would it take to make the real man look as happy as the little boy in the pictures?

The most recent photograph was one Claire had taken of him standing by his pickup, holding a rifle in one hand and a dead wild turkey in the other.

Melody didn't like hunting or his grim expression, but he looked so broad-shouldered and lean in that picture, she'd kept it anyway. Clasping it against her breasts, she opened her patio door and stepped outside into the wild, humid night.

For a long time she stood there, her hair billowing. Frowning, she thought about what that couple had done on the video.

Sexual favors. You know. Show him how much you care.

She bit her bottom lip. Then she poured herself another glass of wine.

What if she called a cab and showed up at his apartment? What if she took the key out from under his flowerpot and let herself inside? What if she slid into bed and made wild passionate love to him?

You tried that once before. You failed miserably.

But the wine sent dizzying sensations all through her. She went back inside and turned on her radio. The thudding beat of the same song she and North had danced to in the bar filled the room. She felt warm and crazy and feminine and needy and wild. She threw herself onto her bed and grabbed her favorite teddy bear and tried to fight the demon in her brain that told her to go to him.

The minutes dragged by. She thought of the stark longing in his eyes when he'd said goodbye. Still, he was stubborn, and he'd made his mind up about her. If only she could stop thinking about him, stop feeling—

Why did she feel so jittery and restless? An hour later and she was up pacing.

If she didn't do something—

What if he threw her out?

What if he didn't?

One minute North was sound asleep and dreaming of Melody. Not the innocent, shy exhibitionist, but a real woman with sultry eyes who knew what to do as she writhed underneath him.

The next minute he heard his front door click open and shut. When he heard the jingle of his truck keys, he knew the intruder must've stepped on them, for it was his habit to leave them on the floor by the front door.

Next he heard the soft whispers of footsteps approaching his bedroom. Springing out of bed, he went for his holstered Colt in his top drawer.

Only it wasn't there. He must have forgotten it and left it in his glove compartment.

Quickly he crossed his bedroom to wait in the dark corner by the door.

The wind was beating against his windowpanes as the ghostly figure stepped inside and glided toward his bed. He heard a faint indrawn breath and then a little gasp right before he lunged.

Even before he knocked her down, he knew the intruder was a woman. Still, he pushed her onto the bed, rolled her over, grabbed her wrists and pinned her there. When she tried to scream, his hand covered her mouth.

"Who the hell—"

"It's me, you big idiot—Melody."

Her face was pale, her hair tousled, her eyes as dark and defiant and sultry as his dream girl's. She still wore that sexy white skirt with the red rickrack that had gotten him so wired.

"What do you want?"

"You."

His jaw knotted. "Whoa!" He let her go.

She sprang free of him, got up and backed quickly toward the window.

"You sure scared me," she said a little shakily.

"Likewise. How the hell did you get in?"

"Ah, Bertie, I know all your secrets—"

His heart began to slam, his body to harden. "I hardly think so," he muttered.

She ran a hand down her throat and fiddled with the low neckline of her red blouse. Her hair was iridescent in the dim glow of the moon. He watched the play of her white fingertips and the flicker of fire those glistening moons made against her breasts.

She seemed to be recovering more quickly than he.

"Well, I know where your secret key is...that flowerpot... I know that your ivy died."

"Because I wasn't here to water it. So—"

She floated soundlessly toward his balcony and leaned against his wall there. Moonlight washed her and made her skin glow like alabaster. Her breasts swelled against her knit top.

His throat went dry. "Melody, we said goodbye—"

"I wouldn't blame you if you sent me away." Her voice was small, young, innocent and yet slow and sexy, too. Her long-lashed, smoky dark eyes were erotic as hell.

"I wouldn't blame me, either," he growled. "Go home before you get into more trouble than you can handle."

"You once told me that you wanted a woman," she purred, her eyes smoldering with promises now. "Not a girl."

The voice, those eyes, everything she did— All of a sudden, fool that he was, she had him panting hard. "More than once—"

"Well, I—I'm here now...."

"It's too late," he muttered thickly. "Way too late."

"What if I want to be your woman?"

"Mel, we tried this before—"

"Again. And again. I know. Please, don't send me away."

"Then make it easy for me. I don't want to hurt you. Just go home."

"But I sent the cab away."

"I'll drive you."

Again her gaze locked with his. "I've got a better idea. Let me prove I'm all grown-up."

She seemed so young and eager, so fragile. What if she went to someone else in this mood? It would be so easy to scare her forever.

"Come here," he whispered helplessly.

When she reached him, he took her in his arms and hungrily kissed her mouth, and reeled with shock and fiery sensation.

She was like a lightning bolt. Liquid fire pulsed in his blood. "You're so beautiful," he said, startled.

"Oh, North—"

"You are." She was warm; she tasted like the sweetest wine. Desire flooded him as it always did when she teased him like this.

When he tried to push free, a low moan escaped her lips. His hands tightened around her waist, and he rubbed her against him. She began to tremble and that got him shaking.

With an effort he stopped. "If I fall for this little seduction game, you'll chicken out—"

"Maybe I'll surprise you."

"It won't be the first time."

"Or the last."

Her lips parted. What if, for once, he let her take the lead? When he stood still, she kissed him.

She did indeed taste of wine.

"You've been drinking, darlin'. You never drink."

"Who says courage doesn't come in a bottle?"

"It's a bad habit—drinking."

"I'm a big girl. Maybe it's time…I acquired a few bad habits. Maybe it's time I found out what big girls do in their spare time."

His gut clenched. "Are you still a—?"

"The V-word?"

He nodded.

She licked her lips. "Sort of."

"What's that supposed to mean?"

"I've always figured that sex was overrated."

"So you've been experimenting."

"Maybe."

"You're lying. This whole thing is a ruse, a setup. Like before."

"There's only one way for you to be sure."

"All right." He fixed her with a hard-as-nails glare. Expecting her to run, he ripped off his pajama bottoms.

But she stepped closer. Taking them from him, she tossed them out of the way. Then while he watched her face, she put her hand on his waist and let it glide lower until her fingers circled him.

He froze.

She stared as if she'd shocked herself, too. He drew in a deep breath and reminded himself to do nothing.

Finally she began stroking him. Her caressing fingers were so skilled that when she squeezed him, he almost came.

"Don't you hurt me, little darlin'," he whispered.

"Had enough, Bertie boy?" Then she giggled and let him go and scampered over to his bed.

He watched the graceful movement of her arms as she pushed her blouse down and pulled her skirt up. When she lay down on his bed, she drew a leg up and began to hum the song they'd danced to in the bar.

"Do you want me to put on some music?" he whispered.

"Why don't you come over here so we can make our own?"

Two long strides had him beside her. "I don't believe this."

Languidly she stretched full length across his bed. "Believe it." She took his hand and pulled him down.

"Melody, why? Why tonight?"

Her eyes were hard and intent upon his face, but she couldn't seem to answer. Instead she rolled into his big tan body and threaded her fingertips into the bristly hair of his chest.

"I—I think I always thought you'd devour me, or that this would give you the upper hand."

He was dark and tough while she was slim and fragile. He'd felt old, grown-up, for nearly as long as he could remember. She was fresh, new—able to bring out a part of him he thought long dead. When she climbed on top of him and straddled him, a throbbing, burning excitement began to build inside him.

Then she closed her eyes and touched his face, his throat, her hands moving as lovingly as a blind woman until he went wild beneath her featherlight strokes. He clenched his teeth, determined not to show it. Somehow, aside from his heavier breathing, he was able to lie still while she made love to him.

When her burning lips followed the path of her hands, he stiffened, gasped, and then closed his eyes, too.

Slowly she eased lower. Always before they'd gotten this far, he'd been overcome by his own passion and had sought to control her and push for more.

Not tonight. Tonight he gritted his teeth, and knotted his fingers, mindless with desire and yet afraid of doing anything to frighten her.

Slowly, ever so slowly her golden head and wet tongue trailed the length of his abdomen. She kissed him wetly, sucking his nipples, kissing him everywhere until she sent tremors coursing through his body.

When she hesitated, he reached for her, his hands tangling in the silken waves of her hair. Her scent flooded his nostrils. His breath grew ragged. Still, he sensed she had to be in control.

He shot her a glance and read alarm in her overlarge eyes. He was gut sure she was about to bolt. But when he didn't try to force her, she gave another of those whispery little gasps and scooting farther down his legs, buried her face in his groin. When her mouth closed over him, he groaned.

Stunned, and yet thrilled beyond words, he sank deeper into the mattress and after a while, her lips began to move back and forth with sensuous expertise proving, that after all, she knew exactly what to do. And yet she wasn't simply going through the motions. Reverently, gently, she was making the most exquisite love to him. Sex like that wasn't possible unless—

Hunger surged through him. From tip to base, her tongue was gentle yet scalding hot. She'd hardly started, and he was about to explode.

"Darlin', let me kiss you, too." He put his hands on her shoulders.

When she shook her head, he nearly lost his mind. She'd been stubborn about not making love. She was just as stubborn now.

A wise voice in the back of his head told him to play it smart and lie back and enjoy it, that he'd waited a helluva long time for what this particular lady was offering, that if tonight was her turn to pleasure him, some night, there would be a night that was his turn to return the favor.

So, he changed position slightly and put his hands in her hair, moving her head to and fro, thrusting until he shuddered in completion.

She gasped. When she lifted her face, he stared at her in wonder. She brought a fingertip to her lips. Then, wrapping her in his arms, so that their bodies touched everywhere, he began to kiss her, to coax her. He'd never been sure of her before this moment.

Why? Why had she done this?

Suddenly, she stopped him and nestled her head against his chest as if to hide. He lay still and held her, stunned, wondering at the sheer loveliness of her, at the loveliness of what she'd done.

He stroked her hair. She was beautiful, and skillful at this, amazingly so. Once he had loved her with all his heart. He had wanted to marry her. He had always sensed how warm and sensitive and exquisite she'd be if he ever got her in bed.

Tonight she had sent him over some wild edge. She was really something. Once—and he was already an addict.

"Look at me, little darlin'." He lifted her chin, but she wouldn't look at him.

He grinned. "You want more. Same as I do."

She shook her head fervently.

Again he wondered why she had come to him? Done this? Tonight? When they'd both agreed it was over? After they'd said goodbye?

Why? Was it some new game?

Smile. It's the second best thing you can do with your lips.

Why had she said that at the door? Who had taught her to think like that?

As he lay in the dark, his happiness and hope gave way to disillusionment and doubt. What had she said earlier when he'd been so dazed by her beauty— That she was only *sort of* a virgin now, that she'd been experimenting.

Sort of? Who else had she done this with? What else had she done with him, with them? Was tonight like her job at the park? Another step in ridding herself of her hang-ups?

"Damn you," he whispered.

Her eyes widened.

He tore himself free of her. He had to know, no matter how unpleasant the truth was. Being a man, quite naturally, he stuck his size twelve foot in his mouth and asked her straight out.

"Why'd you come over here? Where the hell did you learn a trick like that? Were you pretending I was somebody else? Somebody more exciting? Who taught—"

Dark eyebrows arched in confusion and then indignation. "Who taught—"

"Well, you're too damn good to be a rank beginner."

"What?"

"I said you've got quite a knack for it, darlin'."

"Is that what you think?" Her sexy voice was low and choked. She continued to stare at him with those frightened, wide, glazed eyes, as if her emotions tore at her.

"You're too damn good," he repeated levelly. "I'm not the first man you tried this on, am I?"

She went even whiter, as if he'd struck her. Her eyes were wet as she scooted away.

"Well, what of it? You weren't! And I'm glad!" She notched her chin up. "I—I had a great teacher! Lots and lots of them! In Paris, India, Austin... All you did was lie there."

"All I did was lie there—"

Rage howled inside him. Hurt, too. His stomach tightened. As she scrambled even farther away from him, his hand snaked around her wrist and pulled her back.

"Lots and lots of them?"

"I shouldn't—"

"No, you shouldn't have— I don't like being compared unfavorably to other men. Maybe it's time I showed you just how talented I am in bed! You want to get over your hang-ups— Well, I'm just the guy to help you with that project!"

Her head thrashed from side to side, as he pulled her back down. Her skin was hot, and she trembled as if a fever raced through her senses. With one hand he gripped both wrists.

"First you ravaged me. Now I'll ravage you. Isn't this what you came over here for?"

"No." Tears slipped through her lashes.

"I don't believe you, darlin'."

With his free hand he traced a downward path over her breasts, lingering there till her nipples peaked. "You like being held down, don't you?"

She shuddered. When he laughed at her quick response, she kicked at him.

To no avail. He shifted his weight and overpowered her easily. "Your short skirt is definitely a plus."

She squirmed to escape him, but his fingers slid up her leg to that dewy place between her thighs. When he caressed her there, his fingers gentled. She caught her breath and then shivered when the finger probed deeper.

Underneath lime-green panties, she was wet. Hot. He couldn't believe it when he met virginal resistance, and the truth hit him.

She had hang-ups. She was scared. But she'd come to him. This was her first time. And he was scaring her again.

"There weren't any other men—"

"L-let me go," she murmured in broken whispers.

He was so nonplussed, he accidentally loosened his grip on her hands, and she pushed at him and somehow got away.

In a flash she shoved free and was out of bed and deftly rearranging her clothes and then running from him.

He got up and stormed after her. "Damn it, I wasn't trying to scare you!"

"I'm not scared! Not anymore! And you'd better not chase me outside, North Black—'cause you're stark naked!"

"So the hell what?"

So what if she was dressed and he wasn't?

"I'll call 911!"

Only when he heard one of his neighbor's cars outside, did he go back for his jeans.

Before he knew it, she was out of the bedroom. He heard his truck keys jingle in the living room.

"Not my truck!" he yelled. "Don't you dare drive my truck!"

His front door slammed. Footsteps raced down the front stairs.

He was yanking on his jeans and hopping toward the front door when she revved his truck loud enough to wake the whole complex. Bare-chested and barefooted, he was skidding down the concrete steps, shouting her name when she roared out of his parking lot so fast he smelled rubber.

"Those are brand-new tires, Melody! And my gun—"

She threw back her head triumphantly.

Behind him the wind caught his front door and slammed it shut.

"My! My! Mr. Black! That pretty girl is mad at you!" Mrs. Carey, his primmest old lady neighbor, who lived right below him, whom he'd long suspected had an innocent, girlish crush on him, got out of her Cadillac and beamed up at him.

A light went on in Mrs. Cullpepper's upstairs apartment. Damn.

He smiled at the blue-haired Mrs. Carey charmingly.

"Where's your shirt, Mr. Black?"

"Never mind." But his grin tightened.

When at last she headed for her door, he raced back upstairs. He twisted the knob of his apartment, but it was

locked. Even before he knelt to dig his key out of the flowerpot, he remembered Melody had taken his spare key inside.

"Damn. Damn."

"Is anything wrong up there, Mr. Black?"

"Couldn't be better," he hollered. "Good night, Mrs.
Carey."

He waited for the old dear to get inside. Only then did
he pick up the flowerpot and shake black dirt onto the
breezeway. With a weary sigh, he heaved his pot against
the window and then stepped back to avoid the spray of
glass and terra-cotta.

But a shard sliced his heel and got him yelping and hopping until he pulled it out and remembered the day he'd
stepped on a fishhook.

*Smile. It's the second best thing you can do with your
lips.*

And he did smile as he remembered Melody's velvet
tongue moving back and forth at his groin, her mouth hot,
probing, tantalizing him.

She'd been so silky and warm afterward.

Until he'd lost it. And scared her again.

Still, for once she'd certainly followed through. Had she
enjoyed it at all? Would she ever be willing to do it again?

Never, ever had he felt anything so pleasurable as her
hands and her mouth on his skin. He wasn't through with
the impossible Melody Woods after all.

Not by a long shot.

Six

Cathy's house seemed strange and mysterious in the dark with its roof splotched in purple shadows and bits of dazzling white.

Nervy and scared, Melody jumped back every time the pebbles she pitched pattered against the windowpane like shotgun pellets.

"Wake up, Cathy," Melody whispered, hunkering lower in the black hedge outside her friend's curtained window.

Nothing.

Melody's slim fingers fidgeted with the pebbles she held again, causing them to rattle. Again, her gaze swept the lawn to see if anyone was watching her. Above, leaves rustled in the heavy humid wind. She felt the breeze against her hot face. Other than the trees' noise and the distant whir of traffic on some thoroughfare, the neighborhood houses on Cathy's street were dark and silent.

Grimacing, Melody pinged several more handfuls against her friend's window. When still Cathy didn't answer, she raided the flower beds for more. Finally Melody picked up two handfuls and moved closer. When she arched her arms, rocks cracked against the glass.

The curtains were torn apart. The small window burst open, and Cathy's spiked head peeped cautiously above the straggling geraniums in her window box.

"Greg?"

"It's me—Melody."

Cathy's fingertips fluttered and were gone. She reappeared within seconds at her front door.

"I was asleep."

"You've got to help me."

Cathy stared at her blankly.

"This is all your fault you know."

"What on earth are you talking about?"

Melody turned away. "I—I… It's all so embarrassing. I—I stole North's truck. I've got to take it back. I can't see him or talk to him ever again. You've got to follow me in your car—"

"Okay. Okay. Give me a minute."

Five minutes later Cathy reappeared at the door again in shorts and a sweatshirt. She had her car keys in one hand and dangled her square little sparkly purse from the other. "So, how was it?"

Blushing, Melody raced down the front steps. "We'd better hurry—"

Cathy swung the purse back and forth. "You did it, didn't you? You finally had sex?"

"No!" She hesitated. "Well, sort of."

"Sort of?"

"I can't talk about it." How did other girls chatter about something so…so personal?

"You and North. Sort of." Cathy laughed. "That's great, babe. That's just great."

"Great?" They had reached North's white pickup. "It was awful. There is no me and North."

"How come you're in his truck then? You took a cab over there, didn't you? What happened?"

For no reason at all Melody was remembering how bronzed and gorgeous North had been against the tumble of white sheets. And how virile—so broad and brown and muscular at his shoulders, so lean at the waist and narrow at the hips. His legs had been paler. But they had been long and thick with muscle.

Melody blushed.

Cathy shrugged. "Babe, the first time's always the hardest. You'll like it. You'll get used to each other. I promise."

Used to each other? He'd been so furious. She'd felt so hurt. Even now Melody still felt vulnerable, raw, too easy to read—and so out there. "You don't understand," she mumbled.

"Oh, but I do. Trust me. This is going to be wonderful."

"Oh, Cathy—"

"No regrets, okay? Remember that pact we made when you broke up with North last time? We're going to be women of power. We're going to live and do our own thing, just like men do. We're going to know who we are and what we want and we're going to be equal to any man. And that means no regrets. North's a great guy, and you're a great gir...er...woman. This is a win-win, babe."

"It sounds so simple in theory."

"Babe, it's way more fun in reality."

The sea breeze that had roared all night was still gusting in the early-morning dark. Out to the southwest, the clouds were black.

Inside, North tugged a tall black boot on, cursing it until it slid over his heel. Next he tore a shirt off a hanger and pulled it on.

Even though he was in town, even though he hadn't gotten much sleep, he was a man of regular habits. Thus, he was up as early as ever. Although the pleasant aroma of bacon and coffee lingered in his apartment, he'd eaten and had coffee and stuffed the dishwasher over an hour ago.

Was it the city or Melody that had him as edgy as a wild bronc that didn't want to be broken? Melody—for sure.

The white walls of the boxy room seemed to close in on him as he crammed his crisp white shirt into his jeans. For a long moment he stared at his rumpled bed and wished Melody were still there, asleep in his bed, her cheeks rosily aglow. He wished he hadn't pushed, hadn't thought, hadn't started one of their quarrels—hadn't scared her.

What she'd done to him had been a soul-stealing pleasure. He wished he could hold her and kiss her and cuddle close to her till she woke up.

If she had to run out, he was almost glad she'd run off in his truck. It gave him an excuse to go after her.

He picked up the phone. He would've called her first thing, if he'd been sure where she was—at her parents' or her grandmother's. He glanced at his watch. It was still too early to call her at the Woodses', so he dialed Jeff.

He would have preferred not to call Jeff. He wasn't in the mood to deal with his cattle buyer or accountant, either. He wanted his mind to settle down, and for that to happen, he needed to talk to Melody.

But if he didn't call Jeff, Jeff would suspect something. No matter where North was, they always hashed out the ranch work schedule together.

"So—was Melody there last night?" Jeff demanded in a surly tone right after he said hello.

"My life is not some soap opera you can tune into at will. Who you got doing fence in the La Negra division down south?"

"Was the dinner just a ruse to set you up with Melody? I gotta know, buddy."

"She…er… That issue didn't come up," North lied smoothly. "Did you hear anything out of our Midnight Bandit?"

"That issue?" Jeff laughed. "That's a pretty borin' description of a mighty interestin', rabble-rousin' little gal."

"You finished, Mr. Gossip-monger?"

"If you're done with her, can I date her?"

"Shut the hell up!"

"Touch-e-e-e," Jeff drawled. "I wouldn't touch that one with a ten-foot pole."

"Not that you've got one."

"Don't be cruel." Jeff laughed and finished knowingly, "So the issue didn't come up."

"Confound it, Gentry! How the hell's Little Camel?"

"You need to get yourself laid. The sooner the better. Good thing we've got hot dates with Maria and Tina."

"Maria?"

"Saturday, remember?"

"I'm beat. Can I get out of that—"

"So the issue did make an appearance."

North said nothing. When they were done talking llamas, bandits, stretchers, wire, posts and pliers, North kept his voice deliberately casual. "One more thing. Could you call my apartment manager over here? Somebody broke my window last night."

"Did you call the police?"

"Just get him to fix it. Tell him it's on me."

"Now that sounds... What the hell did she do—"

"Get off her, understand! Good thing you're not standing here, or you wouldn't still be standing."

"Hey, I almost forgot. W.T. was burning needles off prickly pears with a butane torch and damned if that slacker didn't set half the north pasture on fire."

North tensed.

"Got it out. Not much damage. A few fence stakes. That's all. Got a little rain, too. Might get more."

"Hey. I saw some clouds this morning. Wow."

When a car honked downstairs, North strode to the front window.

"My cab's here."

"What's wrong with your truck?"

"Gotta go." North was halfway down the outside stairs before he realized the cab was parked right beside a white truck.

His pickup.

"Damn your hide, darlin'. You ran out on me again."

He paid the driver with two crisp ten-dollar bills. Then as a matter of course he walked around his truck inspecting it for new dings, checking the tires, too.

She'd left the windows open. His keys were dangling from the ignition. Anybody could have taken it.

Then he remembered his daddy's Colt.

Couldn't she ever do one thing right?

Smile. It's the second best thing you can do with your lips.

Oh, yeah, she could.

North jumped inside and yanked his glove box open. When his hand closed over the carved leather holster, he breathed a sigh of relief. The holster had been his father's. The Colt had been a gift from him on that last birthday before—

North turned it over and over before replacing it inside the glove box. Then he sat in his truck for a long time. Maybe it was W.T. starting the fire that got him thinking about his father. Maybe Melody had him feeling more vulnerable.

His daddy, Rand Black, had been a real, bigger-than-life cowboy hero. He'd expanded the ranch's acreage, negotiated favorable oil leases and crossbred cattle until he'd come up with a superior breed. He'd been an inventor and a national celebrity—and those accomplishments had only been the beginning.

North had wanted to be just like him when he grew up. Then, shortly after North's twelfth birthday, his father had been killed in a fire that had started in some stacks of wood and then had spread to the barn. His father's office had been in the loft. Nobody knew he was missing until the fire was out.

Gran always said North was Rand's spitting image, that she'd never known a son to be so like his father.

Naturally North's mother, Anne, who'd never had the most harmonious of relationships with her husband or mother-in-law, had disagreed. "Rand wasn't a god."

"In these parts he was," Gran always countered.

"He was mortal. Now he's dead," his mother always persisted.

"He was the most popular person on this ranch. And North is going to be just like him."

"Nobody should have to live up to a legend."

"Is that why you didn't shed a tear at the funeral?"

"I run off, as you put it, because I'm alive and Rand's dead, and I don't want to go out of my mind."

His mother had done her maternal duty. Two years ago on one of her trips to Paris, she'd fallen in love.

North hadn't wanted her to tell him about her German count. On her last visit, which had been short and tense, she had told him anyway.

"I want to visit your father's grave before I go," she'd said that last day.

"Why?"

"Maybe to reassure myself his name is really on the tombstone."

"Are you going to marry your count?"

She'd arched a thin, black eyebrow that was many shades darker than her fluffy bright hair. "No."

"How could you be with somebody else—after him?"

"I'm alive. Rand is dead." She'd knelt before his tombstone and traced the letters of his name. "Really really dead." She'd looked up at North. "For years I lived in his shadow. And then for years I lived here in the shadow of his legend. Everything had to be done according to his wishes."

"He was a great rancher."

"You can't hold back change, North." She'd laid a single red rose on the grave and got up. "Not even in a feudal kingdom like El Dorado. He's gone. Let him go."

"That's easy for you to say."

"Oh, no. You don't know how wrong you are. Don't waste your life the way I wasted mine."

It was sunny when Melody awoke. She'd fallen asleep on the edge of the bed beside her teddy bears and on top of her red spread.

Rubbing her eyes, she realized she was exhausted in body and mind. Her mouth was dry, and she had a headache. At first she was so disoriented, she didn't know what was wrong. Then the memory of what she'd done last night and what North had thought of her afterward hit her smack-dab in the middle of her forehead.

Her cheeks got so hot, she was probably purple. Slowly, avoiding looking at herself in her long mirror, she got out of bed and ran to her bathroom.

Splashing hot water onto her face, she scrubbed and scrubbed. Next she brushed her teeth and then drank a long glass of water. Only when her mouth was all minty and clean did she look in the mirror. Other than the telltale color of her cheeks, her face was as angelic and innocent looking as ever.

Last night had left no visible trace.

Except for North, nobody knew.

Who taught you?

She had a few days before her classes started. Maybe she should hide out in Austin.

She was wondering what to do when her phone rang.

It was exactly nine o'clock.

North never called her at her parents' before that hour. Even before she crossed the room and read his name on the caller ID, her heart was already racing.

More than anything she wanted to talk to him. But she was too scared of what she'd done and he'd said.

Would he apologize? Or would he condemn her? She touched the receiver with trembling fingertips and then jumped back every time it rang.

On the fifth ring she picked it up.

"Melody—"

She lost her nerve and hung up on him.

When it rang again, she picked it up and laid it on her bed. Then she ran outside and buried her face in her hands. After she'd finished loving him last night, she'd lifted her head. She felt breathily on fire when his dark eyes had glinted as he'd stared into hers and then down her body. Terrified, she'd been in heaven and hell when he'd pulled her closer, caressing her temples, his gentle fingertips moving in slow, hypnotic circles.

Ablaze with incomprehensible tenderness and passion and yet fear, too, she'd touched her lips with the back of her hand in wonder, and he'd taken that hand and brought it to his lips. He'd kissed each fingertip, and then he'd kissed her.

He'd wanted more. He'd been gentle, but suddenly her old fears had mushroomed, and she'd buried her face in his throat and held onto him fiercely. And all the while some wanton part of her had secretly craved him.

Why had he gotten so angry? Did he think she was cheap now? He must. She tried to remember every detail, so she could understand. But it was all so new to her, so baffling— so terrible.

"Look at me, little darlin'," he'd whispered, lifting her chin.

She'd shut her eyes.

"You want more. Same as I do."

She'd shaken her head.

As they lain in the dark, his arms around her, she'd felt him gradually tense. When he'd let her go and cursed her and accused her of sleeping with other men, she'd been truly mortified.

You've got quite a knack for it, darlin'.

His face had been so stern and unforgiving, she'd been sure he despised her. Her heart had begun to beat with terror. Hardly knowing what she said, she'd lashed out, too.

Then he'd grabbed her, and low, wicked creature that she was, she'd reveled when he'd said, "Now I'll ravage you."

Oh, dear! She was even worse than he thought she was. In the blazing sunshine, it all seemed so cheap and sordid. And yet...

Last night when he'd tackled her with that voracious hunger, she'd felt so turned on, she could have abandoned a lifetime of inhibitions.

This morning she had a hangover. That was a first, too.

She couldn't face him ever again. As she stepped back into her room, she heard her mother's shrill voice from the hall.

The door opened.

"You could knock—"

"Sorry. Why in the world do you have the phone off the hook?"

"Um...er..."

Dee Dee's eyes moved over Melody in that comprehensive nosy manner all mothers have down to a T. "Darling, what's wrong? You're as white as a sheet."

Melody forced a valiant smile. "Nothing."

"Homesick?"

"I'm fine."

Dee Dee's face grew taut. "All right. If you say so. You get dressed, and I'll fix you a great big omelet. Vegetarian."

"Thank you, Mother."

Dee Dee set the phone on the hook. It rang before she could get out the door.

Melody stared at it. "Don't answer it!"

"But I'm the hostess of that charity ball."

Before Melody could stop her, Dee Dee had picked up the phone. "Why...hello, North..."

"I'm not here," Melody mouthed silently, shaking her head. "I won't talk to him."

All of a sudden Dee Dee saw way too much. "Uh…no… She's…she's not here. Uh…maybe…maybe she went out to the university to see about her classes or over to Nana's to work out her move…. Yes. I'll tell her. It was great seeing you, too, last night, dear."

Dee Dee hung up. "What is going on?"

"Nothing," Melody answered quietly.

Dee Dee stared.

"Nothing! And…and I want to keep it that way."

"Do you have to be rude to him?"

"Yes. Mother, please—"

Dee Dee watched her daughter for a very long moment. "I will never understand you."

Seven

The whole thing happened so quickly.

It seemed to Melody she'd been stuck behind the armored Dodge truck with the tinted windows going twenty, stewing over North for hours. Then something moved in the tangles of brush along the side of the road, and instantly the brake lights in front of her blazed red.

The Dodge pulled over and stopped so abruptly, she nearly rammed it. As she passed the monstrous SUV, half a dozen uniformed men swarmed out and chased running figures through the thorny mesquite.

She was so upset, she didn't really register what the high drama was all about. Her head ached as she remembered all the things North had patiently explained to her about his home and his land the first and only time he'd brought her here to meet his family.

The thick brush was problematic because livestock could hide in it, but it was a paradise for wildlife—for Nilgai antelope, quail, feral hogs, and of course, white-tailed deer.

"Which you keep to kill," she'd said.

"Hunting is an important economic factor in managing El Dorado."

"This is the twenty-first century. Hunting is barbaric."

"City girl..."

"I can't help what I am."

"Neither can I."

She was crazy to come back to Bertie's feudal kingdom.

Suddenly she realized what the big Dodge meant—the Border Patrol was out in force flushing illegal aliens.

She swallowed as she thought of the poor countries she'd visited and the desperate lives she'd witnessed. India and China were a whole lot worse than Mexico. Still, during college she'd spent enough weekends and summers in Mexico translating for an American doctor friend of her father's, who ran a free clinic. The poor patients had been crushingly poor. So poor, Melody was familiar with the raw smell of armpits and feet, of bad teeth and dirty clothes. The patients had wheedled, their voices demanding, obscene, angry, friendly. She'd known that no matter what she gave them, it wasn't enough.

The private narrow ranch road that led to El Dorado's headquarters was ten miles long and lined on both sides with tall palms. Their black shadows were bars of darkness.

Melody turned the volume up. Now that she was past the Dodge, she was driving way too fast again and playing her tape too loud. But that was just because she was so nervous. Even though her fingertips kept time and she was humming, she wasn't really listening to the music. All of a sudden she was remembering that one disastrous weekend she'd spent here.

The big house had been filled with snooty, out-of-town relatives along with a senator who'd been flown in by private jet all the way from Washington D.C. She'd gotten so scared she'd forgotten to change shoes and had come down to dinner in a formal and jogging shoes. When everybody had laughed, and North had suggested she go back upstairs and change, she'd gotten defensive and had pretended she'd chosen the outfit deliberately.

Always, always, who North was had gotten in her way. He was so rich, so big, at least in south Texas. Why, his daddy had been as famous as a movie star.

She hadn't really realized until that weekend that dating North was like dating royalty, that if she married him she would never again be free to just be who she was, whoever Melody Woods was.

Maybe he lived in an isolated ranch house in the middle of nowhere, but when she'd met those people, she'd known that he belonged to a glittering world that was beyond her and above her. When he went to Europe, he played polo with princes. Naturally her socially ambitious mother had been wild for her to marry him.

"You'll get used to it, grow into it. Besides, most of the time, you'll be on the ranch."

"Which is boring. I don't care that he has miles and miles of tight fences or all those thousands of cows he's so proud of."

His family had thought she was as ambitious as her mother, that she was marrying him for who he was and what he had, when those were the very things she'd held against him.

"I know you're not like your mother," North had said to reassure her when she hadn't wanted to wear that huge, ancestral diamond he'd given her for an engagement ring.

"Can't I have a little diamond…one that you bought just for me?" she'd begged.

"That wouldn't be right."

In the end he and Libby, his grandmother, had been offended because she'd so rarely worn his ring.

A wild turkey raced across the road. Melody hit the brakes and then smiled as she waited. The big bird, head bobbing, danced about in zigzagging circles. Finally it took off, flapping clumsily over the fence, vanishing into the thick mesquite brush.

Cathy had put her up to this venture with more of her crazy sex advice when she'd dropped by to swim earlier this afternoon.

They'd lain in the shade by the pool together and sipped lemonade.

"Is your daddy home, babe? Can I take off my top and toast all over?"

"No. And no. Mother would have a fit."

"I've never seen you so glum. You really want Bertie, babe?"

"He's arrogant and…"

"But you want him…. So—go get him."

"What? He's at his ranch. They call him 'King' there. Jeff says he's busy and doesn't want to talk to me."

"So—you've called the ranch?" Cathy remarked dryly.

Behind her sunglasses, Melody had squinched her eyes shut.

"You've got wheels, babe."

"I can't just chase him."

"Who said chase? He won't speak to you?" Cathy sucked the last of her lemonade and grinned. "Give him hell."

"I don't get you."

Cathy ran a fingertip up her wet, cold glass and then licked the condensation off it with lascivious show of pink tongue. "Trust me," she said huskily. "Guys love a change of pace."

"I can't stand the country. It is so boring."

"Think of it as one of your adventures…like a safari or something. Melody's cowgirl adventure."

"Cowgirl, my eye. I fell off a horse the last time I was there! The saddle slipped or something. North got real mad at Jeff later. Said he tied the cinch knot all wrong."

"On purpose?"

"I'm not sure. He doesn't like me. Anyway, when I tried to right myself, I jammed my foot all the way through my stirrup. The horse was going so fast, and I was trapped down between her legs. I got skinned on one side.''

''Oh—''

''Then North jumped in front of the horse and grabbed the reins. He saved my life.''

''Well, just remember the only animal down there you're going to climb on and ride is your hero, King Bertie!''

''You're incorrigible!''

''If you get bored on that ranch with Bertie, it's your fault. Hook him big time!''

So, here Melody was, driving toward North's house like a love-struck fool. This thought was cut off when she saw the ranch's white gatehouse up ahead and the letters that spelled El Dorado shimmering in heat waves.

She tensed when she saw the man inside the little house. Then she realized she was in luck. The gate was wide-open.

As soon as he saw her, the slim, rangy gatekeeper set his Stetson straight, pushed his sunglasses higher, and shoved whatever he was reading under the counter. Pasting on what he supposed was a super-sexy smile, he hopped out of his boxy shack square in the middle of the road. Square in front of her.

His red, mirrored sunglasses so startled Melody, she slammed on the brakes.

Tires shrieked.

''Hey,   hey,   watch   where   you're   going, Miss…Woods.…''

Melody lowered her window and rapped her fingers on her steering wheel in high agitation and stared anywhere but at him.

The un-air-conditioned heat rose from the asphalt like a furnace blast.

''I just bet you've got the prettiest eyes,'' she said, ''under those awful glasses.''

Grinning at her, he removed the offending glasses, and she relaxed a little.

"You're famous around here," he said, "or should I say, notorious? Pretty in pink, too."

Melody burned as if the skin over her heart was emblazoned with a scarlet letter A. Had North told every yokel on the ranch he'd scored?

"Notorious?" She licked her lips. "That's a mighty big word for a little boy who wastes his time reading dirty comics."

He flared instantly. "How'd— I wasn't—"

"You hid that comic book mighty fast. Lemme see."

He blushed tellingly.

"Thought so." She laughed with a great deal more confidence than she felt.

The sun was brilliant. Even though she wasn't wearing all that much—a pink, sleeveless knit top, matching pink shorts that didn't quite meet in the middle—and her window was down, she would still soon be sweltering. If only he'd move a little more to the left—

"How in the world do those black cows over there stand this?"

A rivulet of sweat ran down his smooth cheek. "I've got orders not to let you in, Miss Woods."

"Then I guess we'll just have to get acquainted—handsome."

His eyebrows lifted. Through her windshield, his gaze drilled her belly button. "You are certainly living up to your reputation."

"I'll take that as a compliment."

He was gorgeous, too gorgeous for his own good. Not that his babyish golden looks appealed to her. His heavy eyelids lowered to half-mast and stayed there, giving him a sleepy, rather worthless look.

"Poor boy. You look dog-tired out here in this heat," she said. "We're going to have to think of something to perk you up."

"I know just the thing." Full of confidence, he swaggered around to her door.

Finally. "Cute shorts—"

Men were so hopeful. It was part of their charm.

She hit the accelerator.

"Hey!"

Tires squealed. Melody stopped a safe distance down the road to gloat a little. "You're not too good at your job are you?"

"Now you come back here."

"And you don't know too much about women, either. You keep reading those books. Maybe you'll learn something. And, handsome. Count yourself lucky you're not roadkill. Don't you ever, ever jump in front of another lady's car, understand? She might not be as good a driver as me. Oh! I nearly forgot. You call your boss. You tell King Bertie he's got company."

The boy's lips thinned as he glanced worriedly around. "The king's not gonna like this." He slid his sunglasses back on.

"Then I'll have to put in a good word for you. What's your name?"

"W.T."

Melody laughed and then tromped the pedal with her toe again.

Better to laugh than to give in to her fear or cry.

Melody jumped. There it was again—the sound. The faint creaking of a board in the loft or the crackle of hay under a hoof.

How could a big empty barn seem scary?

Because she was a city girl, out of her element.

A slight moan, high in the eaves. Suddenly she felt so vulnerable, so alone in the big barn as she explored, cracking stall doors and peering into them at the cows and their newborns.

Hot little prickles of alarm raced down her spine. She threw an uneasy glance toward the loft. Was somebody watching her? Or was she just so nervous—

As scared as a little kid, she shut the stall door with trembling hands. After that afternoon when those boys had caught her, she used to lie in her bed every night, sure that something evil lurked in the dark. Sometimes, it didn't take much for those old fears to take over.

She scanned the length of the barn—nothing. Still, she had to fight the urge to run. The house, Sissy, and his grandmother had been bad enough.

The barn, even alone, should be easier.

She pushed another stall door open anyway.

At last, llamas!

She smiled. "Hi, guys—"

Two pairs of soft brown eyes stared uncertainly into hers.

"Don't be afraid." Still shaking, she marched into the llamas' stall as brazenly as she'd stomped across the lush green lawn up to the big house where she'd paused to admire Libby Black's pink oleander and white jimson weed blossoms before knocking on the big front door.

The old lady, her thin mouth agape, had come out on the porch in her big straw hat, muddy boots, holding a tall glass of iced tea.

"Hello?" they'd both said at once.

Then Melody had asked, "How in the world do you make the desert bloom like this, Mrs. Black?"

"Lots of water and two good cowboys." The old lady had frowned. "North didn't tell me you were coming."

"Didn't know I was till I got here. Would you please tell him I'm here?"

"Oh, dear," Sissy had come outside then, her dark, angelic face, concerned. "North has been an absolute bear ever since he got home from Corpus. He didn't tell us you…and he even saw each other."

"Could I see him, please—"

"He's…" Sissy's dark brows had knitted. "We've had a little…" Libby had given her a warning look. "It's nothing really…. Just some trouble."

"He's okay?"

Sissy had nodded. "Our pilot flew him down to the border. Five miles of good fence with fresh holes cut in it. A truck stolen. Missing cattle. He's down there riding fence—"

"Then I'll wait."

"No telling how long he'll be really," Sissy had said.

"How about a glass of tea?" Libby had offered.

The baby llama moved hesitantly toward Melody. When the animal nuzzled her belly button with a warm wet nose, she laughed out loud. "I bet you're thirsty."

Sissy had said there was a refrigerator in the tack room and that she could feed Little Camel while she waited. When Melody left the stall, she heard that same eerie sound echoing in the rafters again.

She stopped, waiting. The barn seemed huge and darker than before. All of a sudden she remembered Rand Black had died in the barn. Her eyes ran over the fifty pound sacks of feed, halters, bridles and saddles.

Not this barn! The other one had been a total loss.

The wood of the stalls glowed a pretty shade of red in the late-evening light. Even though it was late, it was still hot. Melody had been wandering around inside the large building less than half an hour, and already the lingering heat and fierce humidity had her pink knit top plastered to her spine and breasts. Her linen shorts felt limp. The hot, stifling air reeked of horses, feed and leather.

When something big began to stomp and snort and bray in another stall, she nearly jumped out of her skin. She almost wished she were back in the parlor trying to make awkward conversation with Sissy and Libby.

The tack room was at the far end of the barn. She saw North's father's name cut into the door. North had told her all the cowboys had carved their names on the door. Right under Rand's name, North had carved his own. Then she saw Jeff's. Even that lazy W.T. had taken the time to carve his. She was tracing the letters of North's name, when she heard a boot heel again—nearer. Someone else really was in the barn. No ghost! But someone sneaky who didn't want her to know he was there.

Something soft wrapped around her leg.

She screamed, and then sank to her knees laughing when she saw it was only a rotund ginger cat. He began to meow loudly. Swishing his tail, he evaded her outstretched hand and stalked stiffly toward the refrigerator.

"Oh, so you want some milk, too?"

Another demanding yowl.

Not that the yellow monster deigned to turn and glance at her.

She opened the refrigerator. Mr. Ginger swirled around her legs, as she lifted the milk carton. Then the boot heel rang on concrete again, and a deep voice behind her said her name.

"Melody!"

Startled, she peered out the door into the dark barn but saw nothing. No one.

Forgetting the cat and the llamas, she stepped out of the tack room into the darkening barn.

"Who is it?" she whispered.

Still nothing.

She heard a footfall behind her and before fear could spiral through her, she whirled.

Two long shadows covered hers. Two men, one lean and rangy wearing a Stetson; the other burly, his baseball cap turned backward, stared at her. No more than twenty feet away, they seemed to have materialized out of thin air.

"You'd better git, girl. King don't want nothin' to do with you," said the one in the baseball hat.

The light came from behind them, so she couldn't see their faces.

"Jeff?"

"I told you, it was her, Gentry!" said the kid from the gate. "You shouldn't have taken off like that, Miss

Woods,'' he purred, shifting his weight from one high-heeled boot to the other.

"W.T. and me—we got better things to do than play cat and mouse with a troublemaker like you."

They were both wearing mirrored sunglasses as they stalked her.

"You never did like me, did you, Jeff?" she whispered.

The two men exchanged a look.

"You're trespassing, Pinky Pooh," Jeff answered.

When she saw four tiny blondes in pink reflected back at her, dread washed over her. It was almost as if she was that terrified little girl again, and those four boys were chasing her.

She couldn't seem to focus on anything other than their shadowy faces and those sunglasses. "You stay away from me."

W.T. laughed, but his eyes bored through her. "You ain't so sassy now."

Prickles of alarm traced up her spine again. All she knew was that she had to get out of the dark barn and away from them. In her panic, she pivoted too sharply. When she ran, they took off after her. She stumbled over a rake. Then the milk carton slid through her fingers and splashed onto the concrete floor.

She stepped in it and slid, falling, hitting the concrete on outstretched palms so hard, it knocked the breath out of her.

They were leaning down, their brawny arms reaching for her. Blood pounded in her temples.

Then barn doors rolled apart noisily, and more vivid red sunlight exploded behind a tall broad-shouldered man with a gun strapped to his right hip.

There were three of them. She was outnumbered. Like before when she'd been eleven. She started screaming.

"Gentry, W.T., just what the hell is going on?" a deep, familiar voice yelled.

"Bertie," Melody gasped weakly. "Bertie…"

He'd come, just in time, again.

"She fell, King," Jeff said. "I swear. That's all—"

North's heavy boot heels resounded on the concrete, echoing all the way to the rafters as he loped toward her.

"Gran just told me she needs two big boys on that front bed. You two git!" His lazy drawl held an edge of menace.

The two demoted cowboys stayed put and said, "We weren't doing nothin' to her. She was trespassing."

"Git! I said!" North repeated, again, in *that* voice they knew and feared.

When at last they skulked past her out of the barn, North took Melody's hand and helped her up. "My big bozos scare you, did they?"

Staring at his gun, she shook her head. If she admitted the truth, then they would dislike her even more for getting them into trouble.

"And no wonder—they're both as ugly as all get out, aren't they?" he murmured.

She drew a deep breath. "It was a simple misunderstanding."

"So—you're okay?"

Her right knee and her left hand throbbed. She was still too stunned to answer. Embarrassed, she threw herself against him and held on tightly. "I—I didn't mean to cause you any trouble."

He was so tall and strong. He felt good, she clung, burying her nose into his cotton shirt so deeply she got a whiff of laundry detergent along with his own fresh male odor. And that made her remember how he'd tasted, which instantly caused thrilling little jolts of male-female awareness to sizzle through her.

He held her stiffly. She drew back, feeling ashamed of what she'd done the other night all over again. For a long moment, the silence that stretched between them seemed as taut as her nerves.

"I wasn't trespassing," she whispered. "I came to see you."

He frowned. "You're always welcome here, Melody. I told you that."

"I—I just wanted to talk to you. I—I tried and tried... Why...why are you wearing that gun?"

"We've had a little excitement around here. I wear it when I'm out alone. Nothing for you to be scared of. I'm sorry I've been kind of hard to reach." He brushed a loose strand of hair from her cheek and cupped her chin as if to lift her lips to his. "What do you need? You've got my full attention now."

She licked her lips.

His gaze narrowed, and he studied her mouth so lingeringly her heartbeats began to quicken. "What was so all-fired important—"

"You know the other night..."

"Oh, yeah," he breathed. "I called you to say I was sorry and you hung up on me."

"I came out to tell you... About all those other men... I'm sorry, too. There weren't any. I mean I lied when I said there were lots and lots.... I—I really didn't know what I was doing when I kissed you like that. I—I was just following my instincts. If I seemed like I knew what I was doing, I guess I just got carried away."

He stared at her in wonder and confusion. "My God, Melody—"

"North?" floated a silken feminine voice behind them.

At the note of possession in that third voice, North moved, uneasily shifting his weight from one foot to the other. "Damn." There was guilt in his low tone.

Melody jumped away from him.

"What's going on?" the newcomer asked very sweetly.

"She's had a little scare, that's all," North explained a little too awkwardly.

Obviously he had a date with Maria. He'd invited Maria, who was perfect for him, here tonight. Not her. He'd gone from her to—

Of all the miserable, rotten, bad timing...!

Afraid she might cry, which would never do, Melody raised her head and wiped at her eyes.

The dark girl, who stood in the last of the red sunlight, was staring at North as if she owned him. And maybe she did now.

Why, oh why, did Maria have to be as dazzlingly beautiful in her tight jeans and cowboy hat as her own sister Claire? Only Claire was blond while this young woman with the hourglass figure had soft, inky waves of black hair and big black eyes that shone like buttons.

Had North ever made love to her?

"You must be Maria," Melody said, her voice strange and hoarse, not her own.

"This is Melody…Woods, an old…friend."

"I know who she is." After a little awkward interval, Maria smiled. "I don't understand. What is she doing here?"

Suddenly Melody realized she was the intruder, not Maria. Jeff had just been trying to warn her a few minutes ago, so she'd leave and save herself the embarrassment of this little scene.

She had to say something. "I—I was about to feed Little Camel while I waited for North."

"Her visit was probably impulsive," North said, protecting her. "And a surprise to me," he finished, protecting himself. "Would you give us a minute alone, Maria?"

"Sure."

"Why are you here?" he asked when Maria was outside with W.T. and Jeff.

"I—I don't guess it really matters now," Melody said, floundering helplessly. How could she say the things she wanted to say when three people lurked right outside the barn, trying to hear her every word.

"Clue me in for once—anyway."

"I told you I tried to call you to talk to you about—" She broke off. "Several times. Only Jeff wouldn't—"

"Gentry? He didn't tell me you called."

"It doesn't matter. I guess he knew how you felt."

"You're wrong."

"I don't believe you."

"Then maybe you'll believe him, darlin'." Before she could stop him, North called out to his friend. "Gentry, what's this about? Melody here says she called me, and you refused— Gentry!"

When Jeff didn't answer immediately, North repeated himself. "You answer me! I know you're out there snooping like usual."

Jeff stuck his bright red head inside the barn. "King, correct me if I'm wrong. So what if she called? You did say that as far as I was concerned, this little Woods gal no longer existed, am I right?"

North lowered his voice until it wasn't much more than a growl. "That's irrelevant...now," he said to Melody. "That was before—"

"Was it irrelevant? Or was it crazy of me to call you or come here? Crazy of me to think," Melody murmured. More upset than ever, she began backing away from him toward the door. "I see how things are. Forget..."

North grabbed her wrist. He seemed to be having a hard time breathing. "Melody, so help me if you run out on me one more time when we're in the middle of something—"

"It's over," she whispered. "I see that."

"You said I was the first."

"That doesn't matter now. But I'm glad I came. Glad I saw I was right about this place...and...and you. Glad I don't fit in—"

"Your impulsive mind works awful fast." He let her go, crossed his arms. He looked angry enough to explode all of a sudden. "Have you ever wanted to fit in?"

"No! Why would I? This is a tight little boring world. And you're—"

He stiffened. "Boring?" he finished helpfully.

The way he said it, in *that* voice, sent a thread of fear through her. "Yes. Yes. You think you're king here in this macho kingdom of yours. You think you're safe because life hasn't changed for a hundred years."

"What if I wasn't as boring as you're determined to think I am? What then?"

She thought of how thrilled she'd felt in his apartment, and a red flush stole up her slender throat and flamed her cheeks.

"King, she said she wants to go," Jeff yelled.

"Shut up, Gentry!" To Melody, North said softly, "If you'd stick around for once instead of always hightailin' it, you might learn different."

North cast an uneasy glance at his men and Maria, who were all glaring at Melody so mutinously from the opening a few yards away, she felt most unwelcome.

"They don't like me," Melody whispered hoarsely.

"You've never given them a chance. You could start by telling us what was so all-fired important to get you out here?"

Again, she was in the bedroom of his apartment. Again she was on his bed vividly responding to his lovemaking. She'd just told him he was the only man she'd ever done something like that with. How could she talk about any of that now, under these circumstances?

"You big lug, if you really don't know, then you are a real idiot!"

She dived past him and started running. She heard North's shouts behind her.

"Hey, wait one cock-eyed minute!"

He sprinted after her. His men, their mirrored glasses glittering, planted their long legs in front of the opening in the barn, forming a human wall that barred her way.

When North caught up to her, she whirled, determined to fight him, but his hard hands circled her slender waist and held on tight. Crying out in dismay as he pulled her closer, she pounded his muscular back.

"Just tell me, only me then," he repeated inexorably,

breathing hard, tugging her deeper into a private corner of the barn.

Stinging sweat—or was it tears?—dripped into her eyes. Furious, she wiped them away with the back of her hand.

"Why do you upset me so much?" she whispered.

"I don't know. You tell me."

"I lay awake all night long after what I—I did the other night—"

"So did I, darlin'."

"But why?'

"'Cause we liked it too much. 'Cause we want more. And it makes us sad and angry. 'Cause we know it can't ever work in the long run."

"Then please, if you know it won't work," she sobbed, "just let me go."

"Even now…when we both know it, that's not so easy, is it, darlin'?" Holding her frightened glance, he bent his lips to her ear and grinned when she jumped because the warmth of his breath tickled and gave her terrifying pleasure.

"You did come back for more even though you don't think it'll work out, didn't you?"

She sobbed quietly into his hard shoulder.

"Admit it, darlin'."

She shook her head.

"You want me to make love to you, don't you?" His callused fingers brushed the soft hair off her neckline. "I mean really make love. My lips doing all the things you did to me." Even his voice made her quiver. "We could do it just for fun. No strings attached."

"No."

"Would that be so terrible?" he demanded huskily.

"Yes. Yes."

"Yes, to terrible?"

He was holding her so tightly, her breath came unevenly, and she was beginning to tremble.

"Or yes to sex?" he persisted in a velvet, sensual tone that undid her.

She paused for what seemed like a lifetime, and he lifted her chin, as if he needed to read her expression. She was studying the cruelly beautiful shape of his mouth and half opening her own so that he could kiss her as she longed, when suddenly Jeff let out a war whoop and ran away from the barn toward the south pastures. There he began yelling loud enough to raise the next ranch house. Pistol raised, he fired a warning shot.

A horse neighed in the distance.

"Hot damn! If it ain't the Midnight Bandit!" W.T. hollered.

North and Melody shot out of the barn together.

Spurs jingling, a lone, mythical cowboy, whose skin glowed like copper, trotted toward them on a tall black horse. The rider sported a sweeping handlebar mustache and a strange, low-crowned hat.

North hadn't ever seen anyone quite like him. Automatically his right hand went to his gun.

"Don't you dare shoot at him!" Melody screamed, breaking free and running toward the stranger who seemed to float toward them on that magnificent animal in a shimmering haze of blinding red light.

"North, don't you see he's carrying a little boy in his arms?"

Eight

North's eyes narrowed on the stranger. Maybe because Melody was so fascinated by him, his own voice came out more curt than usual. "Can I help you, mister?"

"Don't you dare draw on him or attack him!" Melody flared.

"Draw? Attack?" For years North had dreamed of her coming out to his ranch, dreamed of her wanting him in her bed. Now she had done just that, but damn it, she was second-guessing everything he did in front of his men, especially Jeff, and Maria. "I'm not attacking anybody—yet."

"I know that superior tone of voice. You've used it enough times on me."

W.T. was watching him, watching her, listening to every order she dished out, his young face slack-jawed with amazement.

"Apparently not nearly enough," North growled.

"He wasn't doing anything wrong," Melody persisted.

"He's trespassing. But that's between him and me." He lowered his voice. "If you disagree, darlin', tell me so in private. Not here!"

"Oh, so nobody speaks up to the king in public?" Melody whispered back.

"This could be a dangerous situation."

"Come off your high horse, Rancher Black."

"Bienvenidos," Melody said aloud running up to the mysterious stranger. Her voice and actions were so defiant North wanted to shake her. "Welcome," she repeated sassily in English for all to hear.

Although the rider smiled down at Melody in an affable manner, his expression darkened dangerously whenever he looked at North.

North grabbed her arm and pulled her close, again lowering his voice to an undertone. "Do you have to act so thrilled by this man? He could be anybody—a smuggler, any sort of criminal."

"Don't be ridiculous."

"Tu mujer?" the man demanded with that flashy smile North found too familiar. *Your woman?*

"You're on El Dorado, my ranch." North stared at Melody.

"No." Melody eyed North and the stranger and then chirped tartly. *"Amiga."*

"For the last time, stay out of this, Melody." North sucked in a tight breath.

"I think he's cute and sweet," she whispered. "Maybe El Dorado has possibilities after all."

"He could be dangerous."

"You say that to inflate your...er...own position."

"Go inside—now."

"I can take care of myself."

"Like you did in the barn when you threw yourself in my arms?"

When she didn't budge, North was tempted to sling her over his shoulder and carry her to the house as he'd carried her out of Shorty's. Fortunately the stranger interrupted him in the middle of this furious train of thought with a tone of deep courtesy and abject apology.

"I do not mean to cause trouble. I'm afraid I seeked for water for my horse on your land when I saw the black birds circling. And I find *him*—little Teo in the brush. Very thirsty. Many days. Desert. No water." The dusty stranger glanced affectionately down at the boy in his arms. "He is a fighter."

"Teo?" North quizzed, really seeing the child for the first time. "You two together? *Familia?*"

"*No somos familia.* Teo and I, we camp in a hunting hut. Two days. I feed him there. Give him water." The rider patted a gourd strapped to his saddle. "From your well. I shoot strange pig. Feed him."

Melody gasped and studied the boy. Her eyes shining, she looked up at the man. "Oh, you were so wonderful. You saved his life."

"The kid's wet, Melody. So's your knight in dusty buck-skin," North exclaimed, a little ashamed that his voice had a nasty edge. "Illegals."

"No, the boy's poor and desperate. But because of this wonderful man, he's still alive." Melody breathed in deeply, joy lighting her beautiful face as she regarded the boy's beaming savior and then North.

The stranger's admiring green eyes were glued on Melody. Jealousy and pity mixed in North as she stared at the thin little boy in rags in the interloper's arms with more affection than she ever seemed to feel for him.

Kids were supposed to be cute. Not skinny with an overlarge, round dirty head topped with long and irregularly cut black hair like this one. They shouldn't smell bad nor wear rags, either. They shouldn't cower and hold such wincing pain in their big, dark eyes.

"Delfino must've missed this pair when he made his little raid. Call him, Gentry."

Curious, North stared at the man's canvas sandals and at

the strange spurs buckled to his bare ankles. His multilayered saddle topped with a thick sheepskin fleece was no ordinary Mexican saddle.

"Where are you from?" North murmured, automatically slipping back into Spanish.

"Argentina," the man answered, in a lilting, educated accent. "*Gaucho.*" Jeff slipped his cell phone out of his hip pocket and punched in numbers.

The stranger was tall, golden and slim. He had friendly green eyes and teeth as white as Chiclets. Despite an outer layer of grime, he held himself erect with the unconscious air of an aristocrat. His black horse, for all that it was dirty and thirsty, too, was as noble as his master. In perfect control of this splendid mount, the man gently handed the limp little boy down to North.

"A good bed and a few good meals—he be fine," the stranger said.

"You're a long way from home," North replied, taking the child, whose bony frame was as light as air.

"I made a foolish bet, *señor.*"

The stranger threw a long leg over his saddle. In a single fluid motion the gaucho flung himself to the ground, landing beside Melody as gracefully as a dancer.

Acid churned in North's stomach when the handsome fellow tilted the brim of his dusty hat and smiled down at her. "Hugo Avila. At your service, mees."

"Melody Woods." She actually curtsied. "At yours."

Avila extended a lean brown hand, which she took. She would barely speak to North, but she fell all over this filthy stranger with pretentious airs.

"Call me Manolete...after the famous Spanish bullfighter."

"You must be very brave."

North swallowed hard. "You've never seen a bullfight in your life."

"Do you have to be so rude to him? He is your guest. He saved this child."

"My guest?"

"You two must be deeply in love," Manolete whispered way too knowingly.

"What?" North and Melody both erupted.

"The way you fight. The sparks they shoot, like how you say—fireworks. She looks so pretty, so passionate when she is *furiosa, enojada* with you, *señor.* If she is not your *mujer,* make her so—*muy rapido.*"

A screen door banged. When Sissy came running toward them, Manolete dropped Melody's hand and seemed suddenly transfixed.

"Tu mujer?" Manolete asked.

"My sister."

"Is she married?"

"What are you doing on my ranch? Who is this child?" North nodded at the boy in his arms.

"And who are you, *señor?*" Avila demanded with equal arrogance. "Where am I? I asked you a question. Is your beautiful sister married?"

"Why don't you ask her?"

Manolete couldn't seem to quit staring at Sissy's fine-boned face, dark hair or trim figure. When she joined them, he repeated his courteous bow. Manolete lifted her hand and kissed two fingertips. When he reached for the third, Sissy burst into giggles.

"What's with you?" Sissy demanded.

"Hugo Avila. At your service."

"King, I've got Delfino." Jeff shoved the cell phone into North's hand.

"Delfino?" Melody whispered as the boy's black lashes fluttered open.

"Teo," Melody whispered, "you are safe."

The child stretched out a thin dark hand with dirt-encrusted fingernails and bloody scratches. "Angelita—" The ragged child pressed a tiny piece of paper into her hand.

She lifted her gaze to North. "Who's on the phone?"

"Border Patrol."

"No!" Melody cried.

North covered the mouthpiece of the telephone with his palm. "Go inside and stay out of this, Melody."

"He just gave me a phone number with a Houston area code—"

"This isn't your fight."

"Fight? Does that darling child in your arms look like he's fighting?"

The kid's thin, dark face, his huge fearful eyes pierced North through the throat like the shaft of an arrow. "Down here, it's us against them," North said.

"This kid in your arms isn't a threat to you. But if you tell the Border Patrol about him, what will happen to him? He's what, twelve, at the most? He's all alone. No mother. No father. No country. He gave me a phone number. He's got family in Houston."

He stared at her.

"If it's a good idea to rat to Delfino now," she persisted, "why wouldn't it work to tell him later?"

"There's no way I can explain—"

"So, don't—" She grabbed the phone and punched End.

His men, Maria, the green-eyed stranger, and even the pitiful little boy he held, and no telling who else, were all watching them.

"What are you trying to do here, Melody? You come down here, then you use this kid to push me around in front of my men— Where do you see this going? You want to stick around for good? Hash out a lasting compromise on some very serious issues?"

"Y-you're taking this too far."

"Am I? I was the first. I can't seem to forget that."

Her beautiful voice softened. "This isn't about us. This child's life is in your hands."

The little boy in his arms began to tremble the way Little Camel did sometimes. She loved children. She wanted to save this child, and as he looked into her beautiful blue eyes, he wanted—

The hell he did. He stared at the child and then at her. He eyed his men and Maria who were watching.

"All right. He can stay," North said. "For one night. But only if you stay, too—to take care of him."

"What?"

Maria looked hurt. Jeff's mouth was agape. W.T. looked slack-jawed. North could feel them all grappling to understand him even as he was.

"Give him to me," Melody whispered.

When Melody had the child, Teo smiled. North felt a stab of remorse as he stalked toward Maria and let her slide her arm around him.

"I can't believe you did that," Maria said.

"You want to know something. Neither the hell can I."

"He could be a thief from that bad *ejido*. Or worse, what if he's a drug smuggler or works for the Midnight Bandit? Whatever he is, he's illegal."

"Try telling her that."

"You did it for *her*."

And for a skinny, injured kid. "Can we talk about something else, Maria?"

"When is *she* leaving?"

"Tomorrow. First thing."

"*She's* spending the night? Oh, North, you can't be serious. She made a fool of you."

Dozens of times. "It's only one night, okay? The kid needs a bed, care...."

In Maria's soft, understanding black eyes, North saw all his own doubts about the evening ahead of them magnified ten times over.

Nine

The night, his date with the perfect Maria, had barely gotten started, and already North was in one lousy mood. Maria, the rich ranch girl who understood him, wanted him to romance her, which a sane man with a lick of common sense would want to do.

Here he was hiding out in the kitchen with Jeff, rustling through the liquor cabinet.

She was upstairs, for the first time since forever. Melody hadn't taken his calls after that night in his apartment.

But Jeff hadn't taken hers, either, when she'd finally gotten up the nerve to talk to him. How many times had she tried to call him? She'd driven all the way out here to tell him she'd stayed up all night afterward. So had he.

Why the hell couldn't he stop thinking about it?

All of a sudden their argument over the illegals, the way she'd stood up to him in front of his men, didn't bother him nearly as much as it should have. He was too damn glad she'd finally come back to him. And that's what she'd done. Just as he'd said she would.

He was losing control.

Every time he looked at Maria, he saw Melody instead. He kept remembering Melody's mouth that night, the way she'd crawled all over him and then kissed him as if she was an expert until he'd exploded. He kept remembering how shy and surprised and adorable she'd looked. He was touched by her kindness to the kid, too.

He wanted Maria gone. He wanted Melody here.

He wanted to carry Melody to bed and make love to her. He didn't give a damn what Jeff or Gran or anybody else thought about it, either. It seemed to him that for as long as he could remember, he'd been on his own out here, with the ranch to manage and too many people to look out for, and too many people figuring out his life for him.

Now the woman he'd wanted for most of his life was here, and even though she always seemed hell-bent on making a fool of him, the burden and the loneliness of the ranch didn't feel nearly as heavy as usual. It was crazy. Maybe *he* was crazy. But always, *always* when she was around, he felt alive.

So, how to explain to Maria?

"Forget *her*," Jeff whispered behind him. "You know you said yourself that was the smart thing to do."

"Right." Easier said than done. Especially with him thinking maybe smart wasn't so smart after all.

What bedroom would Melody be in tonight? The one across the hall from his own? Or the one next to his with the door that didn't quite latch, the one that had the connecting balcony, too.

"How many times did Mel call the ranch?"

"Forget her."

North set the wine bottle down hard and glared at him. "Seven!"

Silently North reached across Gran's tattered deck of

cards on the kitchen table for an unopened bottle of Chardonnay.

"Maria said she wanted Merlot."

Melody's wine of preference was Chardonnay.

"Right. Merlot."

"So, open that one for her, why don't you," Jeff grumbled, shoving a bottle with the correct label toward North.

"Me, I prefer straight whiskey," North said to cover his blunder. Grabbing a bottle of whiskey from the cupboard that had a shot or two left, he opened the bottle and drained it in a gulp or two. Then he flung the bottle toward the trash.

He missed. The bottle rolled.

"Why didn't you get rid of *her* when you had the chance? If you aren't careful, she'll be leading you around by the nose again."

"She'll be gone soon enough."

"Will she? I have a mighty funny feeling."

North had more than a feeling. Maybe that's why he clamped his lips together and stared at the window at the barn for a long moment, and all the time he was listening for her light footsteps upstairs or for her impertinent voice calling to him.

She didn't belong here…with him.

What if she did?

"Why don't you concentrate on what's right about tonight—the good music, two beautiful women waiting for us in the den—easy women—and great steaks. The moon's gonna be big and bright, just off full, too. Not to mention wine and whiskey."

Jeff forgot his doubts. "We'll get 'em lit, get ourselves lit, take 'em out to a hunting cabin. The night's gonna be perfect."

Something made of glass exploded upstairs.

North cocked his dark head upward. "What the hell was that?"

"*Her.*"

"She's in Daddy's room. Nobody's supposed to ever stay in that room."

"She's bound and determined to ruin our evenin' with Tina and Maria. Don't you dare go up and see—"

But North had slammed the Merlot bottle down and was already dashing from the kitchen through the den past Maria. When she rushed toward him, her pretty face worried, he quickly shook her off and bounded up the stairs two at a time.

When he flung his father's huge, antique Mexican door open and stormed through the sitting room to the bedroom, everybody froze. Sissy was on her knees before the sofa sweeping jagged bits of silver from the wooden planking. Apparently the ancient mirror his father had brought from Spain as a bridal gift to his mother had fallen off the wall.

North saw his dark face and Melody's paler defiant one when she joined him in the sitting room reflected in those gleaming shards.

"This isn't a guest room," North said. "Pick any other bedroom."

Melody had pulled back the sheets of his father's bed, so Manolete could put Teo there, but the boy was staring at the magnificent room, his big black eyes wide-eyed with wonder. When he saw North, his frail face tightened.

Pity pierced North's heart. "Don't you dare lay him there," North grumbled. "Get out of here. All of you. And you, Melody, I want you gone."

"Really," she said a little too brightly. "You did order me to stay. Am I right?"

"I wasn't in my right mind."

"Are we ever, when we're together?"

"Melody—"

"As you can see, I'm very busy."

"We don't use this room."

"Then it's time you did."

He stared at her.

"Why aren't you downstairs entertaining your beautiful,

perfect girlfriend?'' Melody queried, not in the least deterred by his temper or thunderous commands.

"Girlfriend?'' He drew a blank.

"Maria!'' Melody smiled. "She's perfect, you know.''

"And dazzling,'' he agreed.

"So, why aren't you down there having fun with her?''

"Good question. Perfectly logical.''

She smiled up at him. She'd probably lifted the mirror from the wall and smashed it to the floor to get him up here.

He made a low animal sound. "I heard you up here! He can't stay here!''

"Teo? Why on earth not?''

"Like I said, this is my father's suite.''

"I know.'' She directed her voice toward the bedroom. "Manolete, lay him down on the bed and go.''

"I said no!'' North repeated.

The boy groaned.

An odd pang tugged in North's chest.

"Gently. *Cuidado,* Mano.'' Her voice was soft, imploring.

"Mano? Already you have a nickname for this stranger?''

"Don't be so jealous. Everyone calls him that,'' Sissy said, casting an affectionate glance toward Hugo.

"Jealous?'' North demanded. "Who's jealous!''

"If the green boot fits, my darling—'' This from Melody.

She'd called him *darling.*

Since she had his full attention, Melody ignored him and turned to his sister. "Sissy, take Manolete…leave us, please. I think your darling brother wants to be alone with me.''

"Damn it, that's the last thing I want!''

When they rushed to obey her, Melody pulled the bedroom door shut, and he found himself alone with her in his father's vast sitting room and feeling very uncomfortable.

"Who are you to give orders? In my house? When I told you Teo couldn't stay in—"

Melody moved toward him, and quite imperiously he thought. "Your father is dead, isn't he? Do you think his spirit is still here or something?"

"Have you no respect?"

"Maybe I do...for the living." Her voice softened dangerously. "For you."

"That's bull—"

"Well, if your daddy's spirit really is here," Melody began, "I'm sure he could do with a little company. After all Sissy says your mom's in Europe with a new lover—"

A chill went through him. "Don't you dare—"

"If I were your daddy, I certainly wouldn't want to be entombed for years and years in a musty smelling old room like this when everybody else was out having fun. I think your mother's lucky to be in love."

"How would you know?"

"How do you think? The way I felt...when you were with Claire...bleak and horrible. And then when you carried me out of Shorty's like you'd die if you couldn't have me..."

"That's over."

"Is it?"

Her smoky eyes glittered with a heat so wild and bright it threatened to consume him. He felt a strange pull from her, a mad desire to take her in his arms, to forget everything except her.

"When I kissed you like that...the other night," she said, "I—I never felt like that before."

Neither the hell had he.

Unconsciously she sucked in her lower lip, and a sudden shudder shook him. "You said I came back for more.... What if I did? What if I can't leave you alone? Even when you get impossible like you did with Mano and Teo? Even when you come up here and order us around like a great big bully?"

"I'm not a bully!"

"You can be sweet and cute and wonderful...sometimes. Even sensitive and big-hearted. After all, you let Teo stay." She hesitated. "You let me stay."

"I'm in no mood for your teasing."

"I'm not teasing."

A moment passed. He took a step toward her.

She whirled out of his reach and yanked a cord and the dark drapes swished open, flooding the room with reddish-gold light and a view of Gran's emerald-green front lawn stretching from the house to meet buff-colored desert.

"Oh, how beautiful your ranch is!" she exclaimed as if to change the subject. "When he's better, he'll be able to see Libby's jimsonweed and oleander right beneath this window. I'll tell him how the white blossoms close every night and in the heat of the day."

"He won't be here that long. Neither will you."

"I'm not the only one with hang-ups, now am I? Maybe I'm afraid of sex. But what are you afraid of, big guy?"

"Not a damn thing."

But when she came toward him with that gleam in her eye to know more, he backed against the wall as if he were a coward.

"You've been drinking. For courage? The same as I had to that night? Because you're scared of ghosts? Or scared of me? Or maybe both?"

She stopped within inches of him, so close he could feel the heat of her sweet young body. He swallowed, tasted whiskey and longed for more.

She forced her gaze up to his. "Why do you work so hard, North? Why do you have to be in charge of every-body and everything? Of me? Why do you have to protect? To rule? Why can't you ever just be? Just let me be? What is it with you, North? What makes you so uptight?" She stared around the room, her voice dying. "When I was in the barn, I remembered how your daddy died."

The light was going out of the day. Shadows enveloped the room. He couldn't think with her so near.

"You come out here," he rasped. "You think you know all the answers. You think you can run me and this place.... Because...because you look so damned pretty in that pink, and I have a weakness where you're concerned."

"A big one?" she murmured.

"Well, you can't order me around. We're finished."

"Are we?"

"You'd better call that number the kid gave you—fast. Because in the morning—"

"You shouldn't work so hard, North. You're killing yourself. Just like your daddy did."

"He didn't..."

In the fading light, in that pink outfit, she could have been standing there nude. She ran her hands up and down her slender arms, causing the little silver moons in her fingernails to flicker.

His heart began to pound violently as he stood statue-still, just looking at her.

"What do you want, North? I mean just for yourself? When you're not so determined to prove yourself worthy to your dead daddy?"

Desperately he swallowed. "Don't talk about him."

"You know what I think?" She laughed and then dived straight into his arms, like a child, sure of her welcome. "I think you want me. I think you want your own life! Same as I do. Only we're both too afraid...."

She looped her hands around his thick, muscular neck and reached up onto her tiptoes and kissed him. Her kiss was soft and a little clumsy, but wet and bold, too. The velvet early evening shimmered all around her, and soon he was gripping her to him so fiercely, her feet left the ground, and she gasped with pleasure.

"And I am afraid, North, just like you are."

When her tongue came inside his mouth and timidly explored, he shuddered at her exquisite and yet passionate innocence.

"What if we faced our ghosts together?" she asked.

Finally he managed to let her go. In a thick, barely controlled voice, he said, "I want you and this boy gone come morning."

"This is about your father isn't it? Your whole life is about him?"

"Stop."

"I crossed a line when I mentioned him? When I came in here? Sissy said you loved him very much. You did, didn't you?"

Pain and loneliness and grief consumed him. She saw it, and her eyes filled with tears.

"I don't want to cause you pain," she whispered, reaching a hand toward him.

He didn't want her pity.

"You want the truth? Is that what you want? I'll give you truth. I destroyed him! That's why he haunts me. I destroyed the finest man that ever lived! He was a hero. Everybody loved him. You wanted the truth— If I kill myself working, I'll never be a tenth as good as he—"

"North, I—"

"I have no right to set foot in this room and neither do you. And neither does that filthy kid you had the audacity to put in his bed!"

She went white, as if he'd hit her.

Sudden tears filled her eyes. "He's a precious human being. And so are you. He needs a doctor...."

North winced. "Like I said," he whispered, his voice as raw as his heart, "the sooner you leave, the better."

Quick hot tears spilled down her cheeks. But she didn't speak or cry out. Instead she rushed blindly past him and slammed out of the suite into the dark hall.

As he listened to her flying footsteps growing ever softer on the stairs, he sank down onto his daddy's sofa, the whiskey burning his gut.

The kid made some soft raspy sound.

North picked up the phone and called his doctor, who was a close personal friend.

"I have a big favor…"

Ten

Melody held the phone to her ear and listened as it rang endlessly. The doctor had come and gone, saying Teo needed rest and would be fine. "Come on! Answer the phone, whoever you are! A little boy's future depends on it!"

Melody's pulse throbbed. Her heart ached from her fight with North.

Too bruised to face him or the others anytime soon, she hid in the deep shadows of North's state-of-the-art, downstairs office across from the den. Frantically, for what had to be the tenth time, she punched in the numbers of the Houston phone number Teo had slipped into her hand.

"*Tiá* Irma," he had said as she'd told him good-night. *Aunt Irma.*

As Aunt Irma's phone rang again and again, Melody began to quiver like an overly sensitive antenna when she heard North's deeply melodious voice and Maria's answering laughter from the den. How easily he'd gone from her to Maria.

Feeling stupid and shattered, Melody gazed at the mediocre landscapes of ranch scenes on one wall, then at the stern, black-and-white photographs of his ancestors on the opposite wall. Her eyes fell to his computer, his laser printer and then to his in-basket stacked with dozens of neatly organized bills. When North's voice and Maria's laughter seemed to grow louder, Melody thumbed nervously through his bills, realizing for the first time how much he spent on utilities, tractor tires, bovine antibiotics, irrigation systems and bulls. And those were only the first six or seven bills. Why, just one tractor tire cost a thousand dollars.

North lived such an adult life compared to her. She was still in school, graduate school albeit, but still a child in so many ways, not knowing how to be a woman in his bed and at the same time stuck wondering what to do with the rest of her life.

North didn't have the luxury of wondering. He had the very real burden of running this immense ranch on his shoulders, on his alone, with no one to help him, to stand by him. Everyone at El Dorado looked to him to take care of them. He really did need a wife, a mature woman ready to support him, at least emotionally, a woman who understood his world, a woman like Maria.

On the twelfth ring Melody hung up in utter despair to more of Maria's throaty laughter.

North had told Melody he couldn't wait for her to go.

How happy he seemed to be with Maria now.

Quietly, swiftly, Melody slipped out of the silent office and raced back upstairs. To check on Teo, she told herself.

The scent of mesquite, baking potatoes and meat burning drifted upstairs and soon made Melody's hunger win out over heartbreak, causing her to decide to brave going downstairs and joining the others again.

Not that anybody seemed to notice her when she entered

the kitchen where dinner preparations were well under way. The table was set. Mano was whispering to Sissy in a dark corner while Libby was enjoying a game of solitaire at one end of the huge table while she drank her whiskey straight from the bottle.

North and Maria were outside with Jeff and Tina grilling steaks over an enormous mesquite bonfire. Watching North with his friends from the window above the sink made Melody feel even more than a fifth wheel as she glumly poured herself a glass of Chardonnay.

Since Mano and Sissy seemed so preoccupied with each other, she slipped onto the side screened porch. Sitting in a rocker behind hanging baskets of ivy and ferns, she was hidden from everybody and could enjoy the smell of the fire as she sipped her Chardonnay.

She'd forgotten to close the door. The warm evening breeze carried snippets of conversation from both the kitchen and the terrace.

North and Jeff were thrilling their dates with talk of their adventures with the Midnight Bandit, whoever he was.

"I knew there would be trouble when that Mexican on the other side of the Rio Grande sold his small rancho for at least four times the going price. Then the new owner trucked in all those expensive racehorses, brood mares with good bloodlines and prize stud horses, too. I never saw anyone legitimate in the horse business who could afford to spend money that fast.

"That doesn't make him the Midnight Bandit," Maria said.

"He wasn't there a week before somebody cut our fence and ran a thousand head of our cattle across the river to his place and then demanded ransom," Jeff said. "He set soldiers to guard our herd. North told me to go down there and bring them out, come hell or high water."

"Weren't you afraid of breaking international laws?" Maria asked.

"Not when I was knee-deep in the Rio Grande and I

almost got my horse shot out from under me. I was too damn scared to worry about anything but getting out of that jam alive.''

North looked grim, but he didn't say anything to verify Jeff's incredible story, and Melody couldn't believe it was true. Maria, however seemed to take the story as gospel.

How beautiful she looked, her olive face aglow in the firelight as she looked at North. How beautiful they looked together.

All of a sudden the Chardonnay had Melody's mouth feeling dry and cottony. Setting her empty glass on the wicker table beside her rocker, she curled her feet up under her. She felt left out and lonely as she used to around her own family when everybody was talking to each other and not her.

Her mother had wanted a beautiful daughter who wore makeup, beautiful clothes, a daughter like Claire, who followed the rules and married well. Her father had wanted a son.

But Melody felt even worse out here where she was a clumsy city girl and people expected North to marry a ranch princess...like Maria.

Was there no place Melody would ever belong? Was there no one she would ever belong to?

All her life she had tried so hard, too hard to be popular, to be loved, because deep down, she wasn't sure she was worthy of the kind of love she so desperately needed.

She shouldn't have driven out here.

North. North had always seemed so consumed by her, so addicted to her, so willing to put up with her in spite of her faults, so willing to wait for her to grow up. For years, she had taken his love for granted, even told him he was boring...because she'd been able to count on his predictable, steady, enduring, mature love.

Melody had wanted to be loved in that powerful way even if at the same time that sort of love had felt heavy and controlling and maybe even a little dull for someone of her supposedly free nature.

Maria was mature and beautiful—perfect for a mature man like North. She probably accepted that the bonds of love could limit a woman's freedom, limit her choices. She wanted North enough to make those necessary sacrifices.

Melody pressed her head against the back wall of the house. Life was so confusing. What did she want—really?

When she'd had North, she'd thrown him away. Now that she didn't have him, she felt as if she would die if she couldn't have him again. But if she got him back, would she just throw him away again? Was that fair?

She ran her hands through her hair. What was she doing here?

The group around the fire were speaking so low she couldn't hear them any longer. Now it was Mano's husky voice and Sissy's thrilled replies in the kitchen that held her attention.

"Argentina?" Sissy was saying. "How romantic!"

Mano's voice was husky. "This is more so. You are—"

North used to speak to her in that same sexy, desperate way.

"Don't say things you don't mean. I have been...unlucky in love."

"No more. To think, I would never have seen this pretty face if I had not drunk too much in a bar with my best friend."

"What do you mean?"

"We made crazy bets, he and I. I bet him I could travel from Argentina to New York City on horseback like my ancestor who was a French explorer. I read about him in family diaries. We both pledged that if I did it, we would give much money to the hospital where my father works as a doctor."

"How wonderful. So, what is Argentina like?"

"My father was born a rancher, so we have *estancia*. Very big even now. But the old days are gone forever."

"Here, too."

"Everywhere, *mi vida*."

"North tries so hard. Too hard—"

Why did he work so hard, so urgently? Why did that make her heart tug with a tight little pain?

"Did I tell you, you are very beautiful, Sissy."

"Too many times for me to believe you."

"When I reach New York and send for beautiful Sissy, will you believe me then?"

"We must wait and see what you say then and what I believe then."

"It is so exciting."

"What?"

"You. Me. Love. Like North and Melody."

Melody's breath caught when she heard their names.

"But he's dating Maria now," Sissy said.

"His heart belongs to Melody."

"Is our mysterious gaucho right? Is that really what's wrong with me?" a deep voice said in Melody's ear.

She whirled and then said nothing, her gaze widening as she beheld the blurrily familiar shape of a certain broad-shouldered individual framed by the pointy black leaves of the ivy that dripped from baskets on all sides of him.

"How long have you been out here all by yourself in the dark?" he whispered.

She felt dizzy, excited. "I didn't hear you come up."

"How's the kid?"

"Better by the hour."

He sucked in a deep breath. "I'm sorry," he said, curving his hand beneath her face as if she were infinitely precious.

Her heart had begun to beat in her throat. "Me, too."

"I didn't think." His thumb followed the smooth flesh of her shoulder. When she jumped a little, he hesitated. "I've had a lot on my mind."

"You were upset." He looked surprised when she tilted her head willingly toward his.

"I'm supposed to be with Maria tonight."

"She's beautiful, perfect—"

"All that and more," he agreed, his voice lazy. "And yet—"

"You said you wanted me gone upstairs."

"Yes. But why? That is the question."

There was a strange note in his deep voice that lit her heart. Melody waited, holding her breath.

"I want you gone—because you disturb me." His hand moved through her hair. "Because you can make me more miserable than anyone alive," he whispered, his voice hushed, tender.

"I know the feeling."

He broke away. "But then again—you make me happier."

"What are you saying?"

"I don't know." His free hand closed on hers and pulled it behind her waist, locking it there. Then he lowered his lips to the top of her head. "Everything, I suppose. You make me crazy. We quarrel." His lips were hot against her brow. "Then Maria flatters me when I most need flattering. She is so easy to be with, and yet all I can think of is what we started in my father's bedroom. Of what we started in my apartment."

Suddenly his soft, warm kisses against her forehead weren't enough. Nothing they'd ever shared was enough. She wanted his whole mouth. His whole body. His entire being. Everything—even though the thought of such total surrender terrified her.

She slid her hand instinctively along the white cotton material of his shirt and then lower, down the hard muscles of his thigh. "Oh, North— Me, too."

"Melody, I can't forget how it felt…being in your mouth."

Neither could she.

He whirled her around, so that she faced him. "Why did you do that?"

"I—I don't know. It just happened. I was afraid you would think I was terrible."

"Oh, darlin'—" His lips hovered near hers. For a breathless second she waited for him to kiss her hard.

She pursed her lips expectantly, aware of the elemental chemistry charging the air that separated her mouth from his. With an abandon that amazed her she stood up on her tiptoes and took the initiative.

Her lips met his. The kiss she began was soft, hungry, sweet, but cut short too soon.

"Supper," Jeff yelled right before he barged inside the screened porch with the platter of steaks along with Maria and Tina.

North cursed low under his breath as Melody jumped free.

All through dinner, Maria sat by North and flirted outrageously with him. Jeff pretended that the romantic night he'd set up was going just as he'd intended, that Melody's presence made no difference.

Melody felt North's edgy tension every time his brooding gaze fell on her. What had the near kiss meant to him? Was he as consumed by her as she was by him? Or did he see it as a mistake now?

Maria and he talked ranch stuff. Then the conversation turned to the growing problems they had with illegals. Everybody tried to explain to Mano why they'd been so alarmed when he'd ridden up.

"—They come on our ranches—"

"It's different now. Two weeks ago three of them held the ranch manager at *Rancho Tigre* at gunpoint."

"But Mano is on a mission," Melody said. "And Teo's just a child. How do you know they aren't all—"

Maria was shaking her head, looking at North, sure he'd agree with her.

"Melody has a valid point," North said, his eyes kind as he conceded to her. "We shouldn't mistreat children. There's no excuse—ever."

"Pass the potatoes," Libby said, as if she'd decided that paying more attention to his change of tact wasn't such a good idea.

There were eight people around the kitchen table, and all Melody wanted was to be alone with North again. Why had he taken her side in front of them? Did he feel the same as she—that tonight, if only they found their chance, she and he could bridge the chasm that separated them and make their own safe, cozy little world?

Manolete began to talk about his passion for bullfighting. When Melody got so interested, she began asking him questions, North began to scowl hard from his end of the table.

"I used to fight bulls, too—when I was a kid," North interjected.

"I can't believe that," Melody said with a smile. "You're no daredevil."

North looked at her with an intensity that scared her.

"Oh, but he was," Sissy said, "before Daddy died."

A look passed between brother and sister.

"What does she mean, North?" Melody asked.

"Not a damned thing," he said.

Startled by his harsh, impassioned voice, Maria and Tina turned to stare at him at the same time.

"North used to be wild...impulsive. Everybody said so," Sissy persisted.

"Shut up—" North's face had darkened. His eyes glittered. Slowly, as if he held himself under a tight leash, he got up from the table and poured himself another whiskey. Slamming the cabinet doors, he came back to the table and sat down. "I grew up. I got some sense. It happens to everybody."

"So, how's the kid doing?" Maria asked Melody in a cool, stilted tone, as if she also had decided this topic of conversation was too charged.

"He's okay. He went straight to sleep. I tried to call his aunt."

"And?" Maria queried.

"No answer."

"He ain't got no aunt in Houston," Jeff said matter-of-factly between large mouthfuls of steak.

"How long are you going to let the kid stay here, North?" Maria asked, shaking her head.

Melody's gaze flew to North when the kitchen went ominously silent. Without so much as a glance her way, he shoved his chair back, flung the screen door open, and then stomped outside, scraped his scraps on the ground with a knife and whistled for his dogs.

The screen door banged. When everybody looked at her, especially Jeff, Melody pressed steepled fingers to her mouth. It was a defensive gesture. Jeff blamed her for ruining tonight, for ruining far more than tonight.

"The Border Patrol has fought a lot of battles for us, let me tell you, city girl," Jeff said, a bitter note in his voice. "A lot of illegals are dangerous. We've gotta be careful...and fair. You've put him in a hard place." He hesitated. "But then that's always been your specialty."

Melody's chest tightened. When they, especially Maria, continued to glare at her, she felt heat in her cheeks. But before she could say anything to defend herself, the phone rang.

Jeff grabbed it. Almost instantly, his red eyebrows came together and his ruddy face turned purple.

"The Midnight Bandit?" Jeff exploded from his chair. "He what?" After another minute or two Jeff put a broad freckled hand over the mouthpiece and yelled toward the back door. "Hey, King, W.T. says Arturo called. Says there's a big new hole in our new fence down at La Negra. Signs of heavy trucks—"

North, who was still outside, didn't answer.

"Do you really think it's—the Midnight Bandit?" Maria asked.

Jeff's eyes were like ice. He slammed the phone down.

"So, what's with this Midnight Bandit?" Melody whispered tightly as North pushed the door open and stepped back inside. "Is he a joke or what?"

"You think he's a joke? You would, city girl," Jeff snapped.

"The name alone," Melody said lamely.

Jeff gave her another hard-eyed look. "Obviously we don't know his real name. W.T. made it up till we get a formal introduction in polite society."

"Oh."

"I have a hunch we're going out ridin' tonight, lookin' for him," Jeff said. "And pretty soon. Want to come, city girl?"

North bolted across the room and glared first at Melody and then at Jeff. "Don't you dare invite her on something like this, Gentry."

"Can I go, North?" Maria's voice had a wistful quality.

"Everybody but Melody," North snapped. "You can shoot straight."

"So can I," Melody volunteered.

"You've got the kid to see about, remember?" North said. "Teo needs you."

So, he thought Maria was more useful than she.

Manolete and Sissy decided to stay at the ranch, too.

"We better git," Jeff said, pouring his whiskey into a tall stainless steel mug and screwing the black lid on tightly.

Melody couldn't believe it when everybody sprang up from the table and went to the gun safe in the den and started grabbing shotguns and rifles. North was strapping his Colt revolver onto his hip and shouldering a shotgun. Jeff passed everybody rifles and shotguns and then poured three more stainless steel mugs full of whiskey.

"We'll be driving off road," Jeff explained. "This could be a long night."

"Are you crazy? This isn't the Wild West," Melody cried.

"You sure about that, city gal?" Jeff challenged as North grabbed a box of shells.

"North, you're acting as crazy and macho as Jeff. If you're really worried, why don't you call the Border Patrol?"

"We will—when it's time," North said.

"When it's time?" She stared at them, not understanding.

"You're the one harboring an illegal," Jeff said.

Everybody laughed at her.

Everybody but North.

"You're pathetic, North. And you're drunk, Jeff. You're living in a fantasy world. I don't believe there's any such thing as the Midnight Bandit."

"Then you're the one who's living in a fantasy world," Jeff hollered as he flew out the back door. "We want our cows, and we can't afford an international incident. We'll call the Border Patrol, when we've got the bandit and our cows—on this side of the border." He waited on the others. "Let's go."

North headed across the kitchen after Jeff.

Melody ran toward him, suddenly scared for him. "North, I can't believe you're—"

He slanted a look down at her. Then he walked out the door.

She waited, alone in the house. Outside the truck roared. When she got to the garage, the truck's red taillights were disappearing down a rutted road into the thick brush.

Then she was running, crying North's name until she was choking the clouds of dust billowing from the truck into the grass and weeds.

The truck didn't stop.

North was gone.

With Maria. After the Midnight Bandit. Or some such nonsense.

And she was all alone.

Slowly, wrapping her arms around herself, she mounted the stairs to check on Teo.

Eleven

Melody should have known better than to take a shower in such a big old ranch house in the middle of the night. North had been gone for hours. Her upstairs bedroom with its wall of windows along the upper balcony was bright and warm by day. It would have been cozy by night, if she'd drawn the drapes. But after she'd checked on Teo again she'd come inside and tried his aunt's number again.

Aunt Irma had answered. She'd sounded surprised at first and had said that she didn't own a car, but that she'd come as soon as she could arrange transportation. Melody had told Teo and then read for a while and left the drapes open. Now that she was in the shower and could relax about Teo, she was anything but relaxed as she realized there was a lot of dark glass, a lot of exposure at night.

One minute she was arching her body under the warm spray of the shower spigot, trying to rid herself of the inner chill in her soul North's desertion had caused. Spumes of delicious steam were curling all around her as she hummed haltingly and shampooed her hair with shaky fingers.

Then the hardwood floor beyond the bathroom creaked softly. Terrified, she remembered a twig that had cracked right before those boys had started chanting when she'd walked home.

When a drawer opened and closed, she dropped the bottle of shampoo with a clatter and hugged herself.

North had gone off to chase the Midnight Bandit. What if the rogue was for real? What if he was here? What if there was no one awake in the house but her?

She had locked the hall door, but had she checked all the balcony doors? Shrinking against the back wall, her overactive imagination did a replay of the shower scene in that old horror film, *Psycho*. She saw the killer's horrible shadow against the shower curtain, heard the screams.

Stop it, Melody. You aren't by yourself. Libby's probably still playing solitaire. Teo is just down the hall asleep. Manolete and Sissy are somewhere outside. There's no Midnight Bandit. And even if there was, he's down on the border cutting fences and driving heavy trucks around. She kept talking to herself as she stood under the showerhead to get the soap out of her hair.

A boot heel on wood brought her reassuring self-talk to a standstill. No sooner had she turned off the faucets—the better to hear the big bad wolf or whomever was out there—than the bathroom door creaked and a man's broad-shouldered shadow fell against the opposite wall.

"Who's there?" she squeaked, closing her eyes, not wanting to see.

"Just me," came North's deep undertone, causing her heart to knock against her rib cage with a new kind of excitement and a special kind of fear.

"I didn't mean to scare you," he said, his voice deliberately gentle. "I knocked. You didn't answer. I wanted to make sure you're okay."

She couldn't answer. Her shyness and fears warred crazily with her desires as she opened the shower door and stepped blindly into the mists, almost falling into his arms. He ripped a towel off the rod and handed it to her.

"I looked in on Teo. He has more color. You're amazing." She couldn't stop staring at North. He was so beautiful, heart-stoppingly gorgeous. His damp black hair waved silkily across his forehead; his black eyes were fierce with an emotion every bit as strong as whatever she felt.

"Did you catch your bandit?"

He shook his head. "I kept thinking about you back here all alone. So, I left Jeff to do the dirty work."

She smiled impishly, ignoring the towel in his hand. "Why did you come back?"

"I think you know," he murmured.

"What about Maria?"

"I told her how I felt about you."

Melody studied him. "You did, huh?" She laughed. Instead of taking the towel from his large, brown hand, she continued to tease him breathily. "Then don't just stand there. Dry me off."

"I'm the king but you're giving the orders. Not that I'm objecting."

She was naked, timidly so, but trembling with longing. He was fully dressed in his old jeans and white work shirt, his long sleeves rolled up to his elbows. How dark his amber skin looked against the white material. He was wearing the Colt revolver on his right hip again as if he were dead serious about that bandit.

When his eyes flared, she forgot the gun and the mysterious outlaw that kept him up at odd hours. The way he looked at her made her feel bolder and more beautiful than ever before—and desirable. Maybe she wasn't any good at this, maybe she wouldn't ever be, but he'd left Maria, the perfect lady, and come back to her anyway. Never had he made her feel more precious than now as he slowly, carefully folded the towel around her.

"You are beautiful. Incredible," he whispered, causing her to glow as he dried her.

Enveloping her completely in the thick, fluffy cotton, he began to rub her down. She didn't resist his ministrations, not even when he slid the towel between her legs, not even when he wrapped it around her waist and used it to compel her into his arms.

The minute her body came into contact with his, more sweet, wild yearnings seared her even as new fears threatened to send her flying out of the room.

"Are you sure about this?" he whispered. "You don't have to. If there's any hope I'll wait."

She'd wanted to be with him, wanted this strange, terrifying sweetness, wanted to know the pleasure of his hard mouth against her flesh. She'd been so stricken when he'd left her. But always she was of two minds, and now that he was here, she wasn't so sure as she felt the fever heat of his skin. He was immense, uncompromisingly male, all too capable of overpowering her.

He wanted her.

Like those disreputable boys had wanted her.

Not like those boys.

North loved her.

And if she couldn't prove to him she was ready to be his woman, she might lose him to someone else who would, maybe even to Maria. It was now or never. Melody knew there came a moment, when one simply had to seize what one wanted regardless of the risk...or risk losing far more.

"You stay right here, cowboy," she murmured shudderingly. "Kiss me."

When he hesitated, she knew he was afraid of what she might do. So, she dropped the towel to the floor and threaded her fingertips through the dark whorls of hair beneath his molten throat. Then undoing several buttons, her fingertips traced ever lower until she made hardened nubs of his nipples.

He ripped off his shirt and removed his gun. Carefully

he laid holster and revolver on the tiled floor. Then he rose to his full height and pulled her against him again, mashing her breasts against his hot, bronzed torso.

"You came back," she whispered, beginning to burn for him even as she tingled with fear.

His lips touched her throat. "I kept thinking about what you started the other night. And about you being here...all alone. I thought if you had the nerve to try again, hell, so did I."

Her fingers caressed the ridges of his biceps in terror but in wonder as well. "North, I don't know what I'm doing anymore. I never seem to know. I'm not sure you can count on me. I want to be all grown up, a real woman—your woman. But...I want to be my own woman, too, and I'm not sure that's what you want."

He stood motionless as she stroked him, letting her take the lead as he had at his apartment. "One day at a time. If you give me tonight, we'll have that. If that's all we ever have, at least we'll still have that."

When her arms slid around his neck, she felt his body tense. In a way he was as scared as she was.

She lifted her lips to his. When he began to kiss her, his mouth was soon so hot and urgent she forgot to be brave and pulled shyly away.

"Scared?" he muttered thickly, letting her go.

She hugged him tighter, buried her face against his hot chest. "Even if I am, don't stop," she whispered against his throat. "Promise not to stop. See, I've got to get through it. I've got to."

She heard his harsh indrawing of breath. Then his hand stroked her wet hair. "But I want you to enjoy it. To enjoy me. It's not supposed to be an ordeal."

"I won't know what's on the other side till I get there."

He smiled a slow, warm, sexy smile. "Okay, I don't know the answers. I just want to be with you now, tonight. Maybe someday we'll figure the rest out—why you're scared, I mean, and what to do about it."

"Someday... Tonight, let's just follow your instincts."

He seemed disinclined to argue. Easily he picked her up and carried her to the bed. Then he kissed her there as if he were starving. His tongue came inside her mouth with a greedy passion that threatened to devour her. She returned his kiss with such fierce ardor that it was a long time before he let her go. When he did so, he was trembling just as she was.

Quickly he undressed. As she watched him, she felt his passion building, but when he was done, he took her into his arms and kissed her gently. And slowly, oh, so slowly, turned her to flame.

As his lips moved from her face, down her throat, to her breasts, she forgot her fears. He wasn't forcing her. He loved her. He hadn't said it, but she knew. He wanted her, not Maria. Not perfect Maria. He wanted her, even if she couldn't ever fit into his world. Even if she was lousy at sex.

Lousy or not, an odd sensation began to build, a mysterious pressure that began in her belly, a fierce expanding neediness, for what exactly she did not know. She just lay there beneath him, her heart aflutter, clinging to him, dissolving in him, sighing, waiting, not knowing what to do to pleasure him, only knowing that she seemed to be brimming over with new breathtaking needs, until suddenly she felt near bursting. Still, as he wooed her with controlled kisses, the feeling inside her built until she felt herself near some fatal ecstatic edge that both terrified and thrilled her.

"I want to taste you, too," he whispered.

She didn't understand until he lowered his black head, and kissed her ever so tenderly down there.

A moan escaped her lips, and then it struck her, really struck her where his mouth was, how embarrassing and unladylike what he was doing was, and she tried to squirm free. But he held her legs apart and kissed her until what he did felt too good to fight, so she lay still. And suddenly it seemed that what he was doing made her feel most la-

dylike, and she wrapped her arms around his head as a
fierce wildness consumed her. And he kept kissing her and
stroking her until she had to cover her mouth to keep from
crying out as wave after lava wave of passion swept her
and gave her some mysterious release she'd never dreamed
possible. And in that moment, she felt complete, and she
loved him as she'd never dreamed she could. No other adventure seemed as great as just being like this with him.

Only when he felt her go utterly limp and sigh did he
let her go. Only when he'd reduced her to a puddle of
sensual languor did he circle her with his arms and crush
her to him.

"Put your legs around my waist," he ordered.

When she obeyed she felt him there, poised at the center
of her being to plunge inside and possess her, poised to
mate in the most primal way.

And she wanted him to, more than she'd ever wanted
anything.

"For a girl who doesn't like sex, you're very hot," he
whispered.

"For you. Only for you."

"I love you," he said.

"I love you, too."

"I've waited for you longer than I ever believed I could
wait for any woman."

"I know."

"But it was worth it."

"I was good then?"

"Don't you know?" he whispered.

She beamed, feeling very proud and happy, and very,
very special.

"Was I perfect?"

"We're not through," he whispered. "Not by a long
shot."

All that mattered was that he'd waited for her, that he
loved her and that she loved him.

He thrust into her with the hard urgency of a man who'd

denied his own needs far too long, and then he stilled, their bodies joined.

He was bathing her face with tender kisses when his cell phone rang.

She jumped.

"Shh. Maybe it'll quit," he whispered, staying inside her, holding her.

But it didn't.

"Damn," he growled in an almost painful breath against her hair.

The jarring, electronic beeping was growing louder and more insistent with every ring. Soon he was swearing in a hard, angry undertone and rolling off her.

"Lord." He covered his eyes with his hand and then reached for it.

Melody lay in the dark, her eyes closed, rubbing her temples, impassioned almost to a point of insensibility and yet feeling abandoned, rejected—incomplete somehow. "Who—"

"Jeff." North was pulling out his antenna, pressing Talk. "I promised him I'd leave it on."

"Jeff?"

"In case he ran into trouble—"

"You're going to talk to Jeff now?"

"I'm real sorry, darlin'."

Jeff didn't say much, but before long North was cursing again. Ripping the covers aside like a big angry bear, he jumped out of bed and then yelped when his toe struck something hard.

"Ouch!" He began hopping on one foot. "My God! Where—"

Startled, she sat up as he lumbered clumsily across the dark to her bathroom. Slamming the door, he bolted himself inside, so she couldn't hear the rest of their conversation.

She got up. Running after him, she beat frantically on the locked door. "North, what's going on?"

He didn't answer, so she put her ear to the door. He was in the shower. She could hear the water.

He was going. Leaving her.

Feeling cold with a strange terror and curiously let down, she crawled back into bed. When he strutted into the bedroom a few minutes later, his expression was stern, and he was wrapped in a towel. Wearily he finger-combed his wet black hair back into place.

"What is it?"

"Nothing."

"Nothing? You spring out of bed like a cannon went off, and it's nothing?"

"This isn't any of your business, Melody."

What was she—a grown-up woman he took to bed when it pleased him, but a child he was determined to protect when it came to his real life?

"If it's nothing, you'd better come back to bed and finish what you started."

He grinned, clueless as to the depth of her concern. "For a girl that didn't want to, you're mighty eager all of a sudden. A guy like me could get cocky."

"I want to be your woman—in all areas of your life."

"Darlin' there's nothing I'd like better than to come back to bed."

He tugged on his jeans.

"But you're getting dressed! Why are you leaving me?"

He pulled his shirt on and began to work clumsily at the buttons.

"You can't start this after all your years of badgering me and then quit right in the middle," she added.

He managed a grin. "You used to, darlin'. For years and years, remember? Now you know how it feels."

"That's not fair."

"Fair. I run out one night! For a damn good reason! You made it a habit for years!"

"Because I was scared! You're doing this for some stupid, macho reason!"

"Darlin', I'll be back. I swear. I wouldn't miss tonight with you for anything. You're everything! Everything, do you understand!"

"If I'm everything, take me with you!"

His expression darkened as he approached the bed. "No. I can't risk anything happening to you—not ever. Especially now that we've finally found each other. Understand?"

No, she didn't.

"This is dangerous, isn't it?"

He shook his head. But something dark and alarmed in his voice and eyes as he held her close and petted her hair scared her and told her not to argue, not to make him suspicious.

"Darlin', I know what it is to do something stupid and lose somebody. You've got to stay here, where it's safe. If you don't—" His black eyes were fierce, almost threatening.

"Are you going to be in danger?"

"Who me? Not me." He kissed her hard.

He was lying. She could feel it. But if he read her mind and realized she might do something impulsive, there was no telling what he might do to stop her. She could tell he was very determined. So, instead of accusing him, she smiled obediently.

When he was done with his kisses, she curved her lips sleepily. Languidly she yawned and pulled the covers up and pretended to close her eyes.

"Hurry back," she said. "I can't wait!"

"Neither can I."

Satisfied that she was the obedient child he wanted her to be and would do as he asked, he kissed her lips one final time, held her again as if she were infinitely precious to him and then stalked out of the room.

No sooner had he shut the door, than she threw back the sheets and flew to the bathroom. In the dark she stumbled

over something hard. She flicked on the light and saw he'd
forgotten his gun.

Jeff had been out chasing the Midnight Bandit when he'd
gotten into trouble. She knelt, panic welling inside her as
she picked it up.

Almost she thought of running with it to the door and
calling him back. Instead her hand slowly tightened on the
carved leather holster and let herself grow used to how
heavy and deadly it felt.

Revolvers were the easiest guns in the world to use. At
least her daddy always said so. A girl didn't have to be all
that mechanical to use one. That's why he'd taught Claire
and her how to shoot one. He'd taken them to the bay,
thrown cans out, and told them to shoot.

"That way when you miss, you see where the bullets hit
in the water, so you know how far your aim is off," Sam
had said.

After a miss or two, Melody sunk twelve cans in a row,
and he'd proclaimed her a natural talent.

"You're as good as a man, honey."

"Better," she'd replied.

Easing the black revolver out of the holster, Melody released the cylinder and spun it just to make sure it was
loaded.

It was.

Her eyes drifted along the row of extra bullets North had
jammed into the leather belt. For a minute longer she knelt
there on the bathroom floor, holding the gun—her whole
body was paralyzed, literally so scared at the thought of
what she intended to do, she couldn't move. Could she
shoot a man when all she'd ever practiced on were soda
pop cans?

Then she thought of North going out to face whatever
or whomever it was that had Jeff wild with fear and had
made North leave her bed at a time no man would ever
leave unless he had to—alone.

What if something terrible had happened to him just

when she realized how much he'd always meant to her as well as how much more he could grow to mean? What if he needed her out there?

Idly she played with the leather belt, her fingers fiddling with the extra bullets, moving them up and down in their leather loops. Why did men think they were the only ones who could be heroes? Would she be any more capable of forgiving herself if something happened to him than he would be if something were to happen to her?

She sprang up and got dressed even faster than he had.

He would be furious. Maybe furious enough to storm out of her life forever.

North saw male-female roles in black-and-white terms. He thought women should be sweet and modest and obedient and sexy. He had never approved of her impulsive, adventurous spirit. There were certain areas of his life, he considered a man's domain. But if she was to grow up, didn't she have to become brave and whole and modern in all areas of her life? Not just their bedroom? If she were his equal, she couldn't let him order her around like he was a king and she was a serf. Not tonight—when his life might be in danger.

If she was ever going to really be a woman, North's woman, she had to follow him, no matter what it cost her.

Thus, when he slipped out of the house into the dark, she was right behind him.

Twelve

It seemed to North that he and Timmy Star had been squatting in the plane on the runway for nearly an hour.

"Star, haven't you revved your damn engine long enough?"

North flexed his hands, fisting them and then flexing them time and again. Jeff could be dead by now.

He kept seeing Melody's blue eyes ablaze with desire as she'd lain beneath him. She'd wanted him. Finally. She'd actually reveled in it. More than anything, he had to get back to her—fast.

The gravelly roar of the engine betrayed the fact Star had tampered with the plane to increase its horsepower significantly.

"Hold your horses, Black! I don't wanna just git you into Mexico so you can settle your score with the Midnight Bandit. I wanna git myself back to the civilized world."

When the sound of the big engine suddenly changed,

Timmy almost purred, "The prop's feathered. Ready for takeoff?"

As they taxied down the dirt strip lit by crude kerosene lamps, known as *bombas* in Mexico, in the stripped down, single-engine plane, North cursed the rotten luck that had gotten him out of Melody's soft arms and warm bed on this fool's errand just when she'd finally decided sex might be fun. But at least she was home safe.

He glanced at Timmy. Star was bald and fat. His complexion was baby-pink; his teeth were bad. Except for the gray plastic handle of what looked like a very serious military weapon peeping out from under his seat, Tim didn't look or act like a hotshot pilot turned smuggler. He had a wife, kids and a mortgage. He went to church most Sundays. But in this dangerous business, he was known for nerve.

Star had flown jets in the Gulf War. When he'd gone broke during a peso devaluation, he'd bought an old plane and gutted it down to the bulkheads. Other than the two front seats, there was nothing on board that wasn't necessary to flight. Thus, the large cavity behind their seats could be filled with contraband clear to the tail. He'd smuggle anything but dope—people, weapons—but not dope. Dope was dirty.

North couldn't quit thinking of Melody. Most of all he couldn't quit remembering how good he'd felt inside her.

As soon as they were airborne, they swung to the south toward the shadowy glimmer of the Rio Grande.

"She feels heavier tonight," Tim bellowed over the engine and vibrations.

"What?"

"The plane. I can always tell. You sure all you brought was two shotguns?"

"Maybe you've put on a few pounds."

"Too many tacos?" Star patted his belly.

They laughed, but nervously.

North peered over his shoulder into the gloom. "Just my guns."

"The tail feels heavy."

"Relax."

Tim grunted.

"How come you do this? I mean—you've made enough to quit long ago," North asked.

"Adrenaline. It's a rush. After what I did in the military, watching sitcoms every night won't do it."

They were barely in the air ten minutes before Timmy cut the power and banked sharply to the left. They had to fly low to get under the radar. A minute later had them on a fast sliding descent into utter blackness.

"Better get the lights turned on down there, boys—"

Down. Down. They seemed to fall endlessly into a black hole. North leaned forward, his heart thudding like a drum in his ears as he peered out. Expecting trees to rip into the fuselage any second, he held his breath. Flying at night with no lights, ducking and diving over rough country, there was always the possibility that they were off course, that a set of power lines might loom up suddenly.

North breathed a sigh of relief when a ragged line of *bombas* flashed on, marking the ranch landing strip that seemed to be in the middle of nowhere.

Then they were on the potholed strip, bumping to a standstill. The runway lights were instantly snuffed. North grabbed his guns and waited for the prop to crank down.

North slapped two thousand dollars in cash into Tim's hand, grabbed his guns, kicked the door open and stepped onto the wing. "Thanks."

Star stuffed the cash into the back pocket of his jeans. "Flying into Mexico is nothing compared to what I used to do in the military."

"Okay, so, sit tight. If I'm not back in an hour—"

"You know the rules. Any sign of trouble, and I'm outta here."

"Gotcha."

North was about to jump to the ground when an all too familiar, feminine voice behind them said, "Wait for me, Bertie!"

"What the hell!" Tim had his gun aimed on their stow-away in the dark cavity faster than North could blink.

"Rough landing," Melody said cheerily. "Other than that, great flight!" She smiled at Timmy. "Don't shoot. I'm with Rancher Black."

"You didn't say nothin' about no woman. I ain't waiting, Black. Not if you take her! Won't baby-sit her, either!"

"We had a deal—"

"Yeah—deal was—I'm outta here at the first sign of trouble." He propped his big gun across his legs and stared at Melody. "And I know trouble when I set eyes on it. She's it with a capital *T*. She's the little hellion that did the dance at that bar?"

"How the hell am I supposed to get back if you go?" North growled.

"That's your problem! Fly out now! Or get!"

"I'll settle up with you later. Take her with you."

"No way," Star said.

Melody beamed.

North reached back into the cabin and seized Melody's wrist so hard, she whimpered.

"What did you think you were doing tonight, darlin'?"

"Adrenaline. Maybe I like the rush."

Star laughed. "You've got yourself a real little trouble-some spitfire. You two have fun."

North was so enraged, he could have strangled them both, but he concentrated on Melody and yanked her out of the plane.

"You little fool. You could be jeopardizing everything. The bad guys who have Jeff and my cattle are about as friendly as a den of rattlers."

She whitened and had the good sense to lower her eyes. Then she said, "Sounds to me like you need reinforce-ments."

"Not you."

"You should have told me the truth then."

"Oh, so it's my fault you're here?"

That she blamed him for putting her in danger made him even angrier. "You put yourself in danger, understand? You put Gentry in danger, too."

He jumped from the wing to the ground and reached up for her.

"So what happened tonight? What's wrong?" she asked when she landed lightly beside him.

"After Gentry took Maria and Tina home, he saw somebody messing with the trucks he loaded this afternoon. He went over to see what was going on. The Midnight Bandit and his men got him and the trucks and drove them across a low water bridge into Mexico. They're going to demand a ransom of some sort. No telling where they'd be if one of my trucks hadn't hit a rock. They've stopped to change a tire. They left Gentry in the locked cab. They didn't realize he still had his cell phone."

A dog barked. Suddenly they heard the roar of heavy machinery.

"Big truck at the end of the runway," Tim yelled as he began to rev the plane. "You've got company."

"Notify the border patrol," North said.

As Star taxied down the runway, the truck's high beams caught North in their blinding glare.

North grabbed Melody's hand and took off running for the thick brush.

It was hard for Melody to keep up with North as they marched through the high, dry, prickly grasses.

Once she fell on the rocks and cut her hand. North wrapped his handkerchief around it and told her she wouldn't be in this jam if she'd done what he told her.

"I got scared—for you."

"That's bull. You just acted on impulse. Like you did when you ran down the aisle and left me standing in front

of all those people. Like you did when you danced at
Shorty's and got all those shrimpers in a frenzy. You never
give a damn when you turn my life upside down! What if
you get you or me killed...or Jeff?''

"I couldn't let you go alone," she whispered raggedly.

"Stay close to me, and don't say another word till we
get home.'' He knotted the handkerchief. "Just do exactly
what I say. Understand? They could be anywhere. And not
just them. The border's alive with wets, *coyotes* and all
sorts of unsavory characters who prey on them." He
paused. "You little fool. If anything happens to you, I'll
never forgive myself."

"Ditto, you big macho lug," she said silently as she
trudged after him.

"Do you have a plan? Or... Or we going to walk all
night?" she whispered.

"Keep quiet."

"So, a woman isn't supposed to think? She's just supposed to take orders?"

"Is that so hard?"

"Impossible."

He was cursing low under his breath when they heard a
dozen men cock their rifles.

A line of soldiers stood straight in front of them.

"Levantese los manos."

North grabbed her by the hair and shoved her down into
the grasses. The beam of their flashlights struck North full
in the face.

"Don't move!" Then he used the same voice he had
used in her bed—it was deep, intimate, urgent. "Please—"

He began yelling at them in Spanish, and they yelled
back. Slowly he raised his hands, held his guns high and
walked toward them.

Several of the men fanned out into the pasture with spot-
lights. Melody pressed her head to the warm dirt, scared
they would hear the violent thumping of her heart. When,
at last they gave up their search and rejoined the others,

Melody peeped her head above the grasses and saw that
North was completely surrounded by men in brown uniforms. They were laughing at him now. Even though it was
well after midnight, they all sported mirrored, aviator
glasses. A big man with a flashy gold watch seemed to be
in charge.

For a long time she stayed where she was frozen against
the ground by fear. Only when they stripped North of his
guns, tied his hands behind his back, and marched him
roughly away did she regain enough of her courage to get
up and follow them.

They stopped and she hung back, so scared she bit her
lips and then her tongue. So scared she hadn't realized
she'd drawn blood until they were out of sight again and
she tasted copper.

Dear God, what were they going to do to him?

She loved him. She'd never known how much until now.
He had waited for her to grow up. He would lay down his
life for her. He just had.

He'd gone against his friends and come back to the house
tonight. He'd let Teo stay even though it was against the
law and his deepest principles—for her. He'd called the
doctor for Teo.

She loved him. She couldn't let him die.

They would kill him for sure—if she didn't do something—fast.

But what?

What could one scared girl do against so many?

In Mexico?

Thirteen

Cows mooed and shuffled heavily in the pair of cattle trucks the bandits had parked beside the narrow dirt road. Three Mexicans in uniforms and mirrored glasses were kneeling over a back wheel, running their palms along the heavy tread of the big tire they'd just changed.

Melody stared as one wiped his face with a bandanna. Then her gaze wandered to the others clumped around the fire. They'd butchered one of North's cows and were cooking meat over a spit. North and Jeff were bound and gagged in the cab of their own cattle truck filled with bawling cattle.

She closed her eyes. It seemed she'd stood in the dark here for hours, her heart numb with terror, her mind paralyzed by indecision.

One of the Mexicans opened the cab and started the engine. After he'd carefully backed the big rig out onto the road, he jumped out.

"Lista!" Ready!

"Tienes hambre?" Another Mexican held up a piece of meat and waved it at his friend.

The three men at the truck joined the others.

She stared at the open cab door, mesmerized by the silver glimmer of keys in the ignition. Then she began to shake. Jeff and North were in there. She had to save them.

Without even thinking, she pulled out North's revolver and ran for it.

She was inside the cab when the soldiers began to shout. The truck's steering wheel was too big, too heavy. So was the stick shift. She had to sit on the very edge of the hard seat to reach the pedals.

There was a crash of breaking glass inches from her face when she turned the key and started the big engine.

"Don't shoot!" she screamed, fastening her seat belt. *"Soy dama! Tengo miedo!"*

More bullets. She jumped back when she felt a sharp pain in her shoulder. It wasn't a bullet. It was only a shard.

But she got so mad, she aimed the revolver and fired. Then she headed the big eighteen-wheeler straight at them. There was a paper cup and a pint bottle of tequila on the seat beside her. As the truck banged and rattled along the road, the transmission screaming, probably because she was in the wrong gear, she opened the bottle and gulped down fiery bursts of tequila that were so hot she gagged.

She wiped her mouth. In her rearview mirror she could see the Mexicans climbing into the other truck.

She was picking up speed when North spoke sharply from behind her. "Melody! You've got to turn this baby around. Texas is the other way."

"You're okay?"

"I said—"

"Too bad you got your gag off."

"Turn this baby around, damn it!"

"But there's a fence—"

"Drive over it!"

A funny kind of smile lit her face. "I've always wanted

to do something like this! And I thought ranch life was boring!''

She bounced them over rocks and cacti. By the time she had the rig back on the road heading the right way, the other cattle truck was heading straight at her, swerving into her lane deliberately.

''Damn 'em. Veer off the road or we'll lose both trucks,'' North yelled.

''You're not in charge here, Rancher Black! I am!''

Melody took another pull from the tequila bottle and aimed right at them.

''Damn your crazy hide!''

The two embattled cattle trucks met in a cloud of dark boiling dust. The other trunk honked and honked maniacally.

''This is suicide!'' North screamed.

Melody stomped down harder on the accelerator. Only at the last moment did she swerve, and then just a little. So did they.

It was enough. The cabs missed by inches. Only the cattle trailers scraped, making huge rending sounds like giant can openers peeling off lids. The cattle bawled and stomped.

Then she was free. She hit the horn triumphantly and kept tooting it until she saw their headlights in her rearview mirror again.

She cursed.

They'd turned around and were catching up fast.

North was swearing louder than she was when the bandits pulled alongside her and began screaming at her in Spanish, honking and then ramming her. Then just as the thick-shouldered man in the passenger seat pointed a rifle at her face, she saw a clear track off to the right of the roadbed about eight feet below her.

She downshifted and spilled tequila all over her jeans.

''Oops!''

Above his white gag, Jeff's eyes were as big as blue

soccer balls. Right before she skidded the rig off the embankment, she crossed herself. Then she took a final swig from the nearly empty tequila bottle.

They were bouncing over rocks again and sliding, the trailer fishtailing all the way down the embankment. The cab careened to one side wildly. Somehow, miraculously, they were upright when the front tires hit the lower track.

She floored the accelerator. Above them, the other cattle truck downshifted, attempting to outrun her as they raced for the border.

Jeff's gag had slipped. He began to smile as she got ahead of the other truck. "She's beatin' 'em."

"How the hell does she intend to get back up on the road?" North demanded.

As if in answer the big truck shuddered as she ran it off a high bank into a dry riverbed.

When Melody saw water and shingly river rocks, she began to pray and cross herself.

"We're in the Rio Grande!" North screamed.

Suddenly, up ahead, she saw a ramp where she could get the truck up onto a low water bridge. But there was some sort of fence across the middle of the bridge on the higher road, and the other cattle truck was gaining on her again.

Behind her she heard the spray of gunfire. Then she crashed onto the bridge and sent fence stakes and barbed wire flying as she hurdled through the makeshift fence.

"Good Old Ameri-kee! We're home! Now all we have to do is wait for Delfino to show up." Jeff was babbling excitedly about the Border Patrol being on their way because he'd called them right after he'd called North when she crashed into a mesquite tree.

The other truck roared to a stop behind her and twelve men surrounded the rig with raised guns. She lifted her hands, surrendering.

A man with dark black hair and mustache swaggered up to the truck and yanked the door open. As he stood beneath her, she knew he had to be the Midnight Bandit.

His expensive shirt was tight across his shoulders, tight across his waist, which had thickened some in middle age. Although he was past his first youth, he was still very attractive as only a vital, dangerous man can be.

"Take off your mirrored glasses," she called down to him.

When he did so and then offered her his hand, she noticed his heavy gold watch that had thick links the size and shape of small bulldozer tracks.

"So, are you the famous bandit I've heard so much about?"

"Three things make the heart beat fast, *señorita*—money, danger and a beautiful woman."

Twelve men stood behind him.

This time North was tied up and couldn't save her.

But what could they do to her, even if there were twelve, that the four boys hadn't already done on that long-ago afternoon? Strangely, when she jumped down, she realized her old fears were gone.

This man and his outlaw gang couldn't scare her.

Unless she let him.

"Let North Black and his foreman go," she said.

The Midnight Bandit laughed. "Beautiful and brave, too? Señor Black is luckier than I knew." He paused, tweaking his mustache. "We will go back to Mexico, you and me, and I will build you a fire and roast another cow, and I will think about it. It has been a long time since I dined by candlelight with a very beautiful, a very special woman. The way you drove that truck! Wow!—as you gringos say! You are *muy macha*. Tonight I will show you the real Mexico."

He had her hand in his and was shouting to his men to drive her truck back over the bridge when—

Whoomph! *Zoom!*

"*Qué es eso*—"

The roar of ten Dodge Ramchargers, their lights blazing sent twelve bandits, even Melody's new admirer, the Midnight Bandit, scampering into the thick mesquite or wading back across the river.

"You're late, Delfino," North said as he rubbed the red places on his wrist that had been bound. He was drinking water out of a paper cup.

"What's going on here?" Delfino demanded.

"Those bastards were trying to take my trucks into Mexico again. They were going to hold Jeff for ransom."

"Fence is down on the low water—"

"They cut it."

Delfino leaned behind North and peeled barbed wire off the bumper of the truck Melody had just driven across the river. "How come your tires are wet?"

Both men eyed each other warily. "There's more to this than meets the eye, I reckon," Delfino said. But he smiled.

"Thanks for showing up, Delfino. You damn sure saved the day."

For the first time since North had gotten out of the truck, Melody dared to look at him.

Fury harshened his features as his gaze locked on her pale face. "You sure made a fool of me."

"I-is that all that counts? I—I thought I saved your life."

He crushed his cup and threw it to the ground.

His black eyes were dead even before he turned his back on her and walked off with Delfino.

Although she sat beside North as he drove back to the ranch headquarters, he neither looked at her nor said a single word to her.

Fourteen

North drove the truck home so fast, Melody felt as if she was in a giant eggbeater that was literally pounding her to death over the rough potholes. W.T. and Arturo had been sent to get the other truck.

Straining to see ahead in the flying darkness, North leaned over the steering wheel. His huge body was rigid and silent; his hand was like a claw on the stick shift.

She didn't think she'd ever been in the presence of such raw, naked hostility.

He banged the truck over a cattle guard, and she gasped in anxious relief at the sight of the lights gleaming cheerily from the big house.

North slammed on the brakes, and she was thrown against her seat belt and him when the rig careened to a stop.

"Whoa! I don't know which was scarier—your driving or her partyin' with the Midnight Bandit. Or the way you're acting now."

With a frown Jeff stared at North's belligerent profile and then at the barn. "Didn't think I'd ever see any of this again." He regarded North's dark silent face uneasily. Then he grabbed an armful of shotguns.

"Time to go, huh?" Pulling up the door lock, Jeff scooted his large bulk forward, fumbling with the latch to let himself out.

"You were great, Mel," Jeff whispered, patting her shoulder. "Thanks." The gratitude in his blue eyes made her forgive him everything.

"Thanks," she whispered.

"Better not to talk to him till he has a good night's sleep," Jeff said.

North bristled but said nothing until Melody began to slide across her seat after Jeff.

Then North grabbed her hand, wrenching her back. "You're not going anywhere! Not till we talk!" The command cracked like a bullet.

Startled, she hesitated before daring a glance at him. The dark sensuality of his brutal features made her catch her breath. Then every wary nerve in her body sparked in painful defiance.

Only a few hours ago, he'd been in her bed—been inside her. And she'd loved it, really loved it.

She loved him.

"North," she breathed. "I'm sorry."

"So the hell am I. That's why we settle up now. The sooner I'm done with you the better—"

"Done? How bleak that sounds."

His white face was blank; his black eyes glittered. She began to tremble even before full understanding of what he meant registered.

"As soon as this Aunt Irma, or whoever she is, gets here today, I want you gone. Off my ranch. Out of my life."

Her skin felt hot and cold at the same time.

"You can't mean..." Her heart pumped painfully.

He didn't reply.

He was killing her first with words, now with his silence.

"But I saved your life—"

"Do you want a medal? Do you want me down on my knees licking your hand the way you had Jeff—"

His harsh words were like blows. All of a sudden she hurt all over. "No..."

She sucked in a breath as panic raced through her.

"This is my ranch." His voice was tight and angry. "Everybody who sets foot on my land is my responsibility—including you. You deliberately disobeyed me."

"So, that's it. This is about your stupid macho pride."

A hard blue vein throbbed in his temple. "You made a fool of me."

"You're mad because I saved you. Because you didn't protect me."

His lips were pale with leashed rage.

"Where is it written you're the only person in the universe who can be a hero?"

"Don't give yourself airs!"

"You said you wanted a real woman. Well, we had sex, and I loved it so much I want to do it again and again." She remembered how rosy she'd felt, how warm and sweet when she'd ached for him afterward. "Because... Because I love you with all my heart."

"I don't give a damn about that! It was just physical. Something I could get with any woman."

With three cruel sentences he obliterated the warm, sweet rosy memory that had kept her fighting for him, for them, all night.

Something I could get with any woman.

Her body felt as if it were closing down, shriveling up.

Still, she wasn't about to back down.

"Well, if you wanted me to be your woman in that way, even if it doesn't mean as much to you as it did to me, I *was* your woman. Like you said, no matter what happens, we'll have that time together in bed...in our hearts and our minds. Nothing you can say now can take that away—from either of us." She paused. "But something else happened to me tonight. Something more wonderful even than the sex we shared. I lost my fear. I won't ever be that child those boys chased and you saved. I'm past all that. Because of tonight and you, I can move forward in my life. Even if…if I lose you, I won't lose that."

"You're as crazy as you ever were."

"You were in danger. I saved your life. And Jeff's. And your trucks. And your precious cows."

"Don't forget—you even flirted with that monster while he had me trussed like a pig for his spit."

"That, too. I beat him at your game. And I needed to know I could do something like that…at least once in my life. I'm sorry if you can't forgive me, but I had to do it for you…and for me." She hesitated. "When they took you, I would have done anything…*anything*…to save your life, North. You are that precious to me. And no matter what you say or do to me, I would rather have you hate me now than have you dead in Mexico."

"I want that kid who's upstairs in my father's room gone by tonight, and I want you gone, too, do you understand?"

She'd become his woman.

She'd saved his life.

She'd come into her own power.

But in doing so, she'd lost him.

Melody was sitting cross-legged on a little blanket she'd thrown down in the llamas' stall. Little Camel stood beside her sucking vigorously on the bottle's nipple.

"Why won't his mother feed him?" Teo whispered. "Doesn't his mother like him? If she wasn't locked up, would she run away?"

"Her milk won't come."

In the next breath he demanded, "When will Aunt Irma get here?"

Even with black hair clean and gleaming, even in the brand-new plaid cowboy shirt, jeans and new boots that

North had bought him, even after he'd grabbed a huge breakfast, Teo still looked the waif. He was a quiet, self-controlled little boy. He had a deep, natural reserve. He was even shyer than Little Camel.

"Soon I think," Melody reassured him. "It is a six-hour drive from Houston."

The mother llama seemed to be taking an inordinate interest in her baby sucking at that nipple. All of a sudden she walked over and began pawing straw and then nuzzling her baby.

Little Camel stopped sucking.

"Teo watch—"

The child held his breath as Little Camel cautiously stuck his head under her belly and began to suckle.

"Oh," Melody gaspèd, setting the bottle down. "Aren't they cute?"

Teo smiled for the first time since Melody had met him. She pulled the little boy into her arms where he stayed until the barn doors rolled apart. He jumped when heavy boot heels clacked briskly toward them on concrete.

"Melody—"

"North?"

They hadn't spoken since they'd gotten out of the truck. After all, what was there to say?

"In here," she called.

The door opened, and her gaze climbed long legs encased in pressed denim. Just his nearness gave her a physical ache. It seemed forever since he'd held her and kissed her, since his black eyes had gleamed with hungry desire.

He was bronzed in his white shirt and jeans, as lean and handsome as ever, maybe more so since she'd lost him. Maybe more so, since she'd *had* him.

There were shadows under his eyes, and his expression was worn and sad. His beautiful mouth was thin. He wore the look of a man who'd lost his dreams.

She wanted to tell him that it didn't have to be that way. Instead she pressed her fingertips to her lips. He was as stubborn as she was. There were some things a person had to decide for himself. He'd made up his mind.

"Look who's here, Teo," he said, ignoring Melody as he pushed the door wider.

"Teo. *Precioso*," said a soft feminine voice in Spanish behind North.

Straw crunched as a small brown woman in a black dress and shawl knelt and held out her arms.

"*Tiá?*"

When Melody gave him a little push Teo walked hesitantly up to the older woman with the kind wrinkled face.

"*Sí, precioso. Tu Tiá* Irma." She wrapped him in her arms and held him for a long time. Finally she got up, and leading Teo by the hand, North and Melody followed them outside to the battered car she'd borrowed from her cousin.

Arm in arm, Manolete and Sissy joined them. His eyes wet and shining, Manolete knelt and hugged Teo for a very long time.

"I'm a cook," Irma explained. "I'll take good care of him."

"I know you will," said Manolete, releasing Teo, so the boy and Irma could get inside the car.

"You be good, Teo, you hear," Melody said.

"Take care of Little Camel," he replied.

"He has his mother. He doesn't need me anymore." Melody wasn't looking at Teo, though. She was staring at North who stood next to her.

Then to North the little boy said in a small timid voice, "Can I come back for a visit? I'm real good with animals. I worked on a rancho. I could feed all your sick babies. I can milk the cows—I—I can even feed camels."

Irma laughed.

North reached inside and patted the child's glossy black head. "Anytime. Always. *Mi casa es su casa.*"

North leaned down. To Irma, in English, he said, "If you need any help getting him papers, I know people on both sides of the border."

Irma smiled. "You are a very powerful man. A true hero to save this little boy."

North stood up, his face grim. "I'm no hero. Thank these other people."

Irma started the car. Black smoke belched.

Wrapped in each other's arms, Manolete and Sissy seemed very much in love as they waved goodbye.

Melody felt chilled standing so close to North, both of them waving and smiling until the car vanished behind a wall of thick brush. Then their eyes locked, and North's smile died.

A feeling of apprehension washed through Melody. "I guess it's my turn to say goodbye."

"Don't bother," North muttered flatly, his hard gaze flicking away from Melody before he pivoted and walked away.

Melody felt sick.

"He loves you," Sissy whispered. "He does. And it's killing him. I'm his sister. I know." Then she looked up at Manolete. "Mano leaves me, too, today."

"Really?" Melody could barely concentrate on anything other than North's tall form striding away. "North wrote letters of introduction to all our rancher friends, so Mano will have places to stay on the way to New York. This morning I bought my ticket. I'll be there waiting when he gets there."

"Oh, Sissy."

"We shall see what the future will bring," Manolete said.

He took Sissy in his arms and kissed her full on the lips.

"I'm so happy for you," Melody whispered.

Melody was staring at the awful landscapes in his office. North was seated at his desk shuffling papers.

"North—"

He wouldn't look at her.

"Why won't you listen to me?" she begged.

He wadded a paper and pitched it into the trash. "We already discussed this. You could have died. It would have been my fault. I can't risk that again."

"I saved your life. And I'm not sorry I did. I can't play by your rules all the time. I have to be me. I have to take care of me, too. And sometimes I may have to take care of you, too."

"You could have died."

"That's not a crime. You only think it is because...because of the way your daddy died."

He slammed a file closed.

"You didn't kill him."

"Who said I did?"

"Nobody."

"Then why'd you accuse—"

"You accuse yourself. Nobody else accuses you. Why do you do that? Why can't you let it go?"

He stood up. "You want to know why? If I tell you you'll go—"

She nodded, backing into the hall.

"I was twelve. My daddy smoked, and I wanted to do everything he did. So Jeff and me, we were out behind some stacks of lumber with a package of his cigarettes I'd stolen out of his room. We only smoked one, but we both got so sick. We were throwing up our gizzards in the house when the fire started. Hell, nobody knows how it got started. But all of a sudden this black smoke was billowing so high every neighbor in three counties drove up to see what was the matter."

The dark torment in his eyes crushed her. She knew what it was to love one's family, to want to take care of them.

"I—I wish there was something I could say...do..."

"Little Miss Fix-it! You think this is like some cut you can put a Band-Aid on and make it well. You think you're magic after what you did last night—"

"No."

"You think I'm some worthless, cowardly incompetent

because the Midnight Bandit got the best of me and you came to my rescue.''

''No, North. I just think you're human.''

''Get out.''

In a quiet voice, she said, ''I love you.''

''I love you, too. Get the hell out!''

Fifteen

A big engine outside the barn roared to life.

"What the hell was that?" North muttered, wiping his brow in his shirtsleeve. The relentless drought persisted endlessly. So did the summer. Even though it was still early that morning, North and Jeff were already sweating in the barn as they jotted notes on their clipboards as they went over the day's work together.

"That's W.T. I told him to put the truck on bungee autopilot while he feeds hay in the north pasture," Jeff said.

"Hell! I just put Little Camel and his mother in that pasture!"

North threw his clipboard down. He was already yelling to W.T. to cut the engine as he ran out of the barn.

But W.T. couldn't hear him over the noise of the truck. Instead of watching what he was doing, the rangy, no-good cowboy was lying down in the cab, his Stetson tipped low over his nose, reading a comic book.

Behind the huge truck, Little Camel was cornered.

At the exact moment Little Camel saw North and might
have bolted clear, the steel bumper hit the little animal and
knocked him down.

"Get up!" North yelled. "W.T.," he screamed.

As the big wheels rolled closer to the fallen animal, Little
Camel just lay there, too stunned to move.

Then the truck ground its gears and lurched backward.

North leaped over the fence. "Get up! Get out of the
way!"

Little Camel lifted his head. As he looked at North he
seemed to understand and made a valiant struggle to stand.
He was halfway to his feet when the truck knocked him
down and backed over him. The llama's legs twisted and
jerked under the big black double wheels. Then he disappeared completely.

"No! No!"

W.T. finally heard North banging on the door and
stopped the truck. He jumped out, his comic book still
rolled up in his hand. North shoved past him, hopped inside
the cab and put the gear in first.

When he'd gotten the truck off the animal, he jumped
out and ran back to Little Camel. But the llama was a still
and broken thing in the deep soil. After his mother came
up and got her fill of sniffing and licking his nose, North
knelt and lifted the frail, furry body into his arms.

Before North reached the barn with his pet, Gran had
come running out of the house. Jeff and Sissy were there
too.

Nobody spoke as the hot wind gusted around the house.

"Why don't you bury him under my daisies," Gran offered after a lengthy silent interval. "That's the prettiest
spot on the ranch. I'm going to get W.T. to plant me some
tulips come spring."

"I'll get the shovel for you," Jeff offered.

There were tears in North's eyes as he dug the small
grave.

"Could I take a turn…on the shovel?" W.T. finally whispered.

North turned, his heart dark and blank until he read the bleak despair in the boy's expression and saw the sheen of tears in his eyes.

He swallowed. After a long moment he nodded. "It was an accident. It was just an accident."

North stayed by the grave long after the others had gone.

He thought of his father, of Melody, and the memories of the people he'd loved and lost made him ache.

As he stared at Little Camel's grave, the loneliness he'd thought he could accept suddenly threatened to overwhelm him. The thought of eating alone, of going to bed alone, of waking up every day for the rest of his life without Melody nestled warmly against him brought unbearable pain.

But when he thought of his father and the fire, the ghosts from his past were too real.

What he'd done to his father was too real.

Little Camel's death was a reminder.

He couldn't risk Melody.

It had been a rough month. Not just for North. For everybody on the ranch who had dealings with North.

"Calf breathing okay?"

"Yeah, King," Jeff replied glumly.

North frowned as he dropped more antibiotics into the uterus and then began to sew up the cow. It had been a rough delivery. He'd slipped and the cow had stomped him mighty hard in a lot of tender places a man didn't care to catch a hoof.

"You know, King—"

North could tell by the level of gravel in Jeff's tone what he was up to again, so he cut him off at the pass. "I don't want to talk about *her.*"

"You don't look so good. You're back to killing yourself with work again."

"I'm fine."

"You fell. You damn near got you and me both killed. You aren't some god."

"Never said I was."

"You can make a mistake, too."

"I know that! Don't you think I know that?"

"I was wrong about her, King."

"I said don't."

"So are you. You've been wrong about a lot of things. About your daddy—"

"Damn it."

"She didn't show you up. She was safe. You protected her. You faced those guys alone. Give her credit for having the guts to come back for you. She saved our lives, our cattle and our trucks."

"I know what she did better than you!"

"Give yourself credit for saving her. But, hell, she's the best damn cowhand on the place. We need her. Not just for that. But because you're dying on the inside, North. You're so damn proud and stubborn, you're killing yourself just like you did after Rand died. Everything's not your fault, you know. Little Camel's death was an accident, just like your daddy's. You forgave W.T. Why the hell can't you forgive yourself?"

"It's not the same thing."

"You need her. The ranch needs her. So—go get her."

"Hell, she wouldn't have me, and I wouldn't blame her. So, forget it."

"Track her down, throw her over your shoulder and show her she belongs with you—here."

"This ain't the Wild West anymore."

"You could've damn sure fooled me the night she out-rustled the Midnight Bandit. Why don't you get off your high horse and go get her?"

North frowned as he remembered what she'd said that haunted him every night when he tried to sleep.

You said you wanted a real woman. Well, we had sex, and I loved it so much I want to do it again and again.

And what had he said? He'd lied and said what they'd had he could get with any other woman.

She'd looked so sad, so hurt.

But she'd fought for their love anyway. She'd stood up to him, arguing that he was wrong, that she had a right to be a whole person, too.

She'd saved his life.

"Just because she's a hero doesn't mean you aren't one, too, King. You two are cut out of the same cloth. She's worthy of you, worthy of El Dorado. Don't do something real stupid by being so damn stubborn."

Slowly, as North remembered first the wild sex and then their adventure, his eyes lit up from the inside out.

Jeff read him and smiled. "That's the ticket."

"She sure was something, wasn't she?" North said slowly. "The way she drove the truck. Hell, she couldn't even reach the pedals."

"Go get her, why dontcha?" Jeff whispered.

"It's gonna take a lot of nerve."

"The lady's a hero. The question is do you have as much nerve and heart and gumption as that little gal does?"

"Will you marry—"

North was in the shower trying to work up his nerve. He'd called her, but she hadn't answered. So, he'd left a tongue-tied message on her machine that said he wanted to see her.

Then he'd gone straight to Kingsville and stopped at the first jewelry store he'd come to. Hell, when all the salesgirls had surrounded him, he'd been like a shy teenager.

The manager had beamed when North had said, "I want to see your diamond rings."

"For an engagement ring, Mr. Black?"

North had lowered his Stetson over his face and nodded.

"She must be very special?"

"You've got that right."

"Unique."

North had tipped his Stetson back. "You wouldn't believe—"

The manager had known who he was, right off. Hell, everybody knew who he was. So, he'd pulled out a tray of huge diamonds.

"You don't understand," North had drawled. "I want the smallest diamond you've got."

"But if she's so special—"

"Like I said, you don't understand—I didn't, either, for an awfully long time."

The memory made him frown. When North turned off the water, the bathroom was full of steam. The tiny room, like his house, like the ranch, felt so empty without Melody.

He opened the shower door to reach for his towel.

But the girl he'd dreamed of night and day was there, wearing a black lace bra and thong underwear.

"Do you want to dance?" Melody whispered in her sexy voice as she began to hum their song.

"What are you doing here?"

"You called, Bertie Boy." She snapped her fingers. "I came." She threw back her head and laughed nervously. "I'm afraid I'm playing easy to get."

"It took you long enough."

"You can be pretty stubborn, too, Bertie."

"We're a matched pair."

"I certainly hope so." She hesitated. "I was in class. I called home for my messages…. I—I listened to yours over and over. Then I called the ranch and Sissy said you'd gone into Kingsville to buy me a ring."

"Sissy told you that?"

"She said you would be back before I could drive here. So I hopped in my car…and I flew so fast I couldn't even read bumper stickers."

"We're going to have to talk about your driving…about what you did to my truck…"

"Not for a while…." She stepped forward and pushed

im back against the steaming wall. "You've got some oofprints in lots of interesting places."

"Some people around here have been telling me I've been on a self-destructive tear," he admitted roughly, running his hand through her long hair.

"I wonder why?"

"'Cause I was hell-bent not to see the obvious." He issed her throat.

"Don't you think it's time we finished what we started?" he murmured. "You promised, remember?"

"Way past time," he agreed when she peeled off her anties and tossed them on top of the neat pile of clothes e'd stacked to put on after his shower.

He picked her up, and she circled him with her legs. Suddenly just holding her sent flashes of fire sizzling all through him.

"Oh, Bertie," she moaned softly.

"You're going to marry me this time, aren't you?" he whispered. "'Cause I bought you a ring with the smallest diamond you ever saw."

"Really?"

"It's microscopic."

She laughed throatily. "I don't think I can go through he white dress routine again or people like the governor oming to watch us get married."

"Neither can I."

"Oh, Bertie. I hurt you...when I ran away on our wedding day."

"And I hurt you when I was so pigheaded I sent you way after you saved me and Jeff and my cows."

"So, maybe that means it's time for happily ever after?"

"Sounds like a winner," North murmured.

He kissed her as if he were starving for her. She met his isses with a response that was needy and hot.

They made love, first against the bathroom wall, and then n his bed. And everything they did was exciting and wonerful and absolutely perfect.

If he was wild, she was equally so, and after it was over, he held her in his arms and felt happier than he had ever felt before—even when his father had been alive. It was as if at last, with her at his side, he was complete.

He didn't have to control her. He had to believe in her, to let her be, to trust her. And now that she knew who she was, she didn't have to be afraid of anything—not of sex, not of him, not of their life together. She could teach. She could live at the ranch. She could choose. She was his woman. But she was her own woman, too.

"Show me the ring," she whispered a little breathlessly.

He pulled out a black velvet box.

The ring fit her slender finger perfectly.

"Turn on the light so I can see the diamond."

He did so.

"Oh, Bertie, I think you got a little carried away. I need a magnifying glass."

He took a quick, worried breath.

"But I love it. It's me. Mrs. Rancher Black. What do you say we run down to Mexico tonight—and get married."

He laughed. He felt young and happy. "This time, I'll drive, Mrs. Rancher Black."

*   *   *   *   *

MORE TO LOVE

by
Dixie Browning

DIXIE BROWNING

has been writing for Silhouette since 1980 and recently celebrated the publication of her sixty-fifth book. She has also written a number of historical romances with her sister under the name Bronwyn Williams. An award-winning painter and writer, Browning lives on the Outer Banks of North Carolina. You may write to her at PO Box 1389, Buxton, NC 27920, USA.

To all of us 'generous' women

One

To think she had actually considered slipping peacefully into a midlife crisis, never mind that according to one article she had read there was no such thing. She'd had all the classic symptoms. Worry about her looks, about broken relationships and career disappointments, about the waning importance to her family.

Besides, the alternative seemed so selfish. Wanting something for herself.

But a midlife crisis? At the age of thirty-six? Hardly. And Annamarie was still depending on her, which was the reason she was here. As for her new career, it looked promising, once the electricians and painters and plasterers got finished so that everyone could move in again. Being head housekeeper in an assisted-living home might not be the most glamorous career in the world, but then, Molly was nothing if not a realist. And she was finally doing something about her looks. As for the other symptom—the relationship thing—her one shot at happy-ever-after had given her a genuine distaste for fairy tales.

Only four days ago Molly had caught her first glimpse of the ocean. She had seen a sand dune that was almost as big as one of her own West Virginia mountains. She had collected a bushel of tourist brochures on her way down the Outer Banks, telling herself she would read every one and see everything that looked halfway interesting.

And it all did. The miracle was that for once in her life she had time on her hands. The only thing she had to do was feed and water a couple of birds and clean their cages, and look after one elderly cat.

The ferry ride from Hatteras to Ocracoke had been just the beginning. There was an observation deck, but as it had taken her about twenty minutes of the allotted forty to work up enough nerve to step out of her car, she had never made it up the narrow ladder. Instead she'd grabbed hold of the metal railing and waited to see if she was going to be sick. It had taken a few more minutes to get used to the gentle rolling motion of the deck, but there was so much to take in that she'd soon forgotten all about her queasiness. Flocks of seagulls following the ferry swooped down to catch scraps of bread tossed by three pretty girls standing at the chain across the stern. They passed another ferry headed in the opposite direction, and people waved. Feeling bold and adventurous, Molly released her grip on the railing and waved back.

It had to be fate, she remembered thinking at the time. First, the lightning strike that had caused Holly Hills Home where she worked to be shut down for repairs. Next, the fact that Stu and Annamarie had rented a cottage on Ocracoke Island and then decided to take a week off for a side trip and needed someone to look after Pete, Repete and Shag. Molly couldn't remember the last time she had taken a real vacation. She hadn't even had to think twice when Annamarie called to ask if there was any possible way she could come down and take care of the critters for just a few days. It was only a five-hour drive, one way. Ferry included.

Molly had gone right out and splurged on three new outfits suitable for a beach vacation in late April. If she could have found a T-shirt that said Live For The Moment, or Go With The Flow, she would probably have bought it, never mind that she was built more for tents and tunics than T-shirts.

She remembered singing "Don't Worry, Be Happy" under her breath as she'd stood there on the ferry watching the water of Hatteras Inlet flow past. Where better than an island to adopt that attitude?

The teenage girls had giggled and postured. They were a bit underdressed for the weather, which was still cool. But then, if she'd had their figures she might have done some showing off, too. The ferry had been loaded with fishermen, some of them young and attractive. A few were asleep in their vehicles, a few more were outside comparing fishing gear. Most were watching the girls, except for one who was— mercy, he looked like a young Sly Stallone!—watching her!

Watching *her?*

Pretending she hadn't noticed, Molly concentrated on a big black bird sitting on a post out in the water, his wings spread as if he were about to take off.

"Cormorant," said the Stallone look-alike, edging closer along the railing. "Drying his wings." Up close, he was only a few inches taller than Molly's modest five foot two, and already he was showing signs of a beer belly, but he had a nice smile.

She glanced up at the cloudless sky, then back at Sleepy Eyes. "How did they get wet?"

"Diving for dinner."

She remembered trying to look as if she knew precisely what he meant, but as the whole experience had been so new, she probably hadn't been too convincing.

"First time down here?" he asked.

"Actually, it is."

"Me, I come every year, spring and fall. Me and my buddies enter tournaments all up and down the coast. The weather can turn on you real quick this time of year, though. You shoulda waited a few weeks."

"Fishing tournaments?"

He pointed to the small pennant flying from the antenna of his dark green pickup truck. "O.I.F.T. That's Ocracoke International or Invitational, anyway you want to call it." He went on to describe several such tournaments and his prowess at each while Molly soaked up the novelty of sunshine and seagulls, a moving deck underfoot and the full attention, for the moment at least, of a handsome young man. Could someone have waved a magic wand, turning plain, plump Molly Dewhurst into someone her own mirror wouldn't recognize? Had the lumbering old ferryboat been a pumpkin in a previous incarnation?

"Cut bait's what you want. Some like bloodworms, but me, I like salt mullet best."

All right, so his charm was a little on the rustic side. No one had ever accused her of being a snob.

Reaching into the back of his truck, he took a can of beer from the cooler, offered it to Molly, and when she refused, popped the top and drained half the contents in one thirsty gulp.

Molly fingered a strand of blowing hair away from her eyes. Sunglasses. She should have thought to get herself a pair. Big ones. Then she could ogle all she wanted to without getting caught at it. She'd invested in a new lipstick, a new hairstyle and the new outfits, but spending money on herself took practice. She hadn't quite got the knack of it yet.

"Where you staying?" he drawled. He had one of those raspy voices that went with his sleepy eyes.

Molly swallowed hard and tried to sound terribly blasé. "It's a cottage. My sister's. Actually it's not hers. She's only renting it."

"So maybe I'll see you around?" Was that an opening or a dismissal?

She took several mental steps back. She didn't do casual flirtations. The old Molly had never had a chance to learn, and the new Molly needed to work on self-confidence first. "Maybe so," she said airily. "If I don't see you again, good luck in the tournament."

"When it comes to fishing, I make my own luck." He flashed her a lazy grin. "There's sixty teams in this one, with a mile-long waiting list. If you're a betting woman, put your money on ol' Jeffy Smith."

"Thank you. I'll, uh—do that." Molly remembered thinking at the time that men based their ego on the strangest things. Her ex-husband, for instance, made certain everyone knew he'd gone to Yale, never mind that he'd lasted only a single semester. Jeffy Smith evidently took pride in his prowess as a fisherman—or maybe in being a member of an exclusive group. But he'd been friendly. He'd seemed nice. He was attractive in a rough sort of way. And as she had recently cast off her old persona, determined to take a cue from a recruiting slogan and become all she could become, she'd responded with a smile.

And then Jeffy had tossed his beer can over the side, patted his belly and belched. So much for her ferryboat Prince Charming. He was obviously a man's man. But then, she'd reminded herself, her ex-husband had been a ladies' man. Of the two, she preferred the slob.

Correction. Of the two, she preferred neither. Still, it was a shame. Her very first shipboard romance, and it had ended before it even began.

"We'll be landing in a couple of minutes. Now, remember, if you need any help learning how to hold a rod, you just call on ol' Jeffy." His eyes had twinkled. He had black eyes, black hair and a three-days' growth of beard. Molly hadn't known if it was a fashion statement or one of those things men did when they were off the reservation. With Kenny, it had been just the opposite. When he was home, he never bothered to shave or even comb his hair, but if he'd been going out anywhere at all, it was full-dress parade, from the fancy designer shoes he had charged to her account to the expensive cologne he splashed on his throat before he buttoned his designer shirt and knotted his designer tie.

Once when he'd gone on and on about designer this and designer that, she'd asked him who designed the clothes that didn't bear a designer's label. He'd given her a blank stare and asked for fifty dollars to tide him over.

That was another thing about Kenny Dewhurst. He was totally devoid of a sense of humor. He was equally devoid of any funds except those provided by his doormat of a wife.

Ex-doormat, Molly remembered thinking. Breathing deeply of freedom, diesel fumes and salt air, she had smiled at the semi-handsome slob leaning on the railing beside her while the heavy engines throbbed beneath her feet. Here she was, under a cloudless blue sky, off on an island adventure, and before she even set foot on the island, a friendly man had struck up a conversation with her while only a few feet away three really cute girls, size zilch, were flirting with his fishing buddies.

The engines had changed pitch as the ferry swerved into a narrow channel. Her Stallone look-alike had said, "Guess I'd better load up. So...I guess I'll see you around, huh?"

"Probably. I understand it's a small island." *Nice going, Molly. Not too eager, not too cool.* She had climbed back into her car and watched through the rearview mirror as he rejoined his friends. There were some knowing grins, a few elbows to the ribs, and then they stowed their gear and climbed into their muscle trucks.

"Stowed their gear," she repeated smugly now. Pretty nautical for a woman who had never before set foot on an island. Never even set foot outside West Virginia until four months ago.

She was going to like this new Molly just fine. She had...well, maybe not style. At least not yet. But she had attitude, by heck, and that was the first step!

* * *

That had been four days ago. That very afternoon Stu and Annamarie had caught the last ferry headed north, after writing detailed instructions on how to care for the two African Gray parrots and Shag the cat. The next morning Molly had introduced herself to the next-door neighbor, Sally Ann Haskins, who told her how to find the general store, the post office, and tried to tempt her into taking a puppy off her hands.

"Mama Dog's plumb worn out. I'm going to get her fixed. She had seven this time. Last time it was eleven, poor thing. You sure you couldn't use a nice retriever pup? Your sister said she had too many animals already, but she said you might be interested."

"I'd love one, but—" Mama Dog flapped her tail lethargically, but didn't even lift her head when Molly knelt and reached for one of her squirming babies. "But the place where I live has this rule about animals."

"Reckon I could offer it as a prize in the fishing tournament? Biggest catch of the day gets a free puppy? Fishermen mostly drive pickup trucks, and every pickup has to have a dog to ride in the back. It's a state law."

So then Molly had told her all about the ferryboat encounter with a fisherman in a dogless pickup truck. "Just when I was starting to think he had real possibilities, he threw his beer can overboard."

"You know the old saying, garbage in, garbage out." Sally Ann worked for the ferry department, which Molly considered wildly exciting. "Maybe the jerk'll hook into his own beer can and wreck his gear. They say there's a big low headed up the coast. Last three years in a row, the weather's been so bad, most folks left after the first day. You don't want to try surf fishing in gale force winds—the sand'll cut the skin right off your face.''

"Mercy. Why not schedule it for when the weather's better?''

"You know anybody that can schedule the weather? They set it for when the fish are supposed to be here.'' Sally Ann finished ironing a uniform shirt, unplugged the iron and plopped it on the kitchen range to cool. "Trouble is, if the weather closes in, they wait until too late to get off the island. Once the highway's flooded, they're stuck with nothing better to do than shoot pool and tell lies about the big one that got away.''

"Still, it doesn't sound like good planning to me.''

Sally grinned. A strawberry blonde, she had a weathered face, perfect teeth and the biggest, bluest eyes Molly had ever seen. "Makes for some fun, though. Socializing's a big part of these tournaments. If the weather shuts down and they get tired of baling hay, they head for the pubs. And let me tell you, if this low hangs around too long, there'll be some hot old times down at Delroy's Pub.''

One hand on the doorknob, Molly paused. "Uh— did you say baling hay? I thought they were fishing?''

"Catching eelgrass. With the water so rough, the bottom's all tore up. Seaweed's about all they haul in.''

The next day dark clouds closed in, bringing stiff winds that tore new leaves from ancient trees and set small boats to bobbing like corks at the wharf. It was raining, but not heavily when Molly left the general store with a sack of apples and headed back to the cottage. Rain or shine, she was determined to walk each day as part of her new regime.

Diet and exercise. Ugh! Traffic had tripled since she'd arrived only a few days ago. Idly she wondered what had happened to her ferryboat acquaintance. Had he left? Was he shooting pool and swapping lies, or fishing in the rain?

The fish wouldn't know if it was raining or not…would they?

Remembering Sally Anne's warning, that he might try to score a little something on the side just to make the trip worthwhile, she had to laugh. It was flattering to think a warning would even be necessary. The new Molly must be coming along faster than she'd thought, if she had to worry about men trying to pick her up.

"Hi there, pretty lady."

Molly nearly dropped her apples as the familiar-looking dark green truck pulled up beside her. "Oh, hi. How's fishing, uh—Jeffy?"

"Tournament's over. We drew a lousy spot this year, but at least I didn't get skunked. I'm staying on a few more days, long's I come all this way—headed out now to look over conditions. With the wind like this, the beach'll get cut up some. Might be a few promising new sloughs. Wanna come along for the ride?"

A small voice in the back of her mind whispered, *"Watch it, lady, you might've shed a few pounds, but you're not ready for prime time yet."*

The old Molly was aghast to hear the new Molly say cheerfully, "Well…sure, why not?" She accepted the callused hand and hauled herself up into the high cab. So he was something of a slob. So his grammar wasn't perfect and he belched and tossed beer cans. Back in Grover's Hollow some of the nicest people she knew probably did the same thing when no one was looking. But he was friendly, and after all, she wasn't committing herself to anything more than a drive along the beach, which she certainly couldn't do in her own car.

Rarely did Rafe Webber find himself in an awkward situation, thanks to excellent instincts and an impeccable sense of timing. On the few occasions when he blundered, he usually managed to finesse his way out with the minimum amount of damage. This time things might be different. His instincts had been signaling trouble ever since Stu had called to tell him he was getting married to the most beautiful, brilliant, wonderful woman in the world. Rafe had strongly advised a cooling-off period, meaning, *wait until I have time to check things out, little buddy.* Unfortunately Stu had been too charged up to listen.

Rafe had been on his way out of the country at the time. He'd been held up a lot longer than he'd expected, missing Thanksgiving and Christmas completely. Not that he was sentimental—no way! Still, he'd always made a point of getting together for holidays, just to give the kid a sense of stability. He'd read somewhere that establishing traditions helped ground rebellious adolescents, which Stu had been when Rafe had first got him. For the past ten years, Rafe always cooked his special turkey dinner, regardless of the holiday.

So he'd missed the wedding, too. By the time he made it back to the States, the deed was done. But tomorrow was the kid's birthday, and regardless of the bride and an inconvenient nor'easter, he wasn't going to miss that. He'd checked the weather when he'd filed his flight plan. Two separate low-pressure areas were due to join forces just off the North Carolina coast, but he figured he had plenty of time to slide on in before the weather closed in. What he hadn't figured on was finding the whole damned island foundering under a load of surf fishermen. While it might be good for business, it was a damned nuisance when a guy got in late, needing a decent rental car and a room for a couple of days.

Before leaving Pelican's Cove, Florida, Rafe had cleared his calendar for a week, even though he figured it would take only a couple of days to make things up to the kid and find out how much trouble he'd gotten himself in. Not to mention what it was going to take to get him out of it. Stu's taste in women was notorious. From the time Rafe had taken over the care and feeding of a freckle-faced adolescent with too much money, too many hormones and too little common sense, Stu had been a target for every predatory female in range.

This one had waited until Rafe was headed out of the country on a little unofficial business for the government and then reeled in her catch. Stuart Montgomery Grainger III. Old family, new money. Gullible Grainger, green as his daddy's billions. Rafe had dared hope that, with a college degree and a brand-new teaching job waiting for him, his half brother might have matured enough to be let off the leash. The lady had outsmarted him. She'd sprung her trap before any of the family had had a chance to check her out. Not that anyone besides Rafe would even bother, unless it was Stu's father's lawyers.

Ten years ago Rafe's mother had dropped in out of the blue with a scared, resentful fifteen-year-old in tow and announced that as the two of them were half brothers, it was time they got to know one another. To say Rafe was appalled would be an understatement. The only thing that had kept him from flat-out refusing was the fact that the kid obviously felt the same way. Rafe could remember all too well how he'd felt at that age, being shunted between summer camp and boarding school so as not to cramp his mother's lifestyle.

They'd spent the next five years getting to know each other, with Rafe trying his damnedest to instill a few survival instincts in a kid who hadn't a clue.

Evidently he hadn't succeeded. Those wedding pictures that had been waiting when he'd finally made it back to the States had pretty much told the story. Gorgeous bride wearing a knock-out gown, grinning groom wearing cake on his face. The kid still looked about fifteen. You had to wonder if the bride would have been so determined to tie the knot if his name had been Joe Jones instead of S. M. Grainger III of the shipping and banking Graingers.

About all Rafe could do at this point was damage control. Fly in unannounced, apologize for missing out on all the festivities and cook Stu his favorite holiday dinner, which happened to be the only family-style dinner Rafe knew how to prepare. It would serve as a birthday treat, a reminder to Stu that he had family standing squarely behind him, and a similar warning to the bride. It would also tell him a lot about this paragon the kid had married. If she could be bought off, he'd be better off without her.

Rafe wondered how much Stu had told her about

his wildly dysfunctional family. There was the father who couldn't be bothered to keep in touch. The mother who sent extravagant birthday gifts on the wrong date. Somewhere there were some half siblings who might or might not know him personally—not to mention a big brother who had invested a lot of years into keeping him on the right track.

At the moment Rafe was more concerned with the woman. On the way north he had settled on a test he used often in business: the element of surprise. Setting things up, then observing the way people reacted to the unexpected. Having a stranger drop in out of the blue with an armload of groceries to commandeer a woman's kitchen might not be quite as effective a test as being stranded together in a leaky cabin cruiser, but it should do the trick. He could hardly come right out and ask the bride if she was more interested in the trust fund Stu stood to inherit at the age of thirty-one, or the shy, good-natured guy with a good mind, a heart of gold but damned few social skills.

While he secured the plane, taking extra precautions against the wind, Rafe ran through a few old chestnuts about brothers' keepers and no man being an island in an effort to rationalize his guilty conscience for having dropped out of sight at a time when Stu had needed him. He didn't do guilt well. When he'd found out the honeymooners would be spending a few months on one of the islands off the North Carolina coast, it had seemed like the perfect chance to mend a few fences and at the same time see how much trouble Stu was in with this bride of his and what it was going to take to sort things out. Happy marriages did not run in their family.

Unfortunately marriage did. Stella, the mother they

shared, had been married four times to date. A six-foot-tall ex-Vegas showgirl, she was still a beautiful woman at age fifty-nine-and-holding.

Rafe's father had been married three times to successively younger women, and was currently working out prenuptials with number four. Probably a high school cheerleader this time. Rafe didn't know about Stu's old man, but figured he was probably in the same league, marriagewise.

It was when Stella had been about to set out on honeymoon number three a few days before Thanksgiving that she'd turned up at the door of Rafe's condo with the kid. Once he'd gotten over the shock of finding himself unexpectedly landed with the care and feeding of a half-grown boy, Rafe had scrambled like crazy not to blow it. He'd canceled a nine-day trip to Vancouver with Linda—or maybe it had been Liz. He had taken a crash course in basic cooking and started reading every book on adolescent psychology he could lay his hands on. Over the next few years they had weathered countless minor mishaps and a few major ones. He liked the kid.

Hell, he loved the kid.

He'd done a good job of raising him, too, if he did say so himself. Stu was no athlete—they'd both reluctantly faced that fact after half a dozen or so spectacular failures. He was a fine young man, smart as a whip when it came to books. Trouble was, he was dumb as a stump where women were concerned.

That was where Rafe had always come in. Sifting the wheat from the chaff, so to speak. Unfortunately it had mostly been chaff up to now, but at least he'd managed to keep Stu out of major trouble until the call had come a couple of months ago. Rafe had been

within hours of leaving the country on another unofficial fact-finding trip. As a small-time Gulf Coast
resort developer with a modest charter boat fleet, he
had the perfect excuse to explore the coastal regions
of Central and South America. Having served a hitch
in the Coast Guard before Stu had come to live with
him, he was well aware of the fact that DEA was
undermanned, underfunded and overwhelmed.

Which was how he'd happened to miss the wedding. Thanks to a small misunderstanding with a
bunch of entrepreneurs in a little fishing village in
Central America, he'd been out of circulation for the
next several weeks, but at least he was going to make
the kid's twenty-fifth birthday.

What he hadn't figured on was the size of Ocracoke
Island in relation to the concentration of tourists.
Wall-to-wall fishermen, according to the fellow
who'd driven the rental out to the airport to meet him.
He should have made advance reservations, in case
the honeymoon cottage lacked a guest room.

The airport was little more than a paved landing
strip with a phone booth and an open pavilion, all
within a few hundred yards of the Atlantic. It was
crowded and exposed, but adequate. He'd seen a lot
worse. Knowing the weather was likely to deteriorate
before the low moved offshore again, he took his time
with the tie-downs and chocks. Hatteras Lows were
notorious, even in Florida. Once he was satisfied, he
slung his gear, which included several large grocery
sacks, into the only available rental vehicle, an SUV
with a gutted muffler and rusted-out floorboards.

He dropped the driver off at the rental place after
learning the location of Yaupon Cottage and roughly
how to find it, and toyed with the notion of checking

into a hotel first. He decided against it. The turkey
needed to go into an oven, or else they'd be lucky to
dine before midnight. And while that didn't bother
him at all, Stu and whatsername might have other
ideas.

Mission underplanned.

Traffic was bumper-to-bumper. Locating Yaupon
Cottage wasn't quite as easy as it had sounded. The
village was laid out as if someone had tossed handsful
of confetti into the air and then built something wherever a scrap of paper landed. With the low cloud
cover, there was barely enough light left to see his
way up and down the narrow, winding roads with
vehicles parked haphazardly on both sides.

He managed to find the place, and then had to
squeeze in between a picket fence and a tan sedan.
By then the rain had started coming down in solid,
wind-driven sheets. Hatless, coatless, he jogged up
the path to the front door and knocked. And then he
pounded again and waited. There was no light on inside. It might not be wise to walk in unannounced on
a honeymoon couple, but dammit, his backside was
getting wet. The grocery sacks were melting. So he
pounded a few more times, then tried the doorknob.
Finding the door unlocked, he opened it and called,
"Hey, kids? Stu? Anybody home?"

TWO

Dammit, they couldn't be too far away, or else they'd have locked the place. Pushing the door open, Rafe shoved the groceries and his battered leather bag in out of the rain. He should have called first. He should have called before he'd ever left Florida.

Too late now. After a quick look around, he set to work on the surprise birthday dinner. He preferred to think of it as that rather than as a test for the bride, but he was beginning to have a funny feeling about this whole affair. If things didn't work out, Stu was going to take it hard. From some unknown ancestor, the kid had inherited the genes for vulnerability and sensitivity. Thank God those had skipped Rafe. If there were two things he was not, it was vulnerable and sensitive.

The place was a dump. If there was a level surface anywhere, it wasn't easily discernible. It was small to the point of claustrophobic, and the two refrigerator-size birdcages in the room across the hall didn't help. Stu had mentioned that his bride had a couple of birds. Rafe had pictured budgies. Maybe canaries.

Through the open door, he eyed the two red-tailed gray parrots in the next room. Tilting their heads, they eyed him back. Feeling vaguely self-conscious, he turned his attention back to the turkey he'd bought in Tampa and allowed to thaw on the way north. He probably should've opted for something simpler, but the grand gesture had been part of the plan. Showing up with deli food and a bottle of wine wouldn't do the trick. It had been his experience that wives didn't care much for surprises, and a raw turkey definitely qualified as a surprise.

Rafe had had a wife of his own, briefly. He'd like to think Stu would have better luck, but he wouldn't bet on it. Marital bliss was not a component of their gene pool, on either the maternal or the paternal side, he reminded himself as he rummaged underneath the counter for a roasting pan. If the kid found himself married to the wrong kind of woman, who better than Rafe to lead him out of the wilderness?

Judging strictly from the wedding pictures that had been waiting in his stack of mail when he'd gotten back from his extended stay in Central America, the lady was gorgeous and at least three inches taller than her bridegroom, who'd been grinning like Howdy Doody in every single picture. Knowing Stu, Rafe figured his half brother probably hadn't bothered to draw up a prenuptial agreement.

Knowing women in general, the bride probably would have talked him out of it even if he had. His baby brother all but carried a sign that said Kick Me.

The range was an ancient model, the oven barely big enough to hold a roasting pan and the sweet potato casserole he'd planned. In the years after Stu had gone off to college, Rafe's cooking had been limited to intimate dinners for two, usually followed by breakfast. Other than that, he ate out. Domestic, he was not. A woman he'd once known briefly had called it a defense mechanism. She'd been into pop psychology and thought she had his number.

Defense mechanism? No way. He simply liked his life just fine the way it was, and saw no reason to change it. And dammit, he was *not* lonely, no matter what anyone said! Anytime he wanted company, all he had to do was pick up the phone. Could a man have it any better than that? All the fun, none of the hassles?

There was a row of broken shells on the kitchen windowsill and he wondered if that was a clue to the kind of woman Stu had married. Was there some hidden psychological meaning here? What sort of person would bring home broken shells? Judging solely from the wedding photos, the bride could be a model or a starlet. She had the looks. According to Stu, she was supposed to be working on a degree in linguistics.

What the hell was linguistics, anyway?

A long-haired yellow cat with a wide head and ragged ears stalked into the kitchen and glared at him. Rafe glared back. "Don't even think about it, friend," he growled, plopping the turkey into the sink.

"Balderdash!" screamed one of the two African Grays from the living room.

"Yeah, right," Rafe grumbled as he ran water through the cavity and wondered if he'd remembered to buy prepared stuffing. He was getting a low-pressure headache. Either that, or second thoughts were piling in faster than his brain could process them.

The second parrot tuned up with a creditable imitation of a squeaking door, followed by a realistic smoker's hack. From there, things went rapidly downhill.

Rafe wanted to get dinner in the oven before he started checking around for a hotel room. At least since his first disastrous attempt to create a Thanksgiving feast for a desolate kid, he'd learned to remove the unmentionables inside the bird before cramming in the store-bought stuffing.

"Help! Lemme go! Bad-ass, bad-ass!"

"Shut up, you red-tailed devil, or you're going into the oven with baldie here."

If Stu's lovely linguist bride was responsible for her birds' vocabulary, she was a hell of a lot tougher than she looked. Remembering the pictures of the gorgeous vision in white clinging to a beaming Stu reminded Rafe of another reason why he was here instead of being back in Pelican's Cove, Florida, inspecting his latest acquisition to get some idea of how much was salvageable.

Belle was getting married this weekend. Longlegged, sexy Belle, his mistress of the past eight months, who was every bit as good in bed as she was on the tennis courts. They'd met at a yacht christening and promptly entered into the relationship with both pairs of eyes wide open. Rafe had made a point of sharing his philosophy right up front. Except for the five years when Stu lived with him, his motto had always been easy come, easy go. Work hard, play hard, and avoid encumbrances. If he lost everything today, he'd start over tomorrow. Once he'd launched his kid brother and gotten his own life back on track, he had quickly reverted to his old lifestyle. Life was an adventure, he remembered telling Belle at some point. He made a point of not setting up any false expectations. While he was scrupulously faithful to one woman at a time, the last thing he wanted was an anchor holding him down. When the time came to move on, he simply moved on. When both sides clearly understood the ground rules, moving on was easy.

Both he and Belle were in their late thirties and unencumbered. Rafe had been wildly attracted to her body and Belle had been equally attracted to the life-style of a young, moderately wealthy bachelor. Rafe prided himself on being a generous lover, both physically and financially. And he had been, right up until Belle's biological alarm clock had gone off. Six weeks after she had regretfully handed him his walking papers in exchange for a gold charm bracelet and a block of stock, she'd snagged herself an insurance salesman. The last time he'd heard from her they were shopping for a house near a good school.

Rafe wished her luck because he'd genuinely liked the woman. But he'd been feeling increasingly restless ever since he'd heard the news. He'd had his personal assistant pick out an expensive wedding gift, and then he'd rearranged his calendar and filed a flight plan to an off-the-beaten-track island on North Carolina's Outer Banks.

A mile away, Molly struggled to hide a yawn. They'd spent a few hours driving along the beach, and for a little while she'd felt like the heroine of one of those adventure movies, racing along the beach, splashing through the surf with the wind blowing in her face and an attractive man at her side.

Jeffy liked open windows. Said he could smell a school of fish a mile out at sea. Over the roar of the wind, he had told her about his father's concrete block business and his own high school football career, and the trophy-size channel bass he'd taken a few years ago. He had perfect teeth, Molly noted absently during the monologue, and a really nice smile. Actually, he was good company if she overlooked a few minor detractions. His jokes were a little raw, but then, the new Molly wasn't going to be as big a prude as the old Molly had been.

After driving from one end of the island to the other, Jeffy insisted on stopping off for a seafood dinner at Delroy's Pub. By that time she was too hungry to resist. Which meant she was going to have to starve for days to make up for the fried scallops and French fries, even though she had left one of each on her plate.

And then someone fed the jukebox. As soon as the music started, two couples got up to dance. From a corner booth, Molly watched, tapping time on the tabletop.

"Hey, come on, what do you say we show 'em how it's done?" Jeffy stood and held out his hand. There was a chorus of whistles and catcalls from the bar and he turned and bowed, grinning at his buddies.

"I don't—" she started to say, but he cut her off.

"Sure you do, honey. Everybody does. Just do what comes naturally."

What came naturally was to disappear. To hole up in her room with a book. But that was the old Molly, and she had sworn that once she left West Virginia she was going to reinvent herself.

The music was loud and fast. Even those who weren't dancing were swaying and tapping their feet. It was a convivial group, just as Sally Ann had said. Ready for a good time. Beer was served by the pitcher and everything on the seafood platter was fried. And so far, Molly had enjoyed everything except the beer.

But dancing? "I'm not very good at this," she protested breathlessly while Jeffy twisted and snapped his fingers. She wasn't dressed for it, either. Some women weren't built for snug jeans and T-shirts. She was getting there, but she still had a long way to go.

"Just shake it, honey. That's all you have to do."

She slid out of the booth and tried her best to "shake it" without actually *shaking* it. The music was mostly beat with no discernible melody, but the rhythm was contagious. She was actually beginning to enjoy herself when one of the men at the bar yelled, "Hey, Jeffy, what happened to that gold ring you usually wear?"

Without answering, Jeffy managed to twist around until he was between her and the men at the bar. "Ignore 'em. They're drunk."

They weren't drunk, but neither were they sober. She asked breathlessly, "What ring is he talking about? Did you lose one at the beach?"

"I never wear a ring when I'm fishing."

And then, just like that, it hit her. It was written all over those bedroom eyes of his. Guilt. She should have recognized it, having seen so much of it in the past. "What ring? Jeffy, are you married?"

"Aw, c'mon, honey, do I look married?"

"Not to me, you don't," she said, and he could

take that any way he wanted to. She headed for the table, where she'd left her damp, sandy embroidered denim jacket and her shoulder bag. She would pay for her own darned supper. She was going to be paying for it in other ways, she might as well go all the way.

"Come on, Moll, be a sport." She dug into her bag and came up with her wallet.

Jeffy shook his head. "No way—put your money back. When a gentleman invites a lady out to supper, she don't have to pay her way."

"Then thank you."

"Aw, come on, sugar, be a sport." He was whining. If there was one thing she hated in a man, it was whining.

"You could have told me." She headed toward the door, with Jeffy right on her heels. People were staring, some of them grinning, a few calling out comments.

"You tell him, sugar!"

"Go get 'er, tiger!"

Feeling her face burning, Molly was glad for the dim lights.

"I was going to tell you, honest. See, me and Shirl, we been having a little trouble and I figured on getting to know you better and then maybe asking how you'd handle it if you was me. I mean, a woman like you, I could tell right off you were the understanding type."

"No you couldn't, because I'm not," Molly said flatly. She had done all the understanding she intended to do, and it had gotten her nowhere. She might be a slow learner, but eventually the message got through.

It was dark. The rain was coming down in solid sheets, blowing across the highway. She hesitated, trying to get her bearings, and then Jeffy opened the door of his truck. "I'll drive you home. I owe you that much."

She was tempted to refuse, but even the old Molly had better sense. It was pitch dark and pouring rain. Given her track record she would probably walk right off the edge of the island and drown.

Jeffy drove her home. He was a sullen companion, but then, so was she. She didn't know whom she was angrier with, Jeffy or herself. She should never have gotten into the truck in the first place. So she'd met him once before on the ferry—he was still a stranger. He'd seemed friendly and likable, but he was a man— a married man. She couldn't afford another of those in her life. Her bank balance hadn't recovered from the last one.

His fishing buddies had stood at the bar all evening, drinking beer, laughing, talking. It hadn't struck her at the time, but not once had any of them come over to the table to be introduced. That had to mean something...didn't it?

Feeling more miserable by the minute, Molly wondered if he had done the whole thing on a dare. *Five bucks says you won't pick up the fat girl. Ten says you won't show up with her at Delroy's.* It wouldn't be the first time she'd been the butt of a joke.

She wasn't all that fat, she thought defensively. She had measurements. She might use up a few more inches on the measuring tape than some other women but she had a shape.

Jeff double-parked outside the cottage, blocking the street. The yard light was on, and for the life of her, she couldn't recall if it was automatic or not. There was a beach buggy wedged in next to her own ten-year-old sedan, the two vehicles squeezed between a picket fence and a massive live oak tree. Sally Ann had warned her that parking was a haphazard affair at best, and once the season got underway, it was next to impossible.

"Thank you for supper and bringing me home," she muttered, all in one breath.

"Hey, Moll, I'm sorry. Really."

"Why me?" There was obviously something about her that attracted lying, conniving losers.

"'Cause you're nice? 'Cause you looked sort of lonesome on the ferry, and I just decided, what the hell? You know how it is."

"No, not really."

"Most women—you know, like they expect a man to blow his paycheck on 'em, and then they cut him dead if he wants a little fun."

"And you wanted a little fun, right?" Sally Ann had warned her about that, too, but she hadn't listened.

"If it had worked out that way." He shrugged. "I wish now I'd told you about Shirl—my wife. Like I said, we're having some problems. She wanted me to skip the tournament just so I could go to this reunion thing, and we sorta had us some words before I left. You're a real good listener. You prob'ly could've given me some tips on how to handle situations like that."

Oh, yes, she was a grand listener. She had listened to a description of every fish the man had caught in last year's tournament, legal or otherwise, including the weight and length, and what type of tackle he had used. She had listened three times to the description of his game-winning touchdown against Marcus P. Struthers High in the regional play-offs.

Just as she had listened to another man explaining earnestly why he could never hold a job, or why he needed to dress for success, and what he was going to do for her once his ship came in.

Kenny's ship had never left harbor. The last thing she needed was a man whose only ship was a smelly old ferryboat. And what's more, she didn't care if he never caught another fish in his entire life, she was tired of trying to solve problems for men who didn't have the gumption to solve their own.

"Thanks again for supper." She opened her door and dropped to the ground before he could come around and help her out, not that he made a move to get out of the vehicle. It was raining hard, after all. Head down, she jogged up the path to the cottage, stomped the sand from her feet on the front porch and opened the door.

The kitchen light was on. It had been midafternoon when she'd left, so she wouldn't have turned on any light except for the one by the birdcages. Molly swallowed hard, clutching the plastic bag that held her apples and the broken shells she'd collected earlier. Could Stu and Anna have come home early? Could she have made a mistake and barged into the wrong house?

Hardly. Not with those familiar raucous cries coming from the living room. Not with that smelly long-haired cat wreathing her ankles. She'd gotten lost more than once before she'd found her way around the village, using the map on the tourist brochure, but not this time. This was definitely the right house.

Cautiously she moved inside and peered into the kitchen. The bag fell from her fingers. Apples rolled across the sloping floor. She stared openmouthed at the tall, tanned and sun-streaked guy with a dish towel tucked into his belt and a dead turkey cradled in his arms.

Rafe, on hearing a car door slam outside, had peered out the window to see a woman jump down from a dark green pickup truck and hurry up the path to the front porch. He waited for Stu to join her, but the truck drove off.

But then, Stu didn't drive a truck. He drove an expensive toy his father had given him for his twenty-first birthday to make up for a lifetime of neglect.

It also occurred to Rafe that unless the wedding photographer had used a trick lens, this was definitely not the bride.

Rafe was still standing there with the bird all ready for the oven when the woman appeared in the kitchen doorway. Neither of them spoke for a moment. "Surprise, congratulations and happy birthday, kid," didn't seem appropriate.

No way was this Stu's bride. Somebody had a lot of explaining to do. Even wearing wet denim instead of white satin, there was no resemblance. Stu's bride was a tall, slender beauty. This woman was none of the above.

Housekeeper? Housebreaker? Mother-in-law? Friend of the family? "You want to go first?" he offered.

"I think you'd better go first, starting with what you're doing in my kitchen." Her voice was the most striking thing about her. Husky, but with a hint of firmness that was unmistakable.

"*Your* kitchen?"

"I asked who you are," she reminded him with a take-no-hostages glint in her whiskey-colored eyes.

"Actually you didn't, but I'll tell you anyway. Name's Rafe Webber. And if this is your kitchen, then you must be—?" He was momentarily distracted by seeing her eyes narrow. Eyes that big and slumberous weren't equipped to look suspicious, but she managed it anyway.

"Rafe Webber? Is that supposed to ring a bell?"

Well, hell… He wasn't used to having to explain himself. He'd long since earned the privilege of asking the questions, not having to answer them. "You have the advantage of me, Miss—?" A gentleman to the bitter end, he thought with wry amusement. His headache wasn't getting any better.

"Until I know what you're doing here, I don't have to tell you anything. How did you get in?"

"Front door. It wasn't locked. I figured Stu would be back any minute."

"You know Stu?"

He decided to cut her some slack. Had a feeling it might save time and trouble in the long run. "He's my brother."

"Stu's name isn't Webber. Try again."

The lady was sharp. In no mood to go into the convoluted relationships in his immediate family, Rafe kept it simple. "We're half brothers. Same mother, different fathers."

"Do you have some identification?"

Deep breath. Open oven door, insert turkey, shut door and smile. Turning back, he said, "Dammit, lady, I don't need any identification, I know who I am. And I know you're not Stu's wife, so suppose you produce some identification of your own.''

In clinging wet jeans and a baggy wet jacket it was obvious that she was carrying a few extra pounds. For reasons he didn't even try to dissect, a few of his defenses crumbled. The place wasn't big enough for a full-scale war. It was your bottom-line basic seventy-year-old cottage, with slightly newer appliances. He thought about the wedding gift he'd had shipped to Stu's apartment in Durham, a fancy piece of equipment that did everything from poaching salmon to pouring tea, or so he'd been told by the salesman. With it he'd ordered monthly shipments of salmon and prime beef. God knew where they were now. Rotting in some post office, probably.

The woman stared pointedly at the towel around his waist until he whipped it off and flung it at the counter. It fell to the floor. In the next room, the parrots cut loose with a stream of profanities, which didn't help matters.

''They're next, as soon as I get another pan ready.'' He nodded to the oven.

Her eyes widened without losing the look of suspicion. She glanced down at the apples on the floor as if wondering how they'd got there. Glanced at him as if wondering the same thing.

Rafe had to admit the kitchen was a mess. When it came to cooking he was used to state-of-the-art equipment and someone to clean up after him. He said, ''You're wet.''

Without breaking eye contact, she said in that firm, husky voice, ''It's raining.''

So what now? he wondered. He scooped her apple bag off the floor and discovered it was half full of shells. Sandy, broken shells. At least one mystery had been cleared up, which left only a dozen or so to go.

She slipped off her wet jacket and hung it on a hook by the back door. Rafe let his eyes do the walking. The term Rubenesque came to mind. As for her face, it was…interesting. At the moment she looked as if a smile would fracture her jaw, but her skin was the kind a woman had to be born with. Cosmetics could never achieve that buttery smooth texture. He'd seen too many women come to regret having spent half their lives sunbathing not to recognize the difference.

"I don't suppose you know where they are?" He decided on a flank attack. She still hadn't told him who she was, but that could wait. Once the honeymooners got home, they could do the honors.

"Who, Annamarie and Stu?" The look of suspicion was replaced by a look of puzzlement. Or maybe she was just nearsighted. "They're supposed to be in Jamestown."

"Jamestown," he repeated. And then "*Jamestown?* As in Virginia? What the hell are they doing there? I'm cooking their supper."

"Um…studying the diggings. I guess."

"Studying the diggings. You want to run that by me again?"

"It's Annamarie's birthday present."

He shook his head. "Somebody gave her a trip to Jamestown for a birthday gift?" A change in barometric pressure always did a number on his head. This time it had evidently affected his hearing, as well.

With a majestic sigh, the woman said, "It's Annamarie's gift to Stu. He's the historian, as you should know if you really are who you say you are. While they're down here working on her thesis, she's giving him this side trip for a birthday present."

Rafe pressed his cool fingertips above his eyes and rubbed. With a sigh, he said, "Look, Miss—"

"Dewhurst. And it's Ms., not Miss. Annamarie is my baby sister."

"Ms. Dewhurst," he repeated. Great. He'd come all this way, planning to check out his new half sister-in-law and make up to Stu for all the missed occasions with a belated birthday feast, and now he was stuck here with Ms. Congeniality.

"Actually, it's Molly," she said in that quiet, husky voice of hers that kept getting between him and his anger.

Make that frustration. "Well, Molly, whoever you are and whatever you're doing here, I hope you like turkey. And candied sweet potatoes and spoon bread and whatever green vegetable I can find in Stu's pantry. It'll probably be canned peas, but with enough butter and seasoning, they're not half bad."

"Balderdash, balderdash, balderda—!"

Moving swiftly, Rafe closed the door between the two rooms, making the kitchen seem smaller than ever. The whole cottage would fit nicely into his suite at his latest acquisition, a small resort hotel on Florida's Gulf Coast.

"I think we'd better talk," Ms. Molly Dewhurst said as she shucked off a pair of very wet pink sneakers. "But first I really need a cup of coffee. It might be April, but I'm freezing." As if to prove her point, she sneezed, begged his pardon and said, "You're welcome to a cup if you don't mind reheated."

Three

The coffee was weak and decaffeinated, but it served to wash down a couple of aspirin. "Okay, so talk." His company manners were fading fast.

"Talk. All right. What if I pay you for the groceries and you catch the next ferry out?"

He didn't bother to tell her he'd flown in, and until the weather broke, he wouldn't be flying out again. "I've got a better idea," he countered. "What if you catch the ferry and I stay here and house-sit until the happy couple gets back?"

Slowly Molly shook her head. A few more lengths of damp brown hair worked free to brush her shoulders. Dry and left to its own devices, it would probably pass as a crowning glory. Thick, red highlights and a tendency to curl.

"What was that?" Distracted, he'd missed her reply.

"I said I'm not going anywhere. I promised Annamarie I'd stay here and look after Shag and the birds, and I always keep my promises."

"Always?"

"Practically always."

"Then you're one woman in a million."

"I don't know what to say to that, but I'll tell you this much—I'm staying. So if you want to hang around until they get back, I hope you've secured a room. I know it's early in the season, but with this tournament thing and all, they're probably pretty full."

Rafe never knew what made him dig in his heels. It sure as the devil wasn't the woman's personal attractions. She was a frump with pretty hair, a sexy voice, nice eyes and great skin. Period. "I've got a better idea. Why don't *you* book a room?"

"Because I can't afford it," she said flatly. The last thing he was prepared for was a straight answer. Unless she was angling for a pay-off. "And because I promised I'd take care of things. I've never met you before, never even heard of you. That is, I knew Stu had a brother who didn't bother to show up for the wedding, but for all I know, you could be just another—another beach bum, looking for a place to stay."

Rafe tipped his chair back and closed his eyes. When he opened them again, she was still there. Obdurate. Yeah, that was a good description. "What if I pay the tab? Would you go then?"

Huffy. Another good description.

"I beg your pardon," she said loftily.

He had to laugh. Headache and all. "Well, of course you do, honey. What about, How dare you?

Want to run that one by me while you're dishing up
indignation?'' And then he relented. ''Look, you
don't trust me and I don't particularly trust you.''
Actually he was almost beginning to, which came as
something of a surprise. ''So what do you say we
strike a bargain? I'll check out the room situation, but
if I can't find a vacancy, I'll bed down in the room
with the miserable-looking cot buried under all the
junk, and you can have the queen-size bed with a
view of the cemetery.''

''Oh, but—''

''I'll do the cooking, you look after the birds, we'll
both watch to see that nobody steals the family silver,
and if the honeymooners aren't back by the time the
weather breaks, I'll leave.'' He might. He might not.
''Fair enough? Meanwhile I'll do my best to stay out
of your hair.''

Which was beginning to curl around her face. Half
the women he knew had gone red this year. He'd lay
odds she was the genuine article. Even her eyebrows
were auburn.

Outside, the rain pounded down harder than ever.
The trouble with Hatteras Lows was that they had a
tendency to hang around too long, flooding highways,
cutting new inlets, generally messing things up.

''Well, I guess… I mean, all right, we'll give it a
try. But I'm warning you, if I find out you're not who
you say you are—''

Rafe taught the parrots a new word. ''Look, can
you think of another reason why any man in his right
mind would show up on Ocracoke Island in this kind
of weather when he could be down in sunny Florida
sharing a pitcher of margaritas with a pretty woman
and watching preseason baseball?''

* * *

The truce lasted until dinner was served. Molly had already eaten dinner, but that had been hours ago. Since then she had burned up a lot of emotional energy. She had spent the last few hours trying to ignore the tempting smells permeating the whole house while she shifted stacks of books, tapes and taping equipment off the cot and spread it with clean, if musty-smelling, sheets. After that she'd spent an hour or so trying to concentrate on the paperback novel she'd brought to read on the beach while the stranger in her kitchen slammed pots and pans together and muttered under his breath.

He might or might not be Stu's brother. Men lied. Besides, they didn't look anything at all alike. Stu had freckles, red-blond hair that fell over his forehead and a jack-o'-lantern grin. He claimed to have three sisters and one brother, but none of them had showed up at the wedding. His mother was supposed to be somewhere in Europe, and he wasn't quite sure where his father was. According to Annamarie, they weren't at all close.

As for the volunteer chef, he looked like an advertisement for some tropical resort. Tall, tanned, with sun-bleached hair and a pair of pale gray eyes that were clear as rainwater yet impossible to read. Like a trick mirror. His features were far from perfect—his nose a tad too large, his jaw a bit too strong. His cheekbones were more flat and angular than high and aristocratic.

All of which made it hard to understand why she suddenly found herself redefining everything she had ever considered physically attractive in a man. If she needed to prove how wretched her judgment was when it came to men, she had two perfect examples to refer to. Smooth-talking Kenny and Stallone-look-alike Jeffy. Even their names sounded immature.

Their *names* sounded immature? Oh, for heaven's sake, it must be the weather. On a rainy night like this, with nothing to distract her, her mind obviously had a mind of its own.

"Blue cheese okay?"

Molly glanced up at the man in the doorway and caught her breath all over again. Telling herself to quit staring, she managed to say, "Blue's fine."

Any kind of cheese was fine, since she wouldn't be indulging. She had a feeling she could gain weight just looking at that delectable mouth of his and wondering...

Wondering nothing. All she needed to know was what he was doing here, why he was going to all this trouble and how long he intended to stay. At the rate it was raining, the roads would soon be flooded. Sally Ann had mentioned something about high water tables and creeks backing up. If it got much worse, not even the ferries would run, which meant they would be trapped here together.

What if he was lying about being Stu's brother? Men always lied when it was to their advantage. Her ex-husband was a prime example. As her neighbor back in Grover's Hollow had said when she learned that Molly was planning to marry Kenneth Dewhurst, "You don't want to do that, honey. He talks real pretty but there ain't a speck o' truth in him."

Jeffy of the beer cans and bedroom eyes had lied, at least by omission. This man could be lying, too, but for the life of her she couldn't think of a single reason why he should. There was no reason for him to stay, as Stu wouldn't be back for several days. Let him head on back to Florida and his margaritas and pretty women.

With a restless sigh, she laid her book aside. Her stomach growled, either in protest of the fried food she had consumed earlier or anticipation from the delectable smells issuing from the kitchen. She was accustomed to eating early and going to bed before she succumbed to late-night temptation. Not even to herself would she admit that tonight's temptation might involve more than food.

She wandered over to the birdcages and checked the water cups. There was a grape in one. "Messy, aren't you? I'll take care of it tomorrow. It's your bedtime now."

As usual, her comments were greeted by a cacophony of gutter language and filthy suggestions, "*Stick it up yer arse*" being one of the milder ones.

"Eat soap and die," she growled as she snatched her fingers from the danger zone.

"*Bill-ee, shaddup! Bill-ee, shaddup!*"

"Both of you shut up, or I'll—"

"*Balderdash. Hell-oo, honey!*"

"Don't you honey me, you dirty old man." Their names were Pete and Repete. A little too cute, but then, they were Annamarie's problem, not hers.

Pete—or maybe it was the other one—did a flushing toilet and then a series of noises that reminded her of someone cracking his knuckles. Molly ignored it and reached for the sheets to cover the cages.

"*Belly up, down the hatch, belly up, down the hatch!*"

"Just hush up and go to sleep." Her stomach growled once more as she picked up her book and settled down in the slipcovered easy chair again. It was a grisly murder-mystery, the last thing she needed on a night like this with a stranger in the house.

And she was hungry again. It wasn't fair. Both her sisters, Annamarie and Mary, took after the Stevenses, who were all tall and lean and burned up calories without even trying. Molly had taken after her mother's family. The fact that hips and thighs were supposed to be the healthiest place to store fat didn't help. She'd rather not have to store it at all.

It was almost eleven. Normally she would have eaten a light supper at six and been in bed by now. Shag, the half-Persian, half-coon cat Annamarie had had for years, climbed onto her lap, circled and settled down. He smelled like fish. She'd been buying him special treats at the fish market so that he wouldn't wander away and get lost and break Annamarie's heart.

"Dinner is served, madam. I thought a nice merlot. Okay with you?"

She didn't even know what a merlot was, only that it was a wine, and if she had to use up her daily allotment of calories, she intended to use it on something she liked a lot better than she did wine. "Um...water will be fine."

The kitchen table had been spread with a sheet. There was no dining room. No table linens, either. But there were hurricane candles, and her genial host—a little too genial to be trusted—had stuck them into a pair of red glass holders he'd found somewhere and used them as a centerpiece. There wasn't room on the table for the turkey.

"Oh, no, not candied yams." She uttered a soft moan.

"Butter, coconut, orange juice, pecans and brown sugar. Here, try some." He'd cooked enough to feed a platoon.

"Just a taste," she said, not wanting to hurt his feelings. "I ate earlier." Darn it, she'd come so close to having cheekbones. She had lost weight during the breakup of her marriage, but after Kenny had followed her to her next job and made such a pest of himself that they'd found an excuse to let her go, she had nibbled the pounds back again.

Poor Kenny. It wasn't that he was stupid, because he really wasn't. The trouble was, he worked so hard trying to keep from working that he never got anywhere. It hadn't taken long after they were married to discover that he had fallen for her earning capacity, not her looks or her personality. For years she had worked two jobs to put her sisters through college. By the time she'd met Kenny, she was well on the way to rebuilding her savings account, with every intention of cultivating a whole new Molly Stevens, minus the extra pounds and plus a whole lot more pizzazz.

Just as she was ready to reach out for something of her own, Kenny Dewhurst had appeared on the scene. He'd been briefly employed as a sales rep for a farm implement company at the time, despite the fact that he knew little or nothing about farming. But in a tiny place like Grover's Hollow, he'd created something of a sensation. All the girls were talking about him, but to everyone's astonishment, it was Molly he'd singled out. Smooth, handsome—short for a man, but just right for her—he had called her darling. Not honey, or babe, but darling. She'd been in awe of this man who spent more on one pair of shoes than she spent on her entire best outfit, and he drove a convertible, besides.

The convertible had been repossessed two weeks after their wedding because Kenny had had a falling-out with his boss, quit his job and couldn't make the payments. By that time he was no longer calling her darling, or even honey. His famous-name shoes had lasted a lot longer than his charm, but by then she wouldn't have cared if he wore golden slippers. Her neighbor had been right. Not only was he a world-class liar, he hadn't a grain of ambition. Two jobs were enough for any married couple, and she had both of them.

Besides, he was working on "something big." Kenny was always "working on something big." She hadn't dared quit her home-bookkeeping business because her job at the bank, while the title was nice, didn't pay a whole lot. Meanwhile, Kenny went right on working on his Big Deal. So far as Molly was concerned, his Big Deal was making such a pest of himself that he'd managed to get her fired from the bank, and later on, from a job with a small insurance company before they'd separated. She'd left her next job voluntarily after a break-in, because she suspected him of having something to do with it.

Not that she'd ever voiced her suspicions, either to Kenny or the authorities, because the divorce had come through by then, and the last thing she wanted was another kind of involvement with her ex. She had given him every chance to live up to his promises, but he never had. She had tried to understand his point of view—that he was slated for better things, that he'd had some bad breaks, that nobody understood him. It all boiled down to one thing. Besides being bone lazy, Kenny Dewhurst lacked so much as a grain of integrity. He was a failure. He would always be a failure because he refused to listen to advice or accept help, other than the financial help he demanded.

That was when she'd moved from West Virginia to North Carolina and taken a position as head housekeeper for a small assisted-living home. Two months ago she heard from a friend back in West Virginia that Kenny had been asking about her. That was the main reason she'd jumped at the chance to house-sit for Stu and Annamarie while Holly Hills Home was closed down for renovations. She knew Kenny. He was tenacious as flypaper when he wanted something, but like a child, he was easily distracted. With any luck, he would soon get discouraged and look for some other poor woman to hit on.

"Earth to Ms. Dewhurst."

Molly glanced up at the man seated across the table and was struck all over again by the combination of rugged features, pale gray eyes and a crooked grin. So he was attractive. Okay, so he was devastatingly attractive. For a woman who had any number of marketable skills, she was notoriously bad when it came to judging character, but at least knowing her weakness, she was forewarned.

"More spoon bread?"

"What? Oh, no thanks, I never eat—" Oh, my mercy. He had loaded her plate and she'd cleaned it off without even realizing what she was doing. Fifty thousand calories, gone to waste. Make that, gone to waist.

There was no earthly reason, Molly told herself that night as she lay in bed listening to the rain, why they

couldn't simply ignore each other and go their own
way. Once the rain stopped and the roads were clear,
Rafe would probably be more than ready to move on.
Then she could go on cleaning cages, brushing a
shedding, long-hair cat, counting calories and enjoying her first beach vacation. She'd discovered dozens
of purple shell fragments on the beach that Sally Ann
told her were bits of ancient clam shells. Remembering a book that had come out a few years ago, about
older women wearing purple, she decided to take
everyone at the home a handful of purple shell fragments.

A few hours later in another part of the house, Rafe
moved restlessly from window to window, looking
for a way out. So much for his great instincts and
impeccable sense of timing. The least he could have
done was to call before he'd gotten himself trapped
in an impossible situation.

He switched on the kitchen radio, hoping for news
or a weather forecast. He got static. Lightning noise.
There was no TV, and even if there were, chances
were it wouldn't work any better than the radio.
Which meant he was trapped here until the weather
cleared. Trapped with a wary female who had a sharp
tongue, lambent eyes and the kind of body that would
have made her the toast of the town a hundred years
ago.

The birds were asleep—at least, their cages were
covered. His headache had backed off, but he'd given
up trying to sleep. Restless, he located the phone book
and settled down with the old black rotary phone to
call every damned hotel on the island. Only, instead

of a dial tone, he got a sound like a drunk gargling whiskey.

Wet lines. The whole damned island was drowning.

Little Miss Muffet was probably in there snoring her head off. Dammit, if she weren't here to complicate things, he could have at least had himself a busman's holiday. He currently owned two coastal resorts, one recently renovated and reopened, the other in process of being evaluated. He owned a three-boat charter fleet. A day or two of scoping out the local facilities and the whole trip would be a tax write-off.

Not that he begrudged the cost, but he hated like the devil being made to feel like a fool. And now, whichever way he went, it would be wrong. He could hang around for a day or so and find out what needed doing about the woman Stu had married. Or he could take Molly Muffet at her word and leave her to look after those blasphemous birds, trusting to luck that Stu hadn't made the mistake of his life.

Either way, he was pinned down for the time being, and being pinned down wasn't something he bore up under gracefully.

Four

Rafe served Molly, then helped himself to a filet of trout that had been broiled to perfection. The small refrigerator was filled with turkey leftovers. At this rate he'd have to open up a soup kitchen. Until last night his cooking had consisted of the occasional intimate dinner for two, followed by an equally intimate breakfast. This was neither.

"I don't remember seeing you in any of the wedding pictures." It was a harmless observation, but Molly sensed both irritation and frustration.

She glanced up from her plate. "Hmm? Oh, I was somewhere around. I was the one in blue." Navy blue. Because dark colors were slenderizing. She had hoped to be able to fit into something more festive in time for Annamarie's wedding, but thanks to another unpleasant surprise visit from her ex, she had nibbled herself out of that possibility.

One of three Stevens sisters growing up back in West Virginia, Molly had been called the plump one to distinguish her from the gorgeous one and the brainy one. The brainy one was now an assistant research chemist in St. Louis, and the beauty was currently in Jamestown, exploring the excavations with her new husband.

"How's the fish?"

"Delicious." At least broiled fish was something she could enjoy with a clear conscience. She'd even eaten half a baked potato with salt and pepper only.

"Getting it fresh makes the difference. Squirt on the lemon juice, pour on the melted butter and bingo! You've got yourself a real treat."

"Butter?"

"Don't even think about using margarine." Rafe helped himself to the other half of her baked potato and ladled on the sour cream.

She sighed. "All right, I won't."

He looked at her, a frown shadowing his eyes. "Hey, you're not worried about a little butter, are you? Dairy foods are one of the major food groups."

Shag, the cat, shoved his head against her leg, reminding her that he, too, enjoyed seafood, with or without condiments. "Look, it's not a problem, all right? You go on cooking the things you like to cook, and I'll go on eating the things I want to eat. Better yet, you move out and I'll manage on my own."

"Not an option. Unfortunately."

"Unfortunately," she echoed under her breath.

"You don't eat enough," he said, still with that look of fake concern on his winter-tanned face. And that was another thing Molly hated about men. Hypocrisy. Kenny had been so worried about her when she'd had the flu. Worried about her losing her day job and falling behind on her home bookkeeping business.

Molly carefully folded her napkin and shoved her chair back. "If you'll excuse me, I need to go clean cages. Put away the food and I'll take care of the dishes." The cottage didn't run to a dishwasher, which had been just fine when all she'd had to clean up after were her own simple meals. With Rafe the Wonder Chef doing the honors, it was something else again.

"I made double chocolate parfait for dessert." He gave her a sly look that made her want to grind his baked potato, sour cream and all, into his crooked grin.

Closing her eyes, she prayed for patience, or at least a metabolism that wasn't so laid-back she could gain weight from reading a recipe. "Did you have to do that?" she asked plaintively.

"I could've made key lime pie," he said, all innocence, "but I didn't have the ingredients. I only know three desserts."

And so it went for the next few days while the low hung on, bringing gale force winds and torrential rains. For reasons Molly couldn't begin to fathom, Rafe tried to win her over with calories, while she tried her best to resist. To resist both his irresistible kitchen skills and his unmistakable charm.

Because charming he was, even discounting the attraction of his mismatched features. Molly could have sworn she was immune to all forms of masculine charm, but she'd never been exposed to Rafe Webber. Jeffy the jerk had been obvious once she'd come to her senses. At first she'd been flattered, and then she'd thought, where was the harm in a little friendly flirting? Wasn't a flirtation supposed to be included in any dream vacation package?

But once the novelty wore off, she hadn't liked what she'd seen. An unfaithful husband who whined. So far as she knew, Kenny had never been truly unfaithful to her, for all his other faults. Probably because he loved himself far more than he could ever love any woman. But his whining had been the last of a whole haystack full of last straws.

And now, just when she was beginning to regain her self-confidence, she found herself weathered in with a stealth charmer like Rafe Webber. That thick, sun-streaked hair and the sheer physical presence were striking, but the crooked nose, the crooked smile and the juggernaut jaw should have minimized the effect. Instead, it did just the opposite. Either she was allergic or he was addictive. Now she knew how it felt to be a scrap of iron, with a powerful magnet close by.

Not again, no thank you, no way! She'd traveled that route before. Once her sisters were launched and on the way to paying off the last of the loans, she had reached into life's grab bag for something of her own and come up with a handsome, charming scoundrel. The fact that she'd actually married him just went to show that where men were concerned, she hadn't a clue.

Maybe she should try wearing blinders, like the brick maker's pug mill mule back in Grover's Hollow. She had a feeling, though, that blinders wouldn't help with a man like Rafe Webber. She could cover her head with a pillowcase and still know if he was anywhere near.

"What do you do for entertainment?" he asked as he poured two cups of coffee and handed her one.

"If this rain doesn't end, I might take up boating, only I don't have a boat."

"How about shipbuilding? We might need an ark if it gets much deeper. Did you say this was your first trip to the beach, or did I only imagine it?"

"I probably said it." She said all sorts of things when she was ill at ease, as if running her mouth could forestall facing up to whatever trouble she'd blundered into. "I've got all sorts of plans for when the rain stops and the water goes down."

"Surfing? Kayaking?"

"Um…there's a museum."

"Wreck diving? Sunbathing?" He raised one eyebrow in a way that put her instantly on the defensive.

"I don't know how to dive. I don't even know how to swim. As for sunbathing, in case you hadn't noticed, it's cold, windy and raining." As if she would bare her body in public, on even the sunniest day. After Kenny's first cutting remarks about her figure, she'd cried herself sick and then demolished three-quarters of a coconut cream pie.

"I'm going to make a supply run. Want to go with me, or—"

"I'd better cut up more vegetables for the birds."

She watched him through the window, hatless, but wearing a waterproof slicker. With any luck he'd grow tired of waiting and go back to Florida's high-rent district, where he'd picked up that devastating suntan and the kind of casual sophistication Kenny had tried so hard to imitate. She didn't know which was worse—the imitation or the real thing.

Yes, she did. Imitations were like cheap toys—showy, but quickly broken.

She was beginning to believe the real thing could tempt her in ways she could barely imagine.

"Hey, bitch, wanna grape?"

"Hush up, you foul-mouthed creature," she muttered, viciously chopping carrots into manageable slivers. Raw vegetables didn't tempt her at all. Unfortunately.

After that she marched into the living room and carefully pulled the tray out from the bottom of the cage. Food, feathers and droppings clumped together in the orange litter. "Messy birds," she scolded. They had to be male. Her sisters had been well trained to look after themselves, but she had never known a man, including her own father, who didn't expect a woman to clean up after them.

"Shaddup, shaddup, shaddup!"

And then Pete tuned up with his favorite litany of four-letter words, which Molly did her best to ignore. Once both cages were cleaned and all cups washed and refilled, she stared out the window at the rain and sighed. What now? Wash the dishes, make her bed and then settle down with a boring murder-mystery? One thing she wasn't about to do was stay here alone, with the refrigerator crammed full of temptation. She'd given her powers of resistance a workout these past few days.

Besides, she'd promised Annamarie to check the mailbox every few days to clear out the junk mail. That meant a walk to the post office, as there was no house delivery on the island.

She bundled up in her tan raincoat and pulled a matching hat on her head. Both items had long since lost most of their protective qualities, but an umbrella, even if she'd brought one with her, wouldn't stand a chance in this wind. What she needed was one of those cheap plastic raincoats. Something in a bold color, maybe orange or yellow or neon green.

The roads were flooded. Cars got through by driving slowly and throwing up a big wake. Molly didn't even want to think about what might be lurking under all that murky water. She'd borrowed a pair of Stu's rubber boots, which were several inches too long for her feet but high enough to protect her from whatever yucky creatures swam in the floodwaters. If she'd had a grain of common sense, she would have taken Rafe up on his offer, but she couldn't afford any more of his brand of temptation.

Imagine waffles for breakfast. Served with butter and homemade fig preserves. She could hardly decline without hurting his feelings after he'd gone to so much trouble, but she was going to have to slog three times around the island in knee-deep water to work off all the calories.

From now on, she vowed, her rare indulgences would not include food. A woman needed to feel good about herself, and to do that she had to know she looked her best. Straining side seams and hollowless cheeks weren't going to help. A sagging, wet tan raincoat might describe the way she looked on the outside, but not the way she felt on the inside. A bright orange raincoat was more what she needed. Orange had attitude. It worked for highway workers. It worked for the Coast Guard. Maybe if she got herself a bright orange slicker it would work for her.

Hey, wake up, world! Here's Molly, in all her glory!

Rafe might think she was dull as ditch water—Kenny had considered her only as a convenient meal ticket and a shoulder to cry on until something better came along, but Molly knew who she was. It might not show on the outside, but the *real* Molly was bold and imaginative.

Well...maybe sensible and capable was a better description. And maybe a pretty shade of blue would be better. She would never be as smart as Mary Etta, whose SAT scores had been highest in the state the year she'd graduated from high school, or as beautiful as Annamarie, who'd been queen of the Apple Festival and voted the prettiest girl at GHHS.

Still, it was Molly who had held the family together after the folks had been killed. Long before that she'd been working and squirreling away her earnings to go off to college. Instead, she had seen that her two sisters, seven and nine years younger, respectively, had a shot at the gold ring. Mary Etta had gone to college on a scholarship but even so, Molly's help had been needed. Now that both sisters were secure and on their own, it was her turn. Without Kenny there was no limit to what she could do.

Rain dripped from her limp hat and trickled down the back of her neck. The last time she'd seen her ex-husband, he had tried to appeal to her better nature, claiming that without her steadying influence, which Molly wisely interpreted to mean her steady income, he would never be able to realize his potential.

"You reached your potential when you were seven years old," she'd told him that day after he'd tracked her down at her office in Morganton to ask if he could move in with her just until he got back on his feet. When she'd refused, he'd sulked until she threatened to call security.

That same night he'd turned up on her doorstep. He'd been drinking, and when she refused to let him inside he'd started crying. So of course she'd had to let him in, and then he'd got sick and ruined the new slipcover she'd bought for her thrift-shop sofa.

Poor Kenny. He was a miserable excuse for a man, but she had done her best and it hadn't helped. What was that old Chinese thing about saving a man's life and being responsible for him from then on?

Evidently it was a universal thing.

It was shortly after that that she'd moved to North Carolina, changing jobs and addresses. She hadn't heard from him since then. With any luck she wouldn't. Because, heaven help her, she thought as she turned off onto Fig Tree Lane, she really did feel sorry for the poor wretch for being such a loser. Nobody, given a choice, would choose to be such a bona fide jerk.

After collecting the mail, Molly considered her options. She could head back to the cottage and settle down with her gory mystery, or wade around the village in the rain, which had slowed to a drizzle. She was still standing outside the post office when the rusty SUV with the bumper bracket full of empty pole holders pulled up. There were countless similar vehicles on the island, but she knew who it was even before Rafe swung open the door. That darned magnetism again.

"Want a lift?"

"No thanks." Without even trying, the man frazzled every cell in her body, up to and including her brain cells. "Just going for a walk."

"Hop in, we'll go to the beach. I need to check up on the Baron anyway."

The baron? What was a baron doing on the Ocracoke beach? Another few synapses shorted out as she stood there and tried to think of a good reason to refuse. Wind whipped her hair across her face. A crew cut. That was next on her makeover after the orange raincoat.

Molly had planned to drive herself to the ocean beach one more time before she left, anyway. Her budget didn't allow for too many pleasure jaunts, because she still had to get herself back home once Annamarie and Stu got back. They hadn't asked about her finances, and she hadn't told them, but right now her bank balance was the skinniest thing about her.

"Come on. Except for a few diehard fishermen, we should have the beach all to ourselves on a day like this." He leaned across the seat and offered her a hand up.

Mentally she added a backbone to her list, right between the raincoat and crew cut. "Thanks," she muttered, squirming on the rump-sprung seat. The inside of the vehicle was almost as wet as the outside. There were rust holes in the floorboard and the window wouldn't quite shut all the way.

"Think of it as another adventure," Rafe said, his weathered face creasing in an infectious grin.

"Adventures are a lot more comfortable between the covers of a book."

"Hey, it's no adventure when all you have to do is close the book and walk away."

"You want alligators snapping at your heels? Help yourself, but count me out."

He chuckled, and somewhat to her surprise, Molly did, too, the sound nearly lost in the noisy roar of a rusted muffler.

Shortly after they left the village behind, Rafe turned onto a paved road that led to an airstrip nestled against the dune line. "Ocracoke International," he announced. "Mind waiting a few minutes? I'll be right back."

Ocracoke International? She'd thought that was the fishing tournament. Or had that been Ocracoke Invitational? Through the intermittent flurries, she counted eight small planes tied down, their cockpits covered with tarps. A flock of low-flying brown pelicans followed the dune line, and Molly marveled that anything could be so ungainly and so beautiful.

Rafe, his yellow slicker incandescent against a slate-gray sky, jogged out onto the tarmac and circled a white plane with a pale green palm tree against an orange sun painted on the side. She watched as he touched this and tugged at that, occasionally nodding. Molly huddled inside the vehicle. No wonder he hadn't been interested in catching a ferry.

"Rain's easing up," he said when he joined her a few minutes later.

"Is that the baron you were referring to?"

He nodded. "Ready to hit the beach?"

She peered through the salt-hazed, sand-pitted windshield. "It doesn't look much like beach weather."

"What, you're afraid of getting wet?" Backing out of the parking space, he shot her a teasing glance that made her acutely aware of her bedraggled appearance.

In the yellow slicker he looked more dashing than ever.

Molly vowed silently to ditch the awful raincoat and hat the minute she got back to the cottage. By then he was on the ramp leading over the dunes. Shifting into neutral, he glanced up and down the windswept beach. Even in the rain it was beautiful. Broad, flat, its white sands a dramatic contrast to the dark, angry water and the steely gray sky. "We'll head north. The rain's about to slack off. By late afternoon we might even catch a glimpse of sunshine." At her look of disbelief, he grinned and said, "What's the matter? Don't you trust me?"

"Not particularly." Trust wasn't that easy for a woman with her track record, but he was right about the rain. By the time he'd driven half a mile or so along the empty shore, it had stopped completely. Molly was too awed by the roiling gray Atlantic to notice until Rafe stopped and pointed it out to her.

"See? When I promise a lady something, I always deliver. Sea's still rough, but the sun's already trying to break through."

As if on command, a shaft of sunlight slanted through the clouds, glinting pale gold on the distant horizon. Molly sighed and leaned forward to peer through the pitted windshield. And then she squeaked, "Oh, my mercy, look at all the shells!"

She was out before he could offer to come around and help her down, never mind that big-wheeled 4x4s had not been designed with short people in mind. Soggy raincoat flapping, she jogged toward the surf in the clumsy boots, where several days of mountainous seas had deposited tons of broken shells.

Rafe joined her there, making a mental note to buy

her some decent rain gear before he left. And a pair of boots that fit. The ones she was wearing looked miles too big. "These are all busted up. There's a whole cockleshell, though. And, hey—here's an unbroken Scotch bonnet."

Molly ignored his perfect finds to pounce on a worn fragment of broken clamshell. "Purple," she crowed. "Did you ever see such a rich color? Oh, and look—there's another one!"

And so it went. Rafe soon discarded his modest finds. Most of the tourist shops along the eastern seaboard had bins filled with perfect shells, all imported. He doubted if anyone had ever expressed as much delight over a queen conch or a perfect murex as Molly did over a few thumbnail-size bits of broken clamshells.

"Oh, look—I know what this is, it's an oyster shell." She slipped a small, nondescript shell into her pocket, which was already bulging with wet, sandy treasures. "It reminds me of a raccoon's foot—the shape and all."

Rafe thought about buying her a shell book so she could identify her finds, but decided against it. No point in spoiling her pleasure. *Bless your little heart, honey. I'd like to turn you loose on my stretch of the coast for a few hours.*

By the time they got back to the cottage, Molly was chilled, even though the temperature had reached the high fifties. She must have walked off at least a pound. That was a down payment on cheekbones...wasn't it?

"We need to warm you up. What'll it be, hot chocolate or Irish coffee?"

"No chocolate, please. I didn't know coffee grew in Ireland, I thought it came from South America."

"Trust me, you'll like it," Rafe said solemnly. If Molly hadn't known better, she might have mistaken the twinkle in his eyes for laughter.

And heaven help her, she did. Loved it! Strong coffee, Irish whiskey, whipped cream and all. "Oh, my mercy, this is delicious," she all but purred. Thank goodness he'd used the teacups instead of the big lighthouse mugs.

One of the troubles with alcohol was that it had too many calories. Another was that it seldom fit into her budget. But worst of all, Molly had learned a long time ago at an office party that when she tippled, she had a tendency to chatter. Since then she had made a conscious effort not to. Not to drink, and not to chatter. "No more, thank you, but it was delicious. Honestly." She manufactured a yawn that turned into the genuine article. "I'm not really much of a drinker."

Sprawled in the room's one easy chair, Rafe studied the woman curled up on the sofa, her feet tucked under her, cheeks flushed from a combination of wind and Bushmill's. She looked about sixteen years old. "Tell me about my new in-laws," he prompted. "There's you, Annamarie and another one, right? And you're the eldest?"

She nodded solemnly. "I'm thirty-six. Mary Etta's next. She's the brainy one—she's an assistant research chemist. She always loved chemistry—all kinds of science, really. When she was a little girl, I remember..." Her voice trailed off and she yawned again. "Hmm, where was I?"

"You were about to tell me about my new sister-in-law."

"Annamarie. You wouldn't believe what a beautiful baby she was. I used to take care of her because Mama worked at the doctor's office. Strangers would come up and say how pretty she was. Well, actually, we didn't get all that many strangers in Grover's Hollow. The population stays right around nine hundred. People die, people are born, but almost nobody ever moves there voluntarily." She caught him looking at her with those translucent gray eyes and wished she could read his thoughts.

"You were saying?" he prompted.

"Oh. I talk too much. But about Annamarie, I was only trying to explain what she's like. Everybody loves her. Even when she lost six front teeth at one time, she had the sweetest smile." Pausing for breath, she heaved a sigh that caused his gaze to fall from her face to her bosom. Rafe would have to say that proportionally she was just about perfect. A nice, uncomplicated dumpling of a woman who happened to have her own sweet smile, not to mention beautiful eyes and the kind of skin that invited a man's touch.

Not that he was tempted. Not that she'd done anything to tempt him, he had to admit. Just the opposite, if anything, which in itself was something of a novelty. Women had always gone out of their way to catch his attention. He usually enjoyed it. What man wouldn't?

He had a feeling this one would be a lot happier if she'd never laid eyes on him. There was a certain novelty appeal, he had to admit, in being with a woman who wanted nothing more from him than his absence.

She claimed to have been at the wedding—the wedding Rafe had missed. She knew Stu, so he had to wonder just how much had the kid told her about the half brother who had helped raise him. Had he mentioned that Rafe made and lost more money in a single year than some men saw in a lifetime? When a man could afford to lose, he usually didn't. Had that impressed this woman at all? Did anything impress her...anything besides broken bits of purple clamshells?

"Do you like to fly?" he asked. *Go ahead, jerk, spread it on. She's seen the Beechcraft. Now tell her about the other plane back in Tampa.*

"I don't know, I've never flown."

He blinked twice at that. "Everybody flies. It's a lot safer than getting out on the highway."

"You're probably right, but I've never had any real reason to fly anywhere."

That pretty well took care of that topic. "How about boating?"

"Well, I rode in a boat on the New River once."

He waited. "And?"

"And it turned over and my friend had to drag me ashore. He was worried sick about losing the boat—it was a rental—so I sat in the car and waited while he went downriver to catch it."

"And did he?"

"Oh, sure. It had hung up on a snag. I caught a bad cold."

Lady, Rafe was tempted to say, you are no ball of fire when it comes to conversation. "So, what are your hobbies?"

She frowned. Silky auburn eyebrows puckered into worried lines. "Um...I like to read. I've always done a lot of reading. I taught Mary Etta and Annamarie to read before they were old enough to go to school."

It was like pulling teeth. The less she told him, the more determined he was to get behind that placid façade and discover the woman who lived there. It was the challenge of the thing, Rafe told himself. He'd always been a sucker for a challenge. Besides, he was used to women trying to impress him, trying to seduce him—wanting something from him. In the circles he moved in, that was the way the game was played. And when it came to playing the game, he prided himself on being one of the best, making certain first that everyone knew the rules going in.

Molly probably didn't even know there *were* rules.

"What kind of work do you do when you're not cleaning cages and trying not to blush when a parrot calls you a—"

She held up a hand. "Don't say it. I can't believe— I don't even know half the words they say. One's as bad as the other. They egg each other on once they get started."

"Who taught them to talk? Your sister?"

Molly eased a foot out from under her and flexed her ankle as if her leg had gone to sleep. "Heavens, no! Annamarie said they were rescued from a fraternity house after a fire. Nobody would claim them, and Annamarie's fascinated by the way people talk. Birds, too, I guess. She says some of their words are Chaucerian. She wants to do a study of their vocabulary once she finishes with her Ocracoke project. I don't know about Chaucer—it sounds like pure gutter to me."

"Or impure gutter. What kind of work do you do, Molly?"

"I've done lots of things, most of it pretty dull."

He didn't doubt that. On the other hand, no woman

in his experience was an open book. Even his gorgeous, hedonistic Belle had turned out to have a latent nesting urge. Thank God he'd discovered it in time. "Such as?" he prompted.

Molly stiffened her legs out on the sofa and wriggled her toes. She was wearing socks, as Stu's boots had blistered her heels—and until she bought bandages, she didn't care to risk wearing shoes.

"Such as janitor at a grocery store when I was too young to get a regular job. I got paid off in day-old bread and expired meat and produce, which was legal. I think. Anyway, it came in handy and none of us ever got sick. Once I learned simple bookkeeping I did better, but nowadays there are so many different computer programs, and everyone seems to use a different one. I'm a fast learner, about that sort of thing, anyway, but it seems like every time I tackle a new system, it's obsolete by the time I catch on."

She smiled at him, inviting him to share her amusing dilemma. When she forgot herself long enough to let down her hair, so to speak, she was a surprisingly attractive woman. Friendly, warm, engaging. "And?" he prompted, not particularly interested in a recital of her work history so much as fascinated by the way she spoke, using her hands, her eyes and her full, unpainted lips.

"Well. Next came the bank. I've always been good at math, but mostly you just have to be able to read and understand regulations, but anyway, the branch closed when the bank merged and I was redundant. Then I got a job as a stock clerk for a building-supply place. I like the smell of new wood, but the warehouse was full of wallboard and chipboard, all sorts of fabricated materials, and it turned out I was allergic to some of the glues and chemicals. I do—I did—bookkeeping for some small businesses at home.''

Some women touched their hair. It was a classical female gesture. Molly touched her foot. He didn't have a clue what that meant. "So what happened then? You found an allergy-free zone with an opening?''

She flashed him a quick look that made him feel vaguely guilty. All women liked to talk about themselves. He'd thought he was doing her a favor. It wasn't as if they had a lot to choose from when it came to entertainment.

"I'm sorry. I told you—no, I guess I didn't, but the thing is, sometimes I talk too much. I'm not sure if it's the Irish coffee or nerves, so if you'll excuse me—'' She reached for her book, but he stayed her hand.

"Molly, don't.''

"Don't what? Don't read?''

"Don't make me feel guilty, I'm lousy at guilt.'' He was good at guilt. It was one of the reasons why he was here.

"Oh, for mercy's sake, you're not the one boring *me* to death with a recital of all the dull jobs *you've* ever held in your life.''

"I will if you'll listen. But first tell me the rest of the story of Molly Dewhurst.''

"It'll be Molly Stevens again once I get around to changing it legally, but that's another story.''

"For tomorrow night,'' he said, offering her his most disarming grin. Another thing he was good at—disarming women. Evidently he hadn't lost his touch. He wondered if she'd ever heard of Scheherazade. "Go on with what you were saying.''

Molly couldn't remember what she'd been saying. She wasn't sure if he was interested or merely pretending. They could both sit around and listen to the parrots, but that was more embarrassing than entertaining. There was a weather radio but the automated voice quickly grew boring. The tiny AM-FM radio got mostly static and country music.

"So—well, my current job is a position, with a title and everything. And I love it, I really do. I'm going to stay there forever, if they'll keep me." Unless Kenny found out where she was and made a nuisance of himself again. His usual tactic was showing up at her workplace to ask for money, perching on her desk, spreading his smarmy charm on everyone within range, making a general nuisance of himself until, embarrassed to death, she gave him whatever she had on her just to get rid of him. A loan, he always called it, promising to pay her back as soon as his luck turned around.

"And that is?"

"And what is?"

"Your present job."

"Oh. Well, my official title is head housekeeper at an assisted-living establishment, but actually I do a little of everything. Aside from seeing that the laundry and cleaning staff do their jobs, and that supplies are kept current, I mean."

Rafe held his empty cup in both hands and stared at the rain-lashed window. The break had been short-lived, with the rain starting up again just after dark. The low was supposed to move offshore tomorrow or the next day, but until then, he was tied down as securely as the Baron. The fishing tournament was officially over, but most of the teams were still trapped here. Besides, he wasn't going to be around long enough to go to the trouble of moving, even if he could find a vacancy.

He tried to think of another question to ask, not that he was particularly interested, but he liked the sound of her voice. It was slower than he was used to hearing, but not quite a drawl. Husky, but not artificially so. He'd had a brief fling with a woman once who affected a husky drawl that had driven him right up the wall. Evidently she'd thought it sounded sexy. It didn't.

"So…what do you do in your spare time?"

"Nothing you'd find particularly interesting, I'm sure," she said dryly.

"I'm easily entertained."

Lifting her cup, she inhaled the lingering aroma of rich coffee and Irish whiskey. "I help with shopping and wrapping gifts for some of the women, and write letters for others and take care of house plants and help fill photo albums for those whose fingers aren't quite as nimble as they used to be. In a way it's almost like having a big family."

A big family. Ironically, Rafe thought, he actually had one, for all the good it did him. Maybe he'd look up another sibling or two once he got back. He'd met one of his father's brood once and felt no connection at all. The kid had been a spoiled brat.

"It's getting about that time again," he said, stretching his arms over his head. Rainy days were perfect for sleeping in, and for afternoon naps…all with the right partner, of course. "I'd better think about cooking us up something to eat. Unless you'd rather go out?"

"Mercy, no, not until the sun shines again. Let's eat leftovers tonight."

"Great. I'll have the asparagus salad and you can clean up the candied yams, spoonbread and Crab Alfredo."

She tossed a pillow at him. "You're a wicked man." She smiled, and in the light of two low-wattage lamps, she looked almost pretty.

Pretty? Hell, she looked almost beautiful!

Almost…

She reached for the stack of junk mail she'd tossed onto the table when they'd come in from the beach. "Let me sift out the catalogs and then you can put this in your room on the desk. Annamarie said chances are there won't be anything that can't wait until they get back."

Rafe watched her hands as she dealt with a stack of circulars, solicitations and catalogs. Nice hands. Small, shapely, with short, unpolished nails and dimpled knuckles. Belle had long, bony hands with long, metallic red nails. She was forever complaining that they didn't make artificial nails like they used to.

A soft gasp drew his attention from her hands to her face. "Molly? What's wrong?"

She looked up, and he tried to interpret the expression in her large, honey-brown eyes. Dismay? Fear?

Five

"Molly?" Rafe's voice, rough with concern, broke through her concentration and she managed to smile.

"It's nothing. Did you mention coffee?"

He hadn't. They'd just had coffee, but obviously the effects of the Bushmill's had worn off. She needed to think, though, and she could hardly do that with him looming over her. "Cream and two sugars, no whiskey," she said with a smile that probably looked as forced as it felt.

Kenny had tracked her down.

Wrong. The post office had tracked her down. Kenny had addressed the letter to her old apartment, where she'd lived after they had separated, and the post office had done the rest. From Grover's Hollow to Morgantown to Elizabeth City, and then on to Ocracoke after Mrs. James at Holly Hills scribbled in Annamarie's box number and zip code. It didn't necessarily mean that Kenny knew where she was now. According to the original postmark, he was still back in West Virginia. And even if he'd had the skill to track her down again, there was no reason why he should want to. Her modest salary covered her own needs only because those were equally modest. The trouble with Kenny was that he couldn't stand having his toys taken away, even when he grew tired of playing with them.

Rafe was still there, stretched out in the easy chair, his long legs crossed at the ankles. He ignored her request for coffee with two sugars and one cream, which was probably just as well. She preferred it that way, but took it black and bitter. Penance for lost cheekbones.

He'd left his shoes on the front porch alongside her borrowed boots, as both pairs were too sandy to bring inside. Molly had found a surprising sense of intimacy in the mutual shedding of shoes and the barefooted sipping of Irish coffee. Not exactly sexy, but…intimate.

"Want to tell me about it?" he suggested casually.

"What? Tell you about what?"

"What hit you so hard. You went about three shades paler just then."

"Oh, for mercy's sake, I did not." She shuffled the stack of junk mail off onto the floor, still clutching the forwarded legal-size envelope.

"Go ahead and open it. I'll go make more coffee if you want some privacy."

"Go—stay—I don't care what you do. It's nothing, anyway. Nothing important."

Leaning forward, Rafe pulled a copy of the local newspaper, the *Coastland Times,* from the stack on the floor, and pretended to read. Ocracoke's single page was inside. School menus. Board of fisheries report. A poem by a local high school senior. Not a whole lot to engage his attention. He wondered if there was a newsstand on the island that sold the *Wall Street Journal* or even *USA Today*.

He watched as Molly worked the envelope open incrementally. She was frowning, chewing on her lower lip. Whatever it was—threats from a creditor, a ransom note?—it could hardly be all that bad. She wasn't the type of woman to get mixed up in anything too shady.

Or was she? What did he really know about her? She claimed to know Stu, claimed to be Annamarie's sister, but hell, she could just as easily have claimed to be a reincarnation of Mary, Queen of Scots. He had no proof either way. The first time he'd ever seen her she'd been with some guy who hadn't even bothered to see her to the door. Come to think of it, she'd looked upset at the time, even by the single yard light. And that was before she'd even discovered the stranger in her kitchen.

So she knew how to look after the birds. No big deal. Lots of people knew how to take care of birds, although why anyone would want to be around this particular pair escaped him. The cat liked her, but cats could be bought with a treat and a good ear-scratching. Not that he had any personal knowledge when it came to pets. Until a rebellious kid brother had been dumped in his lap, the only dependents he'd allowed himself were a goldfish and a houseplant. When the plant had turned yellow and died, he'd given the fish to the kid next door. Working on a degree and holding down a job as night watchman at a medical supply house, he'd been too busy for further involvement.

That had been just one of several lean periods in his life. Stella had forgotten to transfer the child-care payments when she'd left Stu on his doorstep, so to speak. Meeting his half brother for the first time had left him too rattled to even think about how he was going to manage financially.

The wind-driven rain attacked another side of the house, which meant the wind had shifted. Which meant the nor'easter might finally be moving offshore. Which meant that with any luck, he could be out of here by tomorrow.

Oddly enough, the thought wasn't particularly appealing.

Without even looking at her, he knew Molly had opened her letter. Whoever it was from, whatever it was about, was no concern of his, he reminded himself. But hearing a soft, shuddering sigh, he relented. "If you want to talk about it, I've got broad shoulders and big ears."

She looked up, as if just realizing she wasn't alone, and choked off a laugh. "You have nice ears—not too big, not too small. But no thanks." Her smile cut through a few more layers of the defenses he'd built up over the years without even being aware of it.

"Your call. Look, instead of more coffee, why don't I make us a couple of turkey sandwiches? The sooner we get that carcass out of the way, the sooner we can start over."

Molly said, "Fine." He had an idea she would have agreed to just about anything at that point. Which made him all the more curious.

In the kitchen he laid out the ingredients and

stepped back to survey the possibilities. Turkey, mayo, horseradish, olives, provolone, lettuce—it was only iceberg, but it would do in a pinch. The bread was whole wheat, thin sliced. He would have preferred croissants, but he could compromise. One of the first lessons he'd learned after being left more or less on his own after Stella had dumped his old man and hooked up with her next prospect, was how and when to compromise.

Bread was easy. He set to work slicing and spreading, and pondered adding butter along with the mayo. He decided against it. The lady had a few pounds she'd like to lose, although she looked fine just the way she was. Better than fine, actually.

Which just went to show that he had a few problems of his own. Despite the fact that he had a full social life on tap whenever he was in the mood for companionship, lately he'd been growing restless. Nothing he could put his finger on, just a feeling that life was moving too fast and he just might be missing out on something important.

He was imagining things. The weather had him pinned down. He was stuck in a four-room cottage with a sexy woman and it was screwing up his mind.

Sexy? Molly Dewhurst?

No way. She was simply a nice, wholesome woman with a pretty face, a disarming sense of humor and a ripe, lush body that any normal male would find…interesting.

He stacked thin slices of turkey breast onto bread slathered with mayo, added a touch of horseradish and then artistically arranged the other ingredients. ''Work of art,'' he muttered smugly.

"Did you say something?" Molly called out from the next room.

Glancing around the door into the living room, he saw that she was staring out the window, the letter still in her hands. "I said, work of art. Constructing sandwiches." He topped off the leftover coffee with milk, poured it over ice and carried the tray into the living room. "Later on I'll make us a special dessert instead of dinner, and we can have an early night."

What other kind was there when there was nothing to do? The local pubs weren't worth the effort on a night like this, with the wind blowing a full gale and the roads flooded. If things didn't break by tomorrow, he might have to settle for one of Stu's history books, or something called *Early English Survivals on Hatteras Island*. One of Annamarie's thrillers, no doubt. He'd given it a quick glance, thinking it might be about shipwrecks, but it had to do with exploring remnants of Elizabethan English phraseology along the Outer Banks.

He'd settle for exploring Molly. If he grew tired of that, he would throw together something scrumptious in the kitchen that would tempt her right down to her pretty pink toenails and entertain himself by watching her try to resist.

No, he wouldn't. She didn't need the hassle, not tonight. Maybe tomorrow…

Carefully she refolded the letter and laid the envelope aside. Silently they ate. Rafe couldn't help but notice the way she enjoyed his creation, closing her eyes and sighing. He wished he'd added butter along with the couple of tablespoons of mayonnaise. There was something amazingly sensuous about a woman who truly enjoyed her food.

Later they talked about politics, and somewhat to his surprise, she was well-informed and not at all timid about voicing her opinions. After a spirited discussion of the pros and cons of voter referenda, he made fresh coffee and they switched to sports. Molly loved baseball. He was a football fan. He occasionally played golf. She occasionally watched stock-car races, explaining that the sport had gotten its start with bootleggers trying to outrun revenuers. "One of my great-uncles once operated the biggest still in Grover's Hollow. They say people used to come from all around to buy his whiskey, but he died when revenuers were chasing him up a mountain road and he lost control of his car and went over the side. The strange thing is, it was less than a mile from where my parents ran off the same road and were killed."

How the hell was a guy supposed to react to something like that? Sympathy? Admiration? He opted for changing the subject. "What about fishing? Ever done much of that?"

She shook her head, causing her hair to slither free of its confinement. "It was never a real big thing in Grover's Hollow. Maybe if I'd had brothers instead of sisters, I might have tried it."

"But then, if you'd had brothers instead of sisters, we wouldn't be having this conversation."

She laughed for the first time since she'd sorted through the mail and found the letter that was bothering her. He'd just as soon keep her mind off whatever problem had followed her here, because a relaxed Molly Dewhurst was surprisingly good company. Relaxed, interesting and attractive enough in her own unique way to add the zest of sexual awareness.

A little too much zest. "Tell me about the rest of your family, Molly."

"I've already told you everything there is, even about Great-Uncle Oliver, the bootlegger."

"You left out the part about changing your name to Dewhurst. Stu's wife was a Stevens before she married, wasn't she?"

She picked up a crumb with her thumb and licked it off. "Oh, for mercy's sake, I've done all the talking. It's your turn now. Your life is bound to be more interesting than mine."

"What makes you think so?"

"Your suntan, for one thing. And you fly a plane. And you're a marvelous cook. Most men can't even operate a can opener without cutting their fingers and having to be waited on hand and foot for a week."

Bingo. Another clue. They were beginning to pile up. For a woman who chattered when she was uncomfortable, she didn't impart a whole lot of personal information. And the more she left unsaid, the more she fascinated him.

Maybe *fascinated* was too strong a term. *Mildly interested* was a better one.

Oh, yeah. Nothing like a mildly interested libido.

Sometime in the night he heard a sharp sound, a thump and a soft, muttered curse. He'd been lying awake, wondering what the devil he was doing here when he could be looking over property along the lower mid-Atlantic coast. The southbound Cedar Island ferry was still running. He'd rented the rust bucket for a week.

"You okay?" he called out softly. He was pretty

sure the sound had originated from inside the house, not outside.

"I'm fine. Go back to sleep," she growled.

The rain had stopped, but the wind was howling harder than ever, whistling under the eaves, twisting the branches of ancient live oak trees to scrape against the house. He rolled out of bed and reached for his jeans. Sand gritting under his bare feet, he made his way to the small bathroom that had obviously been added on after the house was built, probably in the late forties. The door hung open. The only way to keep it closed was to hook it. Molly was on her hands and knees peering under the claw-footed bathtub.

Rafe sucked his breath, his hands moving instinctively to echo the sweet curve of her derriere. "Lost a contact?"

"I dropped a bottle of tea tree oil."

"Tell me what it looks like and I'll help you find it."

"It looks like a bottle of tea tree oil," she snapped, reminding him that some women weren't at their best in the middle of the night.

On the other hand, some were.

Molly was obviously of the former persuasion.

"This it?" He raked a small brown bottle from behind the wastebasket and bent over to pick it up. There was a sealed adhesive bandage on the floor, as well. "What are we doing? Performing a little midnight surgery?" She had rolled over onto her behind and was glaring up at him.

Molly on her feet in broad daylight was one thing. Molly on her rump in the middle of the floor at midnight, with one sock on and one sock off, was something else.

"Need some help?"

She said no first, then yes. "My blasted arms are too short! I can't twist far enough around to reach the back of my heel with both hands, and I've already ruined three bandages trying to stick them on one-handed." She looked embarrassed, angry and so damned sweet, he was tempted to offer to kiss her foot and make it well, and then explore any other possible injuries.

But he didn't. There was something about the woman that affected him in a way he had never been affected before. He didn't know quite how to deal with it, but he had a feeling it was nothing to mess around with. Having shared the water with tiger sharks, barracuda and moray eels, he had quickly learned that looks could be deceiving.

She leaned back on her elbows and lifted her bare foot. About a size-five lady's, he figured. Medium. He'd done a stint in a mall shoe store the summer of his freshman year in college.

"You want some of this stuff on it first?" He indicated the small brown bottle.

"Please," she said through clenched jaws. "Just a tad. If you get too much on, the bandage won't stick. That was part of my problem."

"It's going to burn. You've got a big one here, with the top torn half off. Want a little surgery while I'm at it?"

"Just dab on the oil and cover it with a bandage, never mind the flap. It'll either grow back or fall off."

Holding her ankle in one hand, he anointed the blistered heel, smoothed on the bandage and tried not to stare at the length of rounded female leg on the other end. He was breathing through his mouth, somewhat

more rapidly than usual by the time he set her foot
gently back on the floor. When she started to get up,
he offered her a hand.

"Go back to bed," she said in that oddly husky
voice of hers. "You've done your good deed for the
day. And thank you, Rafe. I could have managed, but
this was quicker."

Maybe it was the intoxicating effects of the astrin-
gent oil, combined with something sweet and pow-
dery that smelled like sea grape, but he refused to
leave her there on the floor. Sheer stubbornness on
his part, knowing she wanted him to leave so she
could get up with no great loss of dignity. Some
women, the long-stemmed ones, could manage to rise
in one flowing, balletic movement. Molly was built
along sturdier lines, her ballast arranged slightly dif-
ferently. He found himself wanting to lift her up and
hold her until she was steady on her feet, and then
carry her back to bed.

His or hers?

Damned if he knew. What he did know was that
he'd better think about moving on, weather or no
weather. He could always come back for the Baron,
or send someone else for it. If he missed Stu he would
catch him later, after Sister Molly had gone back to
wherever she did her head-housekeeping.

Funny woman, he concluded. Nice woman. He
couldn't recall the last time he'd spent this much time
in close contact with any woman, even Belle, and felt
so comfortable.

Only, comfort wasn't exactly what he was feeling
at the moment, which was why he cut it short and
told her good-night.

* * *

Rafe had high hopes of getting off the island, but the wind was still howling the next morning when he pulled on his jeans and closed his bedroom window. He had anchored various stacks of paper with giant quahog shells, or else they'd have been scattered all over the room.

Molly was already up. She'd been on the phone. Her expression was puzzling, to say the least. ''Problem?'' he asked, reaching for the coffeemaker.

She shook her head too quickly. He thought about pressing her, but decided to ease up. Odds were better than even that he'd be able to leave by midafternoon. He'd just as soon not get involved in anything that might mess up his exit.

Once he'd packed his gear, he set about putting the office back in the condition he'd found it. The cot had held stacks of books, notes, audiotapes and·a professional looking recorder. Molly had stacked them neatly in the corner when she'd made up the cot. He pondered whether or not to pile them back on the cot and decided against it, in case he needed to stay another day.

The truth was, he could probably have flown out by now, but given the condition of the roads he'd felt compelled to hang around until the water went down enough for Molly to be able to drive. If she decided to go sightseeing and ended up driving off into Silver Lake, he didn't want it on his conscience,

By midmorning the heavy clouds had blown offshore. The teenager next door waded across the yard to drape several small crocheted rugs over the picket fence. Seeing Rafe, she grinned and shrugged. He lifted a hand in greeting. Knee-high boots and navel rings? Cute kid, but he was just as happy not to have another teenager to raise.

The phone rang an hour later, just as they were sitting down to cheese-and-salsa sandwiches. As Molly seemed reluctant to answer it, Rafe grabbed it on the fifth ring. "Rafe? What the dickens are you doing there? Did I dial your number by mistake?"

"Stu? Hell, no, boy. I came to help you celebrate your birthday." Rafe filled him in on how he'd flown in with the makings of a surprise dinner and gotten trapped by one of the notorious low-pressure storms.

"Yeah, the birds are fine," he said in answer to the next series of questions. "Cat, too. Molly? Blistered heel from wearing your boots for a beach walk, but other than that—yeah, I thought maybe later today. Tomorrow for sure." There was a long pause, during which Rafe listened to a recital of recently unearthed historical data and the bliss of being married to the world's most wonderful woman.

Molly listened to the one-sided conversation, trying to decipher Rafe's few remarks. Later today *what?* Tomorrow for sure *what?*

He was leaving. The news was surprisingly unwelcome. After only a few days of sharing a cramped cottage with a stranger who delighted in playing diet games with her, she had to admit she had enjoyed herself more than she had in years. He didn't whine, he didn't ask for money and he hadn't once complained that nobody understood him.

The sooner he left, the better, before she got used to having him around.

"Going out?" Rafe asked. He replaced the phone in its cradle and looked from her to the window and back.

"The water's gone down some. I thought I might, um—go for a beach walk. I mean, as long as I'm here, I want to take advantage of every sunny day. And I want to collect some more shells so that I can take some to everyone at Holly Hills." What she wanted even more was not to be here when he left. That way she couldn't embarrass herself by begging him to stay until Stu and Annamarie returned. "In case you're gone when I get back, goodbye, have a good flight, and maybe we'll see each other again someday."

She was talking too much again. Overexplaining. She would have preferred to leave him with a better last impression, but the most important thing was to get out of range before she did anything stupid. Like begging him not to leave.

"Beach walking sounds good. First decent day since I got in. Why don't I join you?"

Men. She didn't know whether to cry or throw something. "I thought you were so anxious to leave."

"Stu said they'll be heading back early tomorrow. I might as well stay another couple of days as long as I'm here. Once I get back to the Gulf Coast it might be a while before I can get away again."

So they drove the rusted SUV Rafe called the rust bucket, with the bracket of pole holders on the front that gave it the appearance of a snaggletoothed rhinoceros, and parked across the narrow highway from the pony pen. He switched off the ignition and they sat for several moments, watching another flight of pelicans following the dune line. "What's bugging you, Molly?" he asked out of the blue.

"Bugging me? I don't know what—"

"Cut it out. Look, it's none of my business, but you've been distracted ever since that letter came. If you've got a problem that could use a disinterested perspective, I'm offering my services. I know for a fact that when you're in over your head, an outside view can sometimes be helpful.''

She heaved a sigh that steamed up the windows. Or maybe he was doing that. Or maybe it was a joint effort. Rafe could think of a few more pleasurable ways of steaming up the windows, but in this case they were inappropriate. Which was a damned shame, because it might be interesting to see—

''My ex-husband. The letter was from him. At first I thought he'd found out where I am, but that's silly. There's no way he can find out because the post office won't give out that kind of information. Will they?'' she asked plaintively.

He almost lost it then. Almost reached for her in the pure interest of offering comfort.

Yeah, sure, you're a saint, Webber. All compassion. ''Let's get out and let the sun bake out some of the mildew. We'll take it point by point, okay?''

Not until they were leaning into the stiff southwest wind that blew sand across a deserted beach did he speak again. Without thinking, he'd taken her hand, and now he tucked her arm in his and adjusted his stride to her shorter legs. ''So your husband's written you a letter and you don't particularly want him to know where you are, right? Is he stalking you? There are legal measures against that sort of thing.''

''Kenny's not a stalker, he's more of a—well, a leech.''

''Suppose you start at the point where things went wrong. If we take it from there, we should be able to pinpoint the problem and figure out an efficient way to deal with it. I do it all the time.''

As a businessman he operated that way. On a personal level he made a point of remaining uninvolved. If problems arose, he simply cut his losses and moved on, having learned at an early age to avoid messy entanglements. Over the years he'd had to haul Stu off the reefs a few times—the least he could do was offer Molly the same service.

"Well. Here goes. The life and times of Molly Dewhurst. You can stop me any time by holding up a hand." With a funny little half smile, she lit into a recital that skimmed over falling in love for the first time, marrying in haste, all the way to repenting at leisure. Some of it he'd heard before, but because he liked her voice, liked the feel of her at his side, the occasional whiff of baby powder and something wildly exotic, like hand lotion, he listened attentively, putting in a probing question or two from time to time.

"Did you ever think of getting a restraining order?"

"Restraining him from what? Being a pest? Actually, I considered it, but when I tried to think of what I could tell a judge, it didn't sound all that bad. I mean, he wasn't exactly stalking me. It was more of an embarrassment than a threat. He'd come by where I work and hang around, talking to everyone else in the office, making a general nuisance of himself. I always got lectured once he left. Once the coffee money disappeared, and I'm pretty sure it was Kenny, but that was hardly a felony. Somebody stole a fur-collared men's coat from the cloakroom last November, but if it was Kenny, I never saw him wearing it. There were some other things, little things that hardly seemed important at the time, but mostly it was that he was always hanging around, making a nuisance of himself and whining to anyone who would listen about stupid laws and stupid rules and stupid bureaucrats. First thing I knew, I'd be out of another job.''

"Honey, there are laws against that, too."

"I know," she said with a sigh. "There's a government agency for just about everything, but I hate having to ask some bureaucrat to solve my personal problems. And anyway, I didn't see it as a pattern when it was happening. I'd just get another job and start over again. Things would be all right for a while, and I'd tell myself I'd imagined it, but then he'd show up again, needing money or begging to move in with me.''

"Didn't he have a job?"

"He was always on the verge of something big."

Rafe knew the type. They usually worked harder at avoiding work than most nine-to-fivers ever did at work.

They walked for a couple of miles, passing three groups of fishermen and several vehicles, including a familiar-looking green pickup truck. Molly was reminded all over again that when it came to romance, she'd do better to take up needlepoint. The only men who showed an interest were interested for all the wrong reasons. She didn't know what the right reasons were, but she knew what they *weren't*. And she was tired of being a one-woman support system for losers.

By the time she accepted a hand up into the rust bucket she was already starting to regret having confided in him. Rafe could tell by the way she twisted her hands in her lap and avoided his eyes. Bless her heart, did she think she was the first woman ever to pour out her worries? Sooner or later, most women he knew intimately did. Mostly it was petty stuff, occasionally family troubles. Now and then an earthshaking decision such as whether or not to have plastic surgery, and whether implants would have the same sensitivity as real breasts.

Rafe didn't always know the answer—sometimes there wasn't a definitive answer—but if listening helped, then he was available. He liked women. If a woman he'd once had an affair with came back after several years and asked for his help or his advice, he was glad to do what he could. Usually they didn't, but once in a while someone did.

But this, he reminded himself, was Molly. If Stu stayed married to Annamarie, then they'd be family. It might be smart to go easy here, on account of Molly's idea of family and his own weren't even in the same ballpark.

"Well…thanks for listening," she said as he pulled up in front of the house between her car and a red convertible.

Six

They could hear the parrots all the way out in the yard. Pete's *"Bad-ass, bad-ass!"* fought for airtime against Repete's string of four-letter words. Molly said, "Oh, Lord, the neighbors," and hurried up onto the porch.

And then she stepped back and looked over her shoulder. "Rafe? The front door's open. Did you say Stu and Annamarie were coming today or tomorrow?"

He was beside her by that time. "Tomorrow," he said quietly. "Know anyone who drives a red convertible?"

She shook her head slowly. "But you know how parking is around here. Wherever there's a space, you squeeze in. Anyway, Sally Ann says there's practically no crime on the island, at least in the wintertime."

"In case you hadn't noticed, it's no longer winter. Go next door and stay there until I come for you."

"I'll do no such thing, I'm responsible for those birds. And Shag. Annamarie would die if something happened to that cat. She's had him forever."

Clasping her shoulders, Rafe eased her to one side. His breath was warm on her cool face, but there was no hint of warmth in his eyes. "Humor me, will you? It's probably nothing, but—"

"Molly? Is that you, darling?" The voice came from inside the house.

Even before he saw her reaction, Rafe had a pretty good idea who their intruder was. He had personally locked the front door, but if he knew Stu, his brother had probably left a key stashed outside in the most obvious place. As a kid he used to lock himself out at least once a week.

Still gripping Molly's shoulders, he whispered, "Recognize the voice?"

Wordlessly she nodded.

"The ex?"

Her eyes said it all.

"Shall I invite him to leave?"

She sighed. "Could you just wait outside for a few minutes? I don't want to have to explain you."

His shrug said, "It's your call," but he didn't release her, not until she looked pointedly at his hand on her shoulder. And by then it was too late.

A guy wearing an unseasonable fur-collared topcoat and a politician's smile appeared in the doorway. The smile disappeared. "Moll, who's this?"

Rafe, who had always considered himself fair and unbiased, despised him on sight.

"Just a—a friend of a friend." Under her breath

she hissed, "Don't you dare call me darling! Don't call me anything. Just go away!"

"You wouldn't answer my letter, you wouldn't return my calls—what am I supposed to do when my wife ignores me?"

Rafe shrugged and headed out to the SUV where he raised the hood and pretended to tinker with the battery cables while the other two stood on the porch talking. If they went inside, he'd have to think of something else, but no way was he going to leave her alone with some jerk who followed her down here and claimed they were still married.

Unless they were. Rafe had only her word that she was divorced. She could have lied about the semi-stalking ex-husband. Lied about the letter. She could be faking the whole scenario. Maybe she was just into games, trying to reignite a burned-out marriage. He'd known people who never told the truth when a lie would serve as well.

But Molly? No way.

The guy didn't look dangerous, but Rafe had learned a long time ago that looks could be deceiving. Any man who would sponge off a woman was obviously short on integrity, not to mention pride.

So he pulled out the dipstick and checked the oil while he was under the hood. For whatever reasons, she didn't want the fellow here or she'd have taken him inside. They were still on the front porch. He could hear them talking, but with the parrots running through their X-rated repertoire, he couldn't quite make out the words. The guy was sweating. He'd like to think it was because Molly was royally reaming him out, but it was probably the coat. To say he was overdressed was an understatement.

Molly wore twin patches of pink on her cheeks. In her damp, sandy denim with her hands on her hips, she looked more than a match for any man, but he had a feeling she was the kind of woman who led with her heart instead of her head.

Frowning down at the distributor cap, Rafe spread his hands on the rusted fender and reminded himself that it was none of his business. Just because she'd confided in him, that didn't mean he had to take on her battles. Hell, any cop would tell you that domestic affairs were trickier than an octopus at a pickpocket's convention.

Still, he couldn't just walk away. In the few days they'd been together he'd come to know her pretty well. They had talked about everything from politics to poetry. They both liked limericks, only he didn't know any clean ones and she wouldn't admit to knowing any of the other kind. Along the way he had come to know the woman lurking underneath that plain exterior.

Actually, the exterior wasn't all that plain, merely understated.

Rafe had no way of knowing if women reacted the same way men did when faced with an unexpected situation. The adrenaline rush. How the devil had she managed to hook up with such a loser in the first place? The guy whined, for Pete's sake! He dressed for effect, not comfort, which said a lot about him right up front. Probably caught her at a weak moment and played on her sympathy. With a woman like Molly, it would be a surefire technique.

"Aw, come on, honey, don't be like that." Now that the birds had run down, both the words and the tone were clearly audible. "For better or worse, remember? You promised."

"Kenny, I said no, and I mean it. I have barely enough gas and grocery money to last out the month. I certainly don't have enough to lend you. And if you get me fired from one more job, I'm going to—to—"

Rafe had heard enough. Wiping his hands on his handkerchief, he sauntered back up to the porch. "Molly? Is there a problem?"

Trapped. That was the only way to describe the look on her face as he moved to stand beside her. He slipped his arm around her waist, presenting a solid front, and there it was, right on schedule. Rafe had never run from a fight in his life. Had a few battle scars to show for it, but damned if he was going to stand by and let this creep talk a good woman into anything against her will. "Hi, I don't think I caught your name. Rafe Webber here." Crocodile smile, extended hand. Dewhurst stared at the hand with distrust, but Rafe wasn't about to let him off the hook.

Reluctantly the smaller man accepted the gesture. At the feel of that soft, limp handclasp, Rafe, not usually given to impulse, did something totally out of the blue. "I'm Molly's new husband. Why don't you go on inside, babe, and heat up the coffee. I'll join you in a minute."

Her jaw fell. She stared at him as if he'd suddenly sprouted a horn in the middle of his forehead, then abruptly she turned and fled.

Had Rafe lost his mind? Molly asked herself, standing stock-still in the middle of the tiny kitchen. Or had she? How on earth was she supposed to deal with *two* men, both claiming to be her husband?

Kenny wanted money, of course. Kenny always

wanted money. He used to nag her to get a retail job so he could use her discount. She'd been far more interested in health benefits, only, as things turned out, once she was married she was never able to keep a job long enough for benefits to kick in. To think she had once worked for the same company for seven years. But that was before she'd met Kenny.

She reached for the coffeemaker, changed her mind, and scowling, marched back to the front door in time to hear Rafe say, "If you hurry, you can just about make the next ferry. I wouldn't bother to call first, just show up at the office, tell him Webber sent you and—yeah, wear what you're wearing now. It's perfect."

Halfway down the steps, Kenny glanced over his shoulder. His face was flushed. Molly couldn't tell if it was fear or excitement she saw there, but whatever Rafe had said seemed to have worked. He was leaving.

"I know where you got that coat," she called after him. "You ought to be ashamed of yourself!"

"Ashamed?" Rafe murmured, both dark eyebrows lifting. To the man hurrying down the front walk, he called out, "Do we understand each other, Dewhurst?"

"Yeah, sure thing. No problem. Wish you luck— you don't have to worry about me, I'm outta here."

Rafe draped an arm over Molly's shoulder and smiled benignly. There was nothing at all benign about the way his gaze followed the departing man.

"Did I step over the line?" he asked once the red convertible was out of sight.

"Probably."

"I tend to be impulsive."

"That, I doubt."

His smile broadened into a grin. "Hey, it takes practice. I'm working on it."

"Whatever you threatened him with, it seems to have worked," she said, but for a second she'd glimpsed another side of Rafe Webber. Where men were concerned, she had learned the hard way that what you saw was not necessarily what you got.

"Hey, I made a suggestion, that's all."

She very much doubted if that was all, but she let it go. "I'd have promised anything just to get rid of him. Can you believe he wanted me to cash in my measly little IRA? He says he's in the stock market now, and he has inside information on a sure thing."

"Last I heard, insider trading was against the law."

"I don't think that will slow him down. And I seriously doubt if he's any kind of an insider. Kenny just likes to collect snippets of rumors and weave them into his own little fantasy." She sighed. "Poor Kenny. He knows better than to try threats on me. They won't work, because I know him too well."

"What works?"

"Bribery." Molly sighed again, and then she chuckled. Rafe had forgotten to remove his arm from her shoulder, and she tried to ignore the heat and weight of it. "He knows just how to embarrass me until I give in and let him have whatever money I have on me just to get rid of him. Trouble is, I can't afford to buy him off any longer. I'm trying to build a retirement fund, but it's not easy."

A retirement fund. It had been his experience that women, including his own mother, counted on men to secure their future. But then he'd never met a woman like this one. Not knowing quite what to say, he changed the subject.

"What'd you mean about the coat?"

"Only that I'm pretty sure he stole it."

"Do tell." And then, for no reason at all, they were suddenly grinning like a pair of conspirators.

Molly said, "I don't know how you managed to get rid of him—threats or promises—but I doubt if he believes we're married."

"What's not to believe?"

Lifting her eyebrows, she stared at him. "Me? You?"

Before she could react, he leaned over and kissed her on the tip of the nose. "Don't worry. I didn't threaten to take out a contract on him, I only suggested that a change of climate might work wonders for that flushed skin of his. Mentioned the name of a modeling agency down in Tampa that was always on the lookout for men with his looks and a flair for wearing good clothes."

Molly almost strangled. "You *what?* Kenny can't afford to go to Florida. He probably couldn't even get off the island if it weren't for the free ferry." The funny thing was, though, that she could almost see him as a male model. His favorite sport had always been trying on clothes.

"Depends on the motivation, I suppose. What do you say we eat out tonight?" Rafe suggested, thus changing the subject from the man he had subtly threatened by dangling the carrot, then showing the stick.

"I thought you were leaving this afternoon."

"As long as I'm here I might as well hang around another day. The honeymooners will be back tomorrow, and there's no telling when I'll be able to free up time for another visit.''

Another few hours, then. There were dozens of questions she wanted to ask. It occurred to her that Rafe knew all there was to know about her, from the fact that she was a sucker for a sob story, to every job she'd ever held, to the fact that she could never remember the punch line of a joke long enough to repeat it, and that she had a real weakness for anything containing coconut. He probably knew what size she wore, because she hadn't gotten around to clipping the tags from inside her new clothes.

What did she know about him? Nothing. What he did when he wasn't cooking up temptation or flying around in that fancy plane of his, whether or not he was involved with a woman. Or with several women. She wanted to ask just how he'd talked Kenny into that hasty, red-faced departure, because she had an idea there was a bit more to it than he'd let on.

A modeling agency? What did he know about modeling agencies?

On second thought, it might be better if she didn't know.

Molly spent the rest of the afternoon giving the birdcages a thorough cleaning. Or as thorough as she dared without risking a finger. Rafe went out. She didn't ask where, nor did he tell her. At least he didn't say goodbye, which meant he'd probably be back in time for their dinner date.

Mercy. She had a date with the man. Her fancy denim outfit with the nailheads and embroidery was damp and sandy. The laundry basket was full of clothes waiting to be washed and line dried once the weather cleared up, as the cottage didn't run to a dryer. Which left her with two choices. Her oldest jeans and a ratty sweatshirt, or the only dressy outfit she had brought with her, a flattering gored skirt, ankle length, with a long turtleneck pullover, both in black.

An hour later she fastened small gray pearl studs to her earlobes. She rouged hollows under her cheekbones, or where her cheekbones would be if they ever surfaced again.

Tomorrow Stu and Annamarie would be here and she'd be free to leave. Tomorrow she would go back to her apartment and wait until the renovators were finished at Holly Hills, and then she could throw herself into all sorts of projects. Starting a library or seeing if she could get someone from the college interested in holding a few classes in creative writing, or genealogy. Oh, she had all sorts of creative ideas that didn't exactly fit her job description. Maybe she would see if Holly Hills needed an activity director. They had a physical therapist and once a week, a crafts instructor, but maybe she could—

And maybe she'd do well to keep her feet on the ground and her head out of the clouds, Molly reminded herself.

They met in the living room. Rafe was breathtaking in khakis, a white shirt and a dark blazer. Which was something else she was going to have to deal with sooner or later. Sooner would be better. Sooner might not leave any lasting scars.

They took her car. Rafe drove. The water had gone down considerably, but it was still slow going. They passed Delroy's Pub and Molly thought of her last dinner date. From this moment on, she had a feeling she'd be measuring every man she met against Rafe Webber. It was a depressing thought for a woman who was determined not to be depressed.

"This suit you?" Having chosen one of several restaurants on the island, Rafe tucked her hand over his arm as they waited to be seated. Her smile nearly rocked him back on his heels. He wouldn't have thought black would be her color, not with her muted coloring, but it brought out the red highlights in her hair, the golden tint of her skin and the amber glow of her eyes. She had a lot to offer some lucky man, he told himself. Some deserving nine-to-fiver who would give her a home and children and all the things a woman like Molly needed.

She ordered the cheapest thing on the menu. He ordered a sampler tray for an appetizer. When the platter of shrimp, scallops and seviche came, she looked at it suspiciously. He forked out a grilled shrimp, dipped it in the tangy sauce and held it to her lips. "Open up, Molly."

She snapped the shrimp off the fork and chewed as if she were angry.

"What's wrong. You wanted the fried cheese? We can have that with coffee for dessert."

Reluctant laughter lit her eyes like an unexpected streak of sunlight. He stared, bemused. "I'm sorry. I guess I'm still worried about Kenny. I wish I knew how he located me. It's awful to dislike someone you once cared enough about to marry. Doesn't say a whole lot about my judgment, does it?"

"How well did you know him before you married him?"

"Not well enough, obviously. I saw what I thought was a handsome man with excellent taste who was involved in a lot of important business deals. I couldn't believe it when he asked me to marry him three weeks after we met.''

"Love at first sight.''

"Infatuation. Followed by confusion, followed by disillusionment. Followed by a few other things I'd just as soon forget. At least I learned my lesson.'' *Did you now, Moll? What about Jeffy? What about this man? What do you really know about him after all?*

Rafe fed her another shrimp, and then a scallop dipped in tartar sauce. She closed her eyes, savoring the sweet, tangy blend of flavors. "No more men, hmm?''

"No more marriage,'' she corrected, and sampled the seviche. "I end up feeling sorry for the men I'm attracted to, and it just doesn't—oh, this is so good!— it just doesn't work out.''

"You feel sorry for Dewhurst?''

"Can't help it.'' She took a delicate bite from a golden brown hush puppy. "It can't be easy, knowing you're such a loser, always having to pretend because you're afraid other people will see through you.''

"How did you get to be so wise at your age?''

She laughed outright at that. "Wise? Uh-uh, not me. Mercy, how can you say that when you've just met one of my major mistakes? Here, try this stuff. I don't know what it is, but it's delicious.''

"Raw fish.''

Her eyes widened. "No it's not. Raw fish is sushi, and it's all rolled up in little balls with capers and things sticking out the ends.''

"This was marinated in lime juice. The acid— you'll pardon the expression, coagulates the proto-plasm. No calories involved.'' He didn't mention the oil. He was beginning to enjoy feeding her, tempting her, enjoying her sensuous pleasure. "Conch seviche's a lot better, but this isn't half-bad."

Fascinated, Rafe watched her golden brown eyes widen and then close as she savored another forkful of the cold fish salad. It occurred to him that he had never known a more sensuous woman. Or a more intriguing one. Her appeal, he was beginning to discover, had nothing to do with fancy clothes or being seen in all the right places with all the right people. Unlike most of the women he'd known intimately, she didn't wait to find out what he thought about a subject and then fall all over herself agreeing. Molly argued. She could talk intelligently about a surprising number of topics, expressed curiosity about as many others and wasn't afraid to admit she knew nothing at all about still others.

By the time the waiter brought their dinners, they had demolished the appetizers. Without asking, Rafe lifted two hush puppies, a crab cake and several fried scallops off his plate and onto hers. "You need all the seafood you can get while you're here. It's got all sorts of health benefits."

"It also has a zillion calories when it comes breaded and fried."

"Have I told you how beautiful you look tonight?"

"No, and don't bother." She sampled a fried scallop and closed her eyes in ecstasy. "I'm overdressed, for one thing. Look around. Practically every other woman in here is wearing jeans and big, dangly earrings. Way cool, as Carly would say."

"That's Carly of the belly-button jewelry, right? The neighbour's daughter? Oh, yeah—I'd trust her fashion expertise any day."

Molly helped herself to a bite of his fried sea trout. "She's only fifteen years old. Give her time."

"Stu was fifteen when I got him to raise. We didn't even speak the same language."

"You did a good job. I don't know him all that well yet, but I like him a lot. I trust Annamarie's judgment." Better than her own, she could have said, but didn't.

"You know about his trust fund?"

"Not much. Only that some day he'll probably get some money."

Rafe nearly swallowed a bone. "Yeah. That's about the size of it."

"He's going to be a great history teacher. You can tell he loves his subject, just listening to him talk about it."

Rafe didn't particularly care to speculate on what would happen when his half brother turned thirty-one. Unless he was a hell of a lot stronger than he looked, it was going to make a big difference. His wife would have a lot to do with how things ultimately turned out. "What do you think, fried cheese and coffee or key lime pie?"

"What? Oh—none for me, thanks. You go ahead, though."

"You didn't touch your dinner." Made some pretty big inroads on his, but her broiled chicken and green salad had been barely touched. "What's wrong, Molly? Are you still worrying about Dewhurst?"

"Kenny? No, I think you opened up a whole new world for him. Of course, it probably won't work out, but…"

"But?"

"Rafe, you did all anyone could ask and more. And

I thank you, I really do. If he shows up again, then I'll deal with it, okay? I've certainly had enough practice."

"Just out of curiosity, how do you usually handle it?"

She toyed with the idea of not answering, but he had more or less made it his business earlier. "When I have it, I give him money. I refuse to let him move in with me, not even when he claims he'll have to sleep on the street because he can't afford security and first month's rent on another place. The sad thing is that Kenny's really fairly smart, in a way. He'll get a job, work until the first payday, then quit and look for something better. He's— I guess you could say he's a perennial dreamer."

"I guess you could say he's a perennial hustler," Rafe said dryly.

"He borrows money to buy lottery tickets. Every time he opens the door he expects to see someone from Publisher's Clearing House." She sighed and propped her chin on her linked fingers. "According to someone who used to know his family, he was a beautiful little boy. His mama spoiled him rotten, gave him everything he ever asked for, convinced him he was special and made excuses for him, no matter what he did. It was never his fault, you know? And then, once she was gone, poor Kenny found out that as far as the rest of the world was concerned, he wasn't so special after all."

Rafe watched the candlelight reflected in her eyes. Large, warm, honey-colored eyes.

"You have to feel sorry for someone like that." That soft husky voice undercut the noise of cutlery, china and laughter all around them.

"You do?"

"You can't despise a child," she said patiently. "Kenny just never grew up."

Rafe shook his head slowly in amazement. How the hell did you respond to a statement like that? Instead, he changed the subject by waving a waiter over and ordering a whole key lime pie to go.

By the time they got back to the cottage, Molly regretted having not done justice to her chicken. She had eaten the raw fish thingee and Rafe had made her sample his seafood platter. She couldn't be hungry. But sharing the cottage with a whole key lime pie was dangerous. When her emotions were involved, she couldn't count on her common sense to protect her. In some ways she was no wiser than Kenny.

Rafe headed for the kitchen to put away the pie. Molly draped her shawl over a chair and tucked a few loose tendrils of hair back into her French twist, then decided to change into something more comfortable. Not that she wasn't perfectly comfortable in her black knit outfit, but key lime pie wasn't her greatest weakness. Rafe had told her she looked beautiful. They both knew it wasn't so, but just to be on the safe side, she'd better change into her grungiest everyday clothes. She was who she was and Rafe was who he was, and no matter what he'd told Kenny about being her new husband, that was one twain that would never meet.

If Kenny came after her again and wanted to know where her husband was, she would tell him—

Nothing. She didn't have to tell him one darned thing. In case Rafe was worried, she wanted him to know that she had no intention of perpetuating the lie. Feet on the ground and cards on the table, that was her policy from now on.

Back in her jeans and a sweatshirt that had seen better days, she marched into the living room intent on clearing the air. Rafe beat her to the draw. "Uh-oh, you've got that look in your eye."

"What look?"

"Militant. Is something bugging you? You're not still upset because I told whatsisname we were married, are you? Molly, where've you been for the past fifty years?"

"Not in your circles, obviously. And anyway, he couldn't have believed it."

"Something's on your mind. I haven't seen that Molly-on-the-warpath look in days."

"I told you, there's nothing on my mind. I'm happy as a clam, so happy I'm going to have a bite of that pie. Do you want me to cut you a slice?"

He studied her with curious eyes. "I'll wait a while."

She made it a tiny slice. Just a teensy sample. Crisis food, she told herself now that the crisis had passed. Back in the living room a few minutes later, she chose one of the two straight chairs, set her pie on the bookshelf and launched her attack. "All right, we can agree on one thing—you're leaving tomorrow, but chances are, we might run into each other from time to time. You being Stu's brother and me being Annamarie's sister and all. So—"

"You think the world's going to come to an end if people think we've slept together? And you're how old, Molly—thirty-five?"

"Thirty-six," she snapped.

Touched and amused, Rafe watched her struggle

with the idea. Color bloomed on her cheeks, competing with the twin streaks of rouge. Racing stripes, they were called among the women he knew. "Honey," he said softly, "this is the twenty-first century. Women have the vote, they hold public office—they pretty much do as they please, and no one holds them accountable." Except maybe for their kids, he thought, but the bitterness he'd once felt toward his own mother had long since lost its edge.

"So? What's your point?"

"My point is this. Unless you've got a few more jealous men lurking in your background, I think I can forget having to explain anything. I don't know about your sister, but Stu won't have a problem with our being here together."

"Oh. Well, I wasn't actually concerned. I mean, for goodness' sake, we're both certainly old enough, and—well, people live together all the time and nobody gives it a second thought. It's just that things are different in real small towns, and anyway—"

"Molly."

"And even in Grover's Hollow we have cable, so it's not like we—"

"Molly," he said again, but she was on a roll. Thank God he'd tossed sheets over the cages or the birds would be adding their two cents' worth. Covered, they were somewhat quieter.

Rafe levered himself out of the sagging easy chair. Planting himself in front of her, he said her name again and then he captured her hands and drew her up into his arms. "Is this what's got you so uptight? I believe it's called sexual tension," he whispered just before his mouth came down on hers.

Rafe had it pegged. It *was* called sexual tension, and it had been simmering just under the surface all day.

Seven

She tasted as sweet as she looked. She felt just the way a woman should feel—soft and solid and warm. Resilient. Not fragile and bony, all angles and edges. The novelty of it alone was enough to encourage him, even before her arms crept around his neck and she started making squeaky little noises in her throat.

Incendiary. That was the only word to describe what was happening. At thirty-eight, Rafe thought he had long since passed the age where testosterone overruled common sense. There were plenty of reasons for not getting involved. Trouble was, they weren't getting through to his brain.

Compulsion was another word that applied. This compulsion to go on holding her, tasting her, feeling her warm body pressed against his, inhaling the essence of Molly Dewhurst. A unique blend of sexiness and innocence.

It caught him off guard, the lack of artifice. Granted, she was a desirable woman, and granted, they'd been sharing close quarters. Granted, too, the sexual awareness that had been lurking just under the surface, feeding on itself. Chemistry happened.

The trouble was, there just might be something more than chemistry involved. Not only did he find himself wanting to explore every delectable inch of her body, he wanted to reach inside her mind and explore the warm, disarming, engaging woman that was Molly Dewhurst. That was downright scary.

"Mercy," she whispered breathlessly. She was clinging to his ears with both hands as her eyes slowly opened to stare wonderingly at his face. "Did you just kiss me, or did I imagine it?"

His amused response held an edge of desperation. "If you don't know, then maybe my technique is getting rusty."

"Oh, no—it's just fine! I mean, you do it really well." She closed her eyes and bopped her head against his chest. "Why not just shut up before you make a complete fool of yourself, Molly Lou?" she muttered fiercely.

The cat was sleeping on the sofa. With one hand, Rafe waved him away. The sofa was too narrow for what he had in mind, but then that might be a good thing. With any other woman in these same circumstances, bed would have been the next logical step. But this was Molly, not any other woman. He wasn't exactly sure of the rules here; he only knew that the old rules didn't apply.

One thing was clear—that loser she'd been married to had obviously been too damned self-centered to know how to treat a woman. Rafe knew how to treat a woman. He'd made it something of an art. Trouble was, Molly deserved more than quick, convenient, a-good-time-was-had-by-all sex. And that was all he could offer.

"Uh—maybe I'll have some pie after all," he said, gently disengaging himself. The cat leapt back up on the sofa and glared at him as if to say, *Hey, if you're not going to use this thing, buddy, butt out!*

"Oh. Pie." She shook her head. "I don't know why I feel like crying."

Gut punch. "You feel like *what?*"

"Don't mind me, you go ahead and have your dessert. Mine's around here somewhere. Would you put it in the refrigerator for me? I'm not hungry after all. I should be—I hardly touched my chicken, but... It must be the weather. That and Kenny and—and everything." Her voice spiked dangerously. She was babbling again.

Rafe recognized the signs by now. She was embarrassed. Her voice was too cheerful, her eyes were too bright—her lips were still swollen from his kiss. He didn't know whether to eat pie or make love. He knew which he'd rather do, and it didn't necessarily include meringue. He stood there, watching her as if he were a member of a bomb squad faced with some strange new explosive device.

"Molly?" She waved him away, but it was too late. One fat tear broke the barrier of her thick lashes and slipped down her cheek. "Ah, honey—don't do that," he growled.

It was all she needed. For all of ten seconds she stood there, arms at her sides, sniffling and gasping convulsively. Then Rafe opened his arms and she turned blindly into his embrace.

Molly was beyond embarrassment, but there was no way she could hold back. What she needed more than anything else in the world at this moment was comfort. Pure, physical, nonjudgmental comfort. She had long since outgrown the kiss-it-and-make-it-well stage, but some needs were elemental.

She didn't even want to think about why she so desperately needed comforting. Kenny was only the smallest part of it. It had far more to do with a basic need that had been growing inside her for too long. "Do you mind—would you mind just holding me?" she asked, struggling for some vestige of dignity. There was nothing at all sexual about the request. That had been only a momentary...aberration.

Still holding her, he shooed the cat away again and settled down on the sofa. Still cradled in his arms, she turned so that she was resting against his chest, her arms draped around his shoulders. That way she could hide her ruined face in his throat until she managed to regain control of her emotions.

"I'm so embarrassed," she mumbled into his collar. She was ruining his shirt, getting it all damp.

Something rumbled in his throat. No words, just a comforting sound. She shoved her fists up under his arms, where it was warm and safe and cozy. Then just as she was beginning to get herself in hand again, the dam burst, releasing the flood that had been building for too many years since her parents had been killed driving in a blinding rain on a mountain road.

There'd been no time to grieve then. She'd had to be strong for her sisters, to deal with the funeral home, the lawyer, the preacher and all the people who had tried to smother them with kindness. Then there'd been the woman from social services, and the insurance people. Her father's policy had lapsed when payments had fallen behind. A wonderful man, kind and funny and loving, he had never been good with details. An avalanche of details. She remembered crying, but grieving was far more than crying, and there'd been no time for anything more than tears shed in the middle of the night, wrenching sobs stifled in her pillow so her sisters wouldn't hear.

She'd had to find a second job, which meant working seven days a week to pay off the lawyer and her father's debts. And then there were braces and tuition and all the extras that kept piling up faster than her meager earnings could cover.

Finally, just as her responsibilities had begun to ease, Kenny had come along, and in a moment of inexcusable weakness she had married him.

It hadn't taken long before she'd realized that her charming prince was largely a figment of her imagination, but the deed was done. For better or worse, she'd been determined to stick by her vows. In Grover's Hollow, things like marriage vows were taken seriously. Things might have been different if she hadn't gotten pregnant. They hadn't planned it. Kenny didn't particularly like children. Probably because, as she realized later, he was still too much of a child himself and didn't want competition.

He'd been having trouble holding a job because, as he put it, either he was overqualified, or the boss was unreasonable or there was no room for advancement. Whatever the excuse, none of his jobs lasted more than a few weeks. The more Molly came to know the man she had married, the more she'd worried. Morning sickness struck hard and early, and that hadn't helped. Then in the space of three weeks her employer had gone bankrupt and Kenny had quit his job driving for a vending machine company because it was beneath his dignity. A week later she lost her baby. Riddled with guilt, she'd been unable to cry, afraid that once she started she might never be able to stop.

And now, of all times, she'd had to start. "I'm so sorry," she blubbered.

"It's all right. Just go on and get him out of your system."

He thought she was crying over Kenny. "I wish he'd drive off the end of the ferry and drown," she muttered against his soggy collar.

"I'm not sure you could handle the guilt if it happened," he said, sounding almost amused.

"Have you evermore got me pegged?" She even managed a wet chuckle. "Knowing Kenny, he'd land on a shoal and have to be rescued, and then sue the rescuers and the ferry company for mental anguish and ruining his new coat."

"Sounds like a real prince."

"Don't laugh. If he thought we were really married, he'd probably sue you for stealing his meal ticket."

"I can see it now, The Molly Stakes. Cross lawyers and come out fighting?"

She snickered. And then she burst out laughing. It felt incredibly good, even though her eyes were burning and her nose was stopped up, and nothing had really changed. "It's not funny, you know. Now that he knows where I work, he's probably going to hang around Holly Hills and make a nuisance of himself, and first thing you know, I'll be more trouble than

I'm worth and they'll find some reason to let me go. It's happened too many times in the past.''

"He'd do that even thinking you've remarried?''

She uttered a ladylike snort. "He'd never in a million years believe someone like you would marry someone like me, even though I've been gainfully employed for nearly twenty years and once won a prize for my practically fat-free chicken pot pie.''

Rafe's arms tightened around her. An intoxicating blend of his cedarwood shaving soap and her baby powder, enhanced by the heat generated by two adult bodies, eddied around them. Somewhat to his amazement, Rafe realized that he could easily see himself married to Molly. She was...comfortable. Surprisingly good company. Sexy in a way that was both earthy and innocent.

Get a grip, man. This is your half brother's sister-in-law!

He tried. He thought about Stu, who might be neck-deep in trouble again, depending on what kind of woman this Annamarie turned out to be. That could turn out to be a messy situation if Rafe allowed himself to get involved with Molly.

He thought about certain personnel problems waiting for him back at the Coral Tree Inn. He thought about Belle, his ex-mistress, who was probably busy making babies at this very moment. Which brought him full circle to the problem in his arms.

The way Rafe saw it, Molly's biggest problem, aside from that jerk she'd been married to, was a badly bruised self-esteem. For which the jerk could probably take full credit. And while Rafe was in a position to do something about it, there were certain hazards involved, one of which was the fact that he might not be able to maintain his objectivity.

Her fingers uncurled and slipped around to his back. Couldn't she tell what was happening to him? His heart was thundering like a cattle stampede, he was breathing like a locomotive headed up a steep grade. Not to mention certain other obvious clues.

He really should pull back before things got too far out of control. "Molly?"

"This feels so good. Isn't it the most wonderful feeling in the world, being held by someone bigger and stronger than you are?"

"I wouldn't know," he said with a wry grin.

She laughed, a husky, whispery sound that registered in the pit of his belly. *Patience, man. You're in control here. See that you keep it that way.*

Her knees were drawn up beside her. Beside him. Rafe had a feeling that somewhere a fuse was burning dangerously short. "For just this little bit of time," she whispered, "I don't have to think about tomorrow. I don't have to worry about whether or not Kenny's going to be waiting for me once I go back to Holly Hills. For now, I can just stay right here and…glow."

"Glow?"

"Mmm. That nice, drifty feeling you get just before you fall asleep. Sometimes when I have a big problem, I put it under my pillow just before I fall asleep and when I wake up in the morning, the answer is there waiting for me. It's like leaving a door open in your mind."

"Uh-huh. Yes, well—I've got a little problem, but I don't think I'll find an answer under my pillow."

"Sex, you mean."

Mentally he slammed on the antilock brakes. "I do? I mean, it's no big problem…honestly. Nothing I can't handle." A long, cold shower and a fast flight out at daybreak should just about do it. The honeymooners could wait.

"I'm sorry. I didn't mean to embarrass you, but— well, I couldn't help notice, and if there's anything I can do—"

He swore. Broke it off quickly, not wanting the birds to get any ideas, but— "Dammit, Molly, do you always blurt out the first thing that pops into your mind?"

"Not always—actually, almost never, but it's a good policy. Feet on the floor, cards on the table. It saves misunderstandings."

"Yeah, well, I have to tell you, it just might land you in trouble one of these days. Another man might take you up on your offer."

"I didn't offer—well, I guess I did, didn't I? But you know what I mean."

"No, I don't. Suppose you tell me."

"Well, I meant…that is, I might be partly to blame—I mean, I know how men are about these— um, physiological things?" She tipped her face back far enough to peer up at him. Far enough for him to see the fiery color flare in her cheeks again.

"You mean a man might get aroused just from holding a beautiful woman in his arms and kissing her—feeling her breasts pressed against his chest, breathing in the scent of her skin, imagining what it would be like to—"

She covered his mouth with her hand. "I didn't mean—"

"Feet on the floor, cards on the table, Molly."

"Oh, my mercy, all right! Me, too, for what it's worth. I mean, I was, too—feeling that way. Only, with a woman, men can't tell."

"I can tell." His voice sounded as if someone had a hammerlock on his larynx.

"You can? How?"

"First clue? Your pupils are dilated. Second? Your pulse is too fast. Third? You're breathing as if you've just run a three-minute mile."

"All right, you made your point." And then, "I am?" she asked wonderingly.

"You're still here, right? You could have walked away. And then there's this," he murmured as he lowered his face to hers.

One kiss merged into another. By the time they came up for air, Molly's sweatshirt was on the floor. Rafe's hand-tailored shirt was unbuttoned and tugged free of his belt. Shag had had his way with Molly's pie and was licking the empty saucer across the floor.

No one noticed. No one cared. Somehow they managed to reach the bedroom without barging into anything. Rafe left the door open so that light from the living room fell through the doorway. Molly flung back the quilt just before they collapsed onto the bed, then Rafe tugged it over them both. He was burning up. She was shivering, but probably not from cold.

Fleetingly she considered confessing that she wasn't particularly experienced. She had slept with only one man in her life, and hadn't especially enjoyed it. Cards on the table and all that.

But the thought was lost when she felt his fingers on the buttons of her jeans. Frantically they finished undressing each other. Hands tangled, the quilt ended up in a heap on the floor, but by that time neither of them had need of the additional warmth.

Rafe felt on the floor for his khakis and managed to extract his wallet from the hip pocket. There should be a single condom there, left over from his pre-Belle days. One should do it. It wasn't as if this would lead to anything more, it was just a case of—

Of letting off steam, he told himself. Bleeding the pressure down to a safe level.

And then Molly touched him and his brain shut down. Her hands were small, her touch tentative, but he stiffened and caught his breath.

She snatched her hand away. "I'm sorry, I didn't mean to—it was an accident."

He captured her hand and brought it to his lips. "Molly, Molly, don't apologize. This is for both of us. I just don't want it to end too fast."

"No, of course not, I understand. I won't do anything or say anything to—"

He had to laugh. Here he was, so damned hard he ached with it, and all he could do was lie there laughing. It did nothing at all to relieve the tension. Turning onto his side, he drew her close and eased his knee between her thighs. Her flesh was surprisingly cool. He was hot as an afterburner. She lay perfectly still for several moments, her uneven breathing the only sign that she was as aroused as he was. Rafe slid one hand up between them and tipped her chin up so that he could study her face.

"Molly? We don't have to go through with this if you've changed your mind. A nice, cold midnight swim and I'll be just fine." He vaguely recalled thinking those same thoughts not too long ago. Back to square one. How the hell had that happened?

"I want to."

Her voice was so soft he was afraid he'd misunderstood her. And then he caught on. And swore. "He wanted you silent and passive. Is that it?"

She swallowed hard and nodded, her hair brushing his chin. "Oh, baby—oh, sweetheart, that was his loss. I could almost feel sorry for the poor bastard, but I have an idea he might have put you through some rough times, even more than you let on." He lifted her thigh and eased it over his hip so that they were nestled together in breathtaking intimacy. "Talk. Touch. Tell me what you want, Molly—we're equal partners in this. Your pleasure only doubles mine."

And when she didn't react immediately, he lowered his lips to her breast. "Tell me what you want. Do you like this?" He suckled her gently, and then not so gently. Her nipples were amazingly responsive. "What about this? How does it make you feel?"

He could tell without words how it made her feel. Her toes curled against his shins, her hips moved as if she couldn't get close enough, and when he slipped one hand down between them and found her, she reacted instantly.

And then, somehow, they shifted until it was her lips on his nipples, her fingers toying tentatively with the base of his throbbing erection. As if she were afraid of exploring further.

"Rafe?"

Between clenched jaws, he managed to answer her. "Yeah—oh, yes!"

"Do you feel anything when I kiss your breasts?"

"Let me put it this way, sweetheart—" He could barely control his voice, but in the interests of freeing her of inhibitions, he went on. "Had a house once—lightning struck a tree just outside, ran in on some buried wires. Burned the insulation off the inside wiring, blackened an entire wall and blew off a few switch plates. Feeling your mouth on my nipple is…comparable."

"It's all connected, isn't it?"

"Yes'm, that it is. Breast bone connected to the, uh—other bone. And I have to tell you, if you go on doing what you're doing, you're going to blow a few major circuits."

He moved over her then, and even in the near dark he could see her smile. White teeth, shining eyes. Lowering his face, he murmured against her mouth as he parted her and eased into position. "Molly, sweet Molly, what am I going to do with you?"

Her hips lifted to meet him, welcoming him into her body, and to his amazement she uttered a breathless chuckle. "I hope…that's a rhetorical…question. Oh, yess-s. Please…"

One slow, measured thrust. And then another. And then there was no holding back, for either of them. Molly began to whimper as the fiercest of all pleasures gathered strength and fed on itself like a wildfire inferno, until it ended in one mindless explosion of profound pleasure.

Still holding her sweat-slick body in his trembling arms as the earth slowly settled back on its axis, Rafe became uneasily aware that something had changed. Over the past twenty-odd years he had had sex more times than he could recall, and enjoyed almost every occasion. He always took care to see that his partners shared his enjoyment and he invariably parted on good terms with his lovers.

Except in the technical sense, Molly was not a lover. And that was part of the problem—he didn't know exactly what she was. She didn't fit into any of his neat pigeonholes. Her ego had been bruised. She'd been needy, and he'd been here at the right time. One thing had led to another and they'd ended up in bed.

Where was the harm in that? he rationalized. She had enjoyed it as much as he had, if those kittenlike whimpers and that single, wide-eyed yelp had been any indication. If he'd snapped his fingers and produced a light show on the order of the aurora borealis, she couldn't have looked more dumbstruck. You'd think she'd never climaxed before.

Too exhausted at the moment to locate his clothes and beat a strategic retreat, Rafe lay there beside her in the double bed and stared at the ceiling. This was going to take some careful diplomacy. In the space of a few days they had met, gone from suspicion to armed truce, to guarded friendship…and now this.

Whatever *this* was. He still didn't understand it. Molly wasn't his type. He wasn't in love with her. Liked her, sure, but hell, he liked all the women he slept with.

Could it have been the laughter? Come to think of it, he couldn't remember laughing with a woman right up to the moment when he'd buried himself inside her. He'd have thought laughter would have dampened the fire.

If laughter was all it took, then he'd just made a discovery that would put him right up there with Edison, Fessenden and the Wright brothers.

He needed to get out of here. Needed to go for a

long walk on the beach. Needed to get as far away from the warm, sweet-smelling woman beside him as possible so that he could examine this thing clearly and logically from all angles. Nothing had really changed. They'd slept together, period. As consenting adults, both unattached and in their right minds, where was the harm in that?

She stirred beside him, and her hair tickled his chin. "I was just thinking, Molly. Maybe I'd better not wait around much longer. I can always come back to see Stu later on. We'll probably run into each other from time to time—holidays, maybe. I used to try and make Thanksgiving and Christmas special for the kid—for Stu, that is. Maybe we can—"

"Don't spoil it by feeling guilty, Rafe. It was about the nicest thing that's ever happened to me."

He could almost sense her smiling in the darkness. Her voice took on a special note when she was pleased about something. "Yeah, well..."

"I thought they were making it up, you know? The people who went on and on about how it felt to—well, I don't care for the clinical terms, but you know what I mean. Reading about it is one thing, but actually—you know—experiencing it, that's something else."

He wanted to gather her in his arms and hug her all over again, but didn't dare risk it. His body was already beginning to react to the feel of her warmth beside him, not to mention the heady scent of sex and baby powder. Besides, he'd used his single condom.

"You don't have to stay here. In my bed, I mean. If you'd rather not—I mean—"

"Molly?"

"What?"

"Hush up and go to sleep."

She sighed. It was a smiley kind of sigh. He could tell by her even breathing when she drifted off to sleep. He was on the verge of drifting off himself when the phone rang in the other room.

Eight

Rafe held the phone in one hand, his pants in the other, and listened silently for several minutes. By the time Molly joined him, wearing only his discarded shirt, which was the first thing she'd grabbed, he had managed to get his pants pulled on and was struggling one-handedly with the zipper.

"What's wrong?" she whispered. "Who is it?" Her mind taut with concern, she was struck all over again by the sight of his lean, bronzed body. No matter how often or how rarely she saw him over the years to come, she would never be able to forget the fact that except for a narrow section around his hips, he was tanned all over. That his body hair was several shades darker than the thick crop on his head. Everything about the man was incredibly arousing. From practically her first glimpse, when she hadn't known him, hadn't believed him, hadn't trusted him, she'd been aware at some bone-deep level of that powerful physical attraction.

"Never mind that—I'm here, okay? Yeah, we've met," he said dryly. With one arm he drew her closer to his side and held her there while he spoke tersely into the receiver. "We'll be there in— No, I can't fly out until first light. The landing strip's not—"

"What's wrong?" she whispered.

"You're sure? Level with me. Are you all right?"

"Rafe, what's wrong?" she whispered fiercely. "Who is it?"

He owned a hotel. He probably had dozens of people working for him. Something must have happened back in Florida.

"You said we. Was that you and me, or did I misunderstand?" Of course she'd misunderstood.

He replaced the phone in its cradle and stood for a moment, visibly gathering his thoughts. By this time Molly was truly uneasy. Whatever had happened— wherever it had happened—Rafe was leaving. Going back to Florida at first light. Leaving her here with two birds and a cat and the rest of her life to get through without him.

The thought was devastating.

"How long will it take you to pack?" he demanded.

She stared at him in confusion. "Pack what?"

"Enough for a couple of days. This next-door neighbor—do you think it's too early to wake her up and see if she can take care of the menagerie for a day or so?"

"Sally Ann? She works for the ferry department— she has to get up early. Rafe, what's going on?" Not

Florida, then. Which must mean— "Has something happened to Annamarie?"

Rafe related the bare essentials, which was all he knew. "They were involved in an accident, they're both basically all right, but they're being kept for observation. Save your questions for later, when we're underway. We've got about an hour to wrap things up here. Then I'm headed for the airport, with or without you."

He made another quick call to someone named Mike. Molly didn't wait around to hear what was said. Calling on years of practice, she shoved her emotions into a dark corner of her mind to be dealt with later. First, a quick shower, then she dragged her suitcase out from under the bed and tossed in a few essentials. Every few minutes she would call out another question. "Are you sure neither one of them is seriously hurt?"

"I'm not sure of anything except that they're both able to talk more or less rationally," Rafe called back from the next room. "She said the car didn't catch on fire until after they'd both crawled free."

Catch on fire! In the act of pulling on her one decent pair of jeans. Molly staggered and fell against the bed. "Why didn't you let me talk to my sister?"

"Because she was upset and she kept arguing with Stu on the sidelines, and I figured a four-way conversation would only delay us. Lock the windows and turn off the heat, will you?"

"Down, not off. The birds, remember?" She zipped up her jeans and struggled into her black turtleneck. By the time she had snapped her bag shut and dealt with her hair, the sky was showing a hint of color. Light shone from the kitchen window of the

cottage next door. Molly hurried over to explain to
Sally Ann about the accident. "Stu and Annamarie
are both all right as far as we know, but they've been
admitted to Chesapeake General Hospital for observation."

"Get going, honey, don't you worry about a thing.
Carly and I will take care of everything."

"I'm pretty sure I can be back in a day or so. Even
if Rafe wants to stay on, I'll have him fly me back
here and—"

"And nothing. You just go, girl. We'll play zoo-
keeper for as long as it takes. You just show me
where everything is before you leave."

The two women hurried back to the cottage, where
Molly wrote down the routine, stacked Shag's canned
food on the counter beside two containers of seed mix
and opened the refrigerator to point out the bird's
chopped vegetables. She showed Sally Ann how the
cages worked and told her about washing and refilling
the water cups. "Annamarie says they don't bite, but
I've seen what they can do to a chicken wing poked
through the bars. Watch your fingers."

"I'd take the cat home with me, but with the new
puppies, maybe I'd better not."

"He's fine outdoors as long as it's not raining too
hard. I really owe you for this, Sally Ann."

"You bet you do. You're going to have to take one
puppy for every day you're gone once they're
weaned." She grinned to show she was only half-
serious.

A sleepy-eyed Carly wandered over just as Rafe
tossed the two bags into the rust bucket. Wearing only
an oversize T-shirt and a pair of fur-lined boots, she

looked years younger than the spike-haired, body-pierced teenager he had met once before.

"We'd better get underway before the weather changes again," Rafe said, his gray eyes dark with concern.

Carly yawned, stretched and scratched her neck. "You're flying?"

He nodded. She said, "Coo-wul." And then, "Can I feed the birds while you're gone?"

"It's up to your mother, but I warn you, their vocabulary is X-rated."

"Coo-wul!"

Finally they got away. One look at Rafe's closed face and Molly decided her questions could wait. She tried to focus on Annamarie's situation, but her mind kept straying back to the man beside her.

To think that little more than an hour ago she had been lying in his arms, naked and sated, dreaming warm, fuzzy dreams. Now it was if she didn't even exist. Molly told herself he probably had dozens of women. What wealthy, successful, handsome, charming man didn't? She could hardly expect him to be swept off his feet by a middle-aged, overweight housekeeper from Grover's Hollow, West Virginia.

And yes, she thought dolefully, if seventy-two could be considered elderly, then she was truly middle-aged. The fact that Rafe was even older was immaterial. The rules were different for men.

Her sidelong gaze lingered on his profile. Even frowning, his blunt, angular features redefined male beauty. Hard to believe he and Stu were related. Sweet, shy Stu with his turned-up nose and freckles, who blushed and sometimes stammered under social pressure. By the time he had made it to the altar to stand beside his gorgeous bride in her homemade wedding gown, his boutonniere had been dangling and his bow tie askew. The first time she'd met him, her maternal instincts had stirred to life, though she was only about ten years older than he was.

The instincts Rafe stirred were altogether different, she thought as he slowed down to negotiate a puddle that stretched across the narrow highway. She had a feeling she had just committed a catastrophic blunder. She would like to think that if she had it all to do over again, she never would have slept with him, but an innate sense of honesty refused to let her get away with it. If he were standing before her in a lineup with one hundred of the world's handsomest men, she would have picked him out immediately. There was simply something about the man that got to her. However, this was not the time to analyze it, much less try and deal with it. It would simply have to wait.

The plane was ready to go when they arrived. Rafe checked several things, both inside and out, while a gangly youth lugged their two bags over and shoved them inside. Rafe slipped two folded bills into the hand of the boy, who grinned and said, "Anytime, Cap'n."

Molly didn't even try to breathe as they taxied down the narrow runway, only a stone's throw from the ocean. Eyes closed tightly, she felt the plane lift off and quickly bank around to head north. Opening one eye first and then the other, she clutched her stomach and uttered a soft moan.

"Seat belt too tight? Keep it fastened anyway, okay?"

"It's not the seat belt. It's the breakfast we didn't take time for."

"Open your eyes and look at the horizon. Take a few deep breaths."

Dutifully Molly opened her eyes and peered through the Plexiglas. She drew in a deep breath, and then another.

"Don't hyperventilate," Rafe said over the drone of the engine. "Just look and enjoy."

Remarkably enough, she did just that. Fascinated by the brand-new perspective, Molly forgot all about her queasiness. But before she could appreciate the scenery, she needed answers to the questions there hadn't been time to ask earlier. "Were they on their way back here? What was it, a blow-out? Is Stu a good driver? Because Annamarie's never been all that good. It took three tries before she could even get her license." She covered her mouth. "Don't tell her I told you that. She was so ashamed. I don't know why I did, only—"

He covered her hand with one of his, and she gasped and cried, "Keep your hands on the steering wheel, watch where you're going!"

"Relax, Molly. I won't let anything happen to you. And your secret's safe with me."

"What secret?"

Grinning, he said, "That Annamarie had some trouble getting her license and that you can talk the tail off a kangaroo when you're nervous or uncomfortable."

She was quiet for all of thirty seconds. Then, in a tone of wounded dignity, she said, "Well."

"Here's all I know. There were three vehicles involved. The driver of the dump truck has some broken bones and possible internal injuries, Stu has a mild concussion and three broken bones in his left hand.

Unfortunately he's left-handed. Your sister is basically okay, as far as—''

The plane veered to avoid collision with a flight of geese, and Molly caught her breath and gripped the edges of her seat. Rafe slanted her a quick grin. ''Look down.''

''With my eyes open? Are you crazy?''

But she opened her eyes and looked, and when he pointed out the darker stain on the water and told her it was a school of fish, probably channel bass, she shot him a skeptical look. ''Trust me,'' he said, and she looked again, seeing nothing at all that resembled a fish.

''There. That's not so bad, is it?''

''What, you mean flying with my eyes open? The fact that I'm up here miles above a shark-filled ocean with no visible means of support? Or the fact that your brother has a concussion and a bunch of broken bones and my sister is probably falling apart, even if she's not physically injured?''

Or the fact that we made love, and for the first time I discovered what it's all about, and it probably won't ever happen again?

''How about all of the above?''

''How about concentrating on getting us there?''

The plane was noisy, but surprisingly steady. After a while, Molly relaxed enough to take in the glorious spectacle of sunrise over the chain of narrow barrier islands, an intricate pattern of dark lacework against a background of fiery gold and coral.

Rafe absorbed the scenery as he did every nuance of sound or vibration. He had been flying for more than twenty years. Sometimes he flew as a means of getting from point A to point B. At other times he flew to free his mind of clutter and allow himself to concentrate on the big picture.

Now all he could concentrate on was the woman beside him. Stu's marriage would probably fail; marriages in their families inevitably did, which meant he might never see Molly again. But regardless of what happened in the future, he knew he would never forget her. And that bothered him, because he'd never before had a woman get to him as quickly as she had. Not even Belle, whom he genuinely liked. Certainly not the woman he'd been married to briefly, before he'd wised up and figured the odds.

Molly was…Molly. Feet on the ground, cards on the table.

Her feet might be on the ground, he told himself with tender amusement, but her head was definitely in the clouds. For a thirty-six-year-old divorcée, she was incredibly naive. A sleeping beauty who was just beginning to wake up. The fact that he might have played a part in her awakening gave him an inordinate sense of proprietorship; at the same time it scared the hell out of him.

Noticing how absorbed she was in the panorama below, he banked to allow her better visibility. This time she never even grabbed the seat to hold on. After a while she said softly, "This is a season of firsts for me." Rafe leaned closer to hear, catching a whiff of shampoo and baby powder. She raised her voice and said, "I don't know if I told you, but it's my first trip to the beach. And this is my first flight, and last night was the first time I ever—" She slapped a hand over her mouth.

"The first time you ever what?"

"Nothing."

"You want me to start guessing? The first time you ever *what*, Molly?"

But Molly wasn't about to admit that it was the first time she'd ever slept with any man other than her husband. As for that other thing that had happened, all she could say was that a blaze of sunrise reflected in the water and viewed from the cockpit of a small plane paled in comparison. "The first time I ever met a bird that could curse in three languages."

He laughed. She knew that he knew she was lying, but he was gentleman enough to let her get away with it.

The trip seemed endless. It dawned on Molly that she was moving faster than she had ever moved in her life—another first—yet the earth seemed to creep by below.

"So strange," she murmured. He couldn't possibly have heard her, much less have known what she was talking about. All the same, he reached over and covered her left knee with his right hand, and this time she took comfort in his touch and didn't even yell at him to mind what he was doing.

When they finally landed, Rafe sent her off to find two coffees and a couple of bagels while he took care of the plane. "Meet you at the car rental desk. I'll bring the luggage," he told her, and instructed her on how to get her there.

Airports were another adventure, but by the time she found the ground transportation area, Molly had had her fill of excitement. It had begun to sink in that Annamarie might be more seriously injured than she'd admitted. What about internal injuries? Why else would she be kept for observation?

It didn't help to tell herself that both her sisters

were grown up now. They no longer came running to her to fix every hurt from a stubbed toe to a broken heart. Annamarie had a husband now; she didn't really need her big sister. And Mary Etta was on the verge of getting herself engaged, but then, Mary Etta had always been more independent than Annamarie. In some ways, she was even more independent than Molly was. With Molly, independence had been mostly pretense born of necessity, something she had only recently admitted to herself.

Nevertheless, being accustomed to worrying, Molly continued to worry. By the time she met Rafe at the car rental desk, she was sick with it. "I want you to tell me everything," she said, handing over a cup of weak, lukewarm coffee and a bagel. "I'm strong enough to handle the truth, whatever it is, so don't try to protect me. Besides, I'll find out everything in a little while, and if you've lied, I'll never trust you again. Why did Annamarie insist on talking to you and not me? It's because she knew I'd know, isn't it? I can always tell when she's trying to hide something from me. Her voice sounds different, like she's reading from a script or something."

He dealt with the rental agent, then led her outside, transferred their bags and handed her into the late-model gray sedan. "She talked to me because I answered the phone. As for whether or not she was hiding anything, you know her, I don't. I've never even met her. Whatever we find when we get to the hospital, we can deal with it, all right? Just keep saying to yourself, 'They're the kids, we're the grown-ups.'"

Dutifully Molly repeated, "They're the kids, we're the grown-ups." She drew in a deep, shuddering breath. "Rafe, did you ever get the feeling after your mother left Stu with you that you were just acting the part of an adult? You were scared stiff, but you had to pretend like crazy to keep him from finding out you didn't know all the answers?''

"You, too, huh? Most of the answers I didn't know by then, I found out in a hurry. A few I'm still working on.'' He chuckled softly as he stopped for a red light. "I had a teacher once in the seventh grade who barely managed to stay one lesson ahead of the class. I know how she felt.''

"I can't remember how many times I pretended to be calm and steady and reasonable when I was so scared, I was sick to my stomach.''

He nodded. They followed the signs to the hospital and found a parking space not too far away from the main entrance. When Rafe leaned across her to unfasten her seat belt and Molly caught a hint of his cedarwood shaving soap, it struck her all over again—that stunning affinity she felt for him that she had never felt for another man, not even the one she had married. Dear God, what had she done, besides shattering her concentration just when she needed it most?

A few hours ago she had been naked in bed with this man, doing and feeling things she had never in her wildest dreams imagined doing or feeling. And now, here they were, acting as if it had never happened. As if she didn't know about the scar on his left thigh where a stingray had stuck him and the barb had had to be cut out.

As if he didn't know about all her stretch marks, all the convexities on her body where she would have dearly loved to have concavities. Her rounded belly, for one. Her full cheeks, without a single sign of a cheekbone, for another. She was the plump one, and he was about to meet the gorgeous one. Even as a little girl, strangers would stop to admire Annamarie. Molly had always taken pride in both her sisters, because they were special and she loved them both dearly. They were both enough younger so that sometimes they felt more like her children than her sisters.

Just once, though, she would like to see a man look at her with the same awestruck expression Annamarie never failed to inspire. Just once.

And just this one man.

Please God...

They asked directions and assured Reception they were family. "I'm his, she's hers," he explained. It was enough to get them onto the elevator at least.

Annamarie was pacing outside in the hallway. She rushed forward as soon as the elevator doors opened. "What took you so long? Oh, Molly, I've been so worried—no, no, I'm sorry—I know it must have been awful trying to get through rush-hour traffic, and...you must be Stu's brother. I'm his wife. That is, I'm Annamarie. I'm Molly's sister."

"I would have recognized you anywhere."

"You would?" Both Molly and Annamarie spoke at the same time.

Rafe's smile came on slow and gathered strength. "Yeah, you're a lot alike."

Before Molly could pursue the matter, Annamarie grabbed both her hands and pulled her aside. "I'm sorry, Moll. We should have waited at least until morning." She turned to Rafe and explained. "It's this habit we all have, you know. Not just family, but half the people in Grover's Hollow. Whenever anything goes wrong, everyone calls on Molly to sort it out. When we were growing up, even before Mama and Daddy died, Mary Etta and I used to depend on her. Mama was never what you'd call a hands-on parent. I think Mary Etta and I were afterthoughts—or maybe accidents. Molly was always there, though. She stood up for us and looked out for us—she even made my wedding gown. Did she tell you?'' Rafe opened his mouth to speak, but the exquisite creature with the eggplant-colored bruise on her forehead rushed on. ''Anyway, when all this awful mess happened, naturally the first thing I thought was to call Molly. I just didn't know what else to do. I mean, here we are in a strange city with no car, no clothes— all our notes and the film Stu shot—'' Her face suddenly crumbled and Molly opened her arms.

Over the shoulder of his sobbing sister-in-law, Rafe met Molly's eyes and nodded. ''See what I mean?'' he mouthed silently. ''You're just alike.''

He left her to figure it out while he went in search of his brother's room. He'd recognized Annamarie easily from her wedding pictures. Although she was somewhat the worse for wear at the moment, she looked more like a Hollywood starlet than a linguist. More like a luxury beachfront condo than a two-bedroom cottage with little more than the basic amenities. More like a pedigreed pooch with a rhinestone collar than a pair of ragged, profane parrots and a lazy tomcat.

Rafe decided to reserve judgment on the newest member of the family. When it came to the Stevens women, what you saw was not necessarily all there was. He seemed to remember hearing about another sister who was some kind of research scientist. Hadn't paid much attention at the time because it hadn't seemed important to learn all there was to know about what would probably turn out to be only a temporary alliance.

In the space of a few days it had become vitally important. Molly was what—seven and nine years older than the two youngest sisters? Which meant she'd have been a young teenager when they were just starting school. Their parents had still been alive then. Funny thing though, he had a feeling that however they'd turned out, Molly was largely responsible.

She had made the wedding gown? All that white satin and lace? When the hell had she had time?

Dammit, it was about time people stopped using her and began appreciating her for what she was— one of the sweetest, kindest, most patient, most responsible, most generous women he'd ever had the good fortune to meet.

Not to mention one of the sexiest.

Stu, wearing a thin white turban, was sitting in a chair by the window, staring morosely down at the cast on his left hand. He glanced up when Rafe stepped inside the room. "Boy, did I screw up this time."

"I'm afraid to ask what you mean."

"Old chimneys. You know me and old chimneys. One look at a burned-out hearth and I get to wondering who lived there, and when, and what the living conditions were like when the house was first built. We'd just passed a set of rock ones and I started to say something to Annie, and whamo!"

Whamo. Rafe could remember any number of whamos in his kid brother's past. There were countless skateboard whamos, fortunately with full protective gear, the TR-6 whamo that had doubled his insurance rates, not to mention any number of spectacular surfing wipe-outs. Once Stu had stopped trying to live up to his older brother's example and accepted the fact that he was never going to be an athlete, he'd settled down nicely to become a fairly serious scholar.

Rafe did his best to reassure him that the accident hadn't been his fault, and that even if it had—Rafe hadn't read the report yet, so he didn't honestly know—that these things happened. The kid had enough to deal with without taking on the burden of guilt. "That's what insurance is for. You, uh, you have kept up your premiums, haven't you?"

Glumly the younger man nodded. "Annie sees to all that kind of thing. She's good at paperwork."

"Great. You can trade off, then, because you're good at—"

"Screwing up."

"Knock it off, will you? You must be good at something, to get a beauty like Annamarie to marry you."

Stu's smile started slowly and broadened into a full-blown grin. "Yeah, well...I don't like to brag, but..."

And then the women were there, and there were more formal introductions to be made and plans to be laid. By the time Rafe and Molly left, promising to return during evening visiting hours, Rafe had a pretty good idea of what had to be done. Molly had a list of her own. Outside the hospital, it occurred to Rafe that they hadn't yet secured a place to stay. There were a lot more options here than on Ocracoke Island, but still...

"First priority is finding a bed. I don't know about you, but I didn't get a whole lot of sleep last night."

Molly blushed. Seeing it, Rafe wanted to wrap her in his arms and hold her until the rest of the world went away. Instead, he did his best to ease her embarrassment. "What do you say we hunt up a good restaurant first? I have a feeling we're both going to need to keep up our strength."

She rolled her eyes, and he had to laugh. After a few moments, Molly joined him, and he said, "That's what I like about you—your sense of humor." And then he shook his head. "It's not *all* I like about you—don't misunderstand me. What I meant was—"

"Rafe?"

"Yeah."

"Did anyone ever tell you you talk too much when you're ill at ease?"

"It must be catching."

"That's right, blame someone else. Now hush up and let's go find that restaurant, all right? I'm in the mood for fried chicken and lots of mashed potatoes, with maybe coconut pie for dessert."

There were times, Molly told herself, when calories simply didn't count.

Nine

Molly yawned all the way to the hotel. She was uncomfortably full, because another thing she did besides talk too much when she was upset or worried or ill at ease was eat. She tried to keep pretzels on hand—the fat-free kind—because they crunched so good, but she'd been known to devour a whole bag in one sitting. Pure nerves, but that didn't help the end result.

"A suite?" She gaped at the luxurious surroundings the minute they were alone. "Rafe, that's five whole rooms! It must cost a fortune!"

"Bathrooms don't count."

She shot him the kind of look such a remark deserved, and he shrugged and tossed his jacket at the velvet love seat. "Call it market research if it'll ease your conscience. I'm involved with a couple of hotels—I need to keep up with what the competition is offering.''

''You could have done your market research at Ocracoke instead of moving into a cottage that's not much bigger than this—this—'' She indicated the comfortable lounge that separated the two bedrooms, each with a private bath.

''No vacancies, remember?''

''I wonder how hard you really looked.''

''What, you think I wanted to be stuck there with you?''

She shook her head. They were at it again. Where Rafe was concerned, there was no such thing as a moderate, reasoned response. Almost from the first, every cell in her body had been aware of the man. If she were fifteen years old with typical teenager roller-coaster hormones, it might have been understandable. But she was a thirty-six-year-old divorcée, considered by practically everyone in Grover's Hollow to be seriously, dependably mature. Of the three Stevens sisters, she was said to be the only one with a lick of common sense.

Great. So now the sensible sister had gone and fallen in love with a man who never would have given her a second look if they hadn't been stuck together in a five-room cottage. She would simply have to fall out of love. It might not be easy—it was probably going to hurt like the very devil, but eventually she'd get over it.

At least she could take pride in one thing—her taste in men had improved enormously, she thought as she explored the closets and the bathroom amenities. She was too embarrassed to admit that although she had stayed in motels before—the economy kind where you had to go outside and locate the machines if you got hungry or thirsty—she had never stayed in a real hotel.

Shampoo and conditioner, bubble bath and body lotion, a hair dryer, a sewing kit—and mercy, there was even a phone in the bathroom and a bathrobe hanging on the back of the door. If she'd needed a reminder of the vast gulf between a man who owned an airplane and a hotel, and a woman who had never even been inside either until today, this was it. It made her want to crawl into that massive bed, pull the covers over her head and sleep until she could wake up in her own narrow bed, in her own two-and-a-half-room apartment with the wag-tailed clock in the kitchen and the fake Oriental rug in the tiny living room.

However, that wasn't possible, and Molly was nothing if not a realist. She surveyed the huge, gleaming bathtub. Her apartment held only a cramped shower. The tub in the only cottage Annamarie had been able to rent on short notice was small, rust stained and uncomfortable, the hot-water supply barely adequate. The hotel's water heater was probably the size of a city block.

Besides, there was that lovely basket of toiletries, just waiting to be sampled. And while she might lack sophistication, she had never been short of common sense.

When Rafe called through the door some twenty minutes later, wanting to know if she was all right, Molly could hardly find the energy to answer. Up to her shoulders in scented bubbles, her hair wet, smelling of passionflower and dewberry bodywash, she seriously considered spending the night right where she was. The water was growing cool, though, and what little energy she possessed had gone flat, along with the bubbles. "I'm fine, thank you," she called back, her voice sounding as drowsy as her boneless body felt.

"Good. We need to talk about tomorrow," came the brisk response.

Molly didn't want to talk about tomorrow. She didn't want to *think* about tomorrow. All her life she'd had to think about tomorrow. Just this once she would like to wallow in a cocoon of luxury and think of nothing more serious than whether or not she should polish her toenails.

"We'll talk tomorrow," she called through the door.

Silence. She could picture him standing on the other side of the door, frustrated and unable to do anything about it. It gave her an exhilarating sense of power.

"Are you sure you're all right in there?" His voice was mild, even concerned. "You're not feeling sick, are you? That pie was pretty rich."

Oh, great. She really needed that. Her eyes suddenly started to sting and she blamed it on the highly scented shampoo. "Would you mind calling the hospital to see if Annamarie's thought of anything else she needs?"

In other words, go away and leave me alone with my sweet-scented guilt and my busted bubbles.

"It's too late to call tonight. You need to go to bed, Molly. We got a heavy schedule tomorrow."

"Stop trying to plan my life. I don't want it and I don't need it. I told you—" She broke off with an indignant yelp as the door opened. It had never occurred to her to lock it. What was the point of having two bathrooms if you couldn't count on a little privacy?

He opened the door and flinched as heavily scented steam surrounded him. "God, you need gills to breathe in here." Holding out an enormous bath towel, he said, "Come on, honey. Time to get out before you turn into a prune."

"Do you *mind?*"

Indignation was hard to hang on to when a woman was sopping wet, bone tired and fighting tears. Add to that about ten thousand calories worth of guilt....

"Get out of the bathtub, Molly."

"Get out of my bathroom, Rafe," she snapped back, but her voice lacked conviction.

"Come on now. You're bound to be bushed. We won't talk about tomorrow's schedule until after we've both had a good night's sleep, if you'd rather not. I left a wake-up call for seven."

Using her toe, she opened the drain. Iridescent bubbles clung to her breasts as the water slowly drained from the tub. Rafe stood patiently, holding the towel outspread. "Anytime you're ready, honey."

"I'm not your honey, and believe it or not, I'm perfectly capable of climbing out of a bathtub."

"Humor me. I've got about all I can handle with Stu's busted head and broken hand. I'm not taking any chances on your slipping and breaking your...whatever."

Well, there was that, too. She felt about as steady on her feet as a string of boiled spaghetti. Besides, he had seen it all before. "Then turn off the light."

"No way. Want me to tell you what I see?"

"Don't you dare," she wailed. "And don't look!"

"I see a wet, beautiful woman with skin like vanilla ice cream. I see a woman whose—"

She lunged into the towel and his arms closed around her. "And I see a man who swallowed the whole blooming Blarney stone," she growled. "Vanilla ice cream?"

"French vanilla. Cream and sugar and—" He sniffed her shoulder. "Maybe a few exotic fruits and flowers."

She choked back a laugh that ended with a sob. "It's passionflower. And dewberries."

"See? I knew it was edible."

Her eyes were still burning from the shampoo, but she had to laugh. When Rafe would have held her there, she pulled away and, still clutching the towel, reached for another one, draping it over her head, face and all. She managed to escape into the bedroom without blundering into any furniture. "All right, you saved me from drowning. Now go away."

"Make me," he purred, grinning.

The towel still covered her head. How on earth did she manage to get herself into these ludicrous situations, one right after the other? Why would any intelligent, levelheaded woman marry a third-rate hustler? Why would she allow herself to be picked up by a sexy-looking fisherman she happened to meet on a ferryboat? Why on earth would she then fall head over heels in love with the very next man she met?

There was no hope for her, simply no hope. During the years when she should have been learning about boy-girl relationships, she'd been too busy pretending to be grown-up so that she could hold her family together. By the time she was free to be herself, it was too late. Ignoring the deficiencies in her social development, she had made one blind leap for the brass ring and missed, and now she was scared stiff of jumping again for fear of breaking something irreparable.

He was still there. She could feel his presence, even though she couldn't see him. Shoving the towel off her face, Molly gave up trying to ignore him. "Scoundrel," she muttered. Clutching the bath towel around her torso, she padded across to the luggage rack. While Rafe stood in the doorway and watched, arms crossed over his chest, she dug out her pajamas. Short of a suit of armor, it was the best she could do. There was certainly nothing seductive about yellow flannel and stringy wet hair. "Would you please leave, or do I have to call for help?"

"Come on out as soon as you're ready. I made fresh coffee."

"You told me I needed sleep. You said we'd wait until morning to talk about what had to be done."

"I lied. I'll give you a choice, though—go to bed, turn off the light, and if you're snoring within five minutes, I'll leave you alone. But if you're planning on lying there in the dark, fretting about how four people are going to fit into a five-room cottage, or how we're all going to get there, then you might as well join me in a nightcap while we go over a plan of operations."

Molly sighed. Under cover of the damp bath towel she had managed to pull on her pajama pants, tug them up and tie the drawstring, thankful the waist was adjustable. She couldn't think of anything more embarrassing than eating an enormous meal and then not being able to get into her clothes.

Tomorrow. Absolutely, without fail tomorrow she would start on the diet of her life, with no time-outs, no excuses, no chocolate rewards for losing two pounds that caused her to gain three more. Not one single forbidden bite until she had lost fifteen pounds. It wasn't enough, but it was a start. At Mary Etta's statuesque five-foot-ten, fifteen extra pounds would hardly even be noticeable, but at five-foot two, those pounds made the difference between the upper-end of average for a large-framed woman—which she wasn't—and overweight. All the charts said so. Charts might lie, but Molly's mirror didn't. Nor had Kenny. For a guy who poured on the smarmy charm like maple syrup when it suited his purpose, her ex-husband knew just how to boost his own ego by slicing hers up into small, bleeding bits. Dumbo had been one of his kinder pet names.

"Black, with one sweetener, right?"

She sighed and buttoned her pajama top up under her chin. "One cup of coffee and that's it. We can talk until I finish, but then I'm going to bed."

After he left the room, she used the hotel's hair dryer for a few minutes, but her hair was too thick and she gave up halfway though. She'd been exhausted before the long, hot soak. Now she felt like a flower-scented zombie. Back when she'd been working two jobs, plus a third on weekends, she'd been younger. Now, at thirty-six, she felt old as the West Virginia hills.

When she came into the lounge, Rafe handed her a thin, gold-banded cup and saucer. "I'll be on the phone first thing tomorrow with the insurance people and the DMV. Then I want to check the car ads in the morning paper. While I do that, why don't you take the rental and go shopping? There's a mall not far away—we passed it on the way to the hotel earlier, remember?''

The thought of trying to find her way around a strange city was daunting, however Molly had tackled worst things in her life. "Fine. Have you got a list for your brother? You'd better specify brands and sizes, because I don't know all that much about men's clothes.'' Molly shopped at discount stores. Kenny had insisted on buying his things from the most expensive men's store in Morgantown, or ordering from those fancy catalogs that sold battered milking stools for hundreds of dollars and priced faded cotton as if it were woven gold.

She sipped her coffee, hoping the caffeine would kick in while they discussed plans for tomorrow. "We should be able to get the basics out of the way by about ten,'' Rafe said. "I'll meet you back here when you're through shopping and we'll run out to the hospital and see if we can bail the honeymooners out. After that we'll grab some lunch and then leave them here while you and I check out the car dealers.''

Molly nodded silently. She knew what it was like to be broke. She couldn't imagine what it must be like to have lost everything, right down to driver's license and Social Security card. Some things could not be replaced at the corner drugstore. "Won't Stu want to pick out his own car?''

"He trusts me.''

Leaning back in her chair Molly tucked her bare feet up beside her and studied the man across from her. Mercy, he was beautiful. That sun-streaked hair hadn't come from any bottle, any more than that spectacular tan had. Molly had belatedly developed an excellent instinct for phonies, and whatever else he was, Rafe was no phony—he was genuine to the bone. You could take him or leave him; he couldn't care less. Everything about him practically shouted that message.

And Molly would have given her last earthly possession to take him, but that wasn't a choice she'd been offered, except on a strictly temporary basis. Once Stu and Annamarie were settled, Rafe would go back to the lifestyle of the rich and famous and she would go back to the lifestyle of a head-housekeeper at Holly Hills Home.

"Isn't that right?"

"Isn't what right?"

"Wake up, darling. You haven't heard a thing I've said for the past five minutes, have you?"

"I warned you I wasn't up to a serious planning session tonight."

"You did." He stood and held out his hand. Molly sighed and took it, but only because she honestly didn't think she possessed the strength to resist. He tugged her to her feet and then held her in a loose embrace, his chin resting on the top of her head. "Molly, Molly, what am I going to do about you?" he murmured, his voice almost too soft to be heard over the clumsy thump-ka-thud of her heart.

"I don't know," she said simply. Hopefully. Hopelessly.

"I know what I'd like to do, but let's get this other business sorted out first."

Rafe had been asleep for about three hours. There'd been a time when he could go without sleep for thirty-six hours without losing his edge. Now it was more like twenty-four. He could still fall asleep within minutes, catnap and wake up fresh and ready to meet trouble head on, but he rarely slept so deeply that the slightest sound didn't bring him instantly alert.

He was instantly alert. Silently he slipped out of bed and felt for his khakis. By the time he reached Molly's bedroom door, he was marginally decent. He listened, not knowing what he was listening for, but knowing he would recognize it if it came again.

Thump! The sound of muffled curses. He opened the door a crack and peered into the darkness, wondering how good hotel security was, wishing he had brought along his own protection. Even four star hotels had their share of break-ins.

"Oh, dammit, dammit, dammit." Molly's voice. She sounded as if she were in pain, but not as if she were fighting off an intruder. He'd been in enough tight situations to recognize the difference.

Reaching inside the door, he switched on the entry light, all sixty watts of it. She was sitting on the floor clutching one foot, rocking back and forth and muttering, "Dammit, dammit, dammit" in a dull monotone. Stifling the urge to laugh, he entered, leaving the door open. "Got a problem?"

"My toe—or rather, my leg and my toe." And then she uttered a basic four letter word that was so un-Molly-like he had to laugh.

Kneeling before her, he took her foot into his own hands. "Let me guess. Another blister? You got up to go to the bathroom and stubbed your toe?"

"I got a leg cramp and got up to walk it off and tripped over that—that damn-blasted chair!" She glared at the guilty chair, but as Rafe began to massage her calf and the small, childlike foot, she sighed and closed her eyes. "I can do that myself. I was getting ready to."

"Hush up and let my magic fingers go to work. Your arms are too short, remember?" He was sitting cross-legged on the floor in front of her, beside the bed. The covers were spilling onto the floor, as if the bed itself had been under attack.

"This is getting to be an embarrassing habit," she muttered. "You and my feet."

"You need to take better care of yourself. Is this better?"

"I take excellent care of myself. I always have."

"Right," he said with a knowing look as he gently manipulated the spasming muscles at the back of her leg.

She flinched when he touched a trigger spot, and Rafe smoothed the place with long, slow strokes, watching her mouth tense, then soften. Watching the way her gold-tipped russet eyelashes curled on her cheek when her eyes were closed. After a while she said, "I always walk. Even when I'm tied to my desk all day, I always walk at least a couple of miles. Today I didn't."

"Mmm." There was the faintest dusting of fine, transparent hair on her lower legs, none at all above the knee. She didn't shave, and for some reason, that struck him as incredibly arousing. No polish on her toenails. She was pure, plain Molly. What you saw was what you got.

He very much liked what he saw. And what he felt. And the heady scent of warm, sleepy woman with overtones of some fruity-scented body lotion. Liked it too much…and that was beginning to be a problem.

The trouble with Molly was that she was nothing

at all like the women who had left their mark on his life to a greater or lesser degree, starting with his mother, a Vegas showgirl. Gorgeous even somewhere in her early sixties, Stella loved romance with a capital *R*. She had married often and loved every one of her husbands, but if she'd ever had a maternal bone in her body, it had yet to be discovered.

Molly was purring, her eyes almost closed, but not quite. Funny thing about women. His ex-wife, eighteen at the time they were married, had never liked being touched. He hadn't seen her—had scarcely even thought about her in the sixteen years since their divorce. But he could still remember how he'd felt when she'd announced shortly after their wedding that she would do the Dirty Deed with him whenever he required her to, but she preferred to sleep alone.

At the time he'd been as hormone-driven as any normal nineteen-year-old. Once he realized she meant it, he'd told her she was flat-out crazy. With nothing else to sustain it, their brief marriage had gone downhill from there. It had been years before he'd trusted his judgment with any woman. Even now, he never asked for more than he was prepared to offer, which definitely ruled out any emotional involvement.

Until Molly.

Over the years, he'd run pretty true to type where women were concerned. Invariably he was drawn to brunettes. One of the sexiest women he'd ever known had a sleek cap of blue-black hair and almond-shaped eyes the color of green seedless grapes. Molly's hair was long, reddish brown and inclined to curl. Her eyes were as round and brown as chestnuts.

He'd always been turned on by tall women, athletic types with long legs, lean bodies and small breasts.

Molly was short and well-rounded, generously endowed in every area.

The one thing that was nonnegotiable in the women he guardedly allowed into his life was detachment. No clinging vines. No demands on either side. The only reason he had broken off with Belle, who fit all his requirements to a T, was that, approaching the age of forty she had discovered a long-buried nesting urge.

Molly dropped off the charts in every single category. A woman who had helped raise two sisters? No way. She was one of those women whatsername sang about—people who needed people. If she'd struck out on her own after her folks had been killed, leaving her sisters with other relatives, it might be different, but she wasn't the type to shirk her responsibilities.

Right. Like you didn't take on the care and feeding of a fifteen-year-old kid when you were barely making it yourself.

Okay, so they both had a few weaknesses. All the more reason not to get any more involved than they already were, Rafe told himself.

"Your hands have got to be tired. I'm all right now, honestly. See?" She wiggled her toes. Small, straight toes with nails as pink as the inside of a conch shell.

"You sure? You've got a long list tomorrow."

"Just move that blasted chair on your way out, will you?"

Rafe was grateful for the dim lighting. It didn't take much candlepower to recognize temptation when it was lying back, propped back on a pair of dimpled elbows with one knee bent, one leg resting across his lap. Those flannel pajamas of hers, with the rabbit-print collar and cuffs, were definitely not one of Victoria's secrets. He started to ease her foot onto the floor. She sighed. He slid his hands to the back of her knee and heard her catch her breath.

"You're ticklish," he accused.

"Only when you touch me behind the knees," she gasped.

Well, naturally, he had to test her.

One thing led to another—later, the only conclusion he could draw was that they both wanted what followed. His fingers traced the dimples at the back of her knee and she planted her stubby little foot on his chest and shoved. Like a kid—like a feisty ten-year-old kid. He retaliated by rolling over her and tickling her ribs.

One thing led to another. The bedding was half on the floor by then. So he dragged it the rest of the way. Making love to a woman on even the best grade of commercial carpet simply wasn't his style, and he knew what was going to happen. At some level, he'd known it when he'd opened her door.

Ten

***

Fingering the soft, rumpled fabric of her pajama top, Rafe said, "Is this what you always sleep in?"

"Yes—no—sometimes."

"I like a woman who knows her own mind."

The pajama top came unbuttoned as if by magic. Molly had a stern mental talk with herself about the advisability of deliberately courting disaster. It lasted all of thirty seconds. She tried to tell herself she couldn't possibly be in love with the man, not after less than a week, but it felt more like love than anything she had ever before experienced. Even at the very first, when she'd been suspicious of him and tried to talk him into leaving, it was as if she had recognized him at some deep, subconscious level. If only he had recognized her in the same way....

Still, she would have this much, no matter what.

This time they were equal partners. The same wild

magic that had propelled them headlong into ecstasy the first time they had made love prevailed once more, but now there was the added element of tenderness. The feeling that this would be a farewell gift made her want to weep.

Lifting his mouth from her breast, Rafe moved down her body. "Let me—" he whispered hoarsely.

"Oh, please—you can't," she said as shivers of sheer pleasure raced though her boneless body.

He could, and he did, and long moments later, Molly cried out her pleasure. Then, with the coals of passion still glowing, he came into her and they rocked together, holding on tightly, murmuring soft broken words until they succumbed to an avalanche of sheer, mindless sensation.

Rafe watched her guardedly the following morning. She wouldn't meet his eyes, but he could feel her gaze focus on him the moment he turned away. There was a sense of sadness about her that didn't make sense. God knows, the last thing he wanted was to have her regret what had happened. Briefly he considered bringing it up—cards on the table, so to speak—but sex was something he'd never felt comfortable discussing. Especially when he was still feeling off balance. He couldn't put his finger on what it was; he only knew that some vital element in his life had changed.

Before he thought too deeply about it—if he had to think about it at all—he preferred to put some distance between them. About a thousand miles should put things in perspective. "How're your leg cramps?"

She looked for a moment as if he'd tossed her a

live mouse. Then, ignoring his question, she picked up her list and read off, "Two sets of clothes, under and outer, for both. Toothbrushes, toothpaste, deodorant, moisturizer—Annamarie doesn't need much makeup. Do you know what Stu needs for shaving? Brands and everything? And they'll need pens and a notepad to list things as they think of them and…whatever."

Rafe named a well-known brand of shaving cream and suggested a pack of disposable razors. "Stu had his wallet on him. Your sister lost her purse, so that'll mean a new drivers' license, new Social Security card—"

"New library card."

"Oh, yeah, can't forget library card," he said dryly, and that brought a smile to her lips. It felt as if the sun had just come blazing out after a three-day hurricane.

By the time they finished breakfast they had allocated duties. Molly went over her lists while Rafe scribbled notes on the hotel stationery and waited impatiently for the insurance office to open. Neither of them mentioned the night before, but it hovered like a third presence in the room. They avoided looking directly at each other, avoided mentioning anything even faintly personal.

Molly was all efficiency, dressing quickly in her black top and jeans. She was down to her last clean outfit. Thank goodness the waistband wasn't too tight today. Occasionally she played games with herself, telling herself it was only water weight, but weight was weight. Measurements were measurements. And Molly was nothing if not a realist.

Thanks to her new pomegranate-pink lipstick and

a touch of blusher, the shadows beneath her eyes weren't so noticeable. Glancing at her watch, she said, "The stores should be open now. I want to allow enough time to find the mall—I think it's on this same street, about two or three blocks south. Or was it north?"

Rafe pointed toward a colorful serigraph on the wall beside the door. "Which direction is that?"

Molly blinked. "Out?"

He shook his head. "Just ask directions from the concierge."

"The what?"

"It's a who. Lady in the lobby, behind the stand-alone desk with the big, potted anthurium."

She scowled at him. "I knew that," she said when it was plain as day that she'd known nothing of the kind.

Which might have been what prompted Rafe to cross the floor just as she reached for her purse, take her in his arms and kiss her on the mouth. It was a soft kiss, not at all passionate, yet all the more devastating for that. Because there was that tenderness again. Passion was one thing, she told herself—passion could flare up for purely chemical reasons and burn itself out within minutes.

Tenderness had a way of lingering long after the flames had died down.

He pressed the car keys and several large bills in her hand and said, "Go shopping. If this doesn't cover it, we'll go back later. Meet you back here about noon."

Rafe talked to the insurance agent and got the ball rolling. He had looked at several cars. "Something a damned sight safer than that high-priced cookie tin you were driving,'' was the criterion he described to Stu when he'd called to discuss the matter. After that, he spent a few hours on the phone, most of them on hold, with various offices and agencies.

With a list of sizes, styles and brands, Molly shopped diligently. Stu was easy. Boxers, white socks and clunky sneakers, size ten medium. As long as his clothes fit, he was happy. If he had an ego, it wasn't based on his appearance.

Annamarie was a bit more demanding, but as she'd look gorgeous wearing kitchen curtains, Molly had bought her underwear, two pairs of dark slacks and two pretty tops, sandals and sneakers. Pajamas for both, plus the toiletries, plus two bags of M&Ms. Annamarie would need her favorite comfort food.

Just as they finished comparing notes over the sandwiches Rafe had ordered from room service, Stu called to say he'd already been discharged, but Annamarie was undergoing tests to be sure the recurring pain in her side was nothing more than a strained muscle.

Hearing that, Molly started fidgeting. And then she started listing every known internal injury and a few no one had ever heard of.

"A strained goozle?" Rafe glanced up from his own lists.

"Oh, it's the—you know. The whatchamacallit. I knew a boy who fell off a tractor and they had to take it out, but he got along just fine without it. But it might be— Oh, Lordy, what if they can't have children? That would break her heart.''

"Molly. Look at me. Close your eyes. Take a deep breath and listen. You're probably talking about a spleen. It has nothing to do with having children. If it has to go, she can live without it. Besides, the tests are only a precaution. If there's the slightest chance of a liability suit, the hospital's not going to let her walk out without the appropriate tests.''

Eyes closed, she said, ''I need to be there. She'll need me.''

''She has a husband now. How about letting him take over the responsibility?''

She opened her eyes and looked at him then, really looked at him for the first time since they'd made love. Golden brown eyes, dark now with apprehension. It was all he could do not to reach for her, but it was time to pull back. Time to begin erecting barriers again. ''Trust me,'' Rafe said, and she nodded.

''You're right. I'm just—it's habit, I guess. I told you Mama wasn't exactly—that is, she was always so tired. She worked—did I tell you that? But she still found time to make most of our clothes and teach me to sew when I was growing up.''

''Mine taught me dance routines. Can't tell you what a big help those high kicks were once I started playing football.''

Molly had to laugh. He shook his head—she thought he might have said something under his breath, but then he was holding her, and there was nothing at all sexual about it, only caring. Come to think about it, that was even more terrifying than the other. The knowledge that she cared too much. And that while he might care just a little bit, too, when it came to caring, there was no middle ground. Too much on one side and not enough on the other could never add up to happiness.

*   *   *

Rafe was not the classic loner. He had scores of friends. He had known hundreds of women and enjoyed dozens of them intimately. He'd always considered himself a generous man, both as a friend and a lover.

But deep down, where it counted, he had always held a part of himself aloof. Only once had he broken the rule, and then it was for a lonely, klutzy, resentful kid with a redwood-size chip on his shoulder. Stu had tried his damnedest to prove something to the big brother he'd been dumped on, to the mother who had done the dumping, and to the father who hadn't bothered to see him since he was about four years old. For the first couple of years he'd nearly broken his neck trying to become something he was never cut out to be. Rafe had realized one thing from his own youth—telling a kid didn't work. Keeping him alive while he learned who he was, what he was all about and where his capabilities lay, turned out to be a large order, but somebody had to tackle it. What the hell could a big brother do but love him, try to teach him a few survival skills and keep him out of major trouble?

Now he had a wife. He was no longer lonely or resentful. He might still be something of a klutz, but he was Annamarie's klutz. Neither of them would appreciate Rafe's stepping in and trying to run the show.

Rafe called the hospital room to describe the SUV he had picked out. Annamarie answered and said Stu had gone out to get her something in chocolate, preferably M&Ms. "We've decided on a pickup truck. It's a lot more practical and just as safe."

Rafe figured Annamarie had decided. Stu's inter-

ests ran more to Roman chariots than to modern transportation. "Okay, your call. How about dark green?"

"Orange. You can see it coming from a mile
away."

"I don't think pickup trucks come in orange."

"Maybe not, but paint does."

On the whole, Rafe decided as he hung up with
plans to collect Stu after visiting hours, he liked his
new sister-in-law.

He also liked his sister-in-law's sister, he thought
late that afternoon as he went through the preflight
checkup. And that might be something of a problem.

Summer had struck with a vengeance. Five in the
afternoon on the first day of May, with the temperature hovering in the eighties. Molly was wearing a
new pair of dark pants which hugged her shapely
hips, with a white open-throated cotton shirt. A plain
white shirt that looked sexier than another woman's
thong bikini. Imagination was a hell of an aphrodi-
siac.

Mayday, mayday!

Silently she climbed in and strapped herself down
without speaking a word. She'd hardly spoken on the
way to the airport. She was worrying again. Not about
money, because Stu still had his credit cards. It would
take more than a bottom-of-the-line pickup truck to
max out his credit. They'd bought the truck—it was
red, not orange—and Annamarie would be driving
until Stu's hand healed.

She was probably worried about her sister's driving. Hadn't she mentioned something about the trouble Annamarie had had getting her driver's license?
"Look, they're going to be cautious as the devil after
what happened. I wouldn't worry."

And then he remembered that her parents had gone off a mountain road in a hard rainstorm and both been killed. "Great roads between Norfolk and Ocracoke. Straight, wide, flat. Not a lot of traffic this time of year." He didn't have a clue about the traffic—Memorial Day was coming up—but it was what she needed to hear.

"I know," she said almost too softly to be heard. "And thank you, Rafe. For—well, for everything."

As they lifted off the runway, he concentrated on flying. Not until they reached cruising altitude did he respond. "I'm not sure what everything you're talking about, but you're certainly welcome." He'd given Stu most of the cash he had on him and paid for another night at the hotel, figuring it wouldn't be a bad idea for the younger adults to be within range of medical care for a day or so before heading back. He wasn't sure about the medical facilities on the island.

"I hope the birds haven't taught Carly too many bad words." Molly had been watching the patterns pass below. The geometric patchwork of fields and doll-size farms, and then the lacework of sounds and creeks, rivers and ponds as they neared the coast.

"I wouldn't be surprised if she hasn't taught them a few."

She looked at him then. "Rafe, she's only a child."

"Yeah," he said, and she shook her head and then laughed. For the first time all day—since they had made love, in fact, she seemed visibly to relax. They hadn't slept together last night. Stu, dismissed from the hospital, had shared Rafe's room, then insisted on racing off to the hospital to spring his wife. It had taken a couple of hours, after which they had gone to the dealer's to collect the new truck.

He had a feeling Molly had spent the most of the time while he was gone making a list of every penny he'd spent on her so that she could settle her account. When he'd come back, she'd been on the phone with her other sister—Etta Mary or was it Mary Etta? There was a stack of receipts and several pages of hotel stationary on the desk beside her.

He'd listened in unabashedly while he poured himself a big glass of orange juice from the minirefrigerator. Molly had obviously explained what had happened, and how it was being dealt with, and was in the process of explaining why she'd been free to house-sit while Annamarie was off on a birthday-gift trip with her new husband.

Rafe had already known most of it. He'd learned about two of the three sisters from watching the interaction between Molly and Annamarie at the hospital. For all their apparent differences, they were surprisingly close. They finished each other's sentences. Molly would say, "Remember that time—"

"—when I dressed Miss Daisy's cat up in doll clothes and it got away?"

And then they would laugh, and Annamarie would say, "If it had been anybody else she would have—"

"The finger. She had the biggest forefinger I ever saw," Molly had explained to Stu and Rafe. "She was always shaking it in someone's face, like it was a—"

"—a weapon. When you're only about three feet tall, and—"

"And there's this huge forefinger shaking right in your face, believe me, it makes a big—"

"—impression, even when you know she'd never lay a hand on you." Annamarie had grinned without diminishing the china-doll perfection of her face. "She might have taken a switch to me, but she would never in this world have hurt you." And to Rafe she'd explained, "Everybody loves Molly."

"Annamarie, that's not—"

"Oh, yes it is. There's not a man, woman or child in all of Grover's Hollow who hasn't—"

"For heaven's sake, you're boring everyone to death!" Molly's cheeks were flaming.

"Well, anyway, they all love her," the younger sister had insisted. Barefooted, wearing a hospital gown over a pair of pink plaid slacks, she'd looked all of twelve years old as she proceeded to embarrass and defend her older sister at the same time.

Rafe had listened with half an ear, trying to bring into focus a younger Molly who had helped to raise both her sisters. A woman whose taste in men was on a par with her taste in seashells, collecting broken specimens of both. A woman who was surprisingly naive, considering she had been married and divorced.

And now that her sisters were out on their own, Rafe thought now as he followed the coastline on a southwesterly course, she was probably going to hole up in some retirement home and spend the rest of her life looking after people who would take advantage of her sweet, generous spirit until she was all used up. No more blushes. No more laughter. No more fresh, dewy cheeks and soft sighs and uninhibited passion.

It was a damned shame, too. Not that there was a sentimental bone in his entire body, but a woman like Molly would bring out the protective instincts of a totem pole. What she needed was—

Was none of his business!

* * *

"I guess they'll be here sometime tomorrow," Molly said brightly a few hours later. She had a kink in her neck from watching a spectacular sunset over the broad waters of the Pamlico Sound. They had barely made it back to the island before dark. Rafe had mentioned that there were no lights on the runway and then concentrated on flying, although from time to time she felt his gaze on her. They hadn't tried to talk over the engine noise, and for that Molly was grateful.

Now she swung herself down from the plane without waiting for his help. No point in getting used to something that was about to end. After today, the pets would no longer need her. The cottage was barely big enough for a couple of honeymooners. Four was definitely a crowd.

"I guess you'll be leaving in the morning," she said with every appearance of cheerfulness.

He nodded. "I told Stu not to be in too big a hurry, in case your sister needs more—more time to shop." Rafe had been about to say, more medical attention, but Molly was a world-class worrier.

"She won't. She has clothes here, and more back in Durham."

"But as long as they're near the shops, she might want to indulge."

"She'll be fine with what I bought her. I know her tastes and her sizes."

Personally Rafe had never known a woman, including his own mother, who wasn't a marathon shopper. The more beautiful they were, the more they enjoyed spending his money to enhance that beauty.

All his mistresses had been high-maintenance types. "At any rate, Stu can afford it. He won't come into his trust until he's thirty-one, but he has an interest income that should keep her happy until then."

Molly gave him a curious look. With the plane secured, they were in the rust bucket, headed back to the cottage. "Is that what it takes to be happy? Money?"

"Doesn't it?" It was like having a sensitive tooth. He couldn't leave it alone, he had to keep probing, testing, ferreting out weaknesses in order not to fall any deeper under her spell. He told himself it was only the novelty factor. That's all it could be, because Molly was different in every conceivable way from his usual women.

Under the low branches of two twisted live oak trees, the cottage was dark. Rafe unlocked the door and Molly stepped inside and felt for the light switch. Pete—or was it Repete?—tuned up with the squeaking door imitation, and the other bird made a chattering noise that sounded like a scolding wren. Actually, Molly thought, they were rather nice birds as long as they weren't spouting profanity.

So, of course they had to start. Every indecent four-letter word known to man. Someone—probably the entire fraternity—had taken great delight in corrupting a pair of otherwise beautiful birds.

"It's a wonder they don't blister the paint," Rafe observed.

"*Bugger off, mate, bugger off, mate, bu—*"

"*Bad-ass, bad-ass!*"

"They don't seem to bother your sister."

"Actually they do, but nobody else would claim

them and she was afraid they'd be—well, whatever you do to unwanted birds. Euthanize them, I guess."

Rafe dropped the bags in the two bedrooms, opened windows and then peered into the refrigerator. "They're probably long past frying age, but stewed, they might be—"

"Rafe!"

"Only kidding," he said. "Want a... Let's see, we could have a bacon-and-cheese omelet or—"

Hearing Shag at the door, Molly opened a can of cat food. No wonder the poor creature always stunk. So did his dinner. "Sally Ann wants me take a puppy."

"So?" Rafe got out the ingredients for an omelet and lined them up on the counter.

"The place where I live has a no-pets policy."

"Call it a guard dog."

"I could call it a stuffed duck, but I don't think it would work."

Molly was almost too tired to eat. She couldn't think why, as she'd done little but sit for the past few hours, conscious every minute of the man beside her—his warmth, his strength, the woody scent of his shaving soap mingling with the oil-and-metal smell of the plane itself. "You wouldn't think you could get tired of resting, would you?"

Rafe was whipping eggs. Oddly enough, there was nothing at all incongruous about a large, rugged man wearing tailor-made khakis and a stylish chambray shirt with a flowered tea towel tucked under his belt.

"I'd better get to work, too," Molly said, and jumped up so fast, her head swam. Then she stood there like a fool, not knowing where to start, what to do. "They'll probably be here sometime tomorrow. I should clean the house."

"Why? Did they clean up before you came?"

"That's different."

"How is it different?"

"I don't know!" she cried, flinging out her arms helplessly. "It just is! I've always cleaned when company was coming. It's—it's expected."

The bacon was sizzling on the back burner. Rafe poured the egg mixture into the omelet pan and let it set before he began tilting and lifting. Calmly he said, "Sit down, Molly. They won't be here until tomorrow evening at the earliest. You need to eat a good supper and go to bed. In the morning you can start worrying again. If necessary, I'll help you with a list of things to worry about."

She had to laugh. It was the strangest thing, but when it occurred to her that he was saying exactly the same sort of thing to her that she'd said for years to Annamarie and Mary Etta, laughter bubbled up inside her like antacid tablets dropped in water.

"What, you think that's funny? You want to get started on tomorrow's list now? How about the Middle East situation? Those earthquakes? The price of oil and what it's doing to the economy?"

And then she howled. "I want extra cheese in mine," she said when she could speak again.

"Hmm…it's sort of green," he warned. "I'd better shave off the mold."

"Who cares? I'll put mold on the list of things to worry about tomorrow."

She would worry about more than moldy cheese tomorrow, but meanwhile she intended to enjoy what might be the last few hours she would ever have with the man who had opened her eyes to what love was all about.

It was about laughing together. About sharing. About fitting together body, soul and mind, as if they were two parts of a whole. It was about that scary, thrilling feeling of knowing that for better or worse you're connected in some mysterious way to another being and there's not one blooming thing you can do about it.

And when the worst came, letting go.

Rafe hadn't exactly said when he was leaving, but it would probably be shortly after Stu and Annamarie got here tomorrow. He'd mentioned waiting to see that they got here safely, but after that, if there was enough light left to fly by, there'd be no more reason for him to hang around.

She might even leave before he did, just to prove she could walk away. Meanwhile she had tonight.

By the time she'd finished her half of the omelet and two glasses of wine, she was having trouble holding her eyes open. "That was delicious, but I can't seem to stop yawning. Would you mind if I wait until morning to do the dishes?"

She hadn't made the bed before they'd left. Now she barely managed to peel off her clothes and drag on her pajama top. Tomorrow she would get busy sweeping and dusting and worrying about the rest of her life and how she was going to fill a big hole in her heart.

Maybe Stu and Annamarie would have babies.

Maybe…

Eleven

Hearing Rafe in the shower, Molly stared up at the water-stained ceiling and went over her mental worry list again. Annamarie would be all right; she had Stu now. And Stu had had Rafe for a role model, so how could he possibly not do well? Which brought her back around to the top of the list.

How about Molly? How was she going to keep from bleeding to death when she watched him drive off in that noisy old rust bucket? Or when she watched him fly off in that shiny white plane with the green palm tree and the orange sunset? Could she shrug it off, pretending it didn't matter?

It wasn't as if he had promised her anything, or even asked for anything. She would willingly have given him her heart, but then, why would he want a heart that had another man's footprints all over it?

Babies, she decided, would be a link. He'd be the

uncle, she the aunt. There would be holidays, family reunions—those were real big occasions back in Grover's Hollow. Maybe not so big in Pelican's Cove, but then, it was something to look forward to, which was a whole lot better than nothing.

Outside the open window a mockingbird tuned up and ran through an impressive repertoire. It occurred to her that before the summer was over, the same bird might be showing off an X-rated vocabulary. Maybe she would think about that possibility and laugh, rather than think about impossibilities and cry.

"I saved you some hot water," Rafe called through the door. He poked his head inside, his wet hair several shades darker. His eyes were...*veiled* was the only word she could think of to describe the way he looked at her. "Rise and shine, lazy bones. You've got a kitchen full of dirty dishes that have to be washed before I can make us some breakfast."

Funny, Molly thought, how quickly habits could be formed, rituals established. She washed the dishes and then she stripped the beds. And since the sun was shining, she put in a load of wash. The washing machine protested—its innards were probably full of sand—but being busy was the only way she knew to keep from thinking.

She ate two scrambled eggs and drank freshly squeezed orange juice and Rafe's strong Columbian coffee and thought, *This is the last time we'll share breakfast. Stu and Annamarie will be here this afternoon, and Rafe will want to get back to whatever he left down in Florida.*

Or whoever.

"I'm going to the store. Do you want to come with

me?'' he said, raking his chair back and glancing at his watch.

Even his voice set off her internal seismograph. ''No, you go ahead. I need to hang out the wash.'' They had discussed it yesterday and decided to clean out their leftovers from the refrigerator and restock it with easy meal makings. With one hand in a cast, Stu wouldn't be a whole lot of help for a week or so, and Annamarie had never been particularly domestic.

Through the front window, Molly watched Rafe drive off. She tried to tell herself she was allergic to salt air, but it wasn't salt air that was making her throat ache and her eyes brim over. Maybe it wasn't love—she'd been fooled before—but whatever it was, right now it hurt like the very devil, and she had to start getting over it. No way was she going to waste the rest of her life moping over a man who was probably down in Florida feeding some skinny little bimbo in a string bikini his Irish coffee and sweet potato casserole.

''Balderdash,'' she muttered.

She hung the wash, including two of Rafe's shirts, a pair of khakis and two pairs of briefs, and thought with a wicked sense of satisfaction, *He can't pack up and leave until his laundry dries or it'll mildew.*

Glancing at the sun, feeling the southwest breeze on her face, she felt her spirits droop. So maybe she would simply leave before he did. Dressed in her black skirt and turtleneck. Of course, it would be too hot because today promised to be a scorcher, but it was by far her most flattering outfit. She could drape a scarf over her shoulder so that it would flutter in the breeze as she walked away. Not looking back, leaving behind only a taunting whiff of Je Reviens,

which the clerk had told her meant something like
"I'm coming back" in French. Would that be subtle
enough? Too subtle? Would he even notice?

Go now, and don't look back. She'd heard that cli-
chéd line all her life, and hadn't a clue where it came
from, but suddenly it didn't seem all that melodra-
matic.

"I stocked up on deli stuff and a frozen pumpkin
pie," Rafe told her as he unloaded the rust bucket.
She was in the yard taking in the sheets, which had
dried, and feeling her jeans, which would never dry.
He'd almost caught her testing his briefs, which were
dry except for the elastic.

He handed her a plastic sack. "Brought you a gift,
something to remember me by," he said with that
grin of his that ought to be labeled as hazardous to a
woman's health.

He'd brought her a bright orange plastic raincoat
and matching hat. "Lose the beige," he said.

She didn't know whether to laugh or cry. "I'd
planned to. It doesn't shed water anymore." Clutching the plastic raingear to her chest, she tried to think
of something to give him in return. Something that
would remind him of her when he was back in Florida.

"Think this'll serve as a traveling cage?" He
dragged a banana box out of the back of the rust
bucket. "It's ventilated."

"A cage? You're taking the birds?"

He frowned, and she thought, I'd rather have one
of his frowns than a smile from any other man in the
world. "Pups. I thought I might take a couple. If I

don't, Stu'll get suckered into taking the whole litter. He's got a weakness for animals—always did have.''

''Well, now we know what they have in common,'' Molly said dryly. ''Annamarie dragged home every stray in Grover's Hollow. Did I ever tell you about the dying pony someone gave her? Mama had a fit, but Annamarie was so sure she could cure the poor thing and learn to ride it. It was her dream back then—to be a cowgirl.''

''I'm afraid to ask what happened.'' Rafe shoved the box onto the porch and took a sack of groceries in each hand.

Molly draped the fresh-smelling sheets over her shoulder and lifted out the last sack. ''I buried the poor thing. And let me tell you, it's not easy digging a pony-size hole in our section of West Virginia. Annamarie nailed together a wooden cross and was about to dig up Mama's rosebush to plant on his grave, but I bribed her with three packets of flower seeds and a trip to the library. You do know the puppies aren't even weaned yet, don't you?''

''They're not? Carly never mentioned it. I guess I'll have to come back in a couple of weeks, whenever they're ready to fly.''

Oh, sure. Once she was gone he could come back any old time and stay as long as he liked. There wasn't a single reason in the world why that should make her feel like an outsider, but it did. ''Are you allowed to keep pets?''

''Yes'm, I'm allowed,'' he replied, and his eyes took on that look of gentle amusement that melted her defensive anger before she could dig herself in any deeper. She had slept with the man, for heaven's sake. She was ninety-nine percent in love with him. So? As Carly would say—get over it!

"That's right. You own the hotels, or whatever, don't you?"

"At the moment, one of them could be described as a 'whatever,' but the Coral Tree Inn is completely renovated and ready to go on the block."

"To sell, you mean. Is that what you do? Sell hotels?"

"Buy 'em, renovate or demolish and rebuild on the property, then sell and start all over again. It's an interesting business."

"I'm sure," she said, trying not to sound the way she was feeling, which was left out in the cold. Miffed.

No, not miffed, dammit, devastated!

Loaded with laundry and groceries, she paused just inside the door. "You'd better put the cold stuff in the refrigerator. I've got beds to make and packing to do." As a romantic, dramatic parting line, it left a lot to be desired, but it was the best she could come up with. Some women just weren't cut out for leading roles in any man's life.

While Molly was remaking the bed and straightening the office, replacing the stacks of books, papers, tapes and recording equipment on the cot Rafe had used when he wasn't sleeping in the other bed with her, Stu called from Oregon Inlet to say they'd be getting in by midafternoon.

Plenty of time to get away before dark, Rafe told himself.

Plenty of time to leave before Rafe did, Molly told herself. Meanwhile she would think of some casual, witty farewell line and practice it until the final moment came.

"I was scared to death driving onto the ferry," Annamarie exclaimed. "But Stu, bless his heart, didn't yell at me a single time. Molly, is that your suitcase by the door?"

Within minutes of their arrival, the cottage Molly had taken such pains to leave spotless was littered with parcels, flyers, folders and books. Neatness was not one of Annamarie's attributes.

"I thought I might try and catch the—"

"Oh, honey, you're an angel to put up with my babies. I know how cursing gets to you, but they don't really curse, they just use—well, actually, most of their words have a perfectly legitimate origin if you go back far enough."

"Spoken like a true linguist," Molly said, laughing. She shook her head. She had filled her gas tank and washed the salt from her windshield earlier. She was all ready to leave, while Rafe was sprawled in the easy chair, seemingly in no hurry to go. It was going to work, if only she could remember what it was she'd meant to say to him. Her casual, unforgettable parting line.

"Golly, aren't you hot in that black outfit?" Annamarie was wearing the blue pants Molly had picked out, with the white camp shirt. She had kicked off her sandals the minute she'd come inside.

"No, I—that is, it's more comfortable for driving than—" She was going to say than tight jeans. Instead she turned to Rafe and said, "It was nice, um—meeting you, Rafe."

Nice meeting him? I can't believe I said that.

"Oh, I expect we'll run into each other sooner or later."

"Your chambray shirt's still damp around the yoke and the cuffs. You'll need to take it out as soon as you get home so it won't mildew."

So much for the memorable parting word. Molly the head housekeeper strikes again.

"Honey, you need to take your pills. The doctor said—" Annamarie glanced up from the sofa, where she was cradling Stu's cast on her lap. "Oh, but you two don't have to leave just because we're back. At least stay for supper. We can go out somewhere."

But it was obvious to both Rafe and Molly that they were superfluous. Rafe spoke for both. "It's already after four, We'd better get going. I promised your next-door neighbor I'd take a couple of her pups when they're weaned, though, so I'll be seeing you before too long."

"And you two will be stopping by Holly Hills to see me on your way back to Durham, won't you?" Molly forced a smile and was reaching for her bag when Rafe took it from her.

"How about following me to the rental place so I can turn in the rust bucket? You can give me a lift to the airport since you'll be passing by on your way to the ferry."

The newlyweds beamed their approval, obviously delighted that their respective relatives were getting along so well together.

If they only knew, thought Molly as she hugged them both goodbye.

"See you in a couple of weeks," Rafe said. He hugged his brother and kissed his new sister on the cheek. Pride fought with jealousy as Molly followed him outside.

"You go on, I'll follow. We'll gas up your car when we drop off the SUV," Rafe said.

"Thanks, but I've already taken care of it." The big payoff. An orange raincoat and a tank full of gas. "Be still my heart," she muttered as she backed out onto the narrow, oyster-shell-paved road.

They drove in silence after Rafe turned in the vehicle and climbed into her passenger seat. Molly tried to think of some way to crowd a lifetime into a few minutes. She tried to remember Ingrid Bergman's parting words in *Casablanca,* but then, she'd been the one who boarded a plane, not Humphrey.

"Well," Rafe said as they pulled into the parking space outside the pavilion. There were three planes left on the tarmac. It was Wednesday. By weekend, there might be a dozen, but his wouldn't be among them.

Nor would Molly be waiting for him.

He thought of a dozen things he could say, all of them clichés. Reaching into the back seat he lifted out his duffel bag and opened the door. "Don't get out. I know you want to be on your way. I understand the ferries run often enough so that if you miss one, there'll be another along pretty soon."

Amber eyes. He could have sworn they were too clear to hide behind, only this time he hadn't a clue what she was thinking. "Guess this is it, then," he said jovially, and could have kicked himself when he saw those eyes darken.

"I guess it is. If I don't see you again—" Molly's smile was too quick, too bright.

Rafe cleared his throat. "Yeah, well…"

Molly wanted to cry, *Kiss me goodbye, dammit, I might die if you don't!*

She might die if he did. Worse, she might cry and beg him not to leave her, to take her with him, to find a place in his life for her, even if it was only a small place.

But of course he didn't kiss her. He closed the door, leaned down and gave her that familiar crooked grin. And she didn't cry, and she didn't beg and plead. Instead, she got out and stood there, watching him walk around his blasted airplane, undoing the tie-downs, unscrewing the chocks, testing the various whatchamacallits before he finally climbed inside, gave her one last wave and shut the door.

And still she couldn't leave. She stood there beside the gate and waited while he taxied to the far end of the runway. She watched as he came back again, lifted off, circled and headed southwest. She stood there and watched until he was only a faint speck against a cloudless blue sky.

So much for her new philosophy—feet on the floor and cards on the table. So much for reinventing herself. She might as well go ahead and indulge in a messy midlife crisis.

Rafe checked the gauges. He adjusted the trim and thought about the workload waiting for him, the decisions waiting to be made, decisions he had put off for too long. His particular stretch of Pelican's Cove was exposed to serious erosion. Was it wise to invest more there than he already had?

He could love a woman like Molly. The thought broke through his concentration, and he tried to refocus on the derelict hotel he'd recently bought, that he was going to have to either bulldoze or rebuild.

Correction, man. There aren't any other women like Molly.

For the first time he allowed himself to wonder what would happen if he followed his instincts where a woman was concerned. When it came to business, his instincts were superb. When it came to women…

What if he already loved her? How would he know? Could he trust himself to love any woman, especially a woman like Molly, who'd been badly hurt before?

Rafe knew his strengths and weaknesses. When it came to permanent relationships, he dropped off the bottom of the scale. Hell, even his own mother hadn't sent him a birthday card in three years.

On the other hand, he hadn't done a bad job on Stu. The kid still counted on him to come through in a pinch.

Oh, everybody always counts on Molly whenever they need help. Molly's always there. She always knows what to do and how to do it. She's never let anyone down.

How many people had let Molly down besides that jerk she'd married, who still counted on her to pull his chestnuts out of the fire?

"No way, not if I can help it," he muttered.

With no conscious decision, Rafe banked and came about on a heading that took him over the stubby white lighthouse and back to the landing strip. Not that he expected her to be there. She'd be long gone by now, and without another set of wheels, he was going to feel like a damn fool taxiing up Highway 12, trying to overtake her car before she reached the ferry.

By some miracle, she was still at the airport. After making his worst landing in years, he leapt out while the prop was still turning. "Molly! Wait a minute! Wait right there!" She was getting into her car. Rafe jogged across the tarmac and caught her before she could get away.

"Did you forget something? I was going to leave, but—" She broke off when his arms closed around her, smothering her against the hard warmth of his chest.

"Me, too. I would have followed you."

"What made you—?"

He answered without words. A pickup truck pulled into the airport parking area and they moved aside without breaking contact. The kiss said it all. When eventually they came up for breath, Rafe said, "Listen, this sounds crazy, but I've got to make you understand. The kid you must have been? I love her. And the girl you were when you took over the care of your sisters? Her, too. And the woman you are now, and the old woman you'll be someday, clucking over every stray chick and—"

There was such a rightness about it that Molly didn't even bother to argue. Secure in his arms, she said, "Who was it who promised to come back for a couple of puppies?"

"Who was it who paid top dollar for fresh tuna for a good-for-nothing tomcat?"

"Who told you that? It was only a teeny piece."

"I have my sources," Rafe said with a grin that refused to be suppressed. "Ah, Molly, can it possibly work for us?"

"We'll make it work. You know my motto—feet on the ground, head in the clouds."

He still couldn't quite say those three vital words. It wasn't the lack of practice, although he'd never spoken them before. It was just that his heart was still too full. Once he started, he might not be able to stop, and this was no place for a bent-knee declaration. They were already drawing a few leering grins.

But he would spend the rest of his life, he vowed silently, loving this woman. Loving Molly.

*   *   *   *   *

SILHOUETTE®
DESIRE™

AVAILABLE FROM 15TH MARCH 2002

FORBIDDEN ATTRACTION

GABRIEL'S GIFT Cait London

Part of Gabriel died when he sent Miranda away all those years ago. Now she was back, and pregnant! With a single touch Gabriel broke all his rules and re-ignited their passion…

VICTORIA'S CONQUEST Laurie Paige

Business tycoon Jason Broadrick had wanted Victoria from the instant he'd seen her—the day she'd married his cousin! Now, although free, Victoria was still off limits. And Jason knew better than to risk his most valuable asset—his heart.

MILLIONAIRE MARRIAGES

MILLIONAIRE BOSS Peggy Moreland

Penny Rawley hadn't travelled across the country to have sexy boss Erik Thompson order her around! She'd come to his firm with one thing in mind: marrying the man she'd always loved. Now, he had the nerve to ignore her… Well, *that* was going to change…

THE MILLIONAIRE'S SECRET WISH Leanne Banks

Millionaire Dylan Barrows made Alisa's amnesia much easier to handle. The sexy executive made her feel whole again. Dylan told her they were just friends so why did her instincts tell her that wasn't the whole truth?

HEIRESS IN HIS ARMS

IN BED WITH THE BOSS'S DAUGHTER
Bronwyn Jameson

Corporate tough-guy Jack Manning hadn't laid eyes on Paris Grantham since the night he'd rebuffed her teenage advances. But he'd been more than a little tempted by the boss's daughter—and was relieved when the sweet seductress had retreated to London. Until now…

THE HEIRESS & THE BODYGUARD Ryanne Corey

Undercover private investigator Billy Lucas never expected to fall for his beautiful target, society princess Julie Roper. All Billy wanted was to have Julie in his arms… But could he convince Julie that he wanted her and not her riches?

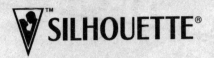

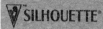

Diana **Palmer**

THE TEXAS RANGER

He has a passion for justice

Published 15th March 2002

**SILHOUETTE
SENSATION**

presents a new heart-pounding
twelve-book series:

A Year of Loving Dangerously

**When a top secret agency is threatened, twelve of the best
agents in the world put their lives—and their hearts—on
the line. But will justice...and true love...prevail?**

SILHOUETTE®

SPECIAL EDITION™

is proud to present

The Stockwells

Where family secrets, scandalous pasts and unexpected love wreak havoc on the lives of the rich and infamous Stockwells!

THE TYCOON'S INSTANT DAUGHTER
Christine Rimmer
January

SEVEN MONTHS AND COUNTING...
Myrna Temte
February

HER UNFORGETTABLE FIANCÉ
Allison Leigh
March

THE MILLIONAIRE AND THE MUM
Patricia Kay
April

THE CATTLEMAN AND THE VIRGIN HEIRESS
Jackie Merritt
May

1201/SH/LC

SILHOUETTE® INTRIGUE™

is proud to present

1201/SH/LC2

TOP SECRET BABIES

These babies need a protector!

THE BODYGUARD'S BABY
Debra Webb - January

SAVING HIS SON
Rita Herron - February

THE HUNT FOR HAWKE'S DAUGHTER
Jean Barrett - March

UNDERCOVER BABY
Adrianne Lee - April

CONCEPTION COVER-UP
Karen Lawton Barrett - May

HIS CHILD
Delores Fossen - June

Unwrap the mystery

SILHOUETTE® INTRIGUE™

*Eden had been named as paradise,
but evil had come to call…*

EDEN'S CHILDREN

A powerful new trilogy by
AMANDA STEVENS

THE INNOCENT	March 2002
THE TEMPTED	April 2002
THE FORGIVEN	May 2002

*Innocent young lives are in danger…
Can the power of love carry them home?*

0302/SH/LC28

SILHOUETTE®
DESIRE™

is proud to present

Millionaires Galore!

Rich, renowned, ruthless and sexy as sin

Millionaire's Club - January

MILLIONAIRE MD *by Jennifer Greene*
WORLD'S MOST ELIGIBLE TEXAN *by Sara Orwig*

Millionaire Men - February

LONE STAR KNIGHT *by Cindy Gerard*
HER ARDENT SHEIKH *by Kristi Gold*

Millionaire Bachelors - March

TYCOON WARRIOR *by Sheri WhiteFeather*
MILLIONAIRE HUSBAND *by Leanne Banks*

Millionaire Marriages - April

MILLIONAIRE BOSS *by Peggy Moreland*
THE MILLIONAIRE'S SECRET WISH
by Leanne Banks

The romance you'd want

Escape into

Silhouette

SENSATION®

Passionate, dramatic, thrilling romances

Sensation™ are sexy, exciting, dramatic and thrilling romances, featuring dangerous men and women strong enough to handle them.

FREE

1 BOOK
AND A SURPRISE GIFT!

We would like to take this opportunity to thank you for reading this Silhouette® book offering you the chance to take another specially selected title from the Desire™ se absolutely FREE! We're also making this offer to introduce you to the benefits the Reader Service™—

★ FREE home delivery   ★ FREE gifts and competitions
★ FREE monthly Newsletter   ★ Exclusive Reader Service discount
★ Books available before they're in the shops

Accepting this FREE book and gift places you under no obligation to buy; you may cance any time, even after receiving your free shipment. Simply complete your details below return the entire page to the address below. *You don't even need a stamp!*

YES! Please send me 1 free Desire book and a surprise gift. I understand that unless hear from me, I will receive 3 superb new titles every month for just £4.99 e postage and packing free. I am under no obligation to purchase any books and may cance subscription at any time. The free book and gift will be mine to keep in any case.

D2

Ms/Mrs/Miss/Mr ....Initials................
BLOCK CAPITALS

Surname..

Address...

....

....Postcode ....

Send this whole page to:
UK: FREEPOST CN81, Croydon, CR9 3WZ
EIRE: PO Box 4546, Kilcock, County Kildare (stamp required)

Offer valid in UK and Eire only and not available to current Reader Service subscribers to this series. We reserve the right to r
an application and applicants must be aged 18 years or over. Only one application per household. Terms and prices subje
change without notice. Offer expires 30th June 2002. As a result of this application, you may receive offers
other carefully selected companies. If you would prefer not to share in this opportunity please write to The Data Manager a
address above.

Silhouette® is a registered trademark used under licence.
Desire™ is being used as a trademark.